Alternative Schools
in British Columbia 1960-1975

A SOCIAL AND CULTURAL HISTORY

HARLEY ROTHSTEIN

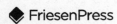 FriesenPress

One Printers Way
Altona, MB R0G 0B0
Canada

www.friesenpress.com

ISBN
978-1-03-913558-1 (Hardcover)
978-1-03-913557-4 (Paperback)
978-1-03-913559-8 (eBook)

1. HISTORY, STUDY & TEACHING

Distributed to the trade by The Ingram Book Company

For my wife, Eleanor Boyle,
and in memory of my parents,
Norman and Annette Rothstein

Table of Contents

Preface

I completed my PhD dissertation *Alternative Schools in British Columbia, 1960–1975* at UBC more than twenty years ago. Finally, I have decided to publish this work in book form. You might ask why I waited so long to publish it. And why publish it now? Both are good questions.

After completing my PhD, I dived into other professional projects and life took over. Besides, I needed a break from alternative schools after working on this subject for almost thirteen years throughout my Masters and Doctoral studies. As well, the manuscript was very long and I was advised to substantially shorten it. I couldn't imagine spending the hundreds of hours that would have been necessary to edit the manuscript, and didn't trust anyone else to do it.

But as the years went by I became increasingly unhappy that this work remained unpublished. No one else in Canada has written this story—of how the alternative schools and programs that we take for granted in the public school system got started in the first place, and how a handful of idealists found the wherewithal to express their values in small private schools. These independent alternative schools of the 1960s and early 1970s were founded by courageous visionaries. They recognized that the public schools could do better in addressing the wide range of students with different needs and interests than the one-size-fits-all system of the time. These pioneers deserve to have their story told. Alternative schools also provide a unique and valuable window into the social and political culture of the 1960s. This relationship has received little attention by scholars, even though interest in the 1960s has remained high.

There are other reasons for wanting this work to be more widely circulated in book form, in addition to the story it has to tell and the analysis it offers of the alternative schools movement. I've noticed over the years that my work has been cited relatively often despite the fact that it is only available in dissertation form. This means that scholars have gone to some trouble to find and reference my research. I'd like the information and insights embedded here to be more easily accessible. I've pulled together vast primary sources on alternative schools during this period, never seen by other researchers. This resource consists of individual school documents (such as enrolment lists, financial statements, newsletters, meeting minutes, prospectuses), letters and personal journals, philosophical statements, school district records, over 150 newspaper articles, and my own 350 original interviews with former alternative school parents, teachers, and students. I'd like future scholars of education, history, and culture to be aware of these resources.

The biggest decision was how much revising, shortening, and editing to do. I finally decided on very little. The book in this form is a retrospective from 1999 of my thinking about the rise of alternative schools, their eventual acceptance into the public school system, and their relationship to the 1960s. As it turns out, my thinking hasn't changed much and an analysis of developments during the last two decades will need to wait for another book.

I'd like to offer a word of explanation about the time period 1960–1975. I chose 1960 as a starting point for several reasons. That year saw the publication, by the Province of BC, of the *Report of the Royal Commission on Education*, otherwise known as the Chant Report. The conservative perspective of that report inspired a group of Vancouver parents to open one of the earliest alternative schools in the province two years later. The year 1960 also ushered in a new decade of both optimism and turmoil, which provided a backdrop for the striking educational developments recounted in this book. I chose 1975 as an endpoint because of the significant and surprising changes that occurred in the public school system between 1970 and 1975. After five years of transformation and excitement, it was clear that the changes were here to stay and that the school system would not revert to its inflexible past. I argue that one of the major factors inspiring that change was the pioneering example of the experimental alternative schools of the 1960s and early 1970s.

Readers and researchers are likely to use this book in a variety of ways. Some might be interested in one individual school, one particular educational theory, or one of the three periods I identify during the years 1960 to 1975: Progressive, Romantic, and Therapeutic. One school, the New School in Vancouver, experienced and evolved through all three, and accordingly its history is presented in three distinct chapters spread through the book. But most of the schools belong to just one category, and I've tried to write the accounts of each school so that they can both stand on their own and also be part of the fuller narrative. Some readers may be most interested in the overview provided in Chapter 1, others may be drawn to the liberalization of the school system described in Chapter 15, others may gravitate to the source materials and bibliography, while still others may be interested in what the book has to contribute to the field of oral history.

My own interest in alternative schools goes back over fifty years. As an undergraduate student I lived with my older cousins who had enrolled their two children in the New School, and I was intrigued. During that time I first heard about Summerhill and was moved to write an article about the school in the student newspaper in 1968. A year later I visited the Barker Free School outside of Vancouver and still have the handwritten letter I received from Bob Barker, confirming his invitation. In 1972 during a visit to London, I convinced some friends to undertake the two-hour drive to the little town where the iconic Summerhill is located. Una Neill, the wife of Summerhill founder A. S. Neill, gave us a tour of the school and the grounds. Neill was in his eighties and wasn't receiving visitors, but I did catch a glimpse of the famous man through a window.

When I became a public school teacher in 1976, I tried to incorporate some of the principles of alternative school teaching into my own class-room. Upon entering graduate school ten years later, it seemed natural to follow this idea and direct my research toward the history of the early alternative schools of the 1960s and 1970s. I couldn't have imagined the richness of people and ideas that awaited me. So as this book ventures out into the world, I hope that you will find this subject as valuable and engaging as I did.

Acknowledgements

First and foremost, I would like to thank my academic mentors, in particular, my PhD advisor, Dr. William Bruneau. Bill, along with dissertation committee members Dr. Jean Barman and Dr. J. Donald Wilson, guided me through those long and sometimes lonely years of graduate studies with extraordinary expertise, intellectual insight, good humour, and equanimity. I could always count on Bill for a valuable idea when I was stuck; Don's interest in the project led him to deliver a relevant document to my mailbox almost weekly; and Jean helped keep me going with her reminder, "the best dissertation is a finished dissertation." The encouragement, support, and friendship of these three outstanding scholars has been invaluable. In addition, I would like to thank my dissertation examiners, Dr. Jim Winter, and Dr. Neil Sutherland, both fine historians who inspired me over the years. Jim helped nurture my love of history when I took his second year course on the twentieth century many years ago, and I learned from Neil the fine art of conducting oral history interviews, which were a key ingredient of my research. Thank you to my outside examiner, respected Canadian historian Dr. Alison Prentice, for offering me valuable commentary on my dissertation.

Thank you to Dr. Ed Hundert whose stimulating evening intellectual history class on the Enlightenment, while I was still teaching in the public school system, inspired me to apply for graduate school. Thank you to historian Dr. Peter Seixas for his encouragement and valuable insights about alternative schools and the 1960s, as well as for several boxes of documents. Thank you to Dr. Peter Maclean of the UBC Department of Psychiatry who inspired me to meet the challenge of comprehensive exams as the deadline loomed with his memorable advice, "Set the date and rise to the occasion." Thank you to lawyer and teacher John Festinger, who gave me valuable advice on intellectual property, image copyright, and several research questions. Thank you to Dr. Nina Bascia, Dr. Esther Sokolov Fine, and Dr. Malcolm Levin, editors of a collection of articles on alternative schools in Toronto, for asking me to contribute an article providing the historical background to alternative schools in Canada. I would also like to thank my three educational mentors, Ms. Sandra Davies and Mr. John Stark who both provided extraordinary guidance as I was establishing myself professionally as a music teacher, and Ms. Cecily Overall who taught me the basic ingredients of effective teaching.

Thank you to my highly skilled editor, Larissa Ardis, for her research into numerous subjects, for editing and formatting the manuscript to send to the publisher, for her technical and software expertise, and for her major role in preparing over seventy images to enhance the text. She was invaluable in both technical and editorial realms. Thank you also to Dr. Patricia Anderson for her professional expertise as a consultant providing publishing advice, and for suggesting the subtitle of the book and two chapter titles. Thank you to research assistant Kathryn Pybus for bringing together valuable bibliographic sources and for transcribing almost one hundred recorded interviews. Thank you also to editor Collette Berg for being available on short notice to help with editing the manuscript and offering advice on communicating with the publisher. Thank you also to editor Catherine Plear for giving me the benefit of her experience and advice. My thanks to James Pugh of Super Suite Digital for transferring more than one hundred interview recordings from cassette tapes to compact discs. Thank you to Jodi Brown at FriesenPress for her beautiful cover design and expert layout. Thank you also to Friesen staff and editors Lee-Ann Jaworski, Leanne Janzen, Gillian Hebert, Elizabeth Siegel, Kerry Wilson, Spenser Smith, Debbie Anderson, Sisilia Zheng, and Janice Logan.

Thank you to Elena Novikova, licensing associate for Post Media, for generously granting me a licence to reproduce a 1967 photograph (New School students David Levi and Katrin Berg) from the *Vancouver Sun* for the book cover, and for arranging licences to use twenty historical photographs from the *Vancouver Sun* and *The Province* in the interior of the book. Thank you also to David Obee, publisher of the *Victoria*

Times-Colonist, for his generous permission to reproduce historical photographs that appeared in the *Victoria Times* and the *Daily Colonist*. Thank you to Andrea Gordon of Canadian Press for permission to reproduce a historical photograph from *The Globe and Mail*, to the *Toronto Star* and agent Stewart Kramer for the use of a historical photograph, and to Douglas Baird of the *Ubyssey* student newspaper for permission to use a 1968 photograph of New School students in Vancouver. Thank you to Lisa Whittington-Hill, publisher of *This Magazine*, for permission to reproduce covers from *This Magazine is about Schools*, and to Lindsey Winstone, of the Archives of Ontario, for permission to reproduce the front cover of an Everdale School brochure. Thank you to Sean Hennessy, the Argenta Friends Meeting, and an anonymous student for permission to reproduce photographs from school brochures. Thank you to Rose Hodwitz, former Principal of the Whole School, for granting permission to reproduce a Whole School prospectus, to Dan Armstrong and Ron Woodward of Pigweed Press for permission to reproduce a photograph taken at the Whole School, and to administrator Valentina Guarneri, for granting permission to reproduce a Whole School group photograph. Thank you to the Vancouver School Board for the use of two photographs from 1970s Total Education school yearbooks. Thank you to photographers Dan Scott, Bill Cunningham, Dave Buchan, Charles Steele, Ralph Bower, Gordon Sedawie, Glenn Baglo, Mark van Manen, Ken Oakes, Brian Kent, George Diack, Ian Lindsay, and Powell Hargrave; and to lawyer Andrew Atkins.

Thank you to Crisanta Sampang for graciously allowing me to reproduce a photograph taken by Daniel Wood on a New School field trip. Thank you also to teacher Daphne Harwood, for granting me permission to reproduce her photographs taken at the New School. Thank you to Meredith MacFarquhar for giving me permission to reproduce her photograph of Bob Davis, and for graciously organizing and hosting a memorable evening in her home with former Everdale students in Toronto in March, 2014.

Heartfelt thanks to friends and family. Thank you to Linda Nading for suggesting the original idea, Kristina Rothstein for discussions on history and culture and Daniel Siegel for reading the manuscript and commenting, and to John Munro, Kelly Foisy, Sam Macklin, Laurie Harris, Bob

Harris, Nicola Kappeli, Karen Clark, Ellen Shapiro, Chuck Nading, Kathy
and Terry Mullen, Janusz Sobuta, Susan Angel, Leonard Angel, and Julian
Wake. Thank you to Lorne Salutin, who first told me about Summerhill,
and to Bill and Sandra Bruneau, Stan Persky, Jon Bartlett and Rika
Ruebsaat, Alan and Annie Sussman, Judy Stoffman, Danny Stoffman,
Jonathan and Heather Berkowitz, Judah Shumiatcher, Andrew Feldmar,
Hanna Tiferet Siegel, Jessica Harris, Zach Dorfman, Lindsey and Travis
Gardner, Buddy Smith, Norma Hamilton, Connie Smith, Gary Smith, Sam
Rothstein, Stan Fisher, Mel Kaushansky, Carol Heaney, Miriam Clavir,
John Donlan, Russell Precious, Mel and Barb Lehan, Rick Nelson, Alan
Matheson, Hillel Goelman, Mary Richter, Steve and Marion Rom, Helen
Wilkes, Rosalind and Howard Karby, Rafi Zack, Irit Tsur, Joanne Zack,
Nadav Blum, Myrna Rabinowitz, Reva Malkin, Barry Rabinowitz, Sheryl
Sorokin, Steve Garrod, Jim Allan, Blaine Culling, Warren Hamill, Susan
and Yom Shamash, Ron and Estarisa Laye, Avi Dolgin, Avril Orloff, Dina-
Hasida Mercy, Michael Welton, Eric Damer, Sheila Hamilton, John and
Ruth Grunau, Joi Freed-Garrod, Stan Garrod, Stephen and Shari Gaerber,
Bernard Pinsky, Daniella Givon, Mark Gurvis, Leah Pomerantz.

My deepest thanks to my wife and life companion, Eleanor Boyle, for
her challenging ideas, insightful editing, and valuable advice as I grappled
with the concepts and writing. Finally, I thank my parents, Norman and
Annette Rothstein, for teaching me the things that are important, and for
instilling in me a love of learning.

Special Thanks to Interviewees

My enduring thanks to the 350 parents, teachers, students, and administrators who agreed to be interviewed, and to the following who I have quoted
directly. They shared with me memories and insights about an experience
that was significant in their lives. This is their story.

I'd like to recognize the many people who contributed by sharing not
only memories, but their materials, their ideas, and their vision. Some also
read chapter drafts. Thank you to John and Helen Stevenson, Tom Durrie,
and Helen Hughes for generous access to their school archives, and thank
you to school founders Bob Barker, Karen Tallman, Bill Sheffeld, Kathy

Sheffeld, Garry Nixon, Dan Meakes, Cathy Meakes, David Hummel, Don Brown, Elliott Gose, Kathy Gose, Rita Cohn, Marilyn Epstein, Joel Harris, Marcia Braundy, Lloyd Arntzen, and Joan Schwartz Ormondroyd. Thank you to Norman Levi, Norman Epstein, Phil Thomas, Julia Brown, Phil Knaiger, Peter Seixas, Nora Randall, Sharon Van Volkingburgh, Hugh Barr, Bonnie Picard, T.C. Carpendale, and Lori Williams for sharing school and personal documents. Thank you to Gloria Levi, Ellen Tallman, Jim Winter, Dan Jason, James Harding, Colin Browne, David Levi, Eric Epstein, Ron Forbes-Roberts, Anne Long, Daryl Sturdy, Daniel Wood, Daphne Trivett, Joan Nemtin, Barbara Shumiatcher, Barbara Hansen, Marty Hykin, Larry Haberlin, Ron Eckert, Bruce Russell, Rob Wood, Greg Sorbara, Hilda Thomas, Valerie Hodge, Patricia Hummel, Jesse Hyder, Jan Fraser, Jacquelin Aubuchon, Charlotte Dauk Herkel, Veronica Doyle, Bob Makaroff, Robert Minden, Gordon Yearsley, and Mary Thomson for their insights

Thank you to the following educational leaders who gave of their time: Olive Johnson, Peter Bullen, Jim Carter, John Wiens, Katherine Mirhady, Elliott Gose, John Wormsbecker, Eileen Dailly, John Young, John Uzelac, Sally Clinton, Thom Hansen, and Starla Anderson.

Thank you to teachers, students, and leaders from other provinces: Bob Davis, Alan Rimmer, Dale Shuttleworth, Murray Shukyn, Patricia Berton, Rico Gerussi, Fiona Nelson, Satu Repo, George Martell, Robert Stamp, Helena Wehrstein, Wally Seccombe, Eleanor Smollett, Carrie Shapiro Greschner, Paul Shapiro, Brian Iler, Vera Williams, Jim Deacove, Gail Ashby, Diana Meredith, Ruth, Shamai, Heather Chetwynd, Naomi McCormack, and Judith McCormack.

Thank you to the following former students for sharing their stories: Pat Lawson, Jack Wells, Jill Tolliday, Paul Nicholls, Laura Jamieson, Galen Bellman, Laura Landsberg, Emily Axelson, Aimee Promislow, Kiyo Kiyooka, Margot Hansen, Diane Brown, Carmen Stavdal, Mary Holland, Miles Durrie, Erin Harris, Kim Maclean, Wendy Maclean, Robin Maclean, Alan Best, Claire Schwartz, Jeff Creque, Barbara Pratt, Megan Ellis, Barbara Stowe, Charles Campbell, Tim Lucey, Monica Yard, Cal Shumiatcher, Tamar Levi, Scott Robinson, Cara Felde, Mark James, Monica Carpendale, John Doheny, Lowell Orcutt, Meghan

Hughes, Susanne Middleditch, Ken Spears, David Spears, Mary Hunt, Mike McConnell, Peter Vogel, Peter Schmidt, Cathleen Bertelsen, Susan Bertelsen, Tony Bertelsen, Marc McDougall, Rick Valentine, Ray Valentine, Jono Drake, Steven Drake, Katrin Berg, Michael Epstein, Dewi Minden, Karen Schendlinger, Dana Long, and Penny Ryan.

Thank you to teachers and parents Mary Schendlinger, Else Wise, Roy Kiyooka, Sandra Currie, Ron Hansen, Ken McFarland, Katherine Chamberlain, Bonnie Evans, David Orcutt, Shirley Maclean, Dave Manning, Jonathan Aldrich, Betty Polster, Brenda Berck, Arnold Porter, Hugh Herbison, Bishop Jim Cruikshank, Charles Hill, Richard Neil, Doug Cochran, Virginia Eckert, Liz Cochran, Annie Simmonds, Kate Barlow, Sharon Wiseman, Georgie Wilson, Barbara Williams, Mona Bertelsen, Kita Ridgeway, Marilyn Carson, Tom Drake, Sally Drake, William Nicholls, Hillary Nicholls, Barbara Beach, Gwen Creech, Kay Stockholder, Barry Promislow, Olive Balabanov, Margaret Sigurgierson, Sharon Burrow, Alan Tolliday, Elma Tolliday, Ed Wickberg, Naomi Growe, Jan Robinson, Philip Hewitt, Aurie Felde, Mervine Beagle, Vance Peavy, Leah Muhleman, and administrators Glen Pope, Bill Simpson, Doug Smith, Colin Dutson, Andy Mikita, and Charles Gregory.

Thank you also to Lyn Bowman, Rob Watt, Lynn Curtis, Donna and Bill Sassaman, Michael Philips, Rini House, Eugene Kaellis, Rhoda Kaellis, Judy Stone, Ian McNaughton, Sharon Mason, John Andrews, Martha Jackson, Lloyd Griffiths, Paul Tillotson, Mary Winder, David Stevenson, Ed Washington, Jane Sheppard, Jason Ridgeway, Michael Carson, Jim Anderson, Jesse Kaellis, John McNaughton, Jonathan Gregory, Mary Jamieson, Kate McIntosh, Katyana Woodruff, David Elderton, Laura Elderton, James Pratt, Steven Pratt, Tom Koltai, Neil Tessler, David Eaton, Carolyn Eaton, Jeremy Carpendate, Polly Wilson,Charles, Dyson, Dan Phelps, Erica Phister, John Rush, Dorothy Wheeler, Judy Rogers, Sally Kahn, Garth Dickman, Ursula Peavy, Erica Peavy, Heather-Jon Maroney, Ann Gregory, Scott Campbell, Dick Pollard, Beth Martin, Darcy Hughes, Sylvia Simpson, Susan Laughton, Pam Douglas, Cindy Williams, Glynis Sandall, Susan Brown, Jenny Laughton, Christina Cepeliauskas, Garth Babcock, Pat Armstrong, Alisha Grey, and Pamela Swanigan. Thank you!

Introduction

Chapter 1

INTRODUCTION: THE MAKING
OF BRITISH COLUMBIA
ALTERNATIVE SCHOOLS

The 1960s was a unique period of idealism, experimentation, and activism. One manifestation of the excitement and innovation of the times was the rise of independent alternative schools. Hundreds appeared across Canada and the United States, including more than twenty in British Columbia between 1960 and 1975. These small pioneering schools were founded by dissatisfied parents or forward-thinking educators who aimed to provide a more humanistic or "child-centred" education than existed in the public schools. Most proponents of alternative schools held some form of idealistic world view. As the 1960s gave rise to many new, creative, and sometimes radical ideas, they wanted their children's schooling to be expressions of those ideas and values.[1]

British Columbia provided fertile ground for alternative schools. Educational thinking in the province was influenced by both the American Progressive and British Romantic movements as well as by the British private school tradition.[2] Other prominent influences were the Canadian socialist and social gospel movements, and the American counterculture

---

1   My use of the term "alternative schools" refers to the non-authoritarian "child-centred" schools that first appeared during the 1960s, as distinct from the socially exclusive or religious private schools that originated much earlier.

2   In Britain these elite schools are referred to as public schools, but for clarity among Canadian and American readers, in this book I will call them private schools. For the best account of British-style schools in BC, see Jean Barman, *Growing Up British in British Columbia: Boys in Private School* (Vancouver: UBC Press, 1984).

of the 1960s. All of these factors combined to encourage the founding of numerous and diverse alternative schools. They were created in disparate regions of the province, including the City of Vancouver, its suburbs, Vancouver Island, the Gulf Islands, and the West Kootenays. Most were governed by parent or teacher co-operatives and varied in their pedagogy from a moderate Progressive curriculum to a laissez-faire Romantic approach with almost no curriculum at all. The goals of alternative schools varied, but in most cases creative exploration, personal growth, and community-building were considered to be as important as academic learning.

Alternative schools in British Columbia passed through three distinct periods. During the early 1960s, alternative schools were inspired by the Progressive ideas of John Dewey and the examples of American Progressive schools. Progressive schools emphasized "learning by doing," project work on interesting themes, co-operative learning, the creative arts, and education for citizenship. Progressive ideas were brought to the province, in part, by liberal American academics recruited by the University of British Columbia during its rapid expansion in the 1950s and early 1960s.

By the late 1960s, alternative schools began to draw on the Romantic tradition inspired by Jean-Jacques Rousseau's naturalistic ideas and A. S. Neill's famous Summerhill School in England. The proponents of Romantic education, or "free schools" as they came to be called, believed that children freed from adult interference would eventually acquire the skills and knowledge they needed while growing up without the constraints and inhibitions imposed by mainstream society.[3] Free schools were closely tied to the rapid emergence of the 1960s counterculture with its emphasis on personal freedom and transformation. Countercultural values and lifestyles in British Columbia were fuelled in part by a second wave of Americans who came to the province in the late 1960s because of their opposition to the Vietnam War.

In the early 1970s, Romantic schools declined with the waning of the counterculture and the radical political movements of the 1960s. Alternative schools became more varied in their methods, and many

---

3   *Romantic education* is my term for what was known as the free school movement in the 1960s.

adopted therapeutic or "rehabilitative" objectives.[4] Therapeutic schools sought to provide a place where the many disaffected young people who emerged from the volatile 1960s could learn basic academic skills in an accepting and supportive environment, meanwhile developing personal characteristics that would help them function more effectively in society. These schools were influenced by the feminist, environmental, and personal transformation movements that grew out of the 1960s. They also acquired a more local quality, staffed primarily by Canadians and at least partly informed by Canadian socialist and humanitarian values.

Individuals of many varied backgrounds and beliefs came together to establish alternative schools. Most shared a common belief in the potential of the individual, the importance of participation in a community, and an optimistic idealism. Some were attracted to alternative education through their experience as teachers or parents. For others, increased rights for young people was a component of a more general quest for self-determination across society.[5] All saw the public schools of the day as representing an outdated political, cultural, and educational outlook: authoritarian, competitive, inflexible, and unimaginative in their pedagogy. They were unhappy that, in the post-Sputnik era, public schools were preoccupied with trying to upgrade their science offerings, and that the recommendations of the 1960 *Royal Commission on Education* (the Chant Report) had relegated the creative arts to "frill" status.[6] Above all, alternative school proponents experienced public schools as unwilling or unable to accommodate the individual differences of children.

The Progressive Movement in Education

The earliest alternative schools of the 1960s were inspired by the Progressive education movement and the ideas of John Dewey.

---

4   "Therapeutic" is my term. The educators of the day most commonly used "rehabilitation."

5   James Harding, "From Authoritarianism to Totalitarianism: Two Winnipeg Schools," *This Magazine is about Schools*, Autumn 1968; reprinted in Tim Reid and Julyan Reid, *Student Power and the Canadian Campus* (Toronto: Peter Martin Associates, 1969).

6   S.N.F. Chant, J.E. Liersch, and R.P. Walrod, *Report of the Royal Commission on Education* (Victoria, BC: Province of British Columbia, 1960).

Progressivism embraced new theories of child development and a human-istic respect for the individual worth of each child. Progressives empha-sized the uniqueness of each student, the importance of educating the "whole child," active rather than passive learning, subject matter aimed at the child's interests, individual progress at the child's own pace, the value of the creative arts, and education for citizenship. Progressives typically advocated a broad, integrated, and "child-centred" curriculum, a stimulat-ing classroom environment, co-operation rather than competition, and an emphasis on self-expression and critical thinking.[7]

John Dewey's educational and philosophical writings were instrumental in shaping and inspiring the Progressive education movement. Underwood & Underwood | Public Domain via Wikimedia Commons

Dewey developed his methods at the University of Chicago Laboratory School, where he was director from 1896 to 1904, and at Columbia

---

7   For the best summary of Progressive ideas and methods at that time, see Harold Rugg and Ann Shumaker, *The Child-Centered School* (Yonkers: World Book, 1928).

University Teachers' College until he retired in 1940. A prolific writer about educational philosophy, Dewey had complex and subtle ideas, many of which have been oversimplified. Dewey believed educators should motivate children by appealing to their genuine "interests." Using a flexible curriculum, teachers would recognize and nurture each child's capabilities, preferences, and attitudes.[8] "Learning through experience," Dewey thought, would give rise to meaningful purpose and change. Teachers should promote critical inquiry and emphasize socially relevant subject material in conjunction with the "handed-down" wisdom and knowledge of Western civilization. Another central principle in Dewey's thought was the education of citizens for democracy. Young people could not be taught in an authoritarian, bureaucratic, and unstimulating atmosphere if they were to become the creative, critical, informed, and socially conscious adults required for an effective democracy.[9] Dewey believed that in a "community-centred" education, children would be active participants in day-to-day school life. His ideal classrooms would be "democratic communities of inquiry."[10]

Progressivism reached its peak in the 1920s and 1930s with the establishment of many private Progressive schools in northeastern United States,[11] such as New York's City and Country School where young children discovered the world through play and the arts. Founded by Caroline Pratt in 1914, the school was located in Greenwich Village and attracted parents who were artists and writers.[12] Lincoln School and Walden School were other well-known New York Progressive schools where traditional

8   For a succinct summary of John Dewey's educational philosophy, see *The School and Society* (Chicago: University of Chicago Press, 1899) and *The Child and the Curriculum* (Chicago, University of Chicago Press, 1902).
9   John Dewey, *Democracy and Education* (New York: Macmillan, 1916), 153.
10   Robert Westbrook, *John Dewey and American Democracy* (Ithaca: Cornell University Press, 1991), 172.
11   See John Dewey and Evelyn Dewey (his daughter), *Schools of Tomorrow* (New York: E. P. Dutton, 1915); Susan Semel and Alan Sadovnik, eds. *"Schools of Tomorrow," Schools of Today* (New York: Peter Lang, 1999); Jane Roland Martin, *School Was Our Life: Remembering Progressive Education* (Bloomington: Indiana University Press, 2018), about New York's Little Red School House; Susan Semel, *The Dalton School* (New York: Peter Lang, 1992); and Susan Lloyd, *The Putney School* (New Haven: Yale University Press, 1987).
12   Caroline Pratt, *I Learn from Children* (New York: Cornerstone Library, 1948).

formal curriculum was dismantled and reorganized into activity units. [13] Although most American Progressive schools were private, two midwestern public school districts developed ambitious Progressive programs in their schools.[14]

Hundreds of teachers were trained in Progressive methodology at Columbia Teachers' College by such scholars as William Kilpatrick, developer of the highly regarded Project Method, and Harold Rugg, a leading educational and social reformer.[15] Teachers could also study Progressive pedagogy at the Bank Street College of Education, founded by Lucy Sprague Mitchell in 1930 in Greenwich Village.[16] Meanwhile, in Italy, Maria Montessori was also developing Progressive ideas at her Children's House, using concrete materials, combining work and play, preferring freedom to compulsion, helping children figure out answers for themselves, and emphasizing "children learning rather than teachers teaching."[17] Some radical Progressives—the "social reconstructionists," exemplified by George Counts—envisioned schools as co-operative communities to bring about the transformation of society.[18]

By the 1930s, however, the humanistic or child-centred Progressives had become overshadowed by a conservative movement called "scientific"

---

13   Lawrence Cremin's pioneering *The Transformation of the School: Progressivism in American Education 1876–1957* (New York: Random House, 1961) is still the most comprehensive source on the history of American Progressive education. He describes many private Progressive schools, including City and Country School, Lincoln School (Abraham Flexner), Walden School (Margaret Naumburg), Edgewood School, Dalton School (all in New York), Oak Lane Country Day School (Philadelphia), Shady Hill School (Boston), Chevy Chase School (Maryland), Putney School (New Hampshire), the Francis Parker School (Chicago), Peninsula School (California), and Marietta Johnson's Organic School (Alabama).

14   Lawrence Cremin, *The Transformation of the School*. The two districts were Gary, Indiana, and Winnetka, Illinois.

15   William Kilpatrick, "The Project Method," *Teachers College Record* 19 (September 1918).

16   Lucy Sprague Mitchell was a Progressive educator with strong connections to many private Progressive schools. Joyce Antler, *Lucy Sprague Mitchell: The Making of a Modern Woman* (New Haven: Yale University Press, 1987).

17   Jane Roland Martin, "Romanticism Domesticated: Maria Montessori and the Casa Dei Bambini," in John Willinsky, ed., *The Educational Legacy of Romanticism* (Waterloo: Wilfrid Laurier University Press, 1990), 161. See also Maria Montessori, *The Montessori Method* (New York: Schocken, 1912).

18   George Counts, *Dare the School Build a New Social Order?* (Carbondale: Southern Illinois University Press, 1932).

or "administrative" Progressivism. Led by Edward Thorndike, it emphasized specialization, expertise, testing, and measurement.[19] Psychological testing and the "cult of efficiency" were, ironically, the most noticeable Progressive legacies in the public schools up to 1960.[20]

In Canada, a coalition of child-centred educators and humanitarian reformers proposed a variety of Progressive ideas as early as the 1890s.[21] Their curricular innovations, called the "New Education" movement, included kindergartens, manual training, domestic science (home economics), school gardens, and physical education. These Canadian Progressives sought to eliminate traditional nineteenth-century teaching methods that relied on memorization, rote learning, and a narrow curriculum. During the 1920s and 1930s, Progressive ideas dominated Canadian educational thinking, particularly in western Canada. The 1925 Putman-Weir Report in British Columbia endorsed Progressive principles.[22] In Saskatchewan a modest curriculum revision along Progressive lines was begun in 1931, and in 1936 the Alberta Department of Education, under the leadership of Hubert Newland, implemented a locally developed Progressive curriculum called the "enterprise system" organized around broad themes.[23] Some Progressives in western Canada were influenced by democratic socialist politics. During the 1940s, radical educators such as Watson Thomson in Saskatchewan combined Progressive educational theory with

19 David Tyack, *The One Best System* (Cambridge: Harvard University Press, 1974).

20 Lawrence Cremin, *The Transformation of the School: Progressivism in American Education 1876–1957* (New York: Random House, 1961).

21 Neil Sutherland, *Children in English Canadian Society* (Toronto: University of Toronto Press, 1976).

22 J. H. Putman and G. M. Weir, *Survey of the School System* (Victoria: Province of British Columbia, 1925).The fact that J. H. Putman, inspector for Ottawa schools and a well-known proponent of Progressive education, was invited to co-author the report, indicates that Progressive ideas were well-established in BC. See B. Anne Wood, *Idealism Transformed: The Making of a Progressive Educator* (Kingston: McGill-Queen's University Press, 1985). See also Jean Mann, "G. M. Weir and H. B. King: Progressive Education or Education for the Progressive State?" in J. Donald Wilson and David C. Jones, eds., *Schooling and Society in 20th Century British Columbia* (Calgary: Detselig, 1980), 91–118.

23 Donalda Dickie, *The Enterprise in Theory and Practice* (Toronto: Gage, 1941); and Robert Patterson, "The Implementation of Progressive Education in Canada, 1930–1945," in Nick Kach et al., *Essays on Canadian Education* (Edmonton: Brush Education, 1986).

socialist communal values to encourage social change based on democratic, participatory, and egalitarian principles.[24]

Unlike in the United States, few private Progressive schools were established in Canada during the 1920s and 1930s—with the exception of St. George's Progressive School in Montreal, a parent-run school founded in 1930 with twenty-two students in a rented house.[25] Perhaps not surprisingly, due to the influence of Canadian communitarian values, Progressive educators in Canada preferred to focus their energy and ideas on the public school system.

Progressive education had fallen out of public favour by the 1940s as the Canadian mood became more conservative. But despite the fact that child-centred and Progressive methods were widely advocated and endorsed by educational leaders during the 1930s, very few of these methods had actually been implemented in the average Canadian classroom. Historian Neil Sutherland vividly described the traditional pedagogy that endured in British Columbia schools well into the 1960s:

> It was a system that put its rigour into rote learning of
> the times tables, the spelling words, the capes and bays,
> a system that discouraged independent thought, a system
> that provided no opportunity to be creative, a system that
> blamed rather than praised, a system that made no direct
> or purposeful effort to build a sense of self-worth.[26]

It was this conservatism and inertia in the public education system that inspired proponents of alternative schools.

---

24 See Michael Welton's biography of Watson Thomson, *"To Be and Build the Glorious World"* (PhD thesis, University of British Columbia, 1983); and Michael Welton, ed., *Knowledge for the People* (Toronto: OISE Press, 1987).

25 Grattan Gray, "What Happens When Parents Start Schools of Their Own," *Maclean's*, November 18, 1961, 57–58. St. George's School still exists with an enrolment of over four hundred students.

26 Neil Sutherland, "The Triumph of 'Formalism': Elementary Schooling in Vancouver from the 1920s to the 1960s," in R. McDonald and Jean Barman, eds. *Vancouver Past: Essays in Social History, BC Studies* 69/70 (Spring/Summer 1986): 182–183. Several articles by Robert Patterson also make this point. Larry Cuban's *How Teachers Taught* (New York: Longman, 1984) makes a similar case for the United States.

The Romantic Movement

Alternative schools of the 1960s were also strongly influenced by the Romantic tradition in education, which can be traced back to the publication of Jean Jacques Rousseau's *Emile* in 1762.[27] Rousseau proposed a naturalistic education that would leave children free to follow their desires, curiosity, and instincts with little adult direction. His ideas found an eager audience among eighteenth-century English Romantics, political radicals, intellectuals, poets, and educators, and Rousseau became a cult figure among his ardent English followers. His influence also extended to continental Europe, where his ideas were developed and applied by Johann Pestalozzi, Friedrich Froebel, Leo Tolstoy, and others.[28]

Romantic ideas remained largely underground during the nineteenth century, but resurfaced in twentieth-century Britain just as Dewey's ideas were gaining prominence in the United States. From 1913 to 1918, Homer Lane, an American educator in England, pioneered the idea of student self-government at the Little Commonwealth in Dorset, a residential school for delinquent teenagers. School rules were made at meetings of the entire school community where everyone, students and teachers alike, had one vote.[29] In Sussex in 1927, the philosopher Bertrand Russell and his wife, Dora Russell, founded Beacon Hill School where experimental inquiry and natural curiosity were nurtured, while academic study, though encouraged, was voluntary. Decisions were made at school council meetings and students had significant freedom "under the supervision of benevolent adults."[30] Beacon Hill had many admirers, but some people disapproved of the socialist, pacifist, and agnostic views of its founders, while others were skeptical of the idea that children might enjoy themselves at school.[31] Dartington, another rural English school and part of an

---

27   J. J. Rousseau, *Emile* (1762), trans. B. Foxley (London: Dent, 1911).
28   John Willinsky, ed., *The Educational Legacy of Romanticism* (Waterloo: Wilfred Laurier University Press, 1990).
29   Homer Lane, *Talks to Parents and Teachers* (New York: Schocken, 1928).
30   Katharine Tait, *My Father Bertrand Russell* (New York: Harcourt Brace Jovanovich, 1975), 74.
31   Ronald Clark, *The Life of Bertrand Russell* (London: Jonathan Cape, 1975); and Brian Hendley, *Dewey, Russell, Whitehead: Philosophers as Educators* (Carbondale: Southern Illinois University Press, 1986).

experimental self-sustaining intentional community in Devon, opened in 1926, emphasizing the creative arts, Progressive methods, coeducation, and co-operation rather than competition. Its long-serving headmaster, William Curry, had developed Dewey's methods during five years teaching at a Progressive school in Philadelphia.[32] Parents included writers, intellectuals, and some from other countries. Beacon Hill and Dartington had elements of both Progressivism and Romanticism, stopping short of complete freedom for students.[33]

A. S. Neill was the founder of the legendary Summerhill school in England.
Keystone | Hulton Archive | Getty Images 1969

The most famous Romantic school was Summerhill, founded in 1927 in Leiston, Suffolk, a small town northeast of London, by A. S. Neill, an admirer of Homer Lane. Throughout his long career, Neill developed several basic principles: that children would be allowed to pursue any

32   W. B. Curry, *The School and a Changing Civilization* (London: John Lane Bodley Head, 1934); and Michael Young, *The Elmhirsts of Dartington* (London: Routledge & Kegan Paul, 1982).

33   For more on schools in Britain, see R. J. W. Selleck, *English Primary Education and the Progressives 1919–1939* (London: Routledge & Kegan Paul, 1972); Robert Skidelsky, *English Progressive Schools* (Harmondsworth: Penguin, 1969); and W. A. C. Stewart, *The Educational Innovators: Progressive Schools, 1881–1967* (London: Macmillan, 1968).

activities that interested them, that they would not be compelled to attend classes, and that school rules would be set by all members of the school community with each person having one vote whatever his or her age. Neill's approach was based on Freudian psychoanalytic techniques as well as his own experience and intuition, and he had a particular genius for working with young people. However, with little theoretical framework, his methods were difficult to duplicate or transfer, particularly from Summerhill's residential setting to day schools in the United States.

With the publication of A. S. Neill's *Summerhill* in 1960, Romantic ideas burst into the popular culture.[34] This was a timely event for those unhappy with the public school system. The widely-read book was an inspiration to many dissatisfied parents and educators who initiated a wave of Romanticism often referred to as the "free school movement." This resulted in an explosion in the number of alternative schools across Canada and the United States, which by 1970 had reached several hundred.[35] Romantic ideas also found a wide following among counterculture youth.

Summerhill ushered in a new era of thinking about education as dozens of books about alternative schooling appeared between 1964 and 1972. Some identified problems in the public school system and suggested directions for change, while others advocated the creation of independent alternative schools. The most influential authors were John Holt, Paul Goodman, Sylvia Ashton-Warner, Jonathan Kozol, Herbert Kohl, James Herndon, George Dennison, Herb Snitzer, Allen Graubard, Neil Postman and Charles Weingartner, Charles Silberman, Joseph Featherstone, and Ivan Illich (who argued for the abolition of schools entirely).[36] The schools

---

34   A. S. Neill, *Summerhill: A Radical Approach to Child Rearing* (New York: Hart, 1960).

35   Allen Graubard, *Free the Children* (New York: Random House, 1972), 41. Graubard cites the following statistics for the United States: 1967: 20–30 new free schools founded; 1968: another 20–30 new free schools; 1969: 60–80 new free schools; 1970: over 150 new free schools; 1971–1972: over 200 new free schools.

36   John Holt, *How Children Fail* (New York: Pitman, 1964); Paul Goodman, *Compulsory Mis-education* (New York: Knopf, 1964); Sylvia Ashton-Warner, *Teacher* (New York: Simon and Shuster, 1964); Jonathan Kozol, *Death at an Early Age* (Boston: Houghton Mifflin, 1967); and *Free Schools* (Boston: Houghton Mifflin, 1972); Herbert Kohl, *36 Children* (New York: New American Library, 1967) and *The Open Classroom* (New York: New York Review, 1969); James Herndon, *The Way It Spozed to Be* (New York: Simon and Shuster, 1968); George Dennison, *The Lives of Children* (New York: Random House, 1969); Herb Snitzer, *Today Is for Children* (New York: Macmillan,

examined in this book were at least partly inspired by these authors and by pioneer schools like Summerhill.

THERAPEUTIC SCHOOLS

With the decline of the counterculture, alternative schools of the 1970s adopted a more therapeutic outlook. The emergence of Therapeutic schools was an attempt to respond to the needs of the thousands of students at risk of dropping out of conventional high schools during the late 1960s and early 1970s. A few of these students had attended alternative elementary schools and found re-entry into mainstream high schools a shock. Others had been immersed in the counterculture as teenagers and found high school overly authoritarian and alienating. Still others were bored with the traditional pedagogy, disregard of creativity, and lack of individual attention that they experienced in the school system. And, lastly, some came from difficult family situations or had learning disabilities, which mainstream schools were not yet equipped to accommodate. Some of the above students had already dropped out of high school and faced an uncertain future. For all these at-risk students, a Therapeutic alternative school could be a literal lifesaver, sparing them from life on the street or worse. The goal of most alternative school teachers during this period was to support their students as they tried to sort out their lives, and to teach them basic academic skills that they would need to support themselves.

Founders of Therapeutic schools in Canada were influenced by the humanitarian and compassionate values of the social gospel movement and Canadian social democracy.[37] Even more significant was the Human Potential Movement growing out of the 1960s. By the early 1970s, thousands of seekers, both professionals and amateurs, were pursuing all manner of personal or group transformation through a combination of psychological therapies and spiritual techniques. These included encounter

---

1972); Allen Graubard, *Free the Children* (New York: Random House, 1972); Neil Postman and Charles Weingartner, *Teaching as a Subversive Activity* (New York: Delacorte, 1969); Charles Silberman, *Crisis in the Classroom* (New York: Random House, 1970); Joseph Featherstone, *Schools Where Children Learn* (New York: Liveright, 1971); and Ivan Illich, *De-Schooling Society* (New York: Harper and Row, 1971).

37   Richard Allen, *The Social Passion* (Toronto: University of Toronto Press, 1973).

groups, Jungian analysis, meditation, yoga, and other Eastern religious practices. Two influential figures in this movement were Fritz Perls, founder of gestalt therapy, who spent his last years on Vancouver Island, and George Leonard whose *Education and Ecstasy* was read widely by alternative school teachers.[38] The combination of personal growth and social reform goals gave the 1970s alternative schools their particular character and tension.

Eventually, in Canada and especially in British Columbia, a combination of parental pressure, new directions in the education profession, and the general ambience of the times caused the public schools to begin offering a wider choice of programs and pedagogy. By 1975 several independent alternative schools had been integrated into the British Columbia public school system, and some school districts began to create their own alternative programs, thus providing facilities and resources for students not succeeding in mainstream schools. With the demand for alternatives at least partially satisfied within the public system, independent alternative schools declined. Their enduring impact was their example, which encouraged the liberalization and diversification of the public school system.

ALTERNATIVE SCHOOLS IN CANADA

The alternative schools movement in Canada began in the early 1960s, a time of economic expansion and public optimism.[39] But amidst this well-being, it was also an era of increasing dissatisfaction with aspects of mainstream society, including the regimented one-size-fits-all nature of the public education system. In response, small groups of parents and educators took the courageous step of starting their own schools. British Columbia led the way, but within a few years alternative schools sprang up in several other regions of Canada, a reflection of the times.

---

38   Frederick Perls, Ralph Hefferline, and Paul Goodman, *Gestalt Therapy: Excitement and Growth in the Human Personality* (n.p.: Gestalt Institute Press, 1951); and George Leonard, *Education and Ecstasy* (New York: Delacorte Press, 1968).

39   Jean Barman, *The West Beyond the West* (Toronto: University of Toronto Press, 1991).

Ontario became one important centre of the Canadian movement.[40] Indeed, the best known alternative school in the country was Everdale Place, an experimental high school located on a farm fifty miles north-west of Toronto. Everdale was founded by Bob Davis and Alan Rimmer in 1966.[41] Mr. Davis had previously been active in a variety of alternative causes, including nuclear disarmament organizations, the Student Christian Movement, and the "new left" Student Union for Peace Action (SUPA).[42]

Bob Davis, the charismatic co-founder of Everdale Place School, was committed to non-coercive education. Photo courtesy of Meredith MacFarquhar

40   Harley Rothstein, "Private to Public: Alternative Schools in Ontario, 1965–1975," in Nina Bascia, Esther Sokolov Fine, and Malcolm Levin, eds., *Alternative Schooling and Student Engagement: Canadian Stories of Democracy within Bureaucracy* (New York: Palgrave Macmillan, 2017), 71–94.

41   The other founding staff members were Jim Deacove, Ruth Deacove, Gail Ashby, and Eleanor Rimmer.

42   Bob Davis, personal interview, October 18, 1996.

THE EVERDALE PLACE
A SCHOOL COMMUNITY

Ontario's Everdale Place was one of the best-known Romantic or free schools in Canada.
Everdale Place School Brochure | Michael Reichmann, c. 1966

Everdale opened with sixteen students and five teachers, growing to thirty-seven students and eleven staff two years later. Opposed to the authoritarian nature of public schools, Everdale's founders believed that students should share in all decision-making, including in the vital areas of student admissions and staff hiring.[43] As at Summerhill, student attendance at classes was voluntary. But although a full slate of courses was

---

43   Bob Davis, personal interview, October 18, 1996. The school deliberately gave students a majority of members on the Hiring and Admissions Committee.

offered, the teachers were disappointed that only a few students showed sustained interest. There were only two compulsory activities: everyone had to do chores and everyone had to be at the weekly meetings.[44] These meetings could be lengthy or even tedious but were considered essential for working out school policy and inter-personal relationships. Memorable activities at Everdale included tending the farm, preparing large communal meals, constant informal music-making, and an ambitious field trip and travel program.[45] As in many alternative schools, Everdale eventually split over how much structure the staff should provide and how much freedom students should be allowed.[46] Freedom won out, but the school declined and eventually closed in 1973. In the ensuing years, Bob Davis wrote several books and became a tireless advocate for noncoercive and humanistic education.[47]

In 1967 George Martell, another key figure in Canadian alternative education, started Point Blank School in Toronto for fifteen teenage dropouts and street kids, many of whom could neither read nor write. Mr. Martell taught them to read late at night through a method he developed, inspired by Sylvia Ashton-Warner's book *Teacher*, based on stories related by the students themselves.[48] These late night educational activities were supplemented during the day with a "little kids' school" for about fifteen neighbourhood elementary children in Mr. Martell's house in the Cabbagetown neighbourhood.[49] His wife, Satu Repo, and another couple also resided in the house and taught at the school.

---

44   Bob Davis, personal interview, October 18, 1996.
45   Bob Davis took groups of students to the Toronto Courthouse, Quebec City, and to Milwaukee, where students observed the trial of a high profile anti-Vietnam war dissident.
46   Alan Rimmer, personal interview, March 29, 2014.
47   Bob Davis, *What Our High Schools Could Be: A Teacher's Reflections from the 60s to the 90s* (Toronto: Our Schools/Our Selves, 1990).
48   Sylvia Ashton-Warner taught Maori children to read and write using her "Organic Method" in which she helped students develop a "key vocabulary" consisting of important objects and concepts from their lives.
49   George Martell, personal interview, April 14, 1997.

Superschool was located in an old house on Beverley Street in Toronto.
Globe and Mail, September 3, 1968

Superschool meetings were based on the Summerhill model: one person, any age, one vote. *Toronto Daily Star*, April 7, 1969

Another alternative, Superschool, sister school to Everdale, was founded in 1968 by teacher Connie Mungall, following a meeting in her living room with a group of local teenagers unhappy with their public school. Superschool opened in a large house in downtown Toronto with twenty-eight students, both secondary and elementary, and three teachers.[50] The school was known for its extensive urban field trip program and its Summerhill-style school meetings. The staff at these three schools were well acquainted with each other and shared a common educational philosophy.[51]

A few of these teachers sought to spread the word about alternative education and created *This Magazine is about Schools* (1966–1973), a radical journal about alternative or free schools that circulated across Canada and the United States.[52] The influential magazine was edited by Bob Davis, George Martell, and Satu Repo, assisted by Gail Ashby, and contained a combination of articles about individual alternative schools along with a broad debate about the future of education, the alternative schools movement, and society.[53] At its height of popularity, *This Magazine* reached an impressive circulation of over ten thousand.[54] Mr. Martell also wrote widely about education and its political implications in a class society.[55]

Numerous alternative schools were established across Canada during the early 1970s, many the result of increased parent activism.[56] These parent groups shared a dissatisfaction with their children's education in the public school system. The Ottawa New School was founded in 1969 by a group of professional and academic parents concerned about the public system's rigidity. The school opened with eighteen students and two teachers, one trained in Progressive methods. The children chose their

---

50 See "28 students off to Superschool," *Globe and Mail* (Toronto), September 3, 1968.
51 Gail Ashby, personal interview, March 29, 2014. Ms. Ashby was a teacher at both Everdale and Superschool.
52 *This Magazine is about Schools* (Toronto), 1966–1973, volumes 1–6.
53 Satu Repo, ed., *This Book is About Schools* (New York: Random House, 1970).
54 Satu Repo, personal interview, March 25, 2014.
55 See George Martell, *The Politics of the Canadian Public School* (Toronto: James Lewis and Samuel, 1974). Also, "Where Have All the Free Schools Gone?" an interview with Bob Davis, George Martell, and Satu Repo, in Douglas Myers, ed., *The Failure of Educational Reform in Canada* (Toronto: McClelland and Stewart, 1973), 75–94. First published in *Canadian Forum*, October 1972.
56 Sharon Kirsh, Roger Simon, and Malcolm Levin, eds., *Directory of Canadian Alternative and Innovative Education* (Toronto: Ontario Institute for Studies in Education, 1973) listed forty-one alternative schools in Canada in 1973.

own activities, and the school was governed by the parents. But the school split during its second year over how much structure the school should provide and eventually closed in 1972.[57]

This Magazine is about Schools was read widely by alternative school advocates and radical educators across Canada and the United States. Cover of Volume 1, Issue 1, 1966, reproduced with permission of *This Magazine*

---

57 Deborah Gorham, "The Ottawa New School and Educational Dissent in Ontario in the Hall-Dennis Era," *Historical Studies in Education* 21, no. 2 (Fall 2009).

Greenhouse School, in Regina, was started in 1971 by a group of parents and teachers led by head teacher Joan Sass. The school opened with eighteen students and met in a large house (it actually was green). School policy emphasized direct parent involvement, small classes, co-operation rather than competition, and the widespread use of community resource people. Students chose their own individualized activities each day and progressed at their own rate.[58] The school affiliated with the Regina Board of Education in 1974 and received some financial support, but with continued shortfalls, exacerbated by declining enrolment, the school closed in 1982.[59]

The Saturday School in Calgary was founded in 1972 by a group of activist parents and opened with twenty-two students, eventually increasing to forty. Emphasizing aesthetic education and the arts, as well as an integrated curriculum, inquiry and discovery, individual progress, co-operative decision-making, and learning in the community, the project generated much excitement among the parents.[60] Saturday joined the Calgary public school system in 1975. One of the founding parents, the historian Robert Stamp, wrote *About Schools*, a guide for parents about how to be more involved in setting public school policy, or how to start their own school.[61]

These three schools all espoused familiar Progressive or child-centred principles. But as in many parent-driven alternative schools, there was often less agreement than the participants originally thought. They all knew what they were against but frequently couldn't agree on what they were for. In particular, tension often arose over how much freedom versus how much structure was optimal for students. Some schools were successful in charting a middle ground, but in others the differences

---

58   Carrie Shapiro Greschner, personal interview, 2015; Greenhouse School Prospectus, 1974, in Carrie Shapiro Greschner document collection in possession of the author. Also, Gillian McCreary, *Greenhouse, 1970–1977: A Social Historical Analysis of an Alternative School* (master's thesis, University of Saskatchewan, 1978).

59   *Regina Leader-Post*, May 24, 1977, 35; and September 10, 1982, 3. Enrolment had dropped from a high of thirty students to only twelve in 1982.

60   Robert Stamp, personal interview, April 9, 1997; and Robert Stamp, *The Saturday School: How It Began* (Calgary: Saturday School Society, 1973).

61   Robert Stamp, *About Schools: What Every Canadian Parent Should Know* (Toronto: New Press, 1975).

were irreconcilable. When parents at St. Norbert Community School in Winnipeg attempted to find a balance between adult direction and student freedom, they discovered that "it is much harder to devise educational practices and environments than it is to state high-minded ideals."[62]

By the late 1960s, public interest in alternative schools was growing in Canada, as evidenced by the Ontario government's Hall-Dennis Report, *Living and Learning*, and the British Columbia Teachers' Federation Report, *Involvement: The Key to Better Schools*.[63] Both published in 1968, these were groundbreaking documents advocating sweeping and radical change.[64] In the 1970s, a few forward-thinking school districts in Canada began to sponsor alternative schools in response to parental demand.[65] This occurred most notably in Vancouver and Toronto, partly due to the election of left-of-centre reformist trustees to these cities' school boards in the late 1960s and their eventual majority on those boards by the early 1970s.[66]

In 1970 the Toronto Board of Education created SEED, a unique alternative high school, offering a wide choice of activities and field trips.[67] This grew out of a creative summer enrichment program proposed by reform trustee Fiona Nelson and started in 1968 for older students who

---

62   Sharon Kirsh, Roger Simon, and Malcolm Levin, eds., *Directory of Canadian Alternative and Innovative Education* (Toronto: Ontario Institute for Studies in Education, 1973), 44.

63   Hall-Dennis Report, *Living and Learning* (Toronto: Government of Ontario, 1968); and *Involvement: The Key to Better Schools* (Vancouver: British Columbia Teachers' Federation, 1968).

64   See J. Donald Wilson, "From the Swinging Sixties to the Sobering Seventies," in Hugh A. Stevenson and J. Donald Wilson, eds., *Precepts, Policy, and Process: Perspectives on Contemporary Canadian Education* (London, ON: Alexander, Blake Associates, 1976), 21–36, for a description of the educational mood in Canada during this period.

65   Harley Rothstein, "Private to Public: Alternative Schools in Ontario, 1965–1975," in Nina Bascia, Esther Sokolov Fine, and Malcolm Levin, eds., *Alternative Schooling and Student Engagement: Canadian Stories of Democracy within Bureaucracy* (New York: Palgrave Macmillan, 2017), 71–94.

66   In Toronto Fiona Nelson was elected as a trustee in 1969 and became Chair of the School Board in 1974. See her article "Community Schools in Toronto: A Sign of Hope," *Canadian Forum*, October/November 1972. Also, Fiona Nelson, personal interview, March 2014. See also, Jane Gaskell and Ben Levin, *Making a Difference in Urban Schools: Ideas, Politics, and Pedagogy* (Toronto: University of Toronto Press, 2012). Gordon Cressey was another well-known reform trustee, elected in 1969.

67   The name was derived from the phrase "Shared Experience, Exploration, and Discovery."

were unable to find summer employment.[68] Under the direction of Murray Shukyn, SEED was aimed at motivated students, identified as "self-start-ers," who had been bored in mainstream schools.[69] Four teachers were assigned to cover the academic subjects, but the heart of the program was delivered by volunteers or "catalysts" who were brought in, most arranged by the students, to teach a wide array of innovative courses. SEED utilized the resources of the urban community, offering over sixty courses taught by the volunteers.[70]

In 1972 ALPHA School was created by the Toronto Board when a group of parents campaigned for an alternative school for their elementary children.[71] The school accommodated a variety of learning styles as well as significant parental involvement. Three more alternative programs, Contact, Subway, and Laneway, joined the Toronto District between 1973 and 1975. Contact was started by a group of teachers, led by Harry Smaller, in 1973 for the benefit of high school students at risk of dropping out. Subway was initiated by Board Office officials in 1974 and had students spending most of their time learning in the community.[72] Laneway, originally founded by a group of low-income activist parents, was taken under the school board umbrella in 1975 and taught basic skills to disadvantaged students. The expansion of Toronto's alternative programs was promoted by administrator Dale Shuttleworth.[73]

---

68   Dale Shuttleworth, *Schooling for Life: Community Education and Social Enterprise* (Toronto: University of Toronto Press, 2010), 151.

69   Murray Shukyn, personal interview, March 26, 2014; Shukyn, "Shared Experience, Exploration, and Discovery," *NASSP Bulletin* 55, 355, May 1971, 151; and Beverley Shukyn and Murray Shukyn, *You Can't Take a Bathtub on the Subway: A Personal History of SEED, a New Approach to Secondary School Education.* (Toronto: Holt, Rinehart, and Winston, 1973).

70   Douglas Yip, *SEED: A Preliminary Report* (Toronto: Board of Education, 1971).

71   The name ALPHA was derived from the phrase "A Lot of People Hoping for an Alternative."

72   Dale Shuttleworth, *Schooling for Life: Community Education and Social Enterprise* (Toronto: University of Toronto Press, 2010), provides a thorough account of the growth of alternative schools in the Toronto School District. Also, personal interview, March 31, 2014.

73   Dr. Shuttleworth chaired the Toronto School Board's Alternative and Community Programs Committee.

The Vancouver School District also responded to demand from parents for alternative programs.[74] Between 1970 and 1975, the Vancouver Board created or supported dozens of small niche programs, some consistent with Progressive child-centred philosophy and others with rehabilitation or therapeutic goals. The rehabilitation programs were an attempt to accommodate the hundreds of Vancouver students identified by the district as at risk of dropping out of school entirely. Among these programs were City School, started by the School District in 1971, and Total Education and Ideal School, both adopted by the Vancouver School Board in 1974. Alternative programs were supported by reformist trustees including Peter Bullen, Olive Johnson, Katherine Mirhady, and Elliott Gose. Equally supportive were innovative teachers and liberal administrators including Alf Clinton, Jim Carter, and John Wormsbecker. Joining them were John Wiens of Victoria and BC Human Resources Minister Norman Levi. They understood the need to open the public schools to a wider variety of student learning needs, a diverse spectrum of pedagogy, and more choice for students.[75]

BRITISH COLUMBIA

The quest for a new child-centred and humanistic education in Canada was born in British Columbia in the first years of the 1960s, significantly earlier than in the rest of the country. Alternative schools in BC were also more prolific and varied than in any other province. By 1966 four alternative schools had already been founded in British Columbia, and by the early 1970s numbered more than twenty. This book examines the development of ten British Columbia alternative schools representing a range of variables, including urban and rural, elementary and secondary, parent-run and teacher-run, as well as Progressive, Romantic, and Therapeutic. The heyday of the alternative schools movement spanned the decade and a half between 1960 and 1975. These schools were all independent, small, and child-centred, and they allowed considerable student autonomy.

---

74 The centre-left civic party, TEAM, won a majority on the School Board in 1972. Olive Johnson, a writer and tireless advocate, chair Peter Bullen, future chair Katherine Mirhady, and Elliott Gose were noted reform trustees.

75 BC public alternative schools are discussed in detail in Chapter 15.

The earliest British Columbia alternative schools were of the Progressive type—the Argenta Friends School founded by two teachers, John and Helen Stevenson, in a remote corner of the West Kootenays in 1959, and the New School in 1962 by a group of Vancouver parents, all UBC professors and their spouses.[76] Craigdarroch School in Victoria, launched in 1966 by David Hummel, was another parent-created Progressive school. Meanwhile, in 1965, the first Romantic or free school in Canada, the Barker Free School, was founded in Greater Vancouver by Bob Barker, a Summerhill-trained teacher. It was followed by two more Romantic schools—Knowplace in Vancouver, initiated by a group of assertive teenagers in 1967, and the Saturna Island Free School, founded by teacher Tom Durrie and Bill Sheffeld on a quiet Gulf Island in 1968.

During the 1970s, most BC alternative schools were Therapeutic or rehabilitation schools. These included Total Education in Vancouver, started in 1970 by Dan and Cathy Meakes to provide an education to teenagers at risk; Windsor House in North Vancouver, founded by teacher Helen Hughes in her own house in 1971; and Ideal School in Vancouver, a more academically oriented alternative school founded by former private school teacher Garry Nixon in 1972. The tenth school, the Vallican Whole School, initiated by Joel Harris, Marcia Braundy, and a group of parents in a back-to-the-land community in the Slocan Valley in 1972, exhibited many characteristics of a Romantic School but began later, during the Therapeutic period.

These ten schools spanned the three periods identified by my research—Progressive, Romantic, and Therapeutic. One of the schools, the New School in Vancouver, was unique in having evolved through all three periods. These ten British Columbia alternative schools and their legacy are the subject of this book.

What was it about British Columbia that encouraged the rapid development of alternative schools? The province was a significant location

---

76 The founding parents of the New School were: Norman and Marilyn Epstein, Don and Julia Brown, Elliott and Kathy Gose, Werner and Rita Cohn, and Mac and Ruth McCarthy. Total Education teacher Larry Haberlin joined the founders within a few months of that school's inception. Head teachers including Lloyd Arntzen (New School) and Joan Schwartz (Craigdarroch) also played important roles in defining their schools.

for alternative schools due to its tradition of individualism and popular opposition to central authority, which led to the establishment of many intentional communities in the province throughout the twentieth century.[77] The social gospel, socialist, co-operative, and labour movements also had a strong presence in BC, where many individuals participating in alternative schools had been active in labour unions, the NDP, or in religious groups oriented to social action. Progressive educational theories were well-established in the province, and Romantic ideas found an eager following by the 1960s. Furthermore, the tradition of private schooling was well entrenched in British Columbia, and until 1977 no legislation whatsoever regulated independent schools. Although philosophically very different, alternative schools shared one common belief with the many private British-style schools in BC: the idea that personal development (or what British schools would have called "character-building") was almost as important as academics.[78] Lastly, British Columbia's geographical location also contributed to its predilection to nurture innovative ideas. Because the province is situated on the West Coast of North America as well as the northwestern edge of the continent's population centres, west- and north-bound reformers, radicals, and seekers of all kinds ended up in British Columbia. As BC was "the end of the road," many of them stayed.

Another factor unique to British Columbia was a large influx of immigrants from the United States. The many academics up to 1965 were followed in the late 1960s by thousands of young Americans who left that country for political reasons, mainly their opposition to the Vietnam War. Many were Californians who brought elements of the counterculture with them. Ideas and values popularized by the political movements and counterculture of the 1960s had a profound effect on the development of alternative schools in British Columbia.

It would be difficult to overestimate the historical importance to British Columbia of the counterculture and 1960s aesthetics and values, particularly in Vancouver, the Gulf Islands, and the West Kootenay region.

---

77   See Andrew Scott, *The Promise of Paradise: Utopian Communities in British Columbia* (Vancouver: Whitecap, 1997) and Justine Brown, *All Possible Worlds* (Vancouver: New Star Books, 1995).

78   Jean Barman, *Growing Up British in British Columbia: Boys in Private School* (Vancouver: UBC Press, 1984), 38, 131.

These influences included drug use, sexual experimentation, rock music and psychedelic art, mysticism and Eastern spirituality, personal growth therapies, and values of participatory democracy, anti-intellectualism, communitarianism, and by the early 1970s, the seeds of feminism and environmentalism. British Columbia was one of two centres in Canada (the other being Toronto) where these influences took hold and flourished. Theodore Roszak, who coined the term "counterculture" in his widely read book on that movement, described it as the cultural expression of New Left politics, an effort to discover "new types of community, new family patterns, new sexual mores, new kinds of livelihood, new aesthetic forms, new personal identities on the far side of power politics, the bourgeois home, and the consumer society."[79] Above all, the 1960s was about personal freedom and social transformation. These were also the primary goals of most alternative schools. The history of alternative schools is, in large part, a story of the 1960s.[80]

SOURCES

Historical evidence for this study comes from many sources. I studied individual school archives and document collections, many of which former teachers and parents discovered in their basements. I consulted numerous public documents, including Vancouver School Board and provincial Department of Human Resources records, and federal government

79   Theodore Roszak, *The Making of a Counter Culture* (New York: Doubleday, 1969), 66.

80   For Canada in the 1960s see: Doug Owram, *Born at the Right Time* (Toronto: University of Toronto Press, 1996); Brian Palmer, *Canada's 1960s* (Toronto: University of Toronto Press, 2009); Myrna Kostash, *Long Way from Home* (Toronto: James Lorimer, 1980); Dimitry Anastakis, *The Sixties* (Montreal: McGill–Queens University Press, 2008); and Lara Campbell, Dominique Clément, and Gregory S. Kealey, *Debating Dissent* (Toronto: University of Toronto Press, 2012). For the United States see Edward Morgan, *The Sixties Experience* (Philadelphia: Temple University Press, 1991); Todd Gitlin, *The Sixties: Years of Hope, Days of Rage* (New York: Bantam, 1987); Maurice Isserman and Michael Kazin, *America Divided* (Oxford: Oxford University Press, 2008); Mark Hamilton Lytle, *America's Uncivil Wars* (New York: Oxford University Press, 2006); David Farber and Beth Bailey, eds. *The Columbia Guide to America in the 1960s* (New York: Columbia University Press, 2001). For other countries see Arthur Marwick, *The Sixties* (Oxford: Oxford University Press, 1998) and Mark Kurlansky, *1968: The Year That Rocked the World* (New York: Random House, 2004).

files in the National Archives of Canada pertaining to the Company of Young Canadians, which funded several schools. I also read more than 130 articles about alternative schools published in British Columbia newspapers and magazines between 1960 and 1975, an indication of just how interested the public was in these unique schools.

I consulted many books written by Progressive school advocates in the early twentieth century, as well as books by thinkers about or founders of alternative schools between 1960 and 1975. These historical accounts provide important background and context to the alternative schools movement and help us understand why these schools developed. I also consulted many valuable secondary-source books.

Another major source was the oral evidence gleaned from my own recorded interviews with over 350 former alternative school students, parents, and teachers.[81] Participation in alternative schools was a significant and formative event in the lives of these individuals, and their memories were extensive and vivid. I selected interview subjects in a "chain of acquaintanceship" technique, developed by Neil Sutherland, to uncover "overlapping memories."[82] Although there was remarkable agreement among the individuals' personal accounts of events, I cross-checked all interview information with the accounts of other participants and with the documentary evidence.

Oral historians are aware that individual memories of the past are fallible and that events are seen with the perspective of hindsight, giving them meaning according to the subject's present point of view. However, as Paul Thompson points out in *The Voice of the Past*, all historical evidence is ultimately created by individuals. The historian's job is to examine every source, oral or written, for internal consistency, confirmation in other sources, and potential bias.[83] According to Neil Sutherland, personal memories of recurrent situations (what he calls "scripts") are usually reliable, even if some details of individual events may be inaccurate.

---

81 I conducted these interviews either by telephone or in person and, with one exception, audio recorded each.
82 Neil Sutherland, *Growing Up: Childhood in English Canada from the Great War to the Age of Television* (Toronto: University of Toronto Press, 1997), 17–18.
83 Paul Thompson, *The Voice of the Past* (Oxford: Oxford University Press, 1978), 102.

Furthermore, the very subjectivity of oral evidence is invaluable in re-creating the emotional context of past events.[84]

This book examines the curriculum, governance, and day-to-day life of these ten British Columbia alternative schools, as well as the underlying ideology or world view of their founders. It endeavours to provide insight into that formative experience for the students, teachers, and parents involved in this enterprise. I also provide figures to give a sense of the educational outcomes for the students, though this is not a sociological or statistical study. As well, it's useful to remember that those involved in the phenomenon called the alternative schools movement were not a representative cross-section of society. The great majority of parents were middle-class educators, professionals, or creative artists. This book tells the story of these extraordinary people and what became of the students after their alternative school experience—an experience that had a profound effect on their lives.

---

84   Neil Sutherland, Growing Up: Childhood in English Canada from the Great War to the Age of Television (Toronto: University of Toronto Press, 1997), 9–15.

Part One

PROGRESSIVE SCHOOLS

Chapter 2

THE NEW SCHOOL: EARLY YEARS

In the fall of 1960, several University of British Columbia professors and their spouses began to talk about opening an alternative school for their children in Vancouver. At a New Year's Eve party that year, five couples—Don and Julia Brown, Norman and Marilyn Epstein, Elliott and Kathy Gose, Werner and Rita Cohn, and Mac and Ruth McCarthy—decided to form a weekly planning group. During these discussions they explored Progressive educational theory and co-operative organizational structure. By the fall of 1961, they believed there was enough agreement among the participants to take the next step. They were joined by Warren and Ellen Tallman, Norman and Gloria Levi, and several other families, and the group began serious planning for the establishment of an independent, parent-operated Progressive school.

The timing was no coincidence. The Chant Report, the end result of a major Royal Commission on Education, had been released on December 29, 1960.[1] The dissatisfied parents objected strenuously to the report's traditionalist approach to the "three Rs" and its relegation of the arts to frill status.[2] They were frustrated by what they saw as a lack of creative teaching and meaningful enrichment in the school system and by a

---

1   John Arnett, "Four Profs Plan Own School: Disenchanted with Chant," *Vancouver Sun*, February 7, 1961, 1. This was corroborated by several parent interviews. S.N.F. Chant, J.E. Liersch, and R.P. Walrod, *Report of the Royal Commission on Education* (Victoria, BC: Province of British Columbia, 1960).

2   Gloria Levi, Marilyn Epstein, personal interviews, April 1987. The encouragement of the creative arts was also a central goal for the parents who founded Saturday School in Calgary. See Robert Stamp, *About Schools* (Don Mills: New Press, 1975): 144.

pervasive unstimulating atmosphere.[3] They concluded that public education in British Columbia was "dull and disagreeable."[4]

These parents saw public school as a bureaucratic, lock-step, and conformist system incapable of responding to students as individuals and lacking a basic respect for young people. They believed discipline practices were inhumane. Rita Cohn described the public schools as "uptight and conventional" places where her children had no personal freedom to move around, not even to the bathroom.[5] Don Brown objected to the schools' curricular conservatism, their neglect of the arts, and their "authoritarian stiffness."[6] Ellen Tallman expressed her dissatisfaction with rigid and unimaginative schools: "Karen hated school so much. Something had to be done!"[7] The result was the founding of the New School.

New School parents held a number of common values influenced by Progressive, Romantic, and socialist ideas. They were particularly drawn to the Progressive educational ideas developed by John Dewey at New York's Columbia University. One parent, Kathy Gose, received her early schooling at Edgewood School, a Deweyan Progressive school connected with Columbia Teachers College.[8] The experience left a deep impression and she subsequently employed Progressive methods as a teacher at a two-room school in rural New York State.[9] Another parent, Barbara Beach, attended City and Country School in New York City, a well-known Progressive school founded in 1914.[10] Another, Rita Cohn, had trained as a teacher in Progressive methods at Columbia,[11] and other parents were

---

3   Neil Sutherland, "The Triumph of Formalism: Elementary Schooling in Vancouver from the 1920s to the 1960s," *BC Studies* 69/70 (Spring/Summer 1986): 182–186.

4   John Arnett, "Four Profs Plan Own School," *Vancouver Sun*, February 7, 1961, 1, and Kathy Gose, personal interview April 1987.

5   Rita Cohn, personal interview, April 1987.

6   Don Brown, personal interview, January 1991.

7   Ellen Tallman, personal interview, April 1987.

8   Edgewood School was associated with Marietta Johnson, a leading proponent of American progressivism.

9   Kathy Gose, personal interview, April 1987.

10 Barbara Beach, personal interview, June 1991. The founder was Caroline Pratt. For more on early Progressive educators see Lawrence Cremin, *The Transformation of the School* (New York: Random House, 1961): 147–152 and 202–207.

11 Rita Cohn, personal interview, April 1987.

familiar with Black Mountain College in North Carolina,[12] and the Putney School in Vermont.[13]

Although only seven of the thirty-two inaugural families were originally from the United States, the American parents had a significant impact on the school's philosophy.[14] Most of the Americans were academics who had come to Vancouver to teach at UBC. They shared a liberal arts, intellectual, "Ivy League" ethos; valued the fine arts; and enjoyed arguing about abstract ideas. Several later taught in "Arts I," UBC's interdisciplinary humanities program.[15] They also placed a high value on individual freedom. Those who had come to Vancouver from northeastern United States or northern California were familiar with alternative schooling elsewhere, and one parent remembered being "shocked by the lack of alternative schools" when she arrived in Vancouver.[16]

New School parents favoured a "child-centred" education that built on each child's interests, creativity, and individuality. They subscribed to the Progressive slogans "learning by doing" and "learning through experience." They wanted a curriculum that would encourage their children to explore at their own pace, develop independent and critical thinking skills, and question authority. They also hoped the school would nurture attitudes of co-operation and self-discipline. Many parents termed themselves educationally Progressive but only a few, such as Don Brown (a Canadian philosopher), had studied Dewey's ideas carefully.

There was also a distinctly utopian vision among some founding parents who expressed a yearning for a closer community and had Romantic notions of the one-room schoolhouse.[17] This coincided with Rousseauian, naturalistic, and anarchistic ideas emphasizing freedom, natural growth,

---

12 Black Mountain College was one of several universities incorporating Progressive ideas into its undergraduate program during the 1930s and 1940s. See Lawrence Cremin, *The Transformation of the School* (New York: Random House, 1961), 308.

13 Jim Winter, personal interview, April 1987. See Susan Lloyd, *The Putney School: A Progressive Experiment* (New Haven: Yale University Press, 1987). Putney was founded by Carmelita Hinton, who also taught at Shady Hill School in Boston.

14 Americans among the inaugural group were the Beaches, Cohns, Goses, McCarthys, Tallmans, Winters, Marilyn Epstein, and Gloria Levi.

15 Discussion with Jean Barman. The American academics were influential in such UBC programs as Arts I and the history undergraduate honours program.

16 Barbara Beach, personal interview, June 1991.

17 Jim Winter, personal interview, April 1987.

and self-expression. The publication of A. S. Neill's *Summerhill* in 1960 generated a great deal of discussion and excitement among the parents.[18] However, most parents did not want a strictly Summerhillian school, and just how far they were prepared to go in this direction was always contentious. Progressives and Romantics never resolved their differences, causing the school serious problems in years to come.

A few New School parents were socialists and saw the school as part of a broader movement encouraging people to take control of their own lives and transform society.[19] However, although generally on the left of the political spectrum, most parents were not Marxist socialists. They were activists when faced with social problems, democrats committed to resolving issues through participation, questioners of traditional institutions and social norms, and egalitarians. In theory many parents were collectivists, but they respected individuality and were primarily interested in developing the potential and interests of each person. In this enterprise they favoured "creative individualism" rather than "competitive individualism" and believed that free individuals would produce a free society.[20] They shared many attitudes and values but often for different reasons. At the New School, Progressives and Romantics frequently referred to each other as "socialists" and "anarchists," which describes something of the style of the two groups.

Their activism took many forms. Some were involved in the New Democratic Party, while others were active in peace, disarmament, or civil rights groups. Several participants had been influenced by politico-religious movements. Some parents had explored non-violence inspired by Quakerism, others were brought up with a Methodist social conscience, still others were active in the Unitarian Church,[21] and several Jewish parents had been active in labour Zionism.[22] There was certainly

---

18   A. S. Neill, *Summerhill* (London: Hart, 1960).
19   Julia Brown, personal interview, April 1987.
20   I am indebted to Hilda Thomas for this idea, December 1991.
21   The Unitarian minister Reverend Philip Hewett was a New School parent in the mid-1960s.
22   About 10 per cent of New School families were Jewish. They were evenly divided among those on the political left and those holding more conservative views. However, there was a perception among some later participants that the school had

something of the kibbutz spirit present in the New School community.[23] Although the precise political orientations of the founding parents varied, the majority believed that Progressive education would lead children to constructive criticism of their society,[24] thus producing individuals who would help bring about social change.[25] These views were in keeping with the intellectual and political climate of the early 1960s in Canada—a time of idealism, questioning, and optimism about the future.

New School parents believed strongly in participatory democratic decision-making and shared an interest in co-operative organization. Some founding parents had originally met at a parent co-operative preschool,[26] while others had met at the Child Study Centre at UBC.[27] Several parents knew Mary Thomson, a consultant to Vancouver's parent co-operative preschools, and her husband, Watson Thomson, a pioneer of adult and co-operative education in Canada.[28] Ms. Thomson[29] was an important resource during the planning stages.[30] In keeping with their socialist and egalitarian values, New School parents developed a sliding fee scale based on each family's ability to pay. This would ensure that no families were excluded for economic reasons and would replace the traditional private school scholarship system.[31] The sliding scale remained a central New School policy throughout its life.

Dissatisfaction with the education system was an important aspect of the parents' social and political outlook. They objected to competitive and anti-social values (such as stereotyping of Indigenous children) they believed were transmitted through the public schools. They distrusted

---

been started by a group of "Jewish professors." There is no evidence that their Jewish backgrounds alone had a significant impact on the life of the school.

23   Jim Winter, personal interview, April 1987.
24   Don Brown, personal interview, January 1991.
25   Norman Epstein, personal interview, April 1987.
26   Rita Cohn, Ellen Tallman, Julia Brown, personal interviews, April 1987.
27   Laura Jamieson, personal interview, June 1991; Reverend Philip Hewitt, personal interview, June 1991.
28   Several founding parents knew Watson Thomson and were familiar with his work (Chapter 6). See Michael Welton's biography *To Be and Build the Glorious World* (PhD thesis, University of BC, 1983).
29   The term *Ms.* was not used in the 1960s, but for the contemporary reader, I have used it in place of *Mrs.* or *Miss.*
30   Ellen Tallman, personal interview, April 1987.
31   Norman Epstein, personal interview, April 1987.

large institutions, governments, and strongly religious or nationalistic sentiments.[32] Individualists among the group believed unquestioning nationalism inhibited independent thinking, while the socialists equated nationalism with capitalism and war.

But despite their opposition to the public school system, the founding parents could not agree on precisely what kind of school they wanted. Some favoured a Deweyan Progressive school, others leaned toward a Summerhillian Romantic school, some envisioned an enriched curriculum, and a few wanted to make a political statement. Some parents investigated the ideas of the pioneering educators Maria Montessori and Rudolph Steiner.[33] The group's educational theories were not clearly defined, and people meant different things by "structure, creativity, interests, and freedom."[34] One parent wondered in 1964 "how many of us are in agreement in our use of the term Progressive?"[35] This lack of consensus would cause serious disagreements throughout the life of the school.

SERIOUS PLANNING

A front-page article outlining the goals of the New School appeared in the *Vancouver Sun* on February 7, 1961, titled "Four Profs Plan Own School."[36] The article reported that the professors were "disenchanted with the Chant Report" and would follow the "Progressive system of education." The school would be "informal, unregimented, non-competitive, and nonconformist" with teaching "geared to the individual needs of each child" on the assumption that "learning is interesting and enjoyable." The fine arts would be central to the curriculum. The school was to be accessible to anyone who agreed with its aims: "Fees will be worked out on

---

32   In his study of alternative schools in the United States, Daniel Duke found a common belief among parents that they had "lost control of their institutions." *The Retransformation of the School* (Chicago: Nelson-Hall, 1978), 115.

33   For more on Maria Montessori, Rudolph Steiner, and their worldwide following, see Chapter 13.

34   Barbara Beach, personal interview, June 1991.

35   Charles Christopherson, "Re: The New School," April 20, 1964.

36   John Arnett, "Four Profs Plan Own School," *Vancouver Sun*, February 7, 1961, 1. It was actually five.

the basis of ability to pay. We don't want it to be a school for university professors' children only."

DISENCHANTED WITH CHANT

4 Profs Plan Own School

By JOHN ARNETT

Four University of B.C. professors, disenchanted with the Chant report, are planning to set up a private school for their children.

They charge that the present school system is dull and disagreeable and recommendations of UBC Dean S. N. F. Chant's commission on education won't change it.

They started planning the school last fall but, said Elliott B. Gose, professor of English: "We felt the Chant report made our efforts more appropriate."

Classes will follow the progressive system of education, said Prof. Gose. They will be informal, unregimented, non-competitive and non conformist.

The Chant report said the primary aim of the school system should be the promotion of the intellectual development of the students, with greater emphasis on the core subjects, mathematics and English, and less emphasis on arts.

The professors' school would include fine arts at the core of the curriculum, said Prof. Gose. Children will have freedom to choose the curriculum best suited to them.

Other UBC professors on the planning committee are: Donald G. Brown, philosophy; Werner Cohn, sociology, and Norman Epstein, chemical engineering. H. R. MacCarthy, an entomologist, is also a member.

The professors' school is expected to have a starting

NORMAN EPSTEIN
...on planning group

enrolment of 30 students in the equivalent of the first three grades, said Prof. Gose. The founders have four children who will attend.

He said the planning committee hopes the school will eventually provide classes from kindergarten to Grade 12.

Fees will be worked out on the basis of ability to pay, said Prof. Gose. "We don't want it to be a school for university professors' children only." he said.

"Everybody who is in agreement with the aims of the school should be able to send their children to it, re-

Please Turn to Page Two
See: "School"

Vancouver Sun, February 7, 1961.

The entire planning process took two years and included long debates about theory and governance as well as detailed committee work on practical matters such as finances, recruitment, and physical space. The New School was incorporated under the Societies Act in February 1962 to "establish and maintain a non-profit co-operative school," to provide an "experimental and Progressive" education, and to "minimize the exclusion of children on economic grounds."[37] The first board was elected with Elliott Gose as President.[38] The board represented a variety of ideologies and included two business people who added some badly needed practical and financial expertise. The co-operative governing structure was based on "individuality, mutual respect, and trust in democratic procedures."

---

37 New School Constitution, February 13, 1962.
38 The New School Prospectus, 1962, 3. Board members in the first two years were Elliott Gose, Don Brown, Charles Christopherson, Gwen Creech, Norman Epstein, Pat Hanson, Ean Hay, Ken McFarland, Alan Tolliday, Ellen Tallman, and Andy Johnston. Elliott Gose became a Vancouver school trustee ten years later.

Parents would share "a fair distribution of the burden" of supporting the school. The prospectus stated prophetically: "The school is for children but parents are also engaged in an educational experiment."[39]

After many hours of discussion, drafts, and position papers, a comprehensive prospectus explaining the New School's approach to Progressive learning was completed in June 1962. Much of the school's educational theory came from John Dewey. Children would be respected for their individual nature and humanity and would progress through the curriculum at their own rates and in their own ways. The school would offer individualized instruction, a flexible curriculum, and small classes. Activities would derive from student interests: "the child must do the work of learning; his activity is most satisfying and productive when it stems from his own interests." The encouragement of artistic expression would be an essential goal: "Through the arts a child learns to express and develop his personality and to approach the basic skills more creatively. The arts are not frills but a basic part of the curriculum."

Developing critical thinking and problem-solving skills was a primary goal, and the New School would encourage students' natural curiosity. The prospectus stated that each student would "actively experience his education rather than passively accept it. The work of a teacher is not only to communicate a body of knowledge but to create conditions under which the students will develop an ability to think through problems and to be creative." This would necessitate an informal classroom atmosphere with interdisciplinary projects and experimentation. Nevertheless, prospective parents were assured that instruction in the basic subjects would be "at least equivalent to that in the public schools over the long run." In this assertion the founders overestimated their capacity to carry this out.

A central goal of the New School was the promotion of co-operation rather than competition, and there would be no examinations or grading systems. Parents believed that competition "aside from demoralizing some and distorting relations among all, introduces irrelevant motives into children's work and confuses their values." The school would encourage growth in self-discipline, self-reliance, and independence. Tolerance and respect for individual differences would be highly valued, and the school

---

39   This and the next five quoted passages are from the 1962 Prospectus, 1–2.

would not promote any religious or nationalistic bias. Lastly, New School parents were determined that school would be an enjoyable experience for their children and that learning would be fun.

One difficult policy issue confronted the group—whether the school should accept children with learning, emotional, or behavioural disabilities for whom there was little assistance available in the public school system. Although the parents were compassionate individuals who did not want to turn away students they thought they could help, this was to be a school for "normal children" and required a careful "balancing act."[40] The school accepted several students with reading disabilities and one autistic child, but the number was kept deliberately low so they could be absorbed without substantially altering the program. Parents worried that too many "problem students," as they called them, would change the basic nature of the school.[41] The 1964 prospectus warned that the school would not accept children whose "problems require special facilities which the school cannot adequately provide."[42]

The teachers had little expertise in handling reading disabilities and there were no diagnostic services. Nevertheless, one parent reported that her child was treated for mild dyslexia that she believed would have been undetected in the public system at that time. Another parent, whose son had a reading disability, thought he would have been in "bad trouble" in public school and praised the teachers who "worked all the time with him and really brought him through."[43] These successes were exceptions, however. The issue was never resolved, and in 1965 the school began to accept a higher proportion of special-needs students.

New families were attracted primarily through word of mouth. Some parents read about the school in newspaper advertisements and articles,[44] while others saw a television interview with Elliott Gose, Don Brown, and Marilyn Epstein on the CBC program *Almanac*."[45] Prospective parents

---

40 Gloria Levi, personal interview, April 1987.
41 Norman Epstein, personal interview, April 1987. Also Charles Christopherson, "Re: The New School," April 1964. Some fears were exaggerated in 1964 but proved to be well founded five years later.
42 The New School Prospectus, 1964, 2.
43 New School parent, personal interview, April 1987.
44 Gloria Levi, personal interview, April 1987.
45 Alan and Elma Tolliday, personal interview, April 1987.

were interviewed at their homes by members of the admissions commit-tee to ensure that the applicants' educational goals and expectations were compatible with those of the New School. By the spring of 1962, thirty-two families had enrolled their children.

Almost half of the parents were professional educators (nine university professors and six teachers), but the school succeeded in attracting families from all walks of life. Seven worked in other professions, four in business, three in trades, and three in the performing arts.[46] Aside from teaching, parental occupations included law, social work, psychology, science, man-agement, architecture, carpentry, theatre, music, and the ministry. Over 60 per cent lived on the more affluent West Side of Vancouver. Another 20 per cent came all the way from West and North Vancouver, and the rest lived in Vancouver's East Side, Burnaby, Richmond, and Ladner.[47] The school had a strong professional and middle-class ambiance typical of Progressive schools. As the historian Lawrence Cremin explained, "The costliness of private schools and the normal pedagogical conservatism of working-class parents tended to make independent Progressive schools middle- or upper-class institutions."[48] The New School fit this pattern.

STAFFING

The most important task of the new organization was to hire teaching staff. In April 1962, the school hired Lloyd Arntzen, a respected West Vancouver elementary teacher and musician, as head teacher. He had been suggested by Ean Hay, a board member and fellow band leader. Mr. Arntzen was attracted to the New School because of its commitment to innovative teaching, individualized student progress, small ungraded classes, and the creative arts. He had been frustrated by the lack of a support system for students with reading problems "left by the wayside in the public system"

---

46   More than 80 per cent of the occupations are known. The percentages are approximations but nevertheless provide a useful picture of the occupational backgrounds of New School parents. Only women working outside the home were included in the figures.

47   New School enrolment and membership lists, 1962–1966. The figures for the 32 families in 1962 were: Vancouver, west of Main Street, 20; North Vancouver, 5; West Vancouver, 2; Vancouver, east of Main Street, 2; Burnaby, 1; Richmond, 1; Ladner, 1.

48   Lawrence Cremin, *American Education: The Metropolitan Experience* (New York: Harper and Row, 1988), 240.

and believed that competitiveness in learning was counterproductive.[49] Mr. Arntzen did not subscribe to any particular educational theory. He considered various methods, implementing whatever he thought would work in a given situation. He aimed to discover each student's unique learning style (verbal, written, dramatic, creative, analytical, introspective). He introduced activities that appealed to student interests but, unlike Romantic educators, he believed teachers should control the curriculum.[50] Parent Julia Brown reported that Mr. Arntzen conveyed "an excitement and enthusiasm about learning" and "was wonderful with kids."[51]

Joyce Beck, a primary teacher with five years' experience in public schools, was hired shortly afterwards. She believed in "students going at their own rate rather than some struggling to keep up while others sit bored." She found her "new freedom an exciting experience."[52] Parents and students remembered both teachers as dedicated individuals with a gift for motivating young people while giving them the freedom to be themselves. Both had British Columbia teaching certificates, but neither had any special training in Progressive methods.

The New School opened in September 1962 with thirty-nine students in grades one through five.[53] Students were organized in two multi-age groups; Mr. Arntzen taught the older class and Ms. Beck worked with the younger children. Attempts to find a suitable location for the school had been unsuccessful, so the board rented two rooms from the Peretz School, a socialist Jewish educational and cultural organization. But it was difficult working in someone else's space and trying to operate a school that encouraged work with concrete materials when everything had to be dismantled and put away at the end of the day.

Seeking to resolve the accommodation problem, parents Ken McFarland and Alan Tolliday combed the city for an appropriate location. One day in October they noticed a building for sale at 3070 Commercial Drive. It belonged to King's College, a former Christian school, and was already licensed for educational purposes. The group had to act quickly,

---

49 Lloyd Arntzen, personal interview, April 1987.
50 Lloyd Arntzen, personal interview, April 1987.
51 Julia Brown, personal interview, April 1987.
52 John Arnett, *Vancouver Sun*, September 10, 1962, 11.
53 New School enrolment and membership list, 1962.

for another school was interested in the site, and several parents inspected the premises by flashlight that very night. The cost of the building was $33,000. The board asked all members to donate what they could in the form of debentures to be redeemable when the family left the school. The campaign raised $6,500 within a matter of weeks, enough to secure a mortgage for the rest.[54] The New School bought the building and moved in on November 1.

Although the building was not ideal and needed a lot of work, the purchase generated great excitement among the parents. The main floor consisted of several classrooms, a science room, music room, office, and lounge. The basement had a large concrete play area for rainy days, an art room, kitchen, and stage with enough room for an audience.[55] There was no outside playground but students could play at Clark Park across the street. The building was expected to be a temporary home until the school outgrew it. But this never happened, and its deteriorating condition caused the school serious problems in future years.

The school population quickly became a close community. School events and committee tasks kept families in constant communication. Because students came from all over the Lower Mainland, carpools and visits to each other's homes were frequent. Students looked forward to school each day, to the astonishment of their public school friends. The first year was so successful that a third class was added in September 1963, and Carol Williams, a beginning teacher, was hired to teach grades three and four. Enrolment jumped to fifty-five students in grades one through six, and the treasurer announced that the school had broken even after one full year of operation.[56] Most of the school's success was due to the dedication of its participants, and it was not until the spring of the second year that any serious problems arose.

With the success of the first year behind them, parents turned their attention to the future direction of the school. They debated what they wanted their children to learn and how to organize individual studies

---

54   New School Budget, 1962/63. A portion of the mortgage was held by an individual, Percy Easthope, and the remainder was a bank loan.
55   Lloyd Arntzen, Annual Report, June 1963, 1.
56   New School, treasurer's report, newsletter, June 1963.

within a larger scheme. They wondered how much the teachers should shape the curriculum and how much should come from the students themselves. Many circulated their views in writing but their opinions were so diverse they were unable to achieve a consensus. Nevertheless, parents were inspired by the intellectual excitement and optimism generated by the New School and the larger values it represented.

Most parents favoured a flexible Progressive curriculum initiated by the teachers.[57] But some held the Romantic view that school should be "a living, organic, built-in participation in life with infinite possibilities of discovery, diversity, individuality, and creative improvisation." Such parents believed the curriculum should promote practical skills and independent judgement while expanding into the home and the community with a "balanced interaction among all elements in a democratic society." One humanistically-oriented parent hoped her children would be "glad they are alive, and capable of expressing their feelings and communicating their thoughts." She believed an environment encouraging rational thought and expression in speaking, writing, and art was more important than any particular content. She did not expect school to teach her children to fit into society:

> If the education I want is successful, it will not make life easy for my children. Often what they experience will be painful, what they think disturbing, and what they express misunderstood. They will, however, be given the opportunity to realize their potentialities as human beings.[58]

Don Brown understood Dewey's ideas about education in the context of broad personal and social issues. In his essay "Are We a Progressive School?" he praised practical and experienced professional teachers who can "relate material to the child's own experience." He stressed the fundamental importance of the arts and a curriculum "related to life, to equip children with the cultural resources for dealing with the future." Dr. Brown believed that a child whose potential has been brought to maturity "will be a force for greater democracy and social change." He saw Progressive education as a way of life equally valued by parents and children:

---

57   Gloria Levi, untitled statement, early 1964.
58   Pat Hanson, "Thoughts Re New School Philosophy," September 1963.

> Progressivism in education is more than another theory
> of how to do it. It is the working out in the school of an
> attitude to life which demands expression in a person's
> family, job, social relations, politics, and religious com-
> mitments. There are live connections between our educa-
> tional practice and our voluntary association as a group
> of parents. Willingness to think and act independently;
> mutual respect and co-operative relations; reliance on
> democratic procedures; a distribution of the financial
> burden which resists a class bias and attempts fairness
> among ourselves—these seem to me to be characteristic
> of people who also want Progressive education, and to
> imply resistance to some of the strongest influences pro-
> ducing conformity in our society. The school is important
> to both children and parents as an oasis in which sounder
> values can develop.[59]

These kinds of communications, using manual typewriters and old-
style mimeograph machines, are typical of the philosophical and passionate discourse that circulated constantly among members of the group.

CURRICULUM

Education at the New School was child centred, individualized, and experiential. Activities were geared to the interests of the students, but unlike
later "free schools," the teachers prescribed a curriculum, flexible though it
was, and expected the students to learn. The school day began at 9:00 and
followed a timetable that included daily reading and mathematics periods.
But there were no bells, the schedule was flexible, and each day began with
one hour of free activity during which individuals could choose to work on
any subject.[60] Students were responsible for completing assigned material
at their level, but "how you did it was up to you." Students busy with special
projects could continue the entire day if necessary, although the missed
work had to be made up. One student remembered working on a science
experiment continuously for three days and doing research interviews out of

---

59   Don Brown, "Are We a Progressive School?" September 1963.
60   Lloyd Arntzen, Joyce Beck, Annual Report, June 1963, 4.

the school.[61] But when he was finished he caught up on the other subjects. The teachers encouraged spontaneity and unexpected projects. Students learned through their experiences and what was meaningful to them.

The New School's Progressive curriculum interested many educators. Neville Scarfe, Dean of Education at the University of British Columbia, visited in 1963 and described the curriculum as "constructive, creative, and adventurous."[62] The teachers developed structured learning situations but in a gentle manner. "Basically I directed things," Lloyd Arntzen explained. "I brought stuff in and if I saw a glimmering of interest I would present the idea. I would pay attention. I kind of knew what they were interested in."[63] The teachers adjusted their expectations to individual students' abilities and interests and "ideally it would be a different program for every kid."[64] They developed a "fluid kind of structure, almost invisible; it was there but it wasn't, it was flexible."[65] One student could "hardly remember any classes at the New School":

> I think time was structured somewhat (it wasn't a free-for-all) but you didn't have to tell anybody what you were doing and you seemed to be able to do whatever you felt like. So as a young kid I just followed and saw what looked interesting and would go and do that. Maybe there was stuff we had to do but I don't remember any sense of pressure.[66]

Students learned at their own pace and textbooks were rarely used. Class sizes of sixteen to twenty students made individualized teaching more manageable. The senior students were tested to determine their mathematics level and then worked through a systematic sequence of exercises emphasizing understanding of the number system that included hands-on activities and learning aids considered innovative in the early 1960s. "We got bushels of Cuisenaire rods," Mr. Arntzen recalled,[67] and students, accustomed to

61 David Levi, personal interview, April 1987.
62 Neville Scarfe, letter to the New School, October 31, 1963.
63 Lloyd Arntzen, personal interview, April 1987.
64 Norman Epstein, personal interview, April 1987.
65 Julia Brown, personal interview, April 1987.
66 Eric Epstein, personal interview, July 1991.
67 Lloyd Arntzen, personal interview, April 1987. Cuisenaire rods had just become popular in the early 1960s, as aids to help students understand place value in mathematics. They were invented by a Belgian educator, Georges Cuisenaire. Considerable research was done with them at UBC. See J. Donald Wilson, Robert

traditional whole-class teaching, had to get used to doing mathematics "out of file boxes."[68] Two students completed the grade eight mathematics course in grade six.[69] They used geoboards, made their own protractors, and even used triangulation to measure the height of trees. Don Brown recalled the satisfaction he felt on seeing Mr. Arntzen and his students outside surveying the school building on the very first school day in 1962.[70]

The reading program was individualized, and students chose their own literature, in consultation with the teacher, during weekly class trips to the public library. Although there was virtually no reading instruction for the older students, many read a great deal. Several girls formed an informal reading club and, assisted by a parent, read autobiographical accounts of the Holocaust. This was an intense emotional experience. Students read advanced and controversial books such as *Catcher in the Rye*, and one student remembered reading novels in secondary school that she had read several years earlier at the New School.[71] Another student recollected the excitement of hearing *The Hobbit* read aloud in grade three and then writing stories about it and making pictures, posters, and puppets.

In the primary class, Ms. Beck tried to ensure that every child would experience success.[72] Students learned to read when they were ready, and most could not wait to get started. Julia Brown remembered her daughter coming home from her first day in grade one, excited because Ms. Beck had asked the students what they would like to learn; they all said they wanted to learn to read and write. Each child was then asked to choose a word they would like to write. "The kids wanted to learn and they were allowed to learn."[73] Hands-on activities were emphasized, and grade one students used Popsicle sticks instead of Cuisenaire rods to help visualize place value. Social studies, science, and art included individual and group projects emphasizing experience and observation. Students dramatized stories, wrote their own plays, and did imaginative writing.[74]

Stamp, and L .P. Audet, eds., *Canadian Education: A History* (Scarborough: Prentice-Hall, 1970), 491.

68   Karen Tallman, personal interview, April 1987.
69   David Levi, personal interview, April 1987.
70   Don Brown, personal interview, January 1991.
71   Jill Tolliday, personal interview, April 1987.
72   John Arnett, *Vancouver Sun*, September 10, 1962, 11.
73   Julia Brown, personal interview, April 1987.
74   Joyce Beck, Annual Report, June 1963, 3.

It's Like Recess All Day
At Vancouver's New School

Vancouver Sun, May 12, 1967

The teachers emphasized conceptual understanding rather than rote skills. Phonics and spelling were taught to individuals if problems arose, but basic skills were frequently missed. One student reported that she could not spell properly because spelling was ignored during her early years at the New School. Later, she learned the experimental International Teaching Alphabet, which caused her difficulty in grade eight.[75] Another student never learned her times tables, although she understood multiplication,[76] and another student recalled being exposed to times tables for the first time when he entered public school in grade four.[77] Grammar and handwriting were virtually ignored and there was little formal writing activity. One parent was initially concerned about the omission of basic grammar, such as parts of speech and sentence structure, but his son had no difficulty picking up those things in secondary school.[78] Most parents were not worried about academic subjects, and Ellen Tallman was just happy her daughter wanted to go to school.[79]

Individual subjects were integrated through themes, special projects, and group activities according to Dewey's ideas. One student remembered spending three weeks building an entire Inca city and learning about Inca mathematics, stories, weaving, and other aspects of that civilization. Northwest Coast culture was similarly studied. Students split their own wood shakes and built cedar boxes, masks, and longhouses in the school basement.[80] Mr. Arntzen believed that learning ought to be interesting and fun, so he encouraged students to build things. "When I teach history I look for what I think will make it memorable."[81]

Science emphasized inquiry, experimentation, observation, and understanding. Students spent several weeks investigating pendulums using frames they built with parental help and tested objects in a variety of shapes, weights, substances, and lengths of string. In another project, the group made hot air balloons out of vacuum cleaner bags and alcohol burning lights.[82] They built and flew kites, discussed the mathematics involved, and

---

75   Karen Tallman, Ellen Tallman, personal interview, April 1987.
76   Rita Cohn, personal interview, April 1987.
77   Eric Epstein, personal interview, July 1991.
78   Jim Winter, personal interview, April 1987.
79   Ellen Tallman, personal interview, April 1987.
80   Karen Tallman, personal interview, April 1987.
81   Lloyd Arntzen, personal interview, April 1987.
82   Karen Tallman, personal interview, April 1987.

wrote poetry about them.[83] When Trout Lake froze over one winter, the whole school dropped everything and spent an entire week building ice-boats. In such instances, the teachers were flexible enough to discard their schedule and respond to the students' sense of excitement. One younger child remembered helping an older student with chemistry projects, such as making hydrochloric acid and electrolysis.[84] Another student developed a knack for research and spent many hours interviewing experts and public figures, including the chief fire inspector and the mayor. He recalled that students were never "spoon fed" information: "You were given questions but you had to find the answers. There was nothing to regurgitate back. We were taught how to find the necessary tools to answer any question or solve any problem."[85]

The teachers encouraged students to develop an interest in world events. They discussed the significance of the Cuban missile crisis as events were unfolding, and when Martin Luther King was assassinated several years later, the students talked and wrote about it. "It wasn't just something they studied about; there was a lot of emotion that they felt and were able to express."[86] Like their parents, many students were aware of social issues. They discussed political questions such as the Vietnam War[87] and devoted an issue of the student newspaper to a discussion of racism in the United States, titled "Jim Crow Must Go." Some students distributed literature for the NDP during an election campaign,[88] and on one occasion a group of future activists organized a sit-in, taking over the teachers' lounge.[89] In the early days of Vancouver's counterculture, several students undertook to make "a tape-recorded study of the marijuana and LSD scene in Vancouver."[90] One student remembered hearing Bob Dylan for the first time at the New School in 1964 and feeling deeply

83 Jim Winter, personal interview, April 1987.
84 Eric Epstein, personal interview, July 1991.
85 David Levi, personal interview, April 1987.
86 Rita Cohn, personal interview, April 1987.
87 Paul Nicholls, personal interview, April 1991.
88 Karen Tallman, personal interview, April 1987.
89 David Levi, personal interview, April 1987.
90 Clive Cocking, *Vancouver Sun*, May 12, 1967, 14.

moved by "The Times They Are a-Changin'." A few parents favoured
formal education in socialist ideas but this was never pursued.[91]

New School head teacher, Lloyd Arntzen, was ahead of his time using the Orff method of
teaching music in 1962. *Vancouver Sun*, September 10, 1962

Students have vivid memories of music and the other creative arts.
Lloyd Arntzen was one of the earliest practitioners of the Orff method
in BC. Students learned to play xylophones that Mr. Arntzen and several
parents had made themselves. He taught rhythm through word patterns
and intricate clapping techniques, forming a clapping orchestra. Students
enjoyed this activity so much that they often sang and clapped the rhythms
on their way home in the car.[92] Mr. Arntzen introduced the students to folk
music and taught sea songs such as "The Golden Vanity" and "Jack Was
Every Inch a Sailor." One student who went on to do a music education
degree claims that this "joy in her life was fostered by Lloyd Arntzen."[93]

91 Norman Epstein, personal interview, April 1987.
92 Rita Cohn, personal interview, April 1987.
93 Jill Tolliday, personal interview, April 1987.

Students engaged in painting, drawing, and pottery, and the school had its own kiln. Cooking was also popular, and students baked bread and made ice cream. One classroom was set up as a workshop, rare in an elementary school. One of the parents built workbenches, fitted them out with tools, and Mr. Arntzen, a skilled carpenter, developed a successful woodworking program. The shop became a refuge for several students with reading difficulties. Cooking and woodworking activities were available to both boys and girls, unusual at that time.

New School parents believed strongly in the importance of self-expression, and drama was a popular activity. Students wrote their own plays and performed them on the basement stage for other students and for parents on theatre evenings. The student-written plays often arose out of other school activities. During the second year, students put on a play about Ms. Beck (who was pregnant) giving birth that had the parents in stitches.[94] One younger student recalled performing in a three-act play about survival on an island.[95] A group of older boys organized one play per week, enhancing their acting, writing, directing, and social skills. Drama was an activity at which students who were not proficient in academic work could excel. One boy was so talented that he started getting parts at the CBC, prompting him to learn to read.[96] Some students also made films. In keeping with New School goals, dramatic activities encouraged creative work but de-emphasized performance.

The school used community resources for physical education, including the Trout Lake gymnasium for indoor games, and the local swimming pool and skating rink. The parents purchased gymnastics equipment for the basement. The school had a soccer team composed of boys and girls and occasionally played games with nearby St. Joseph's Catholic School. Clark Park across the street became the main student playground, and students were called back to the school by an old-fashioned hand-held bell.

Interaction with the outside community was a major goal at all alternative schools. New School students participated in field trips to the harbour, a bakery, and a sewage plant. The school invited professional artists,

---

94 Elma Tolliday, personal interview, April 1987.
95 Eric Epstein, personal interview, July 1991.
96 Lloyd Arntzen, personal interview, April 1987.

musicians, and actors to come in and work with students, and Holiday Theatre offered afternoon classes in creative drama at the school. The parents constituted an extensive pool of talent and were invited into the school to share their expertise with students. One father who was a printer brought in an antique printing machine with a heavy roller and boxes of type, and students produced their own newspaper.[97]

School Life

Informality characterized everyday life at the New School. Students worked at trapezoid-shaped tables (built by parents) rather than desks, an innovation in the early 1960s, and were free to move around the school. There were also carrels that fulfilled some students' wishes for a private space, "like having their own house."[98] Students and teachers dressed as they liked, and girls enjoyed the freedom to wear pants. Strict dress codes were the norm in public schools at that time, and one *Vancouver Sun* reporter, writing in 1967, wondered if the reader could imagine a school "where a mop-headed youngster can swagger around in a poncho embroidered with golden tigers and dragons" and where a teacher "can sport a beard and doesn't have to wear a suit."[99] He was surprised that kids could fly kites in the hall, carry around a transistor radio, and walk in and out of class anytime they wanted. He concluded that it was difficult to tell "when it is recess and when it is not."

New School parents considered freedom of dress and mobility important in developing self-confidence and responsibility.[100] Parents also wanted their children to express their individuality and have fun while they were learning. Lloyd Arntzen recalled going to great lengths to summarize for the first annual meeting how much the students had learned, when one board member interrupted, "I can see they are learning things but are they enjoying themselves?"[101]

---

97 Lloyd Arntzen, personal interview, April 1987.
98 Karen Tallman, personal interview, April 1987.
99 Clive Cocking, *Vancouver Sun*, May 12, 1967, 14.
100 Some New School parents believed that dress codes are often used in more traditional schools to keep young people from being interested in real issues.
101 Lloyd Arntzen, personal interview, April 1987.

Teachers respected student opinion and allowed them to participate in establishing rules of conduct at weekly meetings. Students helped decide how to share equipment, organize sports day, and limit noise in the school building.[102] They learned to negotiate and resolve conflicts. If some children wanted to have water fights outside, they would have to find a way to do so without affecting those who wanted to stay dry.[103] Students were permitted to do whatever they wanted in the school basement and sometimes painted the whole area black or wild colours in paisley or psychedelic style. However, there was an "edge of formality" at the New School.[104] Teachers were addressed by their last names and made all decisions regarding student safety. The adults listened to student suggestions and discussion was open and free, but the New School did not adopt a philosophy of complete freedom during its early years.

Student responsibility and self-discipline took the place of punishment.[105] A *Vancouver Province* reporter visiting the school in 1963 noted that "there's no strap in the school and little formal discipline."[106] This was a major departure from BC public schools where the strap would continue to be used for another decade. There were few rules, and students were taught to set their own limits in regard to personal safety and behaviour toward others. Discipline was indeed gentle. One student remembered "peeing in the waste basket in grade one and Lloyd coming down the stairs and simply saying 'Don't do that.'" Instead of detentions or other traditional methods of discipline, the teachers could rely on genuine respect from students and regular communication with parents to deal effectively with any problems. Nevertheless, teachers exercised their authority when necessary. One student recalled a sanction that was available to control behaviour—he could be prohibited from going out on research projects. He continued, "We were never a Summerhill. Breaking windows didn't go. But it was very much our school."[107]

---

102 Lloyd Arntzen, Joyce Beck, Annual Report, June 1963, 5.
103 Lloyd Arntzen, personal interview, April 1987.
104 David Levi, personal interview, April 1987.
105 Lloyd Arntzen, Joyce Beck, Annual Report, June 1963.
106 Wilf Bennett, *Vancouver Province*, June 12, 1963, 17.
107 David Levi, personal interview, April 1987.

The teachers reported that "on the whole the students exhibited good sense and sensible behaviour at school."[108] This view was echoed by a *Province* reporter who observed that "the school was humming with activity. The discipline was obviously good. Every youngster was busy doing something. There was no sign of horsing around or idleness." Commenting on the wide range of activity, he continued, "One group was busy performing an electrolysis of water experiment; others were painting, reading, composing music, or woodworking."[109] Nevertheless, the energetic and unconstrained New School students could be a handful for the teachers to manage.

New School students collaborated on science and research projects.
The Province, June 12, 1963

108 Lloyd Arntzen, Joyce Beck, Annual Report, June 1963, 5.
109 Wilf Bennett, *Vancouver Province*, June 12, 1963, 17.

Teachers hoped that students would be motivated by their excitement about learning and by the interesting activities offered rather than by examinations and grades. One parent recalled that "the kids would continue their school experience in the car with activities such as mental arithmetic."[110] The absence of exams, grades, and formal report cards was a source of amazement to New School visitors. A 1963 article in the *Province* was headlined "Exams Are Passé for Children at New School," and a similar story titled "No Exams, Reports, at New School" appeared in the *Sun* three years later.[111]

But teachers did write extensive anecdotal comments on each student's academic progress, artistic activities, and social growth, an unusual practice in the public schools at that time. Mr. Arntzen believed in building on student strengths, and his remarks were honest but positive. In one report, after outlining a student's need for remedial work in reading and arithmetic, he devoted an entire paragraph to the child's leadership in creating imaginative plays with "a motley crew of boys down in the basement." In some classes, students wrote their own reports at the end of the year as summaries of what they had learned. Teachers often discussed student progress with parents informally and at scheduled conferences.[112]

The elimination of grades was part of an attempt to de-emphasize competition. Mr. Arntzen opposed competitiveness in learning because "the poor learner was in a race he could not win."[113] The teachers reported that students "worked with interest and enthusiasm without the ulterior stimulus of grades." They believed the absence of grades eliminated frustration and contributed toward a "more friendly, charitable, and helpful atmosphere among the students."[114] Students were fiercely competitive in team sports (A. S. Neill found the same at Summerhill), but individual competitions were discouraged in favour of co-operative races and games.

---

110 Rita Cohn, personal interview, April 1987.
111 "Exams Are Passé for Children at New School," *Vancouver Province*, June 12, 1963, 14; "No Exams, Reports, at New School," *Vancouver Sun*, April 26, 1966, 27.
112 Lloyd Arntzen, student reports, June 1964, Phil Thomas document collection; Lloyd Arntzen, Joyce Beck, Annual Report, June 1963, 5.
113 Lloyd Arntzen, personal interview, April 1987.
114 Lloyd Arntzen, Joyce Beck, Annual Report, June 1963, 5.

This was to become a familiar model for Sports Day in public elementary schools some years later.

Students were encouraged to help each other with their work. The drama groups that functioned without adult assistance exemplified student co-operation. One former student said, "I think we learned how to co-operate without being aware of it."[115] Students of all ages worked and played together and the multi-age classes encouraged co-operative learning.[116] One student reminisced about hanging out with older kids, doing what they were doing: "The thing that strikes me the most is how little I remember the presence of teachers. I don't remember teachers showing us how to do things. I remember much more learning from older students."[117] Most students remembered little fighting or bullying on the playground. They were encouraged to work out social problems without teacher intervention, and this became an important part of everyday learning. In a small school, conflicts could not remain unresolved for long.

Girls and boys played together with little fanfare and generally did "the boys' types of things."[118] Although gender equality was not a conscious component of school philosophy in 1962, the New School was ahead of its time in not segregating activities according to gender. Girls played on teams and worked at carpentry while boys did weaving and sewing. One female student said the girls expected to do the same things as the boys and expected to have the same futures, and she was surprised when she found that this attitude did not exist in public school.[119] Another student remarked, "It was the natural thing; we never thought anything of it."[120]

The school had a relaxed attitude toward personal modesty, and during the second year an intense debate erupted over unisex washrooms. Students took part in the discussions and one parent recalled, "The girls didn't care about the philosophy—they wanted their own washroom!"[121]

---

115 Laura Jamieson, personal interview, June 1991.
116 Daniel Greenberg of the Sudbury Valley School believed "age mixing" creates mature children who are not dependent upon adults. See Greenberg, *The Sudbury Valley School Experience* (Framingham, MA: Sudbury Valley School Press, 1985): 96–112.
117 Eric Epstein, personal interview, July 1991.
118 Karen Tallman, personal interview, April 1987.
119 Laura Jamieson, personal interview, June 1991.
120 David Levi, personal interview, April 1987.
121 Gwen Creech, personal interview, January 1991.

Their wishes prevailed. The school provided sex education evenings for the older students and their parents, another practice not found in the public schools at that time. During their presentations, the health officers had to be on their toes lest a precocious New School student accuse them of being too embarrassed to discuss the subject fully.[122] Parents briefly discussed sexual freedom for young people, but most were uncomfortable with the idea and it was dropped.

Respect for individuals and their differences were taken for granted. One parent praised Mr. Arntzen for creating an "accepting atmosphere," helping her daughter learn to value people as they are.[123] Another wrote that the school extended her son's "human sympathies" toward kids with disabilities.[124] Conformity was not valued at the New School, and students were encouraged to be different.[125] Several were extroverted actors and others were gifted scholars. One student brought his typewriter to school and used it continually from grade one. However, according to Lloyd Arntzen, a pecking order did exist, and teachers had to help the "misfits" gain acceptance.[126]

Several parents appreciated the lack of anxiety and pressure their children experienced at the New School. One parent credits the school with providing a supportive environment for his gifted son. Due to the fluid groupings, he could work with the older students while spending his social time with the younger group.[127] Another parent took his daughter out of public school when she developed hives in grade one; she spent the rest of her elementary years at the New School.[128] One student remembered a friend in public school who "had gotten the strap for sliding down a bannister. It seemed barbaric and frightening."[129] Parents believed that the absence of pressure helped their children become better-adjusted

---

122 David Levi, personal interview, April 1987.
123 Gwen Creech, personal interview, January 1991.
124 Julia Brown, personal journal, December 2, 1964.
125 Tamar Levi, personal interview, April 1987.
126 Lloyd Arntzen, personal interview, April 1987.
127 Barry Promislow, personal interview, January 1991.
128 New School Parent, personal interview, July 1991.
129 Eric Epstein, personal interview, July 1991.

individuals.[130] One student reflected movingly on his first year at the New School after three unhappy public school years:

> I just remember feeling that I liked school again. At the New School I felt like a person. You could walk down the hall and not be afraid. I felt stimulated and interested in what I was doing. I felt like I was learning a lot of things and not feeling like I was failing all the time. I just felt happy. In some ways I think that first year saved my life.[131]

Many children had been similarly unhappy in public school, though most were bright and well-motivated students. At the New School they developed confidence, independence, and a sense of adventure encouraged by teachers who rewarded initiative. One parent described New School kids as "alive and exciting."[132] Creative thinking was encouraged even if it didn't lead to tangible results. One student recalled:

> Drew came in with a copy of *Hamlet* and thought we could do it. I thought it was a great idea—I read the first few pages and there was a ghost and everything. The big problem was how are we going to get scripts. So I got out the carbon paper to type out this copy of *Hamlet*! I didn't get very far. Another time I wanted to create a machine that would make marbles by melting the glass and pouring it into a mold. I don't think it ever materialized but I spent a lot of time thinking about how this marble machine could be made. I think there was a lot of creative activity going on, some of it materializing, and some of it just figuring. There were lots of schemes and ideas.[133]

This creativity was partly due to the students' upbringing in stimulating home environments that encouraged independent thinking, but it also flourished because the teachers made space for it to happen.

---

130 Julia Brown, Hilary Nicholls, and others.
131 Paul Nicholls, personal interview, April 1991. He later became a practising teacher.
132 Ellen Tallman, personal interview, April 1987.
133 Eric Epstein, personal interview, July 1991.

Students rode the buses all over town, developing considerable independence. One student recalled taking the bus down Dunbar Street each morning, "picking up New School kids along the way."[134] Two others rode the bus to school from Deep Cove at the age of nine, and students in grade two or three often took the bus home.[135] In place of baseball cards, New School kids collected and traded bus transfers. One student said, "When we were on the bus, people would ask what school do you go to, and we would say the New School, and they would say which new school, and it got to be quite a joke among us, like belonging to a club."[136] The feeling of independence and "specialness" was a common memory among New School students. Students became very close and often paid extended weekend visits to each other's homes. Most realized their school was unique and were proud of it. One student remembered that "we always had people writing about us," and another recalled feeling more worldly than the other kids when she went back to public school.

Because of the emphasis on thinking skills, the majority of New School students had no trouble adapting later to public school. Norman Epstein said: "Our kids had no problem adjusting to the public schools. The freedom to operate at their own pace, being on their own, was helpful. They didn't need to lean on us for help in high school."[137] Rita Cohn maintains her four children "must have learned all the essentials because they have all done very well in school."[138] Other parents reported similar observations. Many students were surprised at how little they had missed, caught up easily, and achieved high marks. One student who "didn't feel behind at all" described her New School activities as "exercise for the mind":

> I realized what they had been teaching us was how to learn, how to teach ourselves. There were things that they had learned [in public school] that I hadn't learned, yet I didn't seem to have missed anything. Whether we were learning what the other kids had been learning didn't seem to make any difference."[139]

---

134 Paul Nicholls, personal interview, April 1991.
135 David Levi, personal interview, April 1987.
136 Jill Tolliday, personal interview, April 1987.
137 Norman Epstein, personal interview, April 1987.
138 Rita Cohn, personal interview, April 1987.
139 Laura Jamieson, personal interview, June 1991.

However, language skills were a problem for some students. Most New School children had already learned to read at public school or at home and had many family resources to fall back on. As one former student explained, "our parents were well-educated and that made up for anything we might have missed in the classroom."[140] But despite this reassurance, several New School students did not learn to read effectively.[141] One former student said, "I don't remember any reading instruction at all. If I hadn't known how to read already, I never would have bothered to learn."[142] Several former students reported having difficulty with grammar and spelling later in their school careers, and parent Ellen Tallman began to worry by the end of her children's third year at the New School "whether they were going to have to pay too high a price for our experiment."[143]

Nevertheless, students had real choices—what they wanted to learn, how they would organize their time—and most valued this experience in their further educational endeavours. A former student observed, "The most important thing you can learn in school is to be self-sufficient and independent, and that the New School gave me."[144] Another emphasized that she may have missed some skills but "we learned how to motivate ourselves and regulate our own time."[145] Many New School students believed they could do anything they set their minds to. One student described the feeling of empowerment as "a sense of being able to think of something and go and do it; having an idea and being able to follow through on it." Public school did not inspire him: "Once I realized that I could get As, it was just a matter of getting by on what was required. There was much less of a sense of working for myself, whereas at the New School there didn't seem to be anybody else to work for."[146]

140 Jill Tolliday, personal interview, April 1987.
141 Lloyd Arntzen, Ellen Tallman, Kay Stockholder, personal interviews, April 1987.
142 Laura Jamieson, personal interview, June 1991.
143 Ellen Tallman, personal interview, April 1987.
144 David Levi, personal interview, April 1987.
145 Tamar Levi, personal interview, April 1987.
146 Eric Epstein, personal interview, July 1991.

The Parent Co-operative

The New School was governed as a parent co-operative under strict democratic principles. Decisions were made at regular meetings of the entire school community. The founders hoped that most decisions would be reached by consensus, but if necessary, majority votes were taken with each family having one vote.[147] A board of ten members was elected for a three-year term to manage the affairs of the school. Although the school constitution established a detailed decision-making structure, member families never agreed about how much power the board should have. As with curriculum disagreements, the parents' lack of clarity from the beginning about how decisions would be made caused a great deal of dissension.

Some members of the community favoured a less formal system of direct democracy, and Werner Cohn warned of the "inherent inequalities" of any system of representative democracy.[148] Drawing on Rousseau's principle of General Will, he suggested a system with no board, no voting, consensus-style decision-making, and a flexible committee structure in which any interested members could participate. A teacher-administrator would run the school, but all decisions would be made by the general membership. There was never enough support to implement this, but a compromise in the spring of 1964 decreased the term of board members to one year and opened committees to the participation of all members.[149]

Decision-making was contentious. Although the founding parents wielded considerable influence, they disagreed over many issues themselves. The organization was subject to "checks, balances, shifting alliances," and factions.[150] Initially, a high percentage of parents took active part in decision-making, but the level of participation decreased as the years passed. One parent estimates that over three-quarters of the members were active in school affairs during the first year, but that less than one-third took part three years later.[151] There was no procedure for integrating new families

---

147 New School Constitution, February 1962.
148 Werner Cohn, "On New School Governance," November 1963.
149 Amended Constitution, June 1964.
150 Robert Sarti, "Decision Making in a Vancouver Alternate School," unpublished undergraduate paper for William Bruneau, UBC, 1974.
151 Norman Epstein, personal interview, April 1987.

and, as the membership increased, more people were content to remain on the periphery. One parent commented, "When you expand to over a hundred people, you don't even know everybody."[152]

Parents were deeply involved in all aspects of school life and developed a comprehensive committee structure to which all members were expected to contribute. Standing committees included finance, building maintenance, admissions, housekeeping, volunteers, carpool, telephone, secretarial, equipment, long-range planning, "scrounging," teachers' aid, ways and means (fundraising), grants, and teacher relations.[153] The committees became so active that by 1963, board members were unaware of many activities taking place in the school. To facilitate communication, President Ean Hay asked for monthly reports from all committees, and the board produced a regular newsletter for the whole membership.[154]

A tremendous amount of energy was unleashed with the purchase of the school building, and parents felt a sense of pride and community. One described the excitement she felt as similar to that of "fixing up an old house."[155] Building tasks provided an avenue through which parents with practical skills could assume leadership roles, just as the academically inclined members had taken the lead in the educational planning. The building committee convened constant work parties on weekends to fix the roof, paint the building, move walls, and make tables, shelves, cushions, pendulum frames, and musical instruments. Another group of parents located sources for scrounging equipment from books to test tubes.[156] Some of these duties were onerous but all the activity contributed to community spirit. Work parties became social occasions, and many parents remembered experiences like pouring tar and pebbles on the school roof. Parents, teachers, and students all did their share and felt this was indeed "their school."[157]

---

152 Julia Brown, personal interview, April 1987.
153 New School committee lists and newsletters, 1962–65.
154 New School, newsletter, September 1963.
155 Kathy Gose, personal interview, November 1963.
156 Ken McFarland, personal interview, June 1991.
157 This was a common feature of independent schools. See Donald Erickson et al., *Characteristics and Relationships in Public and Independent Schools* (Educational Research Institute of BC, 1979).

Parents also performed janitorial duties according to an elaborate rotating schedule in which everyone participated. The maintenance committee prepared detailed instructions on cleaning, and parents were organized into twelve groups according to task. Alan Tolliday considered building maintenance so central to the group's identity that he attributes the beginning of declining community spirit to the hiring of a school janitor in 1964.[158] Parent volunteers drove students to Oakridge Library once a week, telephoned members about events, put together the monthly newsletter, and performed numerous other tasks.[159] The board acknowledged that the amount of time given by parents was "remarkable."[160]

But the constant work load was difficult to sustain. As early as the fall of 1962, one parent lamented the "sacrifice in time, effort, and money; we like the school, but, oh, it's such an effort!"[161] In an interesting twist to the traditional rhyme, the newsletter announced a school picnic at the end of the first year with:

No more car pool
No more mop
Let's have fun
Before we stop.[162]

Tuition fees were based on each family's ability to pay according to a sliding fee scale. This policy was debated extensively during the planning sessions. Some upper-income families were resentful of the sliding scale at first, but politically committed parents, such as Norman Epstein and Don Brown, insisted on it. They argued that it was consistent with egalitarian values that families ought to pay what they could afford. Furthermore, the school founders had always believed in serving a cross-section of the community and did not want to "cater to children of high or low IQ or to children of rich parents."[163] Once adopted, the policy was never questioned as a central school principle, and even one of the early

158 Alan Tolliday, personal interview, April 1987.
159 New School, newsletters, September 30 and October 29, 1965.
160 Special Bulletin from the Board, 1963, Norman Epstein document collection.
161 Julia Brown, personal journal, November 21, 1962.
162 New School, newsletter, June 1963.
163 Don Brown, quoted in the *Vancouver Sun*, March 29, 1961, 12.

opponents agreed that it "brought terrific people into the group who otherwise couldn't afford to come in."[164]

The fee schedule consisted of a base rate plus a percentage of taxable family income. The finance committee chairperson visited the homes of all members to verify their income tax returns. No one seemed to mind providing the information, and Norman Epstein's visits, though time consuming, were cordial and enjoyable.[165] After several years, the school switched to the honour system for collecting income data, which worked just as well.[166] During the summer, the finance committee sent each family a formal assessment specifying the coming year's tuition. The annual fee was set at $110 plus 6 per cent of taxable income. The formula was revised each year, and in 1965 the fee rose to $150 plus 9 per cent of income.[167] During these early years, the maximum fee was $750 with a 25 per cent reduction for each additional child.[168]

A few parents wanted to exchange work for lower tuition fees, but the majority believed that volunteer work and money were equally essential elements in the healthy functioning of the co-operative. Since everyone was expected to contribute both, it would be unfair to exchange one for the other. As with the financial contributions, some families would be able to provide more work than others.

The sliding scale was successful in producing a healthy balance between those who could afford the full fee and those who were subsidized. In 1964/65 seventeen of thirty-eight families paid the full $750, fourteen families paid between $400 and $750, and seven families contributed less than $400. Fees remained fairly stable during the first five years, with the average fee per child ranging from $360[169] in 1962 to $450 in 1966.[170] Member families were also expected to contribute toward the building mortgage in the form of debentures or loans to be returned when they left the school. School fees caused financial hardship for some

164 Elliott Gose, quoted in Julia Brown, journal excerpt.
165 Norman Epstein, personal interview, April 1987.
166 Gloria Levi, Barry Promislow, personal interviews.
167 Finance Committee, reports and minutes, 1965.
168 Finance Committee, minutes; New School, newsletter, 1964.
169 Financial Report and Fee Schedule, June 1963, Norman Epstein document collection.
170 Finance Committee records, 1962–1966.

families; as one parent wrote, "sending two kids to private school is going to be hard,"[171] but participation in the New School was a high priority for most families.

The sliding scale was an ingenious method for measuring ability to pay. The minimum fee was low enough to prevent undue hardship to any members but ensured that every family contributed. The maximum level was set so that no family would have to shoulder too heavy a burden, and the reduction for additional children kept the fees bearable for large families. Although there were occasional complaints about the system—one year self-employed parents were accused of not paying their share—most members considered it fair. The fee policy generated interest outside the school, and a 1961 story in the *Sun* was headlined "New School Bases Fees on Income."[172] Several later alternative schools implemented similar policies.

Norman Epstein, who was instrumental in conceiving and refining the policy, believed that one of the strengths of the New School was that it exposed students to a wide range of socio-economic backgrounds, which created a "lifelong significant difference" for his own children.[173] One student recalled that she had friends "from the waterfront of West Van to the east end of Vancouver,"[174] and several parents commented on the "wonderful mix of kids" from a variety of backgrounds.[175] Many former parents believed that this social mix increased the students' appreciation of differences among people.

The school undertook to pay its teachers the equivalent of Vancouver School District salaries ($6,000 to $9,000 annually in the mid-1960s) as well as matching payments for medical coverage, insurance, and retirement benefits.[176] Teachers were given one day per month sick leave, and each year the school designated a substitute teacher (usually a parent) to

171 Julia Brown, personal journal, August 24, 1963 and April 1964.
172 *Vancouver Sun*, "New School Bases Fees on Income," March 29, 1961, 12.
173 Norman Epstein, personal interview, April 1987. Of course, public schools do this to some extent as well.
174 Jill Tolliday, personal interview, April 1987.
175 Gwen Creech, personal interview, January 1991.
176 New School, budgets and financial statements, 1961–1966, Norman Epstein document collection.

be on call to fill in for any teacher who was ill. New School teachers were spared most of the bureaucratic paperwork faced by public school teachers.

Teachers' salaries accounted for most of the school's operating expenses. In 1962/63 two salaries amounted to $12,000 out of a total expenditure of $17,000. Two years later, three salaries came to $23,000 out of a total of $31,500.[177] Tuition income covered about 90 per cent of operating expenses. Fundraising activities provided for mortgage payments and any capital expenses.[178] The school owed its members over $6,000 in debentures repayable within twelve months after a family left the school. Parents were asked for additional loans when the school incurred its first deficit in 1966.[179] Debentures averaged between $100 and $150, although some families contributed more if they could afford it, one going as high as $850. Some families allowed their money to remain with the school for several years after leaving, and a few forgave the debt entirely.[180] The school finished the first year with a modest surplus of $1,000 and managed to balance its budget four of the first five years. In the meantime, the building mortgage was reduced by approximately $4,000 per year.[181]

Parents spent hundreds of hours on the "constant fundraising" necessary for the school to survive financially. They held rummage sales, auctions, raffles, bazaars, dinners, and dances. During the fall of 1963, the school held a rummage sale in September, an auction in October, a folk song evening in November, a Christmas carnival in December, and a dinner dance later the same month (with music provided by Lloyd Arntzen and friends).[182] Other activities included a film showing at the Varsity Theatre, classical guitar concerts held at a member's home, a ten-week lecture series in 1964, and several art auctions, including work by Jack Shadbolt, Jack Wise, parents, and friends.[183] Single events often brought

---

177 New School, budgets and financial statements, 1962–1966. In 1963/64 three salaries came to $16,150 out of a total spending of $22,600.

178 Annual financial statements, 1963–1968, Registrar of Companies, Victoria; New School, budgets and treasurer's reports, 1963–1968.

179 Pledge form, June 1966, Norman Epstein document collection.

180 Ron Hansen, personal interview, April 1987.

181 Annual reports and financial statements, 1961–1968, Registrar of Companies, Victoria.

182 New School, newsletters, September to November 1963.

183 New School, newsletter, October 29, 1965; New School Art Auction, price list, November 22, 1968.

in over $500, and until 1967 fundraising activities generated between $3,000 and $4,000 each year.[184]

The New School Thrift and Gift Shop, on West Tenth Avenue, opened in August 1964. Parents spent many hours working in the shop, collecting merchandise, and transporting unsold items to waste material outlets near the waterfront to be made into rags.[185] The shop was open five days a week and depended entirely on volunteer labour and donated clothing.[186] Sales averaged $300 a month, which generated an annual profit of $2,000 for several years.[187] But by 1968, sales had fallen and the shop made only $900.[188] The shop moved to Fourth Avenue in 1965 and to Main Street in 1967. The parents had hoped to find a "draft dodger" to run it, but the shop finally closed in 1969 due to fatigue and declining sales.[189]

Fundraising activities were in harmony with New School values. Events were not prohibitively costly and their success depended on the time, energy, and creativity of the members. Art auctions, theatre evenings, and a lecture series were all natural outgrowths of the parents' interest in the arts and intellectual discussion. Five of the ten lectures in the 1964 series were given by school parents. They covered such diverse topics as "Libertarian vs. Authoritarian Communism," "The Revolution in Contemporary Literature," "The Canadian Indians Today," "The Lesson of Buddhism," "Sexual Mores in an Enlightened Society," and "The Existential Answer."[190] All these activities contributed to community spirit.

Whether school admissions policy should be open or selective generated ongoing debate. Several members criticized the admissions committee for making character judgements of prospective parents; apparently a child had been rejected because his mother had a reputation for being "meddling, manipulating, and generally troublesome."[191] A new committee concluded in 1964 that the school was too young for a "rigid

---

184 Financial reports, 1964–1969, Registrar of Companies, Victoria.
185 Julia Brown, personal journal, May 19, 1964.
186 New School Thrift and Gift Shop, Financial Statement, 1964/1965.
187 Thrift Shop sales records, June 1968 to January 1969, Nora Randall document collection.
188 Income Statement, June 1969, Registrar of Companies, Victoria.
189 New School Annual General Meeting, minutes, June 21, 1968.
190 Lecture Series publicity flyer, 1964.
191 Private letter to the board, September 1964.

formalization" of admissions policy. The report proposed that decisions be made solely by the teachers based on whether they thought they could work with the child profitably.

The committee also recommended that although the school "should admit children who require a greater-than-average amount of the teachers' time, the proportion of such children in the school will probably have to be limited."[192] This compromise worked reasonably well but, as in other alternative schools, the issue of special-needs children was always problematic. As the years passed, many children with learning difficulties came to the New School to escape the pressure they felt in public school and because few public programs for them were available. The increased number of such children eventually strained New School resources severely.

Parents spent a great deal of time debating pedagogical issues. Seeking to increase their knowledge of Progressive education so they could formulate policy and advise the teachers more effectively, they set up a curriculum research committee in 1964. Each committee member agreed to read up on one curriculum subject and report back to the group.[193] One parent remembered a heated argument on the pros and cons of Cuisenaire rods! Parents set up a curriculum library and looked into the feasibility of language laboratories. The committee also organized a series of professional development evenings. These included panel discussions on Progressive education where teachers or parents presented their views on curriculum to the membership.[194] Experts on experimental secondary education, such as Neil Sutherland of UBC on Social Studies, and North Vancouver principal James Inkster, were invited to address these discussion evenings.[195] New School parents turned out in large numbers to attend lectures by visiting educators such as Paul Goodman, and the teachers were encouraged to visit other experimental schools.[196]

Parents and visitors were anxious to observe the instruction at the school. There was so much interest that the board decided to limit parental

---

192 Admissions Committee, Report, October 1964.
193 Curriculum Committee, minutes, 1964.
194 New School newsletters, June and September 1964.
195 New School newsletter, December 16, 1963, Norman Levi document collection.
196 Curriculum Committee, minutes, September 20, 1964.

visits to six per week.[197] The many outside visitors included prospective parents, curious laypersons, student teachers, education professors, and teachers wanting to observe innovative teaching practices. Although the school was accommodating to visitors, there was little attempt to cultivate a relationship with the public school system and relations were "neither friendly nor unfriendly."[198] The New School was never inspected by Education Ministry officials.

Because the founders had envisioned a school including grades one through twelve, in 1964 the planning committee initiated discussions on how to organize expansion. Most members were enthusiastic about plans for a secondary program and thought the school should add one grade per year. The goal was a total enrolment of 250, and parents were already preparing to search for a larger building.[199] The committee discussed the role of specialists, individualized programs, and how to reconcile the school's teaching methods with preparation for government examinations.[200] Teachers would offer tutorials and seminars, and students would have free time for individual study. The school hoped to arrange student placements in community businesses to learn vocational skills. As it turned out, volunteer activities and internal turmoil demanded so much parent energy that the school never seriously considered expansion, and plans for the secondary school did not progress beyond the idea stage.

The planning committee recommended the formation of a kindergarten class to eliminate the adjustment from public kindergarten to the New School and soften the boundary between "play and the acquisition of skills."[201] The committee's sense of urgency was evident: "The less our children become involved in competitive, noncreative, teacher-centred school situations, the better for them as individuals and for the future of the school. The younger the child, the more deeply felt the injury."[202] The school grew to include grades one to seven by the third year, and

---

197 New School newsletters, 1962–64.
198 Norman Epstein, November 1991.
199 Planning Committee, Report, undated.
200 Planning Committee, Report, undated.
201 Planning Committee, Report on Kindergarten, undated.
202 Kindergarten attendance was still optional in BC at this time.

kindergarten was added in 1966. Enrolment increased to sixty-nine students in 1964 and a few years later peaked at eighty students.

There was a strong sense of community at the New School. Parents and children spent many waking hours there—working, meeting, cleaning, carpooling, fundraising, and learning. One student remembered feeling "part of a family; we all participated together, it was really fun."[203] Groups of families took vacations together or made excursions to Bowen Island, and students spent weekends at their friends' houses. Some participants remained close friends years later. Teachers enrolled their own children in the school, and professional boundaries between teachers and parents diminished. Many participants saw themselves as pioneers and adventurers, doing something that had not been done before.[204]

Many parents would have been sympathetic to gender issues, but it was not until the 1970s that the feminist movement raised awareness of women's issues at the New School. Though several women among the founding families were well-respected professionals, some traditional attitudes persisted. Seven out of nine members of the first board were men, and only by 1966 were women equally represented. Even in this highly educated group, most mothers did not work outside the home, listing their profession as housewife.[205] Traditionally female activities, such as convening dinners and running the thrift shop, remained the women's domain, although the men did take an equal part in school cleaning duties.

The New School was a diverse community. Political opinion was predominantly left of centre, but a few more traditional parents were attracted to the school out of frustration with the lack of intellectual or creative challenge provided by the public schools.[206] One parent was simply looking for alternatives because her five-year-old daughter had a January birthday and could not be accepted into the public school system without waiting a year.[207] Another parent had been looking for alternative schools because her learning-disabled child was not given adequate attention in public school. Still another thought her children would benefit from a

203 Jill Tolliday, personal interview, April 1987.
204 Julia Brown, personal journal, Gwen Creech, interview.
205 New School, annual reports.
206 Barry Promislow, personal interview, January 1991.
207 Gwen Creech, personal interview, January 1991.

school with less stress. Teachers and board members had to try to satisfy a broad range of opinion, since the only view everybody shared was dissatisfaction with the public school system. This diversity contributed to the school's decision-making difficulties.

Decision-making was exhausting. Board meetings went on until midnight, and parents spent hours at committee meetings or on telephone conferences. Informal discussions occurred almost every afternoon as parents picked up their children. Serious disagreements were mostly about ideological issues, as the parent body was an unusually articulate group with carefully thought-out opinions. Many held their views passionately, and the pioneer nature of the school made the issues seem even more important. This was particularly true for the founding parents, who had difficulty distancing themselves from the school's ongoing evolution.

Several parents earned a reputation for being difficult, carrying on endlessly at meetings that occasionally degenerated into shouting matches. One parent, new to the school in 1966, felt so intimidated that she stopped going to meetings.[208] On the other hand, another parent recalled how she appreciated "being with people who were so well-educated."[209] Many parents circulated their views in writing on educational, ideological, and administrative topics. New School parents enjoyed the intellectual and political debate and spent a good deal of time arguing. Fortunately for the students, the friction had little effect on day-to-day school life.

Important matters were decided by the entire community. The group agonized over tough decisions and tried to honour minority opinions, but sometimes consensus could not be reached, leaving no alternative but to vote. After a decision had been made, the sense of community was usually strong enough to transcend any bad feeling the disagreements may have generated. This was not the case, though, when it came to disputes about the teaching staff.

---

208 New School parent, personal interview, July 1991.
209 Olive Balabanov, personal interview, October 15, 1997.

SUPERVISING THE TEACHERS

The most difficult function of parental governance at the New School was the hiring, supervision, and evaluation of teachers. The school founders had intended to hire teachers who believed in the school's philosophy and to leave them free to teach without interference. But parents wanted more involvement even though they lacked the skills and experience to supervise effectively. Hiring was based on intuition with little attempt to seek teachers trained in Progressive methods. Once hired, teachers were not left alone to develop their programs. Disagreements about teacher evaluation led to a series of major crises.

In 1963 the Teacher Committee proposed that teachers be evaluated by parent committee, other teachers, and surveys of parent opinion. The committee hoped that better communication between parents and teachers would help both groups "know more accurately what they wanted from the school." Their report suggested evaluators be fully knowledgeable about the school's aims but did not discuss what qualifications they should possess.[210] Another proposal by parents William and Hillary Nicholls maintained that parent observation was not an adequate basis for evaluation, and the most reliable means of assessment would be "the professional judgement of colleagues with tenure balanced by some form of representation by parents."[211] Evaluation by qualified educational consultants was finally adopted in 1965 but not before the lack of a realistic procedure permitted two serious disputes to remain unresolved and almost wrecked the school.

The first crisis arose in April 1964 during the school's second year. Some parents believed the discipline methods used by one teacher, Carol Williams, were too traditional to be effective in a Progressive school. They complained that she was not able to control the behaviour of some students. Despite Lloyd Arntzen's recommendation that Ms. Williams be rehired for another year, the Teacher Committee decided she should be let go and the board did not renew her contract. This decision generated a great deal of controversy ("chaos," according to one parent) and several

210 Teacher Committee, Report on Evaluation, November 1963.
211 William and Hillary Nicholls, open letter, February 1965.

families threatened to withdraw from the school. To make matters worse, Mr. Arntzen informed the board that he thought Ms. Williams had considerable potential, and the decision not to rehire her showed a lack of confidence in his professional judgement. Consequently, he was resigning as head teacher.[212] President Ean Hay also resigned in sympathy.

The general membership convened on April 9 to resolve the dispute. Believing the loss of Lloyd Arntzen would be a "calamity for the school," the board reversed its position. Seeking to improve the teachers' working conditions, the board recommended Mr. Arntzen be offered a principalship with responsibility for staff supervision and authority over the reappointment of new teachers.[213] Mr. Arntzen's supporters admired him for his strong principles, and one parent commented, "If my son took a position like that, I'd be proud of him."[214]

The real issue, however, was who ran the school. Elma and Alan Tolliday wrote to the membership that "granting a principal veto powers over his employers and over parent committees amounts to a dictatorial setup."[215] They argued this would undermine the New School's original ideals and transform it into an "ordinary private school." A majority of parents agreed that they should retain control over all decisions affecting their children.[216] After an emotional debate that continued until midnight, the meeting voted fourteen to nine to uphold the decision to replace Ms. Williams and, consequently, to accept Mr. Arntzen's resignation.[217] The meeting was full of recriminations and personal criticism. Ms. Williams, who had refused to resign quietly, was present and heard every word. The outcome left such bitterness that another meeting was held the following week to reconsider the decision. This time the discussion was calm, and several parents changed their votes in an attempt to reunite the group. In the end, though, the membership reaffirmed its earlier decision by a vote of nineteen to sixteen.

---

212 Julia Brown, personal journal, April 11, April 14, 1964.
213 Board recommendation to the membership, April 1964.
214 Andy Johnston, quoted in Julia Brown, journal, April 14, 1964.
215 Alan and Elma Tolliday, open letter to the membership, April 1964.
216 Most independent schools had individual or corporate ownership structure and were governed by appointed boards.
217 Vote totals from Julia Brown, journal, April 11, April 14, 1964.

Several families left the school in the aftermath of this crisis and two board members resigned. One wrote that Mr. Arntzen had become a "convenient scapegoat" for the mistakes of the parent group. He believed that the problem was due to the "very structure and makeup of the New School's organization," citing the failure of the school to define an "adequate philosophy." He feared the teachers were being "led to the lions."[218] One former parent suggested that "Lloyd was treated badly—not as a professional should be treated."[219] Another who remembered Ms. Williams as a good teacher wondered "what the big fuss was about,"[220] while one student recalled learning a lot in her class.[221] Another parent stated, "You don't treat a beginning teacher that way."[222] In the end "it came down to letting Lloyd run things or having the parents run things. The parents won the battle but they lost Lloyd."[223]

The teachers, working under the watchful eye of a group of high-powered parents, were subjected to unrealistic scrutiny and severe pressure. Even Lloyd Arntzen was not immune to criticism despite the high regard parents had for him, some thinking he was too conservative, others thinking he was not structured enough. Most former parents acknowledged that they did not have enough trust in the teachers' capacity to make educational decisions. Rita Cohn explained that "people take sides in the heat of the moment and sometimes regret it later,"[224] while another parent commented at the time that "democracy is for saints."[225]

In the wake of the controversy, the membership decreased the term of board members from three years to one and strengthened the committee system.[226] The parents hired a part-time secretary to relieve the overburdened teachers and a part-time janitor to decrease their own workload. The constant stream of visitors that had contributed to stressful teaching conditions was limited to one morning per week.

---

218 Charles Christopherson, "Re: The New School," letter to members, April 20, 1964.
219 Gwen Creech, personal interview, January 1991.
220 William Nicholls, personal interview, April 1987.
221 Paul Nicholls, personal interview, April 1991.
222 Elliott and Kathy Gose, personal interviews, April 1987.
223 In Robert Sarti, "Decision Making in a Vancouver Alternative School," UBC, 1974.
224 Rita Cohn, personal interview, April 1987.
225 Don Brown, quoted in Julia Brown, personal journal, April 6, 1964.
226 Constitutional Amendments, June 1964.

Students and parents felt great disappointment and sadness with the departure of Lloyd Arntzen, admired by everyone at the New School as an "inspired teacher."[227] Joyce Beck also left for maternity reasons, and the school was faced with finding three new teachers. The hiring committee placed advertisements for "creative and experienced teachers" in Vancouver daily newspapers and British Columbia Teachers' Federation publications. The committee interviewed eighteen applicants and detailed summaries of each interview were circulated. The three teachers recommended were then interviewed by the full board.[228] To avoid repeating past mistakes, the committee decided that all candidates had to be experienced teachers who understood the principles of Progressive education.

More Staff Challenges

By the end of May, the school had engaged three teachers. Adele Gaba and Mervine Beagle were hired to work with students in grades one to five. They had developed an experimental curriculum at a Burnaby public school and knew parent Marilyn Epstein, a Burnaby school district psychologist.[229] Having worked together for a number of years, they brought a strong and cohesive, if somewhat regulated, style to the New School. Phil Thomas, a teacher with twelve years' experience in the Vancouver school district and an artist and musician, was hired to teach the older students. Parents knew his work from Vancouver's Summer Art program and from a talk he had given at the New School about art methods the previous year. Mr. Thomas was enthusiastic about teaching in "an experimental school committed to a dynamic and Progressive educational philosophy" that he hoped would be of value to public education.[230] He aimed to build a "rich and varied program with a flexible curriculum adapted to the needs of all the children" and to provide "a creative, stimulating, and challenging educational experience based on the belief that each child holds the key

---

227 Jim Winter, personal interview, April 1987. Mr. Arntzen combined periods of teaching in the Vancouver School District with his career as a professional musician.
228 New Teachers Committee, Report, May 1964.
229 New Teachers Committee, Report, May 1964.
230 Phil Thomas, letter to VSB, May 1964.

to his own growth." All three teachers were given two-year contracts to protect them from the pressures of dissatisfied parents.[231]

The New School began the 1964/65 school year with forty-seven families and sixty-nine students in grades one through seven.[232] Despite the divisive events of the previous spring, the growing school community looked forward to opening day with optimism. The three teachers met at the end of the summer to discuss timetabling and pedagogy. But from the first day in September, communication broke down between Mr. Thomas on the one hand, and Ms. Gaba and Ms. Beagle on the other. Ms. Beagle recalled that the teachers thought they agreed on basic principles "but when we started working together we found we didn't agree at all."[233] President Gwen Creech and another board member met with the teachers several times but were unable to help them work out their differences. In November the board informed the membership of "a serious impasse among the staff. The teachers cannot function as a team; fundamental differences have prevented basic co-operation or communication between their classes."[234]

The problem was differences in educational philosophy and conflicting personalities.[235] Mr. Thomas favoured a traditional curriculum and expected students to meet certain standards, while Ms. Gaba and Ms. Beagle preferred ideas for classroom activities to be generated by the children. On the other hand, Mr. Thomas gave his students considerable freedom, interfering only in cases of fighting or serious misbehaviour, while Ms. Gaba and Ms. Beagle followed an Adlerian approach to behaviour management requiring months of disciplined co-operation training.[236] But the most striking contrast was in personal organization.[237] Mr. Thomas was unconcerned about mess and confusion and created a museum-like

---

231 William and Hillary Nicholls, open letter, February 1965.
232 Enrolment and membership list, 1964/65.
233 Mervine Beagle, personal interview, June 1991.
234 Special bulletin to the membership, November 1964.
235 Report from the Board, November 1964.
236 Mervine Beagle, personal interview, June 1991. On the Adlerian approach in education, see Rudolf Dreikurs and Vicki Soltz, *Children: The Challenge* (New York: Hawthorne, 1964) and Rudolf Dreikurs, *Psychology in the Classroom* (New York: Harper and Row, 1968).
237 Many alternative schools, such as the Russells' Beacon Hill, have suffered over the years from criticism about mess and confusion.

classroom rich in materials, whereas Ms. Gaba and Ms. Beagle organized their physical space with precision. As one parent put it, "Phil brought incredible amounts of clutter into the school while Mervine and Adele were pristine. The arguments were not about philosophy; they were about where things were."[238]

Ms. Gaba and Ms. Beagle painted the entire school white with mauve trim and created a quiet, carefully arranged environment with cushions on the floor and little furniture or materials other than books. Students were to remove their shoes, walk barefoot through the classroom, and sit silently on the cushions awaiting the beginning of the school day. The two teachers developed an integrated approach to reading similar to the whole language methods developed later.[239] Students chose their own literature and read silently, read to each other, or wrote stories. Reading and writing periods were scheduled daily; students could choose not to participate but they had to be quiet and couldn't do other work.[240] Some students were uncomfortable with the teachers' eccentricities, such as that boys and girls had to change in the same room prior to gym class.[241] Students enjoyed singing popular protest songs like "We Shall Overcome" and "Little Boxes." Early in the year Ms. Gaba and Ms. Beagle emphasized co-operation and citizenship, but some parents objected to their use of Dreikurs behaviour theories as too manipulative.

Mr. Thomas organized a full schedule of traditional subjects and his students did a lot of work.[242] Students chose their own novels for individualized reading and studied mathematics in small groups. On Mr. Thomas's suggestion, the school hired two part-time teachers to help with remedial reading, though there was little systematic diagnosis of students needing assistance.[243] Students studied world geography and ancient history, the standard BC social studies curriculum for grades six and seven, through open-ended research on such topics as primate evolution and Stone Age

238 Gwen Creech, personal interview, January 1991.
239 Mervine Beagle, personal interview, June 1991. See Victor Froese, ed., *Whole Language: Practice and Theory* (Vancouver: UBC Department of Language Education, 1988).
240 Mervine Beagle, personal interview, June 1991.
241 Cal Shumiatcher, personal interview, April 1987.
242 Paul Nicholls, personal interview, April 1991.
243 Jean Affleck and Doris Gray.

tools. Music activities consisted of folk singing and playing Orff instruments, while art classes included painting, balsa wood design, clay modelling, and pottery. Students were permitted several hours of free time per week to work on individual or group projects. Mr. Thomas expected his students to take responsibility for their own discipline and he reported that "the fundamental feeling is one of understanding and co-operation."[244]

Mr. Thomas was an insatiable collector and his room was full of objects piled from floor to ceiling. He had bottles of animals in formaldehyde, a banana tree, rocks, old machinery, a deer skeleton, a wide variety of art materials, and junk of all kinds that he had picked up from the city dump and other places. Some students found him interesting and liked him a great deal, while others found his expectations too great and his manner overly eccentric.[245]

Soon after school opening, several parents expressed concern about Mr. Thomas's teaching methods.[246] They acknowledged his creativity and enthusiasm but felt he was too directive about academic requirements and not directive enough about behaviour. Mr. Thomas also angered some parents when he reported that many students were not reaching their potential in reading, and that student standards in reading, spelling, and arithmetic were very low.

The board convened a general meeting in November, attended by almost one hundred people, to address the staff problems.[247] Some members pressed for an open and "democratic" discussion of the issues among the entire school community, but most parents dreaded another "public pillorying" based on personalities similar to the previous year. The meeting finally voted to strike an ad hoc committee of three parents to investigate the situation privately.

The committee reported to the membership at another charged meeting the following month and identified co-operation problems ranging from disputes over timetable and facilities to disapproval of each other's programs. The report concluded that the main causes of the impasse "lie in

---

244 Phil Thomas, Teacher's Report, 1965.
245 Ellen Tallman believed many students missed Lloyd Arntzen: interview, April 1987.
246 Julia Brown, personal journal, October 28, 1964.
247 Julia Brown described this meeting in detail: personal journal, November 8, 1964.

the personalities on both sides."[248] The meeting denied a request to partition the school into top floor and basement (one parent wondered if she could "pay lower fees for the basement!"[249]) since most parents wanted the two classes to spend more time together, not less. Mr. Thomas expressed frustration that the other teachers would not meet with him to develop common academic goals and objectives.[250] He proposed school-wide assemblies and interclass reading groups and was anxious to contribute his art and music expertise to the other class. Parents wanted this as well, but it never occurred.[251]

Acting on a committee recommendation, the board appointed Gwen Creech as a temporary administrator to arbitrate day-to-day disputes. But although she was a conciliator, she was unable to bring peace to the staff. After meeting with the teachers, she drafted a new timetable providing for a minimum of interaction between classes. However, she emphasized that "the children should all feel that the building is theirs and should be able to move around freely providing they respect what other people are trying to do. If they can't do so then even a Progressive school has to impose limits so as not to have chaos."[252] No one was satisfied and there was little improvement in overall co-operation.[253]

By January most parents had taken sides in the conflict, and two factions developed. A large group of parents who believed Mr. Thomas's "talents, temperament, and teaching methods were not suitable for the New School" began to organize against him. They conducted a telephone campaign, held meetings in homes, and circulated a petition. They stated that Mr. Thomas was unable to accommodate individual student interests or abilities and that he could not manage simultaneous activities, resulting in "random and disorganized teaching and learning in his class."[254] One story had it that some students lit a fire in the waste basket while Mr. Thomas, busy with another group of students, remained unaware. Despite

248 Ad Hoc Committee, Report, December 1964.
249 Marilyn Epstein, quoted in Julia Brown, journal, December 2, 1964.
250 Phil Thomas, personal interview, April 1987.
251 Maureen Beddoes, Phil Thomas, letters to the board, October 1964, Phil Thomas document collection.
252 Gwen Creech, letter to the membership, January 1965.
253 Gwen Creech, Phil Thomas, letters, December 1964, January 1965.
254 Parents' petition, January 1965.

his two-year contract, opponents of Mr. Thomas hoped he could be convinced to resign at the end of the year. A few parents disapproved of Ms. Gaba and Ms. Beagle's teaching methods, believing their standards were low and students were learning little.[255] One student recalled playing a lot of games in their class.[256] However, this never became a major issue.

Mr. Thomas felt under great pressure from this group of parents who, "acting on their private initiative," were questioning his professional integrity. Although willing to accept assistance from "qualified" people, he maintained that his class was developing a positive spirit and he had no intention of resigning.[257] Ms. Creech regretted the harassment but urged him to accept legitimate concern about the "tone and progress in your class." By this time she believed only an objective outsider would be able to help.[258]

A minority of parents claimed the charges against Mr. Thomas were exaggerated and based on hearsay or unreliable evidence from students. Several thought the children were learning a great deal in his class, and one parent feared, "they just aren't going to give him a chance."[259] One parent described the situation as "an unremitting, unfair, and relentless pressuring of one of our teachers in order to obtain his resignation." She appealed to the school's commitment to co-operation, fairness, and justice in human relationships to bring its practice into line with its principles.[260] In an open letter, William and Hillary Nicholls reminded members of their legal and moral obligations to the teachers and pleaded for restraint. They pointed out that the teachers had taken professional risks to teach at the New School and that the board had a duty to protect them from unreasonable pressure. They maintained that annual staff changes were damaging to the children and urged that no action affecting a teacher's tenure be taken. They warned that to avoid an injustice, the situation must be resolved through proper procedures and suggested that the board obtain an assessment of the teachers by an outside professional:

255 Julia Brown, personal journal, December 15, 1964, January 31, 1965; and Hillary Nicholls, personal interview, April 1987.
256 Paul Nicholls, personal interview, April 1991.
257 Phil Thomas, letter to Ms. Creech, February 1965.
258 Gwen Creech, Phil Thomas, letters, January/February 1965.
259 Julia Brown, personal journal, October 28, 1964.
260 Ruth McCarthy, Open Letter to the Membership, February 1985.

Great self-restraint and wisdom will be needed if the present crisis is not to prove fatal to the school. We continue to believe that the professional judgement of colleagues with tenure in the school balanced by some form of representation of the parents is the most reliable means of assessing a teacher. In the case of the present staff we therefore think it urgent to find some outside professional assessment of all the teachers before their contracts are renewed.[261]

The membership narrowly defeated a motion asking Mr. Thomas to resign, and the board engaged two school administrators from Seattle as consultants.[262] They visited the school in February and were "enthusiastic about the program." They advised the parents about how to achieve better communication in the school, make their expectations clearer to the teachers, and develop a more positive atmosphere.[263] However, day-to-day quarrelling continued, much of it about "trivia."[264] As well, Ms. Gaba and Ms. Beagle were seen by some as generating conflict among parents at an evening discussion.[265] School meetings endured into the early morning hours, and the rhetoric intensified as parents expressed their feelings in letters or position papers. One parent was thought to be "rude and abusive" at a board meeting, while another accused the board of "discourtesy, arrogance, and bureaucratic mindlessness."[266] One parent accused another of "Stalinism."[267] The president stated in a letter to the membership that she "can no longer contribute anything to this organization as long as present attitudes prevail" and cited "a total lack of confidence in any regular forms of organizational structure."[268] Parental governance had reached a complete impasse.

Meanwhile, the two classes avoided each other during the school day and didn't even get together for the Christmas party. One student described

261 William and Hillary Nicholls, Open Letter to the Membership, February 1965.
262 Julia Brown, personal journal, February 17, 1965.
263 Report from the Board, February 1965.
264 Gwen Creech, Open Letter to the Membership, March 1965.
265 Letter from the board to Ms. Gaba and Ms. Beagle, March 1965.
266 Two New School parents, letters, March 1965.
267 Correspondence between two New School parents, January to March 1965.
268 Gwen Creech, Open Letter to the Membership, March 1965.

the situation as similar to being in a war zone.[269] Feelings were so high that some parents transferred their children from one class to the other in the middle of the year, even though this removed them from their appropriate age group. However, although students were aware of the conflict and felt the tension, their lives in the classroom remained relatively uneventful. In retrospect, most parents admit they overreacted. The real pity was that "the school had degenerated to the point where parents can't talk to the teachers and the teachers can't talk to each other."[270]

On April 26, 1965, Phil Thomas resigned, effective at the end of the school year. Mr. Thomas believed there should have been appropriate channels for legitimate parental concern. He urged the parents to appoint a director who would receive their support and co-operation in establishing a firm educational basis for the school and warned that "ways must be found to solve the problems concerning the structure of the school and the role of the parents in its operation. But it seems that many parents are unwilling to accept the limitation that would be imposed on their conduct."[271]

Phil Thomas was misunderstood by many, although a few thought him brilliant and ahead of his time. He was a convenient target for the school's structural and ideological shortcomings, but even his critics agreed that he remained gracious and dignified throughout a difficult situation.[272] He concluded ironically that he was "much freer in the public system."[273]

Adele Gaba and Mervine Beagle also left at the end of the year. Ms. Beagle suggested that the New School was a difficult place to teach despite the good intentions of parents who "felt so strongly that compromise was impossible." Once again the school had to begin in September with a new group of teachers.[274]

---

269 David Levi, personal interview, April 1987.
270 Barbara Beach, personal interview, June 1991.
271 Phil Thomas, letter of resignation, April 1965.
272 Norman Epstein, personal interview, April 1987, Julia Brown, personal journal, October 28, 1964.
273 Phil Thomas, personal interview, April 1987.
274 Phil Thomas taught in Vancouver public schools until the mid-1980s. He remained active in both art and music. Adele Gaba and Mervine Beagle continued to work together on the west coast of Vancouver Island and at Discovery School, an alternative elementary school in the Surrey School District, where Ms. Beagle was principal until 1989.

The turmoil affected the New School deeply. Many parents lost their spirited enthusiasm for the project and questioned whether this kind of school could survive.[275] The arguments had continued for too long and had been too intensely personal. Some parents described how friendships, even marriages, were strained; some close friendships were seriously damaged and remained so for many years.[276] Other parents remembered returning home from meetings with "insides churning" and one parent, Ellen Tallman, remembered meetings that were like *Who's Afraid of Virginia Woolf?*. "The fights were enormous; it was constant drama. The things people said to each other—obsessive, hollering, shouting, losing their tempers! We tried not to talk in front of the children but they heard."[277] Another parent felt that the individuals were "brilliant, but couldn't figure out how to work things out."[278] One board member, Norman Epstein, seriously doubted that the school would carry on:

> It was emotionally all-consuming. In the midst of the conflict people began to behave inconsiderately towards others and didn't spare their feelings. People simply stopped behaving according to normal rules of procedure, and some individuals started to behave very irrationally. Many people got burned out. It looked like the school was coming to an end.[279]

Several founding members, completely exhausted, withdrew their children at the end of the year. Dr. Epstein explained that "when we looked into what was happening in the public schools we found that the difference wasn't as great as we had imagined it to be, and the relief of not having to go to incessant meetings."[280] Another parent, who "sadly decided she couldn't stand it," found that her kids had begun to suffer and were glad to have some structure.[281] Julia Brown, another parent who left, said, "There

275 Ellen Tallman, personal interview, April 1987.
276 Don Brown, personal interview, January 1991.
277 Ellen Tallman, personal interview, April 1987.
278 Phillip Hewitt, interview, June 1991.
279 Norman Epstein, personal interview, April 1987.
280 Norman and Marilyn Epstein, personal interviews, April 1987.
281 Barbara Beach, personal interview, June 1991.

is a limit to what we can put up with. The sacrifice of the school is too much; our kids are strong enough to survive in the public school."[282]

Parents were too directly involved in day-to-day professional matters at the New School and did not live up to their commitment to "protect teachers from arbitrary pressures."[283] Parent evaluation of teachers was unworkable. Every parent had an opinion about the performance of the teachers, and many overstepped reasonable bounds of criticism. Teachers were criticized for "not being creative enough, not being individualized enough, or not giving enough grounding."[284] One parent believed that since it was difficult to find Progressive teachers who "had experience with what we wanted, we expected them to make leaps and bounds that they weren't prepared for."[285] Another concluded that "we as parents were no better at choosing teachers than the public schools were. The teachers weren't given a chance."[286]

Teaching in a parent-run school was difficult, as the ad hoc committee acknowledged: "The New School is a difficult place for teachers to work because they are directly exposed to the criticism of a large group of articulate and aggressive parents. The evaluation of teachers is full of dangers from unnecessary harassment, undue influence of gossip and informal caucusing, and the involvement of students in the discussion of teachers."[287] Norman Epstein echoes this view in a movingly honest farewell letter to the teachers that June:

> The teachers did develop good working relationships with most of the children despite the split between the classes and if we are able to start a fourth operating year of the New School it will be because the teachers served us and our children until the final day. They had every reason to walk out on us many months ago after the way they were treated by us, the parents.[288]

282 Julia Brown, personal journal, November 28, 1964.
283 The New School Prospectus, 1962, 2.
284 Gwen Creech, personal interview, January 1991.
285 Barbara Beach, personal interview, June 1991.
286 Julia Brown, personal interview, April 1987.
287 Ad Hoc Committee, Report, December 1964.
288 Norman Epstein, farewell letter to the teachers, June 1965.

TEMPORARY STABILITY

The New School survived, and the membership decided to install a director with the power to take charge of the school and make all educational decisions. The director would have authority for the school's day-to-day operation in curriculum, staff relations, admissions, and the hiring, rehiring, and dismissal of staff. The director would be expected to promote co-operation among teachers, maintain clear communication with parents, and implement school policy according to the budget. Ironically, this job description was not much different from what the membership had refused to offer Lloyd Arntzen a year earlier.

The school finally adopted realistic procedures whereby the director's performance would be evaluated each year by outside consultants with appropriate educational background. The teachers would be evaluated by the director who would make personnel recommendations to the board.[289] To protect the teachers from the kind of attacks that had been all too common during the first three years, no complaints regarding a teacher would be considered at board or parent meetings. All complaints were to be taken up with the director or the consultants.[290]

Two serious candidates for school director were considered. One candidate was Bob Barker, who had taught at Summerhill and his own school in New York State. His educational theory emulated that of A. S. Neill. He believed in the Summerhill model of student government and would not compel students to attend classes. Rita and Werner Cohn interviewed him in New York and were impressed with his background, honesty, charm, knowledge of Progressive methods, and experience in working with parents.[291]

The other candidate, Graham Smith, had a background in secondary teaching, mostly in the public school system. His experience included teaching in Britain, four years in Nigeria, and the principalship of a two-room high school in Hixon, a small town near Quesnel in northern British Columbia. Although he had little Progressive experience, he had

---

289 "The Position of Teacher-Director at the New School," policy paper, April 1965.
290 New School, newsletter, October 29, 1965.
291 Robert Barker, "Biographical Materials and Educational Statement," April 1965.

taken courses in innovative methods and professed to be conversant with Progressive ideas. He favoured an informal but not permissive style of discipline and a flexible curriculum emphasizing research skills to help students learn to "think and act for themselves." He was a pragmatist who disliked jargon and emphasized the importance of supporting good teachers.[292]

Five parents drove all the way to Hixon to interview Mr. Smith. They encountered a strong character who was not afraid to struggle with difficult situations, such as dealing with abused and neglected students from alcoholic families. He broke up fights, looked after children who did not want to go home in the evening, and even arranged for their dental care.[293] The Teacher Selection Committee described Mr. Smith as self-confident, honest, straightforward, realistic, firm but flexible, with a sense of humour, a broad outlook, and an ability to communicate with adults. He was "not a public relations type but possessed a tolerant, pragmatic attitude to education rather than an incisive educational philosophy."[294] He believed children ought to be able to read by the time they were eight or nine and not just do what they liked when they liked.

Graham Smith's application was approved by a large majority and he was given a two-year contract in May 1965. The choice of Mr. Smith, despite his lack of experience with Progressive methods, was the school's attempt to seek a measure of stability after the previous chaotic year. Mr. Smith was a proven administrator who would deal with situations before they got out of control. Mr. Barker, on the other hand, was too Summerhillian for most parents. One parent recalled that she became suspicious when Mr. Barker talked about "love all the time." Mr. Smith appealed to a wider range of opinion, including a few parents who were more conservative.[295]

Graham Smith turned out to be even more traditional than most parents expected. He believed in a skill-based curriculum with formal English and mathematics classes. Textbooks were used at the New School for the first

---

292 Graham Smith, Educational Statement, May 1965.
293 Hillary Nicholls, personal interview, April 1987.
294 Hiring Committee, Report, May 1965.
295 Barry Promislow, personal interview, January 1991.

time, and students sat in rows, copying pages of notes from the chalk-board.[296] One student recalled that physical education classes included "a lot of slow deep knee bends."[297] Mr. Smith was interesting and compassionate but there was an "English hardness about him."[298] Some students and parents experienced him as aloof, and there were strong disagreements about his methods of discipline.

However, he implemented a definite program and pushed students to achieve academically, and some students "learned a lot from him."[299] He read to the students often and livened up classes with stories and slides of his experiences in Africa. Mr. Smith made some attempt to individualize his program, but he was the most traditional teacher to work at the New School. He was not overly popular but most students accepted him well enough and, compared to previous years, parents gave him room in which to operate.

Mr. Smith was a strong advocate of outdoor education and led his grades six and seven students on a two-week hiking trip to the Rockies. The adventure included an eighteen-mile hike in Yoho National Park, an excursion to the Columbia icefields, and a climb to an 8,500-foot peak near Banff. Students hiked through glacial areas, sighting moose and mountain sheep, walking for hours without stopping, testing their endurance.[300] For one student the trip inspired a lifelong interest: "It was one of the great experiences of my life; my love of hiking stems from that trip."[301]

Else Wise taught the grade one/two class in 1965/66. She had experienced family grouping classrooms and the "free activity method" during two years of teaching at an infant school in London. With this British primary school background, Ms. Wise was one of the few New School teachers to develop a comprehensive reading program. Influenced by Sylvia Ashton-Warner and Maria Montessori, she instilled in her students an excitement for reading and writing. Although she seemed to know

296 Cal Shumiatcher, personal interview, April 1987.
297 Eric Epstein, personal interview, July 1991.
298 Paul Nicholls, personal interview, April 1991.
299 David Levi, personal interview, April 1987.
300 Karen Tallman, personal interview, April 1987.
301 Paul Nicholls, personal interview, April 1991.

when a student was ready to read, she waited for the motivation to come from the individual. She described her program:

> I had my students going at their own speed and teach-
> ing each other. I didn't mention anything about reading.
> I just read them stories and read them poetry and played
> reading readiness games. And finally after a few weeks
> of school one little girl said, "When are we going to learn
> to read?" so I handed her the first pre-primer and didn't
> say anything about it except "here you are." She read all
> the way through it and the next two pre-primers in one
> morning. She was thrilled; nobody had to teach her to
> read, she already knew. It spread like measles. Everybody
> came up and asked and when they asked that's when they
> started reading, so they all ended up doing individual
> reading. I would have two or three children together to
> listen to them read every day and there was only one child
> that I had to encourage.[302]

Students wrote their own stories and built up a collection of spelling words on individual flash cards. Students traded words with partners, eventually learning everybody else's words. Some children began writing poetry and produced a book of poems. One boy completed three years of the English program that year and most others finished two years. The small class size (seventeen students) and the background of the children contributed to the effectiveness of the program.[303] Ms. Wise believed in children learning from each other:

> It was their program. They could talk and move around
> and ask each other for help. If I was busy with one child
> and another one needed help they would have to ask
> another child. I really learned to trust them; the more rope
> you give them the more creative they are. If you don't put

302 Else Wise, personal interview, April 1987.
303 Ms. Wise's methods are reminiscent of the co-operative learning or "natural method" pioneered by Celestin Freinet in Southern France from 1920 to the 1960s. He led children at their own rate through a progression of shared drawing, free writing, and reading activities using student poetry, wall journals, and classroom magazines. Celestin Freinet, *Co-operative Learning and Social Change* (Toronto: Our Schools/ Our Selves, 1990).

any limits on what is possible, and if you show them the next place they can get to, they'll go. I expected something from them too. I did not encourage competition but they pushed each other.[304]

Ms. Wise also taught art classes in which students created their own films and worked extensively with clay. Parents remembered her as a creative, intuitive, and outstanding teacher and were disappointed when she left after one year to pursue a career as an artist.

Doris Gray taught the grade three and four class and also provided individual remedial help in reading and arithmetic. Her previous teaching experience had been in California and with Inuit children in Alaska.[305]

Impromptu music-making among teachers and students reflected the creative atmosphere of the New School. *Vancouver Sun*, July 8, 1965

Ms. Gray had a science background and had become discouraged by the emphasis on rote rather than conceptual learning in the public schools. She initiated microscope work and encouraged groups of students to

304 Else Wise, personal interview, April 1987.
305 Kathy Hassard, *Vancouver Sun*, July 8, 1965, 38.

work together independently. After one successful year Ms. Gray also left the school.

Else Wise and Doris Gray were replaced in September 1966 by Anne Long and Beth Jankola. Ms. Long had become disillusioned with traditional methods during two years in Vancouver public schools. After an "idealistic and impassioned" first year, she was deflated by a district inspector who expected silent classrooms. She was assigned to another school and "toed the line but I was much less inspired; definitely the edge was off."[306] Ms. Long had met several New School parents while studying English at UBC, and when an opening arose to teach the grade 4/5 class she gratefully accepted. Beth Jankola, a recent graduate of UBC's education program, was looking for a job in Vancouver when she met Rita Cohn and accepted a position teaching the primary children. Elisabetta Visscher came in to teach French, and the school's first kindergarten class was taught by Margo Morgan.

The year was relatively uneventful. Anne Long described her experience: "There was much more leeway than in public school, and I was able to get kids involved in creative work. But the days were structured; we had subjects scheduled and we basically followed that schedule."[307] Ms. Long trained her students to be self-directed, and reading was individualized.[308] Students chose their own books and had little whole class instruction due to the range of skill levels. Art activities were memorable, the small class size making innovation more feasible. They did batik work with dye vats in the basement, a tricky process that she "would never have tried in the public school." Ms. Long formed strong bonds with her students and was the first New School teacher to be called by her first name. Later that year a student coined the name Anna Banana, which she has gone by ever since.

Despite the director's more traditional approach, the New School retained its essential elements. Students learned at their own pace and were encouraged to pursue individual interests while the arts and critical thinking skills were emphasized. Curriculum and timetabling were flexible,

306 Anne Long, personal interview, May 1987.
307 Anne Long, personal interview, May 1987.
308 Cal Shumiatcher, personal interview, April 1987.

classes small, and exams nonexistent. Students had freedom of movement throughout the school and could spend time in other classrooms.[309]

Mr. Smith enjoyed working with special-needs students, and many were accepted during his tenure. Ms. Long estimates that almost half of her students had a history of learning or behavioural difficulties, and she feared the New School was becoming "a catch-all for kids with problems in the public schools."[310] But the teachers did not want to turn these children away since there were few public school programs for students with learning disabilities at that time. Some parents saw the New School as a "safe haven for their children" where they would be under less pressure to keep up.[311] The increased number of students with special needs changed the nature of the school and contributed to an exodus of academic and middle-class families by 1970.

Mr. Smith proved to be a capable administrator, and the school was spared the personnel and organizational problems that had occurred in previous years. He supported the methods and teaching styles of the other teachers, and parent meetings were relatively calm. But like his predecessors, Mr. Smith found that teaching in such an intimate, experimental environment had taken its toll, and in early 1967 he announced his intention to resign at the end of his second year. Anne Long wrote that he was "constantly under the gun from the parent body for being overly authoritarian,"[312] and one parent suggested that he was "bowled over by the amount of parental involvement." Whatever he did, half the group would disapprove. Mr. Smith was not a diplomat and made no attempt to parrot the views parents wanted to hear. He would say things like, "If these children don't get some education soon, they'll be sweeping the streets of Vancouver when they're adults."[313] He was accused of having a short fuse.[314] His students could be a handful to manage and some parents

309 Bob Sunter, *Vancouver Sun*, April 26, 1966, 27.
310 Anne Long, personal interview, May 1987.
311 Kathy Gose, personal interview, April 1987.
312 Anne Long, "The New School—Vancouver," in *Radical School Reform*, Gross and Gross, eds. (New York: Simon and Schuster, 1969), 275.
313 Barry Promislow, personal interview, January 1991.
314 Robert Sarti, "Decision Making in a Vancouver Alternate School," UBC, 1974.

suspect the pressure was severe. But he was a fighter and stuck it out until the end of his contract.[315]

As the New School approached its fifth birthday in the spring of 1967, it had achieved a great deal of success. It had grown to seventy-three students from kindergarten to grade seven, employed three full-time teachers, owned a substantial equity in its building, and administered a budget of $36,000. Ideological and personal disagreements had tested the commitment of its members, but the community remained optimistic. Many parents believed what they were doing was important and supported the project with enormous time and energy. They were convinced that the New School was "the best school in Vancouver."[316]

Although many parents found their association with the school emotionally draining, "the kids were having a great time."[317] Rita Cohn described the school as a "wonderful experience" for her children. Most New School graduates from this period entered the public school system without great difficulty and managed to acquire the skills they had missed. Many found that their critical and creative thinking skills made high school easy, albeit boring.

However, some students found it difficult to adjust to a more rigid system than what they were used to. One parent commented that her daughter felt like a "misfit" in grade eight, and a student said, "You weren't supposed to question what the teachers said, but I did. Some teachers had difficulty with that. You didn't speak about issues."[318] Public schools had differing reactions to New School students. One student was put into the bright class when she registered at secondary school, while another reported that the elementary school she transferred to "put me into a remedial class and gave me all kinds of psychological tests."[319] For students who reacted poorly to large authoritarian schools, there were soon to be several alternative secondary schools and a few innovative programs

---

315 Mr. Smith went back to teach in Northern British Columbia. Some believe he later returned to England.
316 Wayne Levi, quoted by Clive Cocking, *Vancouver Sun*, May 12, 1967, 14.
317 Jim Winter, personal interview, April 1987.
318 Jill Tolliday, personal interview, April 1987.
319 Laura Jamieson, personal interview, June 1991.

at such public schools as Point Grey (the Integrated Program),[320] Lord Byng (SELF Program), University Hill, and West Vancouver's Sentinel Satellite.[321] Some former New School students became reunited while attending such programs.

Most New School students from the first five years had successful school careers, attended university, and went on to professional, academic, artistic, and business careers. Although there was no continuity in teaching methods, there was enough good teaching that students learned. Graham Smith, though unappreciated by some, was responsible for filling in gaps for many students. Stimulating home environments where education was valued made up for the lack of a systematic reading program. Even so, a few students did not learn effective reading skills. Later in the school's history, when some students had less educational support at home and others had reading disabilities when they entered the school, the results were more serious.

Effective co-operative governance was difficult for New School members. Power struggles and factionalism among the parents brought the school close to the breaking point. The ongoing crises were partly the result of an inadequate foundation, as the parents never reached a firm agreement on what type of education they would offer. As a consultant wrote in 1968: "The New School came into being as a protest against existing educational opportunities rather than as a positive program with a clear identification of goals."[322] Nor did parents agree on what their decision-making approach would be. Although they created a formal structure, they wanted to operate in an open and non-hierarchical manner. But from the outset the more articulate and politically aware among the group formed an elite that dominated the school.[323] A further problem, typical of co-operative organizations, was the large commitment of time and energy expected of the participants, which could not be maintained over time.

---

320 An interdisciplinary program for students in grades ten and eleven, started by the vice principal, Jim Carter. Mr. Carter, a New School parent in the late 1960s, later became deputy education minister. See Chapter 15.

321 Sentinel Satellite offered a humanities and drama-based program headed by Barbara Shumiatcher, a long-time New School parent. Jim Carter was the school principal.

322 Coolie Verner, Consultant's Report, March 1968. Professor Verner of UBC prepared this report during a later school crisis in 1968 (see Chapter 8).

323 Hilda Thomas, personal interview, December 1991.

Parents greatly overestimated their ability to hire and supervise teachers. Their hiring employed few systematic criteria, and the school's teaching methods lacked continuity. All teachers were formally trained and certified but, aside from their general dissatisfaction with the public school system, the teachers had little in common and teaching styles varied widely. Although the school was based on Progressive principles, not one teacher hired during the first six years had any training in Progressive theory or methods. Even the popular Lloyd Arntzen developed a program based more on intuition than on any firm methodological foundation.

Once hired, the teachers were not given the freedom to exercise their professional judgement without interference. Teacher evaluation was often based on hearsay and carried out by individuals who had no training or experience in supervision until a workable evaluation procedure was finally implemented in 1965. As one English historian, W. A. C. Stewart, suggests in *The Educational Innovators*, parents hiring teachers was the "usual American pattern" in Progressive schools. He describes one headmaster's "exasperation with the assumption by uninformed parents that their views on education and teaching could be pressed upon teachers."[324] Unreasonable pressure from parents was a principal cause of the high teacher turnover at the New School. New School parents spent too much time working out their own political and intellectual interests, often losing sight of the original educational goals.

The New School had come to a crossroads by 1967. The parents were tired and would soon be ready to let the teachers determine the direction of the school. Furthermore, volatile cultural change during the late 1960s would result in pressure on the New School to move away from its Progressive orientation as it was swept along with the Romantic tide.

---

324 W. A. C. Stewart, *The Educational Innovators*, vol. 2 (London: Macmillan, 1968), 140. The comment was made by W. B. Curry, who headed the parent-run Oak Lane County Day School, a Progressive school in Philadelphia, before returning to England to become headmaster at Dartington Hall in the early 1930s.

Chapter 3

ARGENTA FRIENDS SCHOOL: EARLY YEARS

The Argenta Friends School was born in a remote mountainous community in the West Kootenay region of southeastern British Columbia at the end of the 1950s. The first alternative school in BC, it was rooted in American Quakerism, but the school also embodied many important Progressive principles and practices. Argenta began as a prosperous silver mining town at the northern tip of Kootenay Lake in the 1890s. After the mining industry declined around 1910, a number of families originally from Europe settled in Argenta to try their hand at farming the benchland above the lake.[1] They sent their weekly produce down the lake to Kaslo and Nelson on the sternwheeler *Moyie*. But the land was marginal and fewer than six families were left by 1950. Then the community was given new life with the arrival of another wave of settlers, a group of Quaker families mainly from California.

In the 1940s, John and Helen Stevenson were teachers and members of a small Quaker farming community in Tracy, California, along with their friends Bob and Ruth Boyd, John and Anne Rush, and George and Mary Pollard. The Stevensons and their friends were dissatisfied with life in the United States. It was difficult for small farmers to compete with large California "factory farms." They also opposed the growth of militarism, violence, materialism, and the attitude that "it's okay to do anything as long as you don't get caught." The last straws were McCarthyism, which

---

1   The best known pioneer families were the Beguins and the Sawczuks.

grew out of the Cold War and fear of Communism in the early 1950s, and the loyalty oath required of all teachers. Objecting on religious principles, the Stevensons refused to take the oath.

In 1952 they decided to move to British Columbia. They were drawn to Canada because it seemed less materialistic and militaristic than the United States. They appreciated the "world political view" of the future Prime Minister Lester Pearson, Canada's apparent lack of nationalism, and the absence of a military draft.[2] After travelling the province for months looking for a place to settle, the Stevensons chose Argenta for its inexpensive land suitable for agriculture, its magnificent physical setting, and a history of co-operation in the community. They bought an abandoned hotel left over from Argenta's mining days and converted it into their family home. They were joined by the Pollards, Boyds, and Rushes, and within the next five years by non-Quaker families sharing a similar world view: Elmo and Ruth Wolfe, Chuck and Helen Valentine, Hugh and Anna Elliot, Hugh and Betty Ector, and Hugh and Agnes Herbison. By the late 1950s, Argenta was known among North American Quakers and other people looking for a communalist, alternative lifestyle. It was an isolated community with limited transportation links and no electrical power or telephone service. The Quakers saw it as a place where they could develop a large degree of economic self-sufficiency and guard against the effects of a future depression or war. Drawn to the ideas of Mahatma Gandhi, they saw Argenta as a place where they could "live their philosophy" and pursue a "considered life."

Although local old-timers viewed the Quakers with some suspicion, the new group revitalized the community. One of the newcomers developed a water-powered generating system to supply electrical power to the community, and others helped expand and maintain the local crank telephone system. They successfully lobbied the government for a new bridge across the Duncan River, thus making transportation to the village much less difficult. Musicians among the newcomers created an amateur orchestra that played at popular monthly dances for the entire community. The Quakers were well-educated, serious, and concerned about large world problems.

---

2   John Gray, "How Seven Families Really Got Away from It All," *Maclean's*, October 7, 1961, 97.

They added enough children to the area that the local one-room school was reopened. Helen Stevenson was hired by the school district, taught at the school for five years, and was an excellent teacher.

But making a living was difficult. In 1955 six families formed the Delta Co-op, a producers' and consumers' co-operative. They worked on farming, logging, and construction projects, pooled the income, and distributed approximately $75 per month to each participant family.[3] They even secured some local government contracts to build bridges and roads. But although industrious, the group still needed to generate more income. During a discussion in 1957, co-op members realized that over half of the adults in their group had teaching experience. A small independent high school would bring in extra money, and the students could be boarded in homes throughout the community.

John and Helen Stevenson had extensive educational backgrounds and became the driving force behind the school. Helen Stevenson graduated from Whittier College in southern California with a degree in biology and a secondary school teaching certificate. She taught for three years in a rural California high school. John Stevenson studied mathematics at the University of California. After spending the war years in alternative service as a conscientious objector, he also taught high school. Ms. Stevenson helped establish Pacific Ackworth Friends School, a Quaker school in southern California where she taught for three years. During this time, she studied at a Columbia University outreach program in Pasadena, where she learned about John Dewey's ideas of "child-centred classrooms" and "education for democracy." Since the early 1940s, the Stevensons had dreamed about establishing their own school.

Quakers (members of the Religious Society of Friends) believe that each person has an Inner Light that should guide human action.[4] This Light arises during group meditation (Meeting for Worship). Participants "try to use silence for the growth of our inward self" and search for ideas

3   Families received $30 for each adult and $5 for each child.
4   For background on Quaker beliefs and practice see Howard Brinton, *Friends for 300 Years* (New York: Harper, 1952); Michael Sheeran, *Beyond Majority Rule* (Philadelphia: Yearly Meeting, 1983); Margaret Bacon, *The Quiet Rebels* (Philadelphia: New Society, 1985); John Punshon, *Portrait in Grey* (London: Quaker Home Service, 1984); Howard Brinton, *Quaker Education* (Philadelphia, Pendle Hill, 1950); W. A. C. Stewart, *Quakers and Education* (London: Epworth, 1953).

that can be formulated "into something useful in ordering our everyday lives."[5] Friends also seek wisdom through social interaction and emphasize the importance of community: acting in the interests of the group, building trusting relationships, and making decisions by consensus.[6] They oppose hierarchy and encourage each individual to follow his or her own conscience. Quaker practice emphasizes pacifism, social activism, direct and truthful speech, and simple living. The Stevensons hoped to incorporate these principles in a "clock-round educational experience" that would "unhinge the students from preconceived ideas," expose them to alternative political, economic, and religious views, and encourage them to find their own values.[7]

The Friends School would aim to contribute to world peace and to encourage ethical social relationships. The founders asked big questions about the connections between economic and political life:

> We are trying to understand those conditions which lead
> the world to choose ways of violence or of non-violence.
> How do we keep the golden mean between "mine" and
> "ours?" How do we keep our co-operative as a means
> rather than an end? How do we stay clear of economic
> dependence on huge corporations or governments? How
> do we reduce our capital assets so that we avoid special
> economic privileges which are the seeds of war? What
> obligations do we have in the light of world hunger? How
> do we nurture faith in each other that allows us to with
> stand our personal weaknesses and limitations?[8]

5   "Discipline for Argenta," 1964. Unless otherwise noted, all school documents are located in the Argenta Friends School archive, originally in the home of John and Helen Stevenson of Nelson, British Columbia. I wish to express my gratitude to the Stevensons for their hospitality and for the generous access they provided me to this rich collection.

6   Quakers prefer the terms "unity" and "the sense of the Meeting." As they see it, consensus is a secular process in which decisions are made through reason. In seeking the Sense of the Meeting, members search together for the truth and open themselves up to the voice of God. Quaker pamphlet by Barry Morley (Wallingford: Pendle Hill, 1993).

7   John and Helen Stevenson, personal interview, September 11, 1996.

8   "For the Study of Argenta Friends School," August 1958.

The ultimate school objective was to produce citizens who would strive to create a better world. The school prospectus stated: "We attempt to practice simplicity, harmony, equality, and community. We hope that we may be a seed in the larger society."[9] This is similar to John Dewey's emphasis on educating citizens to take part in genuine democratic life.

The Friends School was under the "care" and guidance of the Argenta Friends Meeting. This group included people whose professional or life experience would be an asset to the school. Bob Boyd had trained as a minister at the Chicago Theological Seminary and at the University of Chicago during the 1930s while he and his wife, Ruth Boyd, were doing volunteer work in settlement houses. Concluding that social change in large urban areas was impractical, they moved to rural California, formed an agricultural co-operative, and did organizational work in the community. Elmo Wolfe met Mr. Boyd while studying in Chicago to become a Congregational minister and working in a depressed area of the city. In the meantime his wife, Ruth Wolfe, earned a master's degree in elementary education. Mr. Wolfe was hired by a congregation in central California at the height of the McCarthy period in the early 1950s but was asked to leave after four years because of his pacifism. The Wolfes did not want to raise their children under these circumstances and moved to Canada. George and Mary Pollard had also worked in rural co-operatives and had been among the founders of Pacific Ackworth School in California.

Like the founders of the New School, the Argenta Friends were thoughtful and deliberate and spent over two years outlining the philosophy and practical details of the school. A series of working papers, titled "For the Study of Argenta Friends School," were written in 1958 by John Stevenson, Helen Stevenson, Bob Boyd, and Ruth Wolfe. Discussion continued until the group agreed on the general parameters of the school.

By the spring of 1959, they felt ready to open the school that September. Friends Meeting members contributed a modest $5 each and a wider appeal raised $2,000. The School Committee wrote to everyone they could think of who might be interested in sending their teenagers to the school. The weeks leading up to school opening were exciting but stressful. An American teacher slated to join the staff was disallowed entry

---

9   Argenta Friends School, 1963 Prospectus, 5.

into Canada because of a health condition, and the Stevensons suddenly had to find a replacement. They finally hired Jonathan Aldrich, a recent Harvard graduate from Boston. At the last minute, immigration officials at the border crossing south of Nelson threatened to hold up the arriving American students. The three teachers drove more than one hundred miles armed with diplomas, professional references, and school documents to convince the officials of the school's legitimacy.

The Argenta Friends School opened in September 1959 with three teachers and ten students in grades ten, eleven, and twelve. Tuition was set at $800 per year (including room and board), and teachers would earn $75 per month. The founding families decided not to accept any of their own children for the first year because they wanted to begin with a group of students who did not know them. Students were recruited from among Quaker families and friends of the Stevensons in California. John Stevenson taught mathematics, Helen Stevenson taught biology and Canadian geography, and Jonathan Aldrich taught English, drama, and French.

The school was located in the old one-room public schoolhouse, empty again in 1959 because the district had built a larger school in a village eight miles away. The Friends School rented the building for $5 a month. Since the school was directly across Argenta Creek from the Stevensons' home, they offered their living room, kitchen, and a cabin on their property for extra classes. The old hotel served as the library and office. In the summer of 1961, a group of teachers, students, and Meeting members began constructing the Argenta Friends Meeting House, which would also serve as a large classroom for the school. It was built entirely with volunteer labour, and materials were financed by donations totalling $2,000. Work continued throughout the spring and summer of each year. The school began holding classes in the building when it was enclosed in 1963, but it was not usable in the winter until the heating system was finally installed in 1964. John Stevenson called the building a "monument" to the dedication and generosity of school supporters.

EDUCATIONAL GOALS

The Argenta Friends did not have deeply held educational theories. But they were passionate about helping young people develop a social conscience and learn the skills and wisdom to live together in a community. John and Helen Stevenson hoped above all to provide "education for community-building."[10]

ARGENTA FRIENDS SCHOOL

Argenta School students drew inspiration from the natural environment.
Argenta School brochure 1969

Many Progressive ideas, such as those developed by the educational philosopher John Dewey, influenced the school's philosophy and practice. For example, a primary objective of the Friends School was the growth of the "whole person." The prospectus stated: "Our program is clock-around, and classes, recreation, worship, work, and home life are considered as a

---

10   Helen Stevenson, personal interview, September 11, 1996.

whole."[11] Although the school would cover the basic academic requirements to prepare students to enter university, academics were considered
to be just one component of the program. Whereas many private schools
might claim similar aims, the Friends School had important distinguishing
features. Its students would come to understand the value of "wholesome
rural living" and would learn how to build, plant gardens, and survive
in the woods. They would be affected by the beauty of the mountainous
environment and learn valuable lessons from the pervasive peace and
quiet. Students would live with local families and participate in the economic and family life of their hosts through the numerous chores that are
a part of rural living. Students would have the opportunity to gain spiritual
insights through attending the Friends silent worship services. The exploration of Quaker values of non-violence and consensus decision-making
was another central objective. In summary, the school offered experiences
in spiritual observance, group government, family living, academics,
and awareness.[12]

In contrast to traditional schools where the adults formulate a set of
rules and penalties for breaking them, the Argenta Friends' vision was
for students to participate in most aspects of running the school. John
Stevenson wrote: "We have set out to give students freedom and accom-
panying responsibilities. There has been a minimum of emphasis on
rules and penalties and a maximum on group decision followed by group
evaluation."[13] Students helped set school policies in the areas that affected
their lives, including curriculum, scheduling, daily routines, and personal
relationships. The teachers rejected an authoritarian attitude in favour of a
"hands-off" approach, throwing responsibility for decisions back onto the
students. The goal was to develop "self-regulated people."[14]

The school was governed by the Friends Meeting, which set the basic
patterns and philosophy "within the framework of Friends principles."[15] In

---

11   Argenta Friends School, 1963 Prospectus, 6. The attempt to construct a total
     environment was not unlike traditional British private schools, but the goals
     were different.
12   "Main Experiences of Argenta Friends School," May 6, 1971.
13   John Stevenson, Coordinator's Report, January 1963.
14   John Stevenson, 1961.
15   Report to the Monthly Meeting on School Structure, May 1963.

keeping with the Quaker belief that "there is that of God in everyone," the school rejected a hierarchy or "ladder of command" in which individuals might take an "elevated position."[16] Instead, the founders set out to create a democratic structure in which all students and staff were encouraged to participate.[17] School policy was set by the whole group and students had to take personal responsibility for the group's welfare. For several years the school had no principal and administrative tasks were performed by John Stevenson as "Coordinator." Staff and students based their relationships on trust according to the school motto, "We're In This Together":[18]

> The Argenta Friends School is an attempt to give students the opportunity to live in a situation in which they participate in the decisions which affect almost every phase of their living. In addition they have the responsibility of helping implement those decisions. This works only when each member is seeking for the good of all members of the group and of the group itself.[19]

A fundamental goal of the school was that students would learn to make decisions through seeking consensus or "unity" according to the methods of a Friends business meeting. Decisions could be revised only if the entire group changed its mind in a subsequent discussion. The founders believed that most of the world's problems and conflicts arise from a misunderstanding of the meaning of democracy. They hoped the Argenta Friends School would develop citizens who could make decisions more inclusively. The prospectus recognized that "the world is faced with a need for new skills in resolving conflict before its problems become overwhelming. We seek unity for we feel the world can no longer afford to merely outvote minorities and then ignore them."[20] Another school document stated:

> We believe that differences within all groups have too long been settled by the strong or the majority imposing

16 Annual Report, 1970/71.
17 John Stevenson, "History of Argenta Friends School," 1964.
18 The title of Helen Stevenson's memoir written in 1993.
19 Argenta Friends School, 1963 Prospectus, 3–5.
20 Argenta Friends School, 1969 Prospectus, 2, 4.

wishes on the minority. Our very survival may depend on learning new techniques. Our four years together have shown that young people and adults working together can govern themselves with sensitivity to the welfare of the total group. When anyone does this successfully, he is preparing himself to be a valuable world citizen.[21]

Curriculum was divided into academic and enrichment subjects. The school provided all essential high school courses, and the staff tried to ensure that academic offerings suited students' interests as well as university entrance requirements. Enrichment subjects, usually taught by Argenta residents, covered the arts and rural life skills. Because Quakers valued physical activity and citizenship, physical education and a course called World Problems were compulsory. Unlike in later alternative schools, students were expected to attend class and do their assignments. However, an essential principle of the Friends School was that "different students need to proceed at different rates." For some this might mean taking an extra year of school to "find themselves" in Argenta and explore personal and ethical values.

The school originally accepted both general and university bound students, but by 1961 the staff believed that "there was a limit to the range of abilities we could integrate into our small group."[22] Since most students planned to go to university, the school would specialize in the university program. The school opened with grades ten to twelve, and even included grade nine in the second year, but eventually the staff decided that only students in grades eleven and twelve were old enough to benefit fully from the freedom and responsibility the school offered. Argenta remained a senior high school throughout most of its life.

Although the Friends School did not use the term "Progressive," it shared many principles of educational theory with Deweyan Progressive schools. These included an emphasis on the "whole student," self-paced learning, small and informal classes, "active learning," student decision-making, an emphasis on artistic expression, and education for citizenship.

21   "Discipline for Argenta," 1964. A "Discipline" is similar to a constitution, outlining the basic agreements governing a Quaker community.
22   John Stevenson, Coordinator's Report, January 1963.

As John Stevenson wrote in his 1970 letter to applicants, the school was experimental, informal, and flexible within an overarching structure—all compatible with Progressive theory.

STUDENTS

After the successful first year, enrolment increased to seventeen students in 1960/61. Five were returning students from the previous year, who provided continuity and leadership. The founders hoped that senior students rather than teachers would be the principal source of socialization to the school's values.[23] The majority of students (70 per cent) came from California. In addition, one student came from Vancouver and four were local—three children of founding school families and one student from nearby Johnson's Landing.[24] Enrolment averaged eighteen students throughout the 1960s, reaching twenty-three in 1963/64. As interest in alternative schools grew by the end of the decade, Argenta enrolment rose to twenty-one in 1969/70 and peaked at twenty-six students in 1970/71. But students and staff believed the school would be more cohesive if the student body was limited to twenty students.[25] Enrolment dropped to twenty-two the next year and after 1972 returned to an average of eighteen students.[26] Since by this time public enthusiasm for alternative schools had already declined and the number of applications decreased, enrolment would probably have fallen anyway.

During the first decade, the majority of students were American, as the Argenta Quakers had deep roots in the United States. Moreover, the United States had a strong Progressive private school tradition and pockets of liberal population amenable to alternative education. In 1963/64 fifteen of twenty-three students were Americans, thirteen from California. Of the eight Canadians, four were from Argenta and four from other parts

---

23   Although it was not the intention of the founders, this method of socialization was similar to that of British private schools.

24   Enrolment data from student publication, *The Whittler*, December 1959 and Fall 1960. One student's mother heard about the school through Mary Thomson (see chaps. 1, 7).

25   Annual Report, 1970/71.

26   Enrolment data from enrolment and alumni lists, 1959–1973.

of British Columbia. Californians remained the largest single group until 1971, averaging six per year during the late 1960s. But by the end of the decade, students also came from Oregon, Colorado, Michigan, and New York. Canadian students accounted for one-third to one-half of the total. British Columbia provided most of the Canadian students, an average of four students per year from Argenta and four from other parts of the province. By 1970 some students were coming from other regions of Canada, but only after 1975 did Canadian students outnumber those from the United States (over 60 per cent).[27]

About half of the students had Quaker backgrounds and many American students heard about the school through Quaker channels. Some were friends of the Stevensons, others heard about it through Quaker annual Meetings, and a few had been to other Friends schools, such as John Woolman School in California and Scattergood School in Iowa. One student at John Woolman met a former Argenta student there and was attracted by his account of the school. Some students were drawn by what they already knew about Friends education while others were interested in pacifism or consensus.

Students chose Argenta for other reasons as well. Some were attracted to the rural environment, such as one student who "wanted to leave crowded, smoggy Los Angeles and was attracted to the wilds of British Columbia."[28] Others were looking for the personalized experience that could be offered by a small school. Still others were attracted to anything "alternative" during the 1960s, and a few students were simply looking for adventure.

Some students applied to Argenta because they were having difficulty in mainstream schools or with their parents. In 1963 John Stevenson wrote that many students applied because of unhappiness or "a lack of success scholastically, in home adjustment, socially, with personal problems, or North American culture. The improvement in some of the more severe cases has led to the feeling that we are a rehabilitation centre." Mr. Stevenson worried that "we get many applications from students who have problems beyond the scope of our school. We need the strength of a

---

27   Annual Report, 1980/81.
28   Jack Wells, personal interview, February 28, 1997.

number of fairly normal students to carry the one or two who have more severe deficiencies."[29] The school was not equipped to help students with serious problems. Acceptance of too many troubled students contributed to the downfall of several alternative schools.

This became a bigger problem later in the 1960s when some desperate parents hoped to send their children away from the influence of the counterculture or drugs. In such cases the Personnel Committee tried to ensure that the application to the Friends School was primarily the choice of the student. Students who did not really want to be in Argenta did not last long. Staff and students had to cope with some difficult individuals with emotional or family problems. Some students found it hard to adjust to the rural environment, while others were simply unwilling to go along with school policies. One former student recalled, "Students sent there for the wrong reasons felt like they were in reform school because they couldn't drive their car."[30] Another remembered, "There were problems. Some kids coming from big city life were thrown into an isolated rural environment, either going wild or not knowing what to do with their time. Some urban dissatisfied kids were not adjusting well to the policies of the school and were unwilling to live by them."[31]

The founders wanted the school to be accessible to students of all social and economic backgrounds. As in other alternative schools, most students came from middle-class homes with well-educated parents, but the school did attract some students from modest-income families by keeping the tuition low. The school also attracted students from ethnic minorities. The students formed a close group, like an extended family or "brothers and sisters."[32] They maintained a non-competitive environment, treating each other with respect.[33] The senior students helped the new arrivals adjust to Argenta, and "each year the school would constitute itself anew, each person participating in forming the community."[34] Several marriages and

---

29   John Stevenson, Coordinator's Report, January 1963. The term "North America" will sometimes be used in this book as shorthand to refer to Canada and the United States (excluding Mexico).
30   Ed Washington, personal interview, February 10, 1997.
31   Pat Lawson, personal interview, January 29, 1997.
32   Mary Holland, personal interview, November 10, 1996.
33   David Stevenson, personal interview, February 12, 1997.
34   Mary Winder, personal interview, February 24, 1997.

long-term friendships developed, and Argenta graduates continued to cor-
respond with their teachers and fellow students long after their schooldays
were over. Many former students reported that the experience was of
major importance in their lives—creating, as one put it, "strong friendships, bonding, idealism, dreaming, and high hopes; an all-time high in
our lives."[35]

STAFFING

John and Helen Stevenson were the school's leaders for almost fifteen
years. Other staff members came from three principal sources. Some were
Quakers attracted to the Argenta Friends community and their experiment
in education. Most of these were from the United States and saw Canada as
a refuge from American militaristic attitudes. A second group were adults
in their early twenties who had left the United States specifically because
of the Vietnam War. Most were young idealists attracted to Argenta for its
rural location and reputation for tolerance of unconventional lifestyles.
Thirdly, some part-time staff members were already Argenta residents and
taught electives such as art, music, or construction.

Although the Stevensons and a few other staff members were trained
and experienced teachers, most were not. But almost all staff members
had university degrees and led active intellectual lives. Most were gener-
alists—adaptable, fast learners, people with divergent skills and interests.
Some of the teaching was idiosyncratic, and a few staff members were
ineffective or did not subscribe to the school's values and left after one
year. But the majority of teachers were capable despite their lack of training or experience. Former students reported that most of their teachers
conveyed the necessary course material well, and a few were outstanding. Because the staff was small, teachers had to be able to teach courses
outside their fields of expertise. One individual was hired as the school
secretary and ended up teaching French. She took a crash course in French
the next summer so she could do a better job the following year. A full
staff load was three courses, but many staff members doubled as houseparents, which ensured that their duties would be twenty-four hours a day.

35   David Herbison, personal interview, March 10, 1997.

For new staff members life in tiny, isolated Argenta was "total immersion." Adjusting to rural life was not easy—"learning to use a chainsaw, cooking and heating with wood, just staying warm was a challenge."[36] Some staff thought they were coming to a natural paradise but found it "hard, cold, wet, dirty, and uncomfortable."[37] As the staff handbook suggested, "We need staff with energy, flexibility, commitment, imagination, patience, and a good sense of humour."[38] Staff members also had to adjust to living on a very low income, and the handbook included two full pages of "tips on stretching dollars in Argenta." For some, teaching in Argenta resulted in a financial and personal sacrifice.[39] As one former teacher put it, "We loved the rural setting and the physical life was wonderful, but we couldn't manage on the small income."[40] According to Helen Stevenson, teaching at the Friends School could be a challenging experience for "non-Argenta-rooted staff" in contrast to the "resident" teachers who lived in the community on a permanent basis and had been associated with the school for several years.[41] The "non-residents" were largely young people for whom teaching in Argenta was a satisfying experience for one or two years before moving on to a permanent career or larger community.

A few teachers played an important role in the development of the school. Most arrived in Argenta as young adults and some stayed for many years, becoming long-term members of the wider Argenta community. Besides the Stevensons, these were Jonathan Aldrich, Betty and Norman Polster, Brenda Berck, Michael and Lynne Phillips, Donna and Bill Sassaman, Edith Gorman, and Alaine Hawkins. These key staff members were well-educated, socially conscious, and service-oriented individuals. Many worked with Quaker service or peace organizations and were committed to values of peace, participatory democracy, and social activism.[42]

Jonathan Aldrich was the son of a Boston lawyer and judge. Raised as a Unitarian, he graduated from Harvard in the late 1950s and volunteered

---

36   Dan Phelps, personal interview, November 26, 1996.
37   Michael Phillips, personal interview, March 15, 1997.
38   Staff Handbook, undated but probably 1973.
39   Brenda Berck, personal interview, October 14, 1996.
40   Michael Phillips, personal interview, March 16, 1997.
41   Helen Stevenson, "Some Considerations for the Interim Year," 1975.
42   Biographic material from personal interviews and school brochures.

in Mexico with the American Friends Service Committee.[43] He had no
formal teacher training but was familiar with Progressive ideas and the
writings of John Dewey and William James. He also spent nine years as a
student at Shady Hill Progressive School in Cambridge, Massachusetts.[44]
Mr. Aldrich taught at Argenta for six years between 1959 and 1967, the
last two years as principal. Former students praised his "gifted and flexible" teaching style, his delight in English, and his sense of humour. One
recalled that "he catapulted me into wanting to be a writer."[45]

Betty Polster graduated from the University of Pennsylvania, the
state where she grew up.[46] She was active in the Centre for Intentional
Communities and the Pendle Hill Quaker Study Centre in Philadelphia,
where she met John and Helen Stevenson in 1966.[47] She and her husband,
Norman Polster, a scientist and inventor, were income tax refusers and
welcomed an opportunity to leave the United States. In 1967 they arrived
in Argenta, where Ms. Polster taught social studies, while Mr. Polster
taught mathematics and science. Although Betty Polster had limited
teacher training or classroom experience, she taught at the Friends School
for fifteen years. In 1970 she succeeded John Stevenson as principal, a
position she held for most of the next ten years. She was the school's
leader throughout the 1970s, and students and colleagues considered
her an excellent teacher and problem-solver—energetic, compassionate,
and consultative.

Brenda Berck was one of the few Canadian staff members during the
1960s. She grew up in a United Church family in Ontario and was influenced by the Student Christian Movement and the social gospel in the late
1950s and early 1960s.[48] She was active in the peace movement with the
Friends Service Committee in Toronto, assisting American war resisters

43   Jonathan Aldrich, personal interview, November 16, 1996.
44   Shady Hill School was founded in 1915 by a group of parents, mostly Harvard
        professors, and was considered one of the best American Progressive schools. See
        Lawrence Cremin, *The Transformation of the School* (New York: Knopf, 1961), 278.
45   Mary Holland, David Stevenson, personal interviews.
46   Betty Polster, personal interview, December 28, 1994.
47   Pendle Hill was a Quaker study centre and publishing house that provided useful
        resources to the Friends School.
48   See Richard Allen, *The Social Passion* (Toronto: University of Toronto Press, 1973)
        and Paul Axelrod, *Making a Middle Class* (Kingston: McGill-Queens University
        Press, 1994), Chapter 6.

and sending aid to Vietnam. She met John and Helen Stevenson there and accepted an offer to move to Argenta as Friends School secretary in 1968.[49] A trained teacher, she soon filled a vacant staff position and taught French and English from 1968 to 1973. Ms. Berck became the first single houseparent, an uncomfortable idea for some Argenta Meeting members. She was school principal in 1972.

Michael and Lynne Phillips studied history and languages at the University of Washington in Seattle. They later moved to Berkeley in 1966, where Ms. Phillips did graduate work in psychology. Disenchanted with life in the United States due to "Vietnam, police riots, and Chicago," they felt like "political exiles."[50] They heard about the Friends School while doing Quaker peace and social justice work. In 1968 the couple moved to Argenta where they taught and served as houseparents for five years.

Donna and Bill Sassaman had been active in the anti-war movement in the United States and were "fed up with the political situation" there. Both graduated from the University of New Hampshire, Ms. Sassaman with a degree in education and two years' teaching experience, Mr. Sassaman with a degree in science and forestry.[51] Bill Sassaman taught at the Friends School from 1970 to 1972, and both returned in the late 1970s when Donna Sassaman became a member of the school administrative team.

Alaine and John Hawkins moved to Argenta in 1975. Ms. Hawkins, from Ontario, was one of the few Canadians to play a major role at the Friends School. She studied history and languages at the University of Toronto and taught in Ontario for several years prior to teaching in Argenta from 1975 to 1982. Edith Gorman studied education in Vermont, specializing in English, mathematics, and music. Like Ms. Hawkins, she taught for several years in the public school system before coming to Argenta.

Other teachers had shorter tenures. Dan and Jan Phelps grew up in Oregon and New Hampshire. He had a Unitarian background and had attended liberal Reed College. The couple came to Canada in 1962 because

---

49   Brenda Berck, personal interview, October 14, 1996.
50   Michael Phillips, personal interview, March 15, 1997.
51   Donna Sassaman, personal interview, May 15, 1997.

of their opposition to American militarism and the draft. Mr. Phelps earned a PhD at UBC. Moving to Ontario, they were active in the peace movement and the Company of Young Canadians and, while sheltering draft dodgers, met Helen Stevenson at a Quaker education conference in Toronto. Arriving in Argenta in 1967, the couple served as houseparents while Mr. Phelps taught science. For a young couple, looking after six teenage girls was a challenge. They also found it hard to subsist on the low salary and, though they were valued staff members, left Argenta after two years.[52]

Arnold Porter grew up in San Francisco, graduating from university in the middle of the Vietnam era. He claimed conscientious objector status as a pacifist, did draft counselling with the American Friends Service Committee, and worked with a Unitarian youth group. Mr. Porter experienced "great stress around the war," and he and his wife finally decided to "get out of this country and start a life of our own." He met Helen Stevenson at a Quaker Meeting in San Francisco and accepted a position at the Argenta Friends School in 1967.[53]

Hugh Herbison was a native British Columbian and trained teacher. He grew up in a CCF[54] family and was influenced by the social gospel movement. He became a United Church minister in Alert Bay but left the ministry to become principal of the Quadra Island School.[55] Because of his experience with marginalized communities, UBC appointed him to investigate the Doukhobor school issue in the early 1950s. Mr. Herbison lived in a Doukhobor community for two years, but when relations deteriorated between his hosts and the Social Credit government, he resigned.[56] After serving with the Canadian International Development Agency in Southeast Asia, he and his family settled in Argenta. He taught at the Friends School in 1969/70.

52   Dan and Jan Phelps, personal interview, November 26, 1996.
53   Arnold Porter, personal interview, February 10, 1997.
54   The CCF refers to the Co-operative Commonwealth Federation, the precursor to today's New Democratic Party.
55   Hugh Herbison, personal interview, January 22, 1998.
56   See George Woodcock and Ivan Akumovic, *The Doukhobors* (London: Faber and Faber, 1968). Some Doukhobor families refused to enrol their children in public school, but according to Mr. Herbison, many had begun quietly sending their children to school when the newly elected Social Credit government escalated the conflict.

Mary and Steve Holland taught at the Friends School and served as houseparents in 1965/66. Mary Holland (Wolfe) had been a student at the Friends School and was a member of the first graduating class in 1961. She returned to Argenta after completing a degree at the University of California. The Hollands' acceptance of a position at the school made it possible for the Stevensons to take a much-needed sabbatical.

Besides Mary Holland, several former Friends School students came back to teach during the 1970s—Mary Winder from eastern United States, Ed Washington from California, Lynne Campbell from Oregon, Gillian Davies from British Columbia, and Tom Stevenson (John and Helen's son) from Argenta. The school elders considered alumni to be a large extended family and believed that former students could readily transmit the core values and vision of the school. In the early 1970s, several under-graduate students from a Friends College in Ohio helped at the school for one term to fulfill "field term" requirements. The informal association of Friends Schools provided Argenta with a Quaker network of educators and resources. This kind of established network was not available to most other alternative schools.

Numerous Argenta residents, including several school founders, taught individual courses ranging from the creative arts to rural living skills. An underlying school principle was that "there is merit in having a variety of occupations" and that a well-rounded person could work comfortably with "hands and head."[57] Staff members were encouraged to be active intellec-tually and physically. For this reason, part-time teaching was encouraged at Argenta, and the school provided long-term staff members with unpaid sabbaticals for further education or a different type of employment.

Many other individuals with varied backgrounds taught at the Friends School.[58] That so many educated people were available to teach in a small

---

57   John Stevenson, school newsletter, September 1971.
58   Pat Harroff with a chemistry degree and Judy Harroff, an experienced teacher with a degree in education of the deaf, who left the Midwestern United States because of the Vietnam War; Russ Pannier with a master's in philosophy from Harvard and Ann Pannier with four years' teaching experience in Illinois; Andy Kinnaird, a Scottish baker, and Christine Kinnaird, an Ontario office worker; Wayne Smith with a University of Saskatchewan teaching certificate and Judy Smith, a Regina registered nurse; Gary and Margo Williams, trained teachers from Utah who had done service work in the Virgin Islands; Derryll White, a Nova Scotia poet; Sylvia and Bill Powers who studied at Queens University and Royal Military College in Ontario; Elizabeth

out-of-the-way school was largely due to the exodus of liberal young adults from the United States during the Vietnam period and to the appeal of alternative education and lifestyles during the late 1960s.[59]

Teaching at Argenta was demanding of time, energy, and expertise. During the early years, the staff averaged four full-time teachers and was a fairly cohesive group. But by 1967 the staff had doubled in size as more teachers took part-time positions. The increase in part-time work resulted from the retirement of the original Quaker houseparenting families—most teachers now had to double as houseparents and thus needed smaller teaching loads. Furthermore, an increasingly challenging student population, due to 1960s counterculture influences, stretched staff resources. Other alternative schools, such as the New School in Vancouver, experienced a similar increase in staff size around this time.

In a small school, staff changes have a large impact, and staff chemistry at Argenta varied from year to year. For the most part, staff members respected each other as teachers and as people, and enjoyed camaraderie and "esprit de corps."[60] But a few teachers did not fit in, and major disagreements sometimes occurred. During the late 1960s, when the staff had to deal with contentious lifestyle issues, there was considerable discord as staff members thought each other either too moralistic or too permissive. The teachers worked together best when there was a combination of "older more experienced staff members" and younger adults who understood the world of the students and could bridge the generation gap. However, the dominance and experience of John and Helen Stevenson sometimes "made it difficult for younger members to feel they are really

Tanner with degrees in English and library science from the University of Iowa; Jur Bekker with a degree in soil microbiology from a Dutch Agricultural College and Cornell University and Haru Bekker with a master's degree in education from Putney Graduate School in Vermont, a training centre for Progressive teachers. See Susan Lloyd, *The Putney School* (New Haven: Yale University Press, 1987).

59   Other teachers were Tad Melbin, George Strong, Elmo Wolfe, Doug Greene, Lup and Jean Brown, Tom and Ruth Delackner, Margaret Montague, Hugh Ector, Larry Lees, John Rush, Bob Boyd, Don and Georgia Murray, Mitch Bronough, Phil Wells, Marc Hamilton, Phyllis Margolin, Maydelle Quiring, David Taibleson, Michael and Alison Pirot, Peter Renner, Chuck Valentine, Kathryn and Stan Toprorowski, Bill Gray and Jeanne Shaw, Gary Schell and Corol Wight, Pierre and Vicki Picard.

60   Mary Holland, personal interview, November 10, 1996.

sharing the responsibility of the school."[61] Most younger staff members were less interested in academics, more willing to allow students freedom, more tolerant of drug use and sex among teenagers, and more sympathetic to the 1960s counterculture.

CURRICULUM

The academic program at the Friends School was based on the standard British Columbia public school curriculum for university-bound students. They studied English literature, mathematics, Canadian and world history, geography, biology, chemistry, physics, and French. They had regularly scheduled classes, assignments, homework, exams, and report cards.

The school day began with twenty minutes of silence in the style of a Quaker Meeting. Since a major goal of the school was to provide students with an opportunity to develop spiritually through the use of silence, the daily Meeting was compulsory. Throughout the years daily Meeting was scheduled at different times of the day, but most agreed that 8:00 in the morning was as good as any. Mid-morning interfered with classes, before lunch students were too hungry, after lunch they fell asleep, and at the end of the day they wanted to go home. The Meeting was followed by announcements and decisions about the day's events. Three class sessions were held in the morning with one mid-morning break. Students ate lunch in the Meeting House or outside in the spring and early fall. Electives and study periods were held in the afternoon. Students were permitted to leave when their last class was over, usually between 3:00 and 4:00. Most courses met three to four times per week. The timetable and daily schedule were adjusted many times over the years according to student suggestions. For example, short three-month courses were instituted one year so students could take a greater variety of classes.

As in more traditional schools, there was regular homework and students were expected to be in class on time and to have their work done. Study period was compulsory, but after 1963 students who demonstrated mature study habits were exempted. In 1970 study period became optional for everyone, although students were still encouraged to spend spare periods

61   John Stevenson, Coordinator's Report, January 1963.

studying.[62] Attendance at classes was compulsory until 1964 when the staff finally gave in to student pressure that classes be voluntary. Nevertheless, most students continued to attend classes regularly.

Students were evaluated three times per year and had a choice between a credit/no credit grading system or letter grades on their permanent record.[63] The school was accredited in British Columbia, and students could choose to receive an American diploma or complete the more demanding requirements of BC graduation. Grade twelve students wishing a BC graduation wrote government examinations, while most American students also wrote the SATs for university entrance. According to John Stevenson, students did well above average: "Students who wanted to go to Harvard didn't get in but students were accepted at many different universities."[64] The great majority of graduating students did go on to postsecondary education, in some years as many as 90 per cent.

Academic classes at Argenta were small and informal.
Argenta Friends School Prospectus, 1969

Although traditional in some aspects, the Argenta Friends School was much more informal than mainstream public or private schools. Most classes numbered from three to six students, although English classes could be as large as ten, and physical education and the course "World Problems" included the whole school. A few courses had only one or two students. The small classes encouraged informality. Students called teachers by their first names and student-teacher relations were close, since

---

62   Staff Handbook, early 1970s.
63   Student Handbook, 1974/75.
64   John Stevenson, personal interview, September 11, 1996.

students also knew their teachers as houseparents. Students sat around tables rather than at desks and most teachers encouraged discussion. Teachers seldom lectured and, with such low numbers, students readily worked at their own speed. Classes were interactive and, at times, intense. Although teachers were in charge in their classrooms, they often solicited student input when designing courses and sometimes altered their plans if student suggestions seemed practical. Some teachers, after setting the tone and expectations for a course, asked students to take turns doing some of the teaching. One year Mr. Aldrich allowed his students to organize their own plan for studying English literature. Most teachers wanted students to gain understanding rather than accumulate facts, and classes emphasized themes, problem-solving, and values. Even the algebra class emphasized "real problems useful to the intelligent person in understanding today's and tomorrow's problems." Academic courses often had practical applications: the calculation of beams needed to carry a given load over a certain span; arboreal lichens available as winter feed for deer, elk, and caribou.[65]

Teachers were free to determine the content and teaching style of their own courses, although they were somewhat constrained by government examinations. New teachers often consulted with Helen Stevenson about their courses because of her many years of experience. Some teachers planned elaborate course outlines while others "just tried to keep ahead of the students."[66] Because classes were so small, the teachers could be flexible and spontaneous. One student remembered a beautiful day when the lake had frozen over, and Jonathan Aldrich let his students go skating rather than attend class.[67] One year John Stevenson thought his mathematics course was not going well so he turned the class into a study of auto mechanics, and the students worked on their Model A Ford.

Classes were held in several locations. Larger classes met in the "old school," a former one-room public school renovated by staff and students. After 1963 some classes met in the New Meeting House, built by the school community. A cabin near the Meeting House was used as a laboratory and the "old hotel" housed the school library. Some classes even met in the

---

65   Betty Polster, school newsletter, February 1977.
66   John Rush, personal interview, February 25, 1997.
67   Charles Dyson, personal interview, November 5, 1996.

Stevensons' kitchen and dining room during the first two years. The school buildings were heated by wood, and each week two students were responsible for lighting the stove early each morning. The day-to-day informality made classroom learning enjoyable for students, but the school retained a basically traditional approach to teaching.

Students chose their courses with the help of an adult counsellor according to their interests and the requirements for the university they hoped to attend. In 1963/64 the school offered grade eleven and twelve English, grade eleven and twelve mathematics, grade eleven history, grade eleven science, chemistry, and two levels of French.[68] Despite the small staff, the basic high school courses were usually covered. If a basic course had to be omitted because of unavailable staffing, it would be offered the following year such that students might have to take grade eleven and twelve history in reverse order. Students could also take courses by correspondence, and some arranged supervised "independent studies" on a variety of topics from Russian history to the philosophy of Nietzsche or Martin Buber. Teachers provided instruction in basic English and mathematics skills when necessary. One student remembered that teachers were always available to provide individual attention, to help work through a problem.[69]

English literature courses were similar to those offered in any high school. Teachers' reading lists might include *Oedipus Rex*, *Macbeth*, *Wuthering Heights*, *Tom Sawyer*, *Catcher in the Rye*, *Night*, or *The Edible Woman*. Some students were avid readers. Writing was taught sporadically, and one year all students and staff participated in writing improvement tutorials. John Stevenson guided even the most fearful students successfully through mathematics.

The school offered a full science program even though there was little laboratory equipment and teachers had to be creative. John Stevenson designed courses in "kitchen chemistry" and "pots and pans physics," and Dan Phelps "could make a flask or a Bunsen burner out of anything."[70] Teachers used the nearby streams and lake to study ecology, and one year Helen Stevenson taught biology with nothing more than an old-fashioned

---

68 Curriculum meeting, minutes, spring 1962.
69 Charles Dysen, personal interview, October 21, 1996.
70 Mary Winder, personal interview, February 24, 1997.

microscope that her mother had given her. In later years, an earth science course explored astronomy, oceanography, ecology, land structures, the earth's evolutionary history, ancient astrology, and Velikovsky's catastrophe theory.

Because Quakers believe that individuals have an obligation to be active citizens in their community and in the world, John Stevenson developed a required course called World Problems. He brought newspaper articles to stimulate discussion of world events, and students expressed their opinions on the causes of and solutions to various international problems. Students studied and wrote about the Vietnam War, Quebec separatism, recognition of China, overpopulation, the military draft, totalitarianism, and property expropriation. Students remembered serious discussions about the Cuban missile crisis and the assassination of Martin Luther King. Mr. Stevenson asked students to write about whether they would consider participating in a restaurant sit-in, a vigil at a germ warfare plant, a program for registering black voters, or a peace walk.[71] Students developed critical thinking skills as they evaluated arguments and ideas about subjects ranging from pacifism to capital punishment. The final examination asked students to defend their positions on a variety of issues. Most students found this course valuable, and a teacher who sat in on the discussions remembered that it caused him to question the validity of the Vietnam War for the first time.[72] One student recalled that "John taught us to compare sources, that you can't trust a single source. This was memorable."[73] Students even received special permission from the United Nations to fly the world body's flag in front of the school.

School members also became involved in local issues. The building of the Duncan Dam, just upstream from Argenta, generated considerable local protest in the early 1960s. Students were encouraged to make their own decisions, and some participated in demonstrations while others did not. According to almost all students there was very little proselytizing about political issues but a great deal of discussion and debate. Social

---

71   World Problems, course outline, 1964.
72   Jonathan Aldrich, personal interview, November 5, 1996.
73   Ed Washington, personal interview, February 10, 1997.

and political awareness was an integral part of Quaker life; the Friends' perspective was "definitely a world view."

In 1967 Helen Stevenson designed a course called Social Ecology—an exploration of how people live together in communities and "what patterns of interaction tend to foster the greatest degree of human satisfaction?" Students read Ruth Benedict, Victor Frankl, and Konrad Lorenz, examined the influence of culture, and compared the perspective of different schools of psychology. Students also studied and visited Doukhobor intentional communities and read Watson Thomson, a Canadian communitarian socialist.[74] Another year the school offered a course on communal societies in traditional Africa and revolutionary China. Still another course was called "Conflict—To study the nature of conflict and to better understand ways to work for creative resolutions." Students studied aggression, non-violence, competition, co-operation, authority, law enforcement, punishment, and satyagraha.[75] They examined local conflicts in the school and the community. At the heart of these courses was the Quaker view that taking a moral position on public issues was an obligation for all citizens.

In keeping with its spiritual goals, the school offered courses designed to expose students to the spiritual realm. If there was enough interest, a staff member would teach the history of Quakerism, and one year Bob Boyd taught a course on world religions. As religious pursuits gained popularity in the late 1960s, these offerings were expanded with courses in yoga, meditation, spiritual exercises, and a course called Core/Outer. A comparative religion course studied mysticism and gender roles in the major religions, science and religion, prehistoric and "primitive" religion, prophecies, spiritual trends, and Indigenous spirituality, particularly the teachings of Black Elk. A major objective of this course was to develop an appreciation for diversity.

Courses were also taught in the creative arts. Drama was popular, and Mr. Aldrich directed several successful productions, such as *Androcles and the Lion*, enjoyed by many in the community. Opportunities for music instruction were varied because of the number of musicians in Argenta,

---

74   Social Ecology course outlines 1967/68, 1970/71. For Watson Thomson, see Chapter 7.

75   Gandhi's system of non-violence and spiritual practice.

and in later years music and theatre classes combined to put on musical productions. Art was often taught by a team of local craftspeople. One year the crafts included sketching, pottery, batik, weaving, and leatherwork. Photography was also offered over the years.

The Friends School offered practical courses teaching skills for rural living. These were usually taught by long-time Argenta residents and included machinery maintenance, forestry, livestock management, homesteading, cooking, electricity, child care, camping, and community recreation.[76] Homesteading was taught from an environmental perspective, exploring "ways of living that are less exploitative of the world's resources than the current North American standards of living."[77] Construction courses were popular, often growing out of projects like the construction of the school building itself. One year, John Stevenson offered a course in how to cook for a large group of forest fire fighters. Students in community recreation and child care courses applied what they learned by organizing activities for children in the local elementary school and by working with the children of Argenta residents. Students learned life skills by doing them.

The staff considered physical activity very important. Daily physical education was compulsory for students, and staff members were encouraged to participate as well. The school was located in a "recreational paradise," and students had ample opportunity to pursue such outdoor activities as hiking, mountain climbing, swimming, volleyball, skiing, snow-shoeing, and hockey when the lake froze over. One interesting activity was "balancing," described by one teacher as "a form of gymnastics in which the only equipment required is people." Students practised until they could create formations involving two or more individuals balancing on each other's thighs or shoulders. This was to develop strength, balance, and agility as well as trust and co-operation. A former student remembered:

> One person is underneath and one on top. The person on
> top would do an acrobatic activity with the help of the
> person underneath such as standing on the person's thighs

76 Prospectus,   1964,   1969;   annual   reports,   1971–1982;   *Stopped   Press*, 1977–1979.

77 *Stopped Press*, Fall 1977.

or shoulders. Sometimes three people would be involved, all balancing in various positions on each other. The person on the bottom had to be strong. We always had spotters so it wasn't dangerous.[78]

OUTSIDE THE CLASSROOM

Staff and students organized two major school hikes each year in September and June. These were three-day trips to a local mountain peak or valley—Hamil Creek, Fry Creek, Meadow Mountain, Kokanee Glacier, and many others. Students carried everything they needed on their backs and learned wilderness and survival skills. Besides providing a valuable introduction to the outdoors, the beginning of the year hike was also an important experience in group bonding. One student wrote about the very first school hike in September 1959:

> Our three-day hike was a fine way to begin the school year. It gave students and teachers a chance to get acquainted with each other and with the beautiful country we passed through. On the first morning we arranged our sleeping bags and food on our backs. It was a beautiful day and we set out at a good pace, though we weren't so energetic when we reached our campsite by roaring Clint Creek. The bright autumn colours, ferns, and mushrooms made our hike more interesting and the snow-capped peaks made a majestic background. In the evening, as we sat around the campfire, we discussed the purposes of the school. The next morning John Stevenson explained the history of Argenta and its people. We explored farther up the trail and crossed Hamil Creek on a cable chair. We walked along the bottom of the creek with mountains towering above on both sides.[79]

---

78 Pat Lawson, personal interview, January 31, 1997.
79 Marilyn Armstrong (grade ten), "A Hike to Open School," in *The Whittler* (student newspaper), Volume 1, Number 1, December 1959.

Argenta provided numerous opportunities to explore nearby mountains and the beauties of nature right from the school's back yard. Argenta Friends School brochure, 1976

Some students remembered "amazing Northern Lights." Staff considered the hikes a major component of the program, and for many students these camping trips were a highlight of their Argenta experience. The hikes continued to be popular years later, and one student described the school hike to Meadow Mountain in September 1978:

> We camped in an alpine meadow, just below the summit of the mountain. The first night a group hiked to the top to see the sunset. Later we all sat around the fire singing songs, telling stories, and huddling close together for warmth. The next day we hiked around the area with snowy mountains and ridges towering above us. There was lots of wildlife observed and we heard coyotes howling at the moon. We arrived back in Argenta the next afternoon in good spirits.[80]

80   Monty Yaswen, Debbie Borsos, "Beginning of School Hike," *Stopped Press* (News from Argenta Friends School), Fall 1978.

Physical work was an important component of the school curriculum, and each year up to ten regular school days were cancelled to provide "work days" around the school. One essential task was to prepare for winter by chopping and splitting fifteen cords of wood to feed the school furnace during the year.[81] Students also participated in office work and the maintenance, repair, and upgrading of school buildings. School leaders saw community service as a fundamental component of the curriculum, and work days were also spent helping families in the wider Argenta community.[82] One student remembered how the school brought in firewood for an older community member.[83] School members also helped Argenta residents with building projects, gardening, tree pruning, canning, chicken coop maintenance, window washing, and other jobs. Work crews were managed by local adults, and both students and staff took part in these projects, although at times staff members requested exemption due to overwork and exhaustion. Students received credit for participation in ongoing work crews.

A popular innovation beginning in 1968 was called "intersession." This was a two-week period in February when classes ceased so that groups of students could organize in-depth projects usually away from Argenta. These often involved community service, peace and disarmament work, and social activism.[84] In one memorable project, the whole school participated in a training workshop in non-violence with the Pacific Life Community in Vancouver. The students then used their new skills to take part in non-violent action and "public witness" at the Trident nuclear weapons establishment at Bangor, Washington. Another year the group attended a United Nations symposium on human rights and disarmament in Vancouver, which included workshops, a concert with Pete Seeger, a "Walk to Moscow," and a brief stay at Ground Zero.[85] Other projects were arranged through the Friends Service Committee, a Quaker social service

---

81   Cathy Munn, "Another Autumn in Argenta," *Stopped Press*, Fall 1978.

82   Student Handbook, 1969, 2.

83   Charles Dyson, personal interview, November 6, 1996.

84   One former student emphasizes the importance of social activism to Quakers. He remembered picketing the Oakland Induction Centre as a school project at John Woolman Friends School in California.

85   Annual Report, 1981/82.

organization. One year students volunteered at several Calgary service agencies, including a hospital, a daycare centre, a seniors' residence, an agency for the blind, an Indigenous community services program, and Alcoholics Anonymous. Another year students helped build a hostel for autistic adults on Saltspring Island. Students made extended visits to Indigenous communities, the Blood people in Alberta and the Colville Reservation in Washington, to learn about their culture and history.[86] Argenta students visited and studied Doukhobor communities, since Quakers and Doukhobors share common values of pacifism and simplicity. One student recalled his visits to the Doukhobor communities at Grand Forks and Brilliant as a high point of his school years.[87]

Some intersession projects involved creative arts workshops in writing, silk-screening, printing, flute, recorder, and guitar-making.[88] Students visited the fishing village of Bamfield on Vancouver Island and an ashram on Kootenay Lake, and helped clear a portion of the Earl Grey Trail in the Selkirk Mountains. In 1977 the school spent several days at the Powell Lake Farm, a rural commune associated with a Vancouver alternative school, Total Education.[89] Students also spent a week on an exchange with a school in Trois Rivières, Quebec, in the late 1970s.

For a small school the Argenta Friends offered a remarkably full curriculum. Students were provided with a basic academic education, experience of nature and a rural lifestyle, an appreciation of the importance of physical work and recreation, opportunities to pursue the arts, exposure to spiritual practices, and a solid grounding in service and world citizenship. These were combined with a unique feature of the school—the development of communal values through the experience of living with Argenta families.

---

86   Intersession activities described in annual reports, 1976–1982.
87   Jack Wells, personal interview, February 28, 1997.
88   Annual reports, 1971–1982.
89   The founder of this program, Peter Scheiber, lived in Argenta in the 1950s. See Chapter 9.

Home Life

Living in family homes provided students with valuable support and companionship to help them adjust to an unfamiliar life: "Since students live in homes, their problems are faced in the warmth of a home atmosphere. The give and take of chores, cooking, and family fun are activities which give balance and zest to a young person looking ahead."[90]

Students were treated like members of the family and in return were expected to abide by family practices and to participate fully in the economic life of the household. School guidelines suggested that students work on their host family's homestead for an hour a day during the week and four hours on Saturday. Chores included chopping wood, tending the vegetable garden, milking cows, gathering eggs, pitching hay, picking and canning fruit, cooking, and helping with building projects. Helping secure the winter supply of wood was the most important chore, as all households depended on wood heat, and the amount needed was formidable—up to ten cords per household. Some households canned "massive amounts" of fruit each year. Working in the garden, preparing large meals, and putting away food for the winter were enjoyable communal efforts. One student recalled the typical morning routine at the Wolfe household:

> We would get up at 7:00. One of the chores was to light the fire. Everybody would take a five-minute shower. Ruth made breakfast and a crew of two students would pitch in as much as we could. In good weather we all took the shortcut to school straight down the hill.[91]

Daily student life was highly regulated. Due to the rugged terrain surrounding Argenta, students were responsible for letting their houseparents know where they were going and when they expected to return. Visiting between houses on weeknights was allowed only with prior permission of both sets of houseparents. Otherwise, students were expected to spend the evenings at home. Part of the evening was designated as quiet time for study, while the rest of the evening was spent making music, playing games, or listening to the radio. On weekends students visited other

90   Argenta Friends School, Prospectus, 1963, 6.
91   Pat Lawson, personal interview, January 30, 1997.

households or attended school and community social events but had to be home one half hour after the function ended and were restricted to "one late night a week." Although dress was practical and informal, students were required to wear modest clothing and were not allowed to wear mini-skirts or shorts to school during the early years. Students were not permitted to drive cars while they were in Argenta, although local students could use them for legitimate family business or chores. Hitchhiking was discouraged. In addition to the school's restrictions, parents could prohibit their children from engaging in "hazardous activities" such as using a chainsaw, riding motorcycles, or working with farm animals. Students were permitted to leave Argenta four weekends per year by invitation and with permission from home.[92]

Despite an attempt to develop uniform expectations for houseparents, some had stricter rules than others. Houseparents rarely had time to meet as a group and most worked out whatever system suited their own personal style: "Though students and houseparents bear mutual responsibility for making it a place where love and unity prevail, the houseparents have the final responsibility. Some take almost complete authority while others decide rules by house meetings."[93]

Houseparenting was a demanding job. Houseparents received $50 a month per student, most of which was designated for food. Most Argenta residents had huge vegetable gardens so a few dollars could go a long way. During the first decade, the original Quaker families did most of the houseparenting. The Boyds were houseparents for nine years, the Pollards and Ectors for eight, the Wolfes for seven, the Seamarks for six, the Herbisons for five, and the Stevensons for most of the first twelve years.[94] Most considered it a rewarding experience, but by the late 1960s the original host families had grown weary, and it became more difficult to find houseparents. In 1967 and in several subsequent years, the school almost closed due to a lack of suitable homes for students.

The school hired a young couple without children to look after a student house as early as 1962, but by the late 1960s this became more frequent.

---

92   Student Handbook, 1964/65.
93   Discipline for Argenta, 1964.
94   Cumulative list of students, staff, houseparents, January 1973.

The school built a student home in 1968 and later acquired another local house, both of which were staffed by couples. Many of these young house-parents were also staff members. Most found the twenty-four hour a day job more difficult and stressful than they had expected. Their inexperience as parents also took its toll. Several had to give up exhausted in the middle of the year, and one marriage broke up a short time later. Although teaching in Argenta was hard on relationships, it could strengthen marriages as well. Beginning in 1969, several single women served as houseparents, even though the Friends Meeting frowned on this as inappropriate and too demanding for one person. This did turn out to be a difficult job for one person, but some single houseparents managed well. In general, having teenagers of their own and experience dealing with typical teenage problems and discipline proved to be advantageous for houseparents. One couple suggested the following attributes as helpful for successful house-parenting: prior experience with teenagers, a stable proven marital relationship, objectivity, openness, honesty, reasonableness, patience, ability to keep your mouth shut, nerves of stainless steel, and the conviction to be a good model of Quakerism to young people.[95]

The group living experience was a key educational component of the Friends School. The school founders hoped students would work out solutions for getting along with each other: "In our rural environment we find ourselves living at close quarters where we must learn to live together. Group living results in an examination of ideas and attitudes which need not end in mere conformity."[96] One teacher wrote: "Education takes place on a twenty-four hour a day basis. It is when we attend our Meetings, participate in committees, and share in interpersonal relations that we see ourselves growing. The adults find ourselves challenged to grow as new insights are thrust upon us."[97] John Stevenson observed growth in human relations:

> It is the sometimes abrasive twenty-four hour a day
> contact which is different from a large school where stu-
> dents can dismiss the faculty as impossible and the faculty

95   Anneke and Rob Rensing, "Some Observations on Our Role as a Houseparent," undated.
96   Discipline for Argenta, 1964.
97   Betty Polster, Annual Report, Spring 1970.

can ignore individual differences in the students they see. There are always adjustments for houseparents and students as they struggle to be sensitive to the needs of each. Out of it comes a working relationship which is far from perfect, but most of us have grown in the process. We have gained some experience in the art of conciliation.[98]

Most students enjoyed the group living. Since the host families boarded four to six students in addition to their own children, the large households provided camaraderie and fun. Students remembered large meals around the dinner table and family music making in the evenings. They accompanied their families on outings and close relationships developed. One former student said he "benefited from the family living as much as from the education."[99] Another recalled that "for the first time, I felt I was part of a family." Two other students wrote:

> With six other people in the household I had to adapt my life to make room for the needs of other people. I was only allowed one bath per week because of limited hot water supply. Everyone was assigned household jobs and I found myself being taught how to do things that were strange and unfamiliar to me such as chopping wood and harvesting carrots. The most difficult thing I faced was learning to live with people of varying temperaments, backgrounds, and ideas.

> My home in Argenta consists of seven people crowded into a small wooden structure with an outhouse. You soon learn that there is no such thing as privacy. While there is a lot of bumping into each other which can create tension, there is a strong sense of warmth, love, and caring.[100]

Students were exposed to the skills of a new pair of adults and learned a great deal from this experience. This included how rural families live, how to use tools, how to live with older and younger children, how to adjust to a different family pattern, and how to live with peers twenty-four

98   John Stevenson, school newsletter, October 1968.
99   Jack Wells, personal interview, February 28, 1997.
100 Anonymous students, Student Handbook, 1970/71.

hours a day.[101] One student learned how to play chess from his house-parents. Above all, the houseparent was to be a teacher, "a friendly, firm person who helps students fulfill the agreements they have with the school; seeing that they are in nights and after weekend activities, and quiet when study is supposed to be taking place."[102] As John Stevenson suggested:

> Houseparents should set the tone of the home, provide warm understanding love, be a resource person expert in operating a home in a rural environment, and have some knowledge in the ways people can co-operate. The houseparent is the member of the household who has experience and maturity, but not the one who dominates or decides, nor does the work others have left undone. The houseparent advises and watches for opportunities to step back when the students seem ready and able to take responsibility."[103]

The development of trustworthiness was a major goal of the Argenta Friends School. Difficulties were worked through without punishment. John Stevenson remembered one year when he could hear two girls regularly sneaking out of their upstairs bedroom at night. But when they denied it each morning he accepted their word. Eventually they stopped of their own accord, as they realized they were undermining the system of trust.[104] In another incident, three boys went on a spontaneous hike one evening in the middle of winter. They spent the night in a barn and their worried houseparents found them the next morning having breakfast with a family several miles down the road. Instead of punishing the boys, the adults helped them plan a more practical overnight hike two weeks later.[105] As Helen Stevenson said, "We believed that encouraging people to live with a trusting attitude was the most important education we could offer."[106]

---

101 John Stevenson, Report on Housing, mid-1960s.

102 John Stevenson, letter to Jean Wagner, April 26, 1965.

103 John Stevenson, Report on Housing, mid-1960s.

104 John Stevenson, personal interview, September 1996; and Helen Stevenson, *We're In This Together*, unpublished memoir, 1993.

105 John Rush, personal interview, February 25, 1997, and Helen Stevenson, *We're In This Together*, unpublished memoir, 1993.

106 Helen Stevenson, personal interview, September 11, 1996.

Gender equality was a basic assumption among the Argenta Friends, as the equal voice of men and women was part of Quaker belief.[107] As early as the 1950s, the Friends co-operative considered all work to be of equal value and allocated equal income to each adult regardless of his or her role in production. However, the Quakers maintained a somewhat traditional division of labour with men doing the heavy work and women in charge of the home. Country life can be conducive to traditional relationships because of the physical nature of the work. "The boys spent a lot of time out getting wood"[108] and one female teacher was discouraged from using a chainsaw.[109] However, boys were still expected to help in the kitchen, girls took auto mechanics, and boys learned how to knit and darn socks. By the late 1960s, according to one student, there was "little or no differentiation of chores based on gender."[110] As Betty Polster put it, "Everybody collected firewood, everybody did the cooking, everybody did the building."[111] The school leadership was primarily female throughout the 1970s. Feminist issues were discussed in class, and one year everybody read Germaine Greer's *The Female Eunuch*.[112] Several years later, a consciousness-raising session with female students and women from the community grew into a weekly women's group on gender roles. One staff member wrote that "the sharing of feelings and experiences among women of different ages seems to be very valuable to all involved."[113]

Argenta residents were good at organizing their own entertainment. There was no television before 1970 and the nearest movie theatre was miles away. The school helped organize potluck dinners, National Film Board movie nights, coffee house evenings, and monthly Saturday night dances featuring folk, square, or ballroom dancing. Since there were numerous musicians in the community, Bob Boyd organized an orchestra

---

107 W. A. C. Stewart suggests that early Quakers assumed spiritual and educational equality between men and women. *Quakers in Education* (London: Epworth, 1953), 31.

108 Pat Lawson, personal interview, January 30, 1997.

109 Brenda Berck, personal interview, October 15, 1996.

110 Mary Winder, personal interview, February 24, 1997.

111 Betty Polster, personal interview, December 28, 1995.

112 Germaine Greer, *The Female Eunuch* (New York, 1970). This was one of the most influential feminist books of the 1970s.

113 School newsletter, April 1976.

that often played at these events. Students and teachers enjoyed the social activities. Since almost all Argenta residents attended, the dances were an effective way to build bridges between the Quakers, the earlier settlers, and the later countercultural arrivals. School leaders took seriously the school's role as part of the community. The school was an economic benefit to Argenta, bringing in money and providing employment. In turn, the local community provided the school with an extensive curriculum resource.

Former students cited the rural environment as one of the most memorable aspects of the Argenta Friends School. Since most were from cities, students had to be taught how to use a chainsaw, how to camp overnight, how to garden, and how to cook. Although environmentalism was not overtly emphasized, composting and recycling were integral to the way of life. As one former student said: "In rural areas people have always recycled their garbage; it is economical, sensible, and natural."[114] One teacher recalled that "the wilderness and rural way of life was a profound experience for staff and students; walking by orchards, chickens, sheep, and goats, making apple cider ... we were very touched by that."[115] Students walked to and from school through the woods each day, and many had to adjust to the lack of familiar urban stimulation. Although it was hard for some, most came to appreciate the peace and quiet and the meditative quality of the wilderness. One student's memories were particularly evocative:

> The rural environment was a highlight for me. Isolated, beautiful, close to trees, snow. It provided an ideal setting to grow and mature in a silent way. It opened up my heart and mind to wilderness. I got close to the spirit of nature.[116]

This integration of the natural environment with the emotional development of many students was a noteworthy strength of the Argenta Friends School.

---

114 Jack Wells, personal interview, February 28, 1997.
115 Arnold Porter, personal interview, February 7, 1997.
116 Jack Wells, personal interview, February 28, 1997.

DECISION-MAKING

The Argenta Friends Meeting was the ultimate authority in the affairs of the Friends School. The Meeting set the overall philosophy, oversaw the hiring of staff, arranged student accommodation, had the final say on policy issues, and decided each year whether the school should continue. Several Meeting members were experienced in co-operative ventures and could offer meaningful advice to the school staff. John and Helen Stevenson, Bob Boyd, Mary Pollard, and Ruth Wolfe formed the School Committee, an advisory group that met once a month to provide guidance on student admissions, staff hiring, staff relations, school policy, housing, finance, planning, publicity, and maintenance.[117]

At first, school matters were discussed at every monthly Meeting, since most teachers and all houseparents were committed Meeting members. But over the years, the Friends Meeting became less involved in the everyday affairs of the school and, outside of major philosophical or moral issues, most decisions were made at the school level. The Stevensons provided the main link between the Friends Meeting and the school staff, and their opinions carried a lot of weight. But as early as the second year, John Stevenson observed tensions developing:

> During the second year we expanded to include some
> adults who had not been through the Delta Co-op experi-
> ence with us, and some who were not committed Friends.
> There were different interpretations of the abstract ideas
> in the purposes, different moral standards, and different
> degrees of commitment. These tensions resulted in a less
> unanimous adult position.[118]

By 1962 the founders became convinced that decision-making needed to be more formal. But they were opposed to a hierarchical structure and, instead of creating a principalship, appointed John Stevenson as "Coordinator." He was responsible for overseeing the day-to-day function-ing of the school, meeting with committees, helping to solve individual

---

117 John Stevenson, Report on School Structure, May 1963.
118 John Stevenson, "A History of the Relationship between Argenta Friends School and Argenta Monthly Meeting," 1969.

problems, overseeing the use of buildings, and making recommendations on student admissions. These duties took all the coordinator's time, and other administrative tasks such as office work, finance, and publicity were hardly touched until the school hired a part-time secretary in 1963.

In 1962 a serious rift arose among the teachers. Even though they had talked about education all summer and thought they agreed on basic principles, one new teacher argued for a more traditional academic orientation, a selective admissions policy based on academic ability, and a traditional headmaster. John Stevenson reluctantly agreed to become "headmaster" for the rest of the year. Although the teacher left at the end of the year, the possibility of staff disunity and an increase in daily decisions convinced the school community by 1964 that a principal in charge of basic operations would be helpful. But as Betty Polster later explained: "From the first we have been trying to de-emphasize the Principal as the spokesman and head of the school and have looked on the Principal's role as a necessary function of coordination and administration."[119] John Stevenson was principal throughout most of the 1960s and, according to his colleagues, he was an effective leader and an excellent mediator. He was not afraid to make decisions, but he consulted widely and was quick to call meetings whenever a potentially contentious issue arose. Betty Polster served as principal for most of the early 1970s and was also highly respected. Jonathan Aldrich and Brenda Berck served successful short terms, and after 1976 a committee of four teachers took on the role together.

Weekly staff meetings were often held during the evening in the informal atmosphere of a teacher's home, where the teachers discussed individual student progress, educational theory, and the academic program. Although the teachers had autonomy to design their courses as they saw fit, they frequently sought advice from one another. Staff decisions were made by Quaker-style consensus, but John and Helen Stevenson strongly influenced staff discussions since the school continued to be an embodiment of their vision.

Although the staff often enlisted the talents and skills of Argenta residents, some community members believed the school was insufficiently open to outside input. At a "school vision" workshop in 1965

---

119 Annual Report, 1970/71.

one participant said: "Too little use has been made of local talent. I have the impression that a person must conform to the attitudes and demands of the founding Friends group before one is thought fit to work with the school."[120] This was an exaggeration, but the leadership expected staff to subscribe to basic school philosophy.

In 1963 the school began to develop a more formal structure. Some argued for the formation of a community-wide school board, but the founders rejected traditional models of both public and private schools in favour of a structure "more indigenous to the lives of the Argenta Friends. We are searching for a pattern for governing the school which in essence is similar to a Friends business meeting."[121] Authority would rest in the whole group:

> We value each person's contribution to what is being discussed and go ahead with a decision only when we reach consensus. Meetings make up the institutional life of the school. As they are often tedious, redundant, and seemingly counterproductive, sooner or later everyone reaches a point where another meeting seems unbearable. Yet without them the fabric of the school would disintegrate. From meetings come the deepening of our working relations.[122]

Students were expected to play a key role in virtually all levels of school decision-making. The prospectus stated: "The Argenta Friends School is an attempt to give students the opportunity to participate in the decisions which affect almost every phase of their lives."[123] Or as the school Discipline explained, "Students work closely with adults in a group in which the students have a voice in all matters but the basic framework."[124] The founders believed this was the school's most important contribution:

> The unique characteristic of the Argenta Friends School is the opportunity to experience a method of decision

---

120 "Vision of Argenta School," recorded in minutes, Fall 1965.
121 Report to Monthly Meeting on School Structure, May 1963.
122 Staff Handbook, probably 1973.
123 Argenta Friends School, Prospectus, 1963.
124 Discipline for Argenta, 1964.

> making uncommon in our world today. It depends upon a
> group of people working together to reach the best plan of
> action they can envision.[125]

The student-staff meeting guided the day-to-day running of the school. This group, composed of all staff and students, met once a week to discuss scheduling, work projects, special events, school maintenance, and living together as a co-operative group. The meetings were chaired by a student "clerk" (a valuable learning experience), and students were encouraged to voice their opinions on all matters. As the school brochure stated: "This brochure was written by a group of students and staff who struggled to get unity on the wording, picture selection, and layout. This is just one example of ways in which our small school involves students and staff in the workings of the school."[126] The student-staff meeting developed policies on compulsory classes, smoking, evening visiting, use of cars, sex, drug and alcohol use, and attendance at meetings. Their recommendations had to be approved by the Friends Meeting but were rarely overruled except when it came to sex, alcohol, and drugs, when the Meeting generally disallowed any liberalization of existing policy. The only areas not under the jurisdiction of the student-staff meeting were academics, personnel, and the fundamental school vision.[127]

The student-staff meeting followed the model of a Quaker business meeting, reaching decisions only if there was consensus or "unity."[128] Theoretically all participants were equal, although in a Quaker Meeting the opinions of some individuals may carry extra weight due to their experience or particular expertise. The prospectus explained how the Argenta Friends School applied longstanding Quaker methods for building consensus:

> The method involves searching for the best in each person
> and in the group as a whole. In the Student-Staff Meeting

---

125 John and Helen Stevenson, letter to the monthly Meeting, 1973.
126 School brochure insert, 1969.
127 Student Handbook, 1968/69.
128 For an account of Quaker decision making, see Michael Sheeran, *Beyond Majority Rule: Voteless Decisions in the Religious Society of Friends* (Philadelphia: Yearly Meeting, 1983). Argenta Friends adapted methods from Howard Brinton, *Guide to Quaker Practice* (Wallingford, Pennsylvania: Pendle Hill, 1946).

each individual, regardless of age, has a voice. During the discussion individuals reassess their opinions. To arrive at a group decision it is often necessary for an individual or several people to give way, recognizing the validity in others' opinions. On occasion, a person will feel strongly that the changes involved in a decision would be harmful and his objection will prevent its acceptance. There is enormous pressure felt by this individual but his opinion is respected. Hopefully a consensus will emerge incorporating the best ideas acceptable to the group. This may not be unanimous, but it is a decision to which no one objects strongly.[129]

Respect for the views of the minority was a fundamental principle of consensus building. "An opposing minority, however small, is not disregarded, especially if it contains members whose judgement is highly respected. If an individual lays a concern before the meeting, if he feels it deeply and brings it up again and again in spite of opposition, the meeting may finally acquiesce even though a degree of hesitation is still felt by some."[130] The staff handbook stated:

When a group waits until all are satisfied, the decision will be better than when only a majority are in agreement. It means there are fewer disappointed or disgruntled members after the decision is made. It also means long meetings and delays as a minority struggles to incorporate its concern into the final outcome.[131]

In the winter of 1969, the school planned a two-week visit to an Indigenous community on Lesser Slave Lake in northern Alberta.[132] Students were to live with individual families in unfamiliar and difficult conditions. Helen Stevenson described the decision-making process:

One year the school became excited about a proposal to spend two weeks living with impoverished Indian

---

129 Prospectus, 1964, and "Discipline for Argenta," 1964.
130 Argenta Friends School, Prospectus, 1969, 3–4.
131 Staff Handbook, 1973.
132 The project had been suggested by a Company of Young Canadians staff worker.

families in Northern Alberta. A student/staff committee
had worked out the logistics. Though a bit scary to some
students, it seemed like a challenge that we could handle.
All seemed ready for final approval when one student,
who himself wanted to go, stated boldly that he didn't
believe we should go. Disbelief was a first reaction. It
soon became clear that he had been listening to some of
the less vocal students who were more afraid than they
had been willing to admit. With encouragement from him
they were able to express their fears. We didn't go. Later
we learned that our going could have been a disaster.[133]

During Quaker deliberations, individuals are encouraged to genuinely
listen to each other and try to understand others' points of view ("listening
for understanding"). It was customary that a moment of silence follow
each speaker to guard against interruption and "to hear the echo of the
message in our own souls."[134] Staff members tried to model good listening: as one former student said, "the best way to learn to listen is to be
listened to."[135] If issues were contentious the meetings were often long,
and some students found them tedious. But the underlying objective was
to teach the students responsibility and wisdom in decision-making.[136]

The school tried to balance individual and group needs. Quakers strive
to achieve a "reasonable balance between freedom and order; group
authority tempered by individual judgement. Each year is an experiment
to adjust the delicate balance between allowing people to follow their
own pursuits and providing for that work which we need to do together."
The question is, "Does the individual lose his identity as part of the
community?"[137] The student handbook suggested:

The emphasis of all we do is on the importance and
uniqueness of the individual. Yet emphasis is placed on
integrity, sensitivity, and interdependence of the group.

133 Helen Stevenson, "We're In This Together," 12.
134 Student Handbook, 1974/75.
135 Mary Winder, personal interview, February 24, 1997.
136 Jack Wells, personal interview, February 28, 1997.
137 Annual Report, 1971/72.

Group standards must be upheld and, although one is encouraged to be an individual, one is limited."[138]

The school was governed by "policies" or guidelines rather than rules. These policies could be interpreted flexibly: "Policies can be stretched to cover individual needs whereas rules imply a hard and fast set of penalties if broken." As the Discipline explained:

We believe that students can operate without rigid rules or penalties. The school policies are guides for action flexible enough to be adjusted to individual situations. This results in the young person feeling largely self-governed and in learning that he must take responsibility for his actions instead of blaming an adult imposing rules.[139]

Policies were formulated by the entire community and could be changed at a school meeting. The student handbook stated: "The policies have been drawn up after many hours of group consideration. Changes in policies occur only if all agree that the change seems to better implement the philosophy of the school."[140] Contentious policies were subject to ongoing discussion: "Within the school we have had many policies challenged. In some cases flexibility of interpretation has left the policy intact as a guideline, in others new wording had to be considered. Through it all the important fact has been the growth in individuals as open discussion gave opportunities to understand each other and the school better."[141]

The student handbook listed all school policies, and new students were asked to sign an agreement to abide by them: "I understand that Argenta Friends School has some definite policies that will not change. It also has policies that are open to changes as needed. I have read the policies and I believe they describe a school I should like to be part of."[142] Following the policies was basic to school membership: "The school's aim is to develop a close community of students and staff, experiencing joys and hardships. The policies act as a framework within which the student operates,

138 Mary Winder, Student Handbook, 1968/69.
139 Discipline for Argenta, 1964.
140 Student Handbook, 1964/65.
141 Annual Report, Spring 1970.
142 Student declaration form, August 1966.

patterns of action which must be observed. A student must attempt to learn to live within the rules of the school community."[143]

When policies were disregarded, students were given a second chance. The goal was to develop a commitment to the well-being of the community: "Thoughtfulness and consideration for others make up the foundation upon which our regulations rest. The school is based on a growing degree of trust."[144] In Quaker tradition, "when you break the law you should do it openly for a good reason," and school leaders preferred that students defy a policy openly so that it could be addressed.[145] In rare cases when a student continued to disregard the policies after counselling and numerous second chances, this was taken as an indication that he or she did not really want to be there, and the student was sent home. According to John Stevenson, no more than six students were asked to leave over the years:

> We recognize that when a policy is broken, people not rules are involved. Counselling takes place, and each situation is looked at considering the needs of individuals, the school, and wider circles of people. The effort is to find a new working relationship rather than to blame or punish. Only when we have tried many times do we consider asking anyone to leave.[146]

The school developed an elaborate committee structure, and teachers and students spent hundreds of hours per year on committee work. Committees included: curriculum, ministry and counsel, personnel, building maintenance, finance, secretarial, janitorial, library, publicity, sports, social, work crews, and publications. The Curriculum Committee evaluated all courses and determined the course offerings for the following year. It consisted of any staff members and non-graduating students who wanted to participate. The committee considered the academic requirements and interests of individual students in deciding what would be offered. Student suggestions and requests sometimes led to the development of new

---

143 Student Handbook, 1966.
144 Wendy Mitchell, Student Handbook, 1964/65.
145 Jonathan Aldrich, personal interview, November 16, 1996.
146 Student Handbook, 1970/71.

courses such as Helen Stevenson's Social Ecology course, which studied how people get along with each other.

The Ministry and Counsel Committee's job was to help any student experiencing personal problems. Some students had trouble adjusting to life in Argenta; others had difficulty abiding by school policies, while others simply needed help with normal adolescent problems. Four well-respected students were appointed by the student body to sit on this committee with one staff member, usually the principal.[147] Ministry and Counsel was also expected to keep watch over the "tone of the community" and report to the whole group if they noticed any attitudes prevalent in the school that might suggest a policy meeting was necessary. This pre-emptive problem-solving was invaluable. The committee also provided a liaison between students and staff,[148] attempting to "meet the needs of the individuals and the group."[149] Former students believed that the committee addressed problems in a "caring way" with respect for privacy.[150]

The Personnel Committee consisted of the principal, one or two teachers, and several members of the monthly Meeting. The committee reviewed applications for staff positions and student placements, reviewed present staff, organized student housing placements, and counselled with staff members when necessary. The committee sought teachers and students "who will benefit from the school and will be able to contribute in ways that meet school aims and needs."[151] The Personnel Committee came to include students by the late 1960s as, influenced by the prevailing attitudes of the time, students pressed for a more significant role in school governance. Prospective students were encouraged to visit Argenta, but if this was impractical they were interviewed by former students in their area. John Stevenson recalled that the students themselves were the most effective interviewers of prospective students and staff members.

How much influence students really had in determining policy is debatable. One student described the adult attitude as "we want you to

147 Student members were: student clerk, recording clerk, girls' counsellor, boys' counsellor.
148 Student Handbook, 1968/69.
149 From "Discipline for Argenta," 1964.
150 David Stevenson, Mary Winder, personal interviews.
151 "Personnel Practices in AFS," probably early 1970s.

decide how to run things but we want the last say. This was confusing to many students. When an idea was vetoed at the last moment the students felt 'what was the point?'"[152] One student suggested that decision-making was primarily an exercise in generating creative ideas. Another added, "I didn't realize there would not be a conclusion to those issues—it was the process that was important."[153] Certain issues were non-negotiable, and many students believed that decisions on contentious matters were made in advance by the adults who had their minds made up. One remarked, "We felt we did have a say. But we had the impression that some decisions had already been made by John and Helen, that we were going through the motions."[154] Another said that observers had "the impression that students had more say than they really did."[155] One former teacher confirmed that "the adults made the decisions in the large matters, students in the small matters only."[156] Another teacher summarized his feelings this way:

> I was never entirely comfortable with the way it was done. There was tension between the adults and the students and a suspicion on the part of the kids that the adults had already determined the outcome. Students did have significant input into the policies but I'm not sure how effective it was. There were limits.[157]

However, most students found Argenta a refreshing change from public high schools. They believed that the adults genuinely listened to and considered their views.[158] One said that although the adults' opinions carried more weight, students still had "lots of input."[159] Another recalled, "In the big issues we didn't really have input. But we were young and needed guidance. We understood and accepted the school's position."[160]

The Argenta Quakers, for all their openness and courage regarding political and social problems, were found by some to be emotionally

152 Pat Lawson, personal interview, January 30, 1997.
153 Polly Wilson, personal interview, October 24, 1996.
154 Charles Dyson, personal interview, November 5, 1997.
155 Beth Martin, personal interview, April 17, 1997.
156 Hugh Herbison, personal interview, January 22, 1998.
157 Michael Phillips, personal interview, February 10, 1997.
158 Erica Pfister, personal interview, April 16, 1997.
159 Ed Washington, personal interview, January 8, 1997.
160 David Herbison, personal interview, March 31, 1997.

guarded and puritanical about "moral issues." Decisions were occasionally ambiguous, masking disagreements with hazy expressions like "expected but not compulsory." Furthermore, the adults were not consistent in following through with the consequences of policy violations. Students found this lack of clarity frustrating. One teacher suggested that "consensus was such a long, drawn-out process, the kids got discouraged. Some students wished the school had been more authoritarian, then they could have rebelled."[161] Although the elders genuinely wanted students to share in running the school, their strong world view and high moral standards made it difficult for them to accept student decisions with which they did not agree. Yet they were ambivalent about imposing their wishes directly. This basic contradiction was never resolved.

Another frustration for both students and staff was that once a decision was made, it was difficult to achieve consensus to change it. One former student said, "It took a lot of momentum to change a policy once it was made."[162] The staff handbook acknowledged this dilemma:

> This process can make the school seem inflexible to someone who is here for a year or two. Changes which we all agree need to be made seem to be delayed as the group tries to meet the original needs and the needs of changing times and changing attitudes. We have policies about alcohol, drugs, and sex which we all agree could be improved, yet we haven't reached unity as to how to write them in a better way.[163]

Participants also remembered "too many endless meetings." One student recalled several "crises" that questioned the school's existence. Emotional meetings sometimes went on for hours and hours. "It was horrendous at times. But I did learn to balance my views and the needs of the group."[164]

The staff and monthly Meeting re-examined and fine-tuned the school governance structure continuously over the years. As the system evolved,

---

161 Arnold Porter, personal interview, February 10, 1997.
162 David Stevenson, personal interview, March 13, 1997.
163 Staff Handbook, 1973.
164 Pat Lawson, personal interview, January 30, 1997.

it became more elaborate and unwieldy with overlapping decision-making bodies. Furthermore, since the monthly Meeting had to approve any major decisions, the same discussion would often have to occur more than once. In 1969 yet another committee of students, staff, and Meeting members was formed to streamline decision-making. But in over twenty years the overall structure changed little. Although it never satisfied everyone, and many students resented the amount of time and energy required for decision-making, most former students and teachers believed that the system worked reasonably well and resulted in valuable personal growth. The majority of students did their best to make the system work.

Almost every year there were soul-searching discussions about whether the school should remain open. In 1966 as the small Quaker group began to grow tired and as houseparents became more difficult to recruit, the monthly Meeting considered turning the school over to the wider community. However, they rallied enough commitment among the members to continue as a Friends School. In 1968 there was again serious discussion of "laying the school down." The school elders believed that increased individual freedom and an "anything goes" attitude in contemporary society led to a disturbing trend of disrespect for the welfare of the larger group:

> The growing temper of the times all over North America and particularly in the younger generation is one in which the criterion of action is the moment and the self. The school seems too much of a shock and a jolt for young people who are growing up and coming out of this increasing pattern.[165]

But the uncertainty caused by raising the question of school closure every year had a detrimental effect on morale, and in 1969 the Meeting decided that discussion about whether or not the school should continue would only occur every five years "barring an emergency or major crisis."[166]

---

165 Monthly Meeting School Committee, memorandum, October 1967.
166 Argenta Monthly Meeting, minutes, January 12, 1969.

FINANCES

Like most independent alternative schools, the Argenta Friends School struggled to make ends meet. The school founders did not want lack of funds to prevent students from attending, and when the school opened in 1959, tuition fees were only $800 per year including room and board. Families in need of assistance could apply for even lower fees. This was only possible because staff salaries were just $75 per month. The cost of living was low in Argenta and most residents had ingenious ways of reducing their expenses. But the low salaries were a serious problem for many teachers, and only the most committed stayed more than two years. John Stevenson acknowledged in 1963 that "very few people can afford to come here to teach or act as houseparents."[167]

No one had time to undertake major fundraising or publicity campaigns, so small donations from a wide network of supporters were the school's only reliable means of extra support. The school had a mailing list of over seven hundred people by 1970—Quakers, other friends, and additional interested people. Many made small regular donations of $10 year after year. Donations rose from $1,000 per year in the early 1960s to over $8,000 in 1974, almost 25 per cent of the school's income.

The school facilities had become inadequate by the late 1960s, and in 1970 a crew of six began work on a new building that would contain the school library and office, a classroom suitable for art and science, two seminar rooms, and a print shop.[168] Work continued only as labour and funds were available. The two-storey building was not finished until 1978 but portions were used as early as 1973, even though a heating system was not yet installed. School volunteers also built a student home in 1968 to house some of the students. During the 1970s the school acquired another building to house students, but it required a good deal of renovation. All the school buildings needed constant maintenance.

---

167 John Stevenson, Coordinator's Report, January 1963.
168 School newsletter, August 1971.

Hands-on learning started with construction of the school building by a group of students and teachers. Argenta Friends School brochure, 1969.

Construction, improvement, and maintenance of school buildings was done with student and adult volunteer labour and therefore required little capital. This helped keep the school solvent. Building projects were time consuming, and work proceeded only as donations became available to buy materials and supplies. School leaders were practical enough to realize that the school might close at any time, and they were determined not to go into debt for capital expenses. As John Stevenson wrote: "We are building on a pay-as-you-go basis and will stop when our money does. We wish to remain a debt-free school, with the independence that that entails."[169] Building projects were also slow to be completed because, as one construction teacher wrote: "human interaction tends always to get first priority here—which is to say we have to stop work frequently to go

---

169 John Stevenson, school newsletter, August 1971.

to meetings."[170] Apart from buildings, the only other capital needs were suitable vehicles for school trips and hauling wood, which could usually be found locally.

Fees rose gradually, but with each increase a larger portion of the budget was used to assist families who could not afford the full fee. In 1964 one-third of the students received some tuition relief from the school, and 35 per cent of the school's income went into the scholarship fund.[171] By 1965 tuition had risen to $1,800 per year where it remained for several years. Fees increased modestly in 1969 and again in 1974 to $2,200. School leaders considered implementing a sliding scale based on family income, a system used successfully by the New School. But this was rejected because the group believed each family had unique circumstances. By the late 1970s, tuition fees reached $3,000 but the increased income was partly negated by the fact that the school was subsidizing over half of the student body.

The low school enrolment, which averaged just under twenty students, exacerbated the financial difficulties. Because of its large staff the school could have handled more students without increasing expenses, but it was difficult to maintain a cohesive group with more than twenty students. Housing was another limiting factor, and it was often a struggle to find enough placements. The student house built in 1968 alleviated the problem somewhat, although it still had to be staffed with houseparents. After 1972, as interest in alternative schools declined, the school did not receive enough applicants to increase its numbers above eighteen. Declining enrolment was to become a problem for many independent alternative schools during the 1970s.

The school managed by keeping teacher salaries low. During the early 1960s, teachers worked full-time for $750 per year. This increased to $1,500 in 1965 but was still only $2,000 in 1974.[172] Even in Argenta, where the cost of living was low and where most families grew their own food, it was still a hardship for teachers to make ends meet. Houseparents received $80 per month per student, not much more than when the school

---

170 Michael Phillips, school newsletter, October 21, 1971.
171 John Stevenson, school newsletter, January 1965.
172 Finance Committee, Report, May 1974.

began fifteen years earlier. Although the school was always close to the edge financially, it survived through careful management, the avoidance of debt, the use of volunteer labour, and a solid donor base. Most important, however, was that idealistic staff and houseparents were willing to work for very little money. As John Stevenson put it, the school survived "on the backs of the teachers and houseparents."[173]

CONTENTIOUS ISSUES

Staff and students at the Friends School lived harmoniously and managed to solve most problems within the established decision-making structure. However, questions about lifestyle and day-to-day expectations generated widespread student discontent and were never resolved satisfactorily. Students were expected to attend Sunday Meeting as well as a daily period of silence. Although some students attended enthusiastically, most would have preferred not to go. The weeknight visiting policy also bothered some students. Visiting other households during the week was discouraged because "some students find it difficult to study if others are constantly dropping in, and houseparents need some serenity." In 1969 a committee was struck to "consider what pattern might be proposed to meet the needs," but the policy remained intact.[174]

Compulsory classes and study hall also led to much discussion. The staff believed it was their responsibility to regulate study habits, and students were expected to attend all classes and study periods. In 1963 the policy was relaxed so students who proved they could maintain a good academic performance in their courses were exempted from study hall after the first term. But students wanted more freedom and believed they were old enough to regulate their own schedules. In 1964 they lobbied for non-compulsory classes, and the staff reluctantly gave in. Despite the policy change, students were strongly encouraged to attend classes, and most did. As well, students were expected to continue participating in school work projects, committee duties, and in the many decision-making meetings.[175] There was also some disagreement about academic

---

173 John and Helen Stevenson, personal interview, September 11, 1996.
174 Monthly Meeting for School Business, minutes, September 28, 1969.
175 Argenta Friends School, Student Handbook, 1964/65.

requirements. In 1967/68 four students left the school during the year, "one due to a heavy academic program, one because he feels we are checking up on him too much, and two local students who enrolled just because the school is here."[176]

Smoking was another contentious issue. Meeting members believed smoking was a health hazard and should be discouraged but were prepared to allow it, provided the students had their parents' permission and that they not smoke in the school buildings, the homes of non-smokers, or in the presence of children. The student handbook stated:

> Smoking is discouraged. A number of students smoking tends to act as a pressure toward encouragement. For those few who feel a real need, and are willing to restrict their smoking to a pattern set by the school, smoking is allowed with parent's permission.[177]

In a policy statement in 1962, John Stevenson wrote: "The school discourages smoking. The aim of the policies, and the spirit intended, is to prevent a spread of smoking to other students."[178] He considered this so important that "any future breach of the agreement will result in my recommending that the student involved be sent home. We need to feel that agreements are being kept without setting up a system of policing." Only a few students actually smoked (three in 1962), but several over the years found it difficult to abstain from smoking in their family homes. One student adjusted only with the help of the Ministry and Counsel committee.

But smoking and compulsory classes were minor matters compared to what became known as the "SAD Syndrome"—sex, alcohol, and drugs. For John and Helen Stevenson, the policy on alcohol was obvious: since the consumption of alcohol by minors was illegal, Argenta students must not drink. Students did some drinking on the sly, but mostly in moderation and only occasionally. After the end-of-year graduation ceremony, students would frequently go off on their own to a private house or into the woods to celebrate with alcohol. In 1971 the students decided to bring this matter into the open. They wanted to change the policy to permit an

---

176 John Stevenson, Letter to Alumni, December 10, 1968.
177 School Handbook, 1964/65.
178 Memorandum on Smoking, 1962.

evening party for students and staff after the ceremony at which beer and wine would be available. Although this was a relatively innocent request, staff and Meeting members worried about the sensibilities of the wider community and about the feelings of students who did not wish to partake. They also wondered who would be permitted to attend and feared that something could go wrong. During the three days before graduation, staff, students, and Meeting members met for more than twelve hours of soul searching over this issue. In the end unity was not achieved and the party was not held. As usual, some students drank after graduation anyway.[179]

The sex policy caused even more dissension. In the early 1960s teenage sex was not the socially divisive issue between the generations that it would become a few years later. But Argenta students, living and working together in a close and isolated community, certainly had their share of romantic attachments. The school's position was that students had to agree not to engage in sexual relationships. Teachers were concerned about pregnancy, disapproval of parents, and disapproval in the wider Argenta community. As well, the Stevensons argued that it might be detrimental to the small school community if students paired off in couples, restricting their attention to each other, thus removing their energy from the group as a whole:

> The problem is this: how to maintain the group bonds between people in the larger school group when a coupling bond is taking place? In the larger group, people are interdependent so a group spirit emerges; but when couple bonding takes place one begins to withdraw attention, care, and willingness to be fully a member of the larger group."[180]

Or as the monthly Meeting expressed it, "The school was created as a group experience; an experiment in which young people were invited to participate in the search for truth as a group. Coupling off fragments the group." Since the welfare of the group was paramount, this was enough reason to prohibit sexual relations. Furthermore, "involvement in a deep sexual relationship will make it impossible or more difficult for the acquisition of academic skills and community involvement skills."[181]

---

179 John Stevenson, Letter to Alumni, July 1971.
180 Statement on Sex Policy, May 30, 1974.
181 Monthly Meeting for School Business, minutes, March 31, 1973.

Many students believed they were old enough to make their own decisions about sexuality, and discussion of this issue in staff-student meeting was endless and unresolved. One former student, who came back to Argenta as a teacher in the 1970s, wrote:

> The school should make it clear that it intends to firmly enforce the law of the land regarding alcohol and drugs. However, there is no law stating that it is illegal for a sixteen-year-old to have sex with another sixteen-year-old. A student's love life should be primarily the business of the student and his parents.[182]

Nevertheless, the writer agreed that a couple should not be overly involved in their love life to the detriment of group life, and that they should not "scandalize the general community." One long-time Argenta resident well-known for his liberal views on sexuality felt that "the school should withdraw from standing in loco parentis on matters of sex":

> While not actively encouraging sexual relations among its students, the school should not have its own rules on the subject, nor should it be an enforcement body for rules set up by others. If parents want certain attitudes upheld by their children, that is a matter of agreement and understanding between parent and child. Today there is no way a school can impose actions in this realm on the individual. Universities have had to drop this impossible role; so should the Argenta Friends School.[183]

The sexuality issue created endless tension. Students did agree to a no-sex policy, but not all adhered to it. The proximity of forest, fields, and abandoned cabins made the policy unenforceable anyway. Several students were sent home over the years for engaging in sexual activity, and there were a few pregnancies. One student was expelled in 1962, prompting an exchange of angry letters among the staff, Meeting members, and the houseparent who was accused of undermining school policy by his permissive attitudes. In 1963 teachers and houseparents agreed that "visiting would take place somewhere besides in bedrooms, that permission

182 Ed Washington to Bob and Ruth Boyd, probably 1973.
183 Chuck Valentine, letter to the staff, March 1973.

from houseparents would be obtained before short visits to bedrooms, and when mixed groups were in bedrooms the doors would be open."[184] In 1968 the student-staff meeting worked on a revision of the sex policy and, after studying the issue again in 1970, the school community produced a somewhat more liberal statement:

> Sexual intercourse may stem from a wide variety of feel-
> ings, some positive, others negative, and may have a wide
> range of results. The emphasis should not be on judging
> an act but on considering the effects of acts on people.
> Sexual intercourse may result in a fruitful deepening of a
> person's experience.[185]

The adults acknowledged that it is difficult to generalize about issues of personal morality, but the prohibition remained. The staff did not want to alienate parents or conservative Argenta residents or run the risk of legal problems. They worried that sexual activity could become a status symbol and that "a relationship of this intensity is difficult to carry on without drawing the individual away from the group."

After wrestling with the sex question for over a decade, the staff had reached no resolution and in 1973 seriously considered closing the school. As one former teacher said, "Consensus wasn't possible. There was a line past which most staff members were not willing to go."[186] On the other hand "there was real horror expressed at the idea of closing the school because of the sex policy when so many wonderful things are happening here."[187] Meeting members admitted that, though they felt the policy was right, it was not working.

Finally, in 1974 a compromise statement, which was accepted by the school community, combined the adults' deep reservations about teenage sex with an expression of realism:

> In regard to sexual intercourse, Argenta Friends School
> cannot give its permission to engage in this: it is not given
> such authority by parents, society, or our deepest selves.

184 John Stevenson, Memorandum to Houseparents, probably 1964.
185 Student Handbook, 1974/75.
186 Arnold Porter, personal interview, February 10, 1997.
187 Monthly Meeting for School Business, minutes, March 31, 1973.

> The school cannot permit intense sexual involvement in situations under its control, for example in any school household. However AFS cannot explicitly forbid sexual intercourse and have the prohibition followed. Words that prohibit are often empty shouts, often dare persons to violate them, and cause guilt when they are violated by discerning consciences. And so if AFS cannot say either "yes" or "no," with what does that leave us?[188]

This statement said, in effect: "although we don't approve, we don't prohibit, and we realize we can't stop you anyway." This was, in fact, a recognition of the situation that had always existed.

But despite these many years of attempts to forge a consensus on sex policy, some people were still uneasy with the compromise policy, and the subject was reopened in the late 1970s. Even John Stevenson began to doubt whether it was helpful to the students for the adults to officially prohibit sexual relations and then pretend it was not happening:

> How can early sexual experience be fostered in an atmosphere of acceptance, with opportunities for counselling and emotional support? At present, we in Argenta give signals that we don't want it done in our homes, that we would rather not know what is going on, and that we are ambivalent to the wisdom or positive value of such actions. The result is that each year from one couple up to half of the students in the school are participating in intense sexual relationships without support and counselling from the staff. How can we encourage openness and provide caring supervision so that those venturing into highly charged emotional relationships can get needed support, rather than produce furtiveness and guilt?[189]

The most explosive issue of all was drug use. Drugs were rarely a problem in the relatively peaceful early years. But by 1968 Argenta had become a haven for counterculture individuals and American draft resisters. It is ironic that the political commitment of the Argenta Quakers

---

188 Statement on Sex Policy, May 30, 1974.
189 Letter to monthly Meeting, May 4, 1977.

indirectly caused many of the school's problems. Quakers all over North America opposed the war in Vietnam. Because opposition to military conscription was basic to Quaker principles, Friends were particularly active in assisting and harbouring American men escaping the draft. The Argenta Quakers were no exception, and one former student recalled that "every week someone from the United States would knock on the door looking for asylum."[190]

By the late 1960s, Argenta was full of young, long-haired Americans, many of whom used drugs freely. Since the newcomers were only a few years older, Friends School students readily obtained marijuana and occasionally LSD from these individuals and sometimes attended dope-smoking parties at their homes. One student remembered:

> There was dope smoking going on in the woods or in
> student homes when the houseparents were away. People
> in the local community were very upset about this. The
> dope smoking and rumours of free sex caused problems
> in community relations.[191]

This issue even caused some dissension on the staff, for although most teachers opposed drug use, a few younger staff members used marijuana privately and were sympathetic to the views of the students. One former staff member described "a time of great staff/student conflict":

> Some students were on the sixties path. They would visit
> certain people in the community to do drugs, play music,
> and get high. It was tough for the school—in the middle
> of the acid revolution. I understood the students. I saw
> both sides. A lot of times the student point of view made
> more sense to me.[192]

In 1968 John Stevenson felt it necessary to confirm the school's position on drugs and sex in a letter to alumni and parents: "A rumour has been circulating that we really don't care whether our young people in school use drugs, smoke marijuana, or participate in premarital sexual

190 Mary Winder, personal interview, February 24, 1997.
191 Pat Lawson, personal interview, January 30, 1997.
192 Arnold Porter, personal interview, February 10, 1997.

intercourse."[193] Three violations of these policies occurred in 1967/68, and several students were asked to leave the school because of drug use from 1967 to 1970. The endless deliberations about sex and drugs were exhausting, and almost every year there was an attempt to revise the policy on one or the other. However, not all students resented the prohibitions. For some the school provided "a cooling off from the pressures of dope, sex, and drinking" that they faced in their daily lives back at home.[194]

Sex and drugs continued to cause tension and disagreement between staff and students throughout the 1970s, although to a somewhat lesser extent. John Stevenson wrote in 1976 that "we are still unable to convince students to lay marijuana aside for the school year."[195] Some staff members and community supporters believed it was unrealistic for the school to flatly prohibit sexual activity and drug use and particularly unfair to insist on making this a "collective" decision. Many students agreed to the policies reluctantly and felt guilty when they did not live up to their agreements. Non-enforcement of the rule led to more confusion. One friend of the school wrote that the school should either prohibit sex and drugs and make enforcement a staff responsibility, or the staff should agree to leave those areas to the students.[196] A more liberal policy may have avoided some problems, but given the values of the school and the context of the 1960s, the staff probably did the best they could.

COMMUNITY CHANGES

The wave of "hippies" and "draft dodgers" added a new dimension to the Argenta community. They were disliked by long-time residents who were opposed to their ideology of absolute freedom and unconventional ideas about drugs, sex, and public nudity. They also had a disruptive effect on the school. Furthermore, many "old-timers" blamed the Quakers for encouraging the influx of newcomers. John Stevenson tried to discourage the arrival of young people who openly engaged in drug use and casual

---

193 John Stevenson, Letter to Alumni, June 1968.
194 John Stevenson, Letter to Alumni, July 1971.
195 John Stevenson, letter, January 26, 1976.
196 Charlie Boyd to John and Helen Stevenson, 1975.

sex: "The Argenta community is dubious of variations from the norms they grew up with. Young people who feel that their independence or integrity would be jeopardized by conforming to a pattern the community set would be happier if they went elsewhere."[197]

Yet even though they opposed the drugs and liberal values the new-comers brought with them, the Quakers still felt a responsibility to shelter draft resisters. While discouraging young Americans to settle permanently in Argenta due to the lack of economic opportunity and the "small conservative community which has been here more than fifty years," the Friends School offered to take in a few men for short periods of time to help them become established in Canada. They would work for room and board and then move on. John Stevenson wrote:

> I personally feel a need to help some of these young men
> who have been unable to convince their draft boards that
> they are conscientiously opposed to participating in the
> Vietnam War. At present the school is in a position to take
> on one or two for a week or two.[198]

The monthly Meeting even wrote to the federal government urging the formulation of a "new legal structure" for marijuana and LSD. Despite their concern about drugs and the welfare of the school, the Argenta Quakers never lost sight of the big issues they cared about.

Argenta also became a centre for the back-to-the-land movement in British Columbia. Many young adults arrived between 1967 and 1972, looking for land or cabins to rent where they could cultivate vegetable gardens and raise chickens and goats. Some learned a great deal about farming from the local residents. In 1971 an Ontario native, Gordon Yearsley, organized a land co-operative on a large piece of undeveloped property, bringing in another wave of settlers.[199] Their nontraditional life-style continued to be a significant source of worry for school leaders and "old-timers" alike.

---

197 John Stevenson, school newsletter, March 1968.
198 John Stevenson, letter, March 1968.
199 Mr. Yearsley taught at the Barker Free School, knew many Knowplace families, and was a close friend of Watson Thomson, a pioneer in the Canadian co-operative movement (see Chapters 5 and 6).

Similar to other alternative lifestyle communities during this period, Argenta had its share of amateur therapy or "encounter" groups. In 1969 Chuck Valentine organized a series of all-night "marathon" meetings to help members of the growing Argenta community "get to know each other better." Some students attended these sessions. Participants reported that "defences began to crumble and a new depth entered the relationships," while others noticed growth and "both positive and negative results within themselves."[200] Originally enthusiastic about this activity, John Stevenson became convinced by a visiting psychiatrist that self-exposure without a professional present could be hazardous, and from then on students had to have their parents' permission to participate.

The late 1960s saw the rise of Romantic or "free schools" across Canada and the United States. The Friends School was erroneously included in a list of free schools in *This Magazine is about Schools*, the radical Canadian educational journal. John Stevenson responded to the many inquiries from prospective students and parents:

> Since *This Magazine is about Schools* placed our school's name at the top of a list of free schools, we've been deluged by letters. I am happy there is so much interest in education in North America. However, we are *not* a free school. We have more structure, we have regular classes, and there are a number of activities which are expected of students and staff. The students and staff work together on some things, but the staff has responsibilities not shared by students and students have responsibilities not shared by staff. We administer tests and evaluate work. We are, however, experimental in that there are areas in which students and staff do work together. There is an informality here not found in a school of a thousand. There is flexibility within the structure but this comes with group approval, not on the basis of unilateral action.[201]

---

200 John Stevenson, letter to parents, February 23, 1968.
201 John Stevenson, letter to applicants, 1970. Argenta Friends School appeared in "A Short Listing of Free Schools," *This Magazine is about Schools*, Autumn 1969. Barker Free School, Craigdarroch School, and Saturna Island Free School were also listed.

Demographic and cultural changes in Argenta meant difficult times for the Friends School. In 1967/68 when the controversy about drugs and sex was at its height, Helen Stevenson wrote to the students and staff: "Nearly everyone in the school is tired of the pattern of hassling. I'm convinced that each person cares about every other person but we have not been sufficiently unified in purpose nor sensitive enough to get along without rules."[202] Another year of "struggle and searching" occurred in 1971/72. Principal Betty Polster addressed some of the difficulties:

> We've been searching on the question of openness and trust. Breaking of policies means a separation of one's life into public and private. If that private life is more important to the individual, this directly affects the atmosphere of the school. Part of the problem is that each of us is somewhat dissatisfied with the policies on alcohol, drugs, and sex. They are stated as they are because it's the best formulation we've come up with so far. Are the things we're trying to do here important enough to us to act in agreement with these policies even though we don't fully agree with them?[203]

These difficulties led John and Helen Stevenson to suggest that the school look for young staff members who had "experienced some of the youth culture which present day high school students are growing up in. We hope they can work with the older staff members and the monthly Meeting in determining what direction we should be moving."[204]

Another period of low school morale in 1973/74 coincided with the five-year review of whether the school should continue or close.[205] Although many Argenta residents, parents, and former students believed the school fulfilled a valuable function, there was a "crisis of energy" among staff members. The monthly Meeting agreed that "there is sufficient dissatisfaction with things as they are that we feel the need to make changes if the school is to continue."[206] Meeting members blamed everything from the

202 Helen Stevenson, letter to students and staff, March 5, 1968.
203 Betty Polster and Brenda Berck, Annual Report, 1971/72.
204 John/Helen Stevenson, letter to monthly Meeting, May 9, 1973.
205 Argenta Monthly Meeting, minutes, March 2, 1974.
206 Argenta Monthly Meeting, minutes, May 26, 1973.

influence of television to the "getting away with everything philosophy. Society is changing rapidly, new students and staff are coming out of quite different experiences. It is difficult to know if what we have to offer is right."[207] Teachers even considered changing the program to include other age groups and involve more members of the wider community. In the end, members of the school community believed they still had "the physical, psychological, and spiritual strengths to carry on with this demanding project." The Meeting would keep the school open and continue to seek "people who indicate a willingness to devote the school year to exploring Friends' way of living and Friends' procedures and try to apply them to their lives while they are part of the school." But a major ongoing concern of the school's leaders was whether the evolving Argenta community with all its competing lifestyles could still provide a stable home for the school:

> Argenta has evolved into an essentially urban community in its social mores and values. Many of the school's patterns are under heavy pressure to change, from the community, some staff, and the students themselves who bring with them urban counterculture values. Can we realistically expect to be an island of stability in a society turbulent with change?[208]

The Argenta Friends School did remain open throughout the 1970s, as we shall see in Chapter 13, despite the challenges of outside pressures, financial difficulties, and limited personnel and resources. The school benefited from effective leadership, a competent academic program, a well thought-out and comprehensive philosophy and set of values, and a continent-wide Quaker network that provided moral support and human resources. The school's relative longevity was a testament to the dedication of its teachers and the good will of its students.

---

207 Monthly Meeting School Committee, minutes, March 31, 1974.
208 "Argenta Friends," Report of Argenta Friends Meeting, 1973.

Chapter 4

CRAIGDARROCH SCHOOL

While the New School and the Argenta Friends School continued to thrive in the mid-1960s, a third British Columbia Progressive school was conceived in Victoria in 1966. Unlike those earlier schools, whose founders spent two years planning their organizational structure and debating educational theory, the new Victoria school was established in less than two months. In further contrast to the New School, a group project from the outset, this Victoria school was inspired by one individual and reflected his unique perspective and intuition. Although the founder did not draw from the Progressive ideas of John Dewey, the original school philosophy was very much in the Progressive tradition. The school's leadership and original clientele were drawn largely from Victoria's established class, many of whom had attended traditional private schools themselves.

Craigdarroch School was the creation of David Hummel, a successful lawyer and businessman. He and his wife, Patricia Hummel, had grown up in Victoria with extensive private school backgrounds. Mr. Hummel attended St. Christopher's in Victoria, St. George's in Vancouver, and Upper Canada College in Ontario, all traditional independent boys' schools based on elite British private schools.[1] Ms. Hummel had been schooled at St. Margaret's in Victoria. They were conservative in family background and political views and believed private schools were inherently superior to public schools. Mr. Hummel was an unconventional person who, according to his son, "loves to try things that are different." A

---

1   In Britain, these are referred to as public schools, but to avoid confusion in the North American context, I am calling them British private schools.

"self-starter," he made and lost several fortunes during his career and was not deterred by the daunting task of starting a school from scratch. David Hummel described his moment of decision in June 1966:

> My elder son was reaching the age when he needed to go to school and I ruled out the public school system as being totally inadequate. I considered St. Christopher's but I knew some of the people there and that didn't seem a good solution. I had been giving it some thought and had looked at a little school on Joan Crescent. One day as I was driving down the street, I noticed our gardener in my rear-view mirror. So I stopped him and I said: "We're going to start a school on Monday!" So we painted the place up and we started.[2]

David Hummel had an eclectic, though somewhat unsystematic, educational theory. In an attempt to interest others in his project, he outlined his views about schooling in an essay titled "Ideas Concerning a New School," which he circulated among his friends and business associates. Consistent with his individualism, Mr. Hummel believed that a gifted teacher was more important than a sound educational theory. He wrote that he "would prefer my children to be taught by an excellent, natural, gifted teacher with no clearly defined philosophy of education and somewhat antiquated methods, to having my children taught by a teacher without a gift for teaching."[3] This emphasis was fueled by Mr. Hummel's belief that there were few excellent teachers in Victoria's public or private schools.

Mr. Hummel's ideal school would seek to develop personal values similar to a British private school but in a gentler and less regimented environment. Such a school would encourage students to enjoy life and "awaken the minds and souls of the students so that each would leave the school capable of living life to the fullest with an aliveness, awareness, thinking and reasoning power, and judgment." Students would also develop graceful, coordinated, and healthy bodies through sports and daily

---

2   David Hummel, personal interview, January 7, 1997.
3   David Hummel, "Ideas Concerning a New School," unpublished paper, June 22, 1966, document collection of William Stavdal, Victoria.

exercise. Although the school would provide a "minimum basic education" (presumably the three Rs), character building would be equally important.

Mr. Hummel stressed the importance of encouraging each child to develop his or her individual skills and talents. It is here that he comes closest to Deweyan Progressivism. The school would be ungraded with flexible groups of children advancing at their own rate. Without being "permissive," it would provide maximum encouragement without pushing, and a relaxed form of discipline built upon a "high respect for the individuality and rights of other persons." Mr. Hummel also wanted his school to offer instruction in practical secretarial skills as well as non-traditional school subjects such as philosophy, economics, comparative religion, and politics. These would help students develop "a deep sense of community responsibility" to contribute to the well-being of their society.[4] All these views were consistent with his entrepreneurial background and his active role in community life and service organizations.

Mr. Hummel found a partner in Dr. Charles Gregory, an influential child psychiatrist, whom he had met when he was on the board of directors of the Family and Children's Service in Victoria. Born and educated in Liverpool, England, Dr. Gregory immigrated to Canada after the Second World War. He did research in neuropsychology at the University of Toronto before moving to Victoria in the mid-1950s, where he headed a government agency for child mental health. Several years later he founded and financed the Pacific Centre for Human Development, which operated centres for the treatment of emotionally disturbed, autistic, and brain-damaged children. He also lectured at the University of Victoria, served on its board of governors and senate, and was active in many organizations. Dr. Gregory had been a Marxist in his Liverpool years but gave that up long before arriving in Victoria. Like Mr. Hummel he was not a person to be bound by any overarching theories of life or society.

Dr. Gregory also had a son about to enter school and was "appalled with the rigidity and general level of the school system," as well as what he considered to be poorly trained teachers. He held the school system responsible for many of the "problem children" that showed up at his treatment centres. But like most Craigdarroch parents, Dr. Gregory had

---

4   David Hummel, "Ideas Concerning a New School," unpublished paper, June 22, 1966.

few specific complaints about the public education system other than a general feeling that the schools were poor.[5]

Mr. Hummel wasted no time putting his plan into action. By late July he had rented an empty kindergarten building with two small classrooms located on Joan Crescent at the foot of Craigdarroch Castle. Mr. Hummel took out a personal bank loan to cover the purchase of furniture, rent, and other initial expenses. Together with two business partners and Dr. Gregory, he incorporated the Craigdarroch School Society in August 1966. These four became directors of the society and adopted a constitution a month later.

Andy Mikita, a clinical child psychologist and co-director of Dr. Gregory's Pacific Centre, joined the planning group in August. Born in Hungary and raised in Ontario, Mr. Mikita moved to British Columbia in the early 1960s and became a public health psychologist in North Vancouver, where he initiated and directed the school district's mental health program. He met Charles Gregory at a national conference on child health and joined the Pacific Centre shortly afterwards. Mr. Mikita believed most learning and behaviour problems arose from forcing children "to do what they can't do." He favoured emphasizing student strengths and integrating "the things kids need to know" with their play activities.[6] Mr. Mikita enjoyed new ventures and was enthusiastic about the Craigdarroch project, supervising much of the day-to-day planning due to his prior experience in schools. David Hummel, Charles Gregory, and Andy Mikita were the organizational leaders of Craigdarroch School during its first year.

The directors prepared a detailed prospectus and issued a press release in early August to announce the opening of Craigdarroch School on September 6, 1966. Mr. Hummel was an effective organizer experienced in community and political work. He enlisted influential community leaders to provide political support for his project, and Mayor Alfred Toone was listed as "Honourary Chairman of the Board of Directors." His impressive board of advisors included three doctors, one psychologist, three University of Victoria professors (one a former principal of Saskatchewan

---

5   Charles Gregory, personal interview, February 21, 1997.
6   Andy Mikita, personal interview, June 9, 1997.

Teachers' College, another the head of the psychology department), the chair of the Victoria Board of School Trustees, and the Social Credit member of the legislature for Victoria, Waldo Skillings.

The press release highlighted two innovative features of the school. First, Craigdarroch School was to be bilingual. The directors noted that it would be the "first fully bilingual school that we know of west of Winnipeg. French and English will be used interchangeably throughout the school day and we will make every effort to make sure the children become fully bilingual as quickly as possible."[7] The prospectus cover featured a subtitle in large bold letters:

A Bilingual School
Conducted in Both French and English

Secondly, the press release continued, the school would be coeducational, since "it is natural for both boys and girls to grow up and be educated together in mutual respect and understanding. Craigdarroch School therefore will be the first independent coeducational school we know of on Vancouver Island." The directors made it clear, however, that Craigdarroch would not be an "experimental school or a school devoted to weird or speculative theories" but would be based upon the "soundest possible principles of education now known and understood and accepted by a wide number of thoroughly responsible educators."[8] This statement was intended to reassure prospective parents who may have feared that Craigdarroch would be too unstructured.

The press release described a school that would emphasize individual learning rather than "forced teaching from above." The school would have few formal lectures and students would work on individual tasks in almost all subjects. This individual approach would be made possible by class sizes of not more than twenty children. The directors were confident that "the creative method is known to produce happy, well adjusted, self-reliant, self-confident, and self-disciplined individuals who have a burning

---

7   David Hummel, "Notes for the Press on Announcing Craigdarroch School," August 5, 1966, document collection of William Stavdal, Victoria.
8   "Independent School Will Teach by New Methods," *Victoria Colonist*, August 6, 1966.

desire to continue to develop their thought processes and their education through their whole lifetimes." Through the trendy but vague term "creative method," the directors were trying to describe a Progressive emphasis on individualized learning arising out of the interests and capacity of the students.

The school prospectus, based largely on David Hummel's ideas, described the purpose of Craigdarroch School as providing "each individual child with gentle but steady encouragement to develop to the highest degree possible all of his abilities and talents."[9] The school promised to provide a "minimum basic education," individual progress at each child's optimum rate, the encouragement of varied interests, and instruction in both English and French. Although there would be no set curriculum, the prospectus stated that the traditional subjects would be covered along with such practical skills as shorthand, typing, and speed reading. Teachers would aim to "awaken a deep thirst for knowledge so as to infect the children with enthusiasm for learning, thinking, and personal development." Students would be exposed to comparative religion and philosophy, including the examination of such concepts as "truth, honesty, freedom, and tolerance." The directors hoped these subjects would "develop in each child a strong and sure personal and social conscience" and produce individuals ready to shoulder social responsibilities and thus alleviate the apathy they saw as a serious problem in Canada.[10] Lastly, Craigdarroch would nurture personal qualities including leadership, social conscience, and an "acceptable standard of morals, manners, and techniques for dealing with other people."[11]

Though idealistic and well-meaning, the school's founders did not fully understand Progressive theory, and the prospectus combined various ideas from the elite British private school tradition and American Progressivism. What the prospectus did not address was the pedagogical foundation upon which these objectives would rest. The absence of a solid theoretical base would weaken Craigdarroch School in its later years.

---

9   Craigdarroch School, Prospectus, 1966, William Stavdal document collection.
10   David Hummel, "Notes for the Press on Announcing Craigdarroch School."
11   Craigdarroch School, Prospectus, 1966, William Stavdal document collection.

For the first year of operation, the directors decided to restrict enrolment to twenty students aged five and six. Their intention was to add one grade per year right up to high school graduation. They sought "normal or superior" students and hoped to attract children from a variety of family backgrounds. In order to achieve this, they intended to keep the tuition moderate and to offer a few scholarships for families who were unable to afford it.[12]

David Hummel created a simple system of school governance with a four-person board of directors. But since his two business partners were simply on the board for convenience and fundraising and would take no active part in the school's affairs, the effective administration was left to Mr. Hummel and Charles Gregory. The board appointed the Educational Policies Committee, chaired by Andy Mikita, to work closely with the teaching staff to develop specific educational policies. Membership in the school society was limited to the directors and their wives, an issue that would later become contentious among the parent body. The administration was efficient and worked well during the first year, but eventually parents wanted more of a say in the running of the school than this essentially business model provided.

Mr. Hummel provided most of the school's initial financing. In addition to arranging the bank loan, he and his business partners pledged a total of $8,000 to match donations from other sources. He actively sought donations from the Lions Club and other service organizations as well as from among his network of business associates in Victoria. Tuition fees were $240 per year, but the enrolment of each child had to be accompanied by an annual (tax deductible) donation of $500 paid to the school by the family, or another individual or firm.[13] Although the fees were low by private school standards, they were still beyond the means of families who were not professional or middle class. Salaries were low and, like all Canadian alternative schools at that time, Craigdarroch was run on a shoestring with finances a constant problem.

---

12   Craigdarroch School, Prospectus, 1966.
13   Craigdarroch School, Prospectus, 1966.

TEACHERS AND STUDENTS

David Hummel organized a public meeting in early August 1966 at the Red Lion Motor Hotel in Victoria, which he owned. Over sixty interested parents attended this event. They were addressed by Mr. Hummel, Charles Gregory, Andy Mikita, the school's newly hired head teacher, and a University of Victoria education professor serving on the school's board of advisors.[14] This successful meeting was followed by an open house held at the school a week later.

One interested parent at both events was Joan Schwartz. She had moved to Victoria from California with her family during the summer of 1965. Ms. Schwartz had grown up in New York and Oakland, earning a degree in Spanish from the University of Mexico and another degree in English and history from the University of California at Berkeley. She obtained a teaching certificate from the University of California at Davis and taught high school in California for seven years. She also worked with preschool, elementary, and emotionally disturbed children in a variety of other teaching experiences. During these years Ms. Schwartz became "restless about the public schools" and felt that administrators did not respect students. In her search for more humane ways of teaching children, she was influenced by A. S. Neill's *Summerhill* and Sylvia Ashton-Warner's *Teacher*.[15]

Ms. Schwartz grew up in a left-wing family, her father having been a Wobblie and a member of the American Communist Party until 1938. She was "not enthusiastic about what was happening in the United States," particularly the McCarthy hearings of the early 1950s and the escalation of the Vietnam War during the 1960s. So when her husband was offered a teaching position at the University of Victoria they decided to move to Canada. It was too late in the season to apply for a teaching job, so she accepted a position in the university library.[16]

During their first year in Victoria, Ms. Schwartz grew increasingly disappointed in the Victoria public schools, which she experienced as

---

14   Bill Stavdal, "School Seeks Atmosphere of Freedom," *Victoria Colonist*, August 10, 1966; David Hummel, "Notes for the Press on Announcing Craigdarroch School," 5.

15   Elizabeth Bennett, "Progressive System Used in New School," *Victoria Times*, January 19, 1968, 19.

16   Joan Ormondroyd, formerly Joan Schwartz, personal interview, February 26, 1997.

backward and excessively rigid. Her children were unhappy and she was appalled by the strict and sometimes cruel disciplinary methods used by many teachers. So when in August 1966 she saw a notice about a group of parents opening a new independent school with a "free and liberal atmosphere," she was immediately interested. During the open house she spoke with David Hummel, Charles Gregory, and Andy Mikita. But she was disappointed in her discussion with the head teacher and decided not to enrol her children. She described the sequence of events:

> I read an advertisement in the paper about a group of parents who were forming a school in Victoria. I went to a meeting at the Red Lion Inn and they announced that they had a building, they had hired a head teacher, and that they were going to be accepting applications the following week at an open house. So I went with my two younger children but after talking with the head teacher for some length I decided this was not the school I wanted to put my children in. She spoke condescendingly to the children, there was no creativity, and she didn't seem to have any idea of what a free school was all about. There was little difference between her and any other public school teacher I had ever met. So I just went home. But I got a call that evening from Andy Mikita and he said "I noticed you didn't enrol your children" and he asked me why. I said I don't feel the goals your head teacher described to me and the goals that I have are on the same track. He asked me if I would come in the next day and talk with him about that. So I did and we spent three or four hours discussing education and what schools are all about. Then I left and didn't think too much more about it. About a week later I got a call offering me the job of head teacher at Craigdarroch School. I said, "But you have a head teacher," and he said, "Well, no we don't; we sat down and discussed the goals with her and we decided that her goals really weren't our goals." And that's how I got to be the head teacher of Craigdarroch School.[17]

---

17   Joan Ormondroyd, personal interview, February 26, 1997.

Craigdarroch School opened in September 1966 with sixteen students, aged five to eight years old. The hiring of Joan Schwartz proved to be a most fortunate turn of events, for she was admired by everyone connected with the school community. Craigdarroch quickly became her school, informed by her philosophy and her manner of dealing with children. Ironically, she spoke Spanish but little French, so the English/French bilingual nature of the school was more fiction than reality. But nobody cared and the school quickly developed a happy environment and a close community—all this less than three months after David Hummel's original inspiration.

Ms. Schwartz managed as the only full-time teacher during the school's first year. She was assisted by two part-time teachers, Mary Jamieson (who taught beginning reading and math) and Bett Bugslag. Both were certified and experienced teachers who had taught in the public school system. With the growth of the school to over thirty students in the second year, Ms. Schwartz hired two full-time teachers. From California, they had come to Canada for political reasons and to avoid being drafted for the war in Vietnam. Both had degrees in psychology, but neither had a teaching certificate or any experience. To some degree Ms. Schwartz considered their lack of experience an asset, since they would not be constrained by conventional public school values.

Rod Hyder, originally born in Canada, was hired in September 1967 after arriving in Victoria from outside of Los Angeles. In addition to his immediate concern about the Vietnam War, he believed neighbourhoods and communities in southern California were deteriorating. He was "politically progressive, a supporter of countercultural ideas, and looking for change in society."[18] Mr. Hyder taught at Craigdarroch for over two years and was remembered fondly by many students. John Andrews arrived in early 1968 and became friendly with several members of Victoria's academic and literary community, attending Thursday evening readings at the home of well-known poet Robin Skelton. He met Joan Schwartz through

18   Jesse Hyder, personal interview, February 6, 1997. Rod Hyder later went by the name of Jesse Hyder.

these connections and was hired to teach at Craigdarroch later in the second year. He remembered being received warmly by the school community.[19]

The school attracted a well-to-do and professional parent body, "the Oak Bay crowd." Well over half were doctors, lawyers, and university teachers. Of the twenty or so families involved in the school there were six doctors, four lawyers, and three university professors. Craigdarroch differed from other alternative schools in its primarily upper-middle-class clientele. This was probably due to the British private school character of Victoria during that time and to the moderate philosophy of the school. Few of the original parents were overtly influenced by the new lifestyles of the 1960s.[20]

However, the socio-economic makeup of Craigdarroch was not entirely homogeneous. In sharp contrast to the professional majority, three families lived a mainly subsistence lifestyle in rural Metchosin. One of these families, originally from Ontario, had been early CCF[21] supporters and had been farming organically for many years, long before it became popular. Another family had a history of activism—the husband was a pacifist and conscientious objector, while his wife had been active in the Unitarian Church and the Voice of Women. In all, four families in modest circumstances were allowed reduced tuition fees. The school's leaders were also proud of the fact that they provided a full scholarship for an Indigenous student, a member of the well-known Hunt family of Vancouver Island carvers and artists. Although these families did not socialize with the wealthier parents, by all accounts everyone got along well.

Parents described Craigdarroch as a Progressive, liberal, or creative school. Most parents were conservative in outlook but with enough liberal and individualistic ideas to want for their children more freedom than in the public school system or in more traditional private schools. The individuality of the children was highly valued so that they could (in the language of the day) "be free to become themselves." Craigdarroch parents

---

19   John Andrews, personal interview, February 18, 1997.
20   School families were the Hummels, Gregorys, Browns, Williams, Carrosfelds, Morrissons, Clarks, Frenches, Grahams, Graffs, Stavdals, Dickmans, Peavys, Schmidts, and Goughs.
21   The CCF refers to the Co-operative Commonwealth Federation, the precursor to today's New Democratic Party.

were looking for a school with small classes, individualized learning, and an emphasis on the creative arts, without the rigid discipline or authoritarian outlook encountered in other schools, whether public or private. But other than a general notion that the public schools were inadequate, most parents were vague about what they objected to specifically. Some parents (mostly mothers) came in to help with individualized reading or student supervision, as well as regular tasks such as cleaning the school building. But although parents participated keenly in the life of the school, in contrast to the New School, most were not involved in day-to-day operations, policy decisions, or school finances.

The school building was an old house that had been converted to a kindergarten some years earlier. It had two medium-sized rooms that made effective classrooms, as well as a large kitchen and good-sized playground. The school was informal—students wore whatever they wanted and called teachers by their first names, both unusual practices in those days. One parent wrote: "The tyranny of clothing is unknown at Craigdarroch; our daughter comes home smeared with paint and dirt, in her play clothes."[22]

Craigdarroch grew to thirty-three students aged five to twelve for its second year of operation. The school was full by mid-August and had already begun to compile a waiting list for 1968/69.[23] The increase was due to word of mouth and several positive articles in the two Victoria daily newspapers. The 1967 school prospectus continued to portray Craigdarroch as a school "conducted in both French and English," but this description was now secondary to "A Progressive and Creative School."[24] The school optimistically began its second year with a doubled enrolment, an enlarged and enthusiastic teaching staff, and a supportive parent community. The curriculum became somewhat freer during the second year, partly due to the influence of the younger teachers, but Craigdarroch was much the same as it had been during its successful first year.

22   Bill Stavdal, "She Thrives on Freedom," *Victoria Colonist*, June 9, 1968, 5.
23   "Craigdarroch Booked Solid for Second Term," *Victoria Times*, August 25, 1967, 17; and "Progressive School Classes Full," *Victoria Colonist*, August 25, 1967.
24   Craigdarroch School, Prospectus, 1967, William Stavdal document collection.

The school also moved to a more spacious location on a large piece of property near Fort Street, owned by Ms. Hummel's parents. The school had outgrown the original building, and the new site provided plenty of room for classroom activities and play. There were two flat-roofed buildings, each with two small classroom-sized rooms. The teachers organized the four rooms as activity centres, one for art and music, one for math and science activities, one for a reading centre and the school library, and one room for general purposes. The buildings were situated on a secluded lot almost an acre in size, providing a huge natural playground, and the children spent long periods of time outside. According to one teacher, the site and natural setting helped the school to flourish.

CURRICULUM

Day-to-day life at the school was "free flowing." A typical day began at 9:00 with free play and a discussion of the day's events, and by about 9:15 the teachers started organizing group activities. This was often a spontaneous "I'm going to do a group in math; who's going to join me?" or "Over here we can do some singing, and over there you can read."[25] There were usually three groups of five to ten students. Each activity typically began with a twenty-minute instructional lesson followed by individualized work, and would last up to an hour depending on the students' interest.[26] As one teacher recalled, "If we were on a roll we would stay with it; if they were restless we would stop."[27] As Ms. Schwartz put it, "There are no set periods; the children work at their own pace, and no lesson ever stops until the students want to stop."[28] After a period of play and unstructured work, new groups would form later in the morning, and if the school was not going on a field trip there was usually a third group activity in the afternoon.

---

25   Claire Schwartz, personal interview, April 15, 1997.
26   Jesse Hyder, personal interview, February 6, 1997.
27   Mary Jamieson, personal interview, January 15, 1997.
28   Joan Schwartz, quoted by Guy Stanley, "School Experiment in Freedom" *Victoria Times*, June 1, 1967, 31.

Under the leadership of Joan Schwartz, students learned without pressure at Craigdarroch School. Courtesy of *Victoria Daily Times*, January 19, 1968

Students could decide whether or not to participate in any activity. The teachers encouraged the children to attend lessons regularly, and most did. But, as one student recalled, "They would try to convince us [to do academics] but they would never force us; if we didn't want to they would leave us to what we were doing." Students would fade out of classes they weren't enjoying, and a group of ten- and eleven-year-old boys did little academic work. One of these explained that "we were left to our own devices to ask for tutoring in any subject. I did very little academic work except for math. I loved math."[29] Another student who didn't learn to read until she attended public school in grade four said, "Academic subjects weren't the focus of the school. They weren't ignored but they

29   Tom Koltai, personal interview, February 17, 1997.

weren't pushed either. If you wanted to learn something you sought out a teacher—you had to go and tug on somebody's sleeve."[30] Charles Gregory commented in the *Daily Colonist* in June 1968 as the school was completing its second year: "I think the school is doing what it set out to do in 1966. We've sought a free atmosphere in which kids can learn to like learning. I make no extravagant claims about academic achievement at Craigdarroch. We're not after that."[31]

Nevertheless, the teaching staff issued written anecdotal reports to parents on academic progress several times per year. There were no letter grades; instead, the teachers commented on each child's progress and activities in language arts, mathematics, science, social studies, art, music, drama, dance, and foreign languages. The reports were detailed and encouraging, very innovative at that time.[32] Although progress according to traditional grade levels was not a major school objective and there was little or no testing, parents believed their children were doing well. David Hummel boasted to a Lions Club meeting in May 1967 that six grade one pupils were already working at the upper grade two level. Eight others were working at the upper grade one level, and two students, though behind academically, were doing well in creative and artistic activities.[33] The school's primary academic aim was summed up in the 1967 prospectus:

> Not all children are expected to do the same things at the
> same time, but rather the development of their individual
> skills and talents is encouraged. Each child progresses in
> small ungraded classes with no competitive examinations.
> No rigid curriculum is used since the school provides a
> flexible vehicle for each child's education. The primary
> aim of Craigdarroch is to create an environment where
> children can teach themselves how to learn.[34]

---

30 Diane Brown, personal interview, March 17, 1997.
31 Charles Gregory, quoted by Bill Stavdal, "Self-Disciplined Pupils or Ill-Mannered Brats?" *Victoria Colonist*, June 9, 1968, 23.
32 Teacher reports on Lori-Jean Williams, February 1967 to June 1969.
33 "New School Accents Joy of Learning," *Victoria Times*, May 2, 1967, 23.
34 Craigdarroch School, Prospectus, 1967, William Stavdal document collection.

Joan Schwartz developed two major foundations for her program. The first was nature study. She and the students took two to three field trips every week to the beach, the forest, and local parks to identify plants and to investigate the world of nature. Sometimes she would bring in science professors from the university as resource people, while at other times she would teach the concepts herself. Ms. Schwartz did a great deal of reading about science during her evenings at home. Students examined life in tide pools and observed salmon in streams, and several students recalled how the study of marine life at the beach "made it come to life."[35] The nature study often led to interdisciplinary learning, and the students practised their reading, mathematics, and measuring skills right there in the woods. They were encouraged to work on ongoing projects, and one student remembered "studying the praying mantis for weeks."[36] The school also had numerous pets that children would take turns caring for. There was a school garden and, as one student recalled, "Everyone had their own little plot in the big garden. We tended the garden every day, weeded it and watered it. We could choose what we wanted to grow, vegetables or flowers. Carmen and I grew roses. It was a real source of pride."[37]

A second important theme was food and world cultures. Ms. Schwartz used food and cooking as a window into learning about other cultures. The school had a large kitchen, and students made bread, tortillas, refried beans, wonton soup, and Indian curries. During an extended study of India, a local Indian woman came in and taught the children to make saris and samosas. The unit culminated with a student dramatization of the *Ramayana*. Students studied Indian, African, Japanese, and Inuit cultures and enjoyed being free to spend extensive periods of time on a single subject.

As a former high school teacher, Ms. Schwartz had no training in the teaching of beginning reading. Although she read widely on the subject, she sometimes exhibited more "chutzpah" than sense. She tried different techniques with different students. She successfully taught one child to read using Sylvia Ashton-Warner's methods. Another bright boy only had to be taught the fundamentals of phonics and he was "off and running."

---

35 Jonathan Gregory, personal interview, February 27, 1997.
36 Claire Schwartz, personal interview, April 15, 1997.
37 Diane Brown, personal interview, March 17, 1997.

Although times were sometimes set aside for individualized reading, Ms. Schwartz preferred to incorporate reading into "everything we did" according to her belief that knowledge is interrelated. Students read on their own or aloud, and teachers often read to small groups of students sitting in a circle. Teachers tried to stimulate writing activities with varying degrees of success. These sometimes approximated the "whole language" approach of thirty years later. A child would dictate a story that would be written down by a teacher; the story was then read aloud and illustrated by the student. Some students were taught to spell with the Initial Teaching Alphabet (ITA), though spelling and grammar were not high priorities.

Most students worked through the regular mathematics curriculum at their own pace. One student, who became an accountant, recalled the use of Cuisenaire rods to teach place value and how "they made so much sense to me; they made the math click."[38] Several "math whizzes" spent most of their time on that subject progressing far beyond their grade level.[39] French never did become a regular part of the program, but French and Spanish lessons were offered to interested students by two part-time teachers.

---

38   Carmen Stavdal, personal interview, March 26, 1997.
39   Jonathan Gregory, personal interview, February 27, 1997.

Courtesy of *Victoria Daily Colonist*, June 9, 1968.

Craigdarroch School students were encouraged to follow their interests
in the creative arts. Courtesy of *Victoria Daily Colonist*, June 9, 1968

Creative and artistic activities were emphasized. Many students have
vivid memories of classes in dance and creative movement taught by
Judith Koltai, a school parent. She would put on music and darken the
room to create a meditative mood and then suggest an image, such as a
flower blooming, to encourage the students to move in imaginative ways.
"She had all thirty rowdy kids working on their own at the same time."[40]
One student credited her lifelong interest in dance to the movement
classes.[41] One of the teachers played guitar and students enjoyed singing
together on a regular basis. Students learned folk dances, used rhythm
instruments, and made drums, tambourines, and fiddles. Local musicians
played regularly at the school. Students spent a good deal of time painting, drawing, making clay sculpture, and learning to sew. They also spent

40 Diane Brown, personal interview, March 17, 1997.
41 Kate McIntosh, personal interview, February 23, 1997.

considerable time writing, rehearsing, and performing plays,[42] and one former student said that without her experience at Craigdarroch she would not have become a performing actor.[43]

Like other alternative schools, Craigdarroch made extensive use of community resources, and students visited museums, art galleries, the Parliament buildings, a Greek freighter, a bakery, farms, factories, the observatory, and the fire hall. They also enjoyed picnics, visiting parks, and hiking up local mountains such as Mount Douglas and Mount Tolmie. A favourite student activity was watching National Film Board films; as one student recalled, "We would choose them from the NFB catalogue. We would watch them forwards and then we would watch them backwards. It was a tradition. So films would take twice as long!"[44]

Students spent much of the day playing. They dressed up in costumes, listened to music, and played an assortment of indoor games, but most of their time was spent outside building forts, digging in the sand, and generally hanging out having a good time. The school had a tree-filled playground in the back garden and students spent a great deal of time climbing trees. The tree climbing became a joke among teachers and students, for the adults knew that when the children were in the trees there was no point trying to entice them to come down.

For the most part students got along well together and disputes were usually resolved through discussion with the help of the teachers. But there was some bullying and the occasional fight, and one former student suggested that this behaviour was too often unchecked by the teachers. The staff attempted to teach the children to settle their problems without fighting, and Ms. Schwartz claimed that "kids who used to settle everything by fighting now often settle matters by communication. We want them to join the world with this attitude."[45] Social interaction was considered to be an important aspect of student growth and one former student observed, "You couldn't be a loner. We were always encouraged to participate in a group; we were taken by the hand to become involved

42   Craigdarroch School, Prospectus, 1968, William Stavdal document collection.
43   Diane Brown, personal interview, March 17, 1997.
44   Diane Brown, personal interview, March 17, 1997.
45   Joan Schwartz, quoted by Bill Stavdal, "Self-Disciplined Pupils or Ill-Mannered Brats?" *Victoria Colonist*, June 9, 1968, 23.

in the group dynamic."[46] However, the older boys pretty much had their run of the school, and according to one parent were a "wild bunch," while a former student admits that "we were a rowdy group." Despite this, there were few serious incidents and students were not restrained, as long as they did not harm anyone else.

Craigdarroch avoided one of the most serious problems encountered by many alternative schools—a significant influx of students with behavioural or emotional problems. The board decided explicitly not to take such children, and school enrolment remained large enough that it did not need to do so for financial reasons. A few children with behavioural issues did end up at the school and some former students found them disruptive, but the "problem kids" (as some called them) usually did not stay longer than a few months.

Student and teacher meetings were held once a week, and most decisions were made democratically by the entire group. Students felt they had genuine input into school decisions and on one occasion even influenced a staffing issue. Craigdarroch students learned at an early age to hold their own verbally with adults and with each other. There were "rap sessions" and occasional mock court sessions initiated by the students to deal with misbehaviour as, for example, when a group of older kids threw stones at the guinea pigs.

The school community was close. Some families became good friends, students spent time at each other's houses, and some relationships continued for many years. The togetherness was enhanced by school camping trips that often lasted three to four days with up to forty people in attendance. Mr. Hyder remembered trips to such locations as Ladysmith Park, Ivy Green Park, and Goldstream. He, his wife, and a few students would set up an advance camp and the others would follow later in the day. One student found the school to be an upbeat place where he always felt good.[47] Another recalled, "We were like a family; we felt safe. These people were our community. We knew they would look after us."[48] One parent described the school as a "pleasant, easygoing, happy place full of noise,

46   Jonathan Gregory, personal interview, February 27, 1997.
47   Jonathan Gregory, personal interview, February 27, 1997.
48   Diane Brown, personal interview, March 17, 1997.

activity, confusion, and mess."[49] Students of all ages and backgrounds remembered their Craigdarroch school days as a secure and happy time.

CRISES AND CHANGE

Two pivotal changes occurred during the second year that would alter the direction of the school. First, there was a campaign by some parents for a more democratic decision-making structure. This group was led by Leah Brown who, though far from a radical activist, was influenced by current liberal ideas about participatory democracy. Ms. Brown believed that David Hummel, through his appointed board of directors, was autocratic. She argued that since the school was primarily supported by parents' fees, the parent body should make the decisions.[50] Mr. Hummel maintained that since he had financed the school mainly with his own money, and since the school was running smoothly, they should retain the status quo.

Things came to a head at a contentious meeting in January 1968. The parent body decided to change the constitution to allow all parents to become members of the governing Craigdarroch School Society, and the appointed board of directors was replaced by an elected board of seven members. In elections to fill the new board, Leah Brown was elected president, Charles Gregory was elected vice-president, and David Hummel was ousted from the board entirely.[51] This was a sad end to his involvement in the school. Without his original idea, organizational experience, and courage to try something new, Craigdarroch School would not have become a reality. His son transferred to a traditional private school at the end of the year.

With Mr. Hummel's business interests demanding more of his attention, the family may not have remained for the long term anyway. He relocated to the United States several years later. Andy Mikita left the school at the end of the first year, leaving Charles Gregory and Leah Brown as the dominant members of the group.[52]

---

49 Bill Stavdal, personal interview, March 18, 1997.
50 Leah Muhleman, personal interview, March 12, 1997.
51 "Private School Expands Society," *Victoria Times*, January 31, 1968, 35.
52 Several parents speculate that Andy Mikita may have left the school due to a professional disagreement with Charles Gregory.

This change in leadership did not occur in a vacuum. By 1968 the school's educational philosophy was undergoing a gradual change in direction in keeping with the Romantic ideas of the time. New parents were more overtly idealistic in their political and educational thinking. Typical of this group was Vance Peavy, a professor of psychology, counselling, and education at the University of Victoria. He had recently left the United States, disillusioned by the Vietnam War and political assassinations. Dr. Peavy was a liberal democrat and sympathized with the experimental values prevalent in the late 1960s. A few parents inclined to counterculture lifestyles joined the school community. Others, exposed to the educational and cultural ideas of the 1960s, had become more liberal in their thinking and were more accepting of a laissez-faire attitude in the school.

A second event that would change the course of Craigdarroch School was the resignation of Joan Schwartz in June 1968. This was not due to any dissatisfaction but because her family had decided to leave Victoria. Her husband had been one of three professors fired the previous year after political disagreements, and he had been offered a job elsewhere. This came as a shock to the school community. The board asked Barbara Williams, an original Craigdarroch parent, to take over as head teacher. Ironically, the Schwartz family plans changed at the last minute, but it was too late. Ms. Schwartz eventually went back to the United States and subsequently pursued successful careers as a writer and a library professor in the "art of teaching."

Joan Schwartz's impact on Craigdarroch School was definitive. She turned a collection of haphazard ideas into a unified vision and was described by former parents and students as "inspired," "a natural," "prodigious," and "a born leader." One former student remembered her as "the brains and the spirit" of the school and another said, "She got us involved." She combined a creative and child-centred view of teaching with the practical experience and skill necessary to make it a reality. According to one parent, "She could handle thirty-five kids at all different age levels—she made Craigdarroch an exciting place."[53] According to another, "She was the genius behind the school; she had a way of knowing

---

53   Charles Gregory, personal interview, February 21, 1997.

where all the children were at."[54] Although she gave the students genuine freedom, she made the academic work so interesting as to inspire most of them to take part.[55] She loved the children and had great faith in their judgement and abilities. As one former student put it, "Joan left a big hole; we all wanted her to come back."[56]

One consequence of Mr. Hummel's departure was that the school could not remain on his family's property and would once again have to move. Finding another suitable location was a problem that would never be solved. The school moved to the Browns' house for the summer and then to a large house owned by Dr. Gregory near the university. This was followed by several months at the Boy Scout hall in Cadboro Bay. But none of these locations satisfied the health and fire department licensing codes, and the school had to continue moving. For several months the school split into three separate groups, each meeting with one teacher in a private house.[57] This gave the teachers an opportunity to work effectively with smaller groups, but it was a big responsibility for the three homeowners, and overall it was disruptive to the spirit of the school. As one student put it, "The fabric of the community was damaged." The school finally found a semi-permanent home when head teacher Ms. Williams arranged through her membership in the Unitarian Church for the school to meet in the church hall in James Bay. The physical space was well-suited to the school's activities, but as the school was housed in someone else's building, the teachers felt constrained by their concern about protecting the hall.

Despite the change of leadership and the physical dislocation, Craigdarroch's enrolment increased again to forty-two students aged five to twelve. The teaching staff grew to four full-time members as Ms. Williams, Mr. Hyder, and Mr. Andrews were joined by Sam Le Barron. The school's tuition structure was simplified with a basic annual fee of $600 for the first child in each family, $500 for the second, and $300 for

---

54   Ann Gregory, personal interview, February 28, 1997.
55   Andy Mikita, personal interview, June 9, 1997.
56   Diane Brown, personal interview, March 17, 1997.
57   The three houses belonged to the Williams, the Goughs, and the Morrisons.

the third. The school community looked forward to its third year of operation with cautious optimism.

One unforeseen problem of Joan Schwartz's leadership was that the school became too dependent on her personal skill. Parents didn't much care what her theory of learning was because her system worked with the children. This was similar to the New School, which initially thrived due to the personal qualities of its head teacher rather than a coherent educational plan. During Ms. Schwartz's tenure the parent group did not have to come to terms with the wide range of opinion that existed about how structured the school should be. But after her departure factions and disagreements emerged that would trouble the school for the remainder of its existence. This created a difficult situation for her successor.

Barbara Williams was British and had come to Victoria from Kenya with her family. She was an experienced teacher and had trained in Progressive methods. Her background included significant formal training in the kindergarten and nature-study methods of Friedrich Froebel.[58] Ms. Williams was also influenced by John Dewey's writings and believed in the importance of individualized learning and the creative arts. She disapproved of the large classes in the public school system and of controlling or unimaginative teachers. However, although she supported informal classrooms, she believed in more teacher-directed activities and less freedom than the students were used to. She recalled that her interpretation of freedom was different from that of the other staff members and many parents: "I wanted regulated freedom—freedom to learn."[59]

Craigdarroch entered a troubled and difficult year in September 1968. Ms. Williams remembered that the "three young men" on staff advocated more freedom than she did—they "didn't want to lay a trip on the children."[60] Neither could the parent body agree on how much structure they wanted. Some parents desired a great deal of freedom for their children and, according to Ms. Williams, asked her to discontinue keeping records on the students' progress. But another group of parents was becoming increasingly restless because they believed their children

---

58   Friedrich Froebel was the nineteenth-century founder of the kindergarten.
59   Barbara Williams, personal interview, February 20, 1997.
60   Barbara Williams, personal interview, February 20, 1997.

were not learning anything, even though Ms. Williams implemented numerous formal learning activities. The school was split right down the middle. One parent remembered a serious debate about whether a child should be required to wear a life jacket in a boat, while another recalled being laughed at for arguing that individualized learning and academic rigour could be compatible.[61] None of the teachers were wholeheartedly supported by the parent community.

The problem came to a head in November 1968 when over a dozen parents came to a meeting of the Educational Policies Committee. They were particularly dissatisfied with what they saw as a lack of academic standards and maintained that their children were bored at school. Several parents expressed concern about the "hippie element" and the "slovenly, sloppy situation" in the school, and one parent objected to students addressing him by his first name. Others believed there was a misunderstanding of the meaning of "freedom," and two parents cited instances where their children had come home during the school day without the teachers knowing. The general feeling was that the children were not learning much and were no longer happy at school.[62]

The crux of the issue was a basic disagreement about how much freedom students should be given and how much emphasis should be placed on academic work. One parent commented:

> One terrific thing is that the children are starting to have a capacity to love and a sense of genuineness. But they are ignorant. My eight-year-old cannot write the alphabet and cannot add 8 plus 3. My ten-year-old has forgotten everything he learned at Glenlyon School two years ago. I thought this kind of school would provide an intellectual stimulus. For me it is not satisfactory to have a child who goes through five years of being turned on and happy without learning anything.[63]

---

61   Bill Stavdal, personal interview, March 18, 1997.
62   Craigdarroch School, Educational Policies Committee, minutes, November 20, 1968, document collection of William Stavdal, Victoria.
63   Educational Policies Committee, minutes, November 20, 1968, comments of Mr. Warren.

Another parent objected that "there is very little reading, writing, or projects of interest. The children are reverting to playing only because of lack of interest. It is up to the teachers to interest the children and teach them." Another put it this way: "My feeling is around the word freedom. I am worried because of the lack of academic work. I am realistic enough to feel I have to do a few things I don't like in order to survive. Children have to have a basic minimum of knowledge to go ahead." Still another parent said:

> Freedom of choice between various activities is a good thing. But if a kid continues to opt out there is a problem that should be looked into carefully. A healthy involved child will explore and choose, but freedom of choice is a sham if there is nothing going on to catch his interest.[64]

On the other hand, some parents were content with the amount of freedom offered in the school and criticized the others for hypocrisy. As one put it, "What these parents really want is for their children to learn to read and write. They put their children into a free school hoping they would learn. I want my child to be happy and to learn those things that he wants to."[65]

At the meeting one teacher, John Andrews, admitted candidly, "The complaint about lack of alternatives is valid. I had no teaching experience and it has been a continuing learning process. I am still learning." Barbara Williams suggested the problems were partly caused by the restrictive space at the Scout Hall. More importantly, she acknowledged that she "has been bringing in more structure, which has bothered the boys. The tightening of authority has caused some upset." But in response to being called a weak head teacher, she explained, "It was a very permissive school at the end of last year. To change suddenly would not have worked and therefore I held back."[66]

Parents debated their ideas about freedom, responsibility, curriculum, and how to interest the students in academic work to ensure that they learn

---

64   Educational Policies Committee, minutes, November 20, 1968, comments of Mr. Graff.

65   Educational Policies Committee, minutes, November 20, 1968.

66   Educational Policies Committee, minutes, November 20, 1968, comments of Barbara Williams and John Andrews.

the basic subjects. President Leah Brown suggested that parents decide whether Craigdarroch "is a free school or a Progressive school." Another parent raised the question: "Are learning and being happy somehow incompatible? I do not think they are. This is probably the basic issue." One board member summed up the meeting:

> What are we going to do about the curriculum? How is the academic ability of the child going to be evaluated? Children are bound to move in and out for various reasons. If a child reaches the end of the school year and is behind his options are limited. We cannot, therefore, just dismiss this. Some parents would be content with a happy hobo. Most parents have reacted against the forcing of skills, but surely there is some happy medium.[67]

Although no resolution was reached during the remainder of the school year, the central questions were clarified and the most dissatisfied parents withdrew their children from the school. Ms. Williams believed that imposing a more formal academic program on students who were not used to it would best be done gradually. But she was unable to motivate students sufficiently in the non-coercive environment and was criticized for not providing enough structure. Furthermore, she was hampered by a lack of staff unanimity in support of her views. Without broad-based community support, Ms. Williams had a difficult task, and she did not return as head teacher in September 1969. The constant pressure to do things differently undermined her ability to do an effective job. Disagreement about the program had produced a serious deterioration in the community's ability to work together.

The situation continued to worsen. With Barbara Williams's departure, the school lost those parents who supported her, and enrolment dropped from forty-two to twenty-five. As in other alternative schools, the parents who left were those who had been most able to support the school financially. Furthermore, the Unitarian Hall, which had been provided through Ms. Williams, was no longer available to the school.

---

67 Educational Policies Committee, minutes, November 20, 1968, comments of Dr. French.

Craigdarroch School was left with a reduced enrolment, no location, and financial crisis. A number of parents began to fear that their children's educational future was at risk, and one former student believed the group had lost its sense of purpose. Eventually the school reopened in a rented house near Esquimalt with Rod Hyder as acting head teacher. The school shifted once again in the direction of more freedom. But with the community spirit deteriorating, the teachers disillusioned, and no prospect of the financial situation improving, Craigdarroch School could not continue. It closed for good in December 1969.[68] Most of the students returned to the public school system after the teachers had given them a crash course in the procedures of traditional schools. The school's only assets, the furniture, were sold. And the outstanding bills were sent to David Hummel.

EFFECTS OF THE SCHOOL

The key factor in the school's closure was the "split among parents over educational philosophy." A *Daily Colonist* reporter described Craigdarroch's gradual change from a "liberalized private school stressing the humanities" to a school modelled after "the famous Summerhill" where "children were allowed to progress at their own speeds and to select subjects of study at will. There were no tests, no report cards, no schedules. Most of the few rules were formulated by students."[69]

The main problem was that the founders of Craigdarroch did not have a clear idea of what kind of school they wanted. Some desired a liberal version of the standard British private school without the traditionalist emphasis on rote learning and harsh discipline. Others were looking for a more child-friendly environment than what was being offered by the public schools. But as the 1960s unfolded, innovative educational ideas were everywhere in the air, and the school attracted individuals who wanted far more freedom for their children than did the founding group. These contending ideologies of moderate Progressivism and radical Romanticism eventually brought the school to a standstill.

---

68   Mr. Andrews eventually returned to California, but Mr. Hyder remained in Victoria and became a community school coordinator.

69   Clement Chapple, "'Free' Education Brought to End by Money Woes," *Victoria Colonist*, December 18, 1969, 15.

In relying on the "gifted teacher" rather than on a coherent educational philosophy, the school founders remained fuzzy about what the school stood for. Although they claimed to be a Progressive school, almost nowhere in their literature were the ideas of John Dewey or other Progressive thinkers mentioned.[70] The parents' failure to agree on a consistent pedagogy was nowhere more evident than in their personnel decisions. The teachers varied widely in their philosophical approaches and in their knowledge of innovative methods. Only in a period of crisis were pedagogical issues seriously debated.

Craigdarroch's ideological and staffing problems were similar to those of the New School, also run by parents. Both groups were divided, some parents favouring a Progressive school and others wanting a school more like Summerhill. Neither had a workable system for evaluating teachers. The major difference was that Craigdarroch parents were a less participatory and politically aware group, less intensely involved in day-to-day operation and policy decisions than at the New School. They seldom discussed educational ideas, so disagreements about educational goals were less evident and less contentious until the school's last year.

Whether Craigdarroch fulfilled David Hummel's original vision to offer a "basic minimum education" is open to question. The absence of a compulsory curriculum resulted in a number of educational gaps. Some students reported missing such fundamentals as times tables, while others lacked basics in spelling and grammar. One student never learned to read at Craigdarroch, although she began reading almost immediately when she entered public school in grade four. Two students reported being years ahead in mathematics and science but way behind in grammar, and they "didn't know what a noun was." Another was behind in math but far ahead in everything else. One student, although she enjoyed her year at the school, recalled that she "knew she wasn't learning anything and felt nervous about it." She found herself quite far behind when she returned to public school and "felt I more or less missed a year of school; only missing one year was a kind of grace."[71] One former student said she did

---

70   The only educator mentioned in any Craigdarroch literature was Jerome Bruner, who was quoted in the 1967 Prospectus.
71   Ursula Peavy, personal interview, February 15, 1997.

not develop study habits, while another reported that his return to public school was a good thing because "I was a kid who needed more discipline."

However, most former students reported that the school succeeded in teaching them how to learn, and they received enough of the basics to facilitate their further education. Most also indicated their academic progress did not suffer when they returned to traditional schools, and students pursued a wide variety of careers. Whether this would have been the case if Craigdarroch had been longer lived is debatable.

Many students found public school a shock when they left Craigdarroch. One former student, a successful actor, found it oppressive: "I thought I was in the army; I refused to wear a dress and finally the principal gave in." Another, who became a lawyer, found public school traumatic: "I felt trapped, claustrophobic. The discipline was ridiculous and I was incredibly bored." Still another said: "I hated it—the strap, wearing dresses, lining up, the Lord's Prayer." This type of reaction was common among students from all types of alternative schools. But in the case of Craigdarroch students it did not profoundly affect their academic futures.

Craigdarroch School provided an environment where individual interests and personal values were nurtured. Former students believed that they learned many things that benefited their personal and professional lives. Some of these were creativity and an interest in the arts, an ability to question, a developing sense of self, a strong sense of community, and exposure to 1960s ideals. As one student remarked, "We grew up learning how to set our own boundaries and think for ourselves. I grieved when I had to leave."[72] Another observed, "I was lucky to have gone there. My eyes were opened. I grew up not being afraid of people. Nothing fazed me. I knew I could do whatever I wanted to do."[73]

---

72   Claire Schwartz, personal interview, April 16, 1997.
73   Carmen Stavdal, personal interview, March 26, 1997.

At Craigdarroch School, lessons often developed spontaneously.
Victoria Daily Times June 1, 1967

Several female students believed that the school provided an opportunity for their growth as women. One remembered an equality of expectations; no one was discouraged from any activity because they were a girl or a boy.[74] Another was impressed at an early age by the fact that Craigdarroch was essentially female run in contrast to the traditionally patriarchal society that existed in Victoria.[75]

Almost all former students evaluated their experience at the school as positive, and some were deeply affected by the Craigdarroch community. One student remembered that time as a "two-year period when what I did was different from what most people did."[76] Another said, "I can't imagine three or four years being more profound. It was an intense experience, a strong part of my life, both the people and the situation. We knew the school was different."[77] Another was "devastated to be taken out of

74 Carmen Stavdal, personal interview, March 26, 1997.
75 Diane Brown, personal interview, March 17, 1997.
76 Tom Koltai, personal interview, February 17, 1997.
77 Kate McIntosh, personal interview, February 23, 1997.

the school. I remember to this day the day I left."[78] Still another recalled, "It broke my heart to leave Craigdarroch."[79]

Craigdarroch School was strongly influenced by the prevalent ideas and experimental lifestyles of the 1960s, even though a relatively small minority of parents were political activists or "hippies." One student described how her mother was influenced by the 1960s, "not the trends but the ideas and the ideals,"[80] while another pointed out, "We were taught by Berkeley radicals. Our parents were sympathetic even though they may have lived in the Uplands. They didn't look the part but they were influenced by the ideas."[81] Former parent Vance Peavy saw an obvious relationship between the school and the ambiance of the 1960s: "There wouldn't have been Craigdarroch School if not for the 1960s—it was a unique period of time."

Former participants saw a clear relationship between private alternative schools like Craigdarroch and publicly supported alternative schools. Vance Peavy said: "The schools of the sixties laid the foundation for later alternative schools. Craigdarroch created an environment that supported kids and brought hope into the lives of people who were discouraged."[82] A former student believed that the idea that parents have a right to be actively involved in their children's education was inspired by early alternative schools.[83] William Stavdal, education writer for the *Daily Colonist* during the 1960s and a Craigdarroch parent, reflected on the factors that would lead the Victoria School District to create Sundance School in 1973:

> It was beyond question a response to pressure from all
> sides for a more innovative kind of education. Everything
> was in ferment, everything was being questioned. It was
> in the air. I'm sure the genealogy of much that is occur-
> ring in today's education system can be traced to the chal-
> lenges thrown up by the alternative schools of the sixties.

---

78 Carmen Stavdal, personal interview, March 26, 1997.
79 Diane Brown, personal interview, March 17, 1997.
80 Diane Brown, personal interview, March 17, 1997.
81 Kate McIntosh, personal interview, February 23, 1997.
82 Vance Peavy, personal interview, February 17, 1997.
83 Carmen Stavdal, personal interview, March 26, 1997.

> Even when they appeared to fail they won a moral victory
> in their enduring influence.[84]

Craigdarroch School offered a moderate alternative for parents who believed traditional schools were inhumane and uninspiring. For most students Craigdarroch provided a positive interlude to their traditional schooling—a supportive community and an interesting educational environment. But during its three and a half years, the school became increasingly influenced by the 1960s counterculture. Craigdarroch and the other moderate Progressive schools changed with the times, and all developed some characteristics of a Romantic school by 1967. Inspired by Summerhill and the burgeoning counterculture, the Romantic period was about to begin in British Columbia.

---

84   William Stavdal, letter to the author, March 29, 1997. Mr. Stavdal served as executive assistant to Deputy Education Minister Jim Carter for ten years during the 1980s.

Part Two

ROMANTIC SCHOOLS

Chapter 5

THE BARKER FREE SCHOOL

By the mid-1960s a new educational theory began to appear in Canada, rooted in English Romanticism and inspired by A. S. Neill's Summerhill School. This coincided with the arrival of Bob Barker in British Columbia from New York in the summer of 1965. Mr. Barker was a committed advocate of "free schools" and hoped to establish one in Vancouver, modelled after Summerhill. His school would differ from Progressive alternative schools in its emphasis on considerably more freedom for the children.

Although he spent many years in the United States, Bob Barker was born in Saskatchewan in 1913 into a prominent manufacturing and banking family. His grandfather had been a successful Liberal politician, having served in the House of Commons, the Manitoba cabinet, and the Senate from 1882 to 1929.[1] Mr. Barker's parents moved to the United States in 1921, but he spent his summers back in Canada and later attended Ridley College, an old "establishment" school in St. Catharines, Ontario. He graduated with a BA in English from Cornell University in 1935 and worked as a manager for six years in his father's furniture manufacturing business in Chicago.[2] Mr. Barker travelled extensively and tried many occupations during the next two decades, including furniture design,

---

1 Born in Ontario, Robert Watson (1853–1929) founded a milling and machine shop business in Manitoba in the 1870s. He served as an MP (1882–1892) and in the Manitoba cabinet (1892–1900) and was appointed to the Senate in 1900. Henry Morgan, *Canadian Men and Women of the Time* (Toronto: Briggs, 1912); Ross Hamilton, *Prominent Men of Canada* (Montreal: National, 1931).

2 Robert Barker, "Biographical Materials and Educational Statement," submitted to the New School, April 9, 1965, Phil Thomas document collection.

carpentry, sales, and temporary odd jobs, though he never established himself in a long-term professional or business career.[3]

Mr. Barker developed a social conscience in early adulthood, describing himself as someone who has "been fighting totalitarianism at home and abroad in my own way all my life" with "a deep sympathy for the oppressed and the vanquished."[4] A pacifist, he was sent to prison as a conscientious objector during World War II but was eventually allowed to join the ambulance corps in Italy in 1944.[5] After the war he worked with a United Nations organization in Paris, supervising the shipment of war surplus equipment to third world countries.[6]

Mr. Barker was drawn to education during his university days when he was "entranced by the sounds of the little kids playing outside" in the Cornell Faculty of Education nursery school.[7] A Romantic, his interest in alternative education was inspired by Jean Jacques Rousseau, A. S. Neill, and Homer Lane.[8]

Bob Barker's friendship with A. S. Neill, founder of Summerhill, was a turning point in his life. They met in 1948 during Neill's first visit to the United States when Mr. Barker, having read about Summerhill in *Time* magazine, attended Neill's popular lecture at the New School for Social Research in New York.[9] They corresponded regularly and ten years later, in 1958, Mr. Barker taught for a year at Summerhill under Neill's mentorship while enrolling his two children at the school.[10] Upon returning to New York, he studied Progressive education at the Bank Street College[11]

3   Robert Barker, United Nations Relief and Rehabilitation Association, Application, November 7, 1945, National Archives of Canada, CYC Documents, Record Group 116, Volume 142, File 884.
4   Robert Barker, UNNRA Application, November 7, 1945, National Archives of Canada.
5   Robert Barker, "Biographical Materials and Educational Statement."
6   Robert Barker, personal resume, April 9, 1965, National Archives of Canada.
7   Bob Barker, personal interview, October 23, 1996.
8   Robert Barker, "Biographical Materials and Educational Statement." Homer Lane was A. S. Neill's mentor. See his *Talks to Parents and Teachers* (New York: 1928).
9   Neill's trips to the United States are described in Jonathan Croall, *Neill of Summerhill* (New York: Pantheon, 1983) 345–349.
10 "Biographical Materials and Educational Statement," April 9, 1965.
11 Bank Street College was founded by the Progressive educator, Lucy Sprague Mitchell. See Joyce Antler's biography, *Lucy Sprague Mitchell: The Making of a Modern Woman* (New Haven: Yale University Press, 1987).

and did his student teaching at City and Country School, a well-known New York Progressive school.[12] During the early 1960s Mr. Barker met several of the most significant Progressive and Romantic educators of the day.

Headmaster Robert Barker leads students in a discussion of current events and geography at the Barker Free School (later known as the Collaberg School) in upstate New York, an early Romantic (free) school in the United States. Barker School brochure, c. 1962.
CC0 1.0 Universal public domain | Wikimedia Commons

In 1961 Bob Barker fulfilled a longstanding dream by establishing his own school in Stony Point, New York, in a temporary building loaned to

---

12   City and Country School (originally The Play School) was founded by Caroline Pratt in 1914. See Joyce Antler, *Lucy Sprague Mitchell*, 236–246; Caroline Pratt, *Experimental Practice in the City and Country School* (New York: Dutton, 1924); and John and Evelyn Dewey, *Schools of Tomorrow* (New York: Dutton, 1915).

him by the public school board.[13] The Barker Free School opened with thirty students, and by the third year of operation grew to fifty-five children aged four to fifteen. It was the first "free school" in North America.[14] Mr. Barker adopted two fundamental Summerhill principles: student attendance at classes was voluntary, and school decisions (except on matters relating to health and safety) were made at "community government" meetings where staff and students would all have equal voice. Although the students spent some time studying the three Rs, play was the major school activity. Most staff members were experienced educators, and one teacher had been trained in Progressive methods at Columbia Teachers College and later founded the First Street School in 1964, a well-known free school in a poor neighbourhood of New York.[15]

A group of parents had financed the purchase of a permanent building on thirteen wooded acres and controlled the governing board. By the end of the second year, these parents began to fear that their children were falling behind in academic skills and decided to modify school policy. Although the school continued to offer a Progressive education, two of Mr. Barker's basic practices, non-compulsory classes and community government, were eliminated. Deeply disappointed, he resigned as director in December 1963.[16]

Despite this setback, Bob Barker remained committed to Romantic education. He taught for a term at Lewis-Wadhams School in upstate New York, a school founded in 1963 by Herb Snitzer, another follower of A. S. Neill.[17] Mr. Barker also served as a director of the Summerhill Society, founded in 1961 after the publication of *Summerhill*.[18] The society hoped to popularize Neill's ideas in North America by publishing a newsletter

---

13   Barbara Unger, "The Barker School," *County Citizen* (New City, NY), January 10, 1963, 5.

14   George Dennison writes that the Barker School (later renamed the Collaberg School) "represents, as far as I know, the first full-fledged use of Neill's methods in this country." *The Lives of Children* (New York: Random House, 1969): 299. (In this context, "North America" refers to the United States and Canada.)

15   See George Dennison's *The Lives of Children* (New York: Random House, 1969).

16   Robert Barker, "Biographical Materials and Educational Statement," April 9, 1965. After Bob Barker's departure, the school was renamed the Collaberg School.

17   See Herb Snitzer, *Today Is for Children* (New York: Macmillan, 1972).

18   A. S. Neill, *Summerhill: A Radical Approach to Child Rearing* (New York: Hart, 1960).

and by supporting schools based on Summerhill principles. Several well-known educational critics were among the society's founders, including Paul Goodman who had been a sponsor of the Barker School at Stony Point.[19] The society's literature summarized Neill's views on education:

> We hold that when children are given a responsible freedom, in a climate of understanding and non-possessive love, they choose with wisdom, learn with alacrity, develop genuinely social attitudes, and grow to be non-fearful, warm, and loving human beings.[20]

In the spring of 1965, Mr. Barker saw an advertisement in the Summerhill Society newsletter for the directorship of the New School in Vancouver and applied. Two New School parents interviewed him in New York and were impressed by his honesty, initiative, personal warmth, knowledge of Progressive methods, and respect for parents. They noted that "at a time when the Summerhill Society was just talking about a Summerhill School, Bob Barker started his school by himself. He did everything: teaching, directing, fundraising, purchasing, financing, and registering."[21] But most parents wanted the New School to remain a Progressive school based on Dewey's philosophy, and Mr. Barker didn't get the job. They found his ideas too Romantic, particularly the practice of not requiring students to attend classes.

However, with the encouragement of a few New School parents, Bob Barker decided to move to British Columbia to establish a school based on Summerhill principles.[22] He spoke at a public meeting in downtown Vancouver in June 1965 and was featured in a full-page article in the *Vancouver Times* entitled "This Is School?"[23] That fall Mr. Barker opened a small school in a house at Roberts Creek on the Sechelt Peninsula, where several families had expressed interest. However, enrolment never

---

19   See Jonathan Croall, *Neill of Summerhill* (New York: Pantheon, 1983), 350–363.
20   "Statement of Policy," adopted by the Summerhill Society, March 19, 1961, National Archives of Canada, CYC documents, Record Group 116, Volume 142, File 884.
21   Rita and Werner Cohn, "Robert Barker: Impressions Gained in an Interview," New York, April 11, 1965. In the possession of the author. See Chapter 2.
22   Bob Barker, personal interview, October 23, 1996.
23   *Vancouver Times*, June 7, 1965, 13.

exceeded six students, and in 1966 he decided to open a larger school in North Vancouver.[24]

Journalists were often surprised by how much autonomy children had in Romantic schools, and media coverage reflected that.
Headline from *Vancouver Times*, June 7, 1965, 13.

NORTH VANCOUVER

By the summer of 1966, early manifestations of the counterculture were in full swing. *Summerhill* was widely read, and there was growing interest in a less authoritarian kind of education than that offered by the public school system. In this climate Bob Barker generated plenty of enthusiasm for his unconventional ideas. He was interviewed on Jack Webster's popular radio program and gave well-attended public lectures at the downtown YWCA and the Unitarian Church in West Vancouver. Mr. Barker rented a storefront on First Avenue near Lonsdale in North Vancouver, and the Barker Free School opened in September 1966 with twenty-three students ranging in age from four to thirteen.[25]

24   Bob Barker, personal interview, October 23, 1996.
25   Hugh Dickson, "Students at Free School Just Don't Want to Quit," *Citizen* (North Vancouver), January 12, 1967, 1.

Some parents heard about the Barker School through friends or through Mr. Barker's radio appearances, but the majority were those who turned up at his lectures. Most listeners were impressed by Mr. Barker's gentle and warm personality, his love for children, and his ideas about freedom. Three English parents had experienced "integrated" education in Britain and found Vancouver schools rigid and old-fashioned. Another believed the authoritarian school system would be damaging to her children, while another liked the fact that the kids would be able to "move around without being stuck in their seats all day." As one parent put it, "I was just plain anti-school. We all had our own personal reasons."[26] These parents were seeking a more humane education for their children that would emphasize social harmony, creative expression, and natural growth. They were not particularly concerned about formal curriculum or academic learning, which they thought would happen naturally at its own pace, an idea becoming popular in some quarters by the mid-1960s.

There was a strong unconventional, anti-authoritarian, and individualistic streak among the parents. Two were artists, one practised alternative medicine, and another whose father had homesteaded in the North Vancouver bush described herself as an environmentalist from a "long line of English mavericks."[27] One parent was described by her children as a "free spirit" and another as "unorthodox." But while some parents were influenced by countercultural ideas and were actively questioning traditional notions of authority, most would not have considered themselves "hippies" in 1966.

Almost all active parents in the Barker School were women. Many were questioning cultural values and seeking alternative lifestyles, although these interests were not shared by their husbands. These women were forerunners of the feminist movement, although they were not yet consciously challenging traditional female roles. Within the next few years many marriages would be strained among Barker School parents.

Mr. Barker outlined his educational philosophy in his school brochure: "education of the whole child in an atmosphere of freedom and responsibility; the welcome of all creeds and colours; freedom of worship or

26   Shirley Maclean, personal interview, November 14, 1996.
27   Mona Bertelsen, personal interview, December 9, 1996.

non-worship; foundation upon the principles of A. S. Neill's free school, Summerhill." Mr. Barker went on to describe exactly what he meant by a free school:

> Where children can develop voluntarily as free, loving, thinking, acting human beings in an atmosphere of discovery and delight; where the only pressure comes from within the child; where creativity is kept to a maximum, competition to the minimum; where there is mutual respect between teachers and students; where the heart of the school is in community government, each child and each adult having one vote.[28]

Mr. Barker believed that academic pursuits and basic skills in reading, writing, and arithmetic should be an important component of any school, and he was confident that "free children are eager to learn." But this would be secondary to the development of the child as a person. He staunchly defended the child's right to choose whether or not to engage in academic work, even if that meant some did not learn to read at six years old. It was up to the teachers to make those activities engaging enough to interest the children. Students were encouraged to approach the staff if they wanted to pursue academics. The experience at Summerhill suggested that even if students initially rejected formal learning, they would eventually want to take part. Mr. Barker was confident that when this did happen, learning would proceed speedily. His commitment to voluntary classes never wavered, even when it became clear later on that little academic learning was taking place at the Barker School.

Bob Barker hired two staff members, Chuck and Helen Valentine. Originally from New York, the Valentines had come to British Columbia in 1956 to escape McCarthyism in the United States and to seek a more rural lifestyle. Their Quaker background and their search for a small and meaningful community led them to Argenta in the West Kootenays.[29] Chuck Valentine was an engineer by profession, had a wide range of interests,

---

28 Barbara Unger, "The Barker School," *County Citizen* (New City, NY), January 10, 1963, 5.

29 Rick Valentine, personal interview, November 26, 1996.

and was an eccentric and legendary figure in Argenta.[30] His interest in Progressive education began in 1958 when he discovered San Francisco's long established Peninsula School, and several years later he obtained a master's degree from the Putney Graduate School of Teacher Education, a Progressive school in rural Vermont.[31] For several years during the 1960s, the Valentines operated a small home-based school called "Valentine View Point," for children whose parents wanted them to have a live-in rural experience. Their brochure described "a place where children may broaden their interests and try their capacities in relative freedom from the restricted thinking of our culture."[32] The View Point children did little academic work and spent most of their time engaged in outdoor activities and working on the homestead. Since the Valentines were looking for an alternative school for their own children, they accepted Bob Barker's invitation in 1966 to move to Vancouver and teach at the Barker School while enrolling their children there.

Chuck Valentine believed that parents should have more control over their children's education and that school and community should be more closely connected. Students could study local problems and visit places of work, while parents and other community members could be brought into the school to present experiences from their own lives. Mr. Valentine thought education should be less subject based and more concerned with developing "flexibility, creativity, self-direction, self-reliance, and self-confidence." Students should be given more choice of what to learn; observation and "first-hand" sources of information should replace textbooks; and children should spend more time in physical activity and play. Mr. Valentine also believed schools should promote individuality rather than conformity, replace competition with co-operation, abolish the grading system, and allow each child to experience success through learning at his or her own rate. Mr. Valentine thought that schools should teach "human relations" and prepare children to participate in a democratic society: "We

---

30 Although the Valentines were well acquainted with the Argenta Friends School, they had little formal connection with it.

31 The Graduate School, associated with The Putney School, a Progressive high school founded in 1935, became part of Antioch College in 1963. See Susan Lloyd, *The Putney School: A Progressive Experiment* (New Haven: Yale University Press, 1987).

32 View Point brochure, 1965. In possession of the author.

set the school apart from society and, rather than give training and practice in democratic self-government, expect children silently and unquestioningly to follow the directions of an authoritarian teacher at all times."[33] He thought students should experience democracy in the classroom through group planning, problem-solving, and decision-making.

Like many alternative teachers of the time, Chuck Valentine subscribed to a combination of Progressive and Romantic ideals. His emphasis on "learning by doing" and education for democracy placed him partly in the Deweyan tradition. But he also held such Romantic notions as the educational value of a rural lifestyle and the belief that "the choice of whether to learn at school should be left up to the students, that attendance should be voluntary."[34] However, he attached some importance to skill-based learning and stopped short of complete freedom.

The Barker Free School spent a year and a half in its North Vancouver location. The storefront consisted mainly of one large room that became the play area, meeting space, and an all-purpose room for school activities. Since this room was too noisy for most learning activities, several smaller rooms were used for small-group lessons and for Mr. Barker's office. Staff, parents, and students pitched in to renovate the building. Parents were enthusiastic and took part in cleaning, fundraising, supervising field trips, and attending monthly meetings. The school community was informal and relaxed. One parent remembered dressing her daughter in an attractive dress for the first day of school only to find that all the children were wearing "raggy jeans." Another parent described the excitement of participating in something new:

> Bob was guiding us through something we hadn't done before. A lot of it was learning as you went along. The staff really believed in the kids—in their potential. They asked the kids what they wanted to do – a six-year-old can have a good idea. They really listened. They taught me to do that as a parent.[35]

---

33   C. P. Valentine, "A Request for a New Look at Our Schools," Argenta, BC, 1966, 16–17. Unpublished paper, New School document collection.

34   C. P. Valentine, "A Request for a New Look at Our Schools," 8.

35   Kita Ridgeway, personal interview, November 13, 1996.

From the outset Mr. Barker hoped the kids would develop basic literacy and mathematics skills. Students did a little writing, some children read books on their own, staff members read to small groups, and some students learned to read with the Initial Teaching Alphabet.[36] Most of the teaching was on a one-to-one basis with students proceeding at their own pace. One former student remembered using a few math workbooks, another recalled being tutored in math by Mr. Barker, and several remembered working with Cuisenaire rods.

But for the most part, former students had little recollection of academic work, as the dominant activity was play. The building had no playground so students had to spend most of their time inside. Older students were allowed to leave the school, and one student recalled playing in a vacant lot while another remembered "a big gang of us roaming the streets of North Vancouver," looking for such treasures as copper wire.[37]

The school developed an extensive field trip program. Students visited museums, the art gallery, the library, a bakery, and a cabinet-making shop. They went swimming and skating, visited parks, skied on Mount Seymour, and hiked around the North Shore. A trip to the Burrard Shipyard was so memorable that one student credits his lifelong interest in electrical systems to that visit.[38] Some students and their parents spent a week experiencing rural life on the Valentines' farm in Argenta. On another occasion they camped for a week at Long Beach after students had travelled part way by bicycle. There was at least one field trip per week, consistent with the widespread alternative school practice of using the outside community as a major educational resource, reducing the separation between school and community.

Artistic expression was a large part of the school program, and painting, clay work, lino prints, crafts, and weaving were frequent activities. So were visits to the studios of artists, potters, and candle-makers. Students studied with artist Gordon Yearsley at his studio in Vancouver's Gastown area. Mr. Yearsley, who lived in Argenta but worked in Vancouver, founded

36   Hugh Dickson, "Students at Free School Just Don't Want to Quit," *Citizen* (North Vancouver), January 12, 1967, 1.
37   Galen Bellman, personal interview, November 20, 1996.
38   Ray Valentine, personal interview, December 10, 1996.

the Bhavana Studio Workshop, a small art school based on providing an "immediate and human" relationship between teachers and students.[39] One parent, artist Shirley Maclean, offered regular arts and crafts sessions and another parent, an accomplished Canadian musician, came in to teach music. Students did a great deal of impromptu drama and also enjoyed the weekly National Film Board showings arranged by Chuck Valentine.

STAFF CHANGES

Chuck and Helen Valentine missed their rural life and returned to Argenta after one year. They had some differences in philosophy with Bob Barker, particularly about how much freedom students ought to be given. This was a common source of tension among alternative school teachers and one of the reasons staff turnover was usually high. After the Valentines' departure, the Barker School attracted a different kind of staff—a group of young adults in their early to mid-twenties. Few had any formal background in education, but all had read A. S. Neill and saw freedom for children as a way to change the world. These staff members were deeply affected by the movement for social and cultural change that was sweeping North America. Like many young Canadian adults in 1967, they empathized with disadvantaged minorities, opposed the Vietnam War, favoured a simple life with few material possessions, and above all valued personal freedom.

Jan MacDougall was a single parent living in Kitsilano in 1966 when she read an announcement about one of Bob Barker's lectures. That evening was "like a revelation for me." After attending a subsequent meeting at Mr. Barker's home, she enrolled her daughter in the Barker Free School. She was little influenced by educational theory, although she read *Summerhill* after hearing Mr. Barker's lecture. She formed her views about schooling primarily by listening to her own children—"my children kept opening doors for me"—and by observing what she regarded as their "narrow and deadening public school experience; I knew I wanted

39   Bhavana Studio Workshop, Prospectus, 1968, National Archives, CYC Documents. Like Chuck Valentine, Gordon Yearsley lived in Argenta. He was a close friend of Watson Thomson (see Chapter 7) and founded a rural co-operative in Argenta in 1971.

something different for them."[40] After initially volunteering at the school, Ms. MacDougall became a dedicated staff member for two years.

Dave Manning grew up in Midwestern United States and attended Illinois State University, taking a degree in elementary education. Although he took the teachings of his Protestant upbringing seriously, many aspects of American Christian practice in the mid-1960s seemed sadly incoherent. Mr. Manning was opposed to the Vietnam War and immigrated to Canada, like so many other young Americans, in the summer of 1967. He was drawn to British Columbia because of his love of wilderness and nature. Mr. Manning was attracted to free school beliefs after reading about A. S. Neill's work and had seen a reference to the Barker School in a *Look* magazine article. When he arrived in Vancouver he sought out Bob Barker and, in September 1967, joined the staff of the Barker School.[41]

Sharon Mundwiler was also from the American Midwest. She had been active in the civil rights movement and worked in a camp for children from Harlem. She and her husband were opposed to the Vietnam War and finally renounced their citizenship and left for Canada. Settling in Winnipeg, they were scared off by the hard winters and moved to Vancouver. Ms. Mundwiler had read *Summerhill* and had taken several years of education at a small college in Illinois where she had met Dave Manning. She contacted him upon arriving in Vancouver and fit right in with the atmosphere at the Barker School, where she joined the staff in the fall of 1967.[42] Her sister, Marilyn, arrived in Vancouver in 1968 and taught for one year at the school.

Kate Barlow applied to teach at the Barker Free School at the same time as Sharon Mundwiler. Although Mr. Barker had only been looking for one staff member, he liked them both and, in typical inclusive fashion, asked both to join the staff. Ms. Barlow was from rural Ontario and sympathized with the American civil rights movement and the plight of Indigenous people in Canada. She spent six months working at a nursery school on a Manitoba reserve as a volunteer with the Company of Young Canadians, an organization that would play a significant role in Canadian alternative

---

40 Jan Fraser (formerly Jan MacDougall), personal interview, October 29, 1996.
41 Dave Manning, personal interview, November 14, 1996.
42 Sharon Wiseman (formerly Sharon Mundwiler), personal interview, March 16, 1997.

schools. Upon moving to Vancouver Ms. Barlow was inspired by reading A. S. Neill as well as by her meeting with Bob Barker and joined the staff at the Barker Free School in the fall of 1967.[43]

Dan Jason grew up in Montreal and attended McGill University, where he participated in protests against the Vietnam War, "political discussions into the night," and poetry and theatre events. He had also read *Summerhill* and reflected upon "how deadening traditional education was on people like myself." He moved to British Columbia in 1967 and a year later was living on the beach at Long Beach on the west side of Vancouver Island. "One day Bob Barker came down with a bunch of kids from the Barker Free School. He and I connected immediately and he invited me to come out and teach at his school. And just like that I went!"[44]

These individuals formed the backbone of the Barker Free School from 1967 until its closing in 1969. They shared many values, interests, and lifestyle preferences. They formed a close community, often living as well as working together, and much of their social life revolved around the school. Although they admired Bob Barker, they differed with him on some issues. In particular, they were even more laissez-faire in their educational beliefs and were unconcerned if no formal academic activity took place at the school. Their views moved the school firmly to the centre of the 1960s counterculture.

In the meantime, Bob Barker had made extensive connections with other alternative educators across Canada. One visitor to the Barker School was Bob Davis, a founder of Everdale Place north of Toronto, Canada's best-known free school.[45] Mr. Barker also knew George Martell, a leading educational activist in Ontario who later created a storefront school for street kids in Toronto.[46] Mr. Davis and Mr. Martell were among the founders of *This Magazine is about Schools*, which was widely read by alternative educators across North America.

---

43   Kate Barlow, personal interview, October 16, 1996.
44   Dan Jason, personal interview, October 30, 1996.
45   See Bob Davis, *What Our High Schools Could Be* (Toronto: Our Schools/Our Selves, 1990), 41–98. Mr. Barker's son attended Everdale for a brief period.
46   See George Martell, "What Can I Do Right Now?" in Satu Repo, ed., *This Book is About Schools* (New York: Random House, 1970), 286–307.

Mr. Barker also knew several activists within the Company of Young Canadians (CYC), an organization created by the Pearson government in 1965 to sponsor young idealists in helping local people address social problems in their communities. Encouraged by Bob Davis, Mr. Barker made a formal application in May 1967 to have his school accepted as a CYC project.[47] The Barker School was not like typical CYC projects that sent volunteers to poor neighbourhoods or Indigenous communities. However, although the CYC leadership in eastern Canada preferred political and social projects, the Company did support two Ontario free schools, including Everdale, by providing salaries for the teachers. The Barker application was supported by a local CYC staff worker who had been volunteering at the school once a week.[48] George Martell, a member of CYC Ontario staff, recommended that the Barker Free School was the type of educational project the CYC should support, and the program was accepted.

The school was administered as part of the CYC's Vancouver Youth Project, which included several other schools and youth agencies.[49] The Company provided the Barker Free School with salaries for four teachers for two years. Although CYC volunteer salaries were extremely low ($150 to $200 a month), this allowed the school, which was already having a tough time making ends meet, to continue. The Barker School maintained a low profile within the CYC, but the Vancouver Youth Project would later create a public relations embarrassment for the Company.

ALDERGROVE

By the fall of 1967, teachers at the Barker Free School were becoming increasingly dissatisfied with the North Vancouver location. The cramped facilities were not conducive to the spontaneous atmosphere of a free school. Since play was the principal activity of the school day, the lack of an outside playground was seriously inhibiting. The young staff members,

47 Company of Young Canadians Project Application, Barker Free School, May 12, 1967, National Archives of Canada, Record Group 116, Volume 142, File 884.
48 Letter from Dave Berner to Campbell Mackie in the CYC Ottawa office, May 1967, National Archives of Canada.
49 Letters to George Martell and to Bob Barker from Campbell Mackie, CYC Director of Domestic Programs, May 29, 1967; and to Bob Barker from Dave Berner, CYC staff in British Columbia, July 21, 1967, National Archives of Canada.

influenced by the nascent "back to the land" movement, yearned for a more rural environment for themselves and the children. Early in 1968 Mr. Barker rented an old farmhouse in Cloverdale. The main floor served as new quarters for the school and several staff members lived in the bedrooms upstairs. Although the property wasn't large, there was enough space for the children to play outside and a barn provided an enjoyable place for games and exploring.

Later that spring, Bob Barker found an even better location—a farm in Aldergrove with a modern house on thirty-eight acres of woods and fields with a stream running through them. The house had six bedrooms scattered along a long hallway, perfect for small group activities to occur simultaneously. The rooms were fitted out with art and craft materials, science equipment, and the school library. Mr. Barker bought the property for $40,000 (a $20,000 down payment and a $20,000 mortgage), which seriously stretched him financially.[50] No one lived in the house, but staff members stayed over from time to time and Mr. Barker occasionally slept in his office after particularly long days.

In 1967/68 the school enrolled twenty-six students aged six to sixteen.[51] Since most lived thirty miles away in Vancouver, there was a long commute each morning. Mr. Barker drove out from West Vancouver and met the Vancouver students at a street corner in east Vancouver. Some students travelled to the meeting place by carpool while others rode the bus. They piled into Mr. Barker's large station wagon and everyone arrived at the farm by 9:30.

The students spent a great deal of time outside. Much of this was unsupervised play as the children horsed around in small groups, played on a homemade swing, dug holes and built tunnels, played in the fields, and organized games such as hide-and-seek or kick the can. Time was unstructured and fluid, the primary aim being to enjoy the day.[52] As one student said, "We played all day and basically did whatever we wanted. We didn't hurt anybody or do anything dangerous. We just had fun."[53]

50   Bob Barker, personal interview, October 23, 1996.
51   Olive Johnson, "Free Schools: Tomorrow's Education or Passing Fad?" *Vancouver Life*, April 1968, 17.
52   Sharon Wiseman, personal interview, March 16, 1997.
53   Jason Ridgeway, personal interview, September 24, 1997.

The Barker Free School philosophy was that children learn through play.
The Citizen, January 12, 1967

The few adult-initiated activities arose spontaneously. A staff member might say, "Anyone want to learn to develop photographs?" or "Anyone want to go on a nature walk?"[54] Students also took French lessons, watched films, and participated in frequent drama activities.[55] The children did a lot of cooking and baking, and everyone had a "nice noisy time" preparing large communal lunches together. Mr. Manning and Mr. Jason, keenly interested in literature, read stories and poems to groups or individuals.

Most students have vivid memories of the long nature walks led by Dave Manning and Dan Jason. Both had an impressive knowledge of the natural world and taught students to identify varieties of plant life, fish, bugs under logs, and other creatures. They also pointed out various edible plants.[56] Science projects such as collecting leaves, observing fish in the stream, or looking at organisms under a microscope were usually short-term and spontaneous. But one student remembered more substantial

---

54   Galen Bellman, personal interview, November 20, 1996.
55   Olive Johnson, "Free schools: Tomorrow's Education or Passing Fad?" *Vancouver Life*, April 1968, 16.
56   They later wrote the popular *Some Useful Wild Plants* (Vancouver: Talonbooks, 1972).

projects such as assembling bird skeletons and setting up a terrarium and a fish tank. Mr. Barker taught some children to work at carpentry, while other students learned basic mechanics through experimenting with abandoned cars and old machinery on the property. One student "built a mini-bike from scratch at ten years old. I scrounged the parts and Bob would take me down to the hardware store when I needed something. I was left to my own devices but if I needed a hand there was someone there to help me."[57]

Although students could always go to the adults for help, they were encouraged to be self-reliant—"we were expected to organize our own activities, to use our own heads."[58] The older students ran their own store out of a small building on the Aldergrove property. They sold candy, chocolate bars, potato chips, and toys, and the students organized everything from work schedules to inventory. But the store closed when a few kids started stealing products and money.

Academic activities were rare once the school moved to its rural setting. A few students who were keen on learning worked individually with staff members, but the majority did not. Most students had already learned to read at public school and others had learned at home or from the older children. Not that Mr. Barker didn't regularly try to initiate academics with individual students. "He spent a lot of time going around asking people if they would like to do some math or other things. Usually we said no."[59] A former student described one such occasion:

> I remember being brought into a room with Bob and a
> female teacher and asked if I would like to do math. And
> the first time I said yes. So I was sitting there trying to do
> math and looking out the window and everybody else was
> outside playing. I looked at them and I looked at the math
> and I said I don't think I want to do the math anymore.
> I was told, okay, fine. So the next time they asked me I
> said no! And I don't remember doing any other math the
> whole time I was there.[60]

---

57   Tony Bertelsen, personal interview, April 17, 1997.
58   Galen Bellman, personal interview, November 20, 1996.
59   Susan and Cathleen Bertelsen, personal interview, December 9, 1996.
60   Galen Bellman, personal interview, November 20, 1996.

Most former students remembered everybody getting along well. One recalled a "family atmosphere" and big communal meals. Another said, "We cared about each other." There were always enough children at each age level so that nobody got left out. There was little bullying, and "teachers intervened if kids didn't get along."[61] Conflicts were dealt with by talking them out with the help of the staff: "Okay, you are having a conflict, let's sit down and talk about it." The only significant rule was you could do anything you wanted as long as you didn't hurt anyone else. However, a few students experienced a hierarchy of big kids and little kids and believed that there should have been more adult guidance. One of the "little kids" remarked that "we were pretty terrorized by the big kids—nobody was looking out for anybody."[62]

Mr. Barker convened weekly school meetings where everybody would sit around talking, discussing current events, or organizing future activities. Anyone could call a meeting to address a specific problem and everyone, adults and children alike, had one vote. Meetings were frequent, and students recalled that "anything to do with the school we all decided together."[63] Students were encouraged to express themselves when they "had the floor," and anybody with something to say was heard. This was a valuable experience and the children "developed confidence to express how they felt about things." However, most participants acknowledged that "Bob was the leader, the focal point" and could usually sway a meeting.

Although Mr. Barker valued everyone's opinion, he called the shots on the big decisions. As one staff member put it, "Bob was clearly in charge—we challenged him all the time, but he was in charge."[64] Another suggested that "Bob was never really a team player. He had put lots of energy and money into the school. We had the meetings but we didn't have a feeling that he was open to input."[65] Although staff dynamics were amiable and staff participated fully in decisions about curriculum,

61   Monica Yard, personal interview, May 1, 1997.
62   Kim Maclean, personal interview, November 6, 1996. Of course, bullying also occurred in public schools, but free school teachers were less likely to intervene.
63   Cathleen and Susan Bertelsen, personal interview, December 9, 1996.
64   Jan Fraser, personal interview, October 29, 1996.
65   Sharon Wiseman, personal interview, March 16, 1997.

admissions, and how to manage individual students, an effective procedure for reaching consensus never developed.

During the school's last year, the younger staff began to challenge Mr. Barker's views on discipline and academics frequently, and staff meetings became contentious. "It was always a struggle—the staff constantly trying to push Bob in the direction of more freedom, while he was trying to get the kids more interested in learning."[66] According to one staff member, "We were in a rebellious frame of mind. I wanted the kids to be creative, to love nature. Most already knew how to read. We weren't worried about the basics."[67]

The adult community of parents and teachers was very close. The school was too far out of town for parents to drop in on a regular basis, but many parents and teachers lived in Vancouver's Kitsilano district and spent time together outside of school, forming a cohesive social group. Barker School parents and staff, along with the staff of another alternative school, Knowplace, became close friends and created a community atmosphere similar to that of a large extended family. There was little distinction between teachers and parents, and staff members became like another set of parents for some students.[68] Staff members recalled the good rapport enjoyed by the adults, and one described the school as "one of the most loving and unified groups that I've come in contact with."[69] Some families have maintained lifelong connections and several subsequently moved to the country together, creating informal communities in Grand Forks and the Slocan Valley. Two marriages later took place among the children in their adulthood.

By the late 1960s the school had acquired a countercultural look and feel. Parents were exploring new lifestyles, careers, and communal living arrangements. Personal changes put stress on marriages, resulting in several divorces among the parent group. One student recalled how the 1960s influenced his dad: "He got tired of the rat race and wanted to do something different—he was alive and doing new things." During this

66   Jan Fraser, personal interview, October 29, 1996.
67   Sharon Wiseman, personal interview, March 16, 1997.
68   Marilyn Carson, personal interview, March 9, 1997.
69   Dave Manning, personal interview, November 14, 1996.

period two families moved to the country, another travelled for six months in Morocco, and another left the city to take a job operating a lighthouse in northern Vancouver Island. Some parents developed new careers as artists or writers. Others caught up in the times adopted a "hippie" lifestyle complete with rock music and marijuana. Previous formalities separating the world of adults from that of children disappeared. There was some drug use among the adults but it never became a serious problem as it would in some alternative schools. There was little sexual precociousness among these mostly pre-teenage students.

During the later days of the school, some students with emotional or behavioural difficulties joined the school community. Two boys from Arizona heard about the school and boarded there for several months.[70] One teacher reported that there were some "wild kids," while another recalled that children who arrived "fresh out of public school went hog wild" with their new-found freedom.[71] But compared to some alternative schools, the Barker School avoided taking large numbers of what people then called "problem kids." Most parents chose the school because they genuinely believed in its educational theory and practice, rather than seeing it as a refuge for children in trouble.

Financing the school was always a struggle. Bob Barker wanted the school to be accessible to everyone and bent over backwards to accommodate several low-income families.[72] Tuition was based on the ability to pay, an idea he borrowed from the New School. Fees were reasonable, ranging from a minimum of $165 per year to a maximum of $850, with most families paying about $300 per child.[73] Staff salaries were next to nothing. A 1967 operating report stated that "four full-time teachers work for expenses, one part-time teacher for $5.00 per hour plus expenses, one part-time teacher for a scholarship for his daughter, and one works for nothing."[74] Mr. Barker supported his family by drawing income from a

---

70   Olive Johnson, "Free Schools: Tomorrow's Education or Passing Fad?" *Vancouver Life*, April 1968, 17.

71   Dan Jason and Dave Manning, personal interviews, October 30 and November 14, 1996.

72   Marilyn Carson, personal interview, March 9, 1997.

73   Barker Free School, Prospectus, 1968/69; and Financial Report, 1965/66, 1966/67, and 1967/68, National Archives of Canada, Record Group 116, Volume 142, File 884.

74   Operating Report, 1966/67, National Archives of Canada, CYC documents.

small family trust fund. Still, the school had a deficit that year of over
$3,000, which Mr. Barker made up himself. He also spent $5,000 on
renovations.[75] The deficit disappeared the following year with the help
of the CYC funding. But finances became a problem again in 1968 when
a hoped-for grant from the Vancouver Foundation did not materialize. By
this time Mr. Barker had become seriously overextended by the ongoing
payments on the property.

Financial matters deteriorated in the spring of 1969. The school suffered a break-in and a good deal of equipment was lost. Several families were moving to the West Kootenays and would not be coming back
the following year. Another family decided to send their children back
to public school, and only four students were planning to return to the
Barker School. The school had never grown from its original enrolment
of twenty-five students, and depended on the participation of several large
families—the Macleans, the Ridgeways, the Bertelsens, and the Carsons.
When these families left, the school population was decimated.

Furthermore, by 1969 most staff members had decided to move on to
other pursuits. For many the school had been a pleasant and memorable
interlude in their lives before beginning careers or other permanent commitments. Bob Barker was left with few students, no staff, and no money.
He had little choice but to sell the farm and close the school. All the time,
energy, and money he had committed to the Barker Free School left him
feeling "awfully tired." Although Mr. Barker remained in the Vancouver
area for over thirty years, he never again became involved in an educational venture.

Bob Barker is remembered warmly and affectionately by the vast majority of children and adults connected with the school. One former student
said, "Bob never talked down to us, he didn't treat us like kids. I don't
remember him getting mad, or being angry with me—ever. Bob treated
us with respect."[76] Another student remembered him as "warm, open,
compassionate, loving, and heart-connected."[77] Still another described
him as "easygoing and agreeable; I never remember him raising his voice

75   Operating Report, 1966/67, National Archives of Canada, CYC documents.
76   Galen Bellman, personal interview, November 20, 1996.
77   Monica Yard, personal interview, May 1, 1997.

or not smiling."[78] A former staff member remarked, "Bob was a loving, generous, and kind man. He loved children and wanted the best for them. He had a deep respect for children. The basic premise of the school was mutual respect."[79] And one staff member and parent who was inspired by Mr. Barker said simply, "Bob held the whole thing together."[80]

But those who knew him during those years believed that Mr. Barker was disappointed that his students did not show more interest in academic learning. He wanted to create an "exciting, Progressive, academic environment,"[81] but his dilemma was in attempting to combine academic learning with freedom. In a letter to parents in 1967, he wrote candidly about his own doubts:

> I have always felt it was our duty to offer the curriculum and set aside time for it, and that the public would not support a school which did not do so. I have always felt it was our duty to point out to a child and his parents the consequences of his not following it; that while he might be a much more creative person when he left school, he might be months or years behind those of his age in schools where classes were compulsory, and that it might take months or years to catch up if he wanted one of most jobs or to go to college. Are you willing to have your child leave us at eighteen unable to read, write, spell, or do mathematics, as long as he is happy? Or do you want time set aside so he can learn these things while the rest of the time is made as rich as possible?[82]

Despite these doubts, Mr. Barker did not modify his position on voluntary classes. He believed the freedom of the child was more important than the academic risks. He thought it was the teacher's responsibility to discover what the children were interested in, and if teachers were patient enough, children would eventually participate in scholastic activities.[83]

---

78   Susan and Cathleen Bertelsen, personal interview, December 9, 1996.
79   Dave Manning, personal interview, November 20, 1996.
80   Jan Fraser, personal interview, October 29, 1996.
81   Bob Barker, personal interview, October 23, 1996.
82   Bob Barker, Report to Parents, February 28, 1967, National Archives of Canada.
83   Dave Manning, personal interview, November 14, 1996.

One former staff member said, "His idea was that the kids would come around and ask to do academic work. But I don't remember that happening."[84] Mr. Barker continued to believe this even when his own experience indicated otherwise. His deeply Romantic world view and his commitment to A. S. Neill's theory that children would eventually learn if left to their own devices did not waver.

EFFECTS ON STUDENTS AND STAFF

Former students believed they were profoundly affected by the Barker Free School:

"I learned to be more independent and self-sufficient."
"The attention and encouragement gave me confidence."
"I learned about people being different."
"I learned about dealing with problems and conflict."
"The right to my opinion, I can talk and be listened to."
"I learned to be more outgoing."
"Self-respect, self-esteem, belonging."
"Learning about nature."
"The spiritual aspect was nurtured."
"I learned to be myself."[85]

One student said, "I deal with life and people better. That was part of what the school was. We were able to do what we wanted as long as we didn't infringe on anyone else."[86] Although their family situations and the ambiance of the times played a part in shaping their personalities, former students believed the school was instrumental in nurturing such personal qualities as independence, self-confidence, responsibility, and the ability to solve problems.

A few students achieved academic success. One former student, a successful accountant, commented on her accomplishments despite her lack of formal education:

---

84   Sharon Wiseman, personal interview, March 16, 1997.
85   Wendy Maclean, Laura Landsberg, Michael Carson, Monica Yard, Ray Valentine, Susan Bertelsen, Cathleen Bertelsen, Galen Bellman, personal interviews.
86   Tony Bertelsen, personal interview, April 17, 1997.

I had no formal education beyond grade one. It didn't affect me until I tried to work. I felt out of touch with society as a whole. What I learned about the world I got through reading, travelling, and personal experience. I still know almost nothing about history. I got jobs by exaggerating my education. Finally, I went to Canada Manpower to get my Adult Basic Education. They asked me how much formal education I had had and I said "grade one." They didn't believe me at first. I tested at a grade nine level for English and at a grade two level for math! At the end of ten months I had my grade twelve graduation. I enrolled at UBC and graduated with a bachelor of commerce degree in 1989.[87]

Another former student told a moving story of how she overcame a learning disability, a series of family crises, and a debilitating workplace injury in order to pursue a university education. She became a therapist and learned above all that "anything is possible."[88] Another student who finished her high school education at Ideal School, an alternative high school, became a self-taught bookkeeper and accountant, and later earned a college diploma in music.

However, these stories are not typical, and many former Barker School students regretted that their schooling did not provide them with more academic opportunity. Few have university degrees, and some did not finish high school. Many believed their educational and professional opportunities were limited by their lack of formal schooling and basic skills. One said, "I would have liked to have been pushed a bit in my education."[89] Another thought "a little stricter system would have been good for me."[90] Another student who left public school in grade three and never returned to formal education commented that she was not well-prepared in the free school environment where "you had to make your own structure":

I don't think anyone took the education of the kids into consideration. The kids got left behind and finally got left

87   Galen Bellman, personal interview, November 20, 1996.
88   Barker School student, personal interview, May 1, 1997.
89   Barker School student, personal interview, November 5, 1996.
90   Barker School student, personal interview, December 10, 1996.

out. The adults were following their ideals and their passions but I don't think anybody considered that the kids were going to grow up and have to get a job.[91]

Many students were delayed in their language and mathematics development. Some had fallen behind in their computational skills, and four students between the ages of eight and eleven left the Barker School without knowing how to read. Two of these students eventually learned to read on their own—one learned at another alternative school, and one student was taught to read by his grade seven public school teacher in six weeks. One student described his writing as "rough around the edges" while another said, "I wanted to learn but it was hard because it was left so late. I never did get the grammar, my math was terrible, and I still can't spell. It's a bit embarrassing sometimes. I would like to go back and get my high school."[92]

Some students regretted the lack of connection to a normal school life. One girl who attended the Barker School as a five-year-old wanted to go to public school so much that at age six she walked to the local school on the first day in September and registered herself. Another said: "I would have liked more schooling. I had huge gaps. It left me feeling I missed out. I didn't have the same experience other children did."[93]

Most Barker School students never returned to formal education. Their lack of basic skills and their unfamiliarity with an organized learning structure made public school daunting. One former student was unable to re-enter public school after being in an alternative environment for several years:

> I stayed at home after the Barker School closed. I was too shy to go back to public school. I felt I was too far behind. I tried adult education but found it too hard. I did a lot of reading and writing on my own but math was a big problem. I missed the social group at school. I devoted my life to my horses.[94]

---

91 Barker School student, personal interview, November 6, 1996.
92 Two Barker School students, personal interviews, February 18 and September 24, 1997.
93 Barker School student, personal interview, May 1, 1997.
94 Barker School student, personal interview, December 2, 1996.

Another recalled how difficult it was to fit into an alien system:

> They [staff] should have made us do some reading and
> math, just a little structure for an hour a day. It would have
> made a big difference in the transition to public school.
> You have to learn to fit into society. We didn't fit into
> public school. Everything frightened us. My sister could
> read but they put her back to grade one. They wouldn't
> let her come unless she wore a dress. I quit school after
> two weeks of grade eight and left home. I eventually got
> my high school but we definitely felt different from the
> public school kids.[95]

This statement highlights some of the problems facing alternative
school students attempting to return to a still highly traditional school
system. One student who was successful in public school was nevertheless critical of the lack of structure at the Barker School:

> I wanted to learn to read at eight years old. I transferred
> from the Barker School to the New School for part of the
> year and learned to read in two weeks. I read everything I
> could get my hands on. Later in public school I liked the
> academics and caught up fairly easily. For me it was okay
> because I'm very self-motivated. For some of the others it
> hasn't worked out so well. My mother struggled because
> she didn't want us to be part of the status quo. Her inten-
> tion was to find something better but our schools weren't
> structured enough. There were not enough boundaries or
> daily rhythms. I would have liked a little more consis-
> tency in my life. We had to make decisions at too young
> an age.[96]

Another concluded, "I don't think Bob should have given us as much
freedom as he did."[97]

However, a few students found the lack of structure suited them
well. One student who was completely uninterested in traditional school

---

95   Two Barker School students, personal interview, December 9, 1996.
96   Laura Landsberg, personal interview, December 3, 1996.
97   Barker Free School student, personal interview, November 20, 1996.

subjects explored his own interests at the Barker School without feeling any pressure:

> Being able to learn on my own, that's what I got out of it. This attitude towards learning has helped me through my life. It's the only way I would have learned. I may have had serious problems otherwise. For me it was a good thing, for others it might not have been.[98]

Another student valued his Barker School experience despite subsequent academic difficulties: "I wouldn't change anything. I think the things I learned were more important than academics. They made me the person I am."[99] For these young people the school provided a safe, interesting, and supportive place in contrast to the regimented environment of public school. Most Barker School parents valued their independence and raised their children to question authority. Many of these kids would have been unhappy in the public system and may have dropped out anyway.[100]

The majority of former Barker School students became tradespeople or operators of small rural businesses. Despite the absence of professional careers, many of these individuals were successful in their occupations and content in their family life. Most considered themselves happy and believed the personal qualities nurtured by their schooling and their families contributed to their happiness.

Despite his attempts to interest his students in academics, Bob Barker was unable to create an effective learning program at the Barker Free School. Perhaps the Summerhill philosophy, that given complete freedom children will often choose to do academics, doesn't actually work in most situations. But even if a genuine learning program is possible at a Romantic school, there were many impediments at the Barker School.

Although he had studied with respected Progressive educators and established a warm rapport with his students, Mr. Barker didn't develop a thorough expertise in innovative teaching methods. One former staff member suggested, "Bob wasn't able to convey to us how to provide a

---

98　Tony Bertelsen, personal interview, April 17, 1997.
99　Jason Ridgeway, personal interview, September 24, 1997.
100　Sharon Wiseman, personal interview, March 16, 1997.

different sort of teaching."[101] In fact, Mr. Barker's pedagogical ideas were traditional. In a 1967 report to parents he wrote, "I do not believe there is anything basically wrong with the standard curriculum except that its acquisition is required, and required at a certain time."[102] He didn't realize the importance of replacing traditional teaching practices with creative methods if teachers are to interest and excite their students, particularly in a non-coercive and unstructured environment.

Secondly, the school was significantly influenced by the young staff, who were less interested in systematic academic learning than they were in exploring their own newly discovered personal freedom. A former student said, "The adults didn't encourage academic activities."[103] One teacher, who later taught for a year at the New School where the teaching staff was more experienced, recalled: "I felt out of my league [at the New School]. They were older, wiser. I didn't know as much as I thought I did."[104] Even parents were unconcerned about academic learning; as one remembered, "I didn't worry about the academics. I knew the kids were bright enough to pick it up. I wanted them to be more skilled with people."[105]

Thirdly, and perhaps most important, the Barker School was established at a time when all cultural norms and values were being challenged. As one parent observed, "Bob started out with an ideal based on Summerhill but it quickly turned into the revolution of the sixties."[106] Most of the staff and many parents were deeply influenced by the counterculture. "We were riding a cultural wave," as one staff member put it, while another said, "The sixties culture was the backdrop to everything."[107] If the school had existed during a less volatile period, and had students experienced more stability in other aspects of their lives, there may have been more possibility of educational success.

---

101 Sharon Wiseman, personal interview, March 16, 1997.
102 Bob Barker, Report to Parents, February 28, 1967, National Archives of Canada.
103 Michael Carson, personal interview, March 10, 1997.
104 Kate Barlow, personal interview, October 16, 1996.
105 Kita Ridgeway, personal interview, November 13, 1996.
106 Shirley Maclean, personal interview, November 14, 1996.
107 Dan Jason, personal interview, October, 30, 1996.

OTHER SCHOOLS: BOB BARKER'S LEGACY

Bob Barker's influence extended beyond his school. Several Barker Free School staff members continued to experiment with alternative education after the school closed. Dave Manning became a staff member at the Experimental Education Foundation, "the Floating Free School," initiated in the fall of 1968 by Simon Fraser University professors David Berg and Brian Carpendale for their own children. The school's purpose was to offer educational experiences to teenagers who were unhappy with the public school system. It also provided university credits for some SFU student volunteers who had "feelings and theories about teaching that they would be unable to try out in an ordinary classroom situation."[108] Graduate student Dan Davis, the school's first director, coordinated the volunteers. One volunteer was Margaret Sinclair, soon to become the wife of Prime Minister Pierre Trudeau. The school began in a North Vancouver home, later moving to a storefront on Hastings Street in Burnaby. The dozen or so teenagers who attended, mostly children of SFU professors, organized their own activities in the community and communicated through a chain telephone system.[109] Students spent considerable time on the Simon Fraser campus attending lectures, film workshops, and drama classes offered by well-known local director John Juliani. Students also received an experiential political education, taking part in the student occupation of SFU administration offices in October 1968. Students also spent much of their time just "hanging around." The school folded after eighteen months, with some students moving to other alternative schools. One student who returned to the public system said of the Floating Free School: "I really enjoyed the experience. I met a lot of interesting people and had experiences I wouldn't ordinarily have had. It made me a more self-motivated person. I didn't miss anything but I wouldn't have wanted to do it for six or seven years."[110]

Jan McDougall started "The People," a school for young children, in the basement of her Kitsilano house in the fall of 1969. The People

---

108 Brian Carpendale, "Some Thoughts on Free Schools," in *Free School: The Journal of Change in Education* (Saturna Island: Free School Press), Issue 1 (June 1970).
109 Jeremy Carpendale, personal interview, November 13, 1996.
110 Garth Babcock, personal interview, February 21, 1997.

was conceived as a community of families or a "tribal, street school."[111]
Parents and children spent much of their time in the wider community. The
children also did academic work, learning to read with the International
Teaching Alphabet and studying mathematics with Cuisenaire rods.[112]
Parents paid only $10 per month per child, and the school continued for
two years with up to ten children, including some former Barker students.

Dan Jason and Jezrah Hearne started Sunshine School on the ground
floor of their four-storey house near Trout Lake in East Vancouver
in 1971.[113] This school centred around a community of families who
believed they could do a better job of educating their children than could
the public schools. Sunshine School enrolled twenty students and lasted
for two years.

Several former Barker School students earned their high school
diplomas some years later at the Hardy Mountain School near Grand
Forks. Students spent two days per week (including overnight) at the
remote mountain location and worked hard on the basics.[114] Ultimately,
several staff members and parents from the Barker School moved to the
Slocan Valley in 1970 and became part of a community of people who
in 1973 created the Vallican Whole School, an alternative school that
remained independent.

It is difficult to evaluate the success of the Barker Free School with
conventional educational criteria. Most adherents of the free school movement had broader goals and viewed alternative schools as one component of a wider attempt to transform an unhealthy society. Barker School
parents saw their involvement in the school as part of their quest for new
values and a new type of society that would be less competitive, more
humane, and more in tune with the natural world. One CYC observer
commented on the Barker School in 1967:

> The school is difficult and incomplete. The problems that
> arise from attempting models of self-determination are

---

111 "The People," *Focos*, Spring 1969, National Archives of Canada, CYC documents.
112 "The People," Volunteer Report by Barbara Hughes to Director of the Company of
    Young Canadians, National Archives of Canada, CYC documents.
113 Dan Jason later taught in an alternative school on Salt Spring Island and now owns a
    seed company there.
114 This school was operated by Waldo and Anne Dahl.

endless. But, for a change, they are real problems, tasks worth getting bothered about, conflicts that are productive and fun. The result is pretty clear: not one of those children has failed to become just a little bit more sane and balanced and outgoing and responsible and happy. What any of them has learned that can be fed back is questionable, but that all of them have acquired considerable health is beyond doubt.[115]

Others measured the school's success by noting changes in the public school system. *Vancouver Sun* columnist Bob Hunter wrote about Bob Barker in 1969 in the context of a school system that was showing signs of becoming more flexible and innovative:

Bob Barker's ideas have obviously had considerable influence. Something is happening in the public schools—a heightened awareness, a greater sensitivity, perhaps simply a more other-directed consciousness on the part of the teachers. There appears to be considerably less repression and somewhat less authoritarianism than there used to be.[116]

Mr. Hunter suggested that the success of the Barker School may have led to its own extinction in losing students to a revitalized public school system. Dave Berner, a staff person with the Company of Young Canadians who spent several hours a week at the Barker Free School, also believed the school had a wider influence. He wrote to his program director in 1967:

More and more teachers in the public system are aware of and sympathetic to the basic and operative assumptions of Summerhillian education. The result is that the forms are beginning to alter in the public schools as well. I think Bob's school gives considerable impetus to this kind of formal change and movement.[117]

---

115 Dave Berner, Company of Young Canadians, letter to P. Campbell Mackie, May 12, 1967, National Archives of Canada.
116 Bob Hunter, *Vancouver Sun*, September 5, 1969, 19.
117 Dave Berner to P. Campbell Mackie, May 12, 1967, National Archives of Canada.

The public school system has changed markedly since 1965. Bob Barker's modest replica of Summerhill in British Columbia contributed in a small way to making the public schools more child-centred, flexible, and humane.

Chapter 6

KNOWPLACE

The Barker Free School remained the only Romantic school in British Columbia for two years, and few people paid much attention to the quiet experiment with young children in North Vancouver. But by 1967 counter-cultural youth was becoming big news in BC, and it seemed a whole generation had begun to reject mainstream culture and its traditional dress and music, drug and sex taboos, and its competitive, materialistic, and authoritarian values. Out of this context several free schools even more laissez-faire than the Barker School emerged. The first of these was Knowplace, created by a group of discontented teenagers heavily influenced by the counterculture during Vancouver's famous "summer of love."[1]

Karen Tallman had attended the New School from its founding in 1962 until her completion of grade seven in 1966. She began high school that September at Point Grey Secondary in Vancouver but found almost immediately that she didn't fit in. Her clothing targeted her as a hippie, she was "hassled" by classmates, and her English teacher criticized her poor spelling and her unconventional poetry. School administrators had become concerned about drug use and unusual lifestyles at some Vancouver high schools and were anxious to stamp out any nonconformity before

---

1   For a description of Vancouver in 1967 see Myrna Kostash, *Long Way from Home* (Toronto: James Lorimer, 1980), 121–124; Ron Verzuh, *Underground Times: Canada's Flower-Child Revolutionaries* (Toronto: Deneau, 1989), Chapter 3; and Tina Loo, "Flower Children in Lotusland," in *The Beaver* (February–March 1998), 36–41.

it became a serious problem. At the end of the 1966/67 school year Ms. Tallman resolved not to go back.[2]

In the meantime, a group of students at Lord Byng Secondary School had developed similar feelings about their high school experience. Sonya Makaroff, a grade twelve student, found the strictly controlled public school structure oppressive and envisioned something better: "It was all so repressive. One of us was always in trouble for the way we dressed or wore our hair, or for asking questions instead of just parroting back what the teacher said."[3] Another student, Bruce Russell, had spent his elementary years at a "small non-authoritarian" Catholic school and found the "military environment" of Lord Byng a shock. By the middle of his grade nine year, he was threatened with expulsion and spent most of his time at UBC or on the beach.[4] Still another, Lloyd Griffiths, became disillusioned by the "cruelty, snobbery, and competitiveness" of high school by grade ten and was usually found "hanging out in a big house near Lord Byng" with other disaffected students.[5] Michael Thomas, who like Karen Tallman had earlier attended the New School, found Lord Byng "rigid and repressive." He was sent home for inappropriate clothing and was "constantly getting into trouble despite testing high on standardized tests."[6] And Lowell Orcutt, at Kitsilano High, found school just plain "boring."[7] One student summed up his dissatisfaction with the public school system this way:

> You're put in a desk and told what to learn, how fast to learn it, when to speak, when to be silent. You're told how to have your hair cut, what clothes to wear, what ideas are acceptable. Nobody asks you what you're interested in, how you feel about things, whether you agree or disagree.[8]

2   Karen Tallman, personal interview, October 9, 1996.
3   Sonya Makaroff, quoted by Olive Johnson, "As a Cool School, There's No Place like Knowplace," *Maclean's*, December 1967, 5.
4   Bruce Russell, personal interview, December 11, 1996.
5   Lloyd Griffiths, personal interview, December 5, 1996.
6   Hilda Thomas, personal interview, December 15, 1996.
7   Lowell Orcutt, personal interview, November 21, 1996.
8   Rick Valentine, quoted by Olive Johnson, "Free Schools: Tomorrow's Education or Passing Fad?" *Vancouver Life*, April 1968, 19.

By the spring of 1967, these disaffected students were spending a great deal of time together at the Makaroff home in Vancouver's Point Grey neighbourhood complaining about high school and determined to do something about it. Most of these teenagers had been exposed to unconventional ideas through their parents and were familiar with Vancouver's developing counterculture community. Although their parents had varied backgrounds, there were several common themes. Most were politically on the left with CCF[9] or pacifist backgrounds, had individualistic and unconventional lifestyles, and were highly critical of the public school system. Several had connections to the Unitarian Church and some of their children had been involved in Liberal Religious Youth, an activist Christian organization. Many parents were also connected with the academic or artistic communities.

Bob Makaroff, a well-known Vancouver physician, was raised in Saskatchewan of Doukhobor background. His father, a pacifist lawyer, defended labour organizers during the 1930s and had attended the founding convention of the CCF at Regina in 1933. Party leaders were frequent visitors in the household. Dr. Makaroff later became active in peace and social movements and was a vocal critic of the education system. Another parent, David Orcutt, immigrated to British Columbia from the Midwestern United States during the 1950s due to his pacifist beliefs and opposition to the Korean War. He was an artist, a student of unconventional theories about learning and the brain, and active in Vancouver's countercultural community.

Warren and Ellen Tallman, also from the United States, both taught in the UBC English department and were admired by the growing community of countercultural students at UBC during the 1960s. Warren Tallman was an authority on contemporary American poetry and organized the legendary Vancouver Poetry Festival in the summer of 1963.[10] The Tallmans frequently hosted such well-known poets as Allen Ginsberg for readings

9 The CCF refers to the Co-operative Commonwealth Federation, the precursor to today's New Democratic Party.

10 See George Bowering's colourful description of this event in *Bowering's BC: A Swashbuckling History* (Toronto: Penguin, 1996) 320–321. The Festival was headlined by "Black Mountain" poets Charles Olson, Robert Creeley, and Robert Duncan, as well as Allen Ginsberg, Denise Levertov, and Canadian Margaret Avison.

of their work in Vancouver. Ellen Tallman had been active in left-wing and anarchist politics in Berkeley, California, before coming to Vancouver. Phil and Hilda Thomas were also educators with strong Progressive beliefs. Ms. Thomas, an English instructor at UBC, had been an active member of the Christian Socialist Movement in her youth and would later be an NDP candidate for the provincial legislature. Mr. Thomas was a teacher, artist, and noted collector of BC folksongs and had taught for a year at the New School.

These parents supported the young people in their criticism of the public school system and their desire to experiment with alternative schooling and lifestyles. But they also wanted the teenagers to complete their education. Hilda Thomas, fearing that her children would not return to school, met with several other parents to discuss alternatives. While searching for possible locations for a school, she found several classrooms available at the Unitarian Church. However, the Thomases and Tallmans were still tired from their difficult years at the New School and "didn't have the wherewithal" to take on another project. Furthermore, the parents disagreed about how free-flowing a school should be and concluded that "their kids should go back to public school."[11] But meanwhile, despite their parents' misgivings, the students began talking seriously about starting their own school and drew encouragement from another source.

The educational reformers Watson and Mary Thomson lived in the neighbourhood and were respected by both the young people and their parents. Watson Thomson had founded workers' education organizations in Alberta and had been adult education director at the University of Manitoba.[12] In 1944 he was appointed director of adult education by the new Tommy Douglas CCF government in Saskatchewan, developing projects in populist and socialist education in communities across that province. But his orientation was too radical even for the CCF government, and he was fired two years later.[13] Communitarian socialists, the

11   Hilda Thomas, personal interview, December 15, 1996.
12   See Michael Welton's biography of Watson Thomson, *To Be and Build the Glorious World* (unpublished PhD thesis, University of British Columbia, 1984).
13   Michael Welton, "Mobilizing the People for Socialism: The Politics of Adult Education in Saskatchewan, 1944–45," in Michael Welton, ed., *Knowledge for the People* (Toronto: OISE Press, 1987), 151–169.

Thomsons created a co-operative urban living community in Winnipeg during the 1940s and a rural community in Surrey, BC, in the 1950s. After settling in Vancouver, Mr. Thomson lectured in the philosophy of education at UBC, while Ms. Thomson taught early childhood education there for over twenty years. Director of the Child Study Centre, she introduced such Progressive ideas as "teaching the child rather than the subject" and initiated parent participation preschools. As a consultant to over fifty co-operative preschools in Vancouver, she met several future New School and Knowplace parents.[14] The young people were inspired by informal discussions with Watson Thomson in his basement. As one student remembered:

> Watson and Mary were an inspiration in the early stages.
> Most of our parents idealized Watson and he was able to
> override their objections. He would corner us kids and
> want to know what we were reading, what we were think-
> ing about, what our concerns were ... and what he could
> learn from us.[15]

Another supportive individual was Jim Harding, a graduate student at Simon Fraser University and a well-known Canadian student leader. He grew up in a Saskatchewan socialist family and had been active in the Student Union for Peace Action (SUPA), a radical student organization in Canada during the 1960s.[16] Young activists like Jim Harding and older socialists like Watson Thomson thought authoritarian schools were antithetical to democracy. They were excited by the idea of a student-run school because they saw the realization of student rights as part of a broader struggle for self-determination across society.[17] Mr. Harding advised the students to be assertive in approaching their parents, and

---

14   Mary Thomson, personal interview, November 4, 1996.

15   Bruce Russell, personal interview, December 11, 1996.

16   James (Jim) Harding chaired the Federal Council of the Student Union for Peace Action (SUPA) in 1966 and was an editor of and frequent contributor to *Our Generation*, a left-wing student periodical in Canada during the 1960s. See, for example, his "An Ethical Movement in Search of an Analysis," May 1966.

17   James Harding, "From Authoritarianism to Totalitarianism: Two Winnipeg Schools," *This Magazine is about Schools*, Autumn 1968; reprinted in Tim Reid and Julyan Reid, *Student Power and the Canadian Campus* (Toronto: Peter Martin Associates, 1969).

Karen Tallman remembered a seminal moment when he said, "Don't tell your parents you want to start a school, tell them you *are* a school."[18]

Knowplace brochure, personal archive of the author. Photographer unknown.

The students came up with the memorable name, Knowplace, a pun on the Greek word for Utopia.[19] But the project might have been short-lived if it hadn't been for another development involving the Company of Young Canadians, which would come to play a major role in the creation of Knowplace. The Company of Young Canadians (CYC) was an innovative social service program established by the Lester Pearson Liberal government in 1966 in which young adults were paid modest salaries to do social service work with economically disadvantaged communities. By coincidence, Colin Thomson, the son of Watson and Mary Thomson, had

18   Karen Tallman, personal interview, October 9, 1996.
19   Bruce Russell, personal interview, December 11, 1996.

just returned to Vancouver from a CYC training session in Ottawa during the summer of 1967. The younger Thomson had recently graduated from UBC and wanted to work for social change like his father. He arrived back in Vancouver as a CYC "recruitment officer" and was looking for projects. But what he really wanted to do was work with Vancouver's disaffected youth, so the Knowplace students asked him to help them establish their school.

The CYC Council had recently approved funding for the Barker Free School, so Colin Thomson hurriedly put together an application and, with the students, began planning the implementation of the school. The involvement of Mr. Thomson and the CYC immediately gave the project the legitimacy of being run by adults as well as access to funding. However, it also tied the project to the Company's complex internal political relationships. More seriously, it ensured that education would not be the central occupation of the Knowplace community, since CYC staff workers and volunteers were social activists rather than educators.

More students joined the project that summer. They included Frances Long, whose mother was a well-known artist; John Doheny, son of a UBC English professor; Gary Cramer, son of a BCTV producer and associate editor of the *Georgia Straight*; Monica Carpendale, whose father taught communications at Simon Fraser; and Eda Landauer, daughter of a UBC sociology professor. Two teenagers associated with the Barker Free School also joined the group—Bobby Barker, Bob Barker's son, and Rick Valentine, son of Chuck and Helen Valentine. The Knowplace student body was not just a random group of young people. Almost without exception they were the sons and daughters of intellectuals, artists, and adults leading politically active and unconventional lives. The students themselves were engaged, bright, and curious teenagers.

But although sympathetic to an alternative school in principle, most of the parents opposed the project, fearing their children would cut themselves off from further educational opportunities. At a large meeting in the Thomsons' basement that August, Colin Thomson assured the worried parents that appropriate resource people from the universities and artistic communities would be brought in to offer an exciting educational program. The young people's enthusiasm and determination ultimately won over the majority of parents, and plans went full speed ahead for the school opening in September.

Most parents believed they had little choice but to endorse the project. In some cases their children had already dropped out of school and had no intention of going back, while others who remained in public school were alienated. Furthermore, most parents knew their children were immersed in the Vancouver counterculture. Parents hoped that if the students were attached to a group of responsible young adults in a legitimate educational setting, their children would at least be safe from the dangers of drugs and street life. As one parent reflected, "We felt lucky that there was any place off the streets where our kids could be."[20]

As intellectually and politically aware individuals, these parents had raised their children to be independent thinkers and to act on their own initiative. The young people had watched their parents create alternatives when traditional institutions did not suit them. Most parents realized it would have been intellectually dishonest as well as ineffective to stand in the way of their children's plans. But the students created a far less-structured school than their parents anticipated. As one parent suggested, "The fact that I was progressive wasn't a help to my kids because to rebel they had to go even farther out."[21]

There was a lot to do in a short time. To earn legitimacy as an independent school, the group gave itself an official name, the Voluntary Community School. The Unitarian Church classrooms were never used, and the school set up headquarters in a rented four-storey house at 2426 York Avenue in Kitsilano, a few blocks from Fourth Avenue, the heart of Vancouver's youth culture. Student fees were set at $25 per month and Ministry of Education textbooks were ordered. Relatives and friends of Knowplace students donated books to a school library that eventually numbered over one thousand volumes. But as one observer noted, "Their collection leans more heavily on John Lennon and Henry Miller than it does on Shakespeare."[22]

20 Ellen Tallman, personal interview, October 23, 1996.
21 Ellen Tallman, personal interview, October 23, 1996.
22 Olive Johnson, "As a Cool School, There's No Place like Knowplace," *Maclean's*, December 1967, 5.

COMPANY OF YOUNG CANADIANS

The most pressing task was the hiring of the school staff. The Company of Young Canadians Council initially approved funding for five "volunteer" teachers at $185 per month in addition to Colin Thomson who, as a CYC staff member, received a substantial salary as coordinator of the project.[23] The original teaching staff consisted of Colin Thomson, Rob Wood, Greg Sorbara, Rob Watt, and several part-time staff members, most in their early twenties. In contrast to many BC alternative schools, all Knowplace staff were Canadians. None of the principal staff members had any expertise or experience in teaching, which would prove to be a serious obstacle to the project's success.

Staff members had all been involved in other CYC projects before joining the school. Rob Wood was from Ontario and had been active in the American civil rights movement as well as the Student Union for Peace Action.[24] He worked with the Metis in Northern Saskatchewan to help develop local industry and by 1966 was in charge of training CYC staff members for English Canada. Developing training sessions fueled his interest in education, and he met Colin Thomson at a workshop in 1967.[25] Greg Sorbara, also from Ontario, studied theology at the University of Toronto. He signed up with the CYC after graduation and was sent to a housing project in Vancouver, where he met Colin Thomson just as Knowplace was opening.[26] Rob Watt was a student activist at Simon Fraser University. He joined the CYC as a co-operative housing coordinator, establishing several successful projects in New Westminster. As a teaching assistant in Fred Brown's philosophy of education course, Mr. Watt came to believe that a powerful antidote to contemporary social problems would be to create intentional communities. These rural or urban "communes" would emulate extended families, experiment in co-operative living, and emphasize the importance of education. He had read

---

23   Personnel data in Lionel Orlikow, "The Vancouver Youth Project," an assessment submitted to CYC Acting Director Stewart Goodings, October 5, 1968, Appendix B, National Archives of Canada, Record Group 116, Volume 142, File 884.

24   See Doug Owram, *Born at the Right Time* (Toronto: University of Toronto Press, 1996), Chapter 9.

25   Robertson Wood, personal interview, October 10, 1996.

26   Greg Sorbara, personal interview, October 16, 1996.

about Summerhill and Ontario's Everdale Place and was excited about the Knowplace idea.[27]

Knowplace staff was heavily male-dominated even though several women were associated with the school, including Heather-Jon Maroney, a former SUPA member from Ottawa; Shelagh Day, a UBC English instructor, feminist, and political activist; Elli Gomber; and Lynn Burrows. But the influence of female staff was minimal and there was little feminist presence at Knowplace.[28] It was common during the 1960s for women to encounter almost as much inequality within progressive political organizations as existed in the mainstream culture.[29]

When the federal government formed the Company of Young Canadians in 1965, it had envisioned an organization similar to the Peace Corps in the United States. The intention was to encourage young idealists to work on worthwhile social projects, though some critics characterized it as an attempt to co-opt and channel political activism into acceptable activity.[30] From the outset, the Company was rife with political schisms particularly between "radicals" and "moderates." The radical majority transformed the CYC into an organization primarily concerned with activism and social change.[31] As historian Doug Owram writes, "Instead of taming youth, the government ended up funding criticism. Instead of clean-cut Peace Corps workers they got 'dirty bearded hippies' and 'promiscuous women.' Instead of social service, they got social activism."[32] The CYC was also split across regional lines. The Company was dominated by Ontario, but some of its most notable successes occurred in western Canada, and one CYC leader suggested that the farther away a project was from Ottawa the more autonomy it had.[33]

27 Rob Watt, personal interview, November 19, 1996.
28 Heather-Jon Maroney, personal interview, January 14, 1997.
29 See Edward Morgan, *The Sixties Experience* (Philadelphia: Temple University Press, 1991), Chapter 6.
30 Doug Owram, *Born at the Right Time* (Toronto: University of Toronto Press, 1996), 222–225.
31 See Ian Hamilton, *The Children's Crusade* (Toronto: Peter Martin Associates, 1970), particularly Chapter 5.
32 Doug Owram, *Born at the Right Time* (Toronto: University of Toronto Press, 1996), 225.
33 Ian Hamilton, *The Children's Crusade* (Toronto: Peter Martin Associates, 1970), 77.

The CYC rapidly developed an unwieldy bureaucracy. Company policy was made by a government-appointed council and administered by national, regional, and local staff supervisors. But the real work of program delivery was carried out by field "volunteers" in individual projects. These volunteers received tiny salaries of $200 per month and were on two-year contracts, while staff workers received substantial salaries and had reasonably secure jobs.[34] Although the government promised that the organization would eventually be run by the volunteers, they had minimal influence until the Company's last days. Council members, staff, and volunteers all distrusted one another, and volunteers particularly resented their lack of influence.

These internal dynamics had a direct impact on Knowplace. The Company's Ontario leaders were more overtly political than were those in British Columbia and did not think it was a priority to fund alternative schools attended by rebellious middle-class youth. Knowplace suited the general orientation of the CYC in its challenge to traditional educational thinking, but senior staff believed the project needed a more serious "social change" dimension. Although the CYC was already supporting two Ontario alternative schools, radical Ontario educators like Bob Davis and George Martell were more committed to social action than were Knowplace staff.[35] Nevertheless, in 1967 Mr. Martell, a CYC staff worker, prepared a report recommending that Knowplace and the Barker Free School receive Company funding.[36] This was approved but many CYC leaders never felt completely at ease with Knowplace.[37] They worried that the school's countercultural image was potentially embarrassing to the Company, particularly when the organization came under attack from the mainstream press in 1968 for being excessively influenced

---

34 According to Ian Hamilton, staff workers earned between $10,000 and $15,000 per year. *The Children's Crusade*, 32.

35 Greg Sorbara, personal interview, October 16, 1996. Mr. Sorbara taught for a year at Everdale after leaving Knowplace. This is also the view of Bob Davis, personal interview, October 18, 1996. An Everdale fundraising appeal in *This Magazine is about Schools*, Spring 1969, lists two of the five goals as "to practise real democracy" and "to encourage a critical view of society."

36 Alan Clarke (CYC executive director), letter to George Martell, National Archives of Canada, CYC documents, Record Group 116, Volume 142, File 884.

37 CYC correspondence, Colin Thomson to and from Alan Clarke, Stewart Goodings, Campbell Mackie, Jacques Noel, and others.

by radical activists and "hippies."[38] CYC leaders were unhappy about bad press resulting from controversial projects like Knowplace. Nevertheless, the school continued to develop undaunted on the west coast, away from the close scrutiny of Ottawa.

Knowplace, the Barker Free School, and several other alternative youth organizations were combined under the CYC's "Vancouver Youth Project" with Colin Thomson in charge. The affiliated projects were all oriented toward education and youth. One of these groups was "Kool Aid," an alternative welfare agency formed to help street kids as thousands of free-spirited teenagers descended upon Vancouver during the summer of 1967.[39] Other ventures included the Bhavana experimental art school, the "Floating Free School," "The People" free school, a newly formed high school student union, and the "Free University," a loose collection of individuals offering and taking alternative courses. Overseeing almost ten agencies drew Mr. Thomson heavily into administration. As the months wore on, Knowplace staff members became less involved with day-to-day activities, leaving the leadership to the students themselves.

STUDENT ACTIVITIES

Knowplace opened in September 1967 with twenty-two students. From the beginning it was difficult to be sure who was an officially enrolled student and who was not. Defined school hours were virtually non-existent, groups of students were often away on field trips, and a number of young people whose parents insisted they go to public school would hang around Knowplace after 3:00. Early in September the entire school held a weekend retreat at a farm in the Fraser Valley.[40] Students and staff discussed the kind of program they wanted based on readings about alternative education and alternative communities. The retreat set the tone for the whole year and was summarized in a project submission to the CYC:

38 Ian Hamilton, *The Children's Crusade* (Toronto: Peter Martin Associates, 1970), chaps. 2, 6, and 7.
39 Company of Young Canadians internal correspondence on the Barker Free School, May–July 1967, National Archives of Canada, Record Group 116, Volume 142, File 884.
40 The weekend was held on the campus of an experimental free university.

During this weekend the concept of community was discussed in detail. It was felt by all that learning to relate to
one another on a meaningful level was more important
than learning a subject such as algebra. It was this communication and sense of community, important in terms
of personal development, that the students felt they had
been lacking in the educational system.[41]

The school's aim was "to allow each student to develop his individual
human capacities in a framework of a community in which the interrela-
tionships are of equal concern and value. The student must do the work of
learning and his activity is most satisfying and productive when it stems
from his own interests."[42] Regarding curriculum the document continued:

The student should actively experience his education
rather than passively accept it. The curriculum is not
regarded as a predigested body of knowledge which must
be fed by degrees to the recipients. It is looked upon as a
body of educational activities which must develop gradually from an interplay between teachers and students who
are encouraged to bring their individuality to bear on the
selection of and approach to various subjects.[43]

This statement drew on educational thinkers as diverse as John Dewey,
Watson Thomson, and A. S. Neill. The document also stated that "the
standard BC curriculum will be offered for those who request it."

But it soon became clear that Knowplace was not so much a school as an
experiment in communal living. Students and staff together cooked large
group meals that were eaten around two large doors that served as tables
in the middle of the dining room. Although there had been no provision
for boarding (except for Rick Valentine from Argenta who was permitted
to set up a bedroom in one of the walk-in closets), students often slept

---

41 "Knowplace, A Project Submission to the Company of Young Canadians," September
    29, 1967, National Archives of Canada, CYC documents, Record Group 116, Volume
    142, File 884.
42 "Knowplace, A Project Submission to the Company of Young Canadians," September
    29, 1967.
43 "Knowplace, A Project Submission to the Company of Young Canadians," September
    29, 1967.

over at the house. Some of the young people were having trouble at home with parents, while others simply didn't want to miss out on any group experiences. The floor of one entire bedroom was covered with mattresses and sleeping bags, and sometimes up to a dozen kids would stay over. Students spent endless hours in the evenings talking about themselves and their relationships; as one staff member put it, "Teenagers need to talk and talk and talk."[44]

KNOWPLACE... Public school dropouts take their education the way they like it

22 Disgruntled Students
Open Their Own School

Vancouver Sun, December 16, 1967

The students spent much of their time in the outside community. The Company of Young Canadians had provided a "yellow bus" for the school's use, and staff members constantly drove off with groups of kids. They went to university campuses, beaches and parks, museums and art galleries, the law courts, evening poetry readings, and dances at the Retinal Circus on Davie Street, Vancouver's venue for "psychedelic"

44   Rob Wood, personal interview, October 10, 1997.

music. Groups of students made frequent visits to UBC and Simon Fraser to attend lectures, noon hour dances, or demonstrations against the war in Vietnam. Others went "in adolescent packs" to hang out on Fourth Avenue. Groups of Knowplace students spoke at public high schools and even attended a session of a Vancouver School Board counselling course for teachers.[45] Many people respected them as representatives of a new cultural movement, and they were treated as celebrities wherever they went.

Knowplace students also went on longer trips in the yellow bus to Long Beach, Argenta, the Oregon coast, and the always popular San Francisco. All they needed was a staff member who was willing to drive them. Another popular destination was Storm Bay, a remote inlet near the Sechelt Peninsula accessible only by boat. A group of young Vancouver artists and counterculturalists, which included two Knowplace staff members, had bought a piece of land there, and students were free to go to Storm Bay whenever they liked. It was typical for groups to stay for a week or more.

The educational program was tentative at best. The original idea was for students to organize courses that interested them and arrange for appropriate resource persons to provide instruction. Although there were sporadic attempts to schedule classes, anything resembling a formal curriculum never got off the ground. Jim Harding offered a weekly class in Canadian history, and Garry Nixon, a teacher at St. George's private school, taught late afternoon classes in mathematics and science several times a week. Rob Wood offered instruction in photography and drama. But attendance at classes was often as low as two or three students, and occasionally there were no students at all. The constant field trips got in the way of regularly scheduled classes but, for the most part, the students were not really interested anyway.

Most attempts to organize learning activities were short-lived. The teenagers informally discussed books they had read, and one student started a reading course with several others, beginning with *The Autobiography of*

---

45   Letter of appreciation from Jim Melton, VSB Special Counsellor Program Coordinator, November 26, 1968, National Archives of Canada, CYC Documents, Record Group 116, Volume 142, File 884.

Malcolm X. However, the group stopped meeting after a few sessions. One former student remembered a political science class at which he reported on the diaries of Che Guevara. But the class didn't last, and he spent his time at the UBC library instead.[46] Another recalled unused science equipment and unfulfilled promises to take groups to the science labs at UBC. Still another student remembered several meetings of a mythology and storytelling class presented by a local poet, but otherwise there were "little or no academics the whole time."[47] Several students attended Dr. Mary Wertheim's biology classes for a few months. But according to one participant, these were "occasional stabs at education."[48]

Students justified the lack of an educational program with slogans such as: "We're learning to be, not just to do,"[49] or "We're getting the education we want here; it's not so much an academic education but an education in being with people and learning about people."[50] But one student recalled her disappointment at the lack of a real program:

> I approached it like school. I bussed in from New Westminster and stayed for school hours. I was interested in things. I thought there would be interesting topics and discussions, that we would do challenging activities. But I was often the only one who would show up for classes. It was discouraging for the teachers. I ended up spending most of my time in the library upstairs reading Shakespeare and Tolstoy.[51]

If academics were neglected, "sex, drugs, and rock and roll" played a big part in life at Knowplace. The teenagers spent a great deal of time listening to and playing music. They formed bands and jammed for hours. As one student put it, "That's what we did all day; what spoke to us was

---

46   Bruce Russell, personal interview, December 11, 1997.
47   Rick Valentine, personal interview, November 26, 1996.
48   Lowell Orcutt, personal interview, November 21, 1996. Mary and George Wertheim came to Vancouver from California.
49   Maryann Campbell, quoted by Olive Johnson, "Free Schools: Tomorrow's Education or Passing Fad?" *Vancouver Life*, April 1968, 16–21.
50   Bob Wilson, "22 Disgruntled Students Open Their Own School," *Vancouver Sun*, December 16, 1967, 33.
51   Monica Carpendale, personal interview, November 25, 1996.

music,"[52] while a staff member said, "These kids lived for music and listened to it incessantly."[53] Three former students became professional musicians, and two rock bands, "Brain Damage" and "Doug and the Slugs," got their start at Knowplace.

Some students and some adults used drugs, mostly marijuana and LSD, and one staff person was fired for drug-related activities. The staff tried to control drug use on the premises, but it was easy enough for the kids to go somewhere else to get high. A few students later developed addiction problems with harder drugs and alcohol.

Sex was another difficult issue. Even if the inexperienced staff members had been concerned about the possibility of sex among the students in their charge, in the 1960s personal freedom usually prevailed over other considerations. One problem with the Knowplace experiment was the youthfulness of its staff. There was no one in charge who was a little older and wiser, and willing to put limits on student behaviour.

Staff and students sought to make decisions by consensus, but often problems of policy and day-to-day life went unresolved. To improve communication, the school hired a trainer from Saskatchewan to lead an encounter group (sometimes called Therapy, or "T Group") session lasting several days. Such groups, frequent at the time, were often led by individuals with relatively little training. Several students remembered destructive moments and "a lot of angry people" at these sessions. One said, "I went to one and I never went back." Many of the personal problems of Knowplace students were normal issues of adolescent emotional development, but staff didn't always know how to address them effectively. Furthermore, personal problems were sometimes exacerbated by drug consumption, which was generally accepted among the students.

Parents had little influence on the school's development and spent little time there. During the early months, staff, students, and parents had monthly meetings. Colin Thomson defended the school's practices, and a few sympathetic parents tried to mediate between the staff and other parents who were worried about drugs, sex, and the lack of academics. But even the most supportive lost patience with the school at times. In

---

52   Karen Tallman, personal interview, October 9, 1996.
53   Greg Sorbara, personal interview, October 16, 1996.

the end, however, most parents believed they were powerless to control their kids.

For their part, the students developed a tight community. As one student put it, "The pack of kids was very close and having an amazing time."[54] Another recalled being exposed to a rich cultural life with access to an interesting adult world of avant-garde artists, rock bands, and political activists.[55] The staff, on the other hand, contributed little to the student dynamic and, for the most part, simply acceded to the youth culture. As the 1968/69 prospectus stated, "The teachers have very much in common with the students as they are, in many cases, only six or seven years older. Thus total integration of staff and students has been achieved."[56] One former staff member admits that "the adults were drawn too much into the life of the kids."[57]

Staff members eventually lost interest in the youth culture and spent less time at the school as they became involved in other pursuits. The staff developed a closeness of their own, and most lived together in a house on Point Grey Road not far from the school building. A large house belonging to a parent at 16th and Burrard became another focal point for Knowplace staff and students. As in many alternative schools, the Knowplace community resembled an extended family—"tribal" as one student described it—and many friendships remained strong for years.

COMMUNITY RELATIONS

Knowplace became a point of fascination for political activists, artists, and educators. Many were committed to self-determination for students, as were social Romantics who were interested in co-operative communities. Public figures as diverse as the poet Allen Ginsberg, rock stars Country Joe and the Fish, jazz musician Al Neil, and Vancouver poet bill bissett visited the school. So did an Indigenous chief who impressed students with the concept of a talking stick. Many adults offered to teach, including

---

54   Karen Tallman, personal interview, October 9, 1996.
55   Bruce Russell, personal interview, December 11, 1996.
56   Knowplace Prospectus, 1968/69, National Archives of Canada, CYC documents, Record Group 116, Volume 142, File 884.
57   Rob Wood, personal interview, October 10, 1996.

Alternative Schools in British Columbia, 1960-1975

Watson Thomson, Jim Harding, artist Gordon Yearsley, SFU mathematics professor Art Stone, biology professor Mary Wertheim, Ed McClure (founder of Intermedia, an artists' co-operative), poet Nelson Miller, and Jim Kinzel (a CYC member from Saskatchewan). Garry Nixon, a mathematics teacher at St. George's exclusive private school, was a regular visitor. He was concerned about the large numbers of teenagers disaffected by impersonal and inflexible high schools and offered afternoon math classes to Knowplace students after his St. George's duties were completed. Mr. Nixon would become an important figure in the alternative school movement in the early 1970s as the founder of Ideal School.

Knowplace staff members took part in a high-profile Free School Conference attended by about a hundred people at the New School in December 1967. Colin Thomson and Rob Wood spoke about how difficult it is for free school teachers and students to overcome conditioning caused by traditional notions of authority.[58] Individuals attended from across Canada and speakers included Bob Barker, Bob Davis of Ontario's Everdale Place, and Tom Durrie of the New School.[59] The conference was infused with optimism about the future of the free school movement.[60]

The school's link to counterculture youth led to instant notoriety, and Knowplace was deluged by visitors, media, and "hangers-on." A few visitors were unsavory or predatory individuals looking for a place to "crash" and find free food, drugs, or available females. But most were genuinely interested in Knowplace as a social and educational experiment. Knowplace staff were even invited to a United Way meeting to discuss Vancouver's alienated youth problem.[61] The media and the public were enchanted by the youth movement and Knowplace was featured in prominent publications. *Maclean's*, with its national readership, published an article by Olive Johnson on Knowplace in December 1967, titled "As a Cool School, There's

58 "Boss System Hard to Shake Says Free School Teacher," *Vancouver Sun*, December 29, 1967, 13.
59 "Public Schools Turning Out Slaves or Rebels, Meet Told," *Vancouver Sun*, December 30, 1967, 13.
60 Two schools opened shortly after the conference: one run by Lynn Burrows of Knowplace in the Intermedia building downtown, the other by CYC staff person Lynn Curtis. But these schools were short-lived.
61 Letter from C. H. Naphtali, Executive Director of United Community Services of the Greater Vancouver Area, May 14, 1969.

No Place like Knowplace."[62] *Vancouver Life* featured Knowplace in a lead article, "Free Schools: Tomorrow's Education or Passing Fad?" in April 1968,[63] and the *Vancouver Sun* put Knowplace on the front page of Section Three in December 1967. The article, titled "22 Disgruntled Students Open Their Own School," was accompanied by a large photograph of half a dozen "hippie-ish" looking students and young bearded staff members.[64]

Free schools and "hippie" culture were big news in 1967/68, and reporters or politicians could be assured of headlines if they drew attention to them. A Social Credit Member of Parliament from the interior of British Columbia caused a furor in the House of Commons in late 1967 when he accused the Company of Young Canadians of misusing public money "to subvert BC's public education system" in funding Knowplace and the Barker Free School. He also criticized Knowplace for drawing its student body only from upper- and middle-class families. The CYC's assistant director was forced to respond to the charges, and a letter from Prime Minister Lester Pearson himself assured the MP that "the provincial authorities are fully aware of the CYC's participation in these two schools but as they are classified as private schools, the province plays no part in their staffing."[65]

This story was carried by major newspapers across the country, including the *Toronto Star* and *The Globe and Mail*. In the wake of the controversy the *Vancouver Sun* devoted an entire editorial to Knowplace titled "Knowplace to Go?" The editorial posed a number of questions:

> Is this the sort of project to which CYC members should devote their time and effort? One might wonder if there weren't some poor people the CYC could be helping to better social cause than dissatisfied school students who can afford an extra $25 a month to go to Knowplace.

62 Olive Johnson, "As a Cool School, There's No Place like Knowplace," *Maclean's*, December 1967, 5.
63 Olive Johnson, "Free Schools: Tomorrow's Education or Passing Fad?" *Vancouver Life*, April 1968, 16–21.
64 Bob Wilson, "22 Disgruntled Students Open Their Own School," *Vancouver Sun*, December 16, 1967, 33.
65 Letter from Prime Minister Pearson to MP Howard Johnston, March 13, 1968, and memos from Stewart Goodings, National Archives of Canada, CYC documents, Record Group 116, Volume 142, File 884.

Knowplace students say they are not satisfied with public school, its rules, and its lessons. Perhaps if he does nothing else Mr. Peterson [BC Education Minister Leslie Peterson], should see if this is the fault of the students or of the public schools. These are some of the questions posed by this unusual school.[66]

Knowplace to Go?

There has been a disappointing lack of interest shown by persons of authority in the operation in this city of a dropout school, called in rather unsubtle hip parlance "Knowplace."

The easy way out in commenting on this institution, located in an old house in Kitsilano, is that as a private school where pupils pay it is none of anyone's public business.

This, in effect, is what Education Minister Leslie Peterson has said. The Vancouver School Board says nothing. But there are questions which taxpayers and the authorities ought to be asking.

The students at Knowplace say it offers a better way of learning than public school. "We're getting the education we want here," said one 14-year-old. The first question that ought to be asked about this is whether children have a right to decide how they shall be educated.

The next question concerns the active jurisdiction, and it should also be asked if the CYC has consulted provincial authorities, as suggested in the CYC founding legislation.

Apparently there has been no consultation, since Mr. Peterson dismisses Knowplace as beyond his jurisdiction. His reasoning is the virtual carte blanche permissiveness of B.C.'s Public Schools Act concerning private schools. There are, in fact, no set standards for private schools. However, the Public Schools Act does provide a cumbersome and roundabout route for finding out if Knowplace is giving satisfactory education. Attendance at public schools is compulsory between the ages of seven and 15, the act says, unless it can be proved "the child is being educated by some other means satisfactory" to a judge or tribunal. There are students under 15 at Knowplace. Is it worth the school board's finding out if they get "satisfactory" education?

Criticism of Knowplace for pushing boundaries made news across across the country, including in this *Vancouver Sun* editorial.
Vancouver Sun, December 27, 1967

However, Mr. Peterson dismissed the issue as outside his jurisdiction, since the provincial government did not have authority over independent schools before 1977. Referring to Knowplace as "the same as any other private school,"[67] the Minister told a *Province* reporter that he "[doesn't] think Knowplace School is subverting the BC public school system; we have no jurisdiction in respect of the school."[68] The Deputy Education

---

66   "Knowplace to Go?" *Vancouver Sun* editorial, December 27, 1967, 4.

67   Bob Wilson, "22 Disgruntled Students Open Their Own School" *Vancouver Sun*, December 16, 1967, 33; also Olive Johnson, "As a Cool School, There's No Place like Knowplace," *Maclean's*, December 1967, 5.

68   "Knowplace School Okay, According to Peterson," *Vancouver Province*, December 20, 1967, 14.

Minister added, "We aren't concerned about whether these people are hippies or not. As far as we're concerned, it's just another private school."[69] A Vancouver School Board official invited "school age hippie dropouts" to return to school.[70]

Another controversy erupted in 1968 when a Liberal Member of Parliament from Vancouver publicly criticized Knowplace as a "hippy-looking establishment that serves as a hangout for potential high school dropouts, agitates among high school activist groups, and lures young girls into compromising and undisciplined situations."[71] CYC Executive Director Stewart Goodings once again diffused the situation and later summed up some of the broader issues in a memorandum to a senior civil servant:

> We view the project as an attempt to confront the increasingly large number of young people who are questioning established institutions and patterns of behaviour. It is inevitable that this kind of project will make certain people nervous. Most of the students at Knowplace have long hair and wear clothes of their own choosing. Even these minor examples of individualism often attract violent criticism and it is not surprising that the most lurid and sensational stories and rumours will soon develop about a project as unusual as this.[72]

Knowplace was the most notorious Romantic school of the day, and many politicians and members of the public were concerned about such blatant manifestations of the counterculture. But the Department of Education did not perceive marginal schools like Knowplace as threatening enough in 1967 to warrant any intervention. However, by the early 1970s things had changed, and two free schools outside Vancouver were challenged by local authorities.

---

69   Tony Eberts, "Knowplace: An Answer to Boredom," *Vancouver Province*, October 14, 1967.

70   R. F. MacKenzie, VSB pupil personnel services, quoted by Eberts, "Knowplace: An Answer to Boredom."

71   Grant Deachman, quoted by Stewart Goodings, CYC memorandum, December 23, 1968, National Archives of Canada, Record Group 116, Volume 142, File 884.

72   Stewart Goodings, memorandum to Bob Ravinovitch, December 13, 1968, National Archives of Canada, CYC documents, Record Group 116, Volume 142, File 884.

DECLINE OF THE SCHOOL

Knowplace was evicted from the York Avenue house in the spring of 1968, as neighbours complained about groups of hippie kids lounging around in the front yard. The school moved down the street to the second storey of a warehouse at First and Burrard. This location, which the group named the "Wherehouse," was less inviting but it was spacious and hidden from the public eye. However, the energy that had propelled the school through its first year was waning. Rob Watt left after the first year and was replaced by Dr. George Wertheim, a former Stanford psychology professor who had recently immigrated.[73] The student body expanded to thirty but, as in many alternative schools, some of the newcomers had behavioural difficulties and didn't become integral to the group.[74]

By June 1968 it had become obvious that the academic program at Knowplace was not working. Describing the first year as "stormy and unpredictable," the CYC director explained:

> Since the whole emphasis of the school was on giving students the freedom to choose what they wished to learn, it was inevitable that Knowplace would move into unconventional and unorthodox areas of activity. While the CYC volunteers had hoped for a high academic content, it became clear that what most of the twenty-five students really wanted was simply a place where they could begin to learn and grow at their own speed and in their own way. This made for a very haphazard program. While some students did get involved in detailed and substantial study, many others spent their time simply talking to each other, arguing, hanging around the school building, and generally acting as most normal young people would if they suddenly found themselves faced with freedom after a dozen years in the education system.[75]

---

73   Colin Thomson to Stewart Goodings, October 1, 1968, National Archive of Canada, Record Group 116, Volume 142, File 884.
74   Karen Tallman, personal interview, October 9, 1996.
75   Stewart Goodings, memorandum to Bob Ravinovitch, December 13, 1968, National Archives of Canada, CYC documents, Record Group 116, Volume 142, File 884.

The school published a professional-looking prospectus for the second year, but it was becoming increasingly difficult to maintain the fiction that Knowplace was an educational institution. The prospectus warned: "New students contemplating applying to Knowplace should be aware that the focus of 1968/69 will likely continue to be non-academic although help and encouragement will be given to students wishing to follow particular courses of study on their own."[76]

In an effort to inject some structure into the program, the staff divided the student body into three groups of ten students, each working with a staff member on a specific project. But midway through the second year, most students realized this program was not working either. Though the school never officially closed, in early 1969 students simply stopped coming.

The Company of Young Canadians had provided frequent and supportive communication with its Knowplace project throughout the first year, but relations began to deteriorate by the end of 1968. The Vancouver Youth Project underwent its first major evaluation in October 1968, prepared by Lionel Orlikow of the Ontario Institute for Studies in Education. He was critical of the project's staff selection procedures, its lack of accountability, its individualistic focus, its poor relationship with the educational establishment and the community at large, and its lack of a meaningful academic program.[77] This unsatisfactory report contributed to a change in attitude at the Ottawa office toward the Vancouver Youth Project.

The CYC leadership worried about the negative publicity that Knowplace generated. In addition to the high-profile public controversy reported in the press, the Company received complaints from neighbours, concerned letters from individuals, and critical comments from a local high school vice principal.[78] One Knowplace parent complained about his son's unsatisfactory education to the CYC regional director.[79] Although national director Stewart Goodings claimed that "most of the articles

76   Knowplace Prospectus, 1968/69, National Archives of Canada, CYC documents.
77   Lionel Orlikow, "The Vancouver Youth Project," submitted to Stewart Goodings, CYC Director, October 5, 1968, National Archives of Canada, CYC documents.
78   Stewart Goodings, memo, December 23, 1968, National Archives of Canada, CYC documents, Record Group 116, Volume 142, File 884.
79   Geoff Cue to Stewart Goodings, August 28, 1968, National Archives of Canada, CYC documents, Record Group 116, Volume 142, File 884.

about the Company are overwritten,"[80] CYC leaders grew tired of the bad press that projects like Knowplace created.

Furthermore, Knowplace staff paid little attention to administrative details. Budgets were incomplete, staffing records convoluted, and monthly reports requested by the Ottawa office were never submitted. This was not entirely the fault of the Vancouver staff, for the entire CYC organization had developed a reputation for administrative confusion.[81] Colin Thomson complained to the Ottawa office about the lack of "communications over the Rockies" and the "vagueness as to who exercises what power and who makes what decisions."[82] The lack of efficiency was not surprising, since administration was a low priority among politically active youth. But in 1968 the government cut the Company's budget substantially, and as the national staff attempted to tighten up their procedures they became less tolerant of disorganized projects like Knowplace.

When in early 1969 the government appointed a new national director better known for efficiency than for any social service experience, the writing was on the wall for Knowplace. The project's unsatisfactory evaluation, its excessive controversy, and its poor administrative practices led to a decision that spring not to fund Knowplace or the Barker Free School beyond their two-year terms. In December 1969 the entire Vancouver Youth Project was terminated.

Colin Thomson fought this decision for over six months, arguing that the Vancouver Youth Project had become "an essential part of the Vancouver youth scene" and was at a "critical stage in its development." In a long submission to Ottawa, he described "the benefit derived by students directly involved with the project's network of independent community schools." He also outlined what he saw as the project's wider objectives:

> We have been instrumental in changing and widening the
> local school establishment. But change is a slow business
> and the general issues surrounding youth and education
> become more crucial every day. Consequently it would

---

80   Stewart Goodings to director Alan Clarke, November 22, 1967, National Archives of Canada, CYC documents, Record Group 116, Volume 142, File 884.

81   Ian Hamilton, *The Children's Crusade* (Toronto: Peter Martin, 1970), chaps. 3 and 14.

82   Colin Thomson to director Claude Vidal, April 1, 1969, National Archives of Canada, CYC documents, Record Group 116.

be near disastrous for the CYC to suddenly pull out and
allow these schools to collapse. Their mere existence is
a prime factor in promoting a changing attitude toward
young people in the public system.[83]

A few remaining staff members tried to reorganize the project under
the leadership of Barry Cramer, emphasizing their unique work with street
youth "in a way that few other agencies or organizations have been capable
of doing."[84] Parents and young people sent dozens of letters to Ottawa in
support of various projects.[85] But in the end the CYC terminated all contracts except for one six-month extension to the Floating Free School.[86]

Lack of funding, however, was not the basic issue, for Knowplace had
lost its vitality. The initial enthusiasm had disappeared and the school
simply fell apart; as one former student says, "The school ended with a
fizzle."[87] Karen Tallman reflected that "probably the best thing we could
do was close the school. It had lost most of its energy; a few of us were
keeping it going."[88] As for the staff, they went on to a variety of other pursuits. Rob Wood explained, "The end of the school wasn't very dramatic;
few people had that kind of staying power."[89]

VICTORIA FREE SCHOOL

In 1968, for many of the same reasons that Knowplace was created, ten
high school students established a similar school in Victoria. Called the

---

83   Colin Thomson, Project Report, Vancouver Youth Project, June 1969, National
     Archives of Canada, Record Group 116, Volume 142, File 884.
84   Colin Thomson, Project Report, Vancouver Youth Project, June 1969, National
     Archives of Canada.
85   Numerous letters in CYC documents, National Archives of Canada, most in support
     of the Experimental Education Foundation (Floating Free School) directed by
     Dave Manning.
86   Letter from CYC Director Claude Vidal, December 1969, National Archives of
     Canada, Record Group 116, Volume 142, File 884.
87   Lowell Orcutt, personal interview, November 21, 1996.
88   Karen Tallman, personal interview, October 9, 1996.
89   Former Knowplace staff members pursued a variety of careers. Colin Thomson taught
     for several years in China, Rob Wood taught at Ideal School, public schools, and as a
     Catholic school principal, Rob Watt acquired a small manufacturing business, and
     Greg Sorbara became a lawyer and served as a cabinet minister in two Ontario Liberal
     governments; Rob Wood, personal interview, October 10, 1996.

Victoria Free School and later the Bertrand Russell Academy, the school met in the Unitarian Church hall and in a family home. Some of the students were opposed to the authoritarian school system, others had learning problems or family troubles, and a few just wanted to experience the wider world. Most were the children of politically liberal professors but a few came from other backgrounds. "With the help of Joan Schwartz, former head teacher at Craigdarroch School, the students hired resource people to help them with English, mathematics, music, and art. Students discussed novels, wrote short stories, had occasional math lessons, performed plays, and engaged in political discussions. The school "ran out of steam" in less than a year, but students found it an intense experience. Although the academic component was limited, education was more visible than at Knowplace, partly because Victoria had only a small countercultural community to tempt the students. Most returned to mainstream or liberal high schools.[90]

CONCLUSION

The inadequate educational program was a disappointment to many early supporters of Knowplace. One of these suggested that the ethic of individualism and personal freedom hindered any serious consideration of a meaningful academic component:

> I never sensed that Knowplace had an educational philosophy other than free play—not even a sophisticated understanding of A. S. Neill. Classes were never encouraged or supported by the Knowplace subculture. The staff didn't think it was important. They didn't have a process to develop a learning community.[91]

The main problems were a lack of teaching expertise and a negative attitude toward academic learning. One former staff member regretted that

---

90   Personal interviews: Jeff Creque, February 26, 1997; Sally Kahn, April 9, 1997; Garth Dickman, April 3, 1997, and Erica Peavy, February 20, 1997. Three students were American; one had attended an academic Quaker school, and another had attended liberal schools in the United States. Several had a family connection with Craigdarroch School.

91   Jim Harding, personal interview, November 29, 1996.

there was no viable curriculum, not even a Summerhill model, and suggested the problem was that "none of the staff were teachers."[92] Another remembered that "we desperately tried to think of something to do."[93] Former student Bruce Russell explained that: "There was little education going on besides life experience. If there had been some good pedagogues in the group they could have excited us with special projects or a series of speakers."[94] Another former student expressed her disappointment this way: "There was lots of negative attitude toward education. The role of the adults should have been to provide stimulation and opportunity. I found some things myself, but I couldn't find everything. There were a lot of opportunities for learning and discussion that didn't take place."[95]

Gordon Yearsley, an original supporter of the project, had developed serious concerns by 1969. In a letter to the CYC he wrote:

> I encouraged the young people who started Knowplace in June 1967 and I was associated with the project during its early development. Within a few weeks of opening parents became angry because they saw their young people slipping into total inertia. Self-motivated students were held down and constantly distracted by those who only wanted to goof off. Reaction against the system absorbed the energies of these young people and the leaders were forced to develop a rationale for inertia. I assumed the leaders at Knowplace were conscientiously trying to work out their theories of education and were setting up real opportunities for the young people who were hanging around their school. I did not suspect that most of the verbalizing was window dressing to hide an empty project.[96]

For over a year staff and students successfully maintained the illusion that Knowplace had a real educational program. A *Vancouver Sun* writer

92   Heather-Jon Maroney, personal interview, January 14, 1997.
93   Greg Sorbara, personal interview, October 16, 1996.
94   Bruce Russell, personal interview, December 11, 1997.
95   Monica Carpendale, personal interview, November 25, 1996.
96   Gordon Yearsley, Application for CYC Funding, May 6, 1969; National Archives of Canada, CYC documents.

reported in December 1967 that "courses include most of the basic school subjects such as mathematics, French, history, and English, plus unusual ones like religion, psychedelics, and the study of the public school system itself."[97] Another reporter confirmed the existence of subjects such as "French, Canadian history, cooking, knowledge and understanding, jewelry, art, and fantasy."[98] A third writer, explaining the "independent study" option at Knowplace, described how one student planned to complete the regular curriculum in three months so that she "would be free the rest of the year to do our own stuff."[99] None of this happened but because participants and observers were sympathetic to the goals of the program, there was a reluctance to criticize Knowplace. Many observers looked the other way as long as they could.

Knowplace marked the end of the high school careers of almost all its students. As one parent, Ellen Tallman, explained, "It was too hard for most of the kids to go back to school; Karen always felt behind everyone in math and science and had to work twice as hard."[100] One former student believed that "academically just about everyone was set back."[101] Another remembered a functionally illiterate fellow student at thirteen years old "asking me to write down a telephone message for him and realizing that he couldn't write, and being shocked by that."[102] One student enrolled the following year at Campbell River Senior High School where reforms under Principal John Young had made the school considerably less authoritarian than other mainstream schools.[103] But most drifted until they were old enough to begin adult life.

Few students pursued higher education, although there were notable exceptions. UBC registrar John Parnell had offered Knowplace students

97   Bob Wilson, "22 Disgruntled Students Open Their Own School," *Vancouver Sun*, December 16, 1967, 33.

98   Tony Eberts, "Knowplace: An Answer to Boredom," *Vancouver Province*, October 14, 1967.

99   Jennifer Orcutt, quoted by Olive Johnson, "As a Cool School, There's No Place like Knowplace," *Maclean's*, December 1967, 5.

100 Ellen Tallman, personal interview, October 23, 1996.

101 Lowell Orcutt, personal interview, November 21, 1996.

102 Monica Carpendale, personal interview, November 25, 1996.

103 See J. A. Young, "A Rural High School Tries Freedom," *This Magazine is about Schools*, Winter 1967, 63–70. For more on John Young and the Campbell River school, see Chapter 15.

an opportunity to audit courses and earn credit for them if they did well. Karen Tallman took him up on this challenge and passed her first year of university in the Arts I program. She eventually completed a science degree and earned a PhD in psychology. Another former student did graduate work at the University of Washington and a third earned a master's degree in adult education. Still another trained in art therapy and later owned and directed her own school. Several former students managed to find challenging careers through their own efforts. Bruce Russell, though he never went to university, designed a study program for himself that was so successful he became an art historian with the National Gallery in Ottawa. Lowell Orcutt became a self-taught computer analyst and software designer. Still another former student, a talented professional musician who wrestled with drug use, overcame his addiction and successfully earned a bachelor of music degree. Another student became an accomplished freelance pianist performing regularly in Vancouver.

Their determination as well as their family backgrounds helped these individuals overcome educational deficiencies. But most Knowplace students were at a disadvantage in establishing careers, and some continued without occupations, or in jobs that were below their capacity. One parent speculated that the females fared better than the males, perhaps because girls mature earlier.[104] Another parent concluded, "All these kids have turned out to be good people but many have not been able to reach their [educational] potential."[105]

Knowplace and other Romantic schools were closely bound up with the counterculture of the late 1960s, a diffuse movement that included experimentation with drugs and sexual freedom, new forms of creative expression, communal living, spiritual mysticism, a return to nature, and a distrust of authority, competition, and academic pursuits. Some proponents of this new lifestyle were interested in reforming society and culture. But above all, the counterculture was about individual freedom and personal transformation. Romantic schools would help growing individuals free themselves from personal inhibitions and unwanted cultural or intellectual baggage.

---

104 David Orcutt, personal interview, April 24, 1997.
105 Bob Makaroff, personal interview, February 18, 1997.

Knowplace staff and students were caught up in the anti-intellectual-ism that pervaded countercultural values, or as Bob Makaroff put it, "a rejection of discipline and scientific thinking."[106] Some Romantic school advocates believed that even Summerhill, Everdale, and the Barker Free School were only halfway measures because adults were still in control. As one former staff member said, "At Knowplace the kids didn't want a flexible program, they didn't want innovative courses, they didn't want individualized tutoring. They thought education was learning to live in a more meaningful way."[107]

Staff members had little educational expertise and were not mature enough to be effective role models for a group of questioning teenagers. The staff took few opportunities to stimulate intellectual growth, whether formal or informal. They accepted the Romantic notion, prevalent at the time, that adults had nothing to teach children, that if they simply supported kids in whatever they wanted to do, education and growth would take care of themselves. There were maxims about learning how to relate to people rather than to knowledge. But as Jim Harding wrote in 1970:

> We do not have to abandon intellectual curiosities to have
> human freedoms, in fact, the two are very much inter-
> twined. In letting the kids do what they please and being
> supportive passively, rather than in a challenging way,
> something quite different from education is allowed to
> go on.[108]

Educator Jonathan Kozol saw this as an abrogation of adult responsibility. In *Free Schools* he laments that free school adherents did not recognize the virtues of consistency and discipline. Kozol praises "teachers who are not afraid to teach" and exhorts alternative educators:

> It is time for us to face our own inherent fear of strength
> and of effectiveness head-on. I think we must be pre-
> pared to strive with all our hearts to be strong teachers,

---

106 Bob Makaroff, personal interview, February 18, 1997.
107 Rob Watt, personal interview, November 19, 1996.
108 James (Jim) Harding, "Freedom From or Freedom To: Ideas for People in Free Schools," in *Free School: The Journal of Change in Education* (Saturna Island, BC: Free School Press) (June 1970).

efficacious adults, unintimidated leaders, and straight-forward and strong-minded provocations in the lives of children.[109]

Knowplace was one of the most "Canadian" of all BC alternative schools. It was staffed by Canadians and much of its inspiration stemmed from Canadian socialist idealism and youth activism. The sponsorship of the federal government through the Company of Young Canadians was a particularly Canadian development. It is unlikely that government funding for such a radical experiment could have occurred in the United States. These origins, combined with the influence of the English Romantic tradition and the American counterculture, made Knowplace a uniquely British Columbia experiment.

During its two years of operation Knowplace was unsuccessful in establishing a viable academic program, making it more difficult for students to pursue further education. Nor did Knowplace fulfill a therapeutic or problem-solving objective; the prevalence of drugs and the "anything goes" philosophy prevented this. The school did not achieve its high ideals because the staff had little educational experience or well-conceived structured program, and because of the overriding influence of the counterculture, which questioned the value of academic pursuits. One former staff member reflected that the "kids were at the very edge of danger and we adopted their mindset, immersed ourselves in it." Knowplace was "a bridge for kids rather than a school; a halfway house in a transition of lifestyles."[110]

Many years later, however, a few former students suggested that the Knowplace environment helped them learn to rely on their own resources to acquire skills and information or to solve personal problems. Exposed to unusual people and a rich cultural life, students had experiences that they could not have had elsewhere. One student described Knowplace as a "worthwhile experience. It cracked my world open. I was very shy. I needed a major shock. It was an experience of extreme value to me."[111] Karen Tallman agreed that "there was something there. We had a brash

109 Jonathan Kozol, *Free Schools* (Boston: Houghton Mifflin, 1972), 61.
110 Greg Sorbara, personal interview, October 16, 1996.
111 Martha Jackson, personal interview, December 2, 1997.

confidence; we didn't look to anyone for permission. There were costs but the alternative for many of us would have been worse. I wouldn't have given it up. We were doing things that were uncharted. It changed the face of education. My kids can thank me."[112]

Most Knowplace students had become so alienated from the public school system it is unlikely they would have gone back under any circumstances. But there was nowhere else for them to go in 1967. Recognized alternative programs for high school students would not be established for several years, and the counterculture had created too large a gulf between parents and teenagers for parents to have been a useful support. For these students, Knowplace at least provided a semi-safe environment supervised by sympathetic adults that insulated them from the organized drug trade and life on the street. Other Romantic schools would be established in British Columbia during the next several years, some even farther removed from mainstream society than Knowplace.

---

112 Karen Tallman, personal interview, September 15, 1998.

Chapter 7

THE NEW SCHOOL: MIDDLE YEARS

A few months before the opening of Knowplace made the general public more aware of alternative schools, the New School was quietly completing its fifth year of operation in the spring of 1967. Run by parents, the New School had been based on a moderate Progressive curriculum according to the principles of John Dewey. But by the late 1960s, the parent body had come to include many proponents of Romantic or "free schools." Most of these parents were influenced by the emerging counterculture and the radical educational ideas of A.S. Neill. Progressive and Romantic ideologies became increasingly difficult to reconcile.

With the resignation of director Graham Smith in March 1967, the hiring committee began searching for a new teacher-director to replace him the following September. Tom Durrie, an elementary special class teacher in a Williams Lake public school, saw an advertisement for the position in the Summerhill Society Bulletin and applied for the job. Three New School parents made the long trip north to interview him and spend the day at his school. They were impressed and invited him to come to Vancouver to meet the board and the other teachers.

However, some parents, believing it would be "a great mistake to hire a director who had not taught at the school," opposed bringing in an outsider. They thought the directorship should be offered to Anne Long who, having taught at the school for a year, would provide continuity. One parent, Norman Levi, wrote to President Barry Promislow:

> After five years in the New School I am convinced that
> the teaching staff must produce its own director because

they know the intricacies of the teaching problems and the parent-teacher problems, and have worked out techniques to handle them. We have seen that there has to be a learning process in regard to our somewhat nebulous views on Progressive education. After five years we should realize that directors are made in the system they work. They certainly are not born that way.[1]

Ms. Long did eventually put her name forward for the director's job but, due to her insufficient experience, neither she nor the board took her candidacy very seriously.[2]

Many parents, reacting against the traditional methods of Graham Smith, wanted a director who would introduce considerably more "freedom." The composition of the parent body was changing by 1967 and most parents were more influenced by Neill than by Dewey.[3] "Free schools" were the talk of the day and their proponents, considering Mr. Durrie something of a "messiah," succeeded in selling him to the rest of the group.[4] In an interview with the *Vancouver Sun* in August 1967 titled "Far Out School to Be More Free," Mr. Durrie explained that the school would be "more liberal and free in its approach."[5] He thought that since New School children were less repressed than his special class students, they would be less disruptive when given real freedom. He was just as surprised as their parents when this turned out to be incorrect.[6]

New School parents embraced freedom in theory without having any idea of what that meant in reality. Mr. Durrie questioned whether they really wanted a school resembling Summerhill: "They thought they did. But they weren't prepared for what that meant—their nice well-behaved children running around yelling 'fuck you.' I don't think they knew, any more than I did, what would happen."[7] The freedom Mr. Durrie allowed

---

1   Norman Levi to Barry Promislow, March 20, 1967 and Norman Levi document collection.
2   Anne Long, "The New School—Vancouver," in Gross and Gross, eds., *Radical School Reform* (New York: Simon and Shuster, 1969): 275.
3   This was confirmed by virtually all parents interviewed.
4   Anne Long, "The New School—Vancouver," 275.
5   *Vancouver Sun*, August 17, 1967, 20.
6   Tom Durrie, personal interview, July 1988.
7   Tom Durrie, personal interview, July 1988.

his students in Williams Lake was tempered by the traditional school environment where some outside constraints were in effect. New School parents did not realize what complete freedom in an entire school would be like. Their infatuation ended a few weeks into the school year.

The other teachers were Anne Long, Beth Jankola, and new staff members Rita Cohn and Diane McNairn. Rita Cohn was no stranger to the New School, having been one of the founding parents in 1962. She was an experienced teacher, fluent in French, and looked forward to her new role in the school. All three teachers had expressed misgivings to the parent board about Mr. Durrie's permissive approach, and another teacher resigned when he was hired. But at a meeting that spring, the whole staff agreed that the mornings would be set aside for the teachers to organize whatever "structured lessons" they wished. Afternoons would include creative arts, sports, field trips, and other activities that students would not be compelled to attend.[8] What was misunderstood, however, was that Mr. Durrie intended the morning sessions to be strictly voluntary, whereas the other teachers expected their students to attend.[9] The "compromise" did not work.

Rita Cohn had organized her kindergarten/grade one classroom prior to school opening, and remembered:

> But after the first day, it didn't make any difference who you had in your class, because the kids could go anywhere they wanted. I looked into Tom's class that first day and there was nothing. Not a book, no furniture. I asked him, "What are you going to do, Tom?" He said, "Well, I'll see what the kids want to do." I remember thinking, that's not going to work.[10]

Ms. Cohn reported that although some students enjoyed the freedom given by the director, others simply attached themselves to one of the other teachers. Those who remained with Mr. Durrie "ran rampant and became quite destructive, and the school building suffered greatly." One former student recalled that he "did not open a book all year," and

---

8   Anne Long, "The New School—Vancouver," 275–276.
9   Tom Durrie, "New School Director's Annual Report: 1967/68," February 29, 1968, 6.
10   Rita Cohn, personal interview, April 1987.

another remembered school that year as being "lots of fun."[11] Anne Long described that eventful year:

> With no expectation of class work, an anti-academic atti-
> tude pervaded the school and the students were quick to
> reject anything that even half looked like a regular lesson,
> no matter how skillfully devised. They discovered that
> freedom was limitless.[12]

The Monkey Patrol was a group of four boys who made life difficult for everyone else. Ms. Long continued: "They spent their time building forts, fighting over materials, disrupting activities of other kids, light-ing fires, and wrecking furniture, school equipment, and the very walls of the school itself." Parents on the maintenance committee remembered having to repair holes in the walls as big as basketballs. Mr. Durrie "tried to help these kids work through their problems by accepting all of their anti-social and destructive behaviour, buying them candy and pop, and taking them on exclusive outings leaving the rest of his class to fend for themselves."[13] Students soon learned that Mr. Durrie would never disap-prove of any behaviour. One former student remembered having to fight her way out of a room after being dragged in by four or five boys. She described a "gangland situation with no control over the kids—you had to learn to defend yourself."[14] Ms. Long summed up:

> There were Cuisenaire rod fights, fort fights, paint fights,
> water fights. Student meetings were screaming matches.
> Student artwork was destroyed, chairs broken up, desks
> sawed in half. The ditto machine became a juvenile por-
> nography plant. I began feeling that I was living in the
> land of *Lord of the Flies*.[15]

Students would drift into school in the morning. "There was no par-ticular structure—they would go where they wanted to go and do what they wanted to do. The older kids circulated around the whole place and

---

11   Cal Shumiatcher, personal interview, April 1987.
12   Anne Long, "The New School—Vancouver," 276.
13   Anne Long, "The New School—Vancouver," 278.
14   Laura Jamieson, personal interview, June 1991.
15   Anne Long, "The New School—Vancouver," 278–279.

created a lot of mayhem." The other teachers and the younger students were not prepared for the older kids to be so energetic, rambunctious, or hostile and "were afraid of the madness that burst forth without any structure."[16] Students were not allowed to hurt each other, but for the most part suggestions to control them were ignored.

Tom Durrie remembered one day when a group of students had flooded the basement and spent much of the day running and sliding on their bellies. Upon being picked up and asked by a horrified mother, "Why would you do a thing like that?" the child replied, "Nobody stopped me." Mr. Durrie believed that New School parents, though genuinely anti-authoritarian, were too middle class to accept such uncontrolled behaviour from their kids and that "some of the kids found it difficult to accept in themselves."[17] But the director saw their behaviour as natural. He had lots of fun with the kids building electronic equipment or terrariums for frogs, building dams and rivers at the park, and driving to interesting places in the city.

Several incidents finally caused Anne Long to challenge Mr. Durrie openly. According to Ms. Long, he did not intervene when members of the Monkey Patrol refused to allow other students to come along on downtown outings with him. Shoplifting by students may have also taken place.[18] But the most serious disagreement occurred when students began lighting fires all over the school building—in wastebaskets, washrooms, and in corners of the basement. Ms. Long finally began confiscating matches and telephoning parents, and Mr. Durrie agreed to move the burning outside.[19] Staff relations became increasingly strained.

The majority of parents disapproved of Mr. Durrie's methods. The lack of control over the children caused more concern than the decrease in academic activity, although parents and even a few students began worrying that they were not getting an education. However, a significant minority supported him, including President Jean Kuyt, and the school divided into two camps. According to Anne Long, more than twenty students were

---

16   Tom Durrie, personal interview, July 1988.
17   Tom Durrie, personal interview, July 1988.
18   Anne Long, "The New School—Vancouver," 278.
19   Anne Long, "The New School—Vancouver," 276–277.

withdrawn during the first two months and by November it became difficult for the school to function at all.[20]

The school limped along through a series of crises, intense meetings, and a three-day session with a Simon Fraser University consultant. One solution designated the basement as the area where students could do whatever they wanted while the upstairs would be reserved for academic activities, but this and other "adult generated" plans broke down quickly.[21] Mr. Durrie found himself under widespread criticism but he believed in what he was doing. The situation continued to deteriorate after the Christmas break, and the school closed for encounter groups ("T-Grouping") in January in an unsuccessful attempt to resolve the differences.[22] Finally, at a meeting of the entire school community on March 14, 1968, the parents decided to divide into two schools.[23] The moderate majority retained the school building, while Tom Durrie and his "free school" supporters met in their homes throughout the spring.

The moderate group set out to re-establish itself as the Progressive school it had been prior to 1967. But this would not be as easy as they had hoped. The times had changed significantly since the school's founding in 1962, and the Summerhillian free school ideology had become so pervasive in the countercultural and alternative communities that it was difficult for any alternative school to retain a moderate position. The parent group had never resolved their ambivalence as to what kind of school they were to be, and without a strong vision they were easily pulled along with the times.

The New School reopened in April with just under thirty students. Anne Long was appointed acting director for the rest of the year and explained that "we will not be an unstructured school, but we will be much freer than the public schools. We will teach the basic skills, but the kids will also be involved in academic things outside the classroom."[24] According to Ms. Long, the students responded with enthusiasm to the new structured

20   Anne Long, "The New School—Vancouver," 277.
21   Tom Durrie, personal interview, July 1988.
22   Rita Cohn, personal interview; Anne Long, "The New School—Vancouver," 279.
23   "Parents Split School, Disagree With Methods," *Vancouver Sun*, June 1, 1968, 7.
24   New School General Meeting, minutes, April 11, 1968; *Vancouver Sun*, June 1, 1968, 7.

order because they now understood why it was necessary.[25] Following the resignation of five board members, an interim board under new president Kay Stockholder, a UBC English professor, was elected in April.[26] Parents cleaned, repaired, and painted the school building, and the students completed the year without further incident. Few students or their parents believed that they suffered any serious consequences from the unbridled freedom and academic inactivity of the previous six months.

In May, the teachers petitioned the parents to hand the operation of the school over to them. Having endured unreasonably difficult teaching conditions, they saw the aftermath of the crisis as an opportune moment to gain control over their working environment. There was little resistance to this proposal due to parental fatigue and the frequent strife of the previous six years. In fact, one parent, Norman Levi, had suggested the school become a teacher co-operative more than a year earlier.[27] Parents had no desire to administer the school any longer and approved the plan at a general meeting without a dissenting vote.[28]

When the New School opened for its seventh year in September 1968, it was a different school than it had been in 1962. Few of the original families remained, and a new clientele influenced by the cultural movements of the late 1960s predominated. Even with the leadership of the school secured by teachers who opposed Summerhillian ideology, the New School soon came to resemble a typical late 1960s Romantic school.

THE TEACHER CO-OPERATIVE

Anne Long, Rita Cohn, and Beth Jankola took charge of the school that September. Ms. Long taught the intermediate students, Ms. Jankola worked with the older primary students, and Ms. Cohn taught the very young children. Later that year Daryl Sturdy, a former colleague of Anne Long at Hastings School three years earlier, joined the staff. The two teachers had spent many hours talking about Summerhill and other

---

25   Anne Long, "The New School—Vancouver," 280.
26   Board meeting, minutes, March 21, 1968; general meeting, minutes, April 11, 1968.
27   Norman Levi to Barry Promislow, March 20, 1967.
28   General Meeting, minutes, May 16, 1968.

alternatives to the "repressive" public school system. Mr. Sturdy had also attended a high-profile Free School Conference hosted by the New School the previous December. About one hundred people from as far away as Ontario participated in the three-day event, and Mr. Sturdy grew even more enthusiastic about alternative education. Mr. Sturdy joined Ms. Long in teaching the older class.

The New School was re-incorporated as the New School Teachers Society, a teacher co-operative, in June 1968.[29] The legal details were finally concluded in 1969 when the New School Teachers Society bought the school building for a dollar.[30] The constitution was designed to produce maximum stability by putting strict limits on membership in the new society. Only teachers who had been on staff for two years could become permanent members, thus providing a probationary period, and former teachers could remain with the society for two years after leaving the school.[31] Each spring Society members met to decide whether or not to rehire new teachers on a permanent basis (although the decision was usually already made at a staff meeting). The constitution also provided for parents to elect two representatives to the society, but this rarely happened.[32] The society had two principal functions: administering school finances and supervising staff. The school often fell behind in bureaucratic tasks and was fortunate that the bulk of the legal work was done by two parents at minimal cost.[33]

The teachers made all school decisions and parents no longer participated in administrative functions. Decision-making by the teachers was much less stressful than under the parent organization. Weekly staff meetings and frequent informal discussions were natural extensions of the school day. The teachers were together all the time and became friends as well as colleagues. Evening meetings were often held at a staff member's house over a potluck dinner while the teachers discussed curriculum, philosophy, and day-to-day school operation. Team teaching became the

29   New School Teachers Society, constitution, June 21, 1968.
30   Deed of Sale, June 24, 1969, Nora Randall document collection.
31   Later reduced to one year, Constitution and By-Laws, 1968, 1974.
32   New School Teachers Society, annual reports, 1968–1977.
33   Sid Simons and Marvin Stark, legal correspondence, 1968–1973, Nora Randall document collection.

norm, but individuals were free to develop and implement their own programs as they saw fit. Daryl Sturdy described the atmosphere:

> We weren't just teachers leaving at the end of the day—we ran the school. It humanized the workplace. It wasn't just a job. There was a real feeling of family, of connectedness; it was fun. We didn't have to deal with levels of bureaucracy.[34]

Decisions were reached through consensus and, although some issues required extensive discussion and occasionally had to be brought to a vote, most of the teachers agreed on how they wanted to work with kids.[35] On the other hand, meetings could be long and difficult, and at times there were heated arguments. It was a time of strong beliefs, experimentation, and high emotion. People expressed themselves freely, and sometimes feelings were hurt as everyone took the issues very seriously.[36] Although the teachers formed a cohesive group, personnel problems occasionally arose, and in 1970 and 1971 serious disagreements about whether to rehire particular teachers strained the decision-making mechanism.

The school could not afford any administrative, secretarial, or janitorial staff, so each staff member took responsibility for finance and bookkeeping, admissions, supply ordering, building maintenance, secretarial work, fundraising, volunteer coordination, and fielding telephone calls from concerned parents.[37] Every year one teacher would volunteer for the demanding job of treasurer. Some performed this task well, but at times the books were in a shambles.[38] Administration was tiring after a full day of teaching, and in 1971 the teachers attempted to revive parent committees.[39] But many parents were busy with jobs and enjoying their countercultural lifestyle and lacked the drive and commitment of the founders. Parents were informed of ongoing events and issues through a monthly newsletter and provided informal feedback to the teachers at parent/teacher class

34 Daryl Sturdy, personal interview, April 1987.
35 Daryl Sturdy and Daniel Wood, personal interviews, April 1987 and June 1988.
36 Katherine Chamberlain, personal interview, May 1991.
37 New School Prospectus, 1972/73; staff meeting, minutes, September 6, 1973; Nora Randall document collection.
38 Daniel Wood, Anne Long, personal interviews, June 1988, April 1987.
39 New School, newsletter, May 1971.

meetings. Some parents did volunteer to transport children and help with the endless cleaning. Full-day work parties took place several times a year, and each Labour Day weekend was a marathon of painting, fixing, and cleaning.[40] A group of parents built an adventure playground in the early 1970s, while others assisted in the classroom or with field trip supervision. Several parent volunteers became staff members in subsequent years.

Parents were generally content to let the teachers run the school. However, the controversial dismissal of a teacher in May 1971 led to an uproar among the parent body. Many wrote letters protesting the decision and the way it was made, and several parents withdrew their children from the school.[41] They accused the staff of operating a "secret society" and demanded greater participation in decision-making. Although most decisions were made at weekly staff meetings with little secrecy, the teachers had neglected to communicate adequately to the parent body how the school was governed. Following this incident the staff took steps to "acquaint the parents more fully with the administrative structure of the school" and invited non-permanent staff to attend Society meetings.[42] Barbara Shumiatcher, a parent who supported the teachers, reminded others how disruptive personnel decisions had been under the earlier parent co-operative:

> Some parents are agitating for more participation in decisions at the school. This was disastrous in the past as gossip increased and factions grew: stranglehold was the basic political attitude. Since teachers have to take day-to-day consequences for policy decisions it seems only reasonable that they alone should make those decisions.[43]

While less confrontational than during the parent administration, decision-making was never easy, particularly when it came to personnel matters.

Despite the parents' diminished role in decision-making, the school remained a central part of everyone's life, and parents, students, and

---

40   New School, newsletters, September 1969; September 1970; April 1971.
41   These letters are in a file in the Sharon Van Volkingburgh document collection.
42   New School, newsletter, May 1971.
43   Barbara Shumiatcher, letter to the New School Society, April 1971.

teachers attended many evening social events. There were educational evenings, craft nights, dances, political discussions, singing evenings, potluck meals, and birthday parties. One teacher, Daniel Wood, remembered these evenings well:

> They would get someone in to teach them how to tie-dye. For the next week or two everyone in the school would be tie-dying. Or they would have a film and video night where they would learn how to make films. Parents and teachers would get together and talk about issues. Everybody would sit around and sing folk songs or dance. The lights were on in the school all the time, evenings and weekends, and for many of the adults it was the centre of their social life.[44]

These New School students, celebrating a birthday, considered themselves to be part of an extended family. 1970 Photo courtesy of Daphne Harwood

44   Daniel Wood, personal interview, June 1988.

Most teachers enrolled their own children in the school, adding to the family-like atmosphere. One parent, artist Roy Kiyooka, described the social structure as "tribal, familial, extended family."[45] There was a sense of camaraderie, and participants remembered the New School as a welcoming place. This feeling carried over to the children and one student recalled that "we were a lot closer than kids in a regular school."[46] The New School provided a ready-made community, exactly what many parents wanted. The school became an extension of home.

Students were recruited mainly by word of mouth. However, the teachers also advertised in daily newspapers, Anne Long appeared on a radio talk show, and CKLG radio (the local rock station) aired a full-length interview with two New School teachers and two students in 1972.[47] Prospective parents were required to observe in the school for half a day, after which two teachers interviewed the applicant families. The staff believed this was essential to ensure that they could "support the parents' aims for their children and be able to meet the parents' expectations."[48] The school was popular during this period and enrolment reached a peak of eighty students in 1972, even higher than during the Progressive years.[49]

Most parents were attracted to the school because they valued individual freedom. They perceived the public schools as excessively rigid, unresponsive to individual students, and inhumane in methods of discipline (such as the strap, which was legal in BC public schools until 1973). One parent described being drawn to the school by "warmth and colour and kids running in and out." She "hated and feared the school system and didn't want my energetic four-year-old pounded into a mould."[50] Another parent, who had taught at the Progressive City and Country School in New York, hoped the New School would make her daughter less "conforming."[51] Others wanted to eliminate the pressure their children

45   Roy Kiyooka, personal interview, June 1991.
46   Kiyo Kiyooka, personal interview, June 1991.
47   Tape recording of the original broadcast. The teachers were Daniel Wood and Barbara Hansen, and the students were Michael Shumiatcher and Scott Robinson.
48   New School Prospectus, 1972/73.
49   "Students Do All the Talking at Vancouver's New School," *Vancouver Province*, October 4, 1972, 41; New School Prospectus, 1972/73.
50   Margaret Sigurgeirson, personal interview, November 1991.
51   Aurie Felde, personal interview, December 1991.

experienced in public schools. Some were attracted by what they knew of Summerhill and wanted their children to have the kind of freedom they never had.

Although the teachers hoped to attract self-motivated students and to retain a mix of family income, the school no longer appealed to academic, professional, or higher-income families. Most professional parents ultimately wanted their children to do well academically; when academic learning became a low priority, these families left. Parents who favoured the moderate Progressive education offered earlier in the school's life rarely stayed longer than a year or two, and most were gone by the early 1970s.[52] As the public schools became somewhat less rigid in the 1970s, these families could usually find an acceptable alternative in the public system.

Students with learning, emotional, or behaviour difficulties were admitted to the school in significantly greater numbers after 1968. With few programs for these children in public school, many parents chose the New School as their last resort. Of the twenty students in Anne Long's 1968/69 class, "nine had serious enough problems in the public school system for their parents to look for alternative schooling."[53] Some of these kids exhibited aggressive or anti-social behaviour and others were withdrawn.[54] One student, referred by UBC, was a musical genius who would throw chairs and scissors and wander around in the unconfined area. Sometimes he would go into a storage room and write three- and four-part music. Such students were difficult to work with and strained the teachers' abilities and energy, thus compromising the school's regular program. The school became less discriminating in its admissions criteria as it had to maintain its enrolment level to be financially viable. Furthermore, the teachers' idealism led them to genuinely believe they could work with troubled children. But with few exceptions they were

52   Professor Ed Wickberg withdrew his children after one year, and professors Fred and Kay Stockholder withdrew their son after two years. Interviews, October 1987, April 1987.
53   Anne Long, "The New School—Vancouver," 291.
54   Dewi Minden, Kiyo Kiyooka and Margo Hansen described several such students in personal interviews, August 1988, June 1991 and July 1991.

not trained to help these students other than to provide them with a safe, supportive environment.

The New School continued to receive a constant stream of visitors. The school newsletter reported in 1970 that 150 observers had visited during the previous three months.[55] Education professors interested in the free school phenomenon took their students to observe a free school in action. A group of New School teachers and students was invited by the UBC education faculty to make a presentation in the fall of 1972.[56] The school also attracted students training for other professions. Students in the preschool education program at the Vancouver Night School observed for two weeks in 1970, and a group of counsellors-in-training spent an afternoon at the school. A parent who taught social work at UBC arranged for her students to work with New School children on a regular basis during the early 1970s, and a group of UBC architecture students experimented with design exercises at the New School site. Because it was out of the mainstream, many different people used the New School to broaden their experience.

Parent observers were welcome but their visits were pre-arranged and limited to one specific morning or afternoon per week. Restrictions on observations were a reaction to the parental harassment of teachers during the parent co-operative years. Sometimes the school conducted a formal open house. The staff invited parents in for an entire week in December 1970, culminating with an evening of discussion for all participants.[57]

FINANCES

The New School continued to organize creative fundraising activities but, with parents less intensely involved in the school, events were less frequent and less lucrative. Nevertheless, an art auction in 1968 raised $1,000, in 1969 the school convened a smorgasbord dinner, and the

---

55   New School, newsletter, December 1970.
56   "Students Do All the Talking at Vancouver's New School," *Vancouver Province*, October 4, 1972, 41.
57   New School, newsletter, December 1970.

next year collected newspaper for recycling.[58] In 1971 a Spring Fair "transformed the school into colourful craft areas, a coffee house with a foot-stomping blue grass band, a health food store, and a fun and games room."[59] Teachers and parents used their contacts among local rock musicians to organize fundraising concerts, and one New School teacher who wrote for the *Georgia Straight* arranged for the school and the newspaper to co-sponsor a benefit dance in 1972. The school occasionally rented its premises to like-minded educational or political groups such as the Free University.[60] But after 1969, fundraising activities rarely earned more than $500 per year compared to $3,000 in 1966/67.[61]

The school had to depend on tuition fees for its income. The sliding fee scale remained in place and parents were asked to bring their income tax returns to registration. The fee, 8 per cent of family income (less for a second child), rose significantly by 1972. The minimum was $350 per child, with a maximum (for an income over $15,000) of $1,150.[62] The debenture system continued and new families were asked to provide a small interest-free loan to the school. But the decreased number of higher-income and professional parents meant that more families were paying fees at the lower end of the scale than ever before. With fewer families able to contribute at higher levels, the school suffered a serious financial crunch. Daryl Sturdy recalled that "we were always on the edge":

> Financially, it became more and more difficult as the years went on. The parents were not working-class people, they had hippie-type lifestyles. There were a lot of single-parent families and a certain number of those were on welfare. The public school system had changed a lot. Professional families could find what they wanted in the public system.[63]

---

58   Auction accounting sheet, November 1968; New School, newsletter, October 1969, Nora Randall document collection; New School, newsletters, November and December 1970.

59   New School, newsletter, April 1971.

60   Staff meeting, minutes, October 2, 1973. The Free University offered informal non-credit courses (mainly by SFU professors) in a variety of locations.

61   Financial statements, 1967–1974, Registrar of Companies, Victoria.

62   New School, Prospectus and fee schedule, 1972/73.

63   Daryl Sturdy, personal interview, April 1987.

After managing to break even or keep deficits to a minimum up to 1971, the school suffered a major loss of $8,000 in 1972.[64] It remained in financial difficulty throughout its later years.

The deterioration of the school building added to the financial problems. By 1973 the basement floor, back porch, roof, and outside yard were all in poor condition and there were no fire exits.[65] Frequent work parties and attempts to scrounge replacement furniture and equipment did little to improve the situation. A group of UBC architecture students designed an extensive redevelopment plan in 1970, but the school did not have the funds to pursue it.[66] The state of the building became an increasingly serious problem during the school's last five years.

Teachers now earned far less than in the public school system. Ironically, the parent administration had been able to pay higher salaries than the teachers could afford to pay themselves. Full-time New School teachers earned $6,000 annually in 1968/69 while assistants averaged $2,500.[67] By 1970/71 salaries for long-serving teachers increased to $6,600, while other staff earned between $3,000 and $6,000.[68] But in 1971 salaries decreased to $5,000 when, in the spirit of egalitarianism, teachers began sharing salaries equally regardless of their background and experience. They fell even lower several years later.[69] However, most teachers didn't mind earning less than half of what they could have made in the public system. As one former staff member put it, "It was politically correct. No one worried about money then."[70]

The school opened a licenced daycare centre for twenty-four preschool children in 1969 and added an after-school program the next year. The daycare program managed to make ends meet through Department of Human Resources subsidies. However, due to inadequate facilities the school had trouble renewing its permit each year.[71] The bureaucratic

---

64   Financial statements, 1966–1972, Registrar of Companies, Victoria.
65   Staff meeting, minutes, October 16, 1973.
66   UBC Student Architects, Report, May 1970, 43 pages.
67   Annual Report, July 11, 1969, Registrar of Companies, Victoria.
68   New School Teachers' Society meeting, minutes, March 27, 1970.
69   New School income tax records, 1973–1977, Nora Randall document collection.
70   Joan Nemtin, personal interview, December 1987.
71   New School, newsletter, September 1970.

requirements for daycare centres were a chore, and Rita Cohn had to deal with endless correspondence from Human Resources and the Vancouver health and licensing departments. A summer daycare, which constantly lost money, also operated out of the school building.

The school organization changed dramatically between 1969 and 1971. The size of the teaching staff doubled, mostly due to the increasing number of special-needs students. In 1969 the staff hired teaching assistants to work with each of the four teachers so staff could devote more time to individual students. The teams worked so closely together that in 1970 the assistants were made full-fledged teachers with equivalent salaries. This produced an enviable pupil-teacher ratio but placed a severe financial strain on the school. In 1971 the four classes were reorganized into two larger units with three or four teachers attached to each group. The younger group ranged from four to seven years old, while the older group included ages eight to twelve. The larger classes were conducive to an open-area or team-teaching approach (also becoming popular in the public system) and produced a more informal style of teaching. Most important, the school began hiring non-certified teachers in 1970, a practice that increased throughout the next few years. Most of them had backgrounds working in child care and social work. Although they were certainly capable individuals, their lack of teacher training further weakened the academic orientation of the school.

STAFFING

Of the fifteen individuals who taught at the New School during these five years, most were committed to substantial freedom for children. They were all influenced to some degree by the 1960s counterculture, left-wing political ideals, and the nascent women's movement. Daphne Trivett joined the staff in September 1969. She had trained in Progressive teaching methods and had taught for a year at the University of Chicago Laboratory School founded by John Dewey. Like Anne Long, she had spent an unsatisfying year trying to apply child-centred methods at an east Vancouver public school, only to be told to tighten up her discipline. She gratefully accepted a job at the New School.

Ms. Trivett recalled: "So when I arrived at the New School I encountered a new kind of difficulty. Instead of being perceived as the wild one, I was perceived as the straight one. I was too rigid, I was too formal, I wanted to teach lessons."[72] She had no teaching assistant, and several of her students were the children of other staff members, who didn't always approve of the way she handled them. Nevertheless, Ms. Trivett used her contacts at the two universities to arrange mathematics workshops at the school, and several parents report that her reading and mathematics program served their children well.[73] However, at the end of the year a staff majority decided not to rehire her. This was ironic given that she was one of the few New School teachers actually trained in Progressive methods.

Katherine Chamberlain taught at the New School for two years. She was also familiar with Progressive methods, having been educated at the well-known Peninsula High School in Menlo Park, California, where her mother was head teacher. She heard about the New School while doing graduate work in education at UBC and working at the Child Study Centre. She and Daphne Trivett helped each other develop classroom management techniques suited to unstructured learning environments. Ms. Chamberlain became active in the women's movement and eventually returned to California. Catherine Pye, a child care worker, was hired in 1969 and remained at the school for two years.

Saralee James, an active parent at the school since 1966, was hired in 1970. She was not a certified teacher but had volunteered extensively in the intermediate class. She devoted a great deal of energy to the school and would share the older class with Daryl Sturdy for over three years. Daniel Wood joined the staff in the fall of 1971 and also worked with the older class during his two years at the school. A humanitarian activist, he had helped establish schools for Black children in the American south during the 1960s and assisted in setting up primary schools in rural Borneo during a stint with the United States Peace Corps. Mr. Wood taught for one year in the American public school system before coming

---

72   Daphne Trivett, personal interview, October 1987.
73   Barbara Hansen and Barbara Shumiatcher, interviews, October 1987 and April 1987.

to Vancouver because of his opposition to the Vietnam War.[74] Mr. Sturdy, Ms. James, and Mr. Wood developed a co-operative working relationship during their two years together. Mr. Wood remembered that the "close team spirit" and friendship made teaching easier and concluded simply, "We all liked each other."[75]

Daniel Wood was representative of the wave of young American teachers and parents at the New School after 1969. They had come to Canada not for employment reasons (as had the earlier group of American academics) but rather to escape what they saw as an oppressive and morally unacceptable political climate in the United States due to the war in Vietnam. The Americans were a small minority (about 20 per cent) at the school but exerted a significant influence in bringing with them a whole range of counterculture values in a more intense form than their Canadian counterparts.

Barbara Hansen, who began as a parent classroom helper and teaching assistant, taught the younger group from 1970 to 1977. Although not a trained teacher, Ms. Hansen was an intuitive problem-solver and found effective ways to reach individual children. Her background was in social work and child care, and she played a central role in determining the school's direction throughout the 1970s, becoming the acknowledged leader during the school's later years.

Joan Nemtin became a full-time teacher with the younger group in 1971 and stayed for three years. She was a newly certified teacher, and her background in working with children with emotional challenges proved to be useful as the school admitted increasing numbers of such students.

Claudia Stein was also hired to work with the younger group in 1970 and was remembered for her language arts program, which included drama and puppetry. Jonnet Garner, who had been trained in the Nuffield science method, joined the staff the following year. She emphasized academic subjects and introduced such art activities as weaving and natural wool dyeing, and one year organized a group to paint the entire outside of the school. Ms. Hansen, Ms. Nemtin, Ms. Stein, and Ms. Garner formed the core group who worked with the younger class between 1971 and 1974.

---

74   Daniel Wood, personal interview, June 1988.
75   Daniel Wood, personal interview, June 1988.

Geoff Madoc-Jones and Tim Frizzell taught at the New School in 1970/71. Mr. Madoc-Jones was a charismatic individual appreciated by parents for the creative work he inspired in his students. Several students remembered Mr. Frizzell for helping them with reading skills. One former student remembered them as a well-organized and effective team, providing one of her best years at the school.[76] However, Mr. Madoc-Jones was not rehired at the end of the year. A number of parents were angry about his dismissal, and Mr. Frizzell resigned out of sympathy.

Some teachers participated in professional conferences and raised the profile of the New School through speaking engagements. In 1970 Claudia Stein attended a national environmental conference and spoke to Simon Fraser University education students on the socialization of children.[77] Barbara Hansen spoke to staff at the North Shore Neighbourhood House and was a panel member at a secondary teachers conference on "fostering creativity in teacher and child."[78]

Staff relations from 1969 to 1971 were affected by some personal and professional issues. The lines blurred between teachers and parents, who together formed a large social group. When tensions arose, the staff dynamics were all discussed openly.[79] Finally, the staff hired a facilitator to conduct evening sessions in communications, which eased teacher relations.[80] The next year a rift developed between the senior and junior class teachers, at times leading to vigorous disagreements. One staff member thought the teachers lacked the skills and experience necessary for effective consensual decision-making and that ultimately the "do your own thing" attitude inhibited staff co-operation. However, although staff relations were strained, the school was not paralyzed as it had been during earlier conflicts.

In April 1969, after three years at the New School, Anne Long left to pursue a career as a writer, a small-press publisher, and an artist.[81] Beth

76   Cara Felde, personal interview, December 1991.
77   New School, newsletter, December 1970.
78   New School newsletter, December 1970.
79   New School teacher, personal interview, May, 1991.
80   Barbara Hansen, personal interview, October 1987.
81   After spending time at Esalen Institute in California, Anne Long (Anna Banana) returned to Vancouver as a practising artist.

Jankola left the school in 1970 after four years to pursue a career as a graphic artist, painter, and poet. Teacher Rita Cohn, an original founding parent, left in June 1971 after having also taught at the New School for four years.[82] Despite some contentious issues, the central core of teachers remained unusually constant between 1968 and 1973. This stability was made possible by the teachers' control of school policy and practice, and by their general agreement about the school's direction.

CURRICULUM

Students chose and developed their own activities within a free-flowing, exploratory, and open-ended curriculum.[83] The teachers agreed with John Holt, author of *How Children Fail*, that "we learn best when we, not others, decide what we are going to try to learn, and when, and how, and for what purpose."[84] But the most important aspect of the New School curriculum was not about learning. Teachers were more concerned about "human interaction and rapport, personal motivation, meaningful social relationships, and unplanned spur-of-the-moment experiences." One group of visitors observed, in typical 1970 parlance, that the teachers were reluctant to "define what the school is all about because to define is to limit."[85] The teachers wanted no limits on their students or on themselves.

Barbara Hansen described the social/emotional objectives in an interview with radio station CKLG in 1972:

> Kids are learning to cope with themselves and to cope with the environment. They have to come in contact with themselves as people and with adults as adults. They come in contact with other kids in the school from four to twelve as individual people with needs and joys and angers and highs and lows. It's hard work. They are working at being human beings and finding out about themselves and the people around them. It's the same for

---

82   Rita Cohn later taught French immersion in the Vancouver School District for many years.
83   Roy Kiyooka, personal interview, June 1991.
84   John Holt, quoted in the New School newsletter, April 1971.
85   UBC Architecture Students, Report, May 1971, 3.

the teachers. It's not the kind of place where you can hide behind a desk or behind a role.[86]

The teachers believed learning had to be fun, "whether in academic learning like math or non-academics like cooking or carpentry." One student described the curriculum this way: "At our school you work for maybe two hours in the morning and then we do different things all though the day. It's not exactly what you'd call play. We do what we want or what we know how to do. We ask the teachers, and if they're not busy they'll help us with it."[87] New School students interviewed in 1972 by the *Vancouver Province* agreed that they did not have to work as hard in mathematics and reading as at their former schools. One said, "At the school I went to before we studied harder. But at our school it's kind of a wide field of learning."[88]

There was little formal academic content. Parents and students described the curriculum as loose, "unstructured," or "laid-back," and one parent said, "There was nothing very challenging in a teaching way."[89] Classes were "sort of compulsory."[90] One former student could not remember doing any mathematics or other academic subjects at all.[91] Another commented, "We had to do a certain amount of academics but it wasn't much. We watched a lot of National Film Board films."[92] Another student remembered sitting down to do academic work in the kindergarten/grade one class, but after that she spent most of her time "on the swings at the park." There was some mathematics offered but "we had a choice to do it or not. We could get away with doing nothing."[93] This de-emphasis on academics was consistent with other North American Romantic schools where teachers were reacting against what they saw as too much book learning in the public schools.

86   Tape recording of original CKLG interview, 1972.
87   Daniel Wood and Michael Shumiatcher, CKLG interview, 1972.
88   Ted Heyes and Margot Hansen, quoted in "Students Do All the Talking at Vancouver's New School," *Vancouver Province,* October 4, 1972, 41.
89   Ed Wickberg, personal interview, December 1987.
90   Daryl Sturdy, quoted in *Vancouver Province*, October 4, 1972, 41.
91   Kiyo Kiyooka, personal interview, June 1991.
92   Scott Robinson, personal interview, December 1991.
93   Cara Felde, personal interview, December 1991.

Language learning included innovative techniques such as Words in Colour.
1970 Photo courtesy of Daphne Harwood

Periodically teachers would plan lessons in the standard academic subjects. Anne Long organized writing activities every morning for several months but finally gave up, citing student lack of interest. She also developed an individualized mathematics program for the first hour of each day. Although most students participated, she was disappointed by the lack of enthusiasm for any structured activities, even creative ones.[94] Daryl Sturdy and Daniel Wood organized mathematics, writing, and science classes, but these initiatives rarely lasted more than a few weeks. One year students signed up for academic work on a large piece of cardboard, but there were no consequences for students who did not work.[95] Joanne Garner taught regular reading and science classes. Daphne Trivett implemented a reading program called Words in Colour, which assigned different colours to different sounds. This method allowed beginning readers to proceed with confidence despite the uncertainties of English spelling and was successful with a number of students.[96] Ms. Trivett also made extensive use of Cuisenaire rods in her mathematics classes.

But these were exceptions, and few students remembered doing much academic work at the New School during these years. Reading was

94   Anne Long, "The New School — Vancouver," 282–285.
95   Aimee Promislow, personal interview, June 1991.
96   Daphne Trivett, Barbara Shumiatcher, personal interviews, October 1987, April 1987. Words in Colour was invented by Caleb Gattegno, a widely influential Egyptian educator who developed several innovative programs in reading and mathematics.

individualized but inconsistent—students found their own library books and read when they felt like it. Most teachers read aloud to students during some part of the school day but there was little reading instruction, and students remembered few formal writing activities. Daryl Sturdy recalled "a lot of incidental reading and incidental learning but the academics were never very strong. The teachers presented ideas and possibilities and the kids went on from there. Students looked after things themselves and provided their own activities."[97]

Many primary students taught themselves to read. One parent reported that his oldest daughter taught herself and then her sister to read.[98] Another parent only discovered that her daughter could read upon her transfer to public school the following year.[99] Joan Nemtin described the primary program:

> There were generally quiet activities in the morning. We would set out activities in areas, such as a science area, cut and paste, arts and crafts, fantasy, a little bit of number stuff, and lots of stories. The kids were free to come and go. There were enough of us to do a good reading readiness program one-to-one, but there wasn't a real reading program. Some kids had trouble reading at the New School and we weren't trained to help them. It wasn't an easy setting to sit around and read.[100]

The teachers incorporated play as a valuable aspect of learning.[101] Mr. Wood organized treasure hunts with clues in the form of science, mathematics, and reading questions, while Mr. Sturdy devised science problems and experiments to promote thinking skills. One year he organized the Great Egg Drop. Students were given a raw egg and had to design a package so that the egg could be dropped from the school roof without breaking. Students used cotton batting, wings, parachutes, and other creative solutions.[102] Teachers had to improvise, for the school did not have

---

97   Daryl Sturdy, personal interview, April 1987.
98   Robert Minden, personal interview, August 1988.
99   Daphne Trivett, personal interview, October 1977.
100 Joan Nemtin, personal interview, December 1987.
101 Incorporating play was consistent with neo-Froebelian views of education.
102 Daniel Wood, personal interview, June 1988.

sophisticated science equipment. Students made batteries out of lemons, mixed vinegar and baking soda to see the reaction, observed tadpoles, and cared for class pets. Such imaginative ideas rarely found their way into the public schools at that time.

The New School continued to emphasize creative expression and students participated in art activities almost every day. Ms. Long, herself an artist, taught batik, papier-mâché, painting, collage, and pottery. Students learned popular 1960s crafts like making sand candles. In the early 1970s artists were brought in to teach origami, tie-dying, weaving, and bead work.[103] Students photographed downtown Vancouver sites, developing and printing the film in the school darkroom in the basement.[104] One former student, a professional photographer, said that taking pictures and developing them at age nine was "the spark that got me going."[105] Many parents, such as musician Robert Minden, were pleased their children had so much opportunity for artistic expression and exploration.[106]

Art projects were a frequent activity. 1970 Photo courtesy of Daphne Harwood

Teachers and parents had friends in the arts community, and students attended openings of avant-garde art shows and an arts festival at UBC. They

103 New School, newsletter, early 1971, Nora Randall document collection.
104 New School, student newspaper, early 1971, Nora Randall document collection.
105 Scott Robinson, personal interview, December 1991.
106 Robert Minden, personal interview, August 1988.

enjoyed "interactive art" and the Vancouver Art Gallery invited New School students to help "create an environment" for several special events.[107] The teachers took students' interests seriously. One year several students wanted to learn macramé and a teacher bought the necessary supplies right away.[108]

Dramatic activity thrived during this period and included acting, play writing, designing costumes, and puppetry for the younger children. Students also participated in film-making, animation, and video work. Daryl Sturdy taught them how to write scripts and operate technical equipment. The older class presented a fashion show at the Vancouver Art Gallery, which featured student-designed clothes against a background of Beatles music. But, as in many alternative schools, the music program was weak, consisting mainly of singing North American folk songs.[109] A local dance studio offered creative movement sessions after school to interested students.[110] Some students pursued carpentry in the workshop while others spent time cooking. The afternoons were usually reserved for art, music, and drama activities.

The teachers divided students into groups for special activities one afternoon each week. One teacher often took her group home to do cooking, while other classes sometimes went on "juice trips" to other children's homes.[111] These were valuable experiences in seeing how different students lived. Teachers also organized occasional "sleepovers" at the school to provide students with an opportunity to get to know each other better. At one sleepover a teacher took the group to a horror film and then to the cemetery at midnight.[112]

Students had access to the duplicating machine and produced a school newspaper. They published field trip reports, interviews with teachers and students, commentary on world events, recipes, advice to parents, and reviews of school plays and art work. Two nine-year-old boys produced a professional looking eight-page magazine of cartoons and jokes entitled *FLOP*. They did all the writing and drawings and even took part in the

107 New School, newsletters, November 1970, December 1970.
108 Cara Felde, personal interview, December 1991.
109 New School, student newspaper, 1971, Nora Randall document collection.
110 New School, newsletter, September 2, 1970.
111 New School, student newspaper, 1971, Nora Randall document collection.
112 Cara Felde, personal interview, December 1991.

technical operations at Press Gang publishers. Most of the publications were written and produced entirely by students without adult assistance.

Unstructured learning was typical at the New School.
Courtesy of *The Ubyssey*, March 1, 1968

Many parents were happy their children were free to follow their interests. One parent said he didn't care if his children learned to read at age six and was more concerned that the school be a gentle place.[113] Another parent thought that, "it was a little chaotic but the kids were having a good time. I like the idea of deformalizing our institutions."[114] Still another wrote in a letter to the teachers: "As a result of their New School experience, my children have become more untidy in their appearance, more opinionated, and more argumentative. They have also become more willing to undertake new experiences, more trusting of people, and enormously creative in the projects they undertake and complete."[115]

There were few rules at the New School. One student remembered the only rule being that students were not allowed to play on the roof, "but we broke it anyway."[116] Another student recalled being allowed to do whatever they wanted, even paint on the walls. Students who did not want to go on field trips were sometimes left unsupervised at the school, and supervision on camping trips was relaxed. One student described their behaviour as "pretty wild. Out in the woods we were uncontrolled, attacking other people's campsites with flaming spears."[117] Accidents occasionally happened, but fortunately no one was seriously hurt. Younger students were prohibited from going to the store but, other than attempts to keep children from screaming and yelling in the hall, teachers allowed students to do much of what they wanted.[118]

Ms. Long was frustrated at not being able to enlist student co-operation in tasks like cleaning up.[119] One former student returned to the New School as an adolescent in 1972 with an improvisational theatre group. He reported that "we could barely get an audience because they were all watching television, and the teachers wouldn't tell them that they couldn't do that."[120] Teachers were equally reluctant to impose censorship and

---

113 Robert Minden, personal interview, August 1988.
114 Ron Hansen, personal interview, April 1987.
115 Bob Gilliland, letter to the teachers, June 7, 1971.
116 Dana Long, personal interview, June 1987.
117 Scott Robinson, personal interview, December 1991.
118 Staff meeting, minutes, September 6, 1973, Nora Randall document collection.
119 Anne Long, "The New School—Vancouver," 286.
120 Eric Epstein, personal interview, July 1991.

debated how to handle students reading pornography or drawing swastikas. Some took a strict libertarian position and criticized others for not understanding the ramifications of censorship, while others felt that to allow abusive expression was an abrogation of responsibility.[121]

Teachers expected the students to work out disagreements among themselves, but some former students were critical of this approach. One student described how she had to learn to be resourceful and "fend for herself, defend herself, and disarm bullies because the teachers would not step in."[122] Another student remembered that "the attitude was to let the kids do what they wanted and I don't remember the teachers doing or saying anything."[123] Still another said that a few students were ostracized and teased without sufficient intervention by the teachers.[124] Peer pressure was powerful and, as sometimes happens within groups of children, certain kids were given a hard time. But the adults rarely intervened even when some behaviour should not have been tolerated.[125] They could not develop an appropriate response to student conflict because "there was no commitment to a clear set of principles."[126] Although some teachers tried to minimize bullying and destructive behaviour, no one wanted to be authoritarian, and the only thing the adults could usually agree on was that "you didn't lay your own trip on anybody else."

The teachers believed that students would develop self-discipline if they were given responsibility.[127] Nevertheless, some teachers tried to set a basic tone and convey certain limits. Teacher Katherine Chamberlain remembered that not all behaviour was accepted and that one student was even sent home. But this was a recurring battle. Overall, the idea of establishing consequences for inappropriate behaviour did not receive much support.[128] Daryl Sturdy explained the school's philosophy on discipline:

121 Robert Minden, personal interview, August 1988.
122 Dewi Minden, personal interview, August 1988.
123 Aimee Promislow, personal interview, June 1991.
124 Cara Felde, personal interview, December 1991.
125 Margot Hansen, personal interview, July 1991.
126 Daniel Wood, personal interview, June 1988.
127 Barbara Hansen, quoted in, "Students Do All the Talking at Vancouver's New School," *Vancouver Province*, October 4, 1972, 41.
128 Daniel Wood, personal interview, June 1988.

We had kids who fought or who said fuck or who gave
each other a rough time. But we dealt with those things,
not by calling down the wrath of the principal, but by
talking to the kids and by having school meetings. We
tried not to have the kind of rules that would create
problems in the first place. Then we could deal with real
problems like fighting when they came up. We didn't try
to keep the lid on.[129]

Daniel Wood added that "if an issue arose it was discussed right there
on the spot."[130] There were few secrets at the New School.

The day-to-day atmosphere at the New School was easygoing. Students
called teachers by first names and student-teacher relations were informal.
Dress was casual and one student who transferred from a West Vancouver
school remembered having to buy jeans immediately. Students played
most of the time and many remembered school as lots of fun. One year
several groups of students built forts right in the middle of the school
building. Roy Kiyooka described the atmosphere as "uncontained liveli-
ness" and said that the New School was the only school for which his
children were glad to get up in the morning.[131] The 1972/73 prospectus
summarized school life as "an easy interaction between the kids and their
teachers, between the school and its environment."[132] Mr. Sturdy recalled
that "the kids were fun to be with," while "the teachers didn't have to
teach anything they didn't want to and could afford the luxury of doing the
things they enjoyed doing. We didn't do a great deal of planning. The days
seemed to flow.[133]

As in earlier years the teachers discouraged competition. There were
no marks or report cards, and teachers conveyed information to parents
through individual conferences. Older students were encouraged to help
younger kids, and children of different ages played together frequently
(several students remembered having been teased for playing with
younger children at public school). Boys and girls played together, and

129 Daryl Sturdy, personal interview, April 1987.
130 Daniel Wood, personal interview, June 1988.
131 Roy Kiyooka, personal interview, June 1991.
132 New School, Prospectus, 1972/73.
133 Daryl Sturdy, personal interview, April 1987.

girls had access to all the activities available to boys, consistent with New School philosophy. Children and adults were encouraged to be nonconforming individuals, and one student explained how "you had to develop a tolerance there." Students felt emotionally supported at the New School.

ACADEMIC DEFICIENCIES

The lack of attention to basic skills caused problems for some students. One student said that she "didn't have any math skills" when she went into public school.[134] Another described how her public school teacher was startled when she showed up in grade five without knowing how to read or write. She never caught up in mathematics.[135] A third student recalled that his younger sister had great difficulty with reading,[136] and a parent described how her son struggled to read traffic signs. Several students reported that they could read for information when necessary but did not read for pleasure. According to one parent, whose son was dyslexic, it took him two years to make up the time he had lost.[137] Another parent said, "My preference would have been for more academics. I was expecting something more along the lines of Montessori or Ashton-Warner. It was a frustration for me."[138] A third parent agreed that "there were kids who managed not to learn to read as well as they should have. One of them was one of my kids. Some kids fell through the cracks."[139]

One student, who attended the New School in grade three when she was far ahead in reading, described that year and her difficult transfer back to public school:

> I feel like I took grade three off. When I went back to Shaughnessy for grade four that was the toughest year of my life because I didn't know a lot of the skills that they had learned in grade three. I had forgotten how to write, I didn't know how to use a dictionary, I didn't know how

134 New School student, personal interview, August 1988.
135 New School student, personal interview, June 1987.
136 New School student, personal interview, April 1987.
137 New School parent, personal interview, April 1987.
138 Sharon Burrows, personal interview, December 1991.
139 New School parent, personal interview, April 1987.

296 Alternative Schools in British Columbia, 1960-1975

to read maps. The only thing I wasn't behind in was math. By grade five I had caught up. I think that one year was an interesting experience but two or three would have been dangerous. Once you were that far behind, unless you were very motivated, you'd never catch up.[140]

Another student who spent six years at the school talked about the academics she missed:

I think a lot of kids left the New School with a lack of basic education. I felt lucky that I went to grade one [in public school] because that's where I learned how to read. If I hadn't gone to grade one I don't know how long it would have taken me to grasp that kind of stuff. In the morning they would try to get us to sit around the table and do arithmetic. But I don't ever remember doing any writing or being encouraged to read books. I wasn't able to make up the academics I lost. The kids were given a lot of power and could decide what was going to happen on any day. I knew kids who didn't learn how to read quicker than out loud; they couldn't get through a book without it taking forever. A lot of what we did could have been turned into informative or educational experiences, even if we had just written about it. You get addicted to the fun part. My younger sister didn't get the basics.[141]

Still another student who attended the New School for grades four and five in 1969–1971 remembered her experience:

I had learned basic reading in grades one to three and was quite good at reading and writing. But I don't remember us doing any academics at all [at the New School]. After the New School I went to a regular school in North Vancouver and I was miserable there because I was so far behind. They put me back a year into grade five. Then I failed grade five so I was two years behind. It became a nightmare that I couldn't get out of. I felt bad particularly since it wasn't my fault. I wish I had kept the same

---

140 Aimee Promislow, personal interview, June 1991.
141 New School student, personal interview, July 1991.

level as all my peers. Halfway through my second try at grade five I quit. If I had started my education at the New School I think I would be illiterate now.[142]

This student eventually went to a Vancouver alternative high school, as well as two mainstream secondary schools, but several years later said, "I never graduated. I'm just getting my grade twelve now."

On the other hand, most students acknowledged that the New School's academic deficiencies were partially balanced by other benefits, including increased verbal skills, assertiveness, independence, and self-reliance. As one former student put it, "We learned to make decisions. We had to live by the decisions we made."[143]

Some teachers had misgivings about the lack of skill-based learning, but attempts to teach reading, writing, and mathematics were somewhat unfulfilled. One teacher acknowledged that "we didn't do as good a job as we could have" and another said that, in retrospect, he would probably have done it differently.[144] Still another teacher added, "The desire for knowledge has to be fed and I don't know how well we did that."[145] One teacher took her own child out of the school when she was old enough to read.[146] But despite occasional doubts the teachers, committed to the free school ideology of the day, were reluctant to make significant changes to the program.

Many students in the post-1970 period spent much of their elementary careers at the New School and developed permanent habits. By the time they reached secondary school, they were too far behind to catch up and had lost confidence in their academic ability. Not that the reading program had been much better in the earlier Progressive years, but students then had spent enough time in public school to ensure the acquisition of literacy skills, and most had substantial exposure to academic learning at home.

As for students with learning disabilities, the teachers did not have the necessary expertise, and in most cases could do little more than help the

142 New School student, personal interview, June 1991.
143 Cara Felde, personal interview, December 1991.
144 New School teachers, personal interviews, June 1988 and April 1987.
145 New School teacher, personal interview, May 1991.
146 New School teacher, personal interview, December 1987.

kids feel better about themselves emotionally. However, this could be a considerable service in itself, considering the lack of learning assistance in the public schools at the time. One mildly dyslexic student described how the New School "saved my life in a way, from the labelling, emotional trauma, and hell" he experienced in grade one at public school.[147] But that still didn't help them learn to read. As one former teacher put it, "If a kid wanted to read you couldn't stop them," but if a child arrived at the school with a reading problem, improvement was unlikely.[148] This lack of specialized expertise in handling children with learning difficulties caused problems for almost all alternative schools.

A few parents with the will or the resources sought the expert help of doctors or specialist teachers. One parent, whose son had a severe learning disability, sent him to the Centre for Exceptional Children at UBC where he learned to read in three months. Although she acknowledged that the New School provided a good environment for her child with the teachers' non-judgemental attitude and policy of allowing students to learn at their own pace, she believed he would not have learned to read without this intervention.[149]

Nevertheless, many New School students during this period did learn basic skills and managed to return successfully to the public school system. One parent reported that his children learned reading and mathematics at the New School, and that they experienced no academic or adjustment problems in public school.[150] One student remembered, while at the New School, working on her own through the grade three math textbook and part of grade four in one year.[151] Another student who spent six of her elementary years at the New School went on to a successful career at a mainstream secondary school. This student learned to read at home and travelled a great deal with her parents. Even so, she reported "it took me a year to get adjusted, but I did well in school after that."[152] Many of the

---

147 New School student, personal interview, December 1991.
148 Joan Nemtin, personal interview, December 1987.
149 New School parent, personal interview, November 1991.
150 Gerry Growe, personal interview, June 1991.
151 Aimee Promislow, personal interview, June 1991.
152 Cara Felde, personal interview, December 1991.

successful students were assisted by professional parents; others spent a relatively short time at the school.

Some public schools put students back a year despite the opposition of their New School teachers. Mr Wood asserted, "Many kids are not behind but if they are most will catch up quickly" and Mr. Sturdy believed that "as long as students were average learners they had no trouble catching up."[153] But students who had learning disabilities, came from unstimulating home atmospheres, or who had spent many years at the school, often experienced academic problems. However, they may have had difficulty in any school setting.

Many New School students from this period attended alternative high schools such as City School, Total Education, or Ideal School throughout their secondary careers. One student was "too scared" to go to a mainstream high school because she didn't have the academic background.[154] Some of those who tried became overwhelmed by the rigid structure, except in a few special programs at schools like University Hill.[155] Some New School students from this period later completed their secondary education as adults. But fewer than in the school's earlier years attended university. One parent described how her daughter graduated from Total Education and took two years at Simon Fraser University: "She wanted to take medicine but what she missed at the New School was discipline." Roy Kiyooka added:

> When all of this came unravelled at the other end, the kids
> found themselves faced with the fact that, if I'm going to
> get ahead in the world I still have to go back to the three
> Rs. Years having gone by, it was not easy for them. And
> some of them did and some of them didn't.[156]

FIELD TRIPS

New School teachers believed students should learn from the outside community and developed an extraordinary field trip and recreation

---

153 Daniel Wood, CKLG interview, 1972; Daryl Sturdy, personal interview, 1987.
154 New School student, personal interview, July 1991.
155 Several secondary alternative teachers enrolled their own children at the New School such as Total Education teachers Phil Knaiger, and Richard and Elizabeth Neil.
156 Roy Kiyooka, personal interview, June 1991.

program.[157] Students went to the beach, to parks, on forest walks, and took full-day trips to Lynn Canyon and White Rock.[158] They went swimming, ice skating, skiing, bicycling, horseback riding, and hiking in the local mountains.[159]

Anne Long and one parent organized a series of urban living trips. They visited the police station, warehouses, Chinatown, the Salvation Army, grain-loading facilities, and two freighters.[160] Another year students toured the Vancouver General Hospital maternity ward,[161] Gastown, the airport, a pulp mill, the police-dog training centre, the universities,[162] and a train wreck.[163]

Students were encouraged to organize tours and they used the telephone to gather the necessary information. They developed independence and often rode the busses alone. Teachers responded readily to student suggestions about places to visit, as one former student explained: "If we were interested in something we would bug a teacher to take us. For example, some kid would ask how neon signs are made. We'd jump in the car and go right down to the factory and ask them to give us a tour."[164] Parents also contributed their own expertise to the school program. One parent who was a doctor came in and put casts on students. Parent musicians played at the school, while other parents conducted cooking lessons, and still others taught kids how to run video cameras.[165]

Student awareness of environmental issues was raised through visits to the Delta city dump, Joshua Recycling, an organic garden in Sardis, salmon spawning grounds, and the Reifel Bird Sanctuary in Ladner. Students also participated in political activities. They interviewed civic

---

157 The field trip program resembled John Bremer's Parkway Program in Philadelphia. See *The School without Walls* (New York: Holt, Rinehart and Winston, 1971).

158 New School, newsletter, February 1971, Nora Randall document collection.

159 New School, newsletters, 1969–1971, Nora Randall document collection.

160 Anne Long, "The New School—Vancouver," 284–285.

161 New School, Prospectus, 1972/73.

162 New School, student newspaper, 1971, Nora Randall document collection.

163 CKLG interview, 1972.

164 Scott Robinson, personal interview, December 1991.

165 New School, student newsletter, 1971. Barbara Shumiatcher conducted cooking classes, and Aurie and Max Felde, both professional classical musicians, performed at the school.

election candidates, attended a Vancouver City Council meeting, canvassed for the NDP, attended a "Jewish solidarity rally," and took part in a protest demonstration against the 1971 nuclear test at Amchitka.[166] One year Ms. Hansen took a group of students to "confront the School of Social Work at UBC."[167] Teachers chose activities that coincided with their own political and social interests.

The New School's ambitious outdoor education program was one of its most innovative curriculum developments. As early as 1968 Ms. Long and the older students spent five days on a farm in the Gulf Islands. Students hiked, rode horses, sighted deer, tried their hand at spinning, visited farm families, and worked out problems of living together in close quarters.[168] The camping program went into high gear in 1969 under Daryl Sturdy's leadership when he and Catherine Pye took the students to Alouette Lake at the end of the school year. Students also camped on Salt Spring Island and went on a survival trip to Gabriola Island where they had to make do with only a tarp, some rope, and a few matches.[169]

The next year, Mr. Sturdy took a group of students aged eight to eleven on a bicycling trip to Vancouver Island "in the Outward Bound tradition."[170] They took the ferry to Nanaimo and cycled to Port Alberni where they took the boat, the *Lady Rose*, to Ucluelet. They continued to Long Beach, where they met parents who had brought supplies, and camped for several days. Mr. Sturdy recalled, "I spent most of my time fixing bikes. Some of the kids had done very little exercise and I was pushing them all the time. It was hard—twenty miles on a bike with just one speed going up and down hills!"[171]

Another time Mr. Sturdy and Ms. James took a group of students to an archaeological site on the Olympic peninsula:

166 New School, student newspaper, 1971, Nora Randall document collection.
167 New School, newsletter, December 1970.
168 Anne Long, "The New School—Vancouver," 281–282.
169 Anne Long, "The New School—Vancouver," 281–282; New School student newspaper, 1971, Nora Randall document collection.
170 Outward Bound sought to build character through adversity, unlike the New School.
171 Daryl Sturdy, personal interview, April 1987.

We hiked down to the beach and during the night it abso-
lutely poured and we got soaking wet. So we decided to
hike all the kids back up and drove to Olympia where we
dried them all out in a laundromat. We headed into the
interior of Washington and eventually ended up at Grand
Coulee Dam.

They followed the Columbia River north and, after some trouble at
the border, returned to Vancouver through southern British Columbia.
They were gone for ten days. According to Mr. Sturdy, the kids "took
a large part" in such excursions. "We didn't mollycoddle them. They
had their own tents and were responsible for their own food. They were
great trips."[172]

Even the youngest children participated in the camping program. In
1971 Barbara Hansen and Catherine Pye took the five- to seven-year-olds
to Alice Lake via the PGE Railway, where they slept overnight.[173] In other
years the younger group went tenting at Sechelt and at Camp Alexandra
near White Rock.

On a camping tour of B.C., students from Vancouver's New School set a log adrift at Syringa Park, avoiding as much as possible the cold water of South Arrow Lake.

We took 24 kids 1,500 miles across B.C.

Ambitious field trips were standard procedure at alternative schools. Daniel Wood image
in *Vancouver Sun* July 8, 1972, with permission from Crisanta Sampang.

In June 1972 Daryl Sturdy, Saralee James, and Daniel Wood took
twenty-four students, aged seven to twelve, on a two-week camping trip
to the Kootenays that covered 1,500 miles. This trip, the culmination of
almost a year of planning, was featured in a full-page *Vancouver Sun* story

172 Daryl Sturdy, personal interview, April 1987.
173 New School, newsletter, June 1971, Nora Randall document collection.

written by Mr. Wood.[174] Students looked after their own food and made their own campsites. This didn't just happen haphazardly; student knowledge and skills were developed over several months. Preparation began with sleepovers at the school followed by two weekend survival hikes on Galiano Island, where students learned how to identify edible wild plants, make fires, build lean-tos, and cook over a campfire. Cooking groups of five students each were responsible for planning, shopping, and cooking according to an allotment of $1 per child per day. If a group shopped unwisely or ate too much during the first few meals, they had to live with the consequences. Students accepted the challenge willingly, and careful shoppers with money left over were allowed to buy junk food. Two weeks before departure students made equipment lists, conducted practice shopping trips, and helped decide where to go and what to see. On departure day three cars crammed with students, teachers, and supplies pulled away. They visited the ghost town at Sandon, a communal farm, a naturalist park, abandoned mines at Hedley and Silverton, and the Arrow Lakes. Students learned how to make fires and what to do when it rains on the campsite in the middle of the night. They also learned how to co-operate and the consequences of not doing so.

The camping trips were a metaphor for New School philosophy. The teachers believed that kids are capable of far more than adults normally give them credit for. They saw their task as providing materials, challenges, or stimulation for students to develop and carry out their own goals and activities. Preparing for the trips created an ideal learning opportunity that integrated writing, mathematics, map reading, cooking, and co-operative planning. The result, according to Daniel Wood, was growth in confidence and responsibility:

> Children are too frequently protected from real challenges
> and self-discoveries by the very people whose job it is to
> promote challenge and discovery. Basic to the philosophy
> of the New School is the conviction that children, given
> considerable responsiblilty, can learn to think, choose,
> and act wisely.[175]

174 Daniel Wood, "We Took 24 Kids 1,500 Miles across BC," *Vancouver Sun*, July 8, 1972, 41.
175 Daniel Wood, *Vancouver Sun*, July 6, 1972, 41.

THE COUNTERCULTURE

The New School parent community changed dramatically between 1967 and 1973 as the school increasingly appealed to artists, writers, musicians, craftspeople, "seekers," and "free-living types of people."[176] Parents were strongly libertarian and objected to the authoritarian structure of the public schools. Many questioned the value of academic learning and felt that the public schools were too book oriented. Parents and teachers were exploring new values about education and about life, and the New School provided an environment where they could work them out without interference. Daryl Sturdy explained why he left the public school system:

> I was tired of being a policeman. A lot of the curriculum was irrelevant. This was a chance to give children more responsibility, to let them have more say in what they were doing, to be friends with the children. It was a time to explore different ideas about what education should be.[177]

The New School was enormously influenced by the counterculture of the late 1960s. This was a movement that took many forms in North America, embodied in expressions of the time such as: experimentation with drugs, "free love," long hair and colourful clothing, "do your own thing," artistic expression, "back to the land," an emphasis on feelings rather than reason, pacifism, spiritual mysticism, communitarianism, anti-materialism, and above all, individual freedom. Alternative school teachers and parents saw themselves as participants in a movement to reform schools and reform society.

Some parents lived communally, many were artists or members of local rock bands, and others ran alternative businesses such as an herb and sprout farm. Many of the children were long-haired kids with names like "Lark" or "Sage," typical choices of counterculture parents.[178] One teacher described the atmosphere (that could also have applied to some other alternative schools):

---

176 Daniel Wood, personal interview, June 1988.
177 Daryl Sturdy, personal interview, April 1987.
178 Photograph collections of Scott Robinson and Margot Hansen.

Parent meetings would often turn into "love-ins." Everybody would sit around singing folk songs. There were plenty of affairs and breakups. There were not many stable families, there were plenty of single people, and it was the age of free love. If parents were together when they got involved in the school, it was more than likely that they would not be together when they left. Field trips were great social events for the adults as well as for the kids. There would be caravans of Volkswagen vans. Parents would sit around smoking dope and flirting with each other.[179]

The kids, meanwhile, would be swimming, climbing trees, and telling ghost stories. "We were like a big family and I think the kids felt well-loved. We were very close," Mr. Wood said.

There was little sexual experimentation among these pre-teenage children. But, on one occasion a few kids engaged in some exploration in a confined area under the basement steps. The teachers attempted to respond with their characteristic openness.

When we found out about it we didn't suspend anybody; we realized that the kids were expressing something they needed to express. Some of the kids who got caught up in this didn't relate to the other kids very well and and didn't feel too good about themselves. We ended up having a class meeting and had the kids verbalize what had gone on and got it all out so we could talk about it. We realized that we weren't all that clear about our own feelings about sexuality. We ended up having a weekend workshop for the staff so that we could deal with the kids from a more positive position ourselves. I think that illustrated how differently we dealt with problems.[180]

Children and adults often attended the many evening events together, such as dances at the school.[181] Although these events were enjoyed by most participants, many were adult-oriented and some former students

179 New School teacher, personal interview, June 1988.
180 Daryl Sturdy, personal interview, April 1987.
181 Personal interviews with New School students, 1990.

believed that at times the school community became a vehicle for the interests of the adults, as well as for the students.

Teachers and parents began questioning gender roles by the early 1970s. On one occasion a male teacher initiated a writing exercise on dreams. To stimulate the students' imagination he brought in some images from magazines, including *Playboy*. The teacher was severely criticized at several angry school meetings. Parents' main objections to the photographs concerned their stereotyping and objectification of women. Following this incident, parents encouraged female students to confront teachers whenever they saw examples of sexist behaviour. The contemporary feminist movement in Canada was in its early stages at this time, and responding to sexism became a central concern of the New School community.

The Human Potential Movement also influenced the New School during the early 1970s. Several teachers and parents did personal growth work and group therapy at Esalen Institute in California and Cold Mountain Centre on Cortes Island in BC, and three parents were popular gestalt therapists. In 1970, when staff relations became strained, "someone suggested that we might work together better if we did a communications workshop."[182] A faculty member from Simon Fraser University presented several sessions on listening, expressing feelings, and taking responsibility in an attempt to resolve issues among staff members.

But the teachers wanted something more intense, so Richard Weaver, director of Cold Mountain Institute, was engaged to lead a weekend gestalt therapy session. The interaction "brought up so much personal stuff between people" that in the fall of 1970 the whole staff went to Cortes Island for an intensive weekend retreat. One teacher described how "it shook the school up and brought interpersonal issues and relationships out into the open."[183] These experiences encouraged some participants to continue this kind of personal exploration.[184]

Encounter group jargon became common during daily school life. Teachers taught students how to express their feelings using phrases like

---

182 Daryl Sturdy, personal interview, April 1987.
183 New School teacher, personal interview, April 1987.
184 New School teacher, personal interview, October 1987.

"I have a resentment about ..." or "I have an appreciation about ..."[185] Teachers described the students with typical counterculture adjectives: warm, vibrant, open, fully alive, human, loving people.[186] One former New School student captured the spirit of the times poignantly: "If you can cope in the world emotionally, everything else is a snap. What is most important is to find out what is right for yourself, find your own truth."[187]

The New School from 1967 to 1973 was shaped extensively by the period and moved steadily in the direction of a Romantic school. This was similar to the experience of other Progressive schools in which the example of Summerhill and the pervasive youth subculture of the sixties forced the adults to change with the times.[188] By the late 1960s most alternative school teachers and parents subscribed to countercultural values and Romantic views about freedom for children. It would have been difficult for the New School to follow any other path.

Alternative schools were places of exploration and experimentation. As Daryl Sturdy suggested, "The New School was a place where we were not bound by a school board, ministry, or administrator. It was a place where we could work with kids in a way we felt was right. There was an overall philosophy—we wouldn't have wanted a traditional school classroom."[189] Alternative educators were trying to create new ways to work with children and with each other. Because this approach was a major departure from what it replaced, there were few rules. That allowed the innovators to push boundaries. In some cases they pushed too far. The New School was a celebration of freedom, individualism, and self-expression. It was a community of individuals reflecting the excitement and idealism of the times, an expression of powerful cultural movements during a turbulent period.

---

185 Cara Felde, personal interview, December 1991.
186 Daniel Wood, CKLG interview, 1972.
187 Scott Robinson, personal interview, December 1991.
188 Susan Lloyd, *The Putney School* (New Haven: Yale University Press, 1987): 224–229.
189 Daryl Sturdy, written comments to the author, December 15, 1998.

Chapter 8

SATURNA ISLAND FREE SCHOOL

The Saturna Island Free School was the most profound example of Romantic education to arise in British Columbia. Its founder, Tom Durrie, grew up in Portland, Oregon, and attended Reed College, a liberal arts institution there, and the University of California at Santa Barbara where he majored in music history and graduated in 1956. He received his elementary teaching certificate from UCSB and taught for three years in southern California. But like many idealistic young teachers, Mr. Durrie believed he was "completely unprepared for the realities of classroom discipline, instructional problems, and school politics."[1] From the beginning Mr. Durrie disapproved of what he saw as the coerciveness of public schools. Active in the teachers' association, he eventually lost his job for speaking out against merit pay.[2] Looking for an idyllic rural life, he moved to British Columbia in 1960 and taught in Burnaby, Kitwanga, and Williams Lake. After a successful year teaching grade seven in Williams Lake, he taught an Intermediate Special Class (aged eleven to fifteen) of "slow learners" and students with emotional problems from 1964 to 1967.[3]

Mr. Durrie rejected traditional discipline early in his career after reading *Summerhill* and the writings of Paul Goodman and Eric Fromm. Teaching

---

1   Tom Durrie, Application to British Columbia Teachers' Federation, September 18, 1971. All school documents are contained in the Saturna Island Free School archive, in the author's possession. I wish to thank Tom Durrie for his generosity in granting me full access to this valuable material.
2   Tom Durrie, personal interview, July 1987.
3   The district superintendent wrote: "Mr. Durrie's classes are informative and interesting. The pupils work in a relaxed atmosphere. The learning situation is very satisfactory to good." R. M. Hall, "Report on Teacher," April 15, 1964.

learning-disabled children, he explained, "threw a lot of the problems of education into very sharp focus for me":

> I became more and more permissive and things were really quite outrageous with kids running around scream-ing and yelling all day long. My acceptablility in the public system was deteriorating rapidly. But the changes that took place in the kids were astonishing to me and to everyone else in the school.[4]

Mr. Durrie observed his submissive students begin to take more control over their lives through practical activities around the school, such as lawn mowing, and was amazed to see them become "somewhat civilized." Even the school principal was impressed and wrote in 1966:

> Mr. Durrie has taken an experimental approach to instruc-tion with his Special Class. Very little conventional aca-demic work is done. Pupils are free to do as they wish. The classroom is very noisy with pupils engaging in many activities—discussion, listening to records, making model cars, constructing articles with woodworking tools, and playing indoors or out. At the beginning of the year several pupils were quite aggressive and one disagreement followed another. Much damage to the building occurred. Gradually, however, they learned to live with one another in a much more harmonious group. Throughout the year there has been an observable change in the behaviour of the students. Aggressive and destructive impulses have worked themselves out. The withdrawn children have learned to assert themselves and to associate with others. They all seem happier than they were a year ago. Mr. Durrie has had to withstand opposition and criticism. However, the benefits to his pupils have made it apparent that the program should be continued.[5]

When Tom Durrie became director of the New School in 1967, he drew upon this earlier experience to take it in a direction significantly different

---

4   Tom Durrie, personal interview, July 1988.
5   A. H. Gubbels, "Report on Teacher by Principal to Inspector," Williams Lake Elementary School, June 20, 1966.

from the Progressive approach of its first five years.[6] He believed children should not be forced to study and should be allowed the freedom to solve their own problems. He envisioned no set curriculum and would take his cue from the students themselves. Presented with almost complete freedom, the older children engaged in destructive behaviour, "creating all kinds of mayhem," and almost no academic work was done. The other teachers and most parents were highly critical of his methods, objecting particularly to his apparent lack of control over the students. The New School finally split into two groups in March 1968, and Mr. Durrie left with the children of parents who supported his ideas.[7]

During Mr. Durrie's tenure as director, the New School hosted a high-profile Free School Conference in December 1967, organized by Lynn Curtis of the Company of Young Canadians. Anything to do with free schools was considered big news in Vancouver at that time, and both major newspapers ran stories about the conference for three days.[8] The approximately one hundred participants from as far away as Ontario included Bob Davis of Everdale Place, Colin Thomson of Knowplace, Bob Barker of the Barker Free School, several education professors, and numerous public school teachers. Mr. Durrie saw the conference as an opportunity to make contacts with other free school teachers. The sessions generated a great deal of excitement and conviction among those attending, and the success of the conference convinced Mr. Durrie even more that free schools were the wave of the future.

After leaving the New School Mr. Durrie organized a "floating free school" for the ten children who remained with his group, meeting in homes and taking field trips to points of interest in the city for the remainder of the spring. He planned to open a "free school" the following September and formed a committee of several parents to begin searching for a suitable location. In April 1968 they inspected an old house on the Fraser River near Southeast Marine Drive. The caretakers were Bill and

---

6   For more on Tom Durrie's tenure at the New School, see Chapter 7.
7   New School General Meeting, minutes, March 14, 1968.
8   *Vancouver Sun*: "Free School Surge Called Spontaneous Development," December 28, 1967, 16; "Boss System Hard to Shake Says Free School Teacher," December 29, 1967, 13; "Public Schools Turning Out Slaves or Rebels, Meet Told," December 30, 1967, 13. "Free Schools Swap Ideas," *Vancouver Province*, December 29, 1967, 6.

Kathy Sheffeld, recently arrived Americans who came to British Columbia in opposition to the Vietnam War. Bill Sheffeld grew up in upstate New York and studied political science and art at the University of East New Mexico. Although he was not an activist, Mr. Sheffeld had quietly supported the civil rights and anti-war movements. He was a "hands-on" practical person skilled in many trades including carpentry, mechanics, and electrical work. Kathy Sheffeld grew up in New Mexico and studied philosophy, literature, and music. Planning to pursue a career in teaching, Bill Sheffeld had completed part of a teacher certification program when his plans were interrupted by the United States draft board, leading to his departure for Canada. The Sheffelds were drawn to Mr. Durrie's free school project and joined the group investigating potential properties.

The Saturna Island school building served its purpose but was often in need of repair. *Victoria Daily Times*, May 30, 1969

Shortly afterwards, somebody saw a newspaper advertisement for a farm for sale on Saturna Island, in the southern Gulf Islands of British Columbia. These islands were isolated and often home to religious communities, artists' colonies, and people looking for a quiet lifestyle. Although the group had not been looking for property outside Greater Vancouver, Mr. Durrie realized it would be advantageous to have "a school of this sort in a rural setting." He believed many of the problems at the New School would not have arisen "if there had been room for children to carry out their activities outdoors or in separate buildings."[9] A dozen adults and children took the ferry to Saturna to inspect the site. The property was twenty-eight acres of rolling meadow and forest with sea cliffs and a private beach. The farmhouse had been built by one of the island's original settlers in 1890 but was now owned by the local teacher and her husband. Mr. Sheffeld advised the group not to buy it because the house was in such disrepair "it was beyond fixing up." But most of the group "fell in love with it" immediately. They bought the property in June for $55,000 and began preparing to establish the Saturna Island Free School that September.

The group scrambled to raise the necessary cash for a down payment. Tom Durrie and his wife, Gretel, raised $8,000 through the sale of their Vancouver house. The Sheffelds contributed $7,000, and Jack and Betty Spears, whose two boys would attend the school, provided $5,000. Others contributed smaller amounts, but it would always be a struggle to "keep the place together" and pay the mortgage. Bill Sheffeld and another staff member, Lyn Bowman, made enough repairs on the house that summer to make it liveable and suitable for a group of children. They jacked the house up to repair the foundation and built two dormitory-style bedrooms with two tiers of three bunkbeds to accommodate six students in each room. But the house was crowded and had no central heating, only two poorly functioning bathrooms, and an inadequate sewage disposal system. However, the fields and outbuildings provided unlimited places for kids to play. Adjacent to the property was a large piece of forest land (privately managed by Crown Zellerbach) suitable for hiking, studying nature, building forts, or just being alone.

9   Tom Durrie, New School Director's Annual Report, February 29, 1968, 12.

In 1969 the group formed a limited company to own and direct the use of the property. The original directors were: Tom and Gretel Durrie, Bill and Kathy Sheffeld, Jack and Betty Spears, and staff members Rini House and Lyn Bowman. As school director, Mr. Durrie insisted on 51 per cent of the shares and control of the school, not wishing to repeat his New School experience. The remaining shares were divided equally among the others. Tom Durrie and Bill Sheffeld, the principal partners, had great respect for each other but were very different in personality. Mr. Durrie was charismatic, cerebral, and Romantic, while Mr. Sheffeld was quiet, practical, and "down-to-earth." Their differing approaches would eventually lead to disagreements and divide the community.

EDUCATIONAL PHILOSOPHY

Similar in outlook to Summerhill, the Saturna Island Free School offered students complete freedom to explore their own interests without pressure from adults.[10] The original school prospectus in August 1968 stated that the school "provides children with the opportunity for individual development in a non-directive, child-centred environment." The prospectus goes on to explain the school's philosophy:

> At Saturna Island Free School children choose for themselves what they want to do. They discover their own potentialities and explore a variety of possibilities while seeking out their own directions. We believe it is by nature the function of the child to learn from all experiences. The responsibility of the staff is to respond to the expressed interests and desires of the child and to offer varied alternatives and ideas without coercion. The low student-staff ratio (5–1) allows each child to form close associations with enlightened and responsible adults chosen for their belief in human nature as a positive force. The school provides opportunities for expression and development of the child's intellectual, scientific, and artistic interests. A

---

10   Prospectus, Saturna Island Free School, August 1968.

regular academic program is available; however participation is completely voluntary.[11]

The "available academic program" never materialized, for Tom
Durrie's outlook was even more Romantic and laissez-faire than that of
A. S. Neill. At Summerhill, voluntary classes were held on a regular and
ongoing basis; students were free to attend or stay away from classes as
they wished. The Saturna Island Free School, however, offered no formal
classes at all. Students were to pursue their own activities, and if they
wanted to learn something would ask a staff member to help them. The
other major difference was the absence of regular Summerhill-style staff/
student meetings to regulate school behaviour.

In 1969 the school produced a new prospectus with the tagline *Learning
how to live; learning how to learn*: "Here is a place where children can
learn about life by living, free from the artificial restrictions of classrooms,
rules, autocratic teachers, and timetables; where children become part of
an active, child-centred community; where living and learning are one: a
life of joy, participation, and freedom." The Romantic notion of freedom
is discussed in the prospectus at length:

> Our philosophy is based upon the fundamental belief
> that human beings are constructive and growth-oriented.
> We believe that, if given the freedom to choose, every
> individual will direct himself with maximum efficiency
> toward optimum growth and learning. It is natural for
> children to explore and learn about their physical and
> cultural environments. But we believe that to operate in
> a fully human way one must be free from external pres-
> sures and artificial demands; free to respond to inner
> drives, integrate experiences, and interact with others.
> We do not believe that it is necessary to set limits, make
> rules, steer, or correct children as they grow and learn.
> Traditional education assumes children are lazy and
> destructive savages who require disciplining and guiding
> before they can become civilized and human. We reject
> these assumptions and believe that love, caring, approval,

---

11   Saturna Island Free School brochure, August 1968.

and self-direction will alone enable children to become fully-functioning individuals. Learning to handle freedom means taking responsibility for our own actions rather than simply learning to follow a set of rules determined by someone else. We learn to trust the human responses of sensitivity, intuition, and reason.

Mr. Durrie and the staff assumed that academic learning would develop naturally out of a context of "daily living" and relationships:

There is little emphasis on textbooks, classes, and curricula. The world is full of so many fascinating and wonderful things to see, to do, to read and hear, that learning becomes an integral part of daily living. We do not set aside times for learning and times for playing. To the child play and work and learning are all the same thing. We dare not stifle or distort this; our job is to support real play rather than kill it with interference and external rewards.[12]

Mr. Durrie saw the flexible timetables and creative teaching methods of Progressive schools as mere tricks to get students to do what adults wanted them to do in the first place. He characterized "New School Progressivism" as an attempt to "foster the intellectual, emotional, and moral growth of children in certain predetermined, though enlightened, directions, and to capture the interest of children in approved activities through the use of sophisticated and modern techniques and materials."[13] In an article written in 1969, Mr. Durrie questioned the assumption that children have to be taught anything at all and whether adults really know the best ways of growing up and living. He noted that children learn such complex skills as walking and talking during the first few years of life without prodding or assistance. What schools do, he wrote, is "turn learning into a chore when it should be one of life's greatest delights." Accepting the positive and constructive nature of human drives as fundamental, Mr. Durrie concluded that "we need not direct learning and growth but simply allow them to happen." He wrote to one parent:

12   Saturna Island Free School, Prospectus, 1969, 2–3.
13   Tom Durrie, New School Director's Annual Report, February 29, 1968, 2.

> We believe that humans are basically constructive and
> growth-oriented and that education should be largely a
> process of letting, rather than making growth happen.
> We feel that happiness is a creative state of mind and that
> being free of external pressures liberates one to respond
> to internal pressures to growth and self-enhancement.[14]

His message to children was: "You are free to be yourself and to do what you like. I trust that you know better than I do what is good for you." Responsibility for making decisions was left to each individual.[15]

Social growth would also be achieved without coercion. As he wrote to a parent, "we believe in the kind of incidental learning that springs naturally from daily living in a varied household, and that changes in behaviour result from understanding and allowing for the needs of other people rather than through force."[16] Mr. Durrie believed a wide mix of ages was conducive to learning to get along and solve problems. As one staff member put it, "We wanted to teach kids to make their own decisions and take responsibility for their lives, to develop a decision-making impulse that had been destroyed by the culture. Then they could learn anything."[17]

This Romantic view struck a responsive chord with those young adults and teenagers who spent the 1960s exploring personal freedom and actively questioning authority. Political activists saw freedom for the young as a natural extension of liberation movements, while artists, hippies, and spiritual seekers considered educational freedom a prerequisite for unleashing individual human potential. They all saw coercive education as an integral component of a repressive, violent, and joyless society.

---

14 Tom Durrie, letter to Mr. Hunt, January 15, 1969.
15 Tom Durrie, "Free Schools: Threat to the System or Harmless Lunatic Fringe," in *BC Teacher* (British Columbia Teachers' Federation), May/June 1969. Reprinted in Stevenson, Stamp, and Wilson eds., *The Best of Times/The Worst of Times* (Toronto: Holt, Rinehart, and Winston, 1972).
16 Tom Durrie, letter to Ms. Kollander, n.d.
17 Colin Browne, personal interview, November 7, 1996.

STAFF AND STUDENTS

Tom Durrie, Gretel Durrie, Bill Sheffeld, and Kathy Sheffeld were joined by two other staff members for the first year. Lyn Bowman grew up in Vancouver and after a short stint in university managed a student cooperative housing venture in New Westminster.[18] He was a pacifist and, in the mid-1960s, trained at the Joan Baez Institute for Non-violence in California, after which he participated in draft resistance activities in the United States. Later he would become a strong advocate of the gestalt therapy methods developed by Fritz Perls, which were becoming increasingly popular among counterculture individuals. Mr. Bowman helped organize the 1967 Free School Conference and assisted at the New School for several months.[19] The other staff member was Rini House, a single parent originally from Saskatchewan, who had read about alternative lifestyles. She met Mr. Durrie the previous spring and joined the group because of her belief in freedom and because some of her children were having difficulties in public school.[20] Ms. House was remembered by many participants for maintaining a feeling of calm stability even "in the face of chaos."[21]

The school opened on September 10, 1968, with twenty-one students aged five to seventeen.[22] Students had a wide variety of backgrounds. During the first two years, students came from Edmonton, Saskatchewan (originally from New York), Quebec, two from Seattle, two from Wyoming, five from California, and one all the way from Mexico (parents were American officials).[23] But most students were local British Columbians, including seven from Vancouver, ten from Vancouver suburbs, three from Victoria, two from Nanaimo, two from Powell River, and one from Chilliwack.[24] In addition, the student body included the three Durrie children as well as two local Saturna Island boys who attended as day

---

18   Rob Watt of Knowplace was also involved in this project.
19   Lyn Bowman, personal interview, November 18, 1997.
20   Rini House, personal interview, October 31, 1996.
21   Ron Forbes-Roberts, personal interview, January 30, 1997.
22   "Salt Air, Forest, Seashore: Saturna Free School Riches," *Victoria Colonist*, September 22, 1968, 25.
23   Student applications file, Saturna Island Free School.
24   Student applications file.

students, one while finishing his grade twelve studies and another because his parents were dissatisfied with the local school. All the other students were boarders.

Saturna students and teachers formed a community on the remote and sparsely populated Gulf island. *Victoria Daily Times*, May 30, 1969

Although the school accepted children as young as five, most were teenagers. Of the forty-two students who attended the school between 1968 and 1970, twenty-five were thirteen and older.[25] In January 1970 there were twenty-one students: five aged 6–8, four aged 9–12, and twelve

25   Application forms and school enrolment list, May 20, 1969.

aged 13–16.[26] Despite Mr. Durrie's attempts to encourage younger children to enrol, there was always a preponderance of older students making
life challenging for the largely inexperienced staff. However, the school
was more successful in achieving a gender balance, and in January 1970
there were eleven girls and ten boys.

Students attended for a variety of reasons, but most fell into three
categories. The first group (about 25 per cent) consisted of children of
parents who believed in the free school ideology and wanted their children
educated outside the public school system. Some of these were countercultural types, others saw the school system as oppressive, while some simply
wanted their children to grow up "naturally." One couple, a dentist and
his wife, were Jewish intellectuals from New York who had spent several
years in a socialist artists' colony in New Jersey that had a Progressive
school. They moved to Canada because of their opposition to the Vietnam
War and were "desperate to place their children in a Summerhill-type
school."[27] Another parent wrote on her son's application: "Ah! If
only all schools were operated with your incomparable beliefs."[28] A
Seattle parent wrote: "We are desperate for a Canadian Progressive Free
School conducted upon the philosophy of A. S. Neill's Summerhill. The
American public school system has put our twelve-year-old daughter on
the defensive. We want her to be free to be herself again."[29] Another
wrote about her daughter's boredom and frustration: "I have noticed a
change in her original curiosity and creative interests since public school
came into her life. I have read *Summerhill* and we feel a definite need for
this type of influence."[30] Another parent said she was "enamoured with
the Summerhill model"[31] and a former student thought that his parents
were looking for "an ideal place where we could grow creatively."[32]

The second group, which constituted a majority of students (increasingly throughout the life of the school), were young people having trouble

26   Tom Durrie, letter to Richard Bower, January 22, 1970.
27   Dr. and Ms. Kaellis, letter to Tom Durrie, March 25, 1968; personal interview,
     October 1996.
28   Application from Ms. Anderson.
29   Ms. Jeffery, letter to Tom Durrie, April 16, 1969.
30   Ms. Kollander, letter to Tom Durrie, May 18, 1970.
31   Betty Spears, personal interview, April 1, 1997.
32   Ken Spears, personal interview, April 2, 1997.

in public school for a variety of reasons. Some had emotional or learning disabilities while others came from troubled families. Others were so
caught up in the drug scene that they would not attend public school or,
in some cases, no public school would take them. The parents of many of
these students had exhausted all other avenues for help, and the Saturna
Island Free School was a last resort. One fourteen-year-old student from
the West Side of Vancouver had become estranged from the public school
system and no high school would accept him.[33] His parents, desperate to
get him out of Vancouver, sent him to Saturna Island, "a place that will
take you." No member of his family came to investigate Saturna. In their
inquiry in 1968 his parents wrote, "At this juncture we are more concerned
with our son, the person, than with our son, the student."[34] This student
recalled the image of waiting for the ferry with his father: "I had no idea
where the Gulf Islands were. The whole thing took place at night; there
was a ferry change and I was sitting there waiting for it. A group of people
from the school met me on the second ferry and took me up to the farm."[35]
Another student who was "kicked out of high school in grade nine" stated
simply that her parents "didn't know what to do with me."[36] Still another
said, "My mum and dad figured I couldn't get into any trouble if they sent
me to an island."[37] The mother of a thirteen-year-old Edmonton girl wrote:

> Valerie has never shown any interest in school, reading,
> or learning but does have the ability. We are sure that she
> has some sort of emotional block. We would like to have
> her away from here as this is where a great deal of her
> difficulty arises. From what I've heard this type of child
> is supposed to flourish at a free school.[38]

A third group (10-20 per cent) consisted of students whose parents
were looking for a place to leave their children while dealing with difficult
life circumstances. The school enrolled the daughter of a Vancouver poet
who was debilitated by drugs, ill health, and mental illness in the family.

33   Saturna Island School student, personal interview, January 30, 1997.
34   Saturna Island School parents, letter to Tom Durrie, November 28, 1968.
35   Saturna Island School student, personal interview, January 30, 1997.
36   Saturna Island student, personal interview, December 1, 1997.
37   Peter Vogel, personal interview, April 16, 1997.
38   Saturna Island School parent, letter to Tom Durrie, October 8, 1969.

A five-year-old girl kidnapped by her father spent several months at the school until the authorities could locate her mother in California. Another parent was unable to find satisfactory childcare during her several stays in hospital.[39] A Seattle parent dropped her thirteen-year-old son off at Saturna in September 1969 and disappeared for four months. In an attempt to find her, Mr. Durrie wrote to the boy's grandmother: "It is winter here and the temperature will soon be below freezing. Mike has only light summer clothes, no sweater or coat, and is without shoes or boots. He would appreciate clothes or a clothing allowance from his mother." Finally the boy's mother sent a letter explaining "I"m in jail sentenced to one year for possession of marijuana. [My son] is in protective custody in Juvenile Court."[40] Some of these children were so emotionally distant from their families that they did not go home for holidays. Such children were a great challenge to a young and largely untrained staff.

Many parents were in financial difficulties due to irregular employment, dysfunctional personal lives, or "voluntary poverty." In some cases payments stopped coming within months after students were enrolled as their parents' financial circumstances changed. In a few exceptional hardship cases students were permitted to stay for reduced fees. Mr. Durrie wrote hundreds of letters asking parents to bring their fees up to date or to replace bounced cheques. One student wrote to explain why he could not return to Saturna: "I have to go to the stupid public school. My Mom is sorry she couldn't send the $100 but my Dad still has no job."[41] Another parent wrote: "I appreciate your patience in the matter of Jamie's school payments. As you know, my intentions are good but this summer I've had bad luck."[42] A single parent from California had to withdraw her son after just three months due to the loss of her job.[43] However, not all Saturna families were living month to month. One parent was a dentist, another was a lawyer, one was a Canada Manpower placement officer, one owned a Las Vegas casino, and one parent

---

39 Saturna Island School parent, letter to Tom Durrie, May 20, 1969.
40 Correspondence with the family of a student, 1969 to 1970.
41 Saturna Island School student, letter to Tom Durrie, January 15, 1970.
42 Saturna Island School parent, letter to Tom Durrie, October 13, 1970.
43 Saturna Island School parent, letter to Tom Durrie, October 7, 1968.

was an airline pilot (whose brother was the Mayor of Surrey).[44] Five parents
were public school teachers and one was an elementary principal.

School finances were always on the edge. Mr. Durrie wrote to one
parent: "We run the school on a tiny budget. Our staff receives no salary.
Our budget is kept in a precarious balance if our monthly income remains
constant."[45] Initially, tuition fees were set at $1,000 per year including
room and board.[46] This was a modest fee for a boarding school; tuition
was kept "as low as possible" because many parents had low incomes. In
1969/70 tuition was increased to $1,250, and the following year it rose
to $1,500 for teenagers.[47] However, as the school's financial situation
deteriorated and because many students were staying for short durations,
the staff decided to institute a monthly fee of $160.[48] In early 1971 this
was raised to $200 per month. The increase was justified by the offer-
ing of "sensitivity training groups" and the addition of a "qualified social
worker."[49] Bill Sheffeld did most of the school's bookkeeping.

Staff members essentially worked for nothing, receiving only room
and board (a salary of $10 per month was added in 1970). The school
received one loan from a parent, a few modest donations, and the occasional contribution of such needed items as a freezer.[50] But the school
remained in a state of month-to-month survival, and making ends meet
was always a struggle. Monthly mortgage payments, extensive repairs to
the building, parental default on tuition fees, and an unstable enrolment all
took their toll.

Staffing at Saturna was informal. Since staff members received no
salary and had no specific duties it didn't really matter who was officially
on staff and who wasn't. Individuals would "drift in" and were interviewed
informally by the group. Some would stay for a short time while others
would remain for a year or more. A few individuals considered to be free-
loaders were asked to leave, but the school community was exceptionally

44   The student's grandfather had been a Social Credit MLA.
45   Tom Durrie, letter to Ruth Wolfe, September 24, 1969.
46   Saturna Island Free School, Application Form, 1968/69.
47   Saturna Island Free School, Application/Registration Form, 1969/70.
48   Fee structure data from letters to parents.
49   Tom Durrie, letter to Vancouver Children's Aid Society, November 26, 1970.
50   Correspondence of Tom Durrie with Dr. Kaellis and Ms. Anderson.

tolerant of disruptive or eccentric behaviour, and most people who wanted to stay were allowed to do so.

At the end of the first year in June 1969, Lyn Bowman left the school and his place was taken by Colin Browne. Mr. Browne, in his early twenties, grew up in Victoria and attended Seven Oaks Military College there. He developed an interest in education through teaching grade eleven English in the navy. He was attracted to the folk music, poetry, and art of the 1960s as well as opposition to the Vietnam War: "It felt natural to oppose the military/industrial complex." He eventually left Seven Oaks, lived in a shack, grew his hair, and ended up on Saturna in 1969. Mr. Browne loved the "big family of people," liked the kids, and was more interested in the human relationships than in the Summerhill ideology.[51]

Lynn Curtis grew up in a family of teachers in Vancouver and earned a degree in social work and a teaching certificate from the University of Victoria in the early 1960s. He was influenced by socialism and "Christian compassion," leading him to join the Student Union for Peace Action (SUPA) and later the Company of Young Canadians in 1966. Mr. Curtis was a subject of media attention as a leader of the "radical/hippie" faction of the CYC attempting to politicize the young middle-class volunteers.[52] He hoped to achieve political and cultural change through working with students and saw free schools as a vehicle for the "liberation of youth."[53] He organized the Free School Conference at the New School in late 1967, where he met Tom Durrie, and Mr. Curtis spent two years at Saturna beginning in 1969. However, he was occupied by politics, cultural change, and gestalt therapy, and had minimal interaction with students.

Judy Pruss and Dorothy Wheeler joined the staff in 1970. Ms. Pruss came to British Columbia from California, where she studied psychology and education at UCLA and had been active in the Vietnam War resistance movement. She knew other alternative school teachers and heard about Saturna through Lynn Curtis.[54] Ms. Wheeler grew up in New York and moved to San Francisco where she was drawn to the "openness, possibility,

51 Colin Browne, personal interview, November 7, 1996.
52 Ian Hamilton, *The Children's Crusade* (Toronto: Peter Martin, 1970) 14–37, 46–58.
53 Lynn Curtis, personal interview, November 10, 1997.
54 Judy Rogers, personal interview, December 10, 1997.

and excitement" of the counterculture.[55] She had a degree in psychology and looked forward to working with children and living communally.[56]

Daily Activities

The school opened "in the middle of a construction zone" and renovations continued for over a year. Students slept in two main bedrooms, six to a room, but cabins and outbuildings on the property served as extra sleeping quarters. These were popular with the older students because they were free from any supervision. During the third year a dormitory cabin was built to relieve the crowding in the house. One student recalled that "it was pretty rough, a lot of people just sleeping wherever they could."[57] Another student remembered mud all winter and the feeling of camping out. Some staff lived in the house, but eventually the Durries and Sheffelds had their own cabins, and one staff member slept in his truck. During the first year, before any central heating was installed, the house was very cold. The winter of 1968/69 was particularly severe, and everyone kept themselves warm in front of one of several fireplaces in the house. During the bitter cold spell in January, everyone slept in the kitchen near the fire and many remembered it as quite an adventure. During the warmer months some students slept outside in the hay barn or even in the woods. Students looked after their own rooms, their own beds, and their own possessions and kept them as tidy or untidy as they wished.

Students played in small groups and separated themselves into older and younger age cohorts, and into night people and morning people, so the house was rarely quiet. The young children got up early and breakfast, which lasted all morning, was usually prepared by one of the adults. During the second year Mr. Browne cooked large morning meals and became known as "Uncle Breakfast." The teenagers, having been up most of the night, slept late and fended for themselves as they straggled into the kitchen for breakfast. Dinner was usually a group meal prepared by

---

55 Dorothy Wheeler, personal interview, January 2, 1998.
56 Short-term staff members included education student John Laing, Loren and Janet Miller, and Ian Rowe. Shane McGarrett was the cook for several months, and Peter Wheeler and Rosamonde Hunt helped in the kitchen.
57 Ron Forbes-Roberts, personal interview, January 30, 1997.

an adult, although not everyone participated regularly. Lunch was sometimes eaten together, sometimes not, but there were large quantities of bread, peanut butter, honey, and jam available twenty-four hours a day, and students made their own sandwiches. Food was low budget and at times repetitious, but was usually wholesome. Judy Pruss introduced the students to such healthy items as whole wheat bread and granola, which they eventually accepted.

Domestic activities were irregular, chaotic, and "catch as catch can." One parent who visited in December 1969 remembered the "mess, the squalor, and the cold."[58] Three square meals a day were usually provided on a regular basis, but during periods when the staff was preoccupied with problems, meals became sporadic and students had to manage for themselves. This was also true of housekeeping—staff members sometimes spent long hours doing laundry and at other times the children were on their own for these domestic tasks. Day-to-day living consumed most of the staff time. Groups of students frequently accompanied staff members on shopping trips to Victoria and occasionally to Vancouver to do bulk shopping at Famous Foods. Most children received an allowance of fifty cents per week, which they spent at the local store or on trips to town.

At the Saturna Island Free School, students had opportunities to interact with animals.
Victoria Daily Times, May 30, 1969.

---

58   Rhoda Kaellis, personal interview, October 2, 1996.

Most students spent a great deal of time outside, and especially for the younger children, it was an "active healthy lifestyle."[59] They hiked and explored on the adjacent forest land, walked to the beach, observed tide pools, and spent many hours climbing trees, building forts, and playing in the hay barn. Some children helped out in the vegetable garden or looked after the chickens, cats, rabbits, and goats. Several girls had horses and enjoyed riding them on the farm. One student remembered "lots of wonderful junk, old machinery, and equipment" on the property.[60]

Old farm equipment offered students hands-on opportunities to learn about mechanics.
Daily Colonist, September 22, 1968

Some of the older boys became interested in carpentry, mechanics, or engineering and spent hours with Bill Sheffeld working on house and property improvement projects. One student helped build Mr. Sheffeld's cabin, and several students credit him with teaching them lifelong useful skills. Others learned engine mechanics or how to use hydraulic equipment to move boulders. But most of the teenagers spent the winter inside sitting around the fire talking, smoking, and listening to music. After dinner, staff and students sat around the big dining room table playing cards or board games, doing artistic activities, or making music until late in the evening.

---

59   Tim Lucey, personal interview, November 12, 1997.
60   Miles Durrie, personal interview, April 22, 1997.

Music played an important role at Saturna. Mr. Durrie had a music degree and was a competent pianist, but is most remembered by staff and students for his love of opera. Listening to the Saturday afternoon opera production on CBC radio became a weekly ritual. Mr. Durrie had a comprehensive collection of librettos so students could follow along as they listened. Kathy Sheffeld was a guitarist and sang 1960s folk songs with groups of children. Several older students spent many hours playing guitar. Two former students moved to Victoria and became professional musicians, one a guitarist, the other a vocalist.

Art activities were less prevalent at Saturna than at most other alternative schools. Mr. Sheffeld was an artist and had trained as an art teacher, but he was so busy looking after the physical plant that he only had time to organize artistic ventures in the evenings. Nevertheless, art materials were always available and some students would paint or make collages. Occasionally a visitor would offer to teach such crafts as pottery, tie-dying, or making stained glass windows.

Staff and students organized the school library. *Daily Colonist*, September 22, 1968

Saturna Island Free School founder Tom Durrie believed that conventional education turned learning into a chore. *Vancouver Sun*, November 24, 1969

Unlike at Summerhill, Saturna had no scheduled classes or organized academic activities. Mr. Durrie believed that "informal learning" was more effective, as he explained in a 1969 full-page *Vancouver Sun* article, "Informal Learning Best Way to Knowledge."[61] He cited various examples of spontaneous learning: reading Chaucer due to a chance mention of the author's name, mathematics growing out of cooking from recipes, questions about anatomy arising from observing the animals outside, students learning English through participation in the school paper or writing letters "because they want to communicate, not because they are ordered to write an essay." The school received a full set of textbooks from the

---

61   Robert Sarti, "Informal Learning Best Way to Knowledge" *Vancouver Sun*, November 24, 1969, 16.

Department of Education but they were virtually never used. A few students did a lot of reading as they "ploughed through" the school's large library. Occasionally a staff member would interest a group of younger students in some reading or arithmetic, but this was usually short-lived. The school organized an NFB film series and invited the community at large to the showings.

A few students did pursue serious studies, but they had to be highly motivated and disciplined. Mr. Durrie wrote to one student:

> You can get your grade twelve here with full recognition
> from the department, although in all fairness, I must tell
> you that it is not easy. If you are really determined to do it
> you can cover the material a lot faster than in a classroom
> where you have to spend time waiting for other students
> to catch on and reviewing material you already know.
> You can tailor your studies exactly to your own needs and
> abilities. However, a lot of motivation is required.[62]

One local student completed his grade twelve requirements with the help of tutoring from Mr. Durrie, and one teenage girl made progress in her grade eleven English and mathematics.

But for the great majority of students, life at Saturna Island was far removed from academic activity, and few returned to formal schooling after their experience there. One student said, "There wasn't any academic activity that I ever saw."[63] Another remembered "virtually no academics" other than some private reading, and a third said there was "no teaching at all."[64] One staff member recalled that "every once in a while someone would ask to be taught something," but interest rarely lasted more than a few hours.[65] Another felt she was more a "caretaker than an educator."[66]

Mr. Durrie answered numerous inquiries from public schools about the academic standing of former students. Although the school did not keep "any kind of academic or attendance records," he did supply anecdotal

62 Tom Durrie, letter to Cam Dodds, August 27, 1970.
63 Ken Spears, personal interview, April 1997.
64 Tim Lucey, personal interview, November 12, 1997; David Spears, personal interview, April 2, 1997.
65 Colin Browne, personal interview, November 7, 1997.
66 Dorothy Wheeler, personal interview, January 2, 1998.

comments regarding length of attendance, specific interests, and personal traits. For one student in grade twelve he attested to completion of graduation requirements, and for another he ascribed letter grades for all grade eleven subjects. For another he wrote, "In my opinion Chris would be quite able to function at the grade eight level." However, he only did this in the few instances where students had actually done the work, and in most cases Mr. Durrie recommended that students repeat a grade. Regarding one student he wrote: "While Charles did some work in geography and biology while in attendance here it was not sufficient to constitute completed course work."[67] For another: "Jesse would be suited to a grade nine class in most subjects but I recommend he be given special remedial work or remain on the grade eight level in mathematics. I'm sure he will be found to be an interesting and co-operative student."[68] And for still another: "D'Arcy has done some academic work in grade ten subjects, particularly math. However, his work has been of a sporadic nature and I would not want to say that he has satisfactorily completed any of the course work for the grade. It would probably be best if he started grade ten over again in September."[69]

Decision-making at Saturna Island Free School was very informal. Tom Durrie had ultimate control over the school operation, but only used it in rare cases such as when he asked a staff member to leave in 1971. Like many alternative organizations, the group had difficulty agreeing about how to make decisions and how democratic they should be. Mr. Durrie encouraged individuals to act spontaneously, believing "if you want to do something, go do it."[70] The shareholders only met twice in three years to resolve crises affecting the very existence of the school. But informal discussions about practical questions and sometimes emotional staff meetings about such serious issues as the school's policy on drug use were held frequently. There were no Summerhill-style "self-government" meetings, however. Mr. Durrie believed such meetings only served to

67   Tom Durrie, letter to Mark Twain Junior High School, Los Angeles, September 17, 1969.
68   Tom Durrie, letter to E. D. Feehan Catholic School, February 14, 1970.
69   Tom Durrie, letter to Point Grey High School, May 19, 1969.
70   Lyn Bowman, personal interview, November 18, 1997.

control "anti-social elements," and that issues between individuals were better resolved informally.

One of the most difficult issues for the staff was whether they should ever impose their wishes on students. As Mr. Durrie wrote to one parent about whether the school should enforce a no-drugs policy: "I suppose the problem which confounded us the most was do we, because we are the grown-ups, have the right to make such a decision about the lives of the kids here."[71] This attitude led to problems in areas of drug use, sexuality, and personal safety. Young children were left unsupervised in potentially dangerous situations, and two students took falls while playing on the cliffs. Teenagers were allowed to travel off the property, even off the island, if they wished. A group of students was permitted to burn candles at night in the hay barn and another student set a field of grass on fire. Staff expected the children to settle their own disputes and, according to most students, rarely intervened even when students were cruel or bullying toward others. If some adults wanted to prohibit a particular behaviour, others would disagree on the grounds that "it's a free school." It was difficult to implement discipline if the staff could not agree, and the students soon learned that they could do almost anything. The adults' unwillingness to direct the lives of the children arose partly because staff members, mostly in their early twenties, were caught up in their own exploration of new values and the celebration of their new-found freedom from traditional social standards.

PUBLIC RELATIONS

Throughout his career, Tom Durrie was a tireless and eloquent advocate for the free school movement. He was a prolific correspondent and wrote hundreds of letters to parents, prospective parents, visitors, supporters, and government officials. He published several articles, including "Free Schools: Threat to the System or Harmless Lunatic Fringe?" and "Free Schools: The Answer or the Question?"[72] Mr. Durrie also appeared on

---

71   Tom Durrie, letter to Daniel Elam, July 18, 1969.

72   Tom Durrie, "Free Schools: Threat to the System or Harmless Lunatic Fringe?" *BC Teacher*, (British Columbia Teachers' Federation), May/June 1969; Tom Durrie,

television and radio talk shows and accepted numerous speaking engagements. He was invited to address a teachers' convention in Alberni in 1970 because "you have spoken out against traditional methods and have adopted an exciting, radical, and controversial approach to education. We, as fellow members of the teaching profession, regard your approach with avid interest."[73] The organizers hoped to provoke a "reassessment of educational goals in light of the unrest of the younger generation." Social change was a timely subject in 1970, and Mr. Durrie spoke to large teacher gatherings at professional development conferences in Oliver and Saanich on "The Role of the School in a Changing Society."[74] He was no stranger to teacher organizations, having served on the executive of the BC Association for Teachers of Special Education.

Many university students were interested in free schools and Mr. Durrie spoke regularly on all three BC campuses. He addressed an Education Symposium on "Schools and Free Schools" sponsored by the UBC student society in 1968, and another in 1970 sponsored by Arts I, an interdisciplinary humanities program.[75] At a talk to UBC education students in 1971, Mr. Durrie was billed as the "founder of the most radical free school in North America."[76] He addressed a Future Teachers Conference at Simon Fraser University and spoke to over two hundred students in a second year education course in 1968. The professor wrote to Mr. Durrie that his "students have argued at some length about free schools along the lines of Summerhill and the Barker Free School but we need someone of your calibre."[77] Mr. Durrie took part in a Victoria Youth Conference

---

"Free Schools: The Answer or the Question?" in Byrne and Quarter, ed., *Must Schools Fail?* (Toronto: McClelland and Stewart, 1972), 33–44.

73   J. R. Nelson (Alberni teacher), letter to Tom Durrie, November 10, 1969.

74   Correspondence and program announcements from R. W. Lawson, Secondary Supervisor, Saanich and Gulf Islands School Districts, December 19, 1969. Another speaker at the conference was Dr. Charles Gregory, co-founder of Craigdarroch School.

75   Other participants were Jim Harding (Knowplace), Bob Rowan (UBC philosopher), Martin Loney (SFU student activist), and Alf Clinton (Vancouver School District assistant superintendent, an enthusiastic supporter of alternative schools during the 1970s).

76   Saturna Island Free School publicity materials.

77   MacDonald Burbidge, SFU, letter to Tom Durrie, October 29, 1968. Mr. Burbidge was later a parent at the New School and a school trustee in North Vancouver.

and gave several lectures at the University of Victoria.[78] In 1971 he embarked on a cross-Canada tour that included appearances in Edmonton, the Universities of Saskatchewan and Manitoba, and the Ontario Institute for Studies in Education, in Toronto.[79]

Tom Durrie and Lynn Curtis believed it was part of the school's role to contribute to the growth and development of the "free school movement." In June 1970 Mr. Curtis published one hundred copies of *Free School: The Journal of Change in Education*, a package of articles written by Paul Goodman, Brian Carpendale (SFU instructor), and Jim Harding (student leader). Mr. Curtis also organized two successive summer conferences at Saturna in 1970 and 1971, on one occasion hosting over two hundred people for ten days.[80]

Mr. Durrie communicated with many alternative organizations from the Summerhill Society in New York to the *Georgia Straight*, Vancouver's underground press. He corresponded with staff at other free schools, attended a free school conference in California, and listed Saturna in several North American free school directories.[81] He also maintained liaison with social service agencies. He spoke to the Canadian Mental Health Association, hosted the director of the Maples, a treatment centre for emotionally troubled adolescents in Burnaby,[82] and regularly wrote to the Vancouver Children's Aid Society and the Victoria Family and Children's Service.

These prolific writing, speaking, and networking activities made Saturna Island Free School well-known among alternative schools across North America. As a result the school received a constant stream of visitors. Some planned their visits in advance while others just drifted in. Whenever a "hippieish" looking young person walked off the ferry, local

78   The conference was organized by Lynn Curtis. An entire session was devoted to "The Status of Women," unusual as early as 1968.
79   "Free School Head Plans Nation Tour," *Victoria Times*, January 29, 1971, 35.
80   "School Workshop Marathon Set," *Victoria Times*, June 27, 1970, 12; letter from Tom Durrie to "George," July 30, 1971. David Suzuki participated at this conference.
81   Saturna Island Free School was listed in the "Summerhill Bulletin," in New York; the "New Schools Exchange Newsletter," in California; the "Teacher Dropout Centre," in Massachusetts; and the "Carleton Collective Communities Clearinghouse," in Vermont.
82   Correspondence from Tom Durrie to Peter Lavelle, director of The Maples in Burnaby.

residents immediately directed him or her to the free school. Some visitors stayed for a weekend, some for a month or two, and others never left. There were "so many people wandering the roads in those days, such a parade of people coming through" that who could come and who could stay became a constant issue. In 1970 the staff decided to limit visits to two days per month. Some individuals were helpful, fit in well, and moved on after a short visit, but others were merely looking for a free place to stay. In a few cases unsavory visitors were asked to leave because of drugs, sexual exploitation, or because they were not contributing to the community.

Mr. Durrie was deluged with requests to visit. Some were from teachers at other alternative schools including the Bellingham Community School, the Little School in Seattle, the Putney School in Vermont, and Peninsula School and Pacific High in California. Other requests came from free school students at Knowplace, the Victoria Free School, and as far away as Everdale. A group of Craigdarroch students visited, one of whom later attended Saturna. Letters came from a dissatisfied public school student in Campbell River and a group of grade eleven Alberni students in an "experimental humanities program." Four teachers from California brought nineteen students to camp at Saturna for five days in 1969. Requests also came from public school teachers, a teacher "naive enough to still believe in Summerhill," and a sociology student doing research on "how free schools are affecting the traditional school system."[83]

The school also received numerous requests from education students at UBC and Simon Fraser, and even one from Chicago's Northwestern University to study the "methods and techniques" of free schools. Although Mr. Durrie welcomed most prospective visitors, he disapproved of education programs and strongly discouraged the education students. As he replied to one such request, "When people talk about methods and techniques I am at a loss to know how to answer because we simply do not think in those terms. Since we don't have classes here there would be little opportunity to observe teaching in progress."[84] To an SFU student who wanted to bring her seminar group to Saturna he answered, "Since there are no regular planned activities or scheduled events other than

83   Visitor Request File, Saturna Island Free School.
84   Tom Durrie, letter to Ms. Hoague, Fairhaven College, Bellingham, February 6, 1969.

mealtimes here, most visitors feel that nothing is happening; planning for a group of visitors necessarily brings to a halt all the usual things that might be going on."[85] In another reply he added that "the real learning that happens here involves assuming personal responsibility for one's own life and conduct."[86]

In many ways, Saturna was more like a commune than a school, and the group received many requests from young people "visiting communes around the country." Some intended to start their own communes and wanted to learn from the experience of existing groups. Others were "former communards" or sociologists gathering data for books on the commune movement. Two students from Friends World College, a "Quaker experimental school" in Ohio, asked to visit because of their interest in "intentional communities, free schools, and liberating environments."[87] Mr. Durrie explained that Saturna was a school and rarely discouraged anyone from coming, but he became less patient as the requests piled up. In refusing a visit to two college students he wrote: "Every so-called intentional community runs aground on pretty much the same problem—who's going to do the work. As the dishes pile up and the floor gets dirty, you can have endless meetings, discussions, and work-plans all as a way to stave off doing things."[88]

Parents occasionally visited, and one recently separated parent actually moved onto the property for several months with his trailer and goats. But for the most part, parents played a minor role in the life of the school (other than paying fees) due to the isolation of the community, and, in the case of a few parents, their lack of capacity or opportunity. Some parents didn't visit the school during their children's stay. This contrasts strikingly with the zealous parental involvement at alternative schools like the New School.

The lack of parent participation led to some awkward situations. One California father arranged for his eight-year-old son to spend the Easter holidays with an aunt and uncle in Vancouver. His relatives were shocked

85   Tom Durrie, letter to Ms. Soane, SFU, April 6, 1970.
86   Tom Durrie, letter to Mr. Detzel, November 9, 1970, Saturna Island Free School archive.
87   Mr. Powell and Ms. McClure, letter to Tom Durrie, October 18, 1969.
88   Tom Durrie, letter to "Cindy and Marlin," Manchester College, Indiana, July 24, 1970.

by the boy's appearance and stories about the school and wrote to the boy's grandmother:

> Jamie's hair was long and dirty to the point where it actually smelled. His face and hands had not seen water in many days and his filthy clothing would have stood alone. He proceeded proudly to tell us fantastic stories about his school. "We don't have any grades or classes or books. If you want to know something you just ask. I'll teach myself to write some day. We go to bed and get up whenever we want to and sometimes we fix our own food. We only take a bath if we want to. I never clean my teeth anymore. I play down by the ocean early in the morning before anyone else is up. I smoke cigarettes every day. I buy the kind you make yourself." We decided to see the school for ourselves and everything Jamie had said was true. We were amazed to find the children at the dock preparing to go fishing on a school day. They had their faces painted with psychedelic designs. A boy of twelve was reading one of the filthiest sex paperbacks imaginable and another boy spoke to us in language that made us blush. The school building was run down and the floors were littered with filth. Jamie rarely sleeps in his room. The school is a breeding place for hippies and nonconformists. We feel that the school will be closed down within a short time. It is not a school, it is more like an animal farm.[89]

This description was typical of the general feeling among British Columbians about hippies, communes, and countercultural lifestyles. But despite the cultural gap, relations between the school and the local community were cordial. Tom Durrie served as vice-president of the Saturna Island Community Club and was "a valuable asset at island meetings."[90] Bill Sheffeld was well liked on the island and was valued for his practical skills. Mr. Durrie described the local residents as "kind, friendly, and

---

89 Letter from a Saturna Island School student's aunt to his grandmother, April 9, 1970.
90 R. W. Pillsbury, *Gulf Islands Driftwood*, September 2, 1971.

generous,"[91] and even the local minister was friendly. However, many stories spread about the school among the local residents, some of them undoubtedly true, others probably exaggerations. Stories abounded about teenage girls riding horses around the island naked, and the *Gulf Islands Driftwood* reported in November 1968 that a Saturna resident "really popped both eyes when he saw a naked teenage female swimming and diving for starfish from the local float."[92] The staff's tolerance of almost any behaviour and the lack of a viable academic program left the school vulnerable to criticism and harassment from public officials.

DRUGS AND SEX

As with many other 1960s non-mainstream ventures, drugs became a part of life at the Saturna Island Free School. During the first winter the use of marijuana and LSD among the teenage students usually occurred in a cabin away from the main house and remained relatively discreet, "an open secret" as one student put it. Since the teenagers were permitted to travel at will, drugs could be bought in Vancouver, and when the supply at the school was plentiful, individuals might be high for several days at a time. The staff was aware of the drug problem and consistently disapproved of their use, but "the kids, sensing our ambivalence to imposing our desire upon them, went ahead and used the drugs covertly because, after all, what would we do if we found out anyway?"[93]

In the spring of 1969, a parent informed Mr. Durrie about extensive drug use among students. Mr. Durrie's primary concern was "the ever-present danger of the illegality of their use," for the discovery of drugs on school property by the authorities would result in almost certain closure. He also perceived drug use to be "of questionable value in relation to the school's function."[94] Somewhat older than the other adults, Mr. Durrie

91   Tom Durrie, letter to Mr. Pillsbury, Saturna Island Community Club President, August 25, 1971.
92   *Gulf Islands Driftwood*, November 28, 1968.
93   Correspondence between Tom Durrie and Daniel Elam, July 6, 1969 and July 18, 1969.
94   Tom Durrie, letter to Daniel Elam, July 18, 1969.

told a parent, "I guess I'm just enough of the wrong generation to fail to see any need or use for drugs."[95]

Mr. Durrie wrote to one parent about the problem in April 1969:

> I am in the throes of what seems to be a recurring problem in free schools—drugs. We can't risk the safety of the little kids by tolerating drug use on the property. Those who don't agree have found it necessary to develop elaborate systems of deceit and subterfuge. People have to make a choice between the school and drugs, the two cannot coexist. Therefore, I am asking anyone who feels they cannot live here without drugs to leave.[96]

To a prospective parent he wrote: "It has to be understood that drugs are not used at the school at all. The youngsters who come here have to make a choice: either they live here without using drugs, or they do not live here."[97]

During June 1969 the staff had several meetings about drug use. The essential issue was "do we go on disapproving and being ignored or do we invoke sanctions?"[98] They decided to take a hard line—drug use at the school would not be tolerated. Any staff caught using drugs would be asked to leave, and student drug-users would be suspended for four months (most feeling expulsion was too severe). Late one night in January 1970, Bill Sheffeld discovered nine of the older students using marijuana in one of the upstairs bedrooms. They were suspended and directed to leave the school immediately. When two students asked to be accepted back before the four-month period expired, the staff held firm. In explaining the lack of leniency to one of the students, Tom Durrie wrote, "It is necessary for all of us, once in a while, to say that we're going to do a thing, and then actually do it."[99] Since the nine teenagers accounted for almost half the student body, this was a devastating financial blow for the school, as most did not return.

---

95   Tom Durrie, letter to Ms. Griffin, July 16, 1969.
96   Tom Durrie, letter to Ms. Wolfe, April 19, 1969.
97   Tom Durrie, letter to Ms. Hansen, January 16, 1970.
98   Tom Durrie, letter to Daniel Elam, July 18, 1969.
99   Tom Durrie, letter to Saturna Island School student, April 29, 1970.

The student suspensions resulted in decreased drug use at Saturna and students began to take some responsibility for policing themselves. But the problem never disappeared. Some staff members continued to use drugs off the property and had stashes hidden on the adjacent forest land. Drugs brought in by visitors were even more difficult to control, and some students resented that drug use among visiting adults was tolerated.[100] Although Mr. Durrie and Mr. Sheffeld tried to control drug use at the school, as one former student said, "Drugs screwed things up."[101]

Sexual relations proved to be an equally problematic but less clear issue for the school community. Far from a moralist about sex, Mr. Durrie expressed his views in a letter to a parent: "About sex, our attitude is that people must make their own choices and take responsibility for what they do. However, there is a genuine respect for individuals here."[102]

One student recalled that there was "sexual experimentation" among some of the students. "The attitude was 'don't get caught.' "I don't think the staff quite knew where to stand. It was a fuzzier issue than drugs."[103] As with Knowplace, many of the adults at Saturna were only a few years older than the teenage students and seemed not to have enough experience or wisdom to set and enforce limits. A further complicating factor was the steady stream of visitors who came to Saturna, some of them with questionable motives.

One winter, the school community was shocked when a female staff member in her mid-thirties became romantically involved with a sixteen-year-old male student. This turned out to be far from a casual or short-lived affair and continued for the better part of a year. As the relationship dragged on, the community alternated from pretending not to notice to talking about it incessantly. To make matters worse, the boy's parents were not told of the relationship. Finally, eight months later, Bill Sheffeld asked the couple to end the relationship or leave the community. They moved to a nearby island and eventually married. The boy's family threatened legal action but eventually accepted a financial settlement. These events

---

100 Ron Forbes-Roberts, personal interview, January 30, 1997.
101 Miles Durrie, personal interview, April 22, 1997.
102 Tom Durrie, letter to Ms. Liknaitzky, April 19, 1971.
103 Saturna Island School student, personal interview, January 30, 1997.

were devastating to the young community and it was some time before the school recovered.

POLITICAL DIFFICULTIES

A major setback ensued when the Greater Victoria Metropolitan Board of Health entered into a long running battle with the school. Dr. John Whitbread, Senior Medical Health Officer, inspected the school in May 1969 and found an inoperative sewage system, no central heating system, and overcrowded bedrooms.[104] In a three-page report, the inspector noted many other deficiencies, including kitchen and bathrooms in need of cleaning and redecorating, furniture in poor state of repair, broken and dirty windows, poor lighting, scattered clothing and litter, unacceptable wall and floor coverings, insufficient bedding, and "dark, dingy, and dirty" conditions.[105] Dr. Whitbread described the kitchen as "filthy" and the school as "dirty, untidy, and unfit for students to live in and be taught in."[106] The school was given until August to rectify the deficiencies or face eviction.

Dr. Whitbread's concerns about the sewage system, heating system, and crowded conditions were justified. However, many of his remarks had more to do with aesthetic taste and personal standards of tidiness than with objective health criteria. Dr. Whitbread objected to the educational philosophy and lifestyle represented by free schools. His political point of view was indicated by statements he made to the *Victoria Daily Times* suggesting that "the Saturna Island problem" exists throughout British Columbia. "It was operating as a boarding home for children; it is not, in our opinion, a school. It should be investigated by the health, education, and welfare departments. Unless the education department defines what a school is, somebody has to take action if these schools are going to operate in a proper way."[107] He was quoted again two weeks later: "I

---

104 Dr. J. M. Whitbread, D. G. Anderson, Greater Victoria Metropolitan Board of Health, Inspection Report, May 27, 1969.
105 Dr. J. M. Whitbread, D. G. Anderson, Inspection Report, May 27, 1969.
106 "Threat of Closure Haunts Free School," *Vancouver Province*, May 15, 1969, 22, and "Free School Warned about Health Threat," *Victoria Colonist*, May 14, 1969, 30.
107 "Meet Standards or Close Down," *Victoria Times*, May 14, 1969, 4.

know what action we're taking. This isn't just a matter of the Saturna Free School."[108]

The health board chairperson, a Victoria city councillor, followed up Dr. Whitbread's report with letters to the provincial Health Minister, the Education Minister, and the Attorney-General. He urged the government to take control over private free schools and expressed judgements about educational and moral standards that were outside of his mandate. He wrote to the Health Minister:

> One problem the Metropolitan Board of Health wishes to present to the Ministers is the lack of adequate supervision and control over free schools and private schools. There should be supervision of the qualifications and type of teachers. In the opinion of the Senior Medical Health Officer the Saturna Island Free School does not have a suitable type of teacher, although three have qualifications. The lack of a syllabus and the lack of any evidence of lessons leaves doubt as to whether or not these children are being given schooling. The Public Schools Act requires all children between the ages of seven and fifteen years to attend school. Action might be considered by the Department of Education or School Boards against the parents of children attending this free school. The problem exists in many of the free schools and private schools throughout the province. The lack of modern standards of sanitation together with the lack of control and discipline would lead one to question the moral standards in this school. Action will be taken to close this institution as soon as clarification is obtained.[109]

Over the next two years, conditions at the school would be the subject of over forty articles in Victoria and Vancouver newspapers. Suspecting that the school was drawing so much attention because of its challenge to traditional schools, Mr. Durrie told reporters, "It is surprising to me that a small institution such as ours would receive so much publicity over a

---

108 "Health Chief Hints Free Schools Doomed," *Victoria Times*, May 29, 1969, 23.
109 Alderman R. Elphick, Chair, Greater Victoria Metropolitan Board of Health, to Ralph Loffmark, Minister of Health, May 29, 1969.

matter of this sort," and, "The publicity in this case is so far out of line with reality it's ridiculous."[110] Mr. Durrie wrote a four-page letter to the Health Minister listing "Items found Inaccurate or Misleading" in the health board report. He wrote: "I question statements about matters which are outside their areas of competence and authority. I refer to those parts of the letter expressing their opinions about the teaching staff and educational situation at Saturna Island Free School."[111]

The Minister received a letter of support for the school signed by eight parents.[112] They took exception to inaccuracies, statements of personal opinion unrelated to health matters, and the overall tone of the health board report. They noted that none of their children had ever been ill at the free school.[113] Another parent, himself a dentist, reported that he was "rather fussy about cleanliness and had been completely satisfied when he visited the school."[114] A number of local islanders also expressed support for the school; as one student explained, "Even if they didn't agree with us, they didn't like outside interference."

The Minister also received a letter from J. M. Campbell, President of the BC School Trustees Association, who happened to be a Saturna Island resident. As a public school trustee, Mr. Campbell would hardly be expected to come to the defence of a controversial private school. Nevertheless, his criticism of the health board report was scathing. After visiting the premises himself, he reported that the buildings were shoddy but "very clean." He wrote to the Health Minister:

> It is obvious to me since making my own inspection of the premises that Dr. Whitbread's report creates a grossly false impression of the real situation, so false indeed as to make me suspect serious bias if not outright malice. Alderman Elphick appears to have gone far beyond his terms of reference as Board of Health chairman. I consider

---

110 "Health Standards Now Met, Says Free School Head," *Vancouver Province*, May 23, 1969, 12; "Head Hints Persecution," *Vancouver Sun*, May 23, 1969, 2.

111 Tom Durrie, letter to the Greater Victoria Metropolitan Board of Health, "Items Found Inaccurate or Misleading," June 6, 1969.

112 Copies to other ministers and NDP opposition leader, Tom Berger.

113 Eight parents to Minister Ralph Loffmark, July 5, 1969.

114 "Did Signal Tip-Off School?" *Victoria Times*, September 27, 1972, 1.

his letter offensive to my personal concept of reasonable justice and objectivity.[115]

In the meantime, a second inspection in June 1969 showed "the same rather deplorable conditions as before," and the staff embarked upon a summer renovation program to rectify the deficiencies.[116] A new septic tank was installed with the help of a neighbour who brought in a truckload of gravel, the kitchen and bathrooms were remodelled, and the building was given a thorough cleaning. The health board was silent for the next five months until, finally, after a third visit by four inspectors in November 1969, Dr. Whitbread wrote to Mr. Durrie:

> Conditions of cleanliness, basic sanitation, and hygiene had improved and could be considered satisfactory. Our visit indicated that you have come up to the requirements outlined in our letter of June 1969. Certain requirements which cannot be met (overcrowding, additional bathroom) will not be enforced as long as rigid standards of cleanliness are maintained. Your efforts to bring your school up to the required standards are appreciated. We wish to express our thanks for your co-operation in improving the environmental conditions of your school.[117]

This about-face appears to have been a political decision. As with Knowplace, the provincial government did not consider action against the school worthwhile, and the health board was advised that the school did have a right to exist. But many officials and journalists were surprised that, at that time, private schools were not regulated by the Department of Education and did not have to meet any standards. Since Confederation, the Department of Education had adopted a "hands-off" attitude toward all private schools in British Columbia, and private schools were not even required to register with the government. Religious or "elitist" private schools had never been perceived as a problem, but marginal alternative schools like Saturna or Knowplace were another story. In April 1970 a Social Credit MLA visited the school. Her comments were reported in the

---

115 J. M. Campbell, BCSTA President to Ralph Loffmark, June 5, 1969.
116 "Free School Cleanup Extended," *Victoria Times*, June 11, 1969, 41.
117 Dr. Whitbread, letter to Tom Durrie, November 25, 1969.

press, generating more negative publicity. She described the living conditions as deplorable, and the building as a crowded fire hazard. The MLA is quoted as saying, "Schools like this shouldn't be permitted. There is no curriculum, no discipline, and no rules. This is a loophole in the Public Schools Act which must be plugged."[118] Using the health regulations was one of the only ways the government could exert its authority over such schools. Several years later another free school in the Slocan Valley, the Whole School, would face a similar challenge from municipal authorities.

Conflict with the authorities continued. In late 1970 BC Hydro built power lines across a corner of the property against the wishes of the school community. One teenage student set fire to the cables and severely damaged them. He was apprehended by the police and jailed for ten months.[119] Six months later, acting on rumours of drug use on the property, an undercover RCMP constable spent two nights at the school in the spring of 1971. The officer found "no evidence of drugs on the premises" but did report nude sunbathing and evidence of student sexual activity. The officer also reported bed linen on the floor, dirty washrooms, irregular meals, and "sanitary conditions so bad he refused to eat or drink there."[120] Some stories told about the school were true but others were fabricated, and one teenager drew unwanted attention to the school by telling a series of false stories to the police. These were reported by the press and in 1971 a *Vancouver Sun* columnist severely criticized the school, prompting Mr. Durrie to respond:

> Drugs, sex, lying, cheating, and swearing are common in every public high school and little notice is taken; however, our little school comes under the most critical scrutiny and if one of our students slips up and gets into trouble, even though there may be no history of previous problems, we are subject to immediate condemnation.[121]

118 Agnes Kripps, MLA, "Kripps Attacks Free School," *Victoria Times*, April 17, 1970, 17.
119 Police Warrant to Search, October 18, 1970.
120 "RCMP Agent at School," *Victoria Times*, September 28, 1972, 1.
121 Tom Durrie, letter to Jack Wasserman, May 28, 1971.

FINANCIAL AND ENROLMENT DIFFICULTIES

By the spring of 1970, the end of the school's second year, low enrolment had become a serious problem. This was partly due to the vacancies left by the students suspended for using drugs. As well, some parents became disenchanted with the lack of an academic program. But for most students, a one- to two-year stay at Saturna was enough, and for others, now in their later teens, it was time to move on. But the most important cause of the enrolment drop was simply that the demand for Romantic education was drying up in British Columbia and across North America. This had also been a key factor in the closure of the Barker Free School. Some public school districts had begun to offer innovative programs so that parents and students seeking alternatives did not have to look outside the public system. If the Saturna Island Free School was to survive, it would need to find another source of students.

Like most alternative schools during the 1960s, Saturna accepted more than its share of students with special needs. But by 1970 the school began actively recruiting students that no other institution would take. Mr. Durrie accepted several wards of the Vancouver Children's Aid Society and continued to seek out such children. In late 1970 he advised a Society placement officer that "we have a number of vacancies that we are eager to fill as soon as possible. If you should know of anyone needing the kind of facility we can provide we should be happy to hear from you."[122] Several students were also referred to the school by Dr. Bennett Wong, well-known in Vancouver during the 1960s for his work with seriously disturbed teenagers and those involved in the drug culture. The advantage of accepting such students was that the school could count on the agencies to keep the students' fees current. As Mr. Durrie wrote to one parent, "We're now beginning to get kids from Children's Aid which helps fill our enrolment and secure our income. They pay regularly and they pay well."[123] But some of these teenagers had serious problems far beyond the

---

122 Tom Durrie, letter to Evelyn Henderson, Vancouver Children's Aid Society, November 20, 1970.
123 Tom Durrie, letter to Patricia Henry, December 15, 1970.

ability of the inexperienced staff to handle adequately. Nevertheless, the school "took every kid who was willing to come."[124]

The school accepted several teenage girls whose behaviour could be disruptive and violent. One girl of fourteen from Montreal was supported by the Quebec Social Allowance Commission. She was prone to volatile behaviour toward other children and animals, and many were frightened of her. One described her as "off the deep end," and another said, "She was a terrifying person—the adults were afraid of her as well."[125] Eventually she was involved in an altercation in Vancouver, and Mr. Durrie refused to let her come back. Another girl of fifteen had been a Vancouver gang member. She had been convicted of several "break and enter" offences and had to go to Vancouver frequently for court appearances. Her application from the Catholic Children's Aid Society stated, "She has difficulty in controlling destructive behaviour. Has been sniffing glue and nail polish remover for six years."[126]

Another girl placed at Saturna by the Children's Aid Society had quit public school at the end of grade five, and according to the application filed by the Society, had been sexually abused by the age of eleven.[127] Another had run away from home because of her concern about her mother's ability to stay off drugs. Although such children temporarily brought in some needed money, their acceptance transformed the school into a therapeutic institution, making it even more difficult to attract mainstream students. One former student remembered "a lot of acting out from these social services students. He recalled "anger, property damage, people smashing windows. It was beyond the testing of limits—there were people hurt."[128] Another former student recalled angry children while still another recollected several female students who disturbed the other kids.[129]

The therapeutic orientation of the school coincided with another shift in direction taken in 1970 when several staff members developed a serious interest in gestalt therapy. Lynn Curtis, although he had no professional

---

124 Lyn Bowman, personal interview, November 18, 1997.
125 Tim Lucey, personal interview, November 12, 1997.
126 Application Form, September 1970.
127 Application Forms, 1968–1970.
128 Saturna Island School student, personal interview, January 30, 1997.
129 Saturna Island School student, personal interview, October 31, 1996.

training, organized therapy groups and "sensitivity" sessions. Participants talked about feelings, analyzed their dreams, and worked on emotional issues during these frequently confrontational sessions. Regular evening discussions were held to share personal feelings, and even meetings about practical issues sometimes turned into spontaneous encounter groups. As one student recalled, "In an informal way it was happening all the time."[130] These sessions were mainly of interest to the adults and were seldom attended by students.

Former staff member Lyn Bowman had taken a position at the Centre for Gestalt Learning founded by Fritz Perls at Cowichan on Vancouver Island. Beginning in the fall of 1970, Mr. Bowman was invited to the school every three months to provide weekend gestalt workshops for staff and other interested people. Mr. Durrie supported these therapeutic activities and in 1971 described the workshops as "softer and warmer than ever." He wrote to a prospective parent: "Solving living and personal problems is a major part of what we do. Currently we have a meeting every evening to give everyone a chance to air their resentments and appreciations. We also have a young man trained in gestalt therapy who offers group therapy and sensitivity training."[131] To another parent he wrote: "In spite of the problems the school is better than ever. At least we don't have the usual formalities and procedures to cover up the way people feel."[132] This enthusiasm for encounter groups and expressing "what you feel" was widespread throughout the counterculture in 1970 and surfaced in many alternative schools. But it removed Saturna even further from traditional educational pursuits.

130 Ron Forbes-Roberts, personal interview, January 30, 1997.
131 Tom Durrie, letter to Mina Fishell, April 14, 1970.
132 Tom Durrie, letter to Patricia Henry, March 26, 1971.

SCHOOL CLOSURE

By the fall of 1970, the school was receiving few applications, losing numerous students, and struggling with a budget at an all-time low. The school was kept afloat by social services placements but, since most of these students stayed for only a few months, the school was unable to establish any financial stability. By May 1971, when only six paying students remained, Mr. Durrie wrote to a friend: "We are so short of enrolments and prospects that we are in serious danger of having to shut down. We need at least ten paying students to break even."[133]

Tom Durrie and Lynn Curtis believed that since the clientele had transformed the school into something akin to a treatment centre, the organization would be more financially viable as a conference or workshop centre specializing in gestalt therapy. But Bill Sheffeld and several other staff members opposed this plan and wanted the school to continue. The matter came to a head in June 1971 when the eight shareholders met to decide the future of the community. The first vote ended in a tie, but after more discussion, Lyn Bowman changed his vote and sided with those favouring a school despite his own personal interest in gestalt.

Tom Durrie handed the directorship of the school over to Bill Sheffeld, sold his interest in the property to another shareholder, and in August 1971 left the school for good. Lynn Curtis and Judy Pruss also left to buy land in Nova Scotia. Mr. Durrie moved to Burnaby where he helped found "Opera in the Schools." He went to Hornby Island in 1984, where he directed the Hornby Island Music Festival for many years. He continued to write about education and occasionally directed school musicals but never returned to teaching.[134]

Meanwhile, in the spring of 1971, the Health Department began making life difficult for the school again. Dr. Whitbread, accompanied by four RCMP officers, inspected the building in June but did not advise the staff of any deficient items. Six weeks later, without warning, an RCMP corporal citing the Health Act and Sanitary Regulations served an eviction notice "to each and every occupant to quit the premises" by August

---

133 Tom Durrie, letter to Thora Nelson, May 18, 1971.
134 Tom Durrie, letter to BCTF, June 5, 1971.

30, 1971.[135] The local authorities used the Health Act to do what the Education Act could not. The police told Mr. Sheffeld privately that if he closed the school, the officers would not enforce the eviction order and the residents could remain on the property.[136] Since they were at a crossroads anyway and enrolment was low, Bill and Kathy Sheffeld agreed to close the school and hoped to reopen in the future.

The school appealed the eviction order and the case dragged on for over a year. The story continued to attract high-profile media coverage. In a front-page article, the *Daily Colonist* reported that the school was "shackled by a court eviction order, undisclosed sanitary infractions, and a wall of silence from health authorities."[137] When the school finally won the right to a trial, the *Colonist* featured another front-page story, "Saturna Free School Wins Court Round."[138] The case was heard in September 1972. The school's lawyer argued that Dr. Whitbread paid too much attention to "surface untidiness" and was unable to recognize different lifestyles that did not include "three meals a day, dishes done three times a day, and people sleeping in traditional bed linen."[139] But on October 18, 1972, Judge Drake, citing "overwhelming evidence," ruled that the school closure had been justified and would not be overturned.[140]

Mr. Sheffeld was devastated by the ruling. He told a *Colonist* reporter, "I don't know what we'll do now but we will do whatever we can to keep on living here ourselves."[141] Bill Sheffeld, Betty Spears, Rini House, and two adult children continued to live on the farm and remained good friends for many years. The property was held in common through Saturna Free School—Community Projects Ltd.—and the house was converted into a bed and breakfast resort. Ms. House worked as an artist and Mr. Sheffeld was elected to the Gulf Islands Trust in 1996. In the years after the school

135 Health Act Eviction Notice, served by Corporal Morris Nelson, August 16, 1971.
136 *The Globe and Mail*, January 4, 1991, A3; Bill Sheffeld, personal interview, October 31, 1996.
137 "Wall of Silence Surrounds Closing of Free School," *Colonist*, September 28, 1971, 1.
138 *Colonist*, January 22, 1972, 1.
139 William Sigurgeirson, "School Fate Weighed," *Colonist*, September 29, 1972, 26.
140 "Free School Closure Sticks," *Colonist*, October 18, 1972, 19; "Free School Loses Appeal," *Victoria Times*, October 18, 1972, 33.
141 Barbara McLintock, "Free School Closure Sticks," *Colonist*, October 18, 1972, 19.

closed, former students returned from time to time to find work, friendship, or a roof over their heads.

EFFECTS ON STUDENTS

However genuinely Saturna parents may have supported Romantic principles in theory, some began to worry that their children were not doing any academic work. Inquiring about his son, one parent asked, "I do not intend to put any pressure on him but I am interested in whether he has begun any studies yet."[142] Another parent wrote, "We still have reservations. As long as he makes a serious effort for part of the day on his school work we shall be content. I feel the purpose of the school should be to create a useful member of our world."[143] Another worried:

> I wonder how a girl is going to get along with only a grade nine education for the rest of her life. Do you believe that students will eventually want to pursue their studies of their own free will? I'm afraid I don't. Fifteen-year-olds are far too immature to realize that education is necessary for both their working and their leisure life until they leave school and cannot earn a living.[144]

Another parent wrote that her son "wanted to work on his grade eleven program but according to him no one at the school seemed to want to take the time to help him with his studies. Either you do not have enough teachers or they are unwilling to teach."[145] Another observed:

> We want Denise to have some scholastic work, an hour or two a day at least. We want her to have some obligations to herself, keeping herself clean, washing her clothes, tidying her own room, and some restrictions on the company she keeps. This is going to be a tough age for her if she has no guidance. We want her to stand

---

142 Mr. Elam, letter to Tom Durrie, October 29, 1968.
143 Ms. Proulx, letter to Tom Durrie, December 5, 1968.
144 Saturna Island School parent, letter to Tom Durrie, October 29, 1968.
145 Ms. Brunner, letter to Tom Durrie, October 1969.

on her own, but she has to be prepared before she can accomplish this.[146]

Yet another parent had similar concerns:

> I am not in full agreement with the educational policies of the school. Daphne still has hankerings for a more academic program and a certificate. She admitted that she could get help with math at Saturna if she wanted to study by herself but none of the other pupils was likely to be interested.[147]

A different parent cited a friend's visit to an English Progressive school:

> There was so much going on that the whole place was throbbing. I can picture students getting that excited about learning but I miss that at Saturna. I think they need more stimulation and motivation. Something should be going on all day. No kid is going to lie in bed when something interesting is going on.[148]

On the other hand, some parents were pleased with the personal development they saw in their children. One parent who had initially expressed reservations had this to say:

> I should like to thank you and your staff for the remarkable change that seems to have come over Mary in the short time that she has been with you. When she came home she was a changed girl—it was the first time I have seen her really happy.[149]

Another parent wrote:

> I would like to thank you for what the school has done for Mike. We see many changes in him that make us happy for him. I'm sure he has become more tolerant and less self-centred than he was and he has a better feeling about his own worth. But it frightens me when I think of

---

146 Saturna Island School parent, letter to Tom Durrie, April 21, 1970.
147 Saturna Island School parent, letter to Tom Durrie, July 8, 1969.
148 Joan Liknaitzky, letter to Tom Durrie, February 26, 1971.
149 Mr. Hunt, letter to Tom Durrie, February 28, 1969.

him as an adult discovering that the world doesn't work
like Saturna.[150]

One parent, although critical of the academic program, acknowledged
that, for her daughter, "life at the school has made her more aware of
her relationships with others. The best education she gains at Saturna is
becoming a member of a family."[151] Similar to other alternative schools,
the perceived benefits had more to do with growth in personal traits such
as independence, self-reliance, confidence, and co-operativeness than
with academic achievement.

Student recollections and retrospective opinions of Saturna vary, but
almost all are critical of the inadequate supervision and lack of academic
stimulation. One student commented on the lack of adult supervision:
"For several months dinner would be cooked and served every night.
Then there would be several months when it wasn't. Us kids felt forgotten.
We were pretty much left to run around on our own. The cliffs and water
were dangerous. There should have been more supervision."[152] Another
student believed some children were neglected: "I don't think Saturna
was good for the younger kids. No one was looking after them or taking
responsibility for them. It might have worked if there had been an overriding structure."[153]

Former students thought the staff was too passive in failing to intervene in student relations to protect shy, insecure, or younger children. One
former student felt that the "absolute lack of structure" was a "misguided"
policy that made life difficult for many students, particularly given the
number of troubled children at the school. Another said, "People were
left to their own devices to solve their problems."[154] Another student
agreed that "you had to be able to look after yourself."[155] One student who
experienced a lot of frightening behaviour slept out in the woods with her
dog. "It was not a happy place—you just stayed out of the way."[156] Still

---

150 Saturna Island School parent, letter to Tom Durrie, June 1971.
151 Ms. Griffin, letter to Tom Durrie, July 8, 1969.
152 Saturna Island School student, personal interview, December 2, 1996.
153 Saturna Free School student, personal interview, April 22, 1997.
154 Mike McConnell, personal interview, March 26, 1997.
155 Peter Vogel, personal interview, April 16, 1997.
156 Saturna Island School student, personal interview, November 6, 1996.

another recalled an environment where: "Anybody who couldn't stand up for themselves had a rough time."[157]

Most former students also believed that the lack of academics was detrimental. "It may have harmed me academically, as I might have done more," one said, while another concluded that "it would have been better for me if I had stayed in school. I wasn't harmed at Saturna but it was a waste of time. Some kids need discipline and I was one of them."[158] Still another recalled, "Further secondary education never played a big part in anybody's life. None of us went on to pursue an academic career. I used to feel intimidated by people with academic credentials that I didn't have."[159]

Saturna students found it difficult to re-enter the public school system because they could no longer fit in. One student remembered attending public school at age thirteen and feeling "out of place. I was too mature for the kids there. At fifteen I was going on twenty."[160] Another student was unhappy and left Saturna halfway through his second year. But on returning to public school, he could not relate to his peers: "I had experienced things that the other kids hadn't."[161] Similarly, when another tried high school in Vancouver, "it didn't work out. It was too hard after having all that freedom."[162]

Others found public school difficult because they lacked academic skills. One student recalled, "It was the end of my formal education. I didn't even finish grade school."[163] Another said, "I started public school at age eight in grade one. My reading held me back. I went through four years of elementary school two years behind."[164] His brother was also at Saturna:

> I chose to return to public school. I was concerned about
> the lack of scholastic work. I missed a regular structure.
> I missed my friends. My scholastics suffered, it set me

157 Saturna Island School student, personal interview, January 30, 1997.
158 Saturna Island School student, personal interview, November 12, 1997.
159 Saturna Island School student, personal interview, January 30, 1997.
160 Saturna Island School student, personal interview, October 31, 1996.
161 Saturna Island School student, personal interview, November 12, 1997.
162 Saturna Island School student, personal interview, March 26, 1997.
163 Saturna Island School student, personal interview, February 18, 1997.
164 Saturna Island School student, personal interview, April 2, 1997.

behind in English and math skills. I was in grade six
but I had to go back to grade five. I finally caught up by
grade nine. I regret that I didn't have a better scholastic education.[165]

Less than one-fourth of Saturna students finished high school, although several went back later to obtain adult basic education. Four attended some university courses and one pursued a degree in social work. The few students who successfully completed high school did not find it easy. One wrote, "A great part of my education was informal. It gave me an appre-ciation of the value of a formal education as I had to gain mine through correspondence which required perseverance and self-motivation."[166] She became a Gulf Islands school trustee.

Another student who already knew the basic skills when she began at Saturna and eventually took her general education certificate at a junior college found it easier to reintegrate:

I went back to public school on Mayne Island, sixteen
kids and one teacher. I loved having my own desk and
pens and pencils. I caught up easily, two grades one year
and two grades the next. I could read better than most
kids and the studies were interesting. It would have been
more scary in a big school.[167]

But she believed that at Saturna "some kids needed more structured education. If a kid wanted to learn how to read, someone would teach him, but most kids didn't want to. There should have been more adult-directed activities such as reading with the kids."

One student who never went back to school, later acquired his high school certificate, became a musician, and earned two university degrees: "I virtually dropped out of school in grade eight. I did my grade twelve equivalency in two months. I haven't been held back by my lack of high school." One student thought Saturna should have provided students with more direction:

---

165 Saturna Island School student, personal interview, April 2, 1997.
166 Susanne Middleditch, biographical sketch, October 18, 1996.
167 Emily Axelson, personal interview, December 2, 1996.

> Teenagers like to have structure, a series of accomplish-
> ments. If you leave them to their own devices they would
> never do anything. The younger kids were expected to be
> motivated to do things on their own. There were kids who
> didn't have a bath in two weeks. The staff people were
> awfully young themselves.[168]

Former Saturna students pursued a variety of occupations. They included two professional musicians, two small business proprietors, one physician, one child care worker, one journalist, two contractors, two independent truckers, one concrete finisher, one set designer, one gardener, one housewife/mother, and one unemployed single parent.[169] Most became independent and self-employed. Diverse family backgrounds make drawing conclusions difficult, but post-secondary education was out of reach of most Saturna students.

Saturna did provide a positive experience for some students. One who "felt frustration and pressure" in public school recalled, "Saturna was quite relaxed. I appreciated the lack of pressure, the quiet, being alone in the natural surroundings. My warts disappeared within four months. There is a strength that I gained from there, I can make decisions."[170] His brother said the school gave him "the freedom to choose for myself. It helped me in decision-making. I came out with a lot of confidence."[171] For another, "the most important things were the things between people."[172] Another former student reported that the school taught her self-reliance, self-motivation, compassion, how to compromise, and how to work effectively in a group.[173] Some students enjoyed the freedom:

> For me it was a good experience. I knew how to look after
> myself. I knew how to make myself a sandwich or find
> my way home. It was a positive time in my life. I was
> free to experience the outdoors, the property, the old junk
> and machinery, being able to explore in a safe wilderness

---

168 Ron Forbes-Roberts, personal interview, January 30, 1997.
169 Personal interviews. Students have become widely dispersed.
170 Saturna Island School student, personal interview, April 2, 1997.
171 Saturna Island School student, personal interview, April 2, 1997.
172 Jim Anderson, personal interview, August 3, 1997.
173 Susanne Middleditch, personal interview, October 31, 1996.

setting, touch history, get a 1930s tractor running again.
I read the Greeks, Shakespeare, Chaucer on my own. I
went back to school later. I don't regret missing public
school, but I wish I'd pursued a university education.[174]

Several students, particularly male teenagers, remembered the school
as a positive factor in their lives. It removed them from desperate personal
situations and provided a safe place to work through emotional upheaval.
One former student, who had become a heavy drug user before going to
Saturna, believed the school saved him from ending up in prison or worse:

If I had remained in the situation I was in, in Vancouver
as a teenager, I would have ended up in desperate circumstances. A lot of people in that scene went on to become
heavy drug users, criminals. People I knew from that time
are dead from drugs, in prison, killed in drug transactions,
and women I knew became prostitutes and junkies. If I
had stayed there I would have been swept along with it.
Bill Sheffeld was a guiding figure, lots of support was
really important right then. So for me it was a good experience. It made me appreciate good character. It gave me
confidence that I could actually do something.[175]

Another student had a similar perspective:

For me it was the best thing that could have happened
at that time. I had chronic problems in the public school
system. School was boring. I'm very physical, hands-on,
creative, interested in projects. I went to St. George's
for grades six and seven. It was stimulating but wearing
a uniform was repugnant. Saturna was a last resort. I
needed an environment where I would be free to explore
what I was interested in. I learned by trial and error. The
school allowed me to screw up and learn from that. You
learned to hold your ground in a discussion. I learned
engineering skills from Bill. Working on the farm taught
me how to think on my feet and solve problems. It was a

---

174 Saturna Island School student, personal interview, April 22, 1997.
175 Saturna Island School student, personal interview, January 30, 1997.

> very physical environment. I took responsibility for my
> own life. It either worked for you or it was a waste of
> time. The school was a close community for me. I lived in
> a series of group homes but went back to Saturna later. It
> was like going back to a family, a lifeline.[176]

"For me the school was great," a different student recalled. "It gave me some breathing room away from home. I was left alone, I got to relax and get back on my feet." Another agreed: "It was great for me. There weren't a lot of other options. The conventional system wasn't working for me. It gave me something to do." And yet another student said, "It gave me a lot of life experience. It filled the time until adult life."[177] "My parents were happy I wasn't in jail."

Bill Sheffeld took several of the older boys under his wing and was almost a father figure. He was a patient listener, taught them practical skills, and was a supportive and reliable friend. These students looked up to and admired him. One former student described him as a "guiding light for a lot of the kids" and some former students looked back on him as the "bedrock of the community."[178] One student remembered him this way: "Bill was always available. The teenagers were going through a lot. He had the clearest understanding of what motivates adolescents. He was stable and rational in the face of a lot of emotionalism."[179] Mr. Sheffeld reflected:

> I saw a lot of kids who were disturbed, distressed, out
> of control, develop purposefulness in their lives. It did
> some of those kids a lot of good. But it was irrelevant
> or destructive to other kids because it couldn't provide
> enough emotional support. A lot of the staff were dysfunc-
> tional or they were consumed with day-to-day activities.
> The constant acting out, smashing windows, was disrup-
> tive to the kids who didn't need that kind of experience.

---

176 Saturna Island School student, personal interview, March 26, 1997.
177 Mary Hunt, personal interview, December 1, 1997; Peter Schmidt, personal interview, March 3, 1997; Peter Vogel, personal interview, April 16, 1997.
178 Tim Lucey, personal interview, November 12, 1997.
179 Ron Forbes-Roberts, personal interview, January 30, 1997.

For them it could be a terrifying experience. But for the
other kids it was a life saver.[180]

It is ironic that the students for whom the school was designed, the
children of parents who believed in the free school ideology, had the most
difficulty at Saturna, while those who were helped the most were the
children whom nobody else would take. Despite their educational weak-
nesses, schools like Saturna provided a safe refuge for some teenagers by
keeping them away from the dangers of addiction and street life.

CONCLUSION

Tom Durrie was a central figure in British Columbia Romantic education. Unlike many free school proponents, he had the courage and the
energy to establish a school that remained true to his beliefs about the
value of freedom for young people. He was a talented teacher as well as
an eloquent and tireless advocate for schools that would allow children
to grow up "naturally." He saw Romantic education as part of a larger
picture, a remedy for an unhealthy and repressive society. However, he
was not able to create an exciting or nurturing educational community at
Saturna. Ultimately the day-to-day realities of a school did not suit him.
His broader goal was the end of compulsory education.[181]

The school's increasingly therapeutic orientation without the necessary
staff training was a serious problem. As Tom Durrie wrote to a parent,
"Our problem is choosing youngsters who have their parents' support in
wanting a free school rather than those who have come to us as a last
resort."[182] Bill Sheffeld added, "About 25 per cent of the parents had heard
of free schools, knew what the concept meant, had read *Summerhill*, and
wanted that for their kids. Another 50 per cent wanted a school that would
take their kids away—they were willing to pay not to know anything."[183]
The staff was not equipped to handle children that came from challenging

---

180 Bill Sheffeld, personal interview, October 31, 1997.
181 As early as 1969 his frustration with Saturna prompted him to apply for a job in a
    school district and later with the BCTF (Applications, May 20, 1969, June 5, 1971.)
    In his distrust of formal education, he was influenced by the writings of Paul Goodman.
182 Tom Durrie, letter to Ms. Brunner, August 14, 1968.
183 Bill Sheffeld, personal interview, October 31, 1996.

home environments. They ignored disturbing behaviour because they simply did not know what to do, thus making life difficult for "normal" children. One former student observed, "Social services sent some really disturbed people. There were students who should never have gone there. The responsible thing would have been to say we can't help this person and find a more appropriate situation. But the school took just about anybody. Nobody stepped in with a practical solution."[184]

The lack of a mature staff with educational expertise and a desire to use it was a more fundamental weakness. The adults were either too young, too caught up in the times, or had too many of their own problems to be effective teachers. One former student said, "The adults were seeking something. They were rudderless themselves. It was a time unique to itself."[185] Commenting on questionable behaviour often overlooked at the school, another student said, "For the most part the adults didn't know it was happening, and when they did they allowed it. The adults were pre-occupied with their own issues."[186] A former parent suggested, "People were working out their own problems. You need adults that have matured to be available for kids."[187] One staff member admits to not "going on anything but intuition during that period," while another concluded, "It was a delusion that enthusiasm could substitute for competence. We didn't have the will to become competent."[188]

Nevertheless, some students saw what the staff was trying to do as admirable. "Most of the staff were great people," one said. "The whole thing was from the heart—they believed in it. There were a few bad characters but every organization has its bad apples."[189] Another former student remarked that "the adults were getting high on their own freedom":

> They were wrapped up in their own problems. They didn't inspire a lot of confidence. The idea was right—they wanted kids to grow into their own people rather

---

184 Ron Forbes-Roberts, personal interview, January 30, 1997.
185 Saturna Island School student, personal interview, February 18, 1997.
186 Susanne Middleditch, personal interview, October 31, 1997.
187 Betty Spears, personal interview, April 1, 1997.
188 Colin Browne, personal interview, November 7, 1996; Lyn Bowman, personal interview, November 18, 1997.
189 Peter Schmidt, personal interview, March 3, 1997.

than how society wants to mould them. If surrounded by
the right people it might have worked.[190]

Over half of the staff were American and, as in other alternative
schools, their influence was substantial. The Vietnam War exerted a profound effect on that generation, demanding courage, hard choices, and, for
some, exile.[191] The young men and women who came to British Columbia
were idealistic, educated, and liberal.[192] They were the embodiment of the
idealism and optimism of the 1960s.

The Saturna Island Free School was the epitome of the Romantic education movement in British Columbia. Its rural location and isolation, its
laissez-faire ideology, the type of students it attracted, and its emergence
at the height of the 1960s counterculture combined to produce an unusual
and at times outlandish school community. Whether or not we believe
that children always know what is best for them, the Saturna Island Free
School would have been unlikely to succeed. First, the staff lacked the
kind of teaching expertise that might have inspired the children to become
excited about learning. Second, because some of the young people the
school attracted were troubled, they needed skill and experience beyond
what the staff could provide. Third, by the early 1970s the counterculture was in decline, causing a marked decrease in excitement about
Romantic schools among the general public. Fourth, the growing interest
in Progressive ideas among educators and parents led some public schools
to offer child-centred programs that satisfied liberal parents seeking less
traditional teaching methods. This development, along with the waning
of the counterculture, meant that private alternative schools like Saturna
had difficulty attracting any but the most marginal students and therefore
could not survive financially. Lastly, conservative politicians, officials, and
journalists found the countercultural lifestyle at high-profile communities
like the Saturna Island school threatening. The demise of the school at the
hands of local bureaucrats was probably inevitable. Although Saturna's

---

190 Saturna Island School student, personal interview, April 22, 1997.
191 Colin Browne, personal interview, November 7, 1996. See also Edward Morgan, *The
     Sixties Experience* (Philadelphia: Temple University Press, 1991), Chapter 4.
192 Tom Durrie, personal interview, September 4, 1996.

educational legacy was minimal, it embodied ideals and values of the time that have subsequently endured.

With the closure of the Saturna Island Free School in 1971, the Romantic era in British Columbia all but came to an end. However, there was one exception: a Romantic school that would emerge in the isolated Slocan Valley of southeastern British Columbia in 1972. How this school differed from the earlier Romantic schools of the 1960s, and how it shifted to become more moderate, will be described in Chapter 12. In the meantime, alternative schools in BC were about to enter a new period with a more varied and practical type of alternative: the Therapeutic school.

Part Three

THERAPEUTIC SCHOOLS

Chapter 9

TOTAL EDUCATION

Romantic schools reached their peak during the late 1960s in British Columbia and by 1971 were already in decline. The Barker Free School and Knowplace both closed in 1969, and the Saturna Island Free School would close in 1971. But there were still many bored and alienated students in the public high schools who had been attracted to Romantic schools, and their numbers were growing. Many of these young people had been affected by the political and cultural mood of the 1960s and were no longer willing to automatically acquiesce to traditional school authority. Some left public school, while others continued to attend but with little enthusiasm. The Vancouver School Board reported a rapid increase in the dropout rate that reached almost 6 per cent in 1970/71.[1] As educational authorities wrestled with this problem, several private alternative high schools were established in Vancouver between 1970 and 1972 to address the needs of these teenagers. They were the forerunners of the

---

1   Dan Mullen, "Dropout School Just Too Popular," *Vancouver Province*, February 5, 1972, 15. According to the article 1,582 students left Vancouver high schools during 1970/71.

Therapeutic or "rehabilitation schools" that would proliferate during the 1970s to become the dominant form of alternative school by the middle of the decade. The first such school in British Columbia was Total Education.

In May 1970 Dan and Cathy Meakes, two Anglican Church youth workers in their early twenties, organized an educational program for high school dropouts. The program had grown out of a youth group, a kind of community "drop-in" centre held in the basement of St. Mary's Anglican Church in Vancouver's Kerrisdale neighbourhood. The couple had spent two months working with a summer employment project for university students, seeking to examine social values and organize service initiatives such as medical clinics and legal aid centres.[2] But the Meakeses were interested in visible social change, and believing there had been too much talk and not enough action, they decided to initiate a project on their own. They realized there were significant numbers of young people out of school and believed that to be effective they had to reach out to teenagers, not only on the higher socio-economic West Side of Vancouver but also on the less affluent East Side as well. They began planning a hands-on practical educational program to open as a school in September.

Their first task was to find a suitable venue. May Gutteridge, a "social services matriarch" operating out of St. James Anglican Church on Cordova Street in Vancouver's "Skid Row," provided a large room on the second floor of an unheated and poorly lighted condemned warehouse, a former noodle factory. St. Mary's offered an empty house owned by the congregation directly behind the church. Dan and Cathy Meakes decided to operate the school as two separate programs: one for middle class dropouts mostly on the West Side of the city, and the other for teenagers with social problems mostly on the East Side. The school opened with thirty-six students, twenty-four in the West Side program and twelve in the East. In order to qualify, a student had to have been out of school for a minimum of six months. Mr. Meakes and several volunteers went out knocking on doors looking for disaffected kids who had dropped out of

---

2   The Inner City Service Project, organized by the Anglican Church and the Law Society, was a "student think tank paying subsistence wages to university students."

mainstream schools.[3] These students had "no feeling there was a place for them, no feeling of doing anything that was valued."[4]

Some students were referred by Vancouver school counsellors, the Children's Aid Society, and by the well-known child psychiatrist Bennett Wong. Others learned of the program by word of mouth. Mr. Meakes visited potential students at their homes, accompanied by a teenager on probation who had been assigned to his custody. Although Ms. Meakes had a teaching certificate and Mr. Meakes had attended Arts I, an interdisciplinary humanities program at UBC, neither had much teaching experience. But they did have plenty of energy and enthusiasm and believed the teenagers "were attracted to us because of our youth. We were running on our commitment and our caring for these young people. We showed there was no way of failing. We provided a caring environment."[5]

Dan and Cathy Meakes were joined by Larry Haberlin, also in his early twenties, within a few months of establishing the program. Mr. Haberlin had grown up in an active Anglican Church family and spent six formative months at the Sorrento Centre for Human Development, an Anglican retreat centre on Shuswap Lake that promoted meaningful religious ritual and personal development in a spiritual community. The Centre had been founded by Bishop Jim Cruikshank who, along with other liberal thinkers in the church during the 1960s and 1970s, sought to develop a more meaningful and joyous spirituality based on how to become what he called a "fully alive human being."[6] In the tradition of the social gospel of the 1920s and 1930s, he was also concerned about broader social issues and believed a caring Canadian society should protect its most vulnerable citizens. Bishop Cruikshank, as Dean of Christchurch Cathedral in Vancouver and a faculty member at the Vancouver School of Theology, devoted his energy to social causes that included affordable housing, minority and gay rights, and food for the homeless. He was an important mentor to Dan and Cathy Meakes and Larry Haberlin, imbuing them with a strong sense of social responsibility. Mr. Haberlin left Sorrento with an

3   Ron Eckert, personal interview, October 28, 1996.
4   Larry Haberlin, personal interview, November 12, 1996.
5   Dan and Cathy Meakes, personal interviews, April 23 and April 28, 1997.
6   Bishop Jim Cruikshank, personal interview, April 25, 1999.

enthusiasm for working with teenagers. During the summer of 1970, he assisted the Meakeses and, by the following spring, was hired as a full-time staff member in the program that was to become Total Education.[7]

Although there was a marked socio-economic difference between the West and East Side groups, family instability was a common denominator. The West Side students were influenced by the 1960s counterculture. Many were capable students who had simply become bored by the way subject matter was presented in mainstream high schools. One student remembered: "I quit Point Grey at fifteen years old. I was a good student but I hated being there. I heard about Total Education from a friend. Everybody was talking about it."[8] Other students had single parents, some were living in group homes, and a few were living on their own. Some were experiencing family crises.

Most of the students in the East Side group were from the Raymur housing project near Main Street. Many came from economically disadvantaged families and had little parental direction, while some had been involved in petty theft. Others had learning disabilities, some had emotional or mental health problems, and still others were using alcohol and drugs. Larry Haberlin observed that although many of these students had potential, mainstream schools "didn't provide the personal support; kids would get lost in the crowd." They needed a "personal structure and daily monitoring." Cathy Meakes remarked that "the school system wasn't flexible enough to find ways they could be successful." There were few special programs for students whose learning, social, or emotional problems got in the way of their concentration. However, Ms. Meakes recalled that although the East Side students "may have grown up a little tougher, they were no more difficult to teach" than the West Side students.

Though it sounds today like stereotyping, the West Side program was considered to be more "cerebral," with debates, discussion, and written work, while the East Side group was more physical, engaging in building, and kinesthetic activities. According to one staff member, the East Side students needed a highly structured program. The young people "had a lot of needs and emotional baggage," and Cathy Meakes described that first

---

7   Larry Haberlin, personal interview, November 12, 1996.
8   Valerie Hodge, personal interview, March 8, 1998.

year as "one of the toughest I've ever lived through." The school aimed to provide a rehabilitation program that integrated a more interesting and relevant approach to academics with concern for the students' needs to develop self-confidence and form meaningful relationships. This concern for the whole person gave rise to the name "Total Education." The founders believed all students needed to be further educated in the curriculum, but personal work was also necessary for them to be successful.[9]

Jim Carter, vice principal of Eric Hamber Secondary School in Vancouver, was a strong supporter of Total Education and provided the fledgling program with teaching materials, regular advice, and the use of his farm on Bowen Island. Ms. Meakes remembered his sponsorship and support as "incredible." Mr. Carter was one of several young Vancouver administrators worried that too many capable high school students were either bored in school or dropping out entirely. As an early supporter of innovative programs in Vancouver public schools, Mr. Carter, along with several colleagues, would play a major role in helping to transform the Vancouver School District during the 1970s.[10]

Total Education subsisted throughout 1970/71 on a few private donations and a $2,500 grant from the Anglican Church Foundation, which funded social change projects.[11] The three staff members earned less than $100 per month. In order to manage the finances, the Society for Total Education was incorporated in January 1971 with Dan Meakes and Jim Carter among its six founding directors whose stated purpose was "that students might receive credit for their work as students, and encouragement in their struggle to become mature and responsible persons."[12]

In addition to the staff, thirteen volunteers worked with the students. Most were university undergraduates who came in to teach one course to four to six participants. Some had a religious affiliation but most simply

9   Cathy Meakes, personal interview, April 28, 1997.
10 For more on Jim Carter and Vancouver School Board alternative programs, see Chapter 15.
11 Vancouver Society for Total Education, Financial Statement, August 1971, Registrar of Companies, Victoria.
12 Susan Leslie, Jane Rosettis, and David Kaufman, *Total Education: An Evaluation* (Vancouver: Educational Research Institute of British Columbia; Victoria: Departments of Education and Human Resources, May 1974), 4.

wanted to be of service to young people.[13] One of these volunteers was Ron Eckert, who was finishing his last year of university. He had heard about Total Education while teaching world religions in a youth program at the Unitarian Church. Raised in a family that valued community service, he had been influenced by A. S. Neill's *Summerhill* and by his own experiences in high school. He had always been drawn to education and believed Total Education was "doing something real."[14]

The volunteers taught what they were most skilled at; for example, two engineering students taught mathematics and physics. Dan Meakes taught mathematics, while Cathy Meakes and Larry Haberlin taught English. Classes met twice a week and instructors provided extra help to students who needed it. The program followed the British Columbia curriculum for grades eight to ten with some "funky stuff" thrown in: meditation, Zen Buddhism, foods, and environmental studies. Staff believed almost any topic that interested the teenagers was valuable. "We avoided homework since many students' personal lives were in disarray, but students had to write an examination at the end of each course." Most instructors were thorough and a few were inspiring.

The academic curriculum was reasonably traditional. The major objective was the development of "basic skills," but the teachers attempted to make the material more "integrated and holistic" than in mainstream schools.[15] Students were encouraged to express themselves in writing and to read widely at their level and interest. English class was run like a university seminar—students read such books as *Lord of the Flies* and *Catcher in the Rye,* and the class discussed them. The West Side group had a regular timetable with two-hour classes scheduled throughout the day into the evening. The East Side group, more rigidly structured, met for four solid hours in the afternoon, working mainly on basic English and mathematics skills. There was a wide range of reading levels—the West Side group worked on English 11 and 12, the East Side on English 9 and 10, although achievement was often lower. Classes were small, numbering

---

13 One successful volunteer with cerebral palsy had originally been deemed "uneducable."

14 Ron Eckert, personal interview, October 28, 1996.

15 Dan Meakes had been influenced by his participation in Arts I, an innovative interdisciplinary program at UBC.

from four to ten, but much of the instruction was one-on-one. The staff did not have any professional expertise in dealing with learning problems but attempted to provide firm guidance.

The school took field trips in the city, went to public lectures at UBC, and spent five days in Sorrento. Students and staff spent a weekend in the Fraser Valley woods, experiencing life as early humans—living in "clans" and eating berries. Students got involved in political activities, such as the Amchitka nuclear test demonstrations and the debate on freeways through Vancouver in the early 1970s, and enjoyed political speakers like the long-serving left-of-centre City Councillor Harry Rankin. The staff tried to connect the academic work to meaningful projects relevant to the surrounding community. The photography class participated in a Metro-Media video project that contrasted life in the two neighbourhoods. Making use of learning opportunities in the community was a cornerstone of educational practice at Total Education, similar to other alternative schools.

Total Education School began in 1970/71 with thirty-six students. Photo from *Total Education Yearbook 1970–1980*. For more photographs of Total Education school, see the Vancouver School Board Archives and Heritage website.

The teachers aimed to accept only students who wanted to be there, and once students were accepted, the staff worked hard to get them to live up to their commitments. Students were expected to attend. If they missed class, the teachers would telephone or go out and "track kids down at their homes or in the pool hall." The rules were straightforward: no drugs, no sex, no alcohol, no "bugging" others. Students often stayed at school after hours, drinking coffee, singing, and just "hanging around." Ron Eckert recalled that "the kids were rambunctious" and would "sit around and blab away, drinking, coffee, coffee, coffee ..."[16] Some had challenging mental health problems, and one student became so stressed by examinations, she would burn herself with cigarettes. However, all but two students finished the year, and only one had to be asked to leave for selling drugs. One student completed grade nine in three months.[17] Dan Meakes recalled that they did not have "a lot of philosophy other than reality therapy" and a "truly Canadian pragmatism."[18] Their main concern was to make the curriculum interesting enough to keep the students in the program and to teach them enough to pass grades eleven and twelve provincial examinations. Although building self-confidence was a major objective and "there was lots of communication around interpersonal relations," the teachers did not distinguish between academic and personal goals:

> We had a deep commitment that the school shouldn't waste students' time so they need to get something out of it, like grade twelve. It was pragmatic and the philosophy wasn't for creating an alternate world or for the school to be a tool of political change. All we knew was that in a caring Canadian society our role was to get a few students through. We were committed to students having self-esteem. We knew that students who felt good about themselves would achieve better. That was the extent of it.[19]

16   Ron Eckert, personal interview, October 28, 1996.
17   Valerie Hodge, personal interview, March 8, 1998.
18   Dan Meakes, personal interview, April 23, 1997.
19   Dan Meakes, personal interview, April 23, 1997.

Dan Meakes made most of the early administrative decisions, but once the school was established, all three teachers collaborated on the educational program. From the beginning, the whole student body participated in discussions about rules and the daily operation of the school. Mr. Meakes remembered that "there were no assumptions in 1970 and just hammering out three rules took two weeks. The school became a process for the staff to grow up in. Most of us were simply coming out of our adolescence. It entrenched high ideals. It had a huge impact on the staff."

TRANSITION

After a successful first year, the teachers hoped to expand the program but needed a stable source of funding and a more viable location. The noodle factory was run down, and the West Side group (which included five foster children) had already outgrown the Kerrisdale house. In the spring of 1971, Mr. Meakes and Mr. Haberlin approached Vancouver School District officials, seeking financial assistance for the school. However, during the negotiations, the Meakeses were asked by the church to go north and establish another pioneering venture, the Carcross School in the Yukon, a rehabilitative program for Indigenous youth.[20] Mr. Meakes explained that they were "seen as too radical" by St. Mary's—the youth group was "too ragtag" and there had been complaints from neighbours about the house.[21] Dan and Cathy Meakes saw the Carcross project as a worthwhile challenge and decided to accept the offer. Besides, living their work twenty-four hours a day at Total Education had been very draining. They were confident that the school would continue in good hands under Larry Haberlin's leadership. After successfully establishing Carcross School, the couple continued to be committed activists and eventually moved to Kamloops where they created other spiritual, educational, and social service projects.

With their departure, Larry Haberlin took over the negotiations with the Vancouver School District. The school asked for one teacher, a

20 Poignantly, the Carcross community was created on the site of an abandoned residential school. See J. R. Miller, *Shingwauk's Vision: A History of Native Residential Schools* (Toronto: University of Toronto Press, 1996), 144.

21 Dan Meakes, personal interview, April 23, 1997.

suitable building, school supplies, and access to mainstream high schools for courses requiring specialized equipment or expertise. Jim Carter and other supportive administrators helped convince district officials that such a program was needed in the Vancouver system and desired by the community. After months of discussion and official school visits, the request was endorsed by the school board's Education Committee.

Dr. Alf Clinton, assistant superintendent of Vancouver schools, was another enthusiastic supporter of Total Education. Dr. Clinton, who began his career as a Vancouver high school teacher in the 1950s, believed the public school system should develop a wide variety of alternative programs for high school dropouts and potentially at-risk students. He saw that many of these were capable students but, influenced by the turbulent 1960s, were unhappy with authoritarian school administration. In June 1971 Dr. Clinton was the guiding force behind the establishment of City School, an alternative program developed within the Vancouver school system.[22] He spoke strongly in support of the Total Education proposal:

> This organization has been operating with remarkable success, a school for teenagers between the ages of 15 and 19, who had dropped out of the Vancouver school system because of a feeling that they did not fit in, and assisting them to rehabilitate themselves into the educational sphere. Some of these students have been referred by welfare agencies, and others by Vancouver schools. Educational officials were most impressed with the work being done by this organization, which follows the curriculum of the Department of Education closely, and wherever possible encourages students to re-enter the Vancouver school system. A low pupil-teacher ratio is necessary (22 teachers, volunteer tutors, assistants for 35 full-time students) because a good number of the students need counselling and someone to take a personal interest in them.[23]

22 For more on Alf Clinton's early support of alternative programs in the Vancouver School District, see Chapter 15.
23 VSB Education Committee, minutes, August 24, 1971.

The proposal was approved by the board in September 1971. The trustees appointed one teacher to the Total Education program to be paid on the same scale as all Vancouver teaching staff. The board also designated five bungalows or "huts" on the grounds of the former Model School at Twelfth Avenue and Cambie Street.[24] This was the beginning of the formal relationship between Total Education and the Vancouver School District that would continue to grow over the next four years. Their successful partnership encouraged the integration of other alternative schools into the public system throughout the province.

A year later the board received a favourable report about the school from Dr. Clinton. The trustees were "satisfied that this operation is being run by a responsible group, that it is serving an important segment of the student population not being reached by the schools of the system, and that the Society had met its commitment to the Vancouver School Board for the 1971/72 school year."[25] The trustees renewed their support for the project in 1972/73 and one trustee even suggested that the program be expanded.[26]

The Total Education huts had been built for the Model School in 1912 as practice facilities for teachers destined for one-room schoolhouses.[27] The buildings were minimal but they didn't leak and the toilets worked. Each hut consisted of one large classroom with a high ceiling. Staff, students, and volunteers built partitions out of plywood, constructed lofts, and bought some old stuffed chairs and couches from the Salvation Army. In subsequent years each new group would reconfigure the walls to suit their needs. The huts contained a kitchen, a darkroom, and a small amount of office space, but the facilities were cramped and private work area was at a premium. The run-down condition of the buildings suited the personal taste of most of the students, and staff "didn't have to worry if somebody kicked something." Having staff and students maintain the premises helped keep the school's costs down. Eventually the buildings began to

24 VSB trustees meeting, minutes, September 13, 1971. The Model School was a teacher-training facility established in the early twentieth century.
25 VSB Education Committee, minutes, August 15, 1971.
26 The school shared the Twelfth and Cambie site with the Vancouver Music School and the "Rainbow City Hall," an alternative shadow city government.
27 Leslie, Rosettis, and Kaufman, *Total Education: An Evaluation*, 8.

deteriorate, but not before the school had occupied them for almost fifteen years. The huts were noisy and cold in the winter, but "the kids had fun decorating them and it was a place they made their own."[28]

STAFF

Phil Knaiger filled the Total Education teaching position funded by the school board. Born in Los Angeles, Mr. Knaiger attended UCLA and, during the mid-1960s, participated in civil rights and anti-Vietnam War demonstrations. He remembered the Watts civil rights riots and police breaking up anti-war rallies. Mr. Knaiger decided he "didn't want to raise a family in the United States" and came to Vancouver in 1967.[29] He registered in teacher training at Simon Fraser University and joined the Vancouver School District in 1969. At Point Grey High School he was part of a team of four teachers in the Integrated Program, a pioneer interdisciplinary project.[30] Administrators Jim Carter and Alf Clinton respected Mr. Knaiger's work at Point Grey. Furthermore, he taught mathematics, a subject that needed covering at Total Education.

Total Education began the 1971/72 school year with a full-time staff of four: Larry Haberlin, Phil Knaiger, Ron Eckert, and Rick Bachman, assisted by a large group of volunteers. The following year the staff expanded to ten and remained at between ten and twelve throughout the 1970s. In 1972/73 the staff added Charles Hill, Ginger Maillard, Annie Paterson, Liz Neil, Richard Neil, Bonnie Picard, Tony Simmonds, and Crista Preus. In 1973 employment counsellors Doug Cochran and Glynn Weyler were provided by Canada Manpower, and Peter Seixas joined the staff the following year. These individuals formed the nucleus of a cohesive group that would stay together for several years. Other significant staff members were Gary Miller, Joan Nemtin, Starla Anderson, Lynne Hyndman, Barbara Knox, and Ralph Miller. Most teachers began by volunteering at the school for several months before becoming recognized as staff members, and the extended staff community often numbered well

28   Charles Hill, personal interview, January 8, 1997.
29   Phil Knaiger, personal interview, October 24, 1996.
30   See Chapter 15.

over twenty. Consistent with the egalitarian principles of the school, there were few distinctions made between teachers, teaching assistants, child care workers, and volunteers. Because the school emphasized continuous staff-student interaction, most staff worked full-time, but it was possible to work part-time and some did.[31]

Most staff members were young middle-class adults in their twenties, university educated with a strong social conscience, and profoundly influenced by the political and cultural movements of the 1960s. Each had reasons for ending up at Total Education. Charles Hill came to Vancouver from California because of the Vietnam War. He grew up in a teaching family and volunteered at the school while studying education at UBC. Previously a community health worker on an Opportunities for Youth grant in a free medical clinic, he agreed to teach an astronomy course and volunteered for a year before becoming a staff member in 1972.[32]

Ginger Maillard grew up in New Hampshire and left the United States in the wake of the student deaths at Kent State University in 1970 and the decline of the anti-war movement. She had a teaching certificate and had taught for a year at Alert Bay but, uncomfortable with the racism she observed there, decided to look for a job in an alternative school. She attended the Saturna Island Conference on Alternative Education during the summer of 1971, where she met Larry Haberlin, Phil Knaiger, and Ron Eckert and was offered a job at Total Education.[33] Liz Neil had earned a teaching certificate in Montreal and later taught at Crofton House, a Vancouver private girls' school. She described her world view as a combination of "politically left-wing and counterculture." She spent the summer of 1972 working at the Total Education farm on Bowen Island and joined the staff that fall, becoming one of the district-funded salaried teachers.[34]

Richard Neil grew up in Montreal and earned a master's degree in biology from McGill. After enrolling in a PhD program at UBC, he was

---

31 Other teachers during this period were Steve Nemtin, Nancy Thompson, John Crouch, and Tom Morton. Teachers joining the staff after 1975 were Rick Singer and Doug Ford.
32 Charles Hill, personal interview, January 8, 1997. The free medical clinic was the precursor to Vancouver's Pine Street Clinic.
33 Virginia Eckert, personal interview, April 15, 1999.
34 Liz Cochran, personal interview, April 11, 1997.

drawn into countercultural pursuits and ended up at the Saturna Island conference where, like Ms. Maillard, he met the Total Education staff. He began to volunteer almost immediately. Annie Paterson grew up in Vancouver, left home at seventeen, and became politically active through trying to find daycare for her child. She began volunteering at Total Education in 1972.[35] Bonnie Picard, a single parent on social assistance, noticed Total Education one day in 1972 while taking her daughter to the Vancouver Montessori School, which had just opened on the Model School site. She volunteered for several years before formally joining the staff as a teaching assistant and later as a child care worker.[36]

Doug Cochran grew up in a Vancouver suburb and earned a teaching certificate from Simon Fraser University, arranging to do his practicum at Total Education. He considered himself both a "political person and a countercultural person" and originally joined the staff as an employment coordinator.[37] Peter Seixas grew up in New York and graduated from Swarthmore, a small liberal arts college with a tradition of political activism. He taught for a year in a Black neighbourhood of Philadelphia before deciding to leave the United States for a commune in the forests of British Columbia. Later, after a year as a child care worker with the Children's Aid Society in Vancouver, he joined the staff of Total Education in 1974. Ralph Miller had been a researcher on the LeDain Commission investigating drug use, Joan Nemtin had taught for two years at the New School, and Starla Anderson had taught at City School. An American volunteer, a former member of the radical Weathermen,[38] remained "underground" and low-profile at Total Education. In summary, staff were young, idealistic, and highly engaged in the anti-war movement, social justice causes, and the counterculture.

Staff members favoured a non-coercive style in relating to teenagers and a fiercely democratic and collegial style in dealing with each other. No one cared how much money they were making or how many hours they had to put in. Almost everyone had to supplement their incomes and

---

35   Annie Simmonds, personal interview, April 16, 1997.
36   Bonnie Picard, personal interview, April 25, 1997.
37   Doug Cochran, personal interview, April 11, 1997.
38   The Weathermen was considered an extreme leftist group in the United States.

most had to find summer jobs in order to get by. One teacher taught at a small private school in the mornings so she could spend the afternoons at Total Education, and another sold antiques in her spare time. Several staff members on welfare or unemployment insurance did not even ask for a salary. The school's 1974 advertisement in the *Vancouver Sun* said it well: "Would you like to work in a co-operatively run program with small classes, freedom to innovate and experiment? And would you like to work long hours for a low salary in inadequate facilities with difficult kids?"[39]

As in other alternative schools, staff members formed a close-knit community and developed intense relationships. They were friends as well as colleagues, and several lived together in a large communal house that became "almost another campus." Teachers ate dinner together once a week, and staff meetings were usually followed by some kind of social time. As might be expected in such a close group, relationships developed among staff members; three couples eventually married and two marriages broke up in the late 1970s.

The staff believed Total Education was a unique enterprise—an opportunity to make a difference for a group of young people, to work with each other in a spirit of teamwork, and to create an example of a different kind of politics. As one staff member remarked, "The school became our whole lives, everyone had a real commitment to it. We weren't in it for the money. We felt like we were doing good work."[40] "We were young and fired up and believed in what we were doing," another teacher remembered. "Everybody was passionately interested in what they were teaching—it was an exciting place to be."[41]

Staff brought all the political and cultural expressions of the late sixties/early seventies with them to Total Education. The school was deeply rooted in the counterculture in its early years.[42] Staff members lived communally and were involved in food co-ops, the Kosmic baseball league, free medical clinics, unions, the NDP, and Marxist study groups. Although most did not see Total Education as overtly promoting

---

39 *Vancouver Sun*, May 16, 1974, 72.
40 Phil Knaiger, personal interview, October 24, 1996.
41 Doug Cochran, personal interview, April 11, 1997; Ron Eckert, personal interview, October 28, 1996.
42 Annie Simmonds, personal interview, April 11, 1997.

social change, it was certainly a place where teachers and students could express their political commitment. Teachers organized meetings about socialist education and subscribed to *Ms.* magazine, school vans carried Greenpeace bumper stickers, and students sold "Save the Whales" t-shirts. Some staff were influenced by the Human Potential Movement and brought in individuals to do gestalt therapy, encounter groups, reality therapy, transactional analysis—*I'm OK, You're OK*,[43] blindfolded trust exercises, sensitivity training, communication skills, "group processing," and to help people "express their feelings." Total Education staff did not see their professional lives as separate from their political, cultural, or personal lives, and consequently the boundaries blurred between school and "life."

STUDENTS

Students came to Total Education for many reasons, but all had in common a feeling of being ignored by the system. They were dropouts, kids on probation, countercultural kids, kids with drug problems, kids in foster or group homes, "street kids," bored kids, kids who were rebelling against authority, kids making their own way. A 1974 school evaluation found that 40 per cent of Total Education students attended the school because they "could not hack the regular system." Almost 50 per cent stated that they would have dropped out of school if they had not been accepted at Total Education.[44] The school became a source of stability, keeping students safe and away from homelessness or the drug trade. Total Education provided a therapeutic place "to heal and to reconnect with human beings who cared."[45] The small classes helped encourage academic progress, but for many staff members the academics were never the most important priority. The primary aim was "integrating kids back into some sort of structure in their lives."

---

43   Thomas A. Harris, *I'm OK, You're OK: A Practical Guide to Transactional Analysis* (New York: Harper & Row, 1969).
44   Leslie, Rosettis, and Kaufman, *Total Education: An Evaluation*, 83–84.
45   Phil Knaiger, personal interview, October 24, 1996.

There were several types of students at Total Education. Some were bright but had dropped out because they could not handle authoritarian mainstream schools. These students were mostly middle-class, intelligent and creative, often rebellious and free-spirited young people who were influenced by the counterculture and had difficulty fitting into regular schools.[46] Most had "difficulties with parents, were bored and turned off school, and were looking for a freer atmosphere."[47]

Another group of students consisted of those severely lacking in academic skills. Most were missing the basic academic and social skills needed to succeed in school, and some could barely read or write. These students had few qualifications for work and were often too young to be hired so, if they left school, often ended up on the street.

A third group had emotional problems or violent tendencies.[48] Some had problems at home or felt lost in secondary schools of up to two thousand students. Others were in foster or group homes, some were under the care of psychiatrists or social workers, and a few had been in reform institutions. Some had histories of parental abuse, drug abuse, or prostitution. One teacher had four students in her class from group homes. Some students had supportive parents but many others did not get along with their families.[49]

One typical group of twenty-three students was described by the teachers as "enthusiastic, spontaneous, turned off to formal academia, unfocused, cynical, and highly susceptible to peer group pressure. Four were failing because of lack of basic skills, four wanted a more creative learning environment, fifteen were failing due to lack of interest, nonconformity, or non-attendance. Nine were living with parents, ten on their own, and four in Children's Aid Society placements. Seventeen said they would not have attended school last year were Total Education not available."[50]

Like other alternative schools, Total Education tried to limit the number of students with behavioural or emotional difficulties. But once the school had become part of the public school district, many mainstream principals

---

46   Charles Hill, personal interview, January 8, 1997.
47   Journal of Phil Knaiger, September 1972.
48   Doug Cochran, personal interview, April 11, 1997.
49   Virginia Eckert, Bonnie Picard, Liz Cochran, personal interviews, 1997.
50   Richard Neil and Liz Neil, Group Evaluation, 1973/74.

and counsellors referred difficult students there, since few special-needs programs were available in the early 1970s. The idealistic Total Education staff were reluctant to turn anyone away. Some students had experienced various forms of family problems, and others had learning disabilities. Several students had serious psychological or behavioural problems. One boy referred by the Children's Aid Society broke all the windows one day. A former staff member recalled taking some students with "severe behaviour problems," while another said, "We had kids who were mentally ill that we couldn't handle."[51] Although the school did have access to some psychiatric services, without the expertise on staff to help such students, working conditions were stressful.

Students had a variety of pressing needs, which teaching staff tried to ascertain. Some were bright and capable individuals who had come to Total Education because it offered them a chance to complete school under more flexible conditions. Others were sorting out emotional troubles and learning to survive in the world. Some, with a history of failure and reacting poorly to pressure in public school, enjoyed the smallness, closeness, one-to-one tutoring, and constant support of Total Education. In fact, the school became a substitute home for many students. A hot lunch program of soup and sandwiches was provided. Music, guitars, and singing were always present, and frequent evening activities turned the school into a kind of community centre.[52] As one former student recalled, "We felt like part of a community, we cared about each other."[53]

Still other students, in limbo and uncertain of what to do next, needed a supportive environment in which to consider their future without anxiety.[54] In an information package for prospective teachers, the staff summarized the Total Education student body:

> The idea is to provide an opportunity to learn for kids
> who cannot make it in the public school system. They
> are mostly between the ages of fourteen and seventeen,
> though some are older. Some have talents which have

---

51 Annie Simmonds, personal interview, April 16, 1997; Liz Cochran, personal interview, April 11, 1997.
52 Ron Eckert, personal interview, October 28, 1997.
53 Valerie Hodge, personal interview March 8, 1998.
54 Total Education, Student Type Descriptions, undated.

been frustrated by the public schools. A larger number are
not interested in learning, they're poor attenders, often
they can hardly read or write. They know they don't want
to learn what they've been learning, but most have no
clue what they do want to learn. Some have come back to
school because they want to, some because their parents
want them to, and some because if they don't they'll go
to jail.[55]

When Total Education opened in its Model School location in 1971/72,
it enrolled seventy students with another seventy on the waiting list.[56]
Most students ranged in age from fifteen to eighteen years old.[57] Many
were referred by social workers, counsellors, probation officers, and
Children's Aid societies. The school accepted as many students as possible, and during 1973/74 enrolment reached close to one hundred. But the
staff found that eighty was all they could handle, and enrolment dropped to
eighty-four the next year and remained stable at just over eighty students
throughout most of the 1970s.[58] However, the waiting list reached as high
as 150 students in 1974 and 141 prospective students in early 1976.[59]
Fortunately for those on the waiting list, student turnover was rapid.

By 1976 most students came from the less affluent East Side: "The
majority of our students are aged 15 to 19 and have special problems
which make it difficult for them to learn in regular schools; all of them
have dropped out. They come from all over Vancouver, though there has
been a concentration in the last year of students from northeast Vancouver.
Only 28 per cent come from two-parent families, and half come from
unstable living situations."[60]

55   Total Education, Information for Staff Applicants, undated.
56   Dan Mullen, "Dropout School Just Too Popular," *Vancouver Province*, February
     5, 1972, 15.
57   Vancouver School District, Annual Report, 1973/74.
58   Department of Education, Teacher's Report of Enrolment, June 1975; school
     enrolment list, September 1973, student and staff list, September 1975. Enrolment
     was 88 in 1973/74, 84 in 1974/75, and 80 in September 1975.
59   The waiting list stood at 41 in January 1973 (journal of Phil Knaiger) and 37 on
     October 31, 1974 (staff meeting, minutes); the June 1974 list is reported in Lesley
     Krueger, "Some Alternatives to a World of Endless Defeat," *Vancouver Sun*, June 20,
     1974, 47; see also Vancouver Society for Total Education, "Evaluation 1975/76," 14.
60   Vancouver Society for Total Education, "Evaluation, 1975/76," 28.

Applicants given the highest priority were those for whom no other school was possible: who had been out of school for more than a year, who had been institutionalized, whose family life had disintegrated, who had been expelled from school, who had a physical or learning disability, who were unable to read, who were under psychiatric counselling, who were a year or more behind their age group, or who had been in trouble with the law. Another group of students had voluntarily chosen not to attend public school because they were unable to relate to authority, were bored and looking for more responsibility and stimulation, wanted to work part-time, or simply wanted to graduate more quickly.[61] Such students typically had a high rate of non-attendance and discipline problems, as well as an unsupportive home life.

Almost all students on the waiting list were eventually accepted into the program. They were referred by school counsellors and group homes, or somehow found the school and "just wandered in." The staff tried to ensure that all applicants really wanted to come, and students, parents, and former teachers were asked to fill out lengthy questionnaires. After being interviewed by staff members, applicants were asked how they felt about the interview with the following choices (in the parlance of the day): "uptight, didn't mind it, or pretty good."[62] The only conditions for acceptance were the student's verbal commitment to the program and the willingness of one staff member to act as the student's personal counsellor. Students were largely self-selecting, and even the few who were refused acceptance could eventually get in if they "hung around the school long enough."[63]

Enrolment was always in flux. Seventeen students left the program during the first five months of the 1974/75 school year. Some left to look for work, some registered in other schools, and a few simply found the program was not what they wanted.[64] But other students took their schooling seriously and, although there were no examinations except for graduating students, there were standards of work and credits had to be

61   Total Education, Criteria for Admission, undated.
62   Student application package, 1974/75.
63   Richard Neil, personal interview, April 20, 1999.
64   Total Education student withdrawals, September through January 1975.

earned. A few students stayed right with the program, attended regularly, and worked hard in class. These individuals made rapid progress, and a class of about fifteen graduated every year.

Not all students enjoyed the work or were able to concentrate; some would come and go, and some just drifted away. Those who missed class frequently gave reasons such as "working," "visiting a friend," or just plain "forgot," while others showed up "too late to participate." Daily attendance was sporadic, and teachers had to count on at least 20 per cent absence—"we didn't like it, it was always a struggle."[65] The 1974 school evaluation estimated the average attendance at 65 per cent.[66] The fact that there was never a lack of students wanting to get into the program was sometimes used as a motivating factor: "It was either go there or regular school or reform school."[67] Many students needed more structure and discipline in their lives. The staff came to realize this, but a disciplinary approach did not come naturally to young adults of the 1960s. As Larry Haberlin put it, "I think some of our beliefs got in the way."[68]

GOVERNANCE

Total Education managed to balance its budget during the first three years by keeping salaries low, by employing a dozen volunteers, and through Larry Haberlin's resourcefulness in finding sources of government funding. In 1971/72, the first year of the Total Education/Vancouver School District partnership, the District contributed $7,000 (one teacher salary) to the operation's budget of $31,000. In addition, the school received a federal government Local Initiatives Program (LIP) grant that provided six subsistence salaries totalling $16,000.[69] The school also received funding from the Vancouver Foundation ($4,000), the Children's Aid Society ($3,000), the Junior League, and private donations. Salaries

65   Annie Simmonds, personal interview, April 16, 1997.
66   Leslie, Rosettis, and Kaufman, *Total Education: An Evaluation*, xv.
67   Valerie Hodge, personal interview, March 8, 1998.
68   Larry Haberlin, personal interview, November 12, 1996.
69   Vancouver Society for Total Education, Financial Statement, August 1972.

were the largest expenditure totalling $28,000 in 1972/73.[70] The school finished the year with a surplus of $8,000.

Half of the funding during the first three years came from the school's LIP grant. But by 1973 the federal government had begun to phase out these grants, and the school had to look increasingly to the school district and the provincial government for financial support. A delegation from Total Education approached the school board in March 1973 with a request for more funding. They claimed that the school was serving a distinct need of students who had dropped out of mainstream schools, and pointed out that many referrals to Total Education came from regular school counsellors. The delegation added, "Some Total Education students have re-entered the regular school system without adjustment problems, others have left to find work, students feel better about themselves as individuals, and parents are enthusiastic about the positive effects of the program."[71] Alf Clinton and other Vancouver administrators continued to support the aims and operation of Total Education and believed the school contributed to the district-wide need for alternative programs.[72] Consequently, the board significantly increased the staff allocation for 1973/74 from one teacher and one teacher's aide to three teachers, two teacher's aides, and a part-time secretary.[73]

In 1974 the school found another important source of financial support, the provincial Department of Human Resources, headed by Minister Norman Levi.[74] This department offered substantial support to alternative schools for several years as a result of the NDP government's policy to provide services to needy children in their own homes, schools, and communities.[75] Total Education received $10,000 for three child care workers through the Department's Special Services for Children program.[76] Eventually, the Education and Human Resources Departments

---

70   Vancouver Society for Total Education, Financial Statement, August 1972.
71   VSB Education Committee, minutes, March 19, 1973.
72   "Report from the Advisory Committee to the Administrative Coordinating Team re Alternative Education," Education Committee, minutes, June 5, 1973.
73   VSB meeting, minutes, June 18, 1973.
74   Norman Levi played a key role in establishing public alternative schools. See Chapter 15.
75   Vancouver Society for Total Education, Financial Statement, 1975.
76   This program was headed by Marilyn Epstein, a founder of the New School.

developed a funding formula based on "rehabilitation units" consisting of one teacher, one teaching assistant, and one child care worker. The further addition of two job placement officers from the federal Department of Manpower and Immigration's Local Employment Assistance Program brought the number of paid staff to ten.[77]

Salaries were low. In 1971/72 each of the ten staff members received $250 per month,[78] then $400 per month in 1973,[79] and $600 per month in 1974/75.[80] As the Vancouver School District provided more teachers' salaries, the staff average continued to increase and by 1975/76 reached $865 per month.[81] Although this was an improvement it was still far below what teachers were earning in the public school system. All staff believed their earnings should be equal to mainstream professional salaries.

By 1974 school district policy was to bring all Vancouver alternative programs under the control of the school board.[82] In July the trustees passed a motion to "assume total responsibility for the educational component of Total Education by providing four teachers, four teacher's aides, and related services." The school would retain its separate facility on the Model School site but would be administered by the principal of Eric Hamber Secondary School. The board promised that Total Education would receive standard district support services, increased funding for learning materials, and student access to specialized courses offered at other schools. The trustees commended the school staff associated with Total Education from its inception "for their initiative in implementing and conducting this program."[83]

Phil Knaiger was officially appointed principal, but in practice school decisions were made democratically by the entire staff. All staff members had an equal voice in shaping the program whatever their professional status, and all had identical roles in any case, whether their formal title was

---

77   Vancouver School District, Annual Report, 1973/74.
78   Dan Mullen, "Dropout School Just Too Popular," *Vancouver Province*, February 5, 1972, 15.
79   Journal of Phil Knaiger, November 1973.
80   Vancouver Society for Total Education, Information for Applicants, September 1974.
81   Staff meeting, minutes, December 1975.
82   VSB Education Committee, minutes, July 10, 1974.
83   VSB trustees meeting, minutes, July 15, 1974.

teacher, teaching assistant, or child care worker. Decisions were usually made by consensus, but on rare occasions votes were taken requiring 50 per cent for "simple" items and 75 per cent for major issues: "We will strive for consensus in decision-making. Where, after debate, it is clear that consensus cannot be achieved we will abide by the decision of 75 per cent of the staff."[84] As in other alternative schools, this often resulted in "long and tortuous, endless, and exhausting" staff meetings.

The staff held two meetings per week, one for day-to-day business and one to discuss political, ideological, philosophical, or personal matters. In addition, teachers held several marathon meetings per year to evaluate the school program and the students. Hiring new staff was the most important of all decisions, and prospective new teachers were interviewed by the entire staff. For the most part, new staff members fit in well, but one or two were asked to leave. The school attracted strong personalities, and although all staff members were committed to alternative education, there were significant disagreements sometimes leading to vigorous debate. In 1972 the staff hired a therapist to lead the staff in group therapy, sensory awareness, respectful staff relations, and tolerance of different points of view.[85]

Consistent with their strongly held egalitarian views, all staff members shared their salaries whether they were teachers, teaching assistants, child care workers, or employment counsellors. Since those receiving a Vancouver School District teacher's salary were the highest paid, these individuals ended up subsidizing the salaries of the others. One year staff were delighted when a teacher with a PhD, Ralph Miller, contributed an even larger salary to the common pot. One former staff member recalled that "you had to fight for your position; you had to negotiate for your part of the salary sharing." Another remembered, "Salary sharing always had to be sorted out; it became quite heated at times." Some thought teachers with children should receive a bonus but this was never endorsed. Salary sharing was deeply entrenched and continued until 1982, despite

---

84   Staff meeting, minutes, June 5, 1974.
85   Journal of Phil Knaiger, April 1972. The therapist was Ruth McCarthy, one of the founders of the New School ten years earlier.

considerable pressure from the various funding bodies to make roles and salaries more distinct.

Leadership was an ongoing issue. Larry Haberlin was a highly skilled organizer and was responsible for arranging much of the school's funding through negotiations with school district administrators and government agencies. He often referred to himself as "managing director" but the staff never endorsed that title. Although staff members respected his organizational work on behalf of the school, some resented his leadership style, which they considered not sufficiently collegial. Mr. Haberlin left the school in 1974 to take a position with the Human Resources Department; Ron Eckert and Ginger Maillard also left that June. In assessing Larry Haberlin's role, one long-time staff member said, "Larry was the leader. There were a lot of countercultural types who didn't want any organization at all. Larry had a problem with that. Some staff were unreasonable with him."[86] Mr. Haberlin was responsible for much of Total Education's early organizational success.

Larry Haberlin's departure led the staff to rethink its organizational structure. The growing volume of administrative business allowed some tasks to fall through the cracks, and school record keeping had become inadequate. At a series of meetings in 1974 the staff agreed to create two new positions. The Internal Staff Coordinator was elected each year to chair staff meetings, centralize school records, oversee office work, and coordinate academic decisions. The External Coordinator would represent the school's interests with outside agencies and run the school's work experience program.[87] These positions were taken by Annie Paterson and Doug Cochran but all decisions would still be made democratically.[88] In accordance with a school district request to develop more clearly defined criteria for student admissions, the school formed the Screening Committee (later the School Advisory Committee), which included staff members, the principal of Eric Hamber, and representatives from the

86   Charles Hill, personal interview, January 8, 1997.
87   Staff meeting, minutes, June 3, 1974.
88   Phil Knaiger was the only certified teacher on staff with a permanent VSB contract.

school board, Human Resources, Canada Manpower, and the Metropolitan Health Unit.[89]

Total Education was influenced by the growing feminist movement of the early 1970s and the increasing political consciousness of the women teachers. Female staff members were aware that the school had been led during its earliest years primarily by men. The women worked hard to ensure equality in staff deliberations and to empower the female students with a feminist perspective. Ginger Maillard and Liz Neil organized a Women's Studies course in 1972 to examine traditional female roles and experiences and to form a support group for female students.

From the early days students participated in decision-making through weekly school-wide meetings to discuss school activities, policies, and interpersonal relations. Students and teachers had equal voice in these deliberations, and one former student recalled that "students had a lot of say."[90] But staff members were disappointed that student attendance at general meetings was low and the teachers usually dominated.[91] In 1975 student input was formalized in an elected student committee that acted as a liaison between staff and students and whose members would attend and vote at staff meetings on such issues as school programs and evaluation.[92]

The teachers valued their independence from outside influence and resisted any attempts to make the school more mainstream. Most staff members distrusted authority figures, rarely initiated contact with the school district administration, and "never asked for anything." When a new principal was appointed to Eric Hamber in 1975 and wanted to take a more active role in Total Education decisions, the teachers objected to his assumption that he was in charge.

Staff were also wary of regular district evaluations, even when conducted by friendly administrators like Alf Clinton. In 1974 Dr. Clinton made a series of recommendations to improve the program, including an examination of all courses, a reduction in the number of electives, in-service training in remedial reading and special education, remedial mathematics

---

89   Staff meeting, minutes, May 1974.
90   Valerie Hodge, personal interview, March 8, 1998.
91   Leslie, Rosettis, and Kaufman, *Total Education: An Evaluation*, xiii.
92   Society for Total Education, Student Committee, Constitution, October 17, 1975.

for every student, more "efficient" decision-making, and more funding for upgrading facilities and purchasing teaching materials.[93]

There was a tension: on the one hand, the teachers wanted independence; on the other hand, they wanted support. Staff were frustrated by school board bureaucracy, paperwork, complex ordering procedures, and how long it took to receive supplies. There was no money for extras—field trips, the school lunch program, or the school library, and even basic materials were in short supply. In fact, some staff members believed that Vancouver School District administrators left the school alone in a kind of "benign neglect."

But for the most part, Total Education staff found Vancouver School District officials very supportive. Some administrators, such as area supervisor Charlie Etchell, were grateful that Total Education "was working with kids [that traditional schools] were unable to handle."[94] According to Phil Knaiger, Harold McAllister, principal of Eric Hamber, and Jim Carter, vice principal, were "great to work with." Another staff member felt that Mr. McAllister "understood what we were trying to accomplish."[95] Alf Clinton remained the school's "best liaison to the school board." Former teachers acknowledged that most district officials were well-meaning and saw the value of the program.[96] In addition, the Department of Human Resources child care workers' coordinator worked closely with the staff, and support from Canada Manpower was "invaluable" in developing the vocational program. Parents were supportive and the school held regular open houses, but the parent group was not a major factor in the school.

The Society for Total Education was the legal channel for funding from the Vancouver School District, the Human Resources Department, and Canada Manpower. Board members included two educators, a public health physician, social worker, and Children's Aid Society volunteer

---

93 Administrative Coordinating Team, "Recommendations to Education Committee," 1974.
94 Doug Cochran, personal interview, April 11, 1997.
95 Annie Simmonds, personal interview, April 16, 1997.
96 Charles Hill, personal interview, January 8, 1997.

coordinator.[97] But the board rarely met, and for all intents and purposes the teachers ran the school. After 1977 all ten board members were Total Education teachers.[98]

By 1975 there were enough alternative school teachers in Greater Vancouver to establish an organization to promote their common interests. They sent representatives to the Vancouver Teachers' Association to enlist support in lobbying the school board for higher wages for teaching assistants and for permanent status for alternative programs within the Vancouver School District. The association even organized an alternative school Sports Day, complete with a moon ball and events that emphasized co-operation.[99]

POLICY DEBATES

How strict the staff would be about attendance sparked an ongoing issue. Some teachers were fairly relaxed about students showing up late or not at all, while others were more demanding. Although staff encouraged attendance and punctuality, there were no sanctions for non-attendance. Tremendous energy went into getting kids to attend. One teacher wrote in 1973: "Regular attendance is expected at Total Ed. Every effort is made by the staff to help students sort out their decisions and actions concerning attendance."[100] The general agreement was that if a student wanted credit for a course he or she had to fulfill the minimum requirements, and if a student wanted to remain enrolled in the school he or she had to attend a reasonable number of days. Eventually the staff agreed to clarify attendance expectations and established a rule that students were expected to attend 80 per cent of the time. Students who came rarely or regularly skipped school for no good reason would be asked to leave.

---

97 Society for Total Education, Annual Report, January 1972. Board members Jim Carter and Don Burbidge, a university instructor and North Vancouver School Board chair, had been New School parents.

98 Society for Total Education, annual reports, 1977–1981. The board did not meet once between 1974 and 1977.

99 Society for Learning Alternatives of Greater Vancouver, Constitution and By-Laws, April 1975; minutes, February 2, 1976.

100 Journal of Phil Knaiger, 1973.

The policies on drugs, alcohol, and sex also gave rise to different points of view. In the end, drugs were prohibited at any school activity, but staff knew that most students used marijuana on a regular basis and drugs were present on almost every school trip. Drugs were also a problem at the school's Bowen Island farm, and a meeting of the school community decided that "anyone found with dope at the farm will be asked to leave on the next ferry."[101] There were constant debates about how strict to be and what to do about individual violators. Finally, in 1974, the staff passed the following motion: "No illegal drugs are permitted at the school or on school functions or activities. The consequence is a two-week suspension."[102] Eventually some students were asked to leave the school because of drug use.

School policy on teenage sex was a less clear-cut issue. The staff had to give the appearance of disapproving of sexual relations among the students. In reality, however, many did not object, and sexuality, birth control, and sexual health were frequent topics of discussion.

Total Education staff members were divided on how much time should be spent teaching basic academic skills, and how much time on personal development, life skills, and counselling. This debate went to the core of staff beliefs about the purpose of the school and reflected two different types of adults attracted to Total Education—educators and counsellor/ social workers. Some staff members were particularly concerned about students lacking academic skills and thought it was their responsibility to teach them basic literacy. Others wanted to emphasize counselling to help students develop self-confidence and meaningful relationships. Some staff wanted to make it as easy as possible for kids to get through Total Education. Others believed they should challenge the students. There was an underlying tension around the issue of academic professionalism. A few years later the re-introduction of provincial examinations in British Columbia sparked considerable debate before the school finally decided to offer examinable courses. Ultimately, the staff had to decide whether Total Education was a school or a treatment program and compromised on a "school completion program."

---

101 School meeting, as reported in the journal of Phil Knaiger, January 1974.
102 Staff meeting, minutes, November 15, 1974.

CURRICULUM

The Vancouver School Board officially described the Total Education program as "a combination of upgrading basic skills, field trips, improving decision-making and social skills, with the overall objective of proceeding to further education or training or employment."[103] But the Total Education staff had more ambitious goals for their students: academic (to develop literacy, communication, calculation, and critical thinking), social (to cope with problems and to apply the skills necessary for community co-operation), personal (to develop a positive self-concept), vocational (to develop employment skills and to make meaningful choices), and physical (to develop attitudes conducive to good health):[104]

> Total Education reaffirms the right of every individual to education. It is a school where young people can learn without the stress of competition; where, in a co-operative and self-critical environment, students are encouraged not only to fulfill the academic requirements of grade twelve, but to develop all areas of potential: the intellectual and the physical, the personal and the social.[105]

Several principles underlay all learning at Total Education. The staff believed it was essential that each student find a natural style and rate of learning to build self-esteem, without the competition "which is overemphasized in all areas of our society." Secondly, teachers sought to make all activity at Total Education relevant to the lives of their students and to address rather than ignore emotional problems that got in the way of learning. Thirdly, staff saw as an essential part of their job helping students make appropriate decisions about their learning and about their lives. Above all, the Total Education staff believed that no learning could take place without a quality relationship between teacher and learner:

> One of the most important requirements for learning, particularly with our students who have weak self-images, is the quality of the interpersonal relationships between the

---

103 Vancouver School District, Annual Report, 1973/74.
104 Total Education, "Goals and Objectives," undated.
105 Vancouver Society for Total Education, "Evaluation 1975/76," 3.

student and teacher. The teacher must come across as a real person with trust and respect for the learner, or very little of value occurs in class.[106]

Small classes at Total Education were conducive to discussion in a French class.
The Province, February 5, 1972

Total Education offered a complete high school curriculum from grades eight to twelve. The majority of students were enrolled in grade ten and eleven courses, but several completed grade twelve.[107] Academic courses included English, International Literature, Mathematics, Social Studies, World and Canadian History, Military History, Geography, Classical Philosophy, Science, Biological Life and Consciousness, Astronomy, Psychology, Anthropology, Economics, Business, and Laboratory French. Because the staff considered non-academic courses important in developing student interests, the school offered a wide variety of electives: Going to College, Women's Studies, Male Studies, Current Problems, Yoga, Basic Guitar, Jazz, Chorus, Flute, Musicianship, Drama, Arts and Crafts,

106 Larry Haberlin, "Educational Philosophy," in "Vancouver Society for Total Education," Annual Report, 1972/73, 8–11.
107 Vancouver Society for Total Education, Annual Report, 1972/73, 4.

Film, Life Rhythm, Nutrition and Natural Foods, Physical Education, Guidance, Child Care, Woodwork, Mechanics, Photography, Typing, Life and Study Skills, Sensitivity and Awareness, Human Sexuality, the Third Eye, Go, and the Art of Flying.[108]

The school's offerings portrayed an excitement and innocence that characterized the expansive and exploratory nature of the post-counterculture period. The Third Eye Workshop was a global study of physiology, behaviour, and psychology exploring states of consciousness, drug effects, dreaming, memory and learning, brain function, religious experience, and therapy.[109] One science course highlighted "myths, magic, and reality," while a psychology course studied influential works by Fritz Perls, R. D. Laing, Eric Fromm, and Eldridge Cleaver. Students learned popular crafts of the day, including batik, macramé, candle-making, crochet, sewing, and embroidery. Military history was somewhat of an anomaly in a school largely staffed by anti-war activists, but the social studies teacher believed this was an effective way to interest students in history, and his re-enactments of historical battles sometimes lasted all evening.[110] Most importantly, teachers at Total Education wanted to teach in a different way that encouraged students to discover rather than to be told. As one teacher wrote in his journal in 1973:

> In mathematics we have spent years being conditioned in an atmosphere that stifled rather than stimulated. Doing what the teacher wants and expects has meant success in school. Mathematics is not "getting the answers" but rather discovering patterns, relationships, the beauties of symmetry. No one can make your discovery for you and no one knows what you will discover.[111]

Total Education teachers developed most of their own courses, and the curriculum depended on the expertise and particular interests of the teachers in any given year. Teachers tried to relate their courses to the students' personal lives, incorporated popular topics of the day, and chose material

---

108 Total Education, Course List, Fall 1973.
109 This all-inclusive psychology course was developed by Richard Neil.
110 This course was designed by Charles Hill.
111 Journal of Phil Knaiger, January 1973.

they thought would interest students. One year two teachers designed a psychology course emphasizing the lives of teenagers with readings and discussions about adolescent behaviour, identity, communication, self-confidence, family, and sexuality. The teachers attempted to teach in a "holistic" manner, integrating subject areas as well as the academic and counselling components of the curriculum. If a course was not working with a particular group of students, the teacher changed the format. Few teachers at Total Education had teaching certificates, and even those who did were relatively new to the profession so some courses required a great deal of preparation.

Because almost all Total Education students had been high school dropouts and many had negative attitudes toward learning, the teachers tried to plan courses that would avoid making students feel frightened or overwhelmed. The mathematics course description assured students that although "regular attendance is necessary," no homework would be required, and it guaranteed "success to every person who participates." The Basic Guitar course promised that "a limited amount of instruction will be given and a good time will be had by all."[112]

On the other hand, some courses had ambitious objectives. The Drama course description expressed hope that reading several plays together would lead to students' "greater and deeper understanding of the nature of being." The art teacher expected to cover papier mâché, silkscreening, painting, ceramics, films, puppets, costumes, embroidery, drawing, murals, mobiles, balance, found art, carving, body awareness, art fundamentals, city resources, and "much, much more." The goal of the Jazz Studies course was "to break the individual's reliance on commercialized music by presenting alternative forms." Perhaps the most ambitious of all was a mathematics course that aimed, through a "creative approach, to free the individual to think for himself, to provide opportunities to discover the basic pattern, order, and relationships both in the natural world and within our minds, and to help students learn the skills which they find are necessary for survival in the modern age."[113] Such optimistic goals were indicative of the perspective of these young teachers who continued

---

112 Total Education, Course List, Fall 1973, 3.
113 Total Education, Course List, Fall 1973, 1.

to carry the hopes and dreams of the 1960s. They wanted to remake the world.

The school day began at ten in the morning but even then students were often late. Most classes were scheduled for Monday to Thursday afternoons and met one to two times per week, except for mathematics, which was held every day.[114] Some evening classes were held at the instructor's house. Classes had only ten to fifteen students and were discussion oriented, creating an informal environment that discouraged the kind of behavioural difficulties one might find in a regular classroom. Teachers were free to use whatever methods worked and employed a wide variety of approaches. Some teachers planned their lessons carefully and others preferred classes to be spontaneous. As the years passed, teachers became more thorough in their organization and courses had more structure. One long-time staff member concluded in his course evaluation in 1976: "I greatly enjoyed attempting this approach to more structured learning at Total Ed. Having a detailed plan of activity and study, prepared in advance, had an unexpected benefit: less sleepless nights wondering what will happen the next day!"[115]

The mathematics courses taught by Phil Knaiger provided for all students to work at their own levels. General mathematics was conducted through a self-pacing individualized program helping students work through basic skills, while in academic math students used textbooks and standard exercises. Classes were "small, relaxed, and informal" with "no examinations or schedules to meet, and no harmful competition with each other." Some students explored mathematical concepts and operations through group activities. They investigated geometric relationships through constructing string figures or using geoboards, and reinforced arithmetical concepts with Cuisenaire rods. Mr. Knaiger's "creative math laboratory" contained tools, materials, puzzles, games, and books to be used for special projects such as making domes, geometric models, spirographs, and "soma blocks." The class also visited the Mathematics Museum at the Seattle Science Centre.[116] Most students were successful

---

114 Total Education, timetables, November 1973 and September 1974.
115 Charles Hill, Course Evaluation, June 1976.
116 Total Education, Course Descriptions, September 1974.

and made progress. The few students who were proficient in mathematics progressed quickly but "those that were slower were getting it too."

The school offered several upper-level English courses. One survey of international literature included Middle Eastern cuneiform writing, Egyptian hieroglyphics, North American picture writing, traditional and contemporary ballads, folk music, and anti-war writing. Another literature course presented myths, theatre, and Canadian literature. Total Education students read and discussed everything from *Canterbury Tales* to *The Ecstasy of Rita Joe*, short stories, novels, essays, newspaper articles, Pauline Johnson's legends, and practical books such as *Edible Plants of BC* or *How to Build a Log Cabin*. English teachers tried their best to make the literature personal and relevant to students' individual experience. A creative writing workshop presented open-ended writing projects stimulated by field trips. A lower-level English class emphasized basic writing skills and grammar ("Brute English" the teacher called it) in a highly prescribed format but, according to the teacher, was "too rigid and monotonous" to interest the students.[117]

Humanities and science courses presented traditional material using seminar-style classes and field trips. The geography course covered climate, land forms, and environmental education, and student activities included hiking, mapping, exploring the city, and trips to Brothers Creek, Alouette Lake, and Wreck Beach. Introductory psychology included animal behaviour, the nervous system, social behaviour, and consciousness. The biology course included genetics and physiology, philosophy of science and social responsibility, and ecology and evolution. The school was limited in its science offerings by a lack of equipment, but students had the option of using the laboratory at a neighbouring high school. French courses included an informal conversation group, and in Current Problems the class would "watch the news, do a special project, and see films." The Life Rhythm Project was an experiential anthropology course in which students graphed human history and simulated early human activities.[118] Projects in British Columbia history included students' research assignments at the city archives.

---

117 Course Evaluations, June 1974.
118 This unusual course was developed by Crista Preus.

Drama courses offered improvisation, play production, performance, awareness and concentration techniques, relaxation, voice, movement, mime skits, theatre games, literature of the theatre, and more. The dance class was a combination of improvisation activities and exercises for coordination, release of tension, and self-expression. The school offered a wide variety of arts and crafts instruction, and some music courses were provided each year according to the skills possessed by staff members.[119]

The Women's Studies and Male Studies courses reflected the growing awareness of gender issues, and first women and then men formed discussion and support groups. The Women's Studies course was intended to build confidence and empower the girls to discover their identity as women. Course objectives were "to put in perspective and understand our past and present experiences being brought up female, to examine women's roles, to do a cross-cultural study of women in other societies, and to develop a trust group in which we can share feelings, problems, and co-operation." Other topics studied were the family, sexuality, and birth control. Eventually Women's Studies evolved into a course called Women's Literature, which studied women's writing and the portrayal of women in literature. The Male Studies course was less thoroughly planned, the course prospectus stating: "We will look at what it means to each of us to be a male animal in a complicated society." The course included discussion of sexual behaviour, gender roles, communication and sensitivity, and "male liberation."

Total Education had a strong political commitment. Many staff members wanted to do more than merely help students adjust to a society they believed required far-reaching social change. As the staff saw it, the school system their students had escaped was symptomatic of wider problems in Canadian society. This political component was built into several courses, such as a 1975 course developed by Peter Seixas, called "Living in a Capitalist Society." Topics included the nature of capitalism; class and inequality; alienation in work, school, and the family; commodity fetishism (consumerism); international capitalism; and alternatives.

---

119 During the earliest years most music courses were offered by Tony Simmonds. Arts and crafts were taught primarily by Lynn Hyndman and Bonnie Pickard.

STUDENT LEARNING AND COUNSELLING GROUPS

Beginning in the second year as enrolment increased, the student body was organized into five "Groups" of approximately fifteen students. This was a way to retain the personal contact between teacher and student that the staff believed was so essential to student success. The Group was intended to provide "a smaller unit within the school for which the student comes to feel the sense of familiarity and belonging which he has lacked in the large impersonal atmosphere of the public school."[120] Each Group was led by a team of two teachers, one male and one female, and had a home base in one of the school huts. Unlike "home-room" at traditional high schools, Groups formed the core of the Total Education program and were considered the "main motivational force in the school."[121] The counselling program was organized through the Groups and every student was assigned to one of the Group leaders for individual counselling. Each counsellor had to meet with eight to ten needy students each week in addition to their regular workload. Group leaders also made home visits and, where possible, worked with the families to teach conflict resolution and problem-solving.

Each Group had a different character that reflected the needs and interests of the students. Students were placed in Groups according to age, academic skill level, and personal growth needs. One year the five Groups were called: Basic Skills, Motivation, Social Skills, Graduating Skills, and Work Experience. Another year the Groups were organized around the following themes: 1) basic reading and writing skills, 2) writing as a "tool for the expression of ideas arising from studies in other areas," for students who needed less "structure and less intensive study of English," 3) "experiential learning," personal growth, decision-making, responsibility, and emotional awareness, 4) encouragement of "independence, responsibility, and self-confidence" for older self-directed students completing grade twelve and often living on their own with part-time jobs,

---

120 Total Education, Curriculum Report, January 1974, 1.
121 Total Education, Curriculum Report, June 1974, 2.

and 5) "interaction skills," listening to others, focus and concentration, sensitivity, and fulfilling commitments for students on a work experience program.[122]

Groups met for two hours each morning, students receiving credit for English, Social Studies, Physical Education, and Guidance. The main priorities for Group sessions included instruction in reading and writing, upgrading basic academic skills, correcting learning disabilities, group counselling, and discussion of personal issues. One Group leader initiated a carpentry project and several Groups created a school newspaper. Each Group had weekly physical education at a Mount Pleasant Boys' Club gymnasium where they played floor hockey and volleyball, but motivation for physical education classes was low.

Groups took numerous field trips around the community to factories, parks, the library, the art gallery, the Vancouver Museum, the Children's Hospital, plays, and concerts. There were Group dinners, lunches at the White Spot, shopping trips, and parties. There were so many field trips that the school's two vans were in constant use and had to be reserved in advance.

Group leaders tried to choose study topics that were relevant, practical, and interesting to students and incorporated both academic and personal growth activities. Topics covered a huge range and included: current events, local history, yoga, writing poetry, playing music, mythology, adolescence and family, comparative religion, government and war, art and crafts, growing up male and female, survival skills, nutrition, organic gardening, Indigenous peoples' histories, social class, labour history, automobile repair, utopias, and the limits of science.[123] Students discussed such topical issues as pollution and pesticides, racism, guerrilla warfare, and student protest. They read the LeDain Commission Report on drug use, Eastern religious works, and popular books of the day on alternative schooling.[124]

---

122 Total Education, Curriculum Report, January 1974, 2–6.
123 Total Education, Curriculum Report, June 1974, 3–27.
124 Favourite authors were A. S. Neill, Paul Goodman, Jonathan Kozol, James Herndon, John Holt, Herbert Kohl, and George Leonard.

Many staff members were strongly influenced by the Human Potential Movement, and Total Education offered several courses in sensitivity and awareness training and therapeutic techniques. These included a wide range of popular 1970s practices, including trust exercises, gestalt therapy, bio-energetics, massage, chanting, communication games, breathing and body exercises, focus and concentration, exploration of fears, and expression of feelings. Participants in these courses also discussed self-confidence, motivation, relationships, and personal problems. For example, the Art of Flying course sought to "investigate the idea that we often make life a lot more difficult for ourselves than it has to be. We will consider how we tend to undervalue ourselves and, consequently, accept relationships in our work, family, and friends that are a lot less enjoyable and creative than they could be."[125]

Personal growth was also a major focus of Group sessions through in-depth discussion of emotional issues, family background, gender roles, drug use, dating, and sexuality. Total Education took sex education seriously and supplied students with information on sexuality and birth control as well as "principles of sexual well-being." Students were asked to comment on: "What do you feel a member of the opposite sex notices about you? What do they expect of you on a date? How would you discourage someone who wanted to make it with you? What would your parents say if you were pregnant?"[126] Group sessions were intended to facilitate growth in confidence, trust, tolerance, communication, conflict resolution, awareness of others, decision-making, and the ability to work independently. Students also discussed pertinent issues such as punctuality, commitment, how to criticize and compliment others, self-defeating behaviour, developing a positive self-image, and setting realistic personal goals.

Total Education offered students a variety of practical courses intended to promote success in school and everyday life. A course called Going to College featured field trips to university and college campuses. In Study Skills, students learned outlining, skimming, note taking, researching,

---

125 Total Education, Course List, Fall 1973, 7. This course was developed by Ron Eckert.
126 Journal of Phil Knaiger, October 1973.

reading graphs and charts, filling out forms and applications, using an index, and using the dictionary. A course called Workshop was open to any student "who wants work experience or who wants to improve his/her job skills." The course discussed "creative job search," unions, employers' and employees' rights, "living on and off the land, and living on your own." Students were placed in volunteer positions in the community and took field trips, watched films about work, and compiled a "working world information book."[127]

In a course called Life Skills, students were taught how to find and maintain a place to live, how to find and keep a job, how to handle money, how to set goals, and how to practise good health and nutrition. Activities included exploring different neighbourhoods, meeting with landlords, writing application letters, role playing job interviews, visiting food outlets, preparing a school luncheon, and debating the merits of various diets. There were lectures on anatomy, medical clinic services, and cooking techniques, and outside resource people gave presentations on housing policy, tenants' rights, and job training programs. Another practical course called "How to Survive in Your Native Land" presented activities designed to help students learn everyday skills.[128] Some of these were: "Open a bank account, visit the law courts, be an apprentice for a day, visit Canada Manpower, plan a trip to a foreign country, involve yourself in an election, learn a new craft, list the city's social agencies, write to your MP, investigate renting living accommodations." A course in "living on your own" and "co-operative living" was designed for independent students. Instruction in life skills and long-range vocational planning was a major component of Group sessions.

Total Education and subsequent alternative schools had a distinct rehabilitation objective. Skill levels varied widely and almost half of the students had significant reading problems. Teachers could not use the same methods with everybody and structured their courses to accommodate a wide range of abilities. A team of four teachers provided reading and writing special assistance to any student who needed it, and students could register for weekly individual tutorials. The often untrained English

---

127 Total Education, Course Descriptions, September 1974.
128 This was the title of a popular book about education by James Herndon.

teachers had to be flexible and imaginative. One teacher remembered a student in grade nine English who could not read or write. "I started him on comic books then went to word recognition and whole language. Then I tried phonics, which I learned from my own child's teacher!"[129]

By the mid-1970s the school began to adopt a more professional approach to reading and writing. Teachers worried that students were not achieving acceptable writing standards, and an English Committee was formed to think of solutions to the "English problem."[130] The committee decided that two hours of English instruction per week was not enough and recommended that all students be assessed each year by a reading teacher and that a compulsory writing course be established at the grade eleven level as a prerequisite for grade twelve. Gary Miller, with a strong reading background, helped the staff develop a systematic remedial program offering one-to-one instruction, somewhat like a modern learning assistance centre. But sporadic attendance and inconsistent motivation made progress slow, and how to best meet the students' remedial needs was a frequent topic of discussion. Due to the teachers' lack of expertise, systematic diagnosis of reading problems was often lacking so students did not always receive the help they needed.

One of the major aims of Group sessions was to improve the students' writing skills through regular assignments. These included writing letters, book reports, journals, research projects, and creative stories. Students also wrote about their own personal growth and practical subjects such as "Describe Your Job Interview." Some students needed to learn skills as basic as spelling, sentence structure, paragraph outlines, and using the dictionary. The goal was functional literacy for everyone. Teachers reported an improvement in students' writing, and some students also expressed greater enthusiasm for reading.

Overall the curriculum was ambitious, and the staff worked hard to develop courses and activities that would draw the students in. Most students reported that they liked coming to school, and many expressed increased confidence in learning. On the other hand, some students did as little as possible and attendance was always a struggle. Group leaders

129 Annie Simmonds, personal interview, April 15, 1997.
130 Staff meeting, minutes, May 22, 1974.

were disappointed when students did not show up consistently or failed to follow through on their agreements due to being wrapped up in their own problems. Some teachers felt limited by their lack of skill or experience in counselling or remedial work.[131] Others believed they were hampered by an unrealistic workload, too few staff for effective counselling, inadequate curriculum resources, and few support services. The school received little help from outside agencies during the 1970s except for the Metropolitan Public Health Service, which provided staff to assist with health needs, and a physician who volunteered her services from time to time.[132] Some students were so needy that Group leaders allowed them to stay at staff members' own homes when they had nowhere else to go. Teachers worked long hours, and many found their dual role as teachers and counsellors a strain.[133]

WORK EXPERIENCE

From the earliest days, a major aim of Total Education was to provide students with work experience and the development of skills for engaging in meaningful work. In June 1973 the school, under Larry Haberlin's leadership, took part in the Local Employment Assistance Program (LEAP) in conjunction with the federal Canada Manpower department, which provided a grant of $71,000 to place students in part-time jobs. The department's Special Programs Division provided two employment coordinators, Doug Cochran and Glynn Weyler, to help the school staff place students in appropriate part-time jobs.

This program was particularly significant because a substantial number of Total Education students were living on their own and needed employment. Furthermore, the staff believed that holding down a job would be highly beneficial to young people with low self-esteem. Finally, the social service projects that made up the bulk of the program fit perfectly with the school's philosophy of contributing to a better world. The goals of the program were: to employ young people who are presently unemployed; to

---

131 Charles Hill, Group Evaluation, June 1975.
132 Dr. Danica Holt, a member of the original board of directors.
133 Bonnie Picard, personal interview, April 25, 1997.

help students develop self-esteem through involvement in worthwhile and productive projects; to provide students with work experience, job training, skill development, and employment references; to aid young people in setting realistic and rewarding vocational and life goals; to develop responsibility and reliability in the participants; and to assist students in the completion of grade twelve through a work-study approach. In addition, the program hoped to "aid in the development of the community and to make the area a more liveable and satisfying place to be."[134]

The program organizers hoped students would develop positive attitudes toward work and themselves through helping others. Accordingly, most of the work experience positions were with "community oriented" projects and service agencies such as daycare centres, youth projects, and neighbourhood houses. Students could provide a real service to understaffed programs such as daycare centres, and several organizations asked for replacement workers when students' terms were over. Students were also placed in private businesses, particularly those with a social or environmental mission. Students were placed according to their financial need, school schedule, interests, future goals, personal qualities, and the needs of the organization.

Eighteen students were placed in the first four months of the program. All enjoyed the work and, according to an interim evaluation, almost all had a positive attitude on the job, improved their self-concept, learned useful skills, were clearer about their vocational goals, and improved their academic performance.[135] Only two left their jobs. By June 1974 forty-one students, aged sixteen to nineteen, had worked on the LEAP project, from five to twenty-five hours per week. The next year the program placed another twenty-three students in jobs throughout the community. Students were expected to carry a full load of academic courses in addition to their job placement. The school's flexible scheduling, tutoring sessions, and academic and personal counselling helped facilitate the work program. Teachers encouraged LEAP students to explore topics in their course work relevant to their work experience.

134 Doug Cochran, Glynn Weyler, "The Energy of Youth: An Evaluation Report on the Local Employment Assistance Program at Total Education School," 1975, 1.
135 LEAP, Interim Report, December 1973, 7–12.

The list of participating organizations was extensive. Many were alternative service agencies or businesses but some mainstream organizations also participated. Most participating agencies considered the student workers valuable assets. At the Fairview Information Centre, two students helped build an adventure playground, survey residents, plan community services, and produce a community newsletter. The coordinators of the centre wrote: "Their energies enriched and gave direction to many of our efforts concerning community planning and developing much-needed community services." A student with the Children's Aid Home Care Service helped needy families with housework and looking after children. Her supervisor wrote: "She has been very reliable and does a super job; there is a good possibility that we will hire her." The supervisor at St. Michael's Daycare wrote that the student workers showed maturity and dependability. A student at Intermedia learned a variety of publishing and graphic arts skills and was "really an asset" to the company.[136]

Students learned a great variety of skills in their placements. At the Society for Pollution and Environmental Control, student workers helped with office work and research projects. At the Kitsilano Information Centre, a student provided information on housing and medical clinics, while a student at the Crisis Centre worked on the telephone line. A student with an interest in mechanics learned a great deal as a mechanic's helper at the People's Garage, and a student at the Riley Park Youth Project helped develop a recreational program for directionless neighbourhood kids. Three students worked at the Fed-Up Food Co-op while another worked in the Nature's Path Health Food Bakery. Several students learned office and public relations skills at Greenpeace and Kitsilano Neighbourhood House, while students working in a small private business learned how to manage a retail store operation. One student taught basic skills to children on probation at Operation Step-Up (a recently formed public alternative program in Vancouver), another interested in botany worked at the UBC Greenhouse, still another learned drafting and design at the Urban Design

---

136 Vancouver Society for Total Education, "LEAP Evaluation, December 1974," 3–6.

Centre, and a student at the Sunnyhill Children's Hospital provided occupational and play therapy as well as tutoring.[137]

Most placements were successful and students found the work experience valuable. The student workers were paid a regular, though low,
salary. The experience gave them an opportunity to be self-supporting, to
serve a valuable function in the community, and to receive training and
job experience. One student commented that the incentive of meaningful work "helped me feel good about myself."[138] Students also gained
the capability to relate to people of different ages and backgrounds and
the ability to seek out jobs. For many students, working motivated them
to study in areas related to their job.[139] One of several students at Co-op
Radio, considering a career in broadcasting, wrote that she was "grateful
for the opportunity to explore broadcasting, to develop existing skills as
well as acquire new ones."[140] Several students were so successful that they
were offered permanent employment by these organizations.

Teachers found the program "particularly useful for students who live
on their own and need the money to complete their schooling, as well as
beneficial for all students, preparing them for the difficult task of working
and living on their own." Staff members also noted growth in the students'
responsibility, consistency, enthusiasm, and sense of usefulness as well
as the beneficial effect of "real life experience in expanding students'
awareness of their society." Larry Haberlin believed the program's main
strengths were "the involvement of young people in creative and interesting work situations and the development of independence and control
over their own lives." The supportive job situations resulted in increased
motivation, confidence, and a better grasp of their abilities.[141] The few
unsuccessful placements were usually due to the student's unsuitability

---

137 Others were Kitsilano Neighbourhood House, Kits House Adult Drop-In, Canadian
     Ceramics, Vancouver Art Gallery, Vancouver Taped Books, Vancity Credit Union,
     Kitsilano Community Centre, Women's Centre (an all women's repair garage),
     Vancouver Resources Board, Bayview School Learning Assistance, Selkirk
     Elementary School, six daycare centres, YMCA, Richmond Animal Hospital, North
     Shore Cable Television, North Shore Shopper, Video Inn, two florists, a bookstore,
     and the Vancouver School Board office.
138 Doug Cochran and Glynn Weyler, "The Energy of Youth," 1975, 13.
139 Interim LEAP Report, June 1974.
140 STEP 1975, Total Education, Project Report.
141 Doug Cochran and Glynn Weyler, "The Energy of Youth," 1975, 15, 17, 18.

for, or lack of interest in, a particular kind of work. The program evaluation indicated that the great majority of LEAP graduates were working or attending training programs or colleges. It cited many successes:

> "David" had many problems at home and in the regular school system before attending Total Education. He moved out of his home and became involved in the drug and night-time scene in Vancouver. Beginning at Total Education he was frequently late or absent and was not completing assignments or living up to commitments. David's involvement with LEAP marked the beginning of a change in attitude for him. He began to take school more seriously, to attend more frequently, and to complete assignments. The counsellor noticed him moving away from his night-life involvement and taking an interest in developing the skill he was training at. He responded to the job positively, being punctual, responsible, and energetic. The job is of great value to David, bringing more depth to his relations with others and school.
>
> "Lois" has attended Total Education for two years. She has always been a bright student. However, she has seldom worked to her potential. She seemed to be bored with school prior to her involvement with LEAP and had little direction or conception of her capabilities. She is working with children in a professional capacity and thoroughly enjoys it. Her supervisor is enthusiastic about her work and her counsellor feels that her job is "the most exciting thing in her life." The job has provided a realistic focus for her studies as she now intends to go on to university and train further in the field she now works in.[142]

The LEAP organizers also initiated an outreach program to serve unemployed youth referred by Canada Manpower or other agencies. The outreach staff provided vocational and educational counselling, helped young people upgrade basic employment and job application skills, and in many cases found appropriate volunteer, training, or employment positions.

---

142 Doug Cochran and Glynn Weyler, "The Energy of Youth," 1975, 19–20.

After three years the funding for the LEAP program expired in 1976, disappointing the staff who feared the loss of "a major component of our educational program would be a blow to the school." Teachers worried that self-supporting students would drop out of school thereby weakening the whole program, and one teacher feared there would be an increase in drug use and students in trouble with the police.

In order to continue the work experience program, the school opened a restaurant on Fourth Avenue near Burrard Street called "Theodora's." Doug Cochran provided the leadership for this project and mortgaged his house to raise the necessary capital of $20,000. The operation was staffed by part-time student workers, a few full-time non-student employees, and several coordinators from the Total Education staff. Having its own business gave the school more flexibility in placing students, and a labour intensive restaurant was ideal. It provided students with experience in real life workplace situations, and the staff also liked the restaurant because it was a vehicle through which students could learn about nutritious food. Although the project organizers wanted the restaurant to operate as a democratic co-operative with all staff having control over their working conditions, it was also essential that the business be run efficiently and not lose money, since any losses would have a direct impact on school programs.[143] During the late seventies a large percentage of Total Education students gained valuable work experience at the restaurant, and Theodora's continued to operate for six years.[144] The work experience program was an unqualified success, far ahead of its time.

OUTDOOR EDUCATION

Outdoor and environmental education was another innovative feature of Total Education. In 1971 the school rented a twenty-acre farm on Bowen Island from Jim Carter, Eric Hamber's vice principal, for a nominal fee. The staff engaged two caretakers, Peter Frinton (environmentalist, biologist, and outdoor educator) and Carol Robb. The farm provided an opportunity for

---

143 Doug Cochran, "Theodora's: Not Just Grist for the Mill," in *Working Teacher* 2, no.3 (1979): 16–19.

144 Charles Hill, "A Short History of Total Education School," in *Total Education, 1980* (Yearbook), 3.

personal retreats and for students to learn building skills, gardening, chopping wood, and making fires. The "rustic" facilities were also conducive to survival education.[145] The school also used the farm for regular weekend trips for group bonding—a place "for staff and students to get to know each other through the experience of living together for a short time in an informal setting."[146] Individual students or small groups were permitted to stay at the farm for periods of up to one week, and the farm also took in a few students with more serious mental health problems from time to time. The farm hosted a conference on alternative education in 1973. Farm visits were popular and teachers and students had to reserve their times well in advance. In addition to trips to the farm, the school took numerous groups of students on hiking and camping adventures to nearby recreational areas. These included skiing and snowshoeing excursions as well as camping trips to Alice Lake. In 1975 forty-five students spent a week in a winter lodge near Whistler Mountain,[147] while another year a group spent a snowy November week camping in the Black Tusk meadows.[148]

Young people enjoyed encounters with animals at the Total Education farm.
Vancouver Sun, November 27, 1976

---

145 Vancouver Society for Total Education, Annual Report, 1973.
146 Leslie, Rosettis, and Kaufman, *Total Education: An Evaluation*, 17.
147 Total Education, Yearbooks, 1972, 1975.
148 Richard Neil, personal interview, April, 20, 1999.

When the Bowen Island farm became unavailable to Total Education, the school decided to look for a rural base farther away from the city with more property where students could stay for longer periods of time. In early 1975 the school rented an eighty-acre farm near Powell Lake on the Sunshine Coast. The farm had been the site of a 1960s-style commune formed by a group of Americans who had come to Canada to escape Vietnam, pollution, and materialism. One member of the group was Mark Vonnegut, son of a well-known writer.[149] In *The Eden Express* the younger Vonnegut described his personal voyage through commune and "hippie" life in rural British Columbia.[150] After the commune disbanded, another of its members, Peter Seixas, began teaching at Total Education. His idea

TEACHERS, STUDENTS AT LUNCH . . . by light of kerosene lamp

'Everything's an adventure'

Students learned to prepare large communal meals at the Total Education farm on the Sunshine Coast. *Vancouver Sun*, November 27, 1976

149 Mark Vonnegut was the son of well-known fiction author Kurt Vonnegut.
150 See Mark Vonnegut, *The Eden Express* (New York: Praeger, 1976) and Jean Barman, *The West Beyond the West* (Toronto: University of Toronto Press, 1991), 315.

was to establish an integrated city-based and country-based educational program and, believing the Powell Lake farm would suit the school's needs well, he arranged for the school to lease the property.

The Total Education farm offered an enrichment rural experience and a bonding opportunity for groups of students. Photo from *Total Education Scrapbook*, 1975

The school hired Peter and Linda Scheiber in the spring of 1975 to run the farm program. Mr. Scheiber, originally from the United States, had spent several years in Argenta during the 1950s when John and Helen Stevenson were preparing to launch the Argenta Friends School. The Scheibers had extensive experience in teaching and rural/wilderness living. Under their leadership the old farmhouse was renovated and students built a large log house to serve as the boys' dormitory and a cabin that became the girls' residence. Other building projects included a kiln, sauna and bathhouse, solar-heated kitchen and greenhouse, waterwheel, fencing, two beehives, and a log house to serve as the Scheibers' residence. In addition to the strenuous building work, students tended goats, chickens, geese, and ponies, and worked in the vegetable garden, orchard, and pastures. Students also had time for academic work, particularly literature, writing, drama, and ecology.[151]

---

151 Moira Farrow, "Everything's an Adventure," *Vancouver Sun*, November 27, 1976, 43.

The Powell Lake farm complemented the regular program at Total Education by providing students with an opportunity for an intensive personal and group experience. The farm program had three major objectives, the first of which was the acquisition of practical rural and wilderness skills, including food production, caring for animals, construction, and maintenance of tools and machinery. The other objectives were completion of remedial school work without urban distractions, and personal growth in self-reliance, decision-making, responsibility, perseverance, and self-esteem. The farm accepted a limited number of students for long-term stays who needed a "more intense environment" than the school could offer, as an alternative to "institutionalization."[152] The wilderness and personal growth goals of this program had elements in common with earlier Progressive and Romantic schools.

STUDENT AND TEACHER EVALUATION

The Therapeutic schools of the 1970s were subject to a great deal more scrutiny and accountability than the Progressive or Romantic schools of the 1960s. Because Total Education received public funding, it was expected to evaluate and report on its performance regularly. This was complicated by the fact that funding was provided by a number of different agencies, each desiring a different kind of evaluation. Planning and conducting evaluations was time consuming for staff members. In the spring of 1973, the school produced an annual report for the Vancouver School Board on all aspects of the previous year. When the provincial Department of Human Resources began funding the school in 1973/74, the department financed a thorough evaluation of the Total Education program by the Educational Research Institute of British Columbia. The result was a massive document of over three hundred pages. In 1974 the school completed a seventy-page internal evaluation of the LEAP program that had begun the previous fall.

Although the teachers were committed to regular staff evaluation, they could not agree on how it should be done. Staff members attended meetings and workshops assessing goals and outcomes, and analyzing hard data on attendance and academic achievement as well as "soft" data about student

---

152 "A New Learning Community: Powell Lake Proposal," funding brief, 2–3.

attitudes and personal growth. They agreed that "we require criteria for evaluation of staff," but most teachers preferred anecdotal and "self-evaluation"
to outside reports and statistical surveys.[153] Initially they tried evaluating
each other but by 1974 teachers were writing lengthy self-evaluations of
every course they taught. Despite numerous staff reports about how best to
evaluate the program, this remained an ongoing discussion.

School district officials encouraged Total Education staff to keep
detailed records and to spend more time in concrete assessment of
student abilities and academic needs, but the teachers preferred informal
student evaluation. Individual assessments occupied staff for many hours.
"Initially each student was evaluated by the student's counsellor. Then,
each reporting period the entire staff discussed in detail the academic and
personal progress of every student in the school during three or four days
of very long meetings."[154] Students and courses were evaluated as many
as five times per year since most courses were organized in seven-week
blocks. Many staff members found the evaluations excessive.[155] One
teacher complained about "the long, complex, and exhausting staff meetings where one or two 'problem' students are discussed ad nauseum most
often to little constructive use." He argued that the school's objectives for
students were too obscure to produce any meaningful evaluation: "This
lack of clarity leads to staff doubts concerning whether they have done
enough for students."[156]

Staff were divided about how formal student evaluation ought to be.
In a small school setting where an attitude of trust prevailed, informal
feedback could be effective. In 1973 Phil Knaiger reported that "evaluation occurs on an almost daily basis. When class size is small and contact
between student and teacher is informal, evaluation can be honest, direct,
and prompt."[157] In some courses students even evaluated their own progress. Although detailed record keeping was not a priority for most Total
Education staff, some teachers did try to keep an account of individual
student participation and progress. Mr. Knaiger kept records on each

153 Staff meeting, minutes, June 25, 1974.
154 Peter Seixas, personal interview, April 5, 1987.
155 Staff meeting, minutes, February 1974.
156 Charles Hill, "Total Education Goals and Objectives: Some Thoughts," June 1976.
157 Vancouver Society for Total Education, Annual Report, 1972/73, 12.

student in his mathematics classes, commenting on attendance, achievement, attitude, work habits, and future needs. This data was then used to ascertain whether the student would receive credit for the course.[158]

The amount of work required for credit in particular courses varied widely from simple attendance or participation in class, to the completion of daily and weekly assignments or the production of a journal, notebook, book report, term paper, or major project. At the end of the year, students would negotiate with teachers about exactly what they would have to do to make up missed assignments in order to receive credit for courses and eventually for graduation.[159] Some students signed contracts for work to be done. For the most part, credit for courses was at the discretion of the teacher and, as one teacher expressed it, "If a student is working at apparent capacity, I give credit."[160] Another teacher suggested that "flexibility was the key to meeting students' needs."[161] But by 1974 some staff members expressed concern about the ambiguous requirements in some courses, and teachers agreed to write out clear requirements necessary for obtaining credit in their courses.[162]

Students received report cards indicating credit or no credit for courses and occasional short comments. Students also did regular self-assessment, evaluating their progress in day-to-day tasks such as "come to group on time, complete my assignments, speak during discussions, respect the rights of others." Students wrote detailed responses to personal growth questions: "Do you find it easier to speak to people in groups? Do you get along better with your family? Are you more honest in your feelings? Do you find reasons to like yourself?" and wrote short essays about their development in various areas, from sexuality to appreciation of other people's points of view. Students also evaluated their courses and the entire program regularly.

158 Journal of Phil Knaiger, 1973/74.
159 Peter Seixas, personal interview, April 5, 1987.
160 Phil Knaiger, course evaluation, 1973/74.
161 Bonnie Picard, personal interview, April 25, 1997.
162 Staff meeting, minutes, February 1974.

Conclusion

Total Education changed over the years to become more structured, "a little more like a regular school," catering mostly to remedial students lacking in basic academic skills.[163] The middle-class dropouts who populated the school in its early days had long since found their way back to the regular school system by the late 1970s as mainstream schools became more accommodating. Total Education continued to limit the number of students with emotional problems but accepted some with behavioural difficulties. A number of former free school students from the Barker School, Saturna Island, and the Whole School attended Total Education and other rehabilitation high schools during the late 1970s. But the school's counterculture and political activist days were long past, and the staff collective began to break down by the end of the 1970s. The school district wanted all staff members in defined roles with distinct salaries, and salary sharing came to an end in 1982. Although some former staff and students remained friends, the all-encompassing community became just a memory.

In 1984 Total Education was offered a new facility in a former school annex just east of Main Street. The school was designated as a senior alternative school offering grades eleven and twelve. Most students graduated, and the school continued to provide a valuable service to the school district. Most of the original staff eventually moved on to mainstream schools or other professions but continued to be a friendship community.[164]

Because so many students came and went through Total Education, some for short periods of time, it is difficult to form more than an impression of how successful the school was in enhancing the educational, vocational, and personal prospects of its students. There is little doubt that most students appreciated the school's informal non-threatening atmosphere.

163 Ron Eckert, personal interview, October 28, 1996.
164 Phil Knaiger left in 1976 and taught at Ideal School, a more academically-oriented alternative school. Peter Seixas taught at two Vancouver public high schools, earned a PhD in history, and taught social studies education at UBC. Doug Cochran became a lawyer and judge, Larry Haberlin became a social services administrator, and Annie Simmonds and Ron Eckert went into social work. Liz Neil and Starla Anderson taught at Vancouver public high schools, and Virginia Eckert and Joan Nemtin became school counsellors. Charles Hill and Bonnie Picard taught for many years at Total Education.

One student commented to a *Province* reporter: "I like it here because there's a more friendly relationship with the teachers than you can have when there's someone standing at the front of a classroom telling people what to do." The reporter noted that "students said they like the school's warm and relaxed atmosphere and felt they learn more by not being told they must accomplish certain goals within specific times."[165] Typical student replies to a 1974 evaluation questionnaire mentioned the "relaxed atmosphere," the "comfortable environment," and "learning without pressure." Others found that the school helped them "learn to survive on their own," while others simply appreciated the opportunity to complete school. As one student expressed it, "Total Ed is trying to give students a second chance at a high school education."[166]

Almost without exception, former staff members believed that students benefited from their Total Education experience:

> Most of the students are leading normal productive lives. We had some enormous successes. Total Education provided an environment that was safe. Students I meet say "people listened to us, we mattered."

> It allowed many students to graduate. They would have had difficulty bouncing around mainstream schools.

> Emotional and social progress was the main goal. The academic component was available to those kids who wanted it. Other kids were fragile; they just needed a place of acceptance. We held students until they got over hurdles in their lives.

> The school's success was due to small classes, counselling, relevant courses, an integrated curriculum, a co-operative committed staff. We worked intensively and had a positive effect on those kids. We made a difference in people's lives.[167]

---

165 Dan Mullen, quoting a student, Pat Kennedy, "Dropout School Just Too Popular," *Vancouver Province*, February 5, 1972, 15.
166 Student replies to evaluation questionnaire, 1974.
167 Larry Haberlin, Ron Eckert, Virginia Eckert, Bonnie Picard, personal interviews.

The number of students enrolled in grade twelve was small during the early years, but a significant number of Total Education students graduated. Two students received their grade twelve graduation in 1971,[168] six in 1972, sixteen in 1973, and thirteen in 1974.[169] A minority of 20 to 30 per cent of these graduates went on to higher education, while most of the rest found employment. In 1973, for example, three of sixteen graduates enrolled in postsecondary programs (college, art school), while eleven found jobs. Of the thirty-four non-graduating students who did not return to Total Education after the 1972/73 year, two found their way to post-secondary programs, nineteen found employment, and three returned to mainstream public schools.[170]

Students ended up in all walks of life. A few went to university, one earning a PhD. Many became artists and musicians, including a nationally recognized female vocalist. One became director of the Vancouver Film Festival, another an administrator with a social service agency, another the host of a television program on computers, and yet another a successful journalist specializing in environmental issues. Other students were "free spirits," and a few endured ongoing problems with drugs. As one former teacher put it, "There were some casualties, but most kids have made out pretty well, and have decent jobs and families."[171]

A problem common to most alternative schools was the difficulty in sustaining the personal energy and commitment to keep them going. The teachers earned far less than equitable professional salaries. They were working with demanding students, with few resources at their disposal, and with little counselling or remedial expertise. One teacher referred to working at Total Education as "a young person's job," and another described it as a "recipe for burnout with that kind of intensity."[172] However, most of the teachers would have had difficulty teaching in the

---

168 Linda James, "Students and Teachers Plan Alternative Education," *Mount Pleasant Mouthpiece*, March 12, 1975, 6.

169 From "Present Activity of Former Total Education Students (1972–1974)," but staff-meeting minutes of June 3, 1974, cite a higher figure of nineteen graduating students in 1974.

170 "Present Activity of Former Total Education Students (1972–1974)."

171 Liz Cochran, personal interview, April 11, 1997.

172 Ron Eckert, personal interview, October 28, 1996.

regular system at that time and found their Total Education experience enormously significant:

> Most enjoyable work experience I've had. The most important formative experience of my life.

> A great experience, great friends, a satisfying communal work situation. They were exciting times, you could really make a change.

> Everybody was passionately interested in what they were teaching. It was an exciting place to be.

> I can't tell you how many kids I meet who come up to me who tell me how well their lives are going. We had some really committed staff who were able to exercise their own power and gifts. I got an experience that is a gift of a lifetime. In many ways it was the best experience of my life.[173]

One shortcoming of Total Education was that the academic program was not sufficiently challenging. As two teachers wrote in their 1974 Group evaluation, "In an attempt to not over-pressure students our expectations were sometimes too low; many of the kids were capable of far more than they did."[174] One former teacher acknowledged that he would emphasize "more of a concentration on basics if I had to do it over again" and another said, "We didn't do a great job with the lower-income kids."[175] For students who had the ability or desire to do challenging academic work, it was a difficult environment. Several students from the late 1970s recalled the work being too easy.[176] One student who was unhappy in public school attended Total Education in 1971 with some disappointment: "I worked through math and science on my own after setting up the program with the teacher. There was lots of one-to-one but you really had to be

173 Doug Cochran, Liz Cochran, Ron Eckert, Virginia Eckert, Richard Neil, interviews.
174 Richard Neil and Liz Neil, Group Evaluation, June 1974.
175 Doug Cochran, personal interview, April 11, 1997; Ron Eckert, personal interview, October 28, 1996.
176 David Eaton, Steven Pratt, Scott Campbell, personal interviews, 1997.

self-motivated. Most kids didn't have that. I think it was too informal."[177] Another student, at the school from 1971 to 1973, had "mixed feelings" about her experience:

> I stuck it out but I wasn't really happy. At first it was a great thing for me. But it lacked focus. People were there because they were vulnerable. People's lives were already in chaos, they didn't need chaos in school. Academics and exams should have been highly stressed. It was a great idea to allow people that freedom but there was no way for learning to occur.[178]

The 1974 school evaluation concluded that academic goals were not emphasized as much as they could have been. The staff belief in the close relationship between student self-image and student attitude toward learning led the school to offer many courses "directed toward increasing self-awareness and self-confidence." The report observes that such courses were very successful in "developing positive attitudes toward learning by offering topics and materials that interest students." But the report concludes that "the development of academic skills is sometimes hampered by the lack of pressure placed on students, and by the strong orientation in many courses toward the discussion of personal experiences. Total Education courses are more effective in promoting personal growth than in preparing students for future academic work."[179]

Nevertheless, students rated the skill and effectiveness of their teachers highly, and 60 per cent of the students evaluated their experience at Total Education as "very much a success."[180] The trusting relationship between students and staff remained the biggest strength of the program, and students were "confident that staff were aware of their educational and social needs."[181] Some students even found the school academically inspiring. According to the Mount Pleasant neighbourhood newspaper, one student who had recently decided to go to university said the "close

---

177 Jane Sheppard, personal interview, April 2, 1997.
178 Valerie Hodge, personal interview, March 8, 1998.
179 Leslie, Rosettis, and Kaufman, *Total Education: An Evaluation*, xviii.
180 Leslie, Rosettis, and Kaufman, 98. The great majority of the rest rated the program as "pretty good."
181 Vancouver Society for Total Education, "Evaluation 1975/76," 31.

informal communication fostered by the school has been instrumental to her feeling of success and new interest in education."[182]

A common difficulty for alternative schools was their tendency to attract students with learning and emotional problems. There simply were not enough resources in the mainstream educational system to meet their needs. Some Total Education teachers were aware of this problem, as Larry Haberlin expressed it to a journalist in 1974:

> Alternative schools can too easily become dumping grounds for the kids who can't make it in the regular school system. [Alternative schools] can be regarded as solutions to the system's problems because they effectively remove the kids who don't fit in and make things seem to run smoothly. But they're really short-term stopgap solutions because the problems don't lie in the kids that fail but in the schools that let them fail. Alternative schools won't solve the system's problems until the regular schools start applying the lessons we learn here. That's a lot of what we're here for.[183]

Total Education marked a turning point in the alternative schools movement in British Columbia. Whereas the Romantic schools of the late 1960s had been almost entirely a product of counterculture philosophy, Therapeutic or rehabilitation schools like Total Education served a wide cross-section of disengaged, bored, under-achieving, or troubled youth. Similar schools addressing an undeniable social need would shortly follow. Within five years of Total Education's founding, both the public school system and the provincial welfare system had entered into the alternative schools arena in a major way. Public education in British Columbia would not be the same thereafter. As one Total Education teacher commented in 1974, "Everyone should have the right to pass. No one at all should ever be allowed to fail. But they do, and they shouldn't."[184] Students

---

182 Linda James, "Students and Teachers Plan Alternative Education," *Mount Pleasant Mouthpiece*, March 12, 1975, 6.

183 Larry Haberlin, quoted in Lesley Krueger, "Some Alternatives to a World of Endless Defeat," *Vancouver Sun*, June 20, 1974, 47.

184 Richard Neil, quoted in Lesley Krueger, "Some Alternatives to a World of Endless Defeat," *Vancouver Sun*, June 20, 1974, 47.

once ignored or feared by the public school system were invited back and offered opportunities to succeed. Total Education, "the One True School," designed to educate everyone, played a significant role in encouraging that change.[185]

___

185 Teacher Richard Neil coined this phrase to refer to Total Education. Departing teachers were presented with a piece of the building inscribed with "The One True School."

Chapter 10

WINDSOR HOUSE

By 1971 most of the Romantic schools founded during the 1960s had closed due to bankruptcy, fatigue, or lack of a clear educational vision. Although the initial excitement generated by the "free school movement" had waned, there was still popular interest in a more humane form of education among growing numbers of parents who thought their children were not well served by the public schools. A few school districts had taken cautious first steps to establish innovative programs, but many parents still saw the public system as rigid, authoritarian, and unimaginative. Besides, public schools offered few programs for students requiring academic or emotional help, or for those who simply did not "fit in." Stopping short of the unlimited freedom advocated by the Romantic schools of the 1960s, alternative schools of the 1970s sought to combine "child-centred" education with a therapeutic environment that would benefit students who had experienced problems in public school.

Windsor House School in North Vancouver, one of these new options, appealed to parents who wanted a more humanistic education for their children. But it also provided a therapeutic educational community for both its students and for those parents who were attempting to solve personal problems or make sense of new ideas. Unlike the alternative schools of the 1960s, the emerging Therapeutic schools were the object of considerable interest from public school administrators and teachers who were being pressed by parents to offer more choice in the public system.

In the fall of 1970, a group of North Vancouver parents approached the school board to ask the district to set up a multi-grade parent-participation class for primary children. Distrusting an impersonal and bureaucratic system, these parents wanted to be more closely involved in their children's education and sought a flexible and enriched school environment. Some of the parents knew each other from the neighbourhood, while others had worked together at a local co-operative preschool. The only alternative elementary school in Greater Vancouver at the time, the New School, was too radical for these parents. So when the school trustees had made no decision by June 1971, the group decided to start their own school in September.

One member of this group was Helen Hughes, an experienced teacher. She began teaching at age nineteen and taught elementary public school for five years, followed by three years in a parent-participation preschool. She developed an "experiential learning program" based on play to pique the curiosity and eagerness of her young students. Ms. Hughes was already experiencing many doubts about how children were taught in the public schools:

> When I had been teaching grade five long enough to look around a bit, I noticed that the children in my classes did very little real thinking while in school. One day I experimented by writing some information on one blackboard that was contradictory to the information on the next board. The children copied it into their books and regurgitated it the next day on a quiz. It confirmed my suspicions.[1]

Helen Hughes read *Summerhill* and several books by Maria Montessori. She also visited the New School and the nascent Waldorf School as she began to formulate a new way of thinking about education. She was eclectic and "stole from everything."[2] Meanwhile, Ms. Hughes was impressed with the inquisitiveness of her own children, then in preschool, and their refusal to accept pat answers:

---

1   Helen Hughes, notes on Windsor House history, early 1980s. All school documents cited were examined by the author in the Windsor House School archive, North Vancouver.
2   Helen Hughes, personal interview, September 30, 1996.

> I rubbed a balloon in my hair and it stuck to the wall. "What makes it stick there?" asked Meghan. "Static electricity," I replied. That response had always been accepted by my intermediate students. Meghan was not satisfied, however, and said, "What is static electricity?" I realized that I didn't really know.[3]

What ultimately convinced Ms. Hughes to take part in the daunting venture of starting a school was that her daughter in grade two, though a good student, was bored by public school.[4]

There was a good deal of interest in the neighbourhood, especially from "middle-class young women who were making careers out of being good mothers and good women," remembered Ms. Hughes. "They wanted the joys of 'hippiedom' and freedom from role restraints without the drawbacks of unpalatable food and lack of cleanliness."[5] These women believed in the importance of child-rearing and thought they should stay home with their young children. They were committed participants in parent co-operative preschools, of which there were several in North Vancouver. But they had also read Fritz Perls' works on gestalt therapy and Betty Friedan's *The Feminine Mystique* and wanted to be more than mothers and wives. A number of marriages were breaking up and two parents were living in communal groups. One parent recalled, "We were all very influenced by the times and the ideas. People were living in different ways."[6] As Helen Hughes said, "We tried everything that came down the pipe."[7] Windsor House was almost entirely developed and run by women and, except for two fathers who played a significant role, the men had little to do with the school.

Another member of the group was Susan Foley, who lived in the neighbourhood and ran a parent-participation preschool. Having worked in a Montessori school in Massachusetts before coming to Vancouver, she had helped found a daycare centre at Simon Fraser University while

---

3 Helen Hughes, notes on Windsor House history, early 1980s.
4 Helen Hughes, personal interview, September 30, 1996.
5 Helen Hughes, "Windsor House: A History" (unpublished paper for Jean Barman, University of British Columbia, circa 1984).
6 Susan Lawton, personal interview, January 27, 1997.
7 Helen Hughes, personal interview, September 30, 1996.

completing her teacher training.[8] Local parents were attracted to her view that "when you take down the barrier between school and home, it takes over your life." In many ways Windsor House was to become an experiment in group home-schooling.

Parents joined the group for a variety of reasons. Some believed that children learn best in a humane supportive environment and wanted their children to be free to learn naturally without pressure. They had read John Holt's *How Children Fail*, A. S. Neill's *Summerhill*, and Sylvia Ashton-Warner's *Teacher* and were suspicious of what they saw as the repressive rules of the school system. Other parents joined because their lively young children had been unhappy in public school.

Windsor House was based on three educational principles. The first was direct involvement of parents, who spent many hours assisting students with their learning and play activities. As a parents' manual stated, "Parent and community involvement is the greatest strength of the school. In many cases the children and parents together learn things about themselves in a supportive environment and so are able to let go of the old patterns that have made learning difficult for the child."[9]

The second principle was a unique problem-solving and decision-making technique. This was both "an educational and humane way of resolving matters of discipline" and "a vehicle for encouraging children to assume responsibility for their own education." The school's goal was to develop "internal discipline" and to connect "decision making with accountability. When the children have participated in the making of rules their attitude is far more positive and supportive of the rules."[10] Decisions were made by consensus. Each parent, student, and teacher was considered "an equal and important member of the school" and was to assume responsibility for the decisions made.[11]

The third principle at Windsor House was individualized academic work, in which students would learn at their own pace based on

---

8   Susan Brown, personal interview, March 20, 1997. Ms. Brown's husband, Fred Brown, was a significant figure in the Intentional Communities Movement.
9   Parents' Manual, 1978, 3.
10   Parents' Manual, 1978, 4.
11   Windsor House parents, "A Brief on Alternatives in Education," presented to the North Vancouver school trustees, April 1975, 4.

one-to-one contact with an adult. Each child was encouraged to set his or her own goals within "a truly non-competitive and non-coercive school situation."[12] The school's founders wanted their children to be allowed to grow and learn by their own volition, at their own speed, and in the types of activities the children chose.[13]

Windsor House was organized as a parent co-operative with Helen Hughes as the teacher and everyone else serving as volunteers. Ms. Hughes and her husband offered their large house on Windsor Road for the school headquarters. Family fees were set at $40 per month, and parents would spend as much time at the school as they could, with a minimum of one half-day per week. Ms. Hughes was paid $70 per month for teaching full-time, her own children attended for free, and the Hughes family received $50 per month for rent. Run on a shoestring, the school's initial budget for 1971/72 was only $320 per month.

Decisions were made informally at monthly meetings.[14] However, decision-making would become complicated when, later in the first year, it became clear that parents had widely differing expectations about how much formal learning there should be. As Helen Hughes wrote in 1973, "Windsor House started originally as a desperate alternative to the public school system. Several of us had children that would have been, or already had been, badly demoralized in the public schools. We were united in what we didn't want—grades, group lessons, competition, discipline, punishment, and compulsory attendance—but had little clear idea of what we did want."[15]

School Opening

That summer of 1971 Helen Hughes transformed her house into a school. The dining room became a craft centre, the study a tutoring room, and the living room was set up for music and books. Even the main hall was converted into a stage through the aid of a curtain. The group painted and

12   Windsor House parents, "A Brief on Alternatives in Education," April 1975, 4.
13   Windsor House, "An Interim Report," February 1977.
14   Windsor House executive meeting, September 1, 1971.
15   Helen Hughes, "What Is Windsor House All About?" daycare funding brief, October 1973, 7.

carpeted the basement to serve as an indoor play area and built a large tree fort and swing in the spacious backyard.

Windsor House School, started by Helen Hughes in her own home, was situated in an spacious heritage house on Windsor Road in North Vancouver. Image c. 1974, Courtesy of Helen Hughes

The school opened in September with fifteen children, almost all in the primary grades. Preschool siblings also spent many hours at the school but were not officially enrolled. One parent remembered the first day as "thrilling and exciting."[16] Ms. Hughes scheduled daily twenty-minute individual lessons with each child for reading, writing, and arithmetic. Parents also read aloud to the children such popular books as *The Hobbit*, *A Wrinkle in Time*, and *Charlotte's Web*. The rest of the day was spent on crafts, nature activities, and field trips. A neighbour came in to teach conversational French, and a local architect taught mathematics with Cuisenaire rods[17] and helped the children build a geodesic dome out of cardboard. Parents offered short mini-courses that included dance, animal

16   Sylvia Simpson, personal interview, November 21, 1996.
17   Cuisenaire rods were popular learning aids to help students understand place value.

care, first aid, multiplication tables, singing, batik, beading, braiding, weaving, candle-making, cursive writing, touch typing, and even witch-craft. Part of the main floor was designated for quiet activity but this was difficult to maintain because there were no rules. Parents cleaned up after the children and helped them solve disagreements. Parents also spent a great deal of time driving children from place to place and arranging learn-ing opportunities in the community. The adults took groups of children to the library to borrow books, to Chinatown, to the market to shop for food and supplies, and to the Vancouver Community Music School for Kodaly lessons.[18] They spent time at beaches, parks, and the skating rink, and travelled to Cheakamus, north of Squamish, on the BC Railway.

Despite all these organized activities, what the children really wanted to do was play in the backyard or the basement. Helen Hughes had expected that, in addition to the twenty-minute lessons, the children would vol-untarily engage in learning activities throughout the day. Some students did a good deal of reading but little other academics occurred. Part way through the year, parents began to worry that their children were not learn-ing anything and believed Ms. Hughes should have been more directive about the students' activities.[19] Not that she considered academic work unimportant, but she was convinced that play opens the door to meaning-ful education and that children learn most effectively when they choose to do so. Parents also debated for weeks about whether the children should be permitted to watch television at school. Ms. Hughes believed the chil-dren could regulate their own television-watching, but most parents were strongly opposed.

These fundamental disagreements could not be resolved and the school broke up at the end of the year. Some children went back into regular class-rooms, while others enrolled in a new co-operative class that the school district had finally opened. One former parent explained, "In theory we thought it would be great, but when we watched our own kids do nothing but play we didn't like it. We agreed they were having a marvelous time but we were worried about the curriculum."[20] They did not want their

---

18   Helen Hughes, Day Plans, 1971/72.
19   Sylvia Simpson, personal interview, November 21, 1996.
20   Susan Lawton, personal interview, January 27, 1997.

children to be coerced but did want them to learn the "three Rs"—reading, writing, and arithmetic.

A few parents decided to start another school down the street the following September. Susan Lawton, Susan Foley, and Sylvia Cepeliauskas organized a group of ten children, aged six to ten, that met in the Lawton home. The dining room was turned into a classroom with a blackboard and table borrowed from the school district. Small formal classes were held in the morning with less structured activities in the afternoon. No one from the authorities ever questioned the tiny school's existence. The group continued to meet for two years, after which the parents grew tired, and as one remembered, "the kids were eager to get back to school; they wanted to be with other kids."

RENEWAL

Having lost all her students after the first year, Helen Hughes expected Windsor House to close quietly, like many other small alternative schools conceived in the early 1970s.[21] But one Coquitlam family, the Heikoops, on hearing about Windsor House, had decided to move to North Vancouver in the summer of 1972 so their daughter could attend the school. Not having "the nerve to tell them that the school had folded," Ms. Hughes decided to reopen in September with her own two children and the Heikoops' daughter. She placed an advertisement in the local community newspaper, and a few parents began to show up with their children.[22]

Helen Hughes now had a clearer idea that Windsor House would have limited academic expectations and would instead provide a non-stressful environment in which the children could develop such traits as co-operation and self-confidence. Parents who were attracted to the renewed Windsor House agreed with these goals. Diane Elderton, an advocate of health food and non-traditional healing practices, had studied sociology and education at UBC and read widely in Montessori. She wanted to home-school her children but knew they needed to be with other young

21 Chelsea House in West Vancouver (based on the British Integrated Day) and the Albert Street School in Burnaby both opened in 1972 but closed after less than a year.
22 "Parents Play Key Role in Private Education System," *Citizen*, September 1972.

people. Sharon Priestley was a former teacher and actor. Sharon Dawson, a teacher and artist, along with Judy Stone, another interested parent, were both recently separated and looking for support. Ian McNaughton, one of the few fathers actively involved in the school, had left the business world to become a therapist. After studying human relations, encounter groups, and psychodrama with Fritz Perls at Esalen Institute in the late 1960s, he wanted a "humanistic" school for his son.[23] Almost all the parents were Canadians, about half were single mothers, and few could afford to pay more than minimal fees. Several had private school backgrounds (St. George's and Crofton House) and liked the idea of sending their children to an independent school. They distrusted the public school system and wanted to have more impact on their children's education. Three parents had dyslexic children in the days when such students were usually labelled "slow." Most of these parents were enthusiastic about the popular ideas of the day, especially those referred to as the Human Potential Movement. Everyone in the school community got along well, and this close group remained together for over three years.

Before long, Windsor House had eighteen students enrolled for the 1972/73 school year, most under ten years of age. There was little student turnover and two years later sixteen students attended, of whom fourteen were nine years old or younger.[24] As in the first year, Ms. Hughes planned to give each child one twenty-minute individualized lesson per day. These sessions consisted of reading aloud and working with flash cards in English and mathematics. But the lessons were voluntary and, although some students enjoyed the personal contact, within a few weeks most stopped coming. The children spent their time dressing up, performing skits for whomever would watch, playing "Alligators" in the basement, and taking care of the many school pets. Students built a fort in the attic and enjoyed the adventure playground, tree forts, and cargo nets in the large backyard.

Parents announced activities they wanted to initiate, such as singing or reading aloud, and children would come if they were interested. Sharon

---

23   This was just before Fritz Perls came to British Columbia himself.
24   Windsor House School parents, "A Brief on Alternatives in Education," April 1975.

Priestley taught drama lessons and Sharon Dawson offered art activities and sang folk songs with the students. Other parents introduced crafts and read to groups of children or individuals. One student remembered that she "loved the reading time." Adults and children went on camping trips to Alice Lake and other destinations and visited Sundance School, a new alternative school in Victoria. Students had to organize their own food on camping trips and live with the consequences of their mistakes. After several days some students could be seen desperately trying to trade a chocolate bar for some "real food." Like other alternative schools, the group took frequent field trips to parks, the planetarium, and the Lynn Valley Ecology Centre.[25] The school also invited members of the general community to offer learning opportunities to the students.[26]

Parents were tolerant of student behaviour, and there were no sanctions for swearing or smoking. One parent remembered "a lot of wildness" as the group struggled to achieve a balance between order and freedom.[27] One year the school bought foam bats that the students used in the basement to hit each other, a psychotherapeutic practice at the time. However, both children and adults were expected to respect each other and refrain from rudeness or physical violence. Several of the students during the fourth year had been asked to leave public schools because of "social problems." A few were considered "hyperactive" and a few others were aggressive, and Ms. Hughes spent much of her time trying to get the children to co-operate. Although difficult children took up a great deal of the adults' attention, the students learned to be tolerant of each other, and troubled children were neither so numerous, nor so severe, that they changed the nature of the school.

When not interacting with the children, parents spent most of their time in the kitchen having philosophical discussions, drinking Inka coffee substitute, and preparing elaborate and healthy group lunches. It was not uncommon for twelve children, three or four parents, and several visitors to sit around the communal lunch table, eating soup, sandwiches, and casseroles. The school community provided adult companionship

25   Windsor House parents, "A Brief on Alternatives in Education," 18.
26   "School Tries Experiment," *Citizen*, April 1974.
27   Katanya Woodruff, personal interview, April 2, 1997.

for otherwise isolated single mothers, and one parent recalled Windsor House as a "therapeutic community." Another said, "We were a motley lot. We were unusual individuals. We had to learn to get along too." Helen Hughes provided a "warm, accepting" environment where parents could feel supported in working on their own problems, and many participants cite this as the most important aspect of the school. Some were in financial difficulty, and one single mother was taken into the family and given a room in the basement. At one point there were eleven people living in the house.[28] Parents talked frequently about "empowerment" and, as one observed, "The school was all about how to stop being a victim."[29] With this primarily therapeutic emphasis, the school became "very personal," according to one parent. Another parent said the school helped him work out a better relationship with his ex-wife. Still another remembered, "I was needy myself. It was a wonderful environment for me. It provided as much for the parents as it did for the children. Windsor House gave some women the courage to leave unhappy marriages. It offered safety and support."[30] Discussions about traditional gender roles sowed the "seeds of feminism" for many.

One innovation at Windsor House was "problem-solving," Helen Hughes' self-developed method for achieving consensus in decision-making and in resolving interpersonal disagreements. Whenever a perceived problem arose, one of the participants or a bystander, either child or adult, could call for a problem-solving session. All other activity would stop immediately and those involved, sometimes the entire school, would try to brainstorm a solution. If a student refused to attend a problem-solving session called by someone else, or obstructed problem-solving proceedings by being unwilling to consider reasonable solutions, that student was considered to be "going on power," which usually called for adult intervention.[31] Rules for problem-solving stipulated that:

> The person with the "problem" calls all those concerned
> to a certain place at a certain time; if the other persons do

28   Meghan Hughes, personal interview, October 3, 1996.
29   Sharon Mason, personal interview, November 25, 1996.
30   Judy Stone, personal interview, January 13, 1997.
31   Helen Hughes, "What Is Windsor House All About?" October 1973, 6.

> not come they must be "on power"; during a problem-
> solving session all parties must be genuinely interested in
> solving the problem; everyone must stay until a solution
> agreeable to everyone is reached.

At times it seemed the school was engaged in problem-solving sessions all day long. Occasionally weighty issues were discussed—Ms.
Hughes once called a session because "not very many people come to
lessons anymore." More typical problems were: "telephone calls not
being handled satisfactorily; people jumping on the bed and wrecking the
record player; Helen is tired of doing all the odds and ends of cleaning
up; Christopher doesn't let anybody use the transformer his Dad bought
for the school; people keep running around screaming upstairs, although
downstairs is the place for it; the guests were taking far too big a helping
of the casserole dish; people are leaving orange peels and apple cores
downstairs; and too many problem-solving sessions!" Those who found
problem-solving tedious had added incentive to find a solution so they
could end the session.[32] "People would get tired of sitting there and finally
just agree."[33] One student said she learned through problem-solving that
"there is always a solution. I felt in control, that I could change things."[34]
Another student described the problem-solving approach as a "human-
centred consensus-based experiment that worked out pretty well."[35]

BECOMING A PUBLIC SCHOOL

By the middle of the 1974/75 school year, Helen Hughes was exhausted,
the school was close to bankruptcy, and she was dealing with her recent
divorce. With the majority of parents barely able to make ends meet themselves, they could contribute little financial support to the school. Parent
meetings discussed ways to reduce expenses. Part way through the school
year, parents were asked to increase their $70 per month fees by $20 if
they were able.[36] Ms. Hughes discovered the daycare subsidies recently

32   Darcy Hughes, personal interview, February 6, 1997.
33   Glynis Sandall, personal interview, November 18, 1996.
34   Laura Elderton, personal interview, April 3, 1997.
35   John McNaughton, personal interview, January 22, 1997.
36   Parents meeting, minutes, October 23, 1974.

established by the NDP government and received subsidies for several preschool children and for several older children who qualified for after-school care.[37] For all her work she took a salary of only $100 per month and was now the major source of her family's income. Ms. Hughes kept the school afloat by earning extra money teaching preschool education at night school two evenings a week, on top of a full day of teaching at Windsor House. The other parents were also tired. Finally, in early 1975, the group decided to petition the North Vancouver School District to take over the school. As one parent explained, "We ran out of resources. We had reservations about the public school district but we thought it was inevitable."

With the assistance of Dr. Ray Williams, an educational consultant and alternative school advocate, the parent group presented a brief to the school trustees in April 1975.[38] They argued that the school district had a responsibility to offer parents and their children more choice of educational practices. They cited the example of the Vancouver School District, which had recently incorporated both Total Education and Ideal School into its system in addition to creating over a dozen other alternative programs. The report also referred to the SEED and Alpha alternative programs in the Toronto public schools. The parents' brief quoted from the Vancouver School District Advisory Committee on Alternative Education:

> There is a significant number of students, whose educational requirements are not being satisfied by the present system. The school system must become more adaptive and flexible in order to deal with the diversified demands of the community. The primary goal should be to legitimize alternative learning experiences so that parents and students can select the educational approaches best suited to their interests, needs, and learning styles. This means opening up learning alternatives within the public schools.[39]

---

37 Helen Hughes, "What Is Windsor House All About?" October 1973, 2.
38 Dr. Williams was a member of the Advisory Committee on Alternative Education in the Vancouver School District.
39 Dr. Ray Williams, "Private Alternatives and the School System," a brief to the North Vancouver school trustees, April 1975, 9, citing a 1973 report of the

Led by school board trustee Don Burbidge, himself a former New School parent, the board agreed to accept Windsor House as a district program for a two-year trial period. The trustees assigned the school one room in an elementary school building and hired Helen Hughes as the program's teacher. Enrolment for 1975/76 was set at twenty-five students aged five to twelve. This initiative succeeded because the school delegation presented a convincing case supported by letters from parents, and had effectively enlisted allies within the community. As well, the timing was right. By 1975 many districts were considering offering alternatives in response to parental demand and professional enthusiasm. As one parent said, "What moves the school board is public pressure. The whole society was swinging to the left."

After joining the School District, Windsor House continued to operate according to its philosophy of inclusive decision-making. *Vancouver Sun*, March 13, 1996

Administrative Coordinating Team on Alternative Education advisory committee in Vancouver.

After a positive evaluation by North Vancouver School District officials two years later, Windsor House was accepted as a permanent program. During the first two years under the board's jurisdiction, the school was disrupted by having to move to four different locations within other schools.[40] Of these, none was completely satisfactory, since having one or two rooms within a larger school operating on different rules and behaviour expectations was difficult. However, the district administration left the school free to pursue its aims with little interference. The program became somewhat more academic after 1975 but retained its emphasis on individualized work. Each student had a "folder" containing daily individual assignments in language, mathematics, and social studies.

Joining the North Vancouver School District allowed Windsor House to survive. However, it also led to an increase in special-needs students, as other school principals often sent difficult students to Windsor House. According to a district report in 1976, one-third of Windsor House students had learning disabilities, while another one-third had emotional problems: "In other words, for two-thirds of her pupils she is doing the work of what we would classify as a Special Education teacher."[41] Less than half of the students were enrolled because their parents believed in the school's philosophy. As Helen Hughes wrote to a district administrator in 1980, "Windsor House accommodates many children who have had quite severe difficulties in regular classrooms. These children are often unpredictable and difficult to deal with."[42] This situation was typical of many public alternative programs.

CONCLUSION: EFFECTS OF THE SCHOOL

Former Windsor House students have ended up in many walks of life. Some returned to the public school system, others went to alternative

---

40 Over the years, Windsor House occupied Brooksbank School, St. Catherine's Church, Keith Lynn School, North Star School, Lonsdale School, Queen Mary School, and Cloverly School.

41 North Vancouver School District, "An Interim Report: Windsor House," February 10, 1977; "Windsor House School: A Report," June 14, 1976.

42 Helen Hughes to Mr. Ian McEown, Supervisor of Special Education, June 16, 1980.

secondary schools, and a few were self-taught or home-schooled. They went on to work at diverse occupations, including as a television actor, nurse, accountant, teacher, self-taught audio-visual consultant, and restaurant manager. One earned a PhD in English and two went into business. Whether attendance at Windsor House limited students' later academic and professional opportunities is difficult to determine. As one parent said, "Students who came from strongly academic families tended to go to university. But there was not as much university attendance as in a regular school."[43]

Windsor House students and parents perceived many benefits from their association with the school. Parents wanted to diminish academic pressure on their children and considered inter-personal relations and life experience as important as academic achievement. Most students appreciated the personal attention they received from the many adults around the school. One student liked the accepting atmosphere at Windsor House, the lack of labelling, the personal attention, and Helen's patience.[44] For another, the most important benefit was "learning to communicate and interpersonal skills."[45] One student commented that "public school was torture; the social value of Windsor House was more valuable than anything you learn at public school."[46] Still another said, "Kids from Windsor House felt like they can make a difference."[47] According to one parent whose son had a reading disability, "Windsor House was the best thing that ever happened to my son's life. He had no self-esteem problems. The school was the reason."[48]

Windsor House also provided a learning environment for individuals who were outside the mainstream. One former student, who later lived in a remote area of Indian Arm accessible only by boat, found a place for herself at Windsor House after being unhappy at large public schools. Another student, upon leaving Windsor House, travelled with her mother for two years before starting public school at age nine on Galiano Island.

---

43   Pam Douglas, personal interview, November 25, 1996.
44   Laura Elderton, personal interview, April 3, 1997.
45   John McNaughton, personal interview, January 22, 1997.
46   Darcy Hughes, personal interview, February 6, 1997.
47   Meghan Hughes, personal interview, October 3, 1996.
48   Ian McNaughton, personal interview, January 28, 1997.

Although she had missed simple addition and writing skills, she "caught up in a year and graduated from university with a nursing degree."[49]

When it was time to leave Windsor House most students made the transition to public school without great difficulty. One remembered having no trouble returning to public school after two years.[50] Another student recalled that, although she was stressed because she missed long division (and never learned it), she had no trouble catching up and later became an accountant. She credited the accepting environment at Windsor House with giving her confidence.[51] Numerous students reported being behind when they re-entered public school, often in only one subject, usually English or mathematics. Several were put back a grade but most caught up quickly. One student suffered "culture shock" when she entered grade eight at the local high school with inadequate writing skills. This student and several others chose to complete their schooling at Ideal School or other alternative high schools.

The lack of emphasis on reading, writing, and mathematics skills was a weakness at Windsor House.[52] However, in contrast to the Romantic schools of the 1960s, all Windsor House students did learn to read, even though they were not required to learn at a particular age. According to one parent, her son was "still not reading at age nine. He decided he wanted to read *Treasure Island* and within a year he was reading aeronautics journals. My kids were able to learn how to learn."[53] Her son confirmed that "I had a difficult time reading until grade four because I wasn't interested. I remember picking up *Treasure Island* and it happened almost overnight."[54] He attended university and established his own audio-visual consulting business. Another student who was not reading until age nine said, "When I did learn to read, I worked at it hard, and in the space of a year I went from being very poor to being able to read anything."[55]

49   Cindy Williams, personal interview, February 3, 1997.
50   Glynis Sandall, personal interview, November 18, 1996.
51   Christina Cepeliauskas, personal interview, January 22, 1997.
52   Dr. Ray Williams, "Windsor House School: A Report," April 1975, 2.
53   Katanya Woodruff, personal interview, April 2, 1997.
54   David Elderton, personal interview, January 21, 1997.
55   John McNaughton, personal interview, January 22, 1997.

Parents considered the strengths of Windsor House to be the strong parental involvement, positive interpersonal relationships, the creative problem-solving approach, and the emphasis on affective development. They were particularly attracted to the absence of competition and the lack of academic pressure. One parent wrote, "The children at Windsor House are productive and display a great deal of initiative. The openness and the supportive atmosphere make it very happy and attractive, an ideal place for learning and growth."[56] Another similarly commented:

> Our son has been with Windsor House for two years and the school has played a major part in his development into a self-reliant human being who has respect for the rights of others. He has received strong support there for academic, personal, and interpersonal growth.[57]

Several parents reflected on why they sought an alternative school. One wrote, "The reason my husband and I took the children to Windsor House was simple. They were unhappy in the public school system. Learning wasn't fun anymore."[58] Another described how her son wanted to quit public school after two weeks of grade one. After three years of "headaches, stomach aches, and fights at recess and after school," she enrolled him at Windsor House:

> I don't have words to express how I feel about the changes in my son since he attended Windsor House. He is beginning to come out of his shell and starting to feel confidence in himself. I asked him why he liked going to Windsor House and he said, "Because they understand kids."[59]

Many students and parents believed that Windsor House influenced the school district. One student commented that "public schools have changed a great deal since the early 1970s and schools like Windsor House have

---

56   Letter from Lorne and Sharon Priestley, in the appendix to "A Brief on Alternatives in Education," to North Vancouver school trustees, April 1975.
57   Letter from Ian McNaughton, in "A Brief on Alternatives in Education," April 1975.
58   Letter from Polly Pawley, in "A Brief on Alternatives in Education," April 1975.
59   Letter from a parent in "A Brief on Alternatives in Education," April 1975.

had an effect."[60] One parent said, "We were a gadfly effect on the whole system. Windsor House became well-known to parents who were disenchanted. I think we shook a lot of people up. We broadened people's minds to what was possible."

Meghan Hughes, for whom the school was created, became head teacher when her mother retired. Photo courtesy of Helen Hughes

Much of the school's success was due to the skill and determination of Helen Hughes. A modest person who pursued a remarkable teaching career with little fanfare, Ms. Hughes made a difference in the lives of many adults and children. One parent described her as "a brilliant woman—a highly skilled teacher and a highly skilled motivator."[61] Another said, "Helen was philosophically devoted to child-centred education. She had total determination to make it work." A North Vancouver administrator in 1976 remarked on Ms. Hughes' "ability to involve students, the atmosphere she creates within the classroom, her attention to individual progress, her concern for people, and her industry."[62] One former student

60   Christina Cepeliauskas, personal interview, January 22, 1997.
61   Sharon Mason, personal interview, November 25, 1996.
62   Allan Stables, North Vancouver Assistant Superintendent, "Windsor House School: A Report," June 14, 1976, 2.

remembered her as "fair, kind, and approachable."[63] Another said, "Helen guided, mediated, asked leading questions, but let people make their own decisions. She definitely set the tone."[64] Still another student recalled, "Helen was easy to learn from. The way she presented the material turned me on to learning. She and our parents realized what was wrong with the school system. They were ahead of their time."[65]

Windsor House had its ups and downs after joining the school district in 1975. Formal academic lessons became more prevalent during the 1980s, but in 1989 the school staff made a recommitment to "non-coercive education" modelled after the Sudbury Valley School in Massachusetts.[66] Not all parents agreed with this decision and more than half took their children out of the school, but by the mid-1990s Windsor House had rebuilt its enrolment to about one hundred students from kindergarten to grade ten.[67] Parents continued to be extensively involved as volunteers. Academic activities were provided for students who requested them, but all scheduled classes were voluntary. Aside from safety measures, school rules were set at weekly meetings of staff and students, with decisions made by a two-thirds vote. "Problem-solving" was replaced by a judicial committee of student volunteers and one staff member.[68] After having to move every few years, the school was finally given its own building in 1996. Helen Hughes would continue to teach at Windsor House and provide inspiration until her retirement in 2005.[69] When her daughter, Meghan Hughes (for whom the school was started), became a central staff member and committed proponent of non-coercive education, Windsor House had come full circle.

Windsor House's entry into the North Vancouver School District was successful because it satisfied the needs of both the school and the public system. Windsor House staff and parents, financially drained and

63   David Elderton, personal interview, January 21, 1997.
64   Glynis Sandall, personal interview, November 18, 1996.
65   Jenny Lawton, personal interview, February 4, 1997.
66   See Daniel and Hanna Greenberg, *The Sudbury Valley School Experience* (Framingham, MA: Sudbury Valley School Press, 1985).
67   Meghan Hughes and Jim Carrico, "Windsor House," in Matt Hern, ed., *Deschooling Our Lives* (Gabriola Island, BC: New Society Publishers, 1996), 134–139.
68   "Students Take Charge of Their Learning," in *Public Choice, Public Schools* (Vancouver: British Columbia Teachers' Federation, September 1996), 48–53.
69   Helen Hughes is still active in alternative education as the president of the Transforming Education Society.

exhausted, could not have carried on without the funding and facilities provided by the school district. The district, for its part, acquired an innovative program at a time when parents were demanding more options in public education. It made sense to take in an established program like Windsor House, which had demonstrated the feasibility of parent-participatory alternatives. Similar conditions led to the incorporation of Total Education and Ideal School into the Vancouver public system. During the next few years, numerous alternative programs would be developed and nurtured in school districts across the province, resulting in more educational choice for parents and students.[70]

Windsor House School offered many field trips, such as this one which brought parents and students to a salmon hatchery in North Vancouver. Photo used with permission granted by head teacher Helen Hughes

70 In 2011, after thirty-six years in the North Vancouver School District, Windsor House was phased out because the district decided to consolidate its alternative programs. Fortunately for the program, the Gulf Islands School District agreed to take financial control of Windsor House and rented a location in North Vancouver so that the school could carry on. However, the school continued to run a substantial deficit and finally announced in 2019 that Windsor House was closing for good.

Chapter 11

IDEAL SCHOOL

In the early 1970s there remained many students who felt bored in mainstream high schools but had few alternatives to the large impersonal institutions. Meanwhile, Garry Nixon was a teacher at St. George's School, an exclusive private school on the West Side of Vancouver, offering an education based on the elite British private school model.[71] He was concerned about the many academically motivated students he believed were not being well served by traditional high schools. He had been a frequent visitor to Knowplace in 1968, often spending the late afternoon hours there after finishing his teaching day at St. George's. But his attempts to generate interest in mathematics and social studies at Knowplace were unsuccessful, and he believed the lack of academic structure in Romantic schools was unrealistic. In the spring of 1972, during his sixth year at St. George's, Mr. Nixon decided to open a small independent high school where students could pursue their studies in a less oppressive and more exciting atmosphere than he believed existed in the public schools.

Mr. Nixon's conception was of a "storefront" school for motivated students who were bored with their present high school education. He believed that bright students were usually ignored in mainstream classrooms because teachers feared leaving the rest of the class behind. His school would offer an exciting curriculum with small classes in an informal atmosphere. But he expected students to attend classes and to be responsible for completing their academic requirements. There would

---

71 Although such schools are designated "public" in Britain, I refer to them here as private schools to conform to North American usage.

be no discipline problems because students would want to be there. The school would take advantage of the many community resources. The Ideal School prospectus described "an alternative academic school based on the premise that children are valuable human beings who will best grow and learn in groups that are small enough to enable them to have a close relationship with their teachers and fellow students. The school is designed for enthusiastic students who wish to participate fully in an exciting learning program."[72]

Garry Nixon created Ideal School as an alternative for academically motivated students.
Vancouver Sun, September 7, 1974

Garry Nixon had grown up in Lethbridge, Alberta, and later moved with his family to Victoria, where they owned a cinema.[73] His wide variety of academic interests and his rapport with teenagers drew him to teaching. He had an undergraduate degree and nine years' teaching experience, but he had never completed his requirements for a teaching certificate. As a generally "self-taught" person, Mr. Nixon believed that motivation was the prime prerequisite for successful learning. He was

72   Ideal School Prospectus, spring 1973, Alan Best document collection.
73   Garry Nixon, personal interview, October 16, 1996.

somewhat eccentric, had an infectious sense of humour, and made classes so interesting that student attention rarely wavered.

Garry Nixon didn't hesitate to translate an idea into action, reminiscent of David Hummel who had founded Craigdarroch School in Victoria six years earlier. In May 1972 he placed an advertisement in the *Vancouver Sun* seeking teachers who "want to teach for freedom, fascination, and abject poverty." He was flooded with over sixty applications from teachers attracted by the promise that students at Ideal would be "eager to learn." An article about the school in the *Sun* was headlined "Teachers Flock to School that Offers Life of Poverty" and a staff of six teachers was selected by mid-June.[74] Mr. Nixon formed the Ideal School Society, which would be governed by a board of advisors. He enlisted the support of a number of educators and well-connected community members who agreed to sit on the board chaired by Robert Bacon, a social worker, teacher, and former colleague at St. George's. Among the board members were several teachers, a lawyer, a minister, a YMCA counsellor, and the director of the Vancouver Art Gallery.[75] In July Mr. Nixon took out a five-year lease on a large five thousand square foot building (a former sausage factory) at Sixteenth Avenue and Willow Street in Vancouver.

There was considerable interest in the school from prospective students and parents. Mr. Nixon organized two public meetings, the first in June at the Unitarian Church and the second in August at the school building, each attracting two hundred participants. His straightforward approach was appealing: "The idea is that if you get students who want to learn and teachers who want to teach and small classes and a good atmosphere, a school should work."[76] Mr. Nixon told parents that "bright students are simply not being challenged enough in large-sized classrooms today" and that while Ideal School was not for bright students only, "we do guarantee that no outstanding students will be bored." He also emphasized that "we don't want a school for the wealthy alone."[77] Fees were set at $600

74   *Vancouver Sun*, June 14, 1972, 84.
75   "Board of Advisors," September 1972, Hugh Barr document collection.
76   Alan Daniels, "An Ideal Is Adopted at Last," *Vancouver Sun*, September 7, 1974, 44.
77   Dan Mullen, "This School Looks for Bored Students," *Vancouver Province*, June 21, 1972, 10.

per year, which Mr. Nixon claimed was half the standard rate for existing private schools, and students began signing up immediately.

Mr. Nixon did not require that his staff members adhere to a uniform educational theory, since he did not consider theory particularly important. He was looking for teachers who were versatile, innovative, and academically strong, who would tailor their programs to fit the goals and interests of students, and who were committed to making academic learning exciting. He gathered together a group of teachers with diverse backgrounds and styles. Some had taught in the public school system, others had taught abroad, and others were newly graduated teachers. Rob Wood, who had returned to Vancouver after living in a back-to-the-land community in the Slocan Valley, was hired to teach mathematics and photography. Mr. Nixon knew him from Knowplace where Mr. Wood had been a staff member four years earlier. Hugh Barr saw the newspaper advertisement. He was familiar with child-centred elementary schools in England and had also taught in Nigeria, where he worked with students who "valued education and wanted to learn." Upon arriving in Vancouver from Ireland, he worked as a substitute teacher before accepting an offer to teach mathematics, science, and Russian at Ideal. Georgie Wilson also saw the advertisement and was soon offered a position to teach English and drama. She had just graduated with a teaching certificate from UBC and was enthusiastic about trying innovative methods. Lorna Allan, the school's geography teacher, had taught previously in Scotland, at Simon Fraser University, and at Vancouver City College. Other teachers during the first two years included Robin Inman who taught French, science teacher Terry Kellington, English teacher Bonnie Chernoff, and part-time literature teacher Richard Holmes who came over from St. George's.[78]

Ideal School opened in September 1972 with seventy students. Most were in grades eight to twelve, but the school also enrolled one class of younger children in grades four to seven. Students came for a variety of reasons. Many were precisely the kind of bored or "turned off" high school students Mr. Nixon was seeking. They heard about the school from newspaper articles, advertisements, a radio interview, and word of

---

78 Part-time teachers were Martin Eskanasy, Alan Dobbs, Wayne Richards, Toni Bacon, Dr. Janet Measday, Dr. Leonard Walker, and Andrea Edwards.

mouth. Several of Mr. Nixon's St. George's students followed him to his new school, while others were referred by Robert Bacon of the Catholic Children's Aid Society. A few students had attended alternative elementary schools and, during the middle of the term, several students transferred from another alternative high school. A few were exceptionally academically adept, while others were nonconformists, both of which could cause distress at traditional high schools. The student body was an unusual mix ranging from the St. George's students "who didn't know what they were walking into," to "hippie types" influenced by the 1960s, to students who were simply discontented or bored with public school.[79] Some students were political activists: one was the daughter of a founder of Greenpeace, and another had edited a city-wide dissident newspaper produced by high school students. Despite their differences, most students were engaged and academically motivated.

The majority of students grew up on the West Side of Vancouver. However, 10 per cent came from Vancouver's East Side and 25 per cent from Burnaby, Richmond, Delta, and North Vancouver.[80] Most students were able to pay the fees, although a few scholarships were available, and one student performed secretarial work for reduced fees. All applicants were interviewed for over an hour by Mr. Nixon and other teachers, with the interview more important than the student's academic record in determining acceptance. Almost all students were accepted, although a few were turned away if the staff believed they were simply looking for a "free ride."

The school building had several advantages. It had a variety of large and small rooms conducive to small classes, individualized study, and a flexible timetable. It was centrally located, which made field trips relatively easy. The five-year lease gave the school security for the future, and the owners permitted the staff to do as much remodelling as they wished. The building was large enough that at various times Mr. Nixon and several other financially strapped staff members actually lived at the school. During the summer, teachers and students renovated and painted the building, installed indoor-outdoor carpeting, and built art and science rooms. When

---

79   Barbara Stowe, personal interview, April 17, 1997.
80   Ideal School enrolment list, 1972/73, Hugh Barr document collection.

the school was ready for opening, there were two large and two small classrooms on the second storey, with three classrooms, a meeting room, and a student lounge on the main floor. However, as in most alternative schools, the building lacked specialized facilities for physical education, home economics, industrial education, music, physics, and chemistry.[81] The building was also run-down, which would cause problems later. At first the building inspector withheld approval, but Mr. Nixon was able to secure the backing of a newly elected Vancouver NDP MLA.[82] Some students complained that the smell of sausages remained indefinitely, but by all accounts the building was adequate to the needs of the school.

CURRICULUM AND DAILY LIFE

Ideal School offered the full BC academic curriculum and a varied selection of electives. English, mathematics, social studies, science, geography, and history were taught at all grade levels. Several teachers spoke second languages and the school was rich in its language offerings, which included French, Spanish, German, Russian, and Chinese. Other academic electives included Civilization, Philosophy, Geology, and Law. The school made effective use of community resources to augment the fine arts program. Groups of students attended plays at the Vancouver Playhouse Theatre and City Stage, and the Vancouver Art Gallery supplied artists and craftspeople to visit the school.[83] Students found Georgie Wilson's enthusiastic drama classes particularly memorable, and the school had a well-equipped darkroom for the photography class. Since no one on staff had musical skills, the school offered no music instruction. The physical education program consisted of weekly skiing sessions in winter and other activities such as skating, tennis, softball, and hiking.

---

81   VSB Education Committee, minutes, July 10, 1974.

82   Garry Nixon knew many NDP politicians and subsequently co-wrote *The 1200 Days* with Lorne Kavic, a book about the Dave Barrett government (Vancouver: Kaen, 1978).

83   Ideal School Prospectus, April 1973.

An active class discusses science with teacher Hugh Barr.
Vancouver Sun, January 7, 1977

The school had a regular timetable, and students were expected to show up on time, attend classes, complete assignments, and write government examinations. One of the unique features of Ideal was its small classes that rarely exceeded twelve students and were conducive to individual attention, flexibility, and "meaningful interaction."[84] Another basic principle was that students would progress at their own rate. Some completed several grade levels in one year in subjects in which they were gifted. On the other hand, those having difficulty with a course could take as much time as they needed, and teachers set up individual programs for students when necessary. If students were interested in subjects such as astrology, yoga, film-making, or dance, Mr. Nixon would find a teacher to come in to the school. Intellectual pursuits outside the school were also recognized, and several students were given credit for attending university classes. One journalist described Ideal as a school "for students who want to learn." Mr. Nixon explained that "the teachers are committed to keeping

---

84   Charles Campbell, personal interview, April 24, 1997.

the child from being bored or from feeling stupid while the student is committed to work to the best of his or her ability."[85]

Most courses were enriched beyond the standard curriculum. Georgie Wilson emphasized female authors in her literature course, and one female student recalled that it made a "huge impression" on her. Other students remembered the excitement of reading Chaucer in Old English. Richard Holmes developed a Civilization course that was a combination of history, art, and architecture based on the Kenneth Clark television series.

Teaching styles were diverse. Some teachers were flamboyant, others were funny, and some were subdued. But most adopted a participatory "hands-on" approach in their classes and, according to most students, learning was exciting. In addition to standard lectures, there was a lot of discussion in seminar-style classes held around tables or sitting on the floor. Students read each other's work and explored themes together, students and teachers shared viewpoints, and teachers respected student opinions.[86] Two former students described the learning environment:

> Ideal School wasn't about classrooms. It was an environment where people engaged each other from morning until evening. People would sit around and have discussions. Some of us would hang out at the Starlight Café in the evenings. What made it different was it had a sense of community. The school was populated by visionaries.[87]

Discipline was rarely an issue. There were a few students with emotional or behavioural problems, but because of the school's academic requirements, they usually dropped out. There were occasional instances of theft and, as in all schools at the time, drug use was a recurrent problem, but for the most part Ideal had few of the emotionally distressed teenagers who often came to other alternative schools. The school's message was to "treat people with respect," and most students did.[88] The few rules were common sense: no drugs at the school, courtesy and consideration for others, no violence, respect for other people's rights, and the right to study

---

85 Elizabeth Touchette, "Making Ideal Commitment," *Vancouver Sun*, September 9, 1972, 44.
86 Georgie Wilson, personal interview, November 5, 1996.
87 Alan Best, Megan Ellis, personal interview, March 17, 1997.
88 Georgie Wilson, personal interview, November 5, 1996.

quietly.[89] The school encouraged "a set of attitudes" rather than a set of rules.[90] As in British private schools, older students socialized younger ones into the ways of the school. If a student was continually disruptive he or she was asked to leave, but this rarely happened because, for most students, the only alternative to Ideal—the public school system—was unacceptable. The fact that the students wanted to be there was the best assurance of a smoothly functioning school. Students felt respected: "If you screwed up, smoked dope, or missed class, there was an honest discussion with Garry. We were treated with respect, as people with enough sense to make a decision."[91]

The school made direct use of learning opportunities in the community and purchased a van for the many field trips. Students visited museums and libraries, went hiking in Manning Park, and spent several days in Victoria visiting the legislature and cabinet ministers.[92] One teacher regularly drove students to the UBC library to do research and also arranged for them to use the language laboratories on the campus. Senior students used the science labs at a nearby high school. The school brought in accomplished visitors from the community, including art gallery director Tony Emory, artist Evelyn Roth, environmentalist Irving Stowe, and folksinger Ian Anderson. Friday afternoon was reserved for showing film classics such as *To Kill a Mockingbird* and *Inherit the Wind*, and one student who went on to become a writer recalled that the films "kindled my interest in film and storytelling."[93]

Day-to-day life at Ideal School was informal. Everyone dressed casually, teachers were called by their first names, and students were welcome in the staff lounge. The school day extended from 9:00 to 4:00 but students often stayed well into the evening. Although there was less of a counter-cultural feel than at 1960s alternatives like Knowplace, Ideal was strongly influenced by that period. As former students recalled, "We thought the

---

89   Alan Daniels, "An Ideal Is Adopted at Last," *Vancouver Sun*, September 7, 1974, 44.
90   M. A. Middleton, *An Evaluation of Ideal School, 1974–75*, Research Report 75-22 (Vancouver: Board of School Trustees, November 1975), 23.
91   Charles Campbell, personal interview, April 24, 1997.
92   Sharon Kirsh, Roger Simon, Malcolm Levin, eds. *Directory of Canadian Alternative and Innovative Education* (Toronto: Communitas Exchange, June 1973).
93   Charles Campbell, personal interview, April 24, 1997.

sixties were still on."[94] Many students smoked marijuana out of the school at least occasionally, and at the end of the first year the graduating class all went skinny-dipping together. Most students ended up at Ideal because they felt somehow different from the mainstream, and this encouraged an ethos of inclusiveness. The student population consisted of "some very bright people and a high percentage of eccentrics"; two legendary brothers were "walking history encyclopedias."[95] As one student suggested, "You had to deal with and relate to people who were a lot different from you. Students at Ideal became a pretty tolerant lot."[96] They formed a close community and remained important in each other's lives for years afterwards.

Garry Nixon was the director and, since he financed the school with his own money, he retained control over finances and hiring. By the middle of the second year, this led to some discontent among the young and predominantly "left of centre" staff members who expected decision-making to be democratic. However, decisions about the academic program, admissions, and how to handle students were made collegially by the entire staff at regular meetings. Although there was an understanding that the basic curriculum would be covered, teachers were free to organize their own courses as they saw fit. As one former teacher remarked, "Mr. Nixon "hand-picked" his people and then never interfered."[97]

Students and staff met together regularly and, although the students had no official power at Ideal, in practice they had a good deal of input into the day-to-day functioning of the school. One student remembered that "if we really wanted something it would happen; I can't recall any difficulty that wasn't resolved."[98] Another recalled that "we felt that our opinions were really listened to, that they mattered."[99] Students were encouraged to initiate activities. When some students decided they needed a cafeteria, they established and ran it themselves. One student organized the library, while another who had dance training arranged a dance class for both students and staff. A student who felt strongly about environmental issues

94   Alan Best, Megan Ellis, personal interview, March 17, 1997.
95   Alan Best, Megan Ellis, personal interview, March 17, 1997.
96   Charles Campbell, personal interview, April 24, 1997.
97   Hugh Barr, personal interview, February 24, 1997.
98   Alan Best, personal interview, March 17, 1997.
99   Charles Campbell, personal interview, April 24, 1997.

organized everybody to go out and pick up garbage: "There was room for zealotry; you were allowed to be yourself."[100] Students also helped create their own academic programs, although the overall academic direction of the school was the domain of the teachers.

The first graduating class numbered twelve students. The first year was so successful that enrolment increased from seventy to ninety for 1973/74. Most participants believed that the inclusion of younger children had been a mistake, and grades four and five were dropped for the second year. The core staff remained intact and the school hired several part-time teachers. Morale remained high despite the fact that the teachers were working long hours for low salaries. Although the board of directors rarely met, at the end of the first year a new board was elected that included several of the teachers.

The school managed to make ends meet financially during the first two years. Expenses for the first year were $43,000, with more than half going toward salaries. Student fees amounted to $45,000 and the school showed a modest profit.[101] The following year both revenue and expenses increased to just over $50,000 as the school broke even.[102] But the main reason the school did not lose money was that staff salaries were so low. Teachers were paid an average of $250 per month, far less than they would have earned in the public school system. Although tuition fees increased from $600 to $800 in the second year, the additional revenue was used to hire more teachers to keep class size low. The only way to increase salaries would have been to raise tuition fees significantly. Mr. Nixon was reluctant to do this for fear that the kind of students he wanted to attract might not be able to afford to attend.

---

100 Barbara Stowe, personal interview, April 17, 1997.
101 Ideal School Society, Annual Report, June 30, 1973, Registrar of Companies, Victoria.
102 Ideal School, financial statements, 1972/73, 1973/74.

A Public School

By the end of the second school year, Garry Nixon realized that he could not ask his staff to continue teaching for less than a living wage. The deteriorating condition of the building added to the financial difficulties. After unsuccessful attempts to arrange a government grant, Mr. Nixon concluded that "the only way out of this dilemma is to join the public school system."[103] So in the spring of 1974, he began to negotiate with Vancouver School Board officials in the hope that the district would take over the school.

The timing was opportune. In the early 1970s the Vancouver School District began to develop alternative programs for the many high school students at risk of dropping out because they were unhappy in large traditional schools. The board recognized that many parents and students were demanding more choice within the school system and that some teachers wanted more freedom to develop innovative programs. In 1971 the board established City School as an alternative high school and also entered into a partnership with Total Education. "Mini-schools," with integrated curricula for motivated students, and special-needs programs began to appear with great frequency. A committee under the leadership of assistant superintendent Alf Clinton was charged with creating and supervising alternative programs.

After visiting Ideal and meeting with the teaching staff, Dr. Clinton reported to the board that "Ideal School is a private alternative school and has a strong academic component, its success largely based on the low pupil-teacher ratio of ten to one." It would be "to the advantage of the Vancouver school system to have an academically oriented mini-school."[104] He recommended that Ideal be established as a "mini-school under the wing of the Board" attached to a secondary school. This was endorsed by the school board in July 1974.[105] The board offered to take in the entire school, "staff, students, and philosophy," and promised to let the school operate with "as much autonomy as possible."[106] The only

103 Garry Nixon, letter to parents, July 23, 1974, Alan Best document collection.
104 VSB Education Committee, minutes, July 10, 1974.
105 VSB meeting, minutes, July 15, 1974.
106 Garry Nixon, letter to parents, July 23, 1974.

conditions were that the school not charge fees and that all teachers be certified.

Mr. Nixon wrote to the parents, explaining his decision to join the Vancouver School District. "The agreement with the school board was the best that I could negotiate. We were faced with the prospect of raising fees exorbitantly in a deteriorating building. This would have still left our teachers at the poverty level and we would have had to exclude students not from wealthy families." He described what he saw as the significance of the arrangement:

> This is an experiment. To my knowledge it is the first time in English Canada that a private school has joined the public system *in toto*. The School Board will be watching us to see that their faith in us was justified; and we, in turn, will be watching them to see that we have the necessary autonomy. We have a very good chance to make it work. You, as parents, will have the right and responsibility to make representation to your elected School Board if you think the school is not working as it should. I look forward to continuing to work with them and I will do my best to make this new arrangement work. If we are successful it will have a lasting effect on our school system.[107]

Taking over Ideal School produced significant benefits for the school district. The district gained a unique program, a cohesive staff that had worked together for two years, and an appropriate setting for students unhappy with mainstream schools. The deal was also beneficial for the school. Teachers would be paid according to the Vancouver School Board salary scale. In addition, the school was offered a new location on the top floor of the former Dawson School in downtown Vancouver, which had closed due to declining enrolment in that neighbourhood.[108] The main floor of the building would be occupied by City School.[109]

Ideal School moved into its new location in September 1974. The school had six classrooms, a student lounge, an office, and shared use

---

107 Garry Nixon, letter to parents, July 23, 1974.
108 VSB meeting, minutes, July 15, 1974.
109 "Dawson School to Be Reopened," *Vancouver Sun*, August 22, 1974, 41.

of the auditorium and gymnasium. Although the building was old and needed renovation, the physical space suited the needs of the school well, and the downtown location was convenient for walking to the library and art gallery. Enrolment jumped to 120 students. True to its word the school board hired all the existing teachers. But in an ironic twist, Garry Nixon could not be hired immediately because he did not have a teaching certificate. Mr. Nixon stepped down temporarily from the directorship of the school and enrolled in education at UBC, where he could obtain his necessary qualifications by December. He was assigned to Ideal School for ten weeks of "practice teaching," after which it was understood that he would be appointed as head teacher.

When January arrived, Mr. Nixon was indeed offered a position with the Vancouver School District, but not at Ideal. Although no reason was given, one possible explanation is that the staff may not have wanted him back. The teachers favoured a more collegial decision-making style than Mr. Nixon had displayed in the first two years. As well, although his vision and leadership had been essential to the success of the school, his lack of interest in formal administration and his deliberate de-emphasis of educational theory may not have suited the role of an administrator in the public school system. Mr. Nixon declined the Vancouver job and became director of Columbia College for two years. Following his tenure at the college, he opened a successful Vancouver accounting practice, which he continued for many years. He never returned to teaching.

Rob Wood also went back to UBC to earn his teaching certificate. Like Garry Nixon, he did not return to Ideal but taught for many years in the public school system and later became principal of an independent Catholic school in Vancouver. Georgie Wilson and Hugh Barr became the nucleus of the Ideal staff. They were joined by several new teachers over the next few years, including social studies teacher Marcie Thoms and mathematics teacher Phil Knaiger, an original member of the Total Education staff. No director was appointed to replace Garry Nixon. Decisions were made by staff consensus at long, exhausting meetings.[110]

---

110 Hugh Barr, personal interview, February 24, 1997.

Ideal School students organized protest activities to oppose their forced move to Lord Byng School. *Vancouver Sun*, December 15, 1976

A Lord Byng student makes a poster to welcome Ideal School students.
Vancouver Sun, January 7, 1977

Staff and students enjoyed their time in the downtown building. Ideal was attached to King George Secondary School for administrative purposes, and teachers remembered the principal as supportive and congenial. But the school's use of this site was called into question in late 1974 when the Vancouver School Board considered selling the property to the provincial government.[111] Although the sale did not take place, eighteen months later, in April 1976, the board announced that the Dawson site was too expensive to be used for educational purposes, and both Ideal and City School would have to move. The trustees, also claiming fire regulations made the use of the building untenable, offered to provide three classrooms for Ideal at Lord Byng Secondary. Parents and students protested by addressing school board meetings, picketing the board office, and writing letters to the editor.[112] The teachers presented a lengthy brief arguing that the school's unique features of trust, informality, self-discipline, integrated courses, and student participation in decision-making required a separate building:

> Ideal School involves students whose dissatisfaction with larger schools resulted in declining attendance, social problems, feelings of alienation, and conflicts with teachers. Some students had dropped out entirely. The larger schools with their authoritarian structure, inflexibility, and pressure to conform have left many needs unfulfilled. The strength of Ideal School and the reasons for its success lies in the awareness of the needs of each individual. The development of a supportive atmosphere of trust is directly dependent on the small size of the school. It is essential that rules be kept to a minimum. To place this school with its principles of flexibility within the confines of a large institution would be to destroy it.[113]

---

111 VSB Planning and Building Committee, minutes, August 13, 1974; board meeting, minutes, September 3, 1974.
112 "Students Mount Final Protest over New Home," *Vancouver Sun*, January 4, 1977, 2.
113 Ideal School Staff, "The Case for a Separate Facility for Ideal School," brief to Vancouver school trustees, October 27, 1976.

Though the protests succeeded in forcing a six-month delay, the trustees eventually made a firm decision that the school would have to move to Lord Byng in January 1976.[114] Ideal School became less autonomous, and students were forced to adapt to a formal learning environment and a set of traditional school rules similar to what they had rejected by enrolling in Ideal in the first place.[115] But parents and teachers did not give up and their unhappiness continued to be covered in the daily newspapers. The board promised to reconsider its decision, and at the end of the school year found a new home for Ideal in a former elementary school annex near Sir Winston Churchill Secondary School.[116] In September 1977, the school moved into its new building where it has remained ever since, and maintained a good relationship with the administration at Churchill. Hugh Barr stayed at the school for almost ten years before transferring to a mainstream secondary school, while Georgie Wilson taught at Ideal for many years.

EFFECTS ON STUDENTS

Ideal School was evaluated by a Vancouver School District research official after its first year with the board in the fall of 1975. His report concluded that the school had a "positive influence on students' attitudes toward academic achievement" and "if the students had not been accepted by Ideal School, over one-half would have dropped out of school altogether." The report continued:

> The dedicated teachers, the low student-teacher ratio of
> twenty to one, and the emphasis on mutual respect tend
> to keep classroom problems to a minimum. At the same
> time these factors have helped breed trust and the forma-
> tion of a cohesive working unit oriented to academic
> achievement. Evidence of these effects may be seen in

---

114 *Vancouver Sun*: Letters to the editor, "Ideal School Students Unjustly Treated," and "Parent Feels Betrayed by School Relocation," December 15, 1976, 5.

115 Karenn Krangle, "Situation Is Less than Ideal for Displaced Students," *Vancouver Sun*, January 7, 1977, 28.

116 "Ideal School Move to Byng Changed to Six-Month Test," *Vancouver Sun*, January 8, 1977, 12.

better attendance, improved relationships with others, greater creativity in thinking, and more freedom to make decisions.[117]

Almost 90 per cent of the students surveyed expressed satisfaction with their lives at Ideal School. Students cited improved personal relationships, more participation in decision-making, increased interaction with teachers, and increased confidence, motivation, and responsibility. The majority of students also reported that they were encouraged to pursue their academic interests, work independently, and complete assignments. They considered field trips valuable and learning experiences "positive." Teachers reported good relationships with students, a friendly atmosphere, few discipline problems, a firm base of mutual respect among staff, and a good sense of teamwork. Teachers also reported that the "quantity of work they could complete far exceeds that achieved by regular classes" due to the co-operativeness and willingness of the students.[118]

Most students ended up at Ideal because they "could not hack the regular system." One student said, "Thank God for those schools for creating opportunities for kids like me."[119] Most Ideal students realized they were different: "Students who attend do so for varying reasons, such as feelings of alienation and loss of individuality experienced in a large learning institution."[120] Ideal was very influenced by the 1960s but differed from other alternative schools in that most of its students were motivated by a desire to prepare for further education and a career.[121]

Although parents of students at alternative high schools were far less involved in day-to-day school life than were elementary alternative school parents, Ideal School parents were appreciative of the school's existence. One parent described how her son had been repeatedly beaten up while attending a Vancouver high school. After being advised by a district official that a transfer to Ideal might avoid the "cliquishness and scapegoating prevalent in our local high schools," she wrote, "Enrolled at Ideal School,

117 M. A. Middleton, *An Evaluation of Ideal School, 1974–75* (Vancouver: Board of School Trustees, November 1975), 4.
118 M. A. Middleton, An Evaluation of Ideal School, 1974–75.
119 Neil Tessler, personal interview, April 11, 1997.
120 Ideal School students, letter to the editor, *Vancouver Sun*, December 15, 1976, 5.
121 M. A. Middleton, An Evaluation of Ideal School, 1974–75, 17–18.

my son gradually got over his painful experiences and is now doing well in Grade 10."[122] In 1977 another parent described changes for the better in her son who "had spent two disastrous failure-ridden years in our local high school and had reached the stage of not attending classes at all":

> In the short time he has been at Ideal, I have seen him change from a sullen, withdrawn, unproductive child to one possessing considerable maturity and self-assurance in his whole approach to life and he is now achieving high marks in Grade 9 math which he had failed twice before. The students are a close-knit, articulate little family, sharing with their teachers a mutual respect and awareness.[123]

While the majority of students thrived at Ideal School, a few did not. One former student, who counted himself as one of the school's success stories, pointed out: "There were also a few tragedies. Several of my classmates ended up as alcoholics, heroin addicts, and homeless. Two of those had been classmates of mine at St. George's, and I seriously doubt whether their stories would have been quite the same had they stayed in that structured environment." While some of these students may well have had difficulty in mainstream schools anyway, "others, crying out for greater discipline, floundered where there was none, and still other bright students took a longer time to obtain their diplomas."[124]

Ideal School gave rise to an intimate learning community populated by some highly gifted and unusual individuals. Most Ideal graduates went on to university and believed the school prepared them well for postsecondary education and for their career paths. Several became academics and lawyers, others ended up in the creative arts (dance, animation, poetry), another became a naturopathic physician, and one Ideal graduate was, for many years, editor of the *Georgia Straight*, Vancouver's alternative cultural newspaper. In fields such as senior science students might not have been as thoroughly prepared as in a more traditional school, but most former students considered the gaps to have been minor. Students

---

122 Ideal School parent, letter to the editor, *Vancouver Sun*, December 15, 1976, 5.
123 Ideal School parent, letter to the editor, Vancouver Sun, January 6, 1977, 5.
124 Alan Best, letter to the author, June 29, 1999.

cited the school's major strengths as the emphasis on academics, the small classes, and the flexibility of the program. Individual student goals and interests were taken seriously and respected. Perhaps most important was the attitude conveyed by the director and the teachers that anything was possible. One member of the first graduating class said, "I really blossomed there."[125] Another student credited the emphasis on discussion with teaching her how to argue a position and take chances. In the words of another former student, "the teachers were passionate about what they did and communicated excitement about learning. The school created people who were resourceful, who could cope with life, who could take initiative. It prepared me admirably."[126]

It was perhaps inevitable that Ideal's founder, Garry Nixon, would leave the school. Though he was a natural teacher, he relied on personal qualities rather than cultivated pedagogical skill. He had an ideological commitment to democratic decision-making but wanted to make the important decisions himself. One former student described him as a "benevolent despot," creating tension between himself and the teachers, who believed they should be equal partners in the school. Furthermore, Mr. Nixon had little interest in the details of administration, and one former student characterized him as a "disorganized visionary." Mr. Nixon's leadership strengths were his ability to motivate others and to recognize talent in other people. This was sufficient when the school was small and informal, but as it grew in size and became accountable to the authority of the school district, administrative tasks became more significant. Ideal School provides an example of how, often, the person with the drive and talent to create a project is not the right person to carry it through to its next stage.[127]

Nevertheless, Ideal School owes its success to the vision and creative drive of Garry Nixon, and to the talent, enthusiasm, and dedication of its staff. Many former Ideal students have described Mr. Nixon as an animated and enthusiastic teacher who "likes to teach, likes ideas, and likes

125 Barbara Stowe, personal interview, April 17, 1997.
126 Charles Campbell, personal interview, April 24, 1997.
127 Barbara Stowe, personal interview, April 24, 1997.

people."[128] Throughout his teaching career, he was "passionately inter-ested in his subject, had a way with words, and had a sense of humour."[129] "He appreciated intellectual energy and made [his subject] interesting. He taught his own version of history. Lessons with Garry were never dull."[130] According to students, Mr. Nixon was committed to helping young people achieve their best and learn how to question "the system." He encouraged students to pursue what they were interested in and valued intellectual and artistic accomplishments equally. In the words of one student, "Garry instilled the idea that learning has no boundaries or no end. All learning is worthwhile."[131]

CONCLUSION

Ideal School has thrived as a public school since its entry into the Vancouver School District in 1974. Ideal benefited from the elimination of student fees, increased teacher salaries, administrative assistance, a more functional building, and access to equipment and materials. The only negative consequences were the reduction in the size of the teach-ing staff in order to fit the district formula and the slowness with which the bureaucracy acted on school needs and requests.[132] Former teachers reported that the district administration allowed the school to develop according to its original values with a minimum of interference. Ideal School retained most of its original character and continued to emphasize academic learning in an informal small-school environment that appeals to students averse to large impersonal institutions.

Ideal School provided a home for many students who attended alterna-tive schools in their elementary years. Almost half of the students enrolled in 1975 had previously attended an alternative elementary school, such as the New School, the Barker Free School, Windsor House, or the Vallican Whole School.[133] These students appreciated Ideal's academic emphasis,

---

128 Charles Campbell, personal interview, April 24, 1997.
129 Barbara Stowe, personal interview, April 17, 1997.
130 Alan Best, Megan Ellis, personal interview, March 17, 1997.
131 Alan Best, Megan Ellis, personal interview, March 17, 1997.
132 M. A. Middleton, An Evaluation of Ideal School, 1974–75.
133 M. A. Middleton, An Evaluation of Ideal School, 1974–75, 3.

respect for students, and engaging classes. They enjoyed the opportunity to attend a high school that allowed them the freedom to be themselves but also took learning seriously. One of these former alternative school students said, "I got turned on to learning there."[134] Another described it as "like a real school; I was privileged to be there."[135] Still another who had never been to a public school said, "There was good camaraderie and the teachers were clear about boundaries. I was motivated and excited to be there; my goal was to go to a real school."[136] Another student recalled, "Academic standards were exceptionally high. Teachers taught the material but also sent the kids off in many directions. They expanded my desire to seek out knowledge. They went far beyond—exceptional children were given exceptional opportunities."[137]

Ideal School owed part of its success to the fact that it came along at the right time. By the early 1970s, the school's goals had become recognized as worthy by educational leaders and significant numbers of parents, and was therefore accepted into the public school system. Ideal also benefited from the experience of its 1960s predecessors in the alternative schools movement. By emulating their strengths and avoiding their mistakes, 1970s alternative schools were more lasting ventures. The fact that alternative schools began to thrive within the public school system is an indication of how that system had changed. The pioneering example of the early alternatives contributed to that change. The continuing existence of Ideal School, along with Total Education and many other innovative public school programs, is one of the legacies of the alternative schools movement.

By the mid-1970s few alternative schools could survive any longer as independent entities. Committed to keeping their fees moderate, they were always on the edge of bankruptcy. But large fee increases would have eliminated most of their clientele, and joining the public school system was the only way they could survive. The years between 1972 and 1975 were a pivotal moment. Pressured by parents for more choice in

---

134 David Eaton, personal interview, April 2, 1997.
135 Steven Pratt, personal interview, March 9, 1997.
136 Erin Harris, personal interview, January 15, 1997.
137 Jono Drake, personal interview, February 10, 1997.

the system and encouraged by a few innovative administrators and teachers, larger school districts like Vancouver, Victoria, and North Vancouver sought to develop alternatives. Taking in already established programs like Ideal School, Total Education, and Windsor House made good sense. The school districts gained valuable alternative programs and the energy of the committed teachers who worked in them. The alternative schools gained the financial means to continue teaching young people in an innovative manner. Parents and students gained a wider range of educational options.

Chapter 12

THE VALLICAN WHOLE SCHOOL AND OTHER INDEPENDENTS

Although the counterculture of the 1960s had waned in most parts of British Columbia by the early 1970s, it remained strong in the isolated Slocan Valley in the West Kootenay region of southeastern BC. This community was a major site of the back-to-the-land movement that began in the late 1960s and reached its peak by the mid-1970s.[1] These recent immigrants to the valley were mainly young, well-educated, and idealistic Americans seeking to escape the Vietnam War and the violent politics and pollution of the cities. They were attracted by the prospects of "a personally meaningful and satisfying existence in the countryside."[2] As one newcomer wrote, "There is a new kind of community growing in this quiet, rural valley. Most of us come from the cities hoping to find a different kind of life for our families on the old Doukhobor farms."[3] By the early 1970s, the newcomers in the Valley numbered in the hundreds; by 1976, close to one thousand.[4] It was in the midst of this countercultural community that parents, wanting to educate their children in a manner consistent with their values, created the Vallican Whole School.

---

1   Pat Moan, "Farm Communes Thriving in Flowery Slocan Country," *Vancouver Sun*, August 6, 1971.

2   John Gower, "The Impact of Alternative Ideology on Landscape: The Back-to-the-Land Movement in the Slocan Valley" (master's thesis, University of British Columbia, 1986), ii.

3   Bryan Marrion, LEAP Project Grand Application, "Media and the Rural Alternative," circa 1971, Vallican Whole School archive.

4   John Gower, "The Impact of Alternative Ideology on Landscape," 103.

The Whole School initially had the characteristics of a typical Romantic school, particularly the laissez-faire attitude of the adults toward student learning and the voluntary nature of all classes. However, the school eventually differed from the Romantic schools of the 1960s. Its founding in 1972 places it chronologically in the Therapeutic period, and within a few years the Whole School would develop traits of a Therapeutic school, especially in its increased academic expectations of students. Furthermore, many of its students would later attend Therapeutic high schools in Vancouver. What held the school together, despite the waning of the counterculture in the rest of the province, was the self-contained and supportive countercultural community in the outlying Slocan Valley.

THE NEWCOMER COMMUNITY

These recent immigrants had few opportunities for making a living in the early 1970s. So like the Argenta Quakers two decades earlier, they formed a co-operative, the Rural Alternatives Research and Training Society, to initiate employment projects.[5] One early success was the development of a community library made possible by a generous federal grant. Another local initiative was the *Slocan Valley Community Forest Management Project*, a comprehensive report encouraging small-scale, community controlled, and environmentally sustainable logging ventures.[6] The most important project undertaken by the newcomers was the construction of the Vallican Whole Community Centre begun in 1971.[7] The centre took five years to build and was financed partly by federal grants from the Opportunities for Youth and Local Initiatives Programs, and partly by donations and volunteer labour. The project organizers included former Knowplace participants David Orcutt, Rob Wood, and Greg Sorbara, who had all moved to the Slocan Valley the previous year.

But the newcomers were disliked by some long-term residents who resented the abundant formal education of the new immigrants, their

---

5   Russell Oughtred, "Urban Refugees Will Learn Rural Skills," *Nelson Daily News*, July 8, 1971, 2.
6   Slocan Valley Community Forest Management Project, 1975.
7   The community centre was originally named the Centre for Rural Alternatives.

perceived lack of work ethic, and the ease with which they could access government grants. Other locals were unhappy with the lifestyle of the new residents—their "hippie" appearance, their drug use, their sometimes liberal attitudes to nudity and sexuality, and their communes such as the New Family whose participants engaged in a polyamorous relationship. For their part, the newcomers did not go out of their way to win over the local people.[8] In 1972 and 1973 divisiveness among three groups— Doukhobors, "Anglos," and "hippies"—reached unpleasant proportions, as the *Nelson Daily News* reported in a story headlined "Unrest Sweeps Valley": "There are the long-haired scruffily-dressed hippies who have come across the border seeking solitude and there are the staid, long-time residents who have worked hard in the many years they have occupied the fertile land, to establish a good environment for their children."[9] Local residents were particularly upset that the community centre construction crew did not complete more than the foundation of the building by the time the federal grant was exhausted, and it was two years before the project was resumed. Angry letters appeared in local newspapers and the region's Social Credit MLA also entered the controversy. Even the distant *Vancouver Sun* published several stories in February 1972 with such headlines as "Hippies, Deserters, Cause Real Problem" and "Hippies, Nudies, and Hole in the Ground."[10]

Some of this resentment was taken out on the "hippie" students at the Winlaw local school, who were harassed by children of local residents to the point that many parents in the countercultural community began keeping their children home. There were numerous incidents of students being beaten up after school and put in garbage cans. The well-educated newcomers also had other reasons for being critical of the school. They believed the quality of education in the rural school was poor and attempts to discuss their concerns with the principal had been unsatisfactory. Furthermore, they distrusted public education in the first place and wanted to transmit their own values to their children.[11]

---

8   John Gower, "The Impact of Alternative Ideology on Landscape," 90–97.
9   "Unrest Sweeps Valley," *Nelson Daily News*, June 22, 1973. A similar article, "Freaks along the Slocan," appeared in the *Vancouver Sun*, July 12, 1973, 37.
10   *Vancouver Sun*, February 10, 1972, 12; February 18, 1972, 11.
11   John Gower, "The Impact of Alternative Ideology on Landscape," 92.

In the fall of 1972, several families decided to start their own school. The impetus for what was originally called the Free School was provided by Marcia Braundy and Joel Harris. Ms. Braundy recalled a moment of inspiration when a friend told her: "Joel Harris has a school in his head. I think the two of you can make it happen."[12]

Ms. Braundy had grown up in Massachusetts and New York and earned a degree in environmental education at Antioch West University in San Francisco. She founded several alternative schools in California before coming to British Columbia. Joel and Nancy Harris also came from California. Mr. Harris had a master's degree in philosophy and had taught at Portland State University. Other founding parents were T. C. and Brian Carpendale, Bonnie and Corky Evans, Tom and Sally Drake, Gretchen and Michael Pratt, Dan and Pat Armstrong, Marty and Susan Hykin, and Freye Grey. Many other individuals helped out with the school in its early days, including Fred Eisen, Bob Inwood, Brian and Cathie Marrion, Susan Zander, and Jeannie Neilson. Most were from the United States, particularly California, and lived within a ten-mile stretch of the central Slocan Valley approximately forty miles north of Castlegar.[13] Before moving to the Slocan in 1970, the Carpendales had been associated with Knowplace, the Floating Free School, and housing co-operatives in Greater Vancouver, where Brian Carpendale had taught communications at Simon Fraser University.[14] The Drakes came from Los Angeles where they had been involved in the film and music industries before leaving the United States to escape the Vietnam War, pollution, and the "police state."[15] The Evanses, also Californians, were political activists from Berkeley who decided that their former home was not "a place to raise children."[16]

Although most were determined to become farmers when they moved to the Slocan, school parents had a variety of former careers. There were

---

12   Marcia Braundy, personal interview, January 20, 1997. The school was also called the Slocan Valley Community School and the Centre: An Alternative School.

13   A few parents were Canadian, two were British, and Tom Drake had been born in BC.

14   Brian Carpendale wrote widely on alternative education in the late 1960s. He was one of the instructors fired during the political strife at Simon Fraser University.

15   Tom and Sally Drake, personal interview, January 9, 1977.

16   Bonnie Evans, personal interview, December 12, 1996. Corky Evans, in addition to involvement in the school, served as MLA for Nelson-Creston and as a cabinet minister in the Glen Clark NDP government from 1996 to 2001.

three teachers, three university instructors, two dancer/actors, two film-makers, one professional artist, one Hollywood writer/director, a publicity writer, a theatre set carpenter, a registered nurse, a linguist, and a biologist. Their beliefs and values stemmed from a combination of political activism and commitment to individual freedom. Some simply wanted to escape from mainstream society, while others hoped to change the world through the example of their small community. Despite being highly educated, many had developed doubts about the value of academic learning as prac-tised in mainstream society. They wanted their children to be free to make their own decisions and wanted the school to emphasize artistic activities, an appreciation for the natural environment, and personal awareness.

CURRICULUM AND GROWING PAINS

The Free School opened in December 1972 in the large "Morton" house, temporarily empty after the breakup of a group marriage. The school's twenty-five children, aged six to sixteen, came from as far as five miles away. Tuition was set at the value of the monthly family allowance cheque plus a small percentage of family income, and all parents were expected to volunteer at the school. Students attended four days per week and were divided into two groups, the younger children up to age nine, and older students ten and over. By September 1973 enrolment climbed to thirty-five, and the school rotated among the Drake, Carpendale, and Pratt homes, "the houses that could handle it." One parent remembered that "you had to hide all the food the night before."[17] The students were an exuberant group.

---

17   Tom and Sally Drake, personal interview, January 9, 1997.

In the early years a wood stove kept Whole School students warm in the winter and doubled as informal seating during warmer months. *Vancouver Sun*, November 9, 1973

Although student attendance at classes was completely voluntary, the school offered a full and eclectic schedule of activities. Joel Harris, the school principal, and Marcia Braundy organized courses given by parent volunteers. Parents had expertise in many different areas and offered a wide variety of courses, most meeting once a week for one to two hours. Courses offered in the first year were drama, art, environment adventure, videotape and film-making, basic three Rs, junior science, senior science, mathematics, physics, French, music, health education, environment, sports play, journal, Canadian and Doukhobor history, reading and writing, gardening, arts and crafts, First Aid, pantomime, and ballet.[18] Judo was held in the hayloft of a barn and science was taught in the fields.[19] Students particularly enjoyed making films, writing plays, acting, and Sally Drake's ballet classes.

Before long the local authorities began to question the school's legitimacy. In March 1973, three months after the school opened, the Nelson School District served notice of their intention to prosecute Free School families for not sending their children to public school. One parent, Sally Drake, received a letter from the chair of the board that "it has come to my attention that you are conducting a school which is possibly operating outside the jurisdiction of the Public Schools Act."[20] After an inconclusive meeting between parents and school district officials, school trustees debated the issue at a board meeting on March 26.[21] Over two dozen parents attended the meeting to support a presentation by Tom Drake, listing the teaching credentials and university degrees of the twenty people associated with the school.[22] After delaying its decision, the board decided to drop the matter two weeks later and opened discussions with the parents about the school's possible inclusion in the school district.[23] Although the negotiations did

---

18   School timetable, March 1973.
19   Moira Farrow, "Free School Starts Out in Bind," *Vancouver Sun*, November 9, 1973, 31.
20   M. D. Berg to Sally Drake, February 26, 1973.
21   Four parents travelled to Victoria to meet with Education Minister Eileen Dailly but had to see special commissioner John Bremer instead. Little came of the meeting.
22   "Staff, Tutors, and Consultants of the Centre School, a Preliminary List," March 26, 1973.
23   Peggy Pawelko, "Board Defers Action," *Nelson Daily News*, March 27, 1973, 2; "No Decision Yet on Free School," *Nelson Daily News*, April 4, 1973, 2; "Negotiations

not come to fruition, the school board confirmed in September that it would not take any legal action against the school or the parents.[24]

Most parents believed the trustees acted under pressure from some local residents hostile to the countercultural community.[25] As in the case of the Saturna Island Free School two years earlier, the major opposition to radical alternative schools came from local authorities. It is significant that this issue arose in the same region of the province where Doukhobor children were removed from their families twenty years earlier for not attending public school. Several local reporters noted, in their accounts of the school board deliberations, that members of the Sons of Freedom Doukhobor sect were "watching the school closely." The local opposition to the school had the opposite of the intended effect, making the newcomer community more close-knit and determined to continue operating the school. In the ensuing years the school would play an integral role in the ongoing development of the countercultural community.

Turning their attention to practical matters, the school group sought a permanent facility. They continued to meet in several different homes and, for a brief period in 1974, leased a small public school building that had closed. Meanwhile, the community centre project was renewed in 1973 with a federal grant from the Local Employment Assistance Program and money raised from large-scale benefit dances. Students, teachers, and parents spent many hours working on the building, and the Vallican Whole Community Centre was finally completed three years later. The school, renamed "The Whole School," moved into the Centre in the fall of 1976 as an elementary school with twenty-six students aged five to twelve.[26]

Open on Slocan School," *Vancouver Sun*, April 12, 1973, 22; "Trustees Shelve Court Action," *Vancouver Province*, April 12, 1973, 6.

24   "Public Funds to Be Denied," *Vancouver Sun*, September 27, 1973, 39.

25   Eli Sopow, "Free Schools Meet Heavy Opposition," and "Parents Desire Educational Choice," *Kootenay Miner*, March 29, 1973, 4.

26   John Gower, "The Impact of Alternative Ideology on Landscape," 102.

Welcome to the Whole School!

The spectacular mountains and woodlands of the Slocan Valley provide a fitting environment for the outstanding educational experience found at the Whole School.

The Whole School in the relatively isolated Slocan Valley is one of the few BC alternative schools that has remained independent as well as financially viable.
The Whole School Prospectus, 1996; courtesy of The Whole School

The school's philosophy during its early years was laissez-faire about learning and behaviour. Formal study was less valued than were practical learning and interpersonal relations. Some inquisitive students delved into academics on their own but most did little conventional study. One former teacher recalled, "Whether the kids learned to get along with each other was more important than learning math."[27] The adults engaged in spirited debates about whether students should be allowed to decide if they would

27   Marcia Braundy, personal interview, January 20, 1997.

learn to read.[28] By the late 1970s the school softened its Romantic position and only admitted students who "want to attend and come to school
primarily to learn."[29] But most students remembered that there was little
academic learning during the early years of the school. One former student
said, "I wasn't a very good alternative student. I didn't do any English, I
didn't do any math, I didn't do any art. They tried to interest us in things,
but all I did all day was smoke dope and play guitar."[30]

. If the academic aims were ill-formed, the school's egalitarian social
principles were well articulated. The "School Philosophy," written in
the late 1970s, states: "The Whole School exists to provide an environment where children can learn to understand and counteract the effects
of living in a society which oppresses people because of their sex, race,
age, class, physical and mental disabilities."[31] The school encouraged
co-operation rather than competition, personal responsibility, and respect
for the environment. The empowerment of women was particularly noteworthy. Female students were encouraged to consider such non-traditional
careers as carpentry and welding, and teachers and students discussed
such serious issues as the effects of pornography. Several former students
said that they appreciated the strong female role models at the school. On
the other hand, some male students reported that they have been disadvantaged in their personal development by the lack of a strong male presence among the school's leaders. Students and adults also participated in
numerous gestalt therapy groups and other psychotherapeutic activities.[32]
Feminism, environmentalism, social change, and personal transformation,
fundamental values of the 1970s, provided the foundations of the Whole
School community.

28   Bonnie Evans, personal interview, December 12, 1996. Ms. Evans was one of
     the parents most strongly in favour of being assertive about teaching the children
     to read.
29   "Whole School Policy," late 1970s.
30   Steven Drake, personal interview, March 26, 1997. Mr. Drake's guitar playing
     did have some benefits, however. He became the lead guitarist with one of Vancouver's
     most popular bands of the time.
31   "Philosophy of the Whole School," mid-1970s.
32   Pamela Swanigan, personal interview, December 11, 1996.

GOVERNANCE

The school was governed by the entire school community of parents, teachers, and students, with decisions made at general meetings where "everyone who is able to understand has a vote." Although there were attempts to institute a board of directors, the community resisted, believing such a change would "destroy the democratic nature of our school."[33] Most decisions were made by majority vote, although "in questions with considerable opposition, we strive for consensus."[34] Even teacher hiring was conducted each year by the entire group, and interviews could be a daunting experience for prospective teachers. Student opinion also had an impact and on a few occasions affected hiring or firing decisions. Full democratic decision-making, as in other alternative schools, was difficult. One parent remembered that the "endless" meetings became "increasingly time consuming and impossible."[35]

Joel Harris was the first school administrator followed, in the late 1970s, by Bonnie Evans and Alex Berland. It was under Ms. Evans' tenure that the school began to develop some academic expectations for students. A great deal was expected of the teachers and the Whole School was not an easy place to teach. In a letter to parents, reminiscent of the New School under the parent co-operative, one teacher stated, "Teachers at our school work hard under often impossible conditions, while constantly being subjected to the pressures of philosophical factions and the demands of individual parents."[36]

The school was also prone to other problems, including "noise and overcrowding, financial problems, morale problems, lack of parent participation, and some difficult children that had two teachers in tears."[37] The school had to struggle financially, partly because many parents were on subsistence incomes, and half of the school budget had to come from donations, benefit events, and grants. As in other alternative schools, teachers' salaries were low, $300 per month (for a four-day week) in

---

33   Dick Vission, letter to members, circa 1979.
34   "Whole School Policy," Vallican Whole School archive.
35   Pat Armstrong, personal interview, April 1, 1997.
36   "Letter to Whole School Parents," undated, late 1970s.
37   "Letter to Whole School Parents," undated, late 1970s.

1977 and $500 per month by the end of the decade.[38] Parent fees were based on income and ranged from $40 per month to $135. Parents were also expected to contribute volunteer labour to the school and to serve on committees.

Despite the challenges, by the 1980s the school achieved some financial stability. Enrolment fluctuated between thirty-five and forty-five students, with three to four full-time staff.[39] Financial difficulties were also alleviated when, in 1980, the school applied for funding under the 1977 BC government initiative to assist accredited independent schools. The school retained two fundamental tensions basic to most alternative schools: first, how structured or unstructured the school would be in regulating the academic learning activities of the students, and second, how democratic and participatory decision-making would be. The Whole School has remained on the side of participatory democracy, with all decisions, including hiring, made by the entire school community. However, academically the school's philosophy did become more moderate, with students expected to engage in typical classroom academic pursuits.

EFFECTS OF THE SCHOOL

The Whole School was created to offer a different kind of education. Students felt that they were respected and given the freedom to fashion their own lives. One former student believed that she "learned how to learn,"[40] and others appreciated their involvement in setting school policy. But although some benefited from the freedom, there were costs. The young people were not given much supervision or guidance to determine their own behaviour. As one former student suggested, "Our parents treated us as adults when we were not ready to be adults."[41] One parent reflected, "We were having a wonderful time being political."[42] Education was not always top priority.

---

38   General Meeting, minutes, July 25, 1977.
39   School enrolment registers, 1980–1982.
40   Ailsha Grey, personal interview, April 14, 1997.
41   Jono Drake, personal interview, February 10, 1997.
42   Whole School parent, personal interview, December 12, 1996.

Students remembered few formal classes, many of them missed spelling, grammar, mathematics, or social studies, and a few were poor readers. Those who were not self-motivated or disciplined enough to create their own learning experiences were limited academically and professionally. A few older students who had been to traditional elementary schools managed to sustain their academic skills. One of these eventually earned a PhD in psychology while another obtained a master's degree in planning.[43] The lack of academics was particularly hard on those who came to the school at an early age before they had learned basic reading and mathematics.[44] About half went on to university, and a few worked hard to complete high school. Several students believed that if academics had been encouraged, they would have gone to university. One student who did complete a university degree summed up her Whole School experience: "We felt loved and important. The interpersonal skills were invaluable. I just wish I had a better academic foundation."[45]

Many Whole School students eventually entered local public high schools. But returning to the school system was difficult, and many students felt out of place in mainstream schools. As one former student said, "I was taught to be marginal. We all had a difficult time fitting in."[46] Former principal of Mt. Sentinel Junior Secondary in Nelson, Tomo Naka, wrote in 1984 that Whole School graduates were strong in the arts and oral communication skills, but "their written work would be weak, their science would be weak, their math would be weak."[47] Given these difficulties, a significant number attended alternative secondary schools. So many Whole School students went to Vancouver to attend Ideal School in the late 1970s and early 1980s that they formed a miniature community in the city.

43 Jeremy Carpendale, James Pratt, personal interviews, November 13, 1996; April 11, 1997.
44 Carolyn Eaton, personal interview, April 2, 1997.
45 Vallican Whole School student, personal interview, January 15, 1997.
46 Vallican student, personal interview, March 13 1997.
47 Tomo Naka, quoted by Adrian Chamberlain, *Castlegar News*, October 10, 1984.

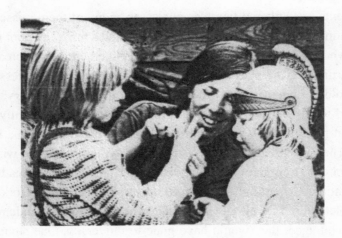

Students and teachers frequently wrote and performed plays at the Vallican Whole
School. Pigweed Press 1979; photographer unknown

The Vallican Whole School continues to operate as one of the few
independent alternative schools in British Columbia. From its origins as
a typical Romantic school allowing children to do as they pleased, the
school adopted a more formal approach to education by the late 1970s.
The school's survival was aided by an increased emphasis on academics
and the expectation that students would engage in structured learning. The
Whole School also benefited from the stability gained by having a permanent home in the community centre from 1976, and by the government
funding that became available to BC independent schools after 1977.
Most important, the school survived largely because it grew out of a self-
contained and cohesive countercutural community that retained its distinct identity for many years. The back-to-the-land community that settled
in the Slocan Valley in the early 1970s continued to support the school in
large enough numbers to maintain its financial viability and organizational
vitality. In 2008 the school moved from the community centre to its own
building in nearby Winlaw and remains independent.[48]

---

48   For more on the Whole School, see Nancy Janovicek, "'The Community School
Literally Takes Place in the Community': Alternative Education in the Back-to-the-
Land Movement in the West Kootenays, 1959–1980," *Historical Studies in Education*
24, no. 1 (Spring 2012).

OTHER INDEPENDENT ALTERNATIVES: RELEVANT HIGH SCHOOL

Similar to the Vallican Whole School, a few additional alternative schools carved out unique niches and were able to remain independent after 1975. One such school, Relevant High, developed a program centred on social responsibility, co-operation, and world citizenship. The school's beginnings were similar to that of Total Education and Ideal School, rising out of an attempt to accommodate students who had dropped out of high school. Relevant High School was founded by Robert Sarginson, who had taught at private Catholic schools in Burnaby and North Vancouver. Prior to teaching he had been in the merchant marine, had excelled at athletics and coaching, and had been active in the trade union movement. Mr. Sarginson, commonly known as "Sarge," believed that many students disliked public high schools due to "boredom, irrelevancy, and being treated like children," which often led to drug use and anti-social behaviour.[49] He sought to present courses in an "interesting and exciting manner" and develop "teaching methods aimed at making courses more relevant to the lives of students."[50] Relevant became Vancouver's first "school without walls" with its own bus to aid in the field trip program.[51] Professionals, educators, politicians, and experts in various fields were brought in to speak at the school, and students spent a great deal of time visiting newspapers, laboratories, industrial sites, the CBC (English and French), and the art gallery.[52]

Relevant High School opened in September 1970 with six teachers and seventy-five students in grades seven to eleven. The school headquarters was located in a downtown office building on Burrard Street across from the old YWCA building, where some of the classes were held. The school moved several times during the early years to another office building on

---

49 "New Downtown High School to Use Community Resources," *Vancouver Sun*, June 29, 1970, 27.

50 "Turning on—without Drugs," *Vancouver Province*, June 24, 1970.

51 See John Bremer and Michael von Moschzisker, *The School without Walls* (New York: Holt, Rinehart, Winston, 1971). City School would later use this idea.

52 Leslie Peterson, "Classroom Tradition Challenged," *Vancouver Sun*, August 23, 1971, 28.

Alberni Street and later to the YMCA building. During the second year, the school acquired a forty-acre farm in Langley where students spent one day per week. The student body was composed partly of countercultural youth and partly of students having difficulty at traditional schools. In the second year the school added grade twelve and expanded to 120 students. Student fees were $400 per year in 1970, increasing to $600 the following year, and teacher salaries ranged from $300 to $400 per month. Despite low salaries, the school lost an average of $5,000 per year for the first four years until it began to break even.[53]

Relevant High students experienced learning in an alternative environment. Although there was a timetable, classes were very informal, with students sitting on the floor or on couches.[54] Students did research at the Vancouver Public Library and some studied languages at the Berlitz Language School. Although there was no competition for grades and no formal testing, graduating students had to write government examinations in order to earn their diplomas. Teaching students how to cope with the advancement of science and technology was one of the school's primary academic goals. To this end, the school emphasized the integration of subject matter, creative thinking, and a good grounding in the humanities and the aesthetic arts.[55]

Although Mr. Sarginson placed a high value on academic learning, other values, particularly group co-operation and involvement in democratic life, were paramount at Relevant. The student body was divided into multi-age learning groups of eight to fifteen students who were responsible for each other's attendance, academic progress, and behaviour using "common sense and consideration for others" as guidelines.[56] Contrary to most alternative schools, Relevant was "group focused" with the group taking precedence over the individual, and group pressure bordering on the coercive at times. According to some students, Mr. Sarginson ran the school "with an iron fist." By 1974 the school had developed an intricate committee structure.

53   Relevant School Society, annual financial reports, 1971–1980.
54   Wilf Bennett, "New School Teaches 'Four Rs,'" *Vancouver Province*, September 30, 1970.
55   Relevant High School, Constitution, "Philosophical Statement," September 1974.
56   Lorraine Shore, "The Best Way to Build a Barn Is in French," *Vancouver Sun*, September 2, 1971, 13.

Every student and staff member participated in running the school through compulsory membership in committees that included academics, attendance, communications, community relations, and classroom management.[57] According to former teachers and students, Mr. Sarginson's personal energy and commitment contributed significantly to the school's success. A long-time teacher at the school recalled his "amazing gift for working with teenagers." He respected students and "changed a lot of kids' lives," many of whom "would not have finished school" otherwise.[58]

Relevant School left downtown Vancouver in 1978. It rented four classrooms in the Peretz School in South Vancouver and later rented a former Catholic school building in New Westminster. Although discussions took place between the school and the Vancouver School District in 1980, the staff feared that the school's philosophy would be lost within the public school system, and Relevant remained independent.[59]

OTHER INDEPENDENT ALTERNATIVES: WALDORF AND MONTESSORI

Two additional well known schools that remained independent were Waldorf and Montessori. The Vancouver Waldorf School was founded in 1971 as part of a worldwide network of schools based on the ideas of Austrian philosopher Rudolf Steiner. Waldorf education is based on Steiner's developmental stages, and one unique aspect is that the classroom teacher remains with the same group of children for eight years as they progress through the elementary grades. Spiritual development is an important foundation, as students are taught to balance "head, heart, and hands." Waldorf schools also emphasize artistic development, and art is incorporated into every academic activity. Students study eurythmy (a form of movement), crafts, and organic gardening. Waldorf schooling has a number of common elements with Progressive education. It emphasizes "education for the whole

---

57   Relevant High School, Constitution, September 1974.
58   Doug Smith, personal interview, March 6, 1997.
59   Doug Smith, personal interview, March 6, 1997. In 1992 and 1994 Relevant bought premises in Surrey to house the elementary and high-school programs, which by now had developed a more Christian orientation. Enrolment has reached as much as three hundred.

child," favours an interdisciplinary approach to learning, minimizes formal examinations, tries to develop flexible thinking, and seeks to maximize the individual development of each student through producing "free human beings." The school opened in West Vancouver with two full-time teachers and twelve children in grades one and two, before moving to its permanent home in North Vancouver in 1972.[60] Each year one grade was added until the school spanned kindergarten to grade ten by the early 1980s.[61] The Vancouver Waldorf School remained independent because the school was committed to underlying beliefs that its teachers feared would be diluted if it entered the public school system.

In her Casa Dei Bambini (Children's House) in Rome, Dr. Maria Montessori revolutionized education for children, including those with special needs, through the use of concrete materials and sensory awareness. 1913 photo from Wikimedia | Creative Commons BY-SA 4.0

Another international educational movement that spread to British Columbia during the 1970s was the Montessori School network inspired

---

60   Vancouver Waldorf School, brochure, February 1997.
61   Colin Dutson, personal interview, March 5, 1997. Today the school includes grades eleven and twelve, and enrolment is over three hundred students. There are now eight Waldorf Schools in British Columbia, including those in North Vancouver, Duncan, Nelson, Kelowna, Whistler, and Squamish.

by the teachings of the Italian educator Maria Montessori. Many of her ideas became an integral part of Progressive educational thought throughout the 1920s and 1930s, particularly her emphasis on the use of concrete materials.[62] During the 1960s, founders of British Columbia Progressive schools drew some of their ideas from the Montessori method. The Vancouver Montessori School was founded in 1972 with eight preschool students in a rented room in the Vancouver School District's Model School building on Twelfth Avenue. The school shared this facility with Total Education and the fledgling Vancouver Music Academy. The Montessori School continued to grow, and five years later added an elementary program, eventually moving to a more permanent building in the Marpole district of Vancouver. Many other Montessori elementary and preschools have been established in British Columbia since 1980, including over twenty in Greater Vancouver. A few have become part of the public school system, but most Montessori Schools are small-scale independent ventures. The Vancouver Montessori School has remained independent and enrols more than two hundred students.

The Vancouver Waldorf School and the Vancouver Montessori School were able to remain independent, supported mainly by tuition fees, even though most alternative schools were not. Several factors explain why these schools survived and eventually thrived as independents. Similar to the Vallican Whole School and Relevant High, the Waldorf and Montessori schools appealed to a unique and committed clientele and teaching staff. Since the teachers were willing to continue working for relatively low salaries, the schools were able to make ends meet. Beginning in 1977 they were also eligible for government financial support to private schools, which allowed them to supplement their budgets with Ministry of Education funding. Waldorf and Montessori schools also had the benefit of outside support systems from their respective worldwide educational organizations that provided teacher training, teaching resources, and curricula, making it easier to remain independent.

---

62   See Maria Montessori, *The Montessori Method* (London, 1913).

Chapter 13

ARGENTA FRIENDS
SCHOOL: LATER YEARS

Similar to the schools in the previous chapter, the Argenta Friends School managed to remain independent throughout its life. The school had some characteristics in common with these other independents. Like the Vallican Whole School, the Friends School had a committed local community to draw upon for staff, students, and moral support. Similar to the Waldorf and Montessori schools, the Argenta School had a wider network of support (in this case the North American Quaker community) as a source of personnel and teaching resources. But the school was small, located in a remote area, and subject to tensions that were a byproduct of the 1960s. At times it was difficult to sustain the necessary energy to keep it viable through the 1970s.

Renewal

By the early 1970s John and Helen Stevenson were ready to step down as leaders of the Argenta Friends school. After more than a dozen years of nurturing their dream, they were tired. They were of the "old school," and though they never stopped listening to and respecting the views of their students, they found adapting to the values of the late 1960s difficult. John Stevenson gave up the principalship to Betty Polster in 1970, and he and Helen spent two years in Toronto directing a Quaker retreat centre from 1971 to 1973. Upon returning to Argenta, they taught for another two years but at a reduced load. Finally, in 1975 their house burned to the ground, and to put the required energy into rebuilding, they retired from the school. After another ten years in Argenta, the Stevensons eventually moved a hundred kilometres down the valley to Nelson.

Beginning in 1973 the Friends School community struggled to reach a new consensus on the purpose and direction of the school. There was no longer agreement about the relative importance of the major components of the school experience—spiritual exploration, academics, rural life, and community-building. The location of the school on Stevenson property and their role as the school founders made some indirect influence unavoidable. In such a small community people found it difficult to change longstanding relationship patterns. The monthly Meeting was still dominated by its original members and had been unable to attract many younger members for the long haul. All agreed that the school needed younger staff who possessed the energy to "work in the discipline which has been the essence of the Argenta Friends School."[1]

In an attempt to renew the school's vision, the teachers declared 1975/76 an "interim year" during which they and a group of motivated students committed themselves to in-depth discussions about changing the school's direction and goals. Full-day workshops generated many ideas: growing more food to maintain a "low-cash lifestyle," devoting two months per year to physical activity and work projects, more credit for out-of-classroom work, intensive academics during the winter months, interdisciplinary work, better "group process skills," more staff orientation, and more attention to building staff/student community.[2]

By the fall of 1976, there was a renewal of commitment. A cohesive group of teachers, Betty Polster, Donna Sassaman, Alaine Hawkins, and Edith Gorman, provided leadership and direction for the next seven years. Ms. Polster suggested these core staff members share the principalship, and they formed a team of "Administrative, Financial, and Academic Principals," while Ms. Polster held the group together as "Coordinating Principal." They made decisions about courses, finances, and day-to-day administration with a minimum of dissension. Assisting the core staff was a large number of part-time teachers, houseparents, and volunteer work

---

1   Argenta Friends education meeting, Notes, December 28, 1973.
2   Report to the Argenta Friends Meeting, April 8, 1975.

coordinators, and in 1978/79 nineteen adults were associated with the school. Although most staff members were still from the United States, there was a significant Canadian influence. In contrast to the earlier years, most were professional educators well aware of contemporary ideas in education. This was consistent with other alternative programs that by the late 1970s had adopted a more professional outlook.

They remained committed to core Quaker values of non-violence, consensus building, and strong community orientation. They reaffirmed the spiritual, communal, and academic goals of the school expressed in a "Core Package" that included Meeting for Worship, academic study, physical work, play, and community decision-making. Betty Polster described it this way:

> Many students and some staff came to Argenta with only a
> partial understanding of what we are trying to offer. Some
> came for academics, some for the beautiful scenery and
> life in the country, and some for the fellowship offered in
> a close community. We view the meeting for worship as
> the basic core of the school with the fellowship of study,
> work, play, and decision making as interrelated parts. We
> have Student-Staff Meetings which are decision-making
> occasions for the school. We work together in work crew
> times; we play together as a group, too. We study Quaker
> philosophy and practice, ways of building community,
> ways of functioning well with each other, and what's
> going on in the outer world. All of this, plus regular aca-
> demic courses, make a full and integrated whole.[3]

The school continued to offer a full complement of basic academic courses including English, mathematics, history, geography, biology, physics, earth sciences, economics, French, Spanish, and Western civili-zation. In 1980/81 the school offered nine academic courses, a long list for a small school. In keeping with a revival in Canadian nationalism in the 1970s, Canadian content was emphasized, particularly in the literature and history courses. Ms. Sassaman and Ms. Gorman taught English as a team, offering a series of modules from which students could choose. English

---

3   Betty Polster, "The Core Package," School Brochure, 1976/77.

eleven and English twelve were offered in alternate years so all students could take these courses together. Most school graduates placed well on province-wide tests, and many continued on to university, but fewer than in the early 1960s. Ms. Hawkins commented in 1976 on the decline of interest in academics:

> The big question is one of motivation. The school offers a great deal for the highly motivated student; however not all students are highly motivated and self-directed in academics. This may be a reflection of the age of television or a general North American trend against the value of higher education.[4]

Although grades eleven and twelve continued to be the school's primary emphasis, the staff decided to experiment with a junior high school in 1978. This was mainly to provide for the teachers' own children who otherwise would have had to commute twenty miles each day to Kaslo. The program enrolled six students in grades six, seven, and eight. Their teacher, Kathy Brunetta, was from Ontario and had completed her teacher training at UBC the previous year. The program was successful and continued for three years until the local need disappeared.

Students enjoyed studying outside in fine weather.
Argenta Friends School Prospectus, 1976

4   Alaine Hawkins, school newsletter, April 1976.

Several important construction projects were undertaken during the 1970s. Students and adult volunteers constructed a new school building begun in 1970 but not completed until 1978. Classes were held in the unfinished building as early as 1973; as one student remembered, "It was freezing. We had small electric heaters and we put plastic on the walls to keep out drafts. Finally we put in a wood furnace system with a hopper of wood that kept going for twenty-four hours."[5] The completion of the building became even more essential when the school office and library burned to the ground in 1975 along with part of the school mailing list, supplies, equipment, and seven thousand books.[6] The school community also built a student home during the early 1970s and acquired several old buildings including the old "Beguin House," built by one of the earliest Argenta residents in 1915. These houses were used to accommodate students and houseparents. Since most of the original Quaker houseparents had retired by 1970, this was the most certain and efficient way to provide student housing. Students and adults took part in a remarkable number of other projects. In the school building they constructed a biology laboratory, built library shelves, and installed a fire alarm system. At the Beguin House, they built a new roof and porch and installed new water lines and wood furnaces in both the school building and the student home.[7]

The school owned a printing press and over the years expanded its publishing activities. Originally established by Michael Phillips, "Root Cellar Press" moved into a building renovated by the school in 1975, where it was managed by John Hawkins. The graphics and publishing program became an important curriculum activity and a vehicle for fundraising. The school published *The Whittler* (school yearbook), *Stopped Press* (school newspaper), a calendar featuring the work of local artists, and the *Argenta Cookbook*. The press also supplemented the school's income by accepting contract work from local groups and individuals as well as from Quaker groups across Canada.

The school remained true to its world service mission. In 1980 the foods class organized a dinner to raise money for "people starving in

---

5   Paul Tillotson, personal interview, October 10, 1996.
6   School newsletter, May 8, 1975.
7   Annual report, 1976/77, 1977/78.

Cambodia." The menu, to demonstrate how Cambodians eat, consisted of rice and stir-fried vegetables, one cup per person.[8] The school also brought in a speaker on nuclear power, an issue then hotly debated in British Columbia. Students gathered information from anti-nuclear organizations and spoke about the subject on CBC radio. The school sponsored a talk by two Friends who had been on a peace mission to Iran during the hostage crisis, and showed a powerful film about the military dictatorship in El Salvador.[9] Students discussed how they could contribute to peace in those regions.

Achieving an effective balance between freedom and responsibility was an ongoing struggle. Alaine Hawkins commented on the general tone of the school:

> The staff feels that the students are often unresponsive and unwilling to take leadership, while students feel that the staff is often manipulating them, "laying heavy trips," or interfering with their initiative. Fortunately, most students take their work responsibilities in the households seriously. All students are concerned about their relationships with peers and others and spend much time and energy in this direction.[10]

In the school's primary goal of community-building, she believed the school continued to be a success: "We have worked especially hard on community-building skills and during the time we were on intersession in Vancouver, it became clear how well we have succeeded. There was a really caring, supportive feeling throughout the group, even when faced with the vicissitudes of adapting to city life."[11]

Public Funding

After 1975, financing the school became increasingly difficult. Expenses rose from $36,000 in 1974 to a high of $90,000 in 1981.[12] The largest

---

8   *Stopped Press* (Argenta Friends School News), Winter 1980.
9   *Stopped Press*, Fall 1981.
10   Alaine Hawkins, school newsletter, April 1976.
11   Alaine Hawkins, school newsletter, May 1977.
12   Financial reports, 1974–1982.

cost was salaries, which increased from $12,000 in 1974 to $36,000 in 1981, while room and board expenses doubled from $12,000 in 1974 to $22,000 in 1981. The only way to keep pace with expenses was to raise tuition fees, which increased rapidly during the late 1970s. From $2,200 per year in 1974, tuition (with room and board) rose to $3,000 in 1977/78 and reached $4,000 by 1981/82.[13] With enrolment at only sixteen students, the school was stretched beyond its means.

Because the school was to be accessible to families of all incomes, tuition increases meant that more students had to be subsidized. After 1975 over half of the students received some financial assistance—60 per cent of the student body by 1978.[14] By 1980 subsidies totalled $16,000.[15] Although the school had a small surplus throughout the 1970s, it would probably not have survived without the donations from its many supporters that amounted to $15,000 in 1980/81.

By 1981 the full-time salary reached $3,200. But teachers were overworked and most doubled as houseparents. In 1978 all teachers taught an extra course for no extra salary to eliminate a budget shortfall. This solved the immediate financial problem but at considerable cost to the teachers, who became overtired by the end of the year.[16] As a result, four teachers left the school or reduced their teaching load.

In 1977 the British Columbia government passed Bill 33, which made public funds available to independent schools. It also, for the first time, brought private schools within the jurisdiction of the Education Ministry and provided for minimum standards. This generated a vigorous debate among the Friends School staff and the Argenta monthly Meeting about whether to apply for the ministry grant. Accepting government funding would have added close to $5,000 to the budget and would have allowed the school to provide a needed salary increase.[17]

However, members of the Friends Meeting had serious reservations. They believed that "the acceptance of government funds would undermine

13   School brochure, 1977/78; Annual Report, 1980/81; Budget, 1982.
14   *Stopped Press*, Fall 1978.
15   Betty Polster, school newsletter, February 1981.
16   Annual Report, 1979.
17   The grant provided 30 per cent of the cost of educating a student in the local public school system, about $500 for each Friends School student from British Columbia.

our independence" and feared the school would become vulnerable to government interference in its practices.[18] Some Meeting members also believed that if the school accepted government funding, supporters would feel their donations were no longer needed and the school would not be much farther ahead. Others feared local resentment of a private school receiving tax money, and a few individuals believed the school might be taking funding away from public schools if they accepted the money.

Most of the teachers and many local parents were in favour of applying for the government grant. Parents believed it was their democratic right to allocate the use of their education tax dollars. Furthermore, requirements contained in the new bill, such as ministry inspection and audited attendance records, would not have posed problems for the school, and some staff members believed they could benefit from external evaluation. The requirement that all teachers be certified would not be a barrier, for although less than half of the teachers were certified, they had five years to obtain their qualifications. The staff proposed that the government money would only be spent on items outside the basic education budget so the school would not become dependent on the grant. Therefore, if the government put too many conditions on the money, the school could change its decision without serious consequences.[19]

Most thought government funding was essential for practical reasons. The extra money could be used to lower tuition, raise teachers' salaries, and upgrade laboratory equipment, physical education facilities, and library holdings. As one letter stated, "Philosophical reservations will not put books on the shelf."[20] Many individuals thought it was unfair for Meeting members to stand in the way of extra funding when teachers were earning so little. As one Argenta resident put it: "It is wrong for people who are not directly involved in the day-to-day operation of the school to veto additional funding for those who are working hard to run a school and support their families on the pittance of $3,200 a year."[21]

---

18   "Argenta Monthly Meeting Rejects Government Funding for Independent Schools," *Stopped Press*, Fall 1978, 6.
19   Letters from local parents, *Stopped Press*, Fall 1978, 8–11.
20   Letters from local parents, *Stopped Press*, Fall 1978, 8–11.
21   Chuck Valentine in *Stopped Press*, Fall 1978, 11.

The school community could not come to a consensus and so did not go ahead with the proposal. However, the issue was reconsidered every year and finally, in 1981/82, the school reached agreement to apply for the grant. Evaluation by a team from the Federation of Independent Schools Association resulted in a positive assessment of the school's academic program.[22] Ironically, though, the Argenta Friends School closed at the end of the year and never did enjoy the benefit of the government grant.

The End of the School

During the winter of 1982, a group of teachers and Meeting members held ongoing discussions about the future of the school. As usual the school was having trouble finding houseparents, and staff were divided and extremely tired. Furthermore, it was becoming increasingly difficult to attract students, and enrolment in 1981 had dropped to fifteen. But the school had weathered crises in the past, and in February the teachers remained optimistic that the program could continue, provided enough staff, suitable students, and appropriate houseparents could be found. However, the group believed the school could only continue with "substantial staff unity" and if a "suitable program can be agreed upon."[23]

Two committees were struck to study possible directions for the school. As early as 1973 staff had considered transforming the school into an adult study centre, a teacher training school, or a postsecondary program.[24] One committee proposed a continuation of the high school program with an emphasis on rural living skills and the winter term devoted to academics. The other group discussed the development of an "outreach program" outside Argenta, offering adult education in peace studies, Quakerism, and mass media. However, this could not be ready for at least a year. At a pivotal meeting in March, the staff concluded that "there is no enthusiasm for a high school program" and regretfully recommended that the school be closed for at least a year so that teachers could regroup, build a unified

22   Annual Report, 1981/82.
23   Meeting on School Future, minutes, February 14, 1982.
24   Argenta Friends education meeting, notes, December 28, 1973.

base, and develop a new program.[25] The staff explained the decision in the 1982 Annual Report:

> We felt that a few meetings or even one summer was not enough time to discover the process of our continued outreach; that we need to take a year off to better establish our roots in order to find our goals and directions. The staff will work together to try to build what we want to share. The main difference for next year is that we are not inviting students.[26]

The teachers helped the grade eleven students find suitable placements in another school for September. A small group continued to work together to develop and plan an alternative program of courses to begin in 1983, possibly outside Argenta. However, this never came to fruition and the school remained permanently closed. The school's small cash surplus reverted to the Argenta Friends Meeting.[27] Betty and Norman Polster as well as Edith Gorman remained in Argenta. Donna and Bill Sassaman left for Victoria in 1980, and Alaine and John Hawkins went back to Toronto to become "resident Friends" at a Friends House.

There were many factors contributing to the decision to close the school. The school's leaders were tired. The perpetual problem of finding enough suitable houseparents in such a small community was never solved. Achieving unity among the staff and the Friends Meeting continued to be an ongoing challenge. As a school visitor wrote in 1979:

> The problems of communal living are ever-present and must be ceaselessly struggled with, particularly when a majority of students entering the school each year are new and may know little of the spiritual ethos of the community and its ways of growing. Staff, therefore, are faced yearly with reinterpreting and renewing the meaning and form of the school community. This dedication to the process of community building, while an invaluable

---

25 *Stopped Press*, "Whither AFS?" Winter 1982, 1.
26 Annual Report, 1981/82.
27 Financial Statement, June 30, 1982.

498   Alternative Schools in British Columbia, 1960-1975

experience for youngsters, can continually tax and drain
the reserves of the faculty."[28]

The school was also affected by a disagreement within the Argenta
Quaker community. When the Friends Meeting decided in the early 1960s
to build a permanent Meeting House and school classroom, the Stevensons
agreed that the building could be located on their land. But they did not
believe they were relinquishing their rights to the property. This was a
verbal agreement among individuals who trusted each other, and no one
questioned the wisdom of the arrangement. But in the 1970s when the
Stevensons asked one of their sons to return to Argenta to manage their
homestead for them, misunderstandings developed and eventually the
Friends Meeting gave up their claim to the building. This produced divisions in the community and further lowered school morale.

Another significant factor was the dramatic change in the Argenta community and the makeup of the student body since 1959. The community
had more than doubled in size; most of the newcomers were young and
brought countercultural attitudes with them. Students had become more
sophisticated, less respectful of adult authority, and more liberal in their
values. They expected to have a good deal of freedom, and some staff
members were sympathetic to the students' opinions. John and Helen
Stevenson wrote:

> When we were planning the Friends School we had
> certain standards about the use of alcohol, sexual activ-
> ity, marijuana use, study halls, hours for being home at
> night, and tobacco use. Some of these standards have
> changed, others have not. Some changed so slowly that
> they were not really examined. Changes have taken place
> among staff members over the years. Within the last few
> years many staff members have willingly (or grudgingly)
> enforced the rules for students but for themselves have
> felt comfortable about premarital sex, smoking tobacco
> and marijuana, using alcohol with students present.[29]

28   Douglas Heath, Report on Visit to Argenta Friends School, November 1979.
29   John/Helen Stevenson, letter to monthly Meeting, May 4, 1977.

Shared decision-making was the genius of the Argenta Friends School, but also partly its undoing. Although students appreciated having input into school policy and being taken seriously, most did not feel their opinions were considered on certain key issues. The staff always lived with a tension between wanting the students to take responsibility for decision-making on the one hand, but wanting definite behavioural standards on the other.

But the most significant factor in the demise of the school was that the times had changed. By the late 1960s the school's leaders were having difficulty adjusting to student expectations, conflicting moral standards, a society that emphasized individualism, the waning of the idealism and optimism of that period, and a shift in demographics in Argenta itself. Furthermore, the rise of alternative programs in mainstream school districts offered parents far more choice in the public school system than had been available in the 1960s. There was therefore less interest in private alternatives. These factors forced the leaders of the Argenta Friends School to question whether their original vision was still appropriate. One staff member expressed this well:

> A number of people are wondering if the school can survive the changes pressed upon it by the demands of a changing community. Argenta is very different from what it was. And the problems of society at large are also increasingly felt here, more and more directly as the population grows and gets statistically younger. The whole cultural climate, including the culture that the students bring with them, seems to have changed radically in the last few years.[30]

CONCLUSION

Most students had an overwhelmingly positive experience at the Argenta Friends School. They cite the close friendships, warm family life, the natural environment, deliberation skills, and the emphasis on personal responsibility as important elements that helped shape their adult lives.

---

30   Michael Phillips, school newsletter, September 18, 1972.

Although few former students believed that they received an outstanding academic education at Argenta, most consider it to have been good enough. Betty Polster acknowledged that "there were times when the academics wasn't as challenging as it might have been because so much else was going on. We didn't want to stress academics too much. But Argenta students went to college knowing how to think."[31]

Most graduates went on to postsecondary education and almost all students who wanted to attend university did so. According to John Stevenson's Coordinator's Report in 1963, only one student in two years failed a government exam. He wrote: "There have been no brilliant results academically but those who have gone on to other schools have had no trouble doing comparable or better work." Of the twenty-nine students attending during the first three years, "twenty-three went on to higher education or are planning to do so."[32] According to 1968 school figures, over 80 per cent of students in the first nine years went to university, and the 1970 Annual Report claimed that "90 per cent of our graduates have gone on to higher education or plan to."[33] One student who graduated in 1965 said: "I was adequately prepared for college at Cal State and got good grades. All six students in our graduating class went to university."[34] Another said, "I went to university in California and I was way ahead," while still another claimed that she received "a very good education, was well-prepared for university, and learned how to study."[35] Students appreciated the small classes and individual attention, and one said she learned "to think, consider, and discuss."[36] John Stevenson wrote that "many students have commented on the growth they experienced in learning to take responsibility rather than being spoon-fed. This has been most keenly felt by the graduates as they entered college."[37]

31   Betty Polster, personal interview, December 28, 1994.
32   John Stevenson, Coordinator's Report, January 1963.
33   John Stevenson, school newsletter, October 1968; and Annual Report, Spring 1970.
34   Erica Pfister, personal interview, April 16, 1997.
35   Ed Washington, personal interview, January 8, 1997; Beth Martin, personal interview, April 17, 1997.
36   Polly Wilson, personal interview, October 24, 1996.
37   John Stevenson, Coordinator's Report, January 1963.

But some former students would have preferred a more rigorous academic program. One observed, "The focus was off to one side just enough that it wasn't a great preparation. But in terms of social and personal life skills it's stood me in good stead."[38] Another student said:

> The Quakers valued academics and the teachers were dedicated, but they had other agendas that were equally important. There wasn't as much pressure to do well academically as I encountered in other schools. I personally needed that pressure. I think if I had gone to a more academically oriented school I probably would have gone to university. At first I regretted not going to university but I'm happy with what I'm doing.[39]

Among Friends School graduates were nineteen teachers; eight doctors or lawyers; eight nurses; six social workers or counsellors; nine environmental or wildlife managers; nineteen artists, musicians, or writers; twelve carpenters or mechanics; seven farmers; eight administrators or business persons; fifteen stay-at-home parents; three political activists; four bus or truck drivers; two loggers or tree planters; and four other professionals.[40] These graduates spanned a wide spectrum of career attainments, but the large number of professionals indicates that most students were not held back in their academic aspirations, as occurred frequently in later alternative schools. As well, the large number of musicians and artists suggests that the school successfully nurtured creative work. The high number of farmers, environmental workers, and carpenters is probably a result of the hands-on experience of rural living at Argenta. Finally, the emergence of three political activists could be credited to the Friends' emphasis on citizenship.

The school helped students become conscientious citizens, empowered to shape their own lives. One former Argenta student suggested that "some of the Quaker principles have stuck with me and they are valuable

---

38   Dick Pollard, personal interview, April 15, 1997.
39   Argenta Friends School student, personal interview, January 30, 1977.
40   Data from alumni lists and John and Helen Stevenson, personal interview, September 11, 1996. Data covers graduates from 1960 to 1976. Seventy-eight careers are unknown.

elements of my life."[41] Another said the school "taught me how to debate and see other people's point of view. We were listened to, treated like responsible adults."[42] A third student credited the Friends School with her "self-confidence and belief in myself."[43] Another said the school taught him self-reliance, trust, responsibility for his actions, how to get along with people, and to "become a better person."[44] One student recalled the support, loving-kindness, and acceptance she received that allowed her to "be who I was."[45] As one former teacher put it, "We taught students that they make a difference, they knew they mattered."[46] A former student agreed, saying, "I felt they esteemed us as people, as young adults. We were looked upon as individuals in our own right. I was trusted, valued as a person."[47] However, one student cautioned that, after leaving Argenta, there was "a kind of culture shock":

> When you come into the real world you try to apply the ideals that you've come to value. You think you are going to change the world with revolutionary ideas like pacifism. But you quickly discover that society has its own set of norms, many of which you might be uncomfortable with.[48]

During the 1960s, American influence on the Friends School was substantial, as it was with other alternative schools. Students from California brought a liberal, casual attitude and an interest in folk music, drugs, left-wing politics, and countercultural values (sometimes before those ideas reached Vancouver). As one former student observed, "Americans are doers."[49] Students and teachers had varying perceptions of their time in Canada. Some students hardly noticed they were in a different country, but most staff members saw it as a "Canadian experience, leaving many

41   Pat Lawson, personal interview, January 30, 1997.
42   Paul Tillotson, personal interview, October 3, 1996.
43   Erica Pfister, personal interview, April 16, 1997.
44   Charles Dyson, personal interview, November 5, 1996.
45   Mary Winder, personal interview, February 24, 1997.
46   Brenda Berck, personal interview, October 15, 1996.
47   Mary Holland, personal interview, November 15, 1996.
48   Pat Lawson, personal interview, January 30, 1997.
49   Jonathan Gregory, personal interview, March 21, 1997.

American values behind."[50] Although Quakers are not nationalistic, John and Helen Stevenson appreciated Canadian values and hoped students and teachers would develop a "Canadian sensibility."[51] In her Canadian history class Ms. Stevenson emphasized differences between Canada and the United States, such as parliamentary government, the settlement of the west, and the role of a "superpower." Most staff members have remained in British Columbia along with a significant minority of students.

The school founders never resolved a basic contradiction in their practice. They had a well-developed and cohesive life philosophy along with a well-defined idea about how the students in their charge ought to structure their studies, their recreation, and their day-to-day interactions. But they wanted the students to reach these conclusions themselves and to take responsibility for decisions that were not really of their choosing. The adults were genuine in their encouragement of student participation, but one former student suggested that the Stevensons were "strong leaders who wanted to appear not to be leading."[52]

The 1960s was a mixed blessing for the Argenta Friends School. While the heightened political and social consciousness of the decade fit with Quaker ideals, the individualistic lifestyle did not. The inability of the Friends Meeting to adjust to the "sixties values" brought by many students during the second half of that decade was not surprising. John and Helen Stevenson were wise enough to realize that they had to make some accommodation to their students' lifestyles, but were often pushed beyond their comfort zone. Despite their limitations, they were admired by their students as "great teachers," while one former student described them as "visionaries."[53] Given the school's reliance on the energy of a small group of people, its small financial base, its idealistic governance structure, and the challenging decade in which it began, it is highly unlikely that it would have survived more than a few years had it not been for the dedication and commitment of John and Helen Stevenson. In the words of one former student, their contribution was "an incredible piece of work."[54]

---

50   Jonathan Aldrich, personal interview, November 16, 1996.
51   Mary Holland, personal interview, November 15, 1996.
52   Polly Wilson, personal interview, October 24, 1996.
53   Mary Winder, personal interview, February 24, 1997.
54   Mary Holland, personal interview, November 7, 1996.

The Friends School sought a delicate balance between freedom and responsibility, between innovation and tradition. Some of its values of simplicity, non-violence, silent worship, physical work, and service dated back to early Quaker schools of the seventeenth century.[55] Argenta added social activism, the nurturing of individual conscience, and consensual community-building. But the school was also an embodiment of many of the principles of Progressive or "child-centred" education developed by John Dewey and his colleagues in the early twentieth century. These included individualized and active learning, an emphasis on the "whole person," and education for citizenship. The Friends School was a bold experiment that broke new ground in British Columbia.

Argenta School students benefited from the experience of a rural village lifestyle.
Argenta Friends School brochure, 1969

The Argenta Friends School was successful in fulfilling most of its objectives. It provided an adequate academic education, good enough to send most of its graduates to university. It gave its students a rural, wilderness, and sometimes spiritual experience. It provided a large, warm family atmosphere where students learned to solve problems in human relations. It introduced the young people to consensual decision-making in which

55   See W. A. C. Stewart, *Quakers and Education* (London: Epworth Press, 1953).

they played a significant part. It fostered a keen sense of citizenship, pacifism, and social activism.

The Argenta Friends School remained an independent alternative
school for twenty-three years. Compared to many of its contemporaries, it
was successful in its longevity, its competent academic program, and the
cultivation of well thought-out personal and communal values. There were
several reasons for this success despite constant financial pressures and
the tensions produced by the cultural upheaval of the 1960s. The school
had effective leaders. John and Helen Stevenson guided the school with a
clear vision throughout the first twelve years, while Betty Polster and her
colleagues had equally strong goals for the school during the 1970s. The
school provided explicit values and standards that allowed it to avoid the
excesses of some alternative schools that developed later in the 1960s. The
school's roots in the Society of Friends provided a network of financial
and moral support as well as a source of students. As the years progressed,
the alumni themselves became an important part of that support network.
Lastly, the foundation of Quaker spiritual heritage provided a solid and
consistent set of shared standards and values. As one visitor to the school
wrote in 1979, "It avoids to some degree the adverse effects of the dilem-
mas and perils that have faced more secularly based communal efforts,
like those associated with the 1960s." Reflecting on the significance of the
Friends School, he continued:

> Quakers have always been outsiders to their society
> if only because they seek to change it. Contemporary
> society needs diverse models of living and of education
> that are deeply characterological as well as more nar-
> rowly academic. The types of changes we face tomorrow
> require qualities I do not see being developed in many
> of the schools that I know. I felt the Friends School was
> grappling honestly with the future. Argenta is not without
> its human problems but it is a place where the word and
> spirit are more closely one.[56]

---

56 Douglas Heath, visit to Argenta Friends School, November 1979.

Chapter 14

THE NEW SCHOOL: LATE YEARS

Like the schools described in the previous two chapters, the New School remained independent. During its first ten years as an independent alternative school, it underwent many changes, mirroring the trajectory of the alternative schools movement and, in some ways, society itself. Originally founded as a Progressive school in 1962 (Chapter 2), it displayed many elements of a Romantic school by 1967 (Chapter 7). During the early 1970s the New School transformed itself once again, this time into a therapeutic community emphasizing personal and political empowerment.

The New School underwent a major shift in membership and philosophy around 1973. The academic families had long since departed and the counterculture parents who had dominated the school since 1968 also began to leave. Some had children who were ready to begin high school, others no longer endorsed free-school methods, and still others were re-entering society's mainstream. Most of the students who remained had experienced trouble coping in the public school system, and almost all came from single-parent families and families on low incomes or welfare. Although a few parents were social workers and one was a civil service manager, most were unemployed or marginally employed. The parent body had become a mix of former hippies, political activists, and "downwardly mobile" people. One teacher described the remaining clientele as poor, single parent, or low-income families.[1]

---

1   Sharon Burrows, personal interview, December 1991; Margaret Sigurgeirson, quoted by Robert Sarti, *Vancouver Sun*, March 15, 1976, 25.

As in earlier years at the New School, pictured above, students engaged in individualized learning. 1970 Photo courtesy of Daphne Harwood

The shift from a middle-class to a lower-income population is borne out by demographic information. When the school opened in 1962, only three out of thirty families (10 per cent) lived east of Main Street (then the perceived border between middle- and working-class Vancouver). By

1969 this had increased to 20 per cent (nine of forty-six families), and in 1971 to 35 per cent. In 1973 the figure rose to 50 per cent, and by 1975, 72 per cent (eighteen out of twenty-five) of New School families lived on Vancouver's East Side.[2] Many now lived in the immediate school neighbourhood, in sharp contrast to the days when carpooling from the West Side of town was such a part of school life. A 1975 fundraising brief described the shift from a "school founded by a group of university professors" to a "work-oriented, East End school."[3]

Family structure had also changed dramatically by 1973. Of thirty-nine New School families in 1975, thirty-three (87 per cent) were headed by single parents. In twenty-six of these families, the second parent (in most cases, the father) had all but disappeared from the children's lives and a few had no contact with the child at all.[4] In most of the single-parent families children were in the custody of the mother, but in three families the father had custody and several separated couples had joint custody agreements. Some of these custodial arrangements were informal, and in one family the child "moved organically" between the two homes.[5] The living situations of New School families were far from traditional.[6] Several parents lived in communal houses and two students were cared for by "four women with equal responsibility for the children."[7]

The acceptance of large numbers of special-needs children with learning disabilities and emotional problems began transforming the New School into a Therapeutic institution by the early 1970s. The school accepted two students from Browndale, a centre for troubled children, and one teacher remembered having to learn how to do the "Browndale

---

2   School enrolment lists: 1962, 1965, 1969, 1971, 1973, and 1975. West and North Vancouver were included with "west of Main Street," and Burnaby and New Westminster were considered to be east of Main Street, the traditional dividing line between the West and East Sides of Vancouver.

3   New School Teachers' Society Brief, "Request for Neighbourhood Improvement Program Funds," September 1975, 2. Some of the low-income parents differed from their eastside neighbours in that they were middle-class in origin.

4   New School tuition records, 1975/76.

5   Student applications, September 1973, Nora Randall document collection.

6   This concurs with Daniel Duke's findings in *The Retransformation of the School* (Chicago: Nelson-Hall, 1978): 79–81. Over half of the non-public alternative schools he studied in the United States had predominantly single parent families, and parents shared "a pattern of living marked by social experimentation."

7   Student applications, September 1973.

hold."[8] There were few mainstream schools offering programs for such children in the early 1970s.

The acceptance of emotionally troubled students was partly an attempt to solve some of the school's financial problems. Teacher Barbara Hansen arranged for the New School to receive Department of Human Resources subsidies if the school took additional special-needs children.[9] The subsidies were a temporary financial benefit of several thousand dollars per year, but in the long run, the increased number of kids with special needs weakened the school.[10] Parents of other students began to withdraw their children because they were not receiving a regular educational program. Eventually, the shift toward special-needs students became irreversible. One teacher, Joan Nemtin, noted that "a lot of new parents had personal problems and their children were quite disturbed. As a child care worker I knew what an emotionally disturbed kid looked like":

> They were badly behaved. Kids would throw rocks at one another and run right into the middle of what you were doing. There were several acting out boys and it was difficult to teach them anything. You could sit around a table and talk, but you couldn't teach them to read. It was discouraging. Barb Hansen was the only one strong enough to provide the disturbed kids with the structure they needed. It was a harrowing experience for the quieter kids. The problem kids had too much power and bullied the others. They were too disturbed to be with normal kids; they needed a more therapeutic setting. We didn't have the training to deal with at least five kids who were there but we felt that if we turned them away there would be nobody else. I felt it wasn't fair to the other kids.[11]

Another teacher estimates that over 20 per cent of the students had serious behaviour problems and that close to 40 per cent had learning disabilities. One girl, whose mother wrestled with alcohol, was stealing cars

8   Staff meeting, minutes, January 8, 1974. Browndale was founded by John Brown.
9   A funding request to the Children's Aid Society was unsuccessful. Staff meeting, minutes, September 24, 1974.
10 Financial statements, 1970–1977, Registrar of Companies, Victoria.
11 Joan Nemtin, personal interview, December 1987.

at age thirteen. Another child "just showed up at our door one day. Her mother was so out of it on drugs that we never even found out her last name."[12] One former student recalled the younger kids being picked on by "a lot of weirdos."[13] Another remembered "destructive kids with bad tempers who should have been in halfway houses—kids I was deathly afraid of."[14] The staff did not have the training to handle children with serious problems, and a group of aggressive boys was particularly difficult for the teachers to control. Teachers attended a conference on special-needs testing, but for the most part assessment was simply done by intuition. Parents desiring a formal assessment had to arrange and pay for it themselves. One teacher, in recalling a boy who was eventually asked to leave the school, said, "His name strikes fear into my heart still!"[15]

Some students ended up at the New School because the public school system could do nothing for them. Desperate social workers placed children there, knowing the school would not turn kids away when there was no other place for them to go. Teacher Barbara Hansen had a vision of the school as a "caring community," a concept she developed through her association with Unitarianism, and the school became a refuge for local kids who needed help. Many of these students received little emotional support from their families. Some kids didn't get enough sleep or enough food, several spent much of their time destroying property, and a few were violent and bullying. Ms. Hansen's daughter remembered how her mother would "bring kids home that needed a break from their parents":

> She took in the ones who couldn't fend for themselves and looked out for them. I also remember picking up a couple of kids whose parents were heroin addicts. The only way they could get to school was if we drove, so we did.[16]

---

12   Sharon Van Volkingburgh, personal interview, November 1991.
13   Karen Schendlinger, personal interview, May 1991.
14   Cara Felde, personal interview, December 1991.
15   Jan Robinson, personal interview, December 1991.
16   Margot Hansen, personal interview, July 1991.

The school's principal function had become therapeutic rather than educational. In a brief to the Human Resources Ministry the teachers listed the kinds of troubled families they served:

> "A pregnant woman on social assistance with three children, who is attempting to get a restraining order on her husband."

> "An unemployed single mother with five children who has just completed a course in welding."

> "A girl referred from Transition House who was not attending school because she was looking after her mother on drugs."

> "A native [Indigenous] single parent with a child who was kicked out of a public school. She thinks it did not respect her culture."

> "A woman with two children who had reading problems in public school found the New School in desperation."

> "A child labelled hyperactive by the school system whose single mother is on social assistance."[17]

In another funding proposal in 1975 the teachers stated, "We provide a program for sixty to seventy children who for a variety of reasons cannot succeed in the school system. It is also a program for these children's parents."[18] The document elaborates on the school's therapeutic and political function in a description of parent and family support groups:

> The program provides an environment where children and their parents learn life skills and responsibility for their lives. It is a preventative program that helps families out of the poverty cycle and social services dependency. The program gets children and their parents in touch with their competence and stresses the importance of taking

---

17 Funding Proposal to Ministry of Human Resources, December 3, 1975.
18 New School Teachers' Society Brief: "Request for Neighbourhood Improvement Program Funds," September 1975, 2.

care of oneself physically, mentally, and emotionally, and
taking care of one's environment.[19]

The brief emphasized the development of practical work attitudes:
"There is a familiarization for the children of different occupations in the
community (printing, woodworking, retail stores, factory work) to give
them concrete employment experiences so that they can begin to see
themselves making choices and have a clear connection of the skills they
work on and how they can be used in life in the community." Education is
mentioned only once: "The basic skills are taught on an individual basis
and in small groups to ensure competence in these areas."[20] This was
more modest than the educational goals of earlier years.

Barbara Hansen, the acknowledged school leader, was admired by
teachers and parents for her ingenuity and intuitive skill in working with
children who had behavioural or emotional problems. But most New
School teachers did not have the skill or the training to help these students, other than to make them feel loved and worthwhile. The effects of
a positive attitude could be considerable, however. One parent credited
the school with restoring her son's self-esteem and saving him and others
from delinquency: "Any other school would have kicked them out or
made their lives hell, but the New School just loved them to death."[21]

The staff was primarily concerned with the emotional rather than academic development of their students and put a great deal of energy into
working with families. This took the form of social work to solve immediate personal or economic problems, and political work in an attempt
to organize the individuals to take collective action. This approach was
developed by Barbara Hansen and Sandra Currie, an American parent
committed to working for social change. Ms. Currie saw her work in the
school as a natural extension of her political interest in "empowering poor
people" through collectivist organizations.

The New School maintained a strong communal atmosphere and
became an extended family for many of the participants. Social evenings

---

19   NIP Fundraising Brief, September 1975, 2.
20   NIP Fundraising Brief, September 1975, 2.
21   New School parent, personal interview, December, 1991.

at the school featuring potluck meals, dancing, or films were frequent.[22] The school provided emotional support for parents with financial or marital problems, and some students would move in temporarily with other families. It was empowering for the kids to feel that they had choices. One parent remembered nights when she took home six kids: "I never knew who was going to be at the dinner table. There were always between five and seven kids, but not necessarily mine. Somebody would move in for six months and I'd see different clothes in one of the drawers. And I'd think, 'Oh, Robin's living here now.'"[23] A long-time New School parent who lived on the North Shore recalled "kids staying in our house every night":

> Sometimes they'd come every night for three weeks. They'd think they lived at our house after a while. Then my kids would disappear for a week or two and live in Kitsilano at somebody's house. There was a community, even though it changed from year to year with new kids coming and people moving away.[24]

TEACHERS AND PARENTS

The New School Teachers Society continued to govern the school in matters of finance, personnel, and long-range planning. Society membership consisted of permanent teachers, former staff members, and two elected parent representatives.[25] One member was responsible for managing school finances with the help of a professional accountant from time to time. Decisions were made by consensus but votes were taken when necessary. The parent representatives played an important role in Society business, as parents wanted significant input in school affairs.

Teachers made decisions collegially at weekly staff meetings. They discussed programs and scheduling, problems with individual students, and communication with parents. Staff members divided up tasks such as building maintenance, purchasing supplies, secretarial duties, screening

22 Staff meeting, minutes, November 13, 1973, Nora Randall document collection.
23 Sandra Currie, personal interview, May 1988.
24 Ron Hansen, personal interview, April, 1987.
25 New School Society meeting, minutes, April 22, 1974.

admissions, and janitorial work. Most staff members became plumbing experts. Salaries were equitable, although teachers with dependent children received a monthly bonus when finances permitted.[26]

The parent body once again became a powerful group in the school. From 1974 to 1977 only two staff members out of ten were certified teachers, and staff and parents often performed similar roles. Some parents volunteered in classrooms and one parent attended staff meetings. Several times a month parents and teachers met together to discuss the children or to attend workshop sessions on such issues as aggression or discipline.[27] Staff/parent meetings sometimes resulted in intense conflict over the direction of the school, and discussions could drag on until late at night. The school was run as a collective and became very politicized. There was "a lot of rage" expressed, and according to one teacher, meetings were draining and decision-making often became a case of the "survival of the fittest."[28] There was a sense of desperation in the belief, voiced by some, that "the school got better (more authentic), the poorer it got."[29]

Co-operative organizations flourished throughout British Columbia in the early to mid-1970s, and the "co-op movement" became an important feature of New School politics. Many parents and teachers belonged to other co-operative and collectivist organizations such as food co-ops, daycare co-ops, and housing co-ops. This high level of social/political activity was balanced by a continuing quest for individual self-actualization, and parents were busy participating in "radical therapy" groups, a blend of individual transformation and political analysis.

Feminism emerged as a significant aspect of New School life during its last few years. Most of the women were single parents, many on welfare, who saw the school as a place they could afford where their kids would be treated well. For many the school also formed an important element of their social, political, and emotional life. The feminist group grew so strong that from 1973 to 1976 the school became a focus for feminist activism throughout the city, and several important women's organizations

---

26   Staff meeting, minutes, October 22, 1974, Nora Randall document collection.
27   Staff meeting, minutes, September 6, 1973, and September 10, 1974.
28   Joan Nemtin, personal interview, December 1987.
29   Sandra Currie, personal interview, May 1988.

had close connections with New School participants. These included the Women's Health Collective, Press Gang publishers, *Makara* magazine, Women's Inter Art Co-op, Women's Emotional Emergency Centre, and the BC Daycare Federation.[30] Several parents were also active members of Southhill Daycare, which took a leading role in advocating for children's rights and increased government funding for daycare.

Feminist theory and practice dominated New School activities during these early years of the women's movement, just as counterculture attitudes had consumed participants a few years earlier. Discussions were sometimes directed against indiscretions of male teachers, such as the use of sexist and degrading language. Several teachers recalled groups of parents walking down the hall, tearing off the walls any material that could be construed as sexist. Whether or not this constituted censorship was a hotly debated question. Parents and teachers also worried about the lack of teacher attention to the girls because of the anti-social and destructive behaviour of several of the boys.

One parent remembered how they were often referred to as the Feminist Mafia: "We were extremely prickly in the seventies. There really was a sexist pig under every bed."[31] But more moderate women had mixed feelings about the school's direction. They agreed with feminist goals but also believed that several fathers and the one male teacher contributed significantly to New School life. Barbara Hansen said that the feminist orthodoxy had everyone "looking over their shoulder" for fear they were not politically correct.[32] One former student recalled dances where men were not allowed; she also remembered how younger girls were teased if they played with dolls or wore dresses.[33] Nevertheless, one of the girls rebelled and insisted on wearing a dress to school for several months. Meanwhile, most overtly sexist behaviour at the New School disappeared within two years.

Sandra Currie organized a women's support group for parents and teachers. Members supported each other both as women confronting sexism

---

30   Mary Schendlinger and Nora Randall, personal interview, June 1991.
31   Mary Schendlinger, personal interview, June 1991.
32   Barbara Hansen, personal interview, October 1987. Most former parents now agree with this assessment.
33   Margot Hansen, personal interview, July 1991.

and as poor people aspiring to meaningful occupations. Women talked about personal experiences with sexism and how they were affected by soft-core pornography.[34] The group helped one parent, a welfare recipient, realize her ambition to become a welder. Another parent credited the emotional support she received at the New School with "helping her get out of a bad marriage and into a career."[35]

Female students were encouraged to confront male teachers whenever sexist behaviour arose, and several parents conducted sessions with the girls about female social conditioning.[36] The boys' response to feminism varied. One former student recalled that the "male energy of the boys was shut down."[37] One parent described how her son became a "militant anti-feminist" (her daughter was a "militant feminist") but pointed out that "although the boys did not get the usual male privilege, they were still cherished even when being outrageous."[38] Nevertheless, adult preoccupations dominated the activities.

A major staff turnover occurred in 1973. Daryl Sturdy, Saralee James, and Daniel Wood all left to pursue other careers, and Claudia Stein, Joan Nemtin, and Jonnet Garner left a year later.[39] Barbara Hansen, along with the new teachers Margaret Sigurgeirson and Dan Morner, worked closely together with the older students for the next three years. Ms. Sigurgeirson had been a long-time parent at the school and Mr. Morner had come to Canada as a draft resister from the United States. As the only male teacher on staff, he spent many hours with the rambunctious boys, some of whom were difficult to control. Sharon Van Volkingburgh, another new teacher, had been active as a community organizer with the Company of Young

---

34   Sandra Currie, personal interview, May 1988.

35   Sandra Currie, personal interview, May 1988; Nora Randall and Mary Schendlinger, personal interview, June 1991.

36   Daniel Wood, personal journal, 1972.

37   Scott Robinson, personal interview, December 1991.

38   Sharon Burrows, personal interview, December 1991.

39   Daryl Sturdy returned to the Vancouver School District in 1974, where he taught for many years and found more freedom for teachers in the public school system than there had been in 1968. Saralee James left to pursue a career in film and the visual arts. Daniel Wood worked with John Bremer, author of *The School without Walls*, on an Educational Research Institute grant and later worked with the Community Education Program in the UBC Education Faculty. Joan Nemtin taught for several years at Total Education. Jonnet Garner moved to Ontario.

Canadians and in an interfaith church association. She met New School parents and teachers through her work with anti-poverty and welfare rights groups and the community woodworking classes she taught. Other staff members were Ellen Nickels, a classical musician; Jan Robinson, a former New School student; Judy de Barros; and Kathy Stafford. Several staff members had social work and child care backgrounds, thus strengthening the therapeutic orientation. Only Linda Proudfoot and Jill Fitzell were certified teachers.

The staff became more cohesive than at any other time in the school's history. The teachers had uniform objectives and a strong leader in Barbara Hansen. Staff members also shared a common political orientation that included the co-operative movement, the women's movement, grass roots community associations, children's rights groups (such as co-operative daycare), and left-of-centre political organizations (including the NDP). Staff members were also drawn together by the almost insurmountable obstacles they faced. They were inadequately trained to work with special-needs children and confronted an increasingly grim financial situation. Staff had to be administrators and custodians in addition to their roles as teachers and caregivers, often cleaning and maintaining the school building after a full day of teaching. Ms. Van Volkingburgh and Ms. Sigurgeirson described the challenge faced by the teachers:

> It was often uncomfortable for adults—it was so much of a kid's place. We had no adult space, no place to take refuge. The New School was very physical—kids were moving all the time. You were living with those kids. I used to spend my Saturdays washing the floor. It wasn't just your job—it was your life.[40]

CURRICULUM

The teachers did not believe in separating "playing, learning, and working" and offered "lots of individual attention and ungraded work with no pressure." The curriculum de-emphasized academic work, as the teachers

---

40   Margaret Sigurgeirson, Sharon Van Volkingburgh, interviews, 1991.

believed future success would depend more on children's attitudes than on skills.[41] Nevertheless, the first two hours of the morning were scheduled for academic subjects followed by play time until lunch. Art, creative activities, and special projects were done in the afternoon, while swimming and physical education took place outside the school two mornings per week. Though there was some structure, much of the classroom day "went according to whatever came up."[42]

As with some other alternative schools, reading instruction was inconsistent. It could range from teachers writing down student stories to reading aloud to groups of children. Some teachers believed reading was less important in a highly technological society, and some students who did not learn to read effectively continued to have difficulty later.[43] Some students learned to read on their own or at home. One parent described the approach toward her son: "He liked to help the younger students because he learned while he was doing that. He had a learning disability so he never really sat down and learned anything. He just sort of picked it up as he was wandering around." [44] Another parent felt "no one noticed" that her daughter struggled with reading,[45] and still another reported that her oldest son was reading at a grade two level at twelve years old.[46] One student who learned to read at home remembered little academic instruction at school.[47] In the late 1970s a teacher at City School, an alternative high school, observed that some former New School kids had difficulty reading.[48] Some students were dyslexic, and although the teachers did provide generous individual attention and understanding, they didn't have the training to really help them.

Ms. Hansen taught a regular mathematics program emphasizing practical skills. One parent remembered that "she used to take ten kids down to

41 Fundraising letter, 1977.
42 Barbara Hansen, personal interview, October 1987.
43 Dana Long and Karen Schendlinger each cite several classmates who did not learn to read at the New School; interviews, May 1991, and June 1987. Several parents interviewed cite similar examples.
44 New School parent, personal interview, May 1988.
45 New School parent, personal interview, June 1991.
46 New School parent, personal interview, May 1988.
47 Karen Schendlinger, personal interview, May 1991.
48 Starla Anderson, personal interview, April 1987.

the bank and say 'this is how you fill out a deposit slip so you won't get ripped off.'"[49] The younger students did little math other than counting things out and sharing. There were occasional science experiments with makeshift equipment or social studies lessons with second-hand textbooks from the school board. The teachers encouraged students to work on individual and group projects. On one occasion, after a visit from a geology professor, students painted floor-to-ceiling dinosaurs and made a geological time line around the inside walls of the school.[50] Academic work was individualized and teachers set minimum standards that varied with each individual.[51] In theory, students had to finish their work before doing anything else, but in practice they could get away with doing very little. Thinking about the value of a regular routine, one teacher said, "I thought kids needed creative stimulation; I didn't think the routine was as important as I do now."[52]

A change in thinking about academics occurred in 1975 as the teachers and some parents realized that sending kids from lower-income families into the world without basic literacy skills would double their disadvantage. Barbara Hansen told a journalist, "There is an expectation of some kind of work being done. Reading, writing, and arithmetic are survival skills in this society, and kids have to learn them, and the job of the teacher is to teach them as efficiently as possible."[53] This view was consistent with a general rethinking of laissez-faire Romanticism and the importance of literacy, initiated by the writings of Jonathan Kozol in the United States and George Martell in Canada by the mid-1970s.[54] As well, the conservative back-to-basics movement was in full swing by 1975.[55]

49 Mary Schendlinger, personal interview, June 1991.
50 Professor Roy Blunden of UBC, the last academic parent at the New School. His son left the school in 1975.
51 Margaret Sigurgeirson, personal interview, November 1991.
52 Sharon Van Volkingburgh, personal interview, November 1991.
53 Barbara Hansen, quoted by Audrey Grescoe in "Working Classrooms: Alternate Education in Vancouver," *Vancouver Magazine* (January 1975): 29.
54 See George Martell, *The Politics of the Canadian Public School* (Toronto: James Lewis and Samuel, 1974) and Jonathan Kozol, *Free Schools* (Boston: Houghton Mifflin, 1972).
55 J. Donald Wilson, "From the Swinging Sixties to the Sobering Seventies," in Stevenson and Wilson, eds., *Precepts, Policy, and Process: Perspectives on Contemporary Canadian Education* (London, ON: 1977): 21–36.

In 1976 the teachers initiated a serious program to teach the younger kids to read. "We got a set of textbooks and worked one-to-one with the kids—we had enough teachers that we could do that. We had check-lists and worked on phonics and keywords. We felt we were making progress."[56] Teachers spent twenty minutes per day with each child while one staff member supervised the others at play or doing individual projects. Teachers were enthusiastic about the program despite the lack of quiet areas or carpets to sit on comfortably. Unfortunately, the school closed before any significant results could be achieved.

Students participated in weekly swimming and skating sessions, played floor hockey and soccer, and exercised on the school's modest gymnastics equipment. Sharon Van Volkingburgh revived the woodwork shop, and some students built forts and even their own desks out of wood lying around in the playground. There were crafts sessions one afternoon per week and occasional art gallery workshops. Ellen Nickels played the piano or led students in singing, and one parent, a Vancouver Symphony musician, performed at the school from time to time, but there wasn't a comprehensive music program.

The New School accepted many visitors, including student teachers, and for several years counsellors in a Vancouver School Board training program spent one afternoon each year at the school.[57] Social work students from Simon Fraser University visited the school once a week and organized interest groups on photography, theatre, cooking, arts and crafts, music, sports, exploring Vancouver, and visiting parents' workplaces.[58] During the school's last months, Ms. Hansen initiated a comprehensive legal rights and awareness program for students and parents, utilizing experts from the field. This program was consistent with the school's commitment to children's rights.

Field trips with small numbers of students were easy to arrange and often occurred spontaneously. Students went to the beach frequently and set up a saltwater aquarium back at the school. One year students were

---

56   Sharon Van Volkingburgh, personal interview, November 1991; also mentioned in Audrey Grescoe, "Working Classrooms," 29.

57   Staff meeting, minutes, February 12, 1974.

58   Staff meeting, minutes, October 9, 1973.

given rides on a hot air balloon; after the experience they made miniature balloons and flew them outside the school. The school provided a student "feast" on Fridays and everyone looked forward to this event, often held at Stanley Park.

The teachers organized regular camping trips, and one parent donated a cabin at an old mine site in a remote area near Anderson Lake south of Lillooet. The only access was via a BC Rail stop, and campers had to climb four and a half miles of steep mountain switchback trail to reach the campsite.[59] Adults and children spent up to a week at the cabin learning basic survival skills in the bush, including cooking, hauling water, and chopping wood. Several adults remembered learning how to use a chainsaw. Students as young as six were expected to do their share of the work and were responsible for getting along with each other.

By 1973 teachers were increasingly willing to set minimal expectations and rules for student behaviour and participation. For example, younger children were not permitted to go to the store or cross the street without an adult, students were not permitted to smoke in forts or burn paper, and no more than two students were allowed on the tire swing. School equipment was not to be taken home, all students were required to go skating, and students were to vacate the staffroom if asked to do so by an adult.[60] Even these few rules were far stricter than the teachers would have imposed a few years earlier when Romanticism was at its height.

Despite the rules, one student remembered the school as "totally free— kids could do what they liked."[61] Attendance was difficult to enforce, and some students missed a great deal of school. Students were permitted to smoke in restricted areas. One former student said that younger kids were often bullied in the unsupervised basement.[62] The only rules consistently enforced concerned violence or property damage, and fights were usually dealt with immediately by several staff members. But the basic stance was to promote student autonomy in almost all situations and teachers expected students to solve most of their own problems. One teacher said

---

59 Nora Randall, "Can You Wear Earrings in the Wood?" (unpublished short story, 1975).
60 Staff meeting, minutes, September 6, 1973, February 12, 1974, April 1975.
61 Karen Schendlinger, personal interview, May 1991.
62 Penny Ryan, personal interview, January 1992.

in retrospect, "We thought the world was a safer place than it was and we exposed kids to scary situations. Some of them developed a pseudo-maturity that made adolescence unnecessarily hard."[63]

In the Summerhill fashion, the school held monthly student/staff meetings, with students setting the agenda and chairing the meetings.[64] New School children learned how to express themselves and debate issues, and were not shy around the adults, who they called by their first names. Students of all ages played and worked together, and older students looked after younger children, contributing to the family atmosphere. Many of the students were going through divorce in their families and living chaotic lives that, according to one parent, would have challenged even the most structured school setting. She pointed out that the students learned to take care of themselves and that the refuge they found at the New School kept some from ending up in the drug subculture or other destructive environments.[65]

FINANCIAL CRISES

The financial situation at the New School continued to worsen. Salary expenditures were high due to the large teaching staff, and revenues from tuition were low because of dropping enrolment and an influx of low-income families. Many parents were unemployed or under-employed and few could afford even the minimum fee, which rose to $500 a year in 1973 and $600 per year in 1975.[66] Families who could have afforded to pay more left the school, unhappy that the therapeutic program had taken precedence over educational activities. The New School, in these last years, could barely afford to pay the staff's salaries, even though the teachers were earning only $5,000 per year, far less than they would have in the public system.[67]

---

63   Sharon Van Volkingburgh, personal interview, November 1991.
64   Staff meeting, minutes, September 10, 1974.
65   Sharon Burrows, personal interview, December 1991.
66   New School Society meeting, minutes, June 22, 1973, and school fee assessments, 1975/76 financial records.
67   Annual Financial Report, 1973–1977; New School Teachers' Society Fundraising Brief, 1975.

By 1973 parents looking for a less-structured school setting could choose from a number of alternative programs emerging in the public school system. Bayview Elementary School in Vancouver's Kitsilano district had a reputation for innovation, and some New School students transferred there. Bayview offered multi-age classes similar to the "open classroom" and Integrated Day practices pioneered by British primary schools. Charles Dickens primary annex in East Vancouver was another school offering a more individualized program, and one former New School student had good memories of Dickens after transferring there. Irwin Park Elementary School in West Vancouver developed an Alternative Intermediate Program in the early 1970s, attended by two former New School students. The existence of these alternatives hastened the departure of the very families necessary for the New School's financial solvency.[68]

The school could have become financially viable through integrating into the Vancouver public school system as Total Education and Ideal School did during the mid-1970s. But there were serious obstacles—the teachers were not certified, the building was substandard, and most participants were too tired to muster the energy to convince the school board that the New School was respectable enough. Furthermore, the group felt a general "hostility" toward the school system.[69] Parents and teachers distrusted large institutions and feared that the school would "lose everything it stood for."[70] They believed the New School's function was fundamentally different from that of alternative programs within the school system, which they saw as merely rehabilitative. New School leaders saw their primary goal as political: the prevention of problems through a kind of education that would empower children rather than teach them to fit into a system.[71]

Barbara Hansen and Sandra Currie applied for grants from numerous organizations and agencies. They applied to the federal Opportunities for

---

68   See Starla Anderson, "Mainstreaming Progressive Education," in *Working Teacher* 2, no.3 (1978): 12. The author also pointed out that by this time "progressive" parents wanted their children to learn academic skills.

69   Margaret Sigurgeirson, personal interview, November 1991.

70   Nora Randall, personal interview, June 1991.

71   Sharon Van Volkingburgh, personal interview, November 1991, and New School Teachers' Society, minutes, November 16, 1980.

Youth and Local Initiatives Programs for assistance to the after-school program and a summer camping experience. They made numerous requests to provincial government agencies up to 1975, hoping that their political orientation would give them some clout with the NDP government. A grant request to the Department of Education for science equipment and supplementary salaries was denied because the government opposed grants to private schools. In the proposal the applicants had referred to the school as "a real independent school, not one subsidized by a religious organization."[72] A similar request to the Vancouver School Board was also denied. However, a 1974 request to Norman Levi, Human Resources Minister and former New School parent, managed to produce some funds to assist the school in caring for children of families on welfare.

The daycare and after-school care program was one New School operation that managed to break even because parents were eligible for government subsidies. However, the daycare was engaged in a running battle with the health department, and visits from health and fire inspectors often resulted in repair requirements such as upgrading the washrooms and kitchen.[73] In 1973 the daycare gave up trying to meet licensing standards and closed. This did not affect parents, since by then the school accepted children as young as four years old into its regular program. But the closure hurt the school financially, as parents of preschoolers no longer received government subsidies.

The school began losing money consistently from 1971 at an average of $5,000 per year, and managed to balance its budget in only two of its last seven years.[74] There was a brief period of optimism when the original mortgage was retired in 1973, and a staff reduction led to a surplus. But a large loss in 1974/75 forced the school to borrow $15,000.[75] In 1976/77, the last year of operation, the school was virtually kept afloat by half a dozen families with average or above incomes. Yet despite an uncertain future, as late as 1975 the New School enrolled fifty-one students and employed six teachers.

---

72   Funding Request to Education Minister, Eileen Dailly, July 7, 1975.
73   Staff meeting, minutes, November 13, 1973.
74   Annual Financial Report, 1971–1977.
75   Annual Financial Report, 1973–1975.

Parents had little energy for fundraising, and occasional benefit concerts and rummage sales rarely brought in more than $500 per year.[76]
The debenture system was abandoned because no one could afford to pay.
Starting in 1974 parents were asked to pay their June tuition at the beginning of the school year and to sign a legal agreement promising regular fee
payments and a partial payment if a child withdrew part way through the
school term.[77] Of course, such agreements were impossible to enforce.

Many families had difficulty paying tuition fees. Of thirty-eight families
registered in 1975, fourteen (37 per cent) were assessed the "minimum fee"
of $600 per year. But twelve families (32 per cent) were assessed far less
(five were charged as little as $200) and one parent was assessed no fees at
all. On the other hand, a few families carried most of the financial burden,
demonstrating how badly they wanted to send their children to the New
School. Five families paid between $600 and $1,000 and four others paid
the maximum fee of $1,150 per child. Two other families paid a total of
$1,800 while one family of five children contributed a total of $3,150.[78]

Despite subsidized fees, some families could not manage to pay,
creating financial uncertainty for the school. Only twenty-three families
managed to pay their assessments in full by the end of the year while five
others paid 80 per cent of their fees. Six families paid less than half of their
assessed fee, and another five withdrew during the year. Yet the teachers
were not about to abandon families in financial trouble and fought hard
to keep them in the school. As several teachers commented, "We were
carrying a lot of families."

The financial problems were exacerbated by the deteriorating state
of the school building. The basement floor and back porch were in poor
condition, and the roof began to leak badly in 1974.[79] The exterior was
shabby, the inside dark and dingy. The outside play area was inadequate
but there was never extra money to develop it. Work parties were held
every six weeks, and during the 1973 Christmas holidays alone, three
rooms were painted and the stage floor, kitchen wall and linoleum, and

76   Financial statements, 1971–1977, Registrar of Companies, Victoria.
77   Fee Agreement, Nora Randall document collection.
78   New   School   accounting   book,   1975/76,   Sharon   Van   Volkingburgh
     document collection.
79   Staff meeting, minutes, October 16, 1973, September 17, 1974.

curtains were repaired.[80] Teachers found their work harder than ever with materials scarce and equipment falling apart. Attempts to scrounge replacement furniture had some success but there was no money for badly needed repairs:

> The building was slowly dissolving into a junk heap and getting more and more unattractive so we were losing the ability to generate the parents that would have been beneficial to the school's financial needs. There is a level of slum living that becomes really hard and produces emotional strain on everyone—a building that you can't keep clean because the building itself makes it impossible.[81]

To make matters worse, the school began to suffer from considerable vandalism. In June 1975 an arsonist set a fire that left the basement a "charred wreck."[82] The following year break-ins became a weekly occurrence: "Mostly, it's neighbourhood kids who throw stuff around, spill paint, break windows, upset displays, and steal equipment such as tape recorders and slide projectors. They destroy the students' work when they can find it. Our kids can't even leave their things here overnight. They're liable to find them stolen the next day and have them turn up in the second-hand store down the block."[83]

Theft and hooliganism were not the only motives for these incidents, for there was some resentment toward the school in the local community. One teacher noted "a basic antagonism in the neighbourhood to the school: The local kids pick it up from their parents. They don't like the kind of school we are, they think we're too free. They don't like the school's run-down appearance."[84] Barbara Hansen also believed the vandalism resulted from the fact that some neighbourhood residents disliked "the unconventional school."[85] The *Vancouver Sun* reported "substantial

80 Staff meeting, minutes, September 6, December 18, 1973.
81 Barbara Hansen, personal interview, October 1987.
82 *Vancouver Province*, June 11, 1975: 7.
83 Sharon Van Volkingburgh, quoted by Robert Sarti, *Vancouver Sun*, March 15, 1976, 25.
84 Margaret Sigurgeirson, quoted by Robert Sarti, *Vancouver Sun*, March 15, 1976, 25.
85 One long-time neighbour, Ms. Mai Lai Wong, recalled being concerned that the children were allowed to "play in the street." She also remembered "hippie people

opposition within the community to the New School because of its unorthodox approach to education."[86]

Attempting to improve the school's shabby appearance and make it more secure against vandalism, the teachers applied to the Vancouver Planning Department for a Neighbourhood Improvement Program (NIP) grant to finance painting, landscaping, and the installation of vandal-proof windows and doors. The application was supplemented by letters of support from parents, members of the local community, and education officials and was approved in late 1975 for just over $5,000.[87] However, the grant was conditional on repairs being made to the roof of the building, which the school could not afford.[88] The situation reached crisis proportions when the building was heavily damaged by a severe fire in March 1976. The students had to move to temporary quarters and spent the next six weeks on field trips to museums and parks. According to Robert Sarti of the *Vancouver Sun*, the break-ins continued even while the school was being repaired and parents had to take turns sleeping in the building.[89]

The school reopened six weeks later. The teachers invited the public to an open house in May to establish better relations with the community. Barbara Hansen said, "If they still don't like us, at least they'll know what they don't like. All our kids will be there and the people from the neighbourhood will be able to see how we go about our business."[90] Teachers went door to door to talk about the school.[91] The New School was back in its building but it was short of supplies, short of money, and low in morale. One parent put it well: "I held the values but I couldn't live the

going in and out," children with old and torn clothing, and the poor condition of the building. She didn't allow her son to play there (interview, November 1991).

86 Ms. F. Simatos of the Canadian Mortgage and Housing Corporation, quoted in *Vancouver Sun*, March 15, 1976, 25.

87 Those sending letters included one neighbour, several local merchants, and Gary Onstad, Education Ministry consultant to the NDP government and later a Vancouver school trustee (September 3, 1975).

88 Letter from the Cedar Cottage Planning Office of the Vancouver City Planning Department to the New School's lawyer, April 15, 1976.

89 Robert Sarti, *Vancouver Sun*, April 30, 1976, 30.

90 Barbara Hansen, quoted by Robert Sarti, *Vancouver Sun*, April 30, 1976, 30.

91 Nora Randall, personal interview, June 1991.

marginal life. The chaos and burnout was not beneficial to the kids. David [her son] wanted out. I wanted out."[92]

The New School was a target of vandalism in its later years, and students pitched in to clean up. *Vancouver Sun*, March 15, 1976

THE END OF THE NEW SCHOOL

The school never recovered from the fire or from its precarious financial situation, but it did begin its fifteenth year in September 1976 with thirty

---

92   Sharon Burrows, personal interview, December 1991. Ms. Burrows was atypical of parents from this period. She managed to go back to university to acquire a profession.

students and a staff of five teachers. Work parties were convened to paint the building, plant shrubs, and clean up the playground.[93] The school received a grant from the Vancouver Foundation to cover the roof repairs that finally allowed the NIP grant to be released.[94] Security improvements, including steel doors and unbreakable windows, were underway by October.[95] School life returned to normal for a few months and parents held regular pub nights and a Hallowe'en potluck party.[96]

However, part way through the year the financial situation became desperate. The school was running a deficit of almost $1,000 per month, and $2,000 was owing in tuition.[97] The shortfall further reduced the teachers' incomes, and several had to take evening jobs to make ends meet. Some parents were so far behind in fee payments after several months that the teachers, already working for less than a living wage, were receiving their salaries two to four weeks late.[98] Food for the Friday feast was often bought straight out of one of the teacher's pockets.[99] The school appealed for help in an advertisement in *Makara* magazine in October 1976:

> The New School assumes that both children and adults are people. Our needs are the same. We need to eat. We need to have shelter. We need to care for ourselves. We need to care for others. We need to do meaningful work. We need to be with other human beings. We need to be alone. We need to learn. We need to teach. We need to change. WE NEED FUNDS.[100]

Parent/staff meetings discussed fundraising ideas, and March was declared "responsibility month" for parents to bring fee payments up-to-date. The March 1977 edition of the school newsletter informed the school community that some parents had not paid any fees since the previous September and announced an immediate 20 per cent fee increase. This

93 New School, newsletter, September 1976.
94 Letters from the Vancouver Foundation, June 30, 1976, and September 28, 1976.
95 New School, newsletter, October 1976, Nora Randall document collection.
96 New School, newsletter, October 1976.
97 Parent/staff meeting, minutes, February 1977.
98 Payroll records, 1976/77, Sharon Van Volkingburgh document collection.
99 Sharon Van Volkingburgh, personal interview, November 1991.
100 *Makara*, October/November 1976, 48.

was a futile request given most families' financial circumstances, and the "parent difficulty" committee reported simply that "parents who aren't paying are broke." A committee tried to brainstorm new fundraising projects such as renting out space, movie showings, bingo, and soliciting businesses or foundations.[101] Teachers and parents distributed leaflets and posters explaining the school's plight throughout the community in an appeal for money, furniture, and equipment. They even requested help from founding parents who had not been active for years. Some support did materialize, but it was not enough.

The school managed to limp through to the end of June, and as late as March the teachers were busy planning for the coming year. They received seven replies to an advertisement in the *Vancouver Sun* for a staff position promising "minimum salary and maximum satisfaction at a co-operatively run elementary school."[102] However, the school could not even pay its teachers by the end of the year, and Sandra Currie had "half the staff living and eating at her house" during the last few months.[103] No matter how strong their political commitment, the teachers could not continue to work under these conditions.

Parents admired the teachers as heroic. One parent, Mary Schendlinger, reported that half of the parents were not contributing anything in the last year and most others were paying little:

> We were asking the teachers to work for almost nothing.
> By the mid 1970s there weren't any more grants or subsidies and there was no other way to finance the operation than from parents. There were a few of us paying what we could afford. We were paying a couple hundred a month which was a lot, but it was worth it to us. The teachers would divvy up whatever came in. Everybody was good-natured about it but it was demoralizing.[104]

The teachers served notice at the end of March that "the entire staff may be leaving at the end of this year."[105] Parents were urged to attend a

---

101 New School, newsletter, March 1977.
102 Applications to advertised staff position, April 1977.
103 Sandra Currie, personal interview, May 1988.
104 Mary Schendlinger, personal interview, June 1991.
105 New School, newsletter, March 1977.

meeting in April "to talk about what kind of school we want—if you have something to say, this is the time to say it."

The school did not officially close in June 1977 but had neither the money nor the spirit to reopen in September. During meetings that summer it became clear that the burnout was debilitating and everyone was just too tired to keep the school running. The teachers decided to sell the school building and expressed sorrow as well as relief that the struggle was finally over. Some hoped the school would resurface in a "new, revised, sensible, workable form."[106] Mary Schendlinger talked about the fatigue and poverty that caused the school's demise: "We were desperate, hanging on by our fingernails. We had faith and a belief that things could be better for our kids. We were really crushed about losing our school."[107] She expressed gratitude to:

> the dedicated women who, for little or no pay helped with
> my mothering, to the parents who spent long hours paint-
> ing and fixing the place up, and to the kids who have been
> such a pleasure for me. I have been so turned on by the
> sights and sounds of children doing their work in ways
> they think are important.[108]

The students returned to a public school system that had become more flexible, but many students had difficult transitions and were too far behind in academics to make catching up easy. Some struggled with traditional high schools, and even those who could meet the academic standards found the size and formality daunting. One teacher estimated that 70 per cent of New School students from the mid-1970s went to alternative secondary schools: Total Education, City School, or Ideal. The following parent's description of her daughter's experience is typical: "She wasn't learning at the New School but when she went to a public school in the neighbourhood she was worse there. She used to come home from school and cry every day. She was miserable until she was old enough to go to Ideal School."[109]

---

106 Mary Schendlinger, personal journal, entry for July 1977.
107 Mary Schendlinger, personal interview, June 1991.
108 Mary Schendlinger, personal journal, entry for July 1977.
109 New School parent, personal interview, June 1991.

Sharon Van Volkingburgh reported that at least ten students in the older class were "entrenched non-readers who had learned to get by without reading." She believed that if students "could read when they got to high school they were okay" for their research skills were well-developed from doing so many projects.[110] However, one former student whose reading ability was well advanced said the New School's de-emphasis of other skills was one reason she did not finish secondary school: "I did no school work for three years and went into grade six with a grade three education. High school was overwhelming because I didn't have any mathematics or writing skills. I just gave up."[111]

But despite the New School's academic deficiencies, it was a positive experience for many students. Students were empowered to take responsibility for their own decisions and learned that they did have choices in their lives. One parent referred proudly to her "uppity, sassy, no-nonsense kids," while another characterized the students as "undisciplined but spirited."[112] In 1976 the *Vancouver Sun* published a letter from a parent whose son was diagnosed as hyperkinetic. She described how an alternative program had been recommended by a physician, psychiatrist, and school counsellor, but the few public school programs that could help him had long waiting lists. She enrolled her son at the New School even though he had to travel two hours a day on the bus:

> In the past year at the New School, I have found an approach to education which I wish I had given to both my children. There is no separation between learning, working, and playing. In those walls he has developed into an outgoing, energetic, and responsible young human being, no longer on medication. I am relieved that neither he nor his skills will become obsolete in an ever-changing world because learning as a part of living means his education will not stop at the end of his school days.[113]

---

110 Sharon Van Volkingburgh, personal interview, November 1991.
111 New School student, personal interview, January 1992.
112 Mary Schendlinger, personal journal, entry for July 1977.
113 New School parent, "New School Changes View of Education," *Vancouver Sun*, March 23, 1976, 5.

Other than in a few such cases, the New School had outlived its purpose. Its appeal had become too marginal, its financial base had disappeared, and at least some students had not learned basic academic skills. As the public school system offered more options, the New School either had to find a place in that system or carve out an even lonelier position on the fringe. Its only other role could have been as a Therapeutic institution within the Human Resources Department. In the end, fatigue, bankruptcy, and a fierce streak of independence left the New School with no option but to close.[114]

In April 1978, less than a year after the school's dissolution, the New School Teachers' Society sold the building for just over $100,000. Official financial reports had to be brought up to date before the sale could go through, and Sharon Van Volkingburgh "stayed up all night with boxes full of receipts."[115] Another teacher tried to locate the many former parents who had allowed their building shares to remain with the school. Some families had forgiven the loans but debentures of almost $10,000 were still owed to more than eighty families.

A fund of approximately $50,000 was left after repayment of the mortgage, creditors, and the NIP grant the school had worked so hard for.[116] The New School Teachers' Society's directors continued to administer the fund for many years. Each year interest earnings were donated to educational projects involving children from low socio-economic backgrounds or with special educational needs. For example, the society's assets were used to guarantee loans to a co-operative daycare and to Theodora's restaurant, run by students at Total Education.[117] The society also supported a tutoring service for special-needs children, a school for dyslexic children, Isadora's co-operative restaurant, Arts Umbrella, Family Place, and a variety of projects at Sunrise East, an alternative public school in east Vancouver. The society donated $10,000 to the Alternate Shelter Society to purchase land on Nelson Island for the use of the adolescents in its

---

114 None of the teachers remained in education after the school closed. Barbara Hansen worked for many years with troubled adolescents and headed the Alternate Shelter Society.
115 Nora Randall, personal interview, June 1991.
116 New School Teachers' Society, Financial Statement, 1977/78.
117 New School Teachers' Society meeting, minutes, 1978–1984.

care. The New School Teachers' Society also continued to maintain the Anderson Lake mine property and funded the purchase of a van so that Dan Morner could keep taking young people to the site, which was to be used exclusively for children.[118]

118 The society also paid for a moon ball for use by alternative schools, provided a scholarship for the Kenneth Gordon School for dyslexic children, and supported Maple Tree Preschool, Imagination Market, a student concession at the Children's Festival, and a walkathon to raise money for children with cancer. True to their commitment to co-operative structures and social change, the directors kept most of the funds at the Community Congress for Economic Change Credit Union (CCEC).

Part Four

PUBLIC ALTERNATIVE SCHOOLS

Chapter 15

THE RISE OF PUBLIC ALTERNATIVE SCHOOLS AND PROGRAMS

In 1968 the British Columbia Teachers' Federation (BCTF) convened a Commission on Education to study the public school system and make recommendations. The commission's report, *Involvement: The Key to Better Schools*, recommended that "education should be humanized and personalized, that programs should be specifically designed for individual children, recognizing the unique way in which each learns, and that active involvement of students will result in the development of real scholarship." This was a trailblazing document with an innovative philosophy of education, similar to Ontario's Hall-Dennis report released the same year. The BCTF report recommended sweeping changes in public schools, including "individualized programs for every student, continuous progress, accommodation of different learning styles, de-emphasis on large group instruction, and education not confined to school buildings." The report also emphasized human relations and communication skills, more student responsibility for planning learning activities, greater student choice in secondary school courses, elimination of corporal punishment, student participation in the running of their schools, active parent involvement, and experimental schools in every district. In summary, the Commission recommended a thorough revamping of the public education system into what would be, in essence, a Progressive model.[1]

---

1 British Columbia Teachers' Federation, *Involvement: The Key to Better Schools*, Report of the Commission on Education (Vancouver: BC Teachers' Federation, 1968).

These recommendations were a product of the times, responding to the demands of parents wanting more choice for their children and the desire of teaching professionals to offer a wider range of options. The recommendations were also partly inspired by the experimental schools of the 1960s and the political and cultural movements of the times. By the early 1970s many of the report's recommendations were gradually being implemented in Vancouver and a few other forward-thinking BC school districts.

VANCOUVER SCHOOL DISTRICT

Despite the rise of the independent alternative schools described in this book, public schooling in British Columbia changed little in structure and curriculum throughout the 1960s.[2] There was minimal official interest in innovative programs in Vancouver, the only exception being the rapid growth of open-area classrooms where several teachers shared a large open space. These numbered forty-six by 1969, and one school, MacCorkindale Elementary, was designed and built as an "open-area school" in 1967.[3] But by the end of the decade, some Vancouver teachers and administrators had become aware of the individualized learning methods pioneered in elementary classrooms in Britain during the 1950s and 1960s. By 1968 references to "continuous progress," "open education," "ungraded class-rooms," "individualized instruction," and "discovery science" began to appear in Vancouver School District publications.[4] The annual report that year suggested that "gradually the spirit of change is moving through Vancouver's school system with a growing trend toward individualization of instruction and involvement of students and a resultant lessening of the use of traditional teacher-dominated methods with their emphasis on memorization of content."[5]

---

2   See Neil Sutherland, "The Triumph of Formalism: Elementary Schooling in Vancouver from the 1920s to the 1960s," *BC Studies*, nos. 69/70 (Spring/Summer 1986): 175–210.

3   Survey of Open-Area Teaching Staff, VSB Education Committee, minutes, May 29, 1969.

4   VSB, Annual Report, 1967/68 to 1974/75.

5   VSB, Annual Report, 1967/68, 2.

But significant numbers of parents and students desired even more choices in the public school system. In July 1969 the Vancouver board of trustees heard a delegation called Citizens Action to Reform Education (CARE), a parent group that grew out of the Social Action Committee of the Unitarian Church. This group was typical of the growing number of parents who believed that learning should be "exciting, interesting, and relevant" and urged the board to develop more innovative programs in Vancouver schools.[6] This increased demand by parents for educational alternatives for their children, and the growing number of professional educators interested in innovative methods, resulted in the rapid development of alternative programs in Vancouver public schools during the next five years.

In the fall of 1968, several modest experimental programs were inaugurated. At Point Grey Secondary, two hundred grade ten and eleven students took part in an Integrated Program that adopted a thematic approach to interdisciplinary learning.[7] Partly inspired by "Arts I," a new integrated initiative at UBC, the Integrated Program was staffed by six teachers from the English, social studies, and counselling departments.[8] The program had the enthusiastic support of Point Grey's vice principal, Jim Carter. Mr. Carter, who later became Deputy Minister of Education in the 1980s, had been one of the authors of the BCTF report. He was struck by the number of "bored, disaffected, and uncommitted young people" at Point Grey. Mr. Carter was one of several young Vancouver administrators and teachers who believed that public education should be based on student responsibility and should accommodate a wider variety of learning styles.[9]

A similar program offered at Prince of Wales and Lord Byng schools, called Project SELF, involved seventy-five students in grades nine to eleven with two teachers. The school district advertised the project as "an individualized program in which an effort is made to place as much responsibility as possible on the student, to develop his interests, to expect a maximum amount of original research, to give him certain freedoms, and

6   VSB meeting, minutes, July 14, 1969.
7   VSB Education Committee, minutes, March 10, 1970.
8   Arts I director Dr. Ian Ross provided considerable moral support to the Point Grey program.
9   Jim Carter, personal interview, December 13, 1996. See also Chapter 9.

to permit students to move more freely about the school and out into the community."[10] Like the Point Grey Integrated Program, Project SELF followed an interdisciplinary approach drawing from English, social studies, physical education, music, and art.

These projects continued as quiet experiments for several years. But in 1971 the number of alternative programs in Vancouver began to increase dramatically. District officials worried about the number of capable students dropping out of high school, and a majority of trustees believed there should be a choice of schooling available for every child. The board's Education Committee suggested that the district implement a system of "continuous progress, non-grading, and flexible grouping," as "there is no evidence to justify keeping pupils in a lock-step arrangement according to age."[11] In March 1971 the board accepted a recommendation from district officials "encouraging the creation of alternative programs throughout every school" and created a fund of $72,000 for teacher-initiated innovative projects. Beginning that year, Vancouver School Board annual reports featured an entire section on alternative programs, explaining that "the emphasis on alternative programs recognized that no one kind of education suits all pupils, parents, or teachers."[12]

This growing commitment to alternative programs in Vancouver was promoted enthusiastically by the Director of Education, Alf Clinton. As a vice principal during the mid-1960s, Dr. Clinton had encountered many students "who didn't fit into the school system and he realized it was highly unlikely they would succeed in the system the way it was."[13] In 1968 he completed a doctorate in "educational change" at the Ontario Institute for Studies in Education and became committed to decentralizing the school system and creating alternatives.[14] Dr. Clinton provided valuable leadership, drawing on his theoretical and practical background, to make a strong case for the district's rapidly developing alternative programs.

---

10   VSB, Annual Report, 1967/68, 12.
11   VSB Education Committee, minutes, March 10, 1971.
12   VSB, Annual Report, 1970/71, 8.
13   Sally Clinton, personal interview, January 28, 1999.
14   Dr. Clinton also worked with Mario Fantini, a leading American advocate of innovative programs.

City School

In May 1971, Dr. Clinton unveiled a proposal to the trustees for "An Ungraded Continuous Progress School" to be known as City School:

> The City School Project is designed for students whose educational growth requires experiences beyond those found within existing school programs. Each student will design, carry out, and evaluate his own learning program. By having to decide what he wants to learn and through finding out how and where this can be done, each learner should develop habits and skills which may better enable him to continue learning through life. The City School experience is designed to develop a healthy sense of responsibility for one's actions and for the community through active involvement in it.[15]

Students would be encouraged to use the resources of the entire metropolitan area, similar to several high profile programs in the United States, including the Parkway Program in Philadelphia and the Metropolitan Learning Centre in Portland. One of the initiators of City School was Dr. John Wormsbecker, assistant superintendent in charge of secondary schools. He had been particularly influenced by the Parkway Program, described by John Bremer and Michael von Moschzisker in their well-known book *The School without Walls*. In that program, students spent most of their time in the community.[16] Another impetus for City School was the example of Toronto School District's SEED program, begun in 1968, which utilized outside resource people from throughout the community.[17] Dr. Clinton and others worked hard to convince district officials and elected trustees that programs like City School would make a

---

15 Alf Clinton, "A Proposal for an Ungraded Continuous Progress School," presented to Vancouver school trustees, May 31, 1971.

16 John Bremer and Michael von Moschzisker, *The School without Walls* (New York: Holt, Rinehart, and Winston, 1971).

17 For more on SEED and other Toronto School District alternatives, see Harley Rothstein, "Private to Public: Alternative Schools in Ontario, 1965–1975," in Nina Bascia, Esther Sokolov Fine, and Malcolm Levin, eds., *Alternative Schooling and Student Engagement: Canadian Stories of Democracy within Bureaucracy* (New York: Palgrave Macmillan, 2017), 71–94.

significant difference in students' lives and were therefore a reasonable use of taxpayers' money.

City School emphasized collaboration rather than competition.
Vancouver Sun, October 2, 1971

The curriculum aimed to develop a "sound general education" through an ungraded and interdisciplinary approach. Although there was a core content of required courses in English and mathematics, the primary emphasis was on the "learning process" and the solution of "relevant problems."[18] Students would decide what they want to learn, find out how and where in the community to do it, and evaluate their efforts. City School teachers wanted students to "gain experience in making real decisions affecting their lives." One explained: "There was nothing artificial or hypothetical about it. Everything students had to learn was based in

---

18   Alf Clinton, "A Proposal for an Ungraded Continuous Progress School," presented to Vancouver school trustees, May 31, 1971.

a context of reality." Another former City School teacher said: "We saw ourselves as resource people rather than teachers. Our hope was that we would be able to guide students in *how* to get educated."[19]

The proposal was approved by the board, and City School opened in September 1971 with one hundred students aged ten to fifteen and four teachers in the former Edith Cavell School annex on Tenth Avenue.[20] There was no formal timetable, and students planned their programs in consultation with a staff "sponsor" who monitored the students' progress. In addition, the school offered classes in basic literacy and computational skills, but attendance was only optional.

City School had two major goals. One was to help students develop independent research skills, and during the first year research topics included genetics, ecology, electronics, drama, photography, film-making, cooking, and organic gardening.[21] The school's other goal was to "use the city as its classroom," and City School developed an extensive field trip component using public transit and rented vans. Students visited the universities, the public library, the art gallery, the law courts, and the Women's Health Collective. One year, some students interviewed judges, police, Family Court workers, and Legal Aid Society representatives, while other students helped establish a co-operative radio station, and still others made costumes and sets for a production at the Frederic Wood Theatre. Another year groups of students surveyed their neighbourhoods and produced socio-economic, cultural, and architectural maps.[22] Students and teachers camped at Long Beach, went hiking in the Rocky Mountains, and learned about nature at the Evans Lake Outdoor School near Squamish. In addition to the outdoor trips, students also visited urban centres including Calgary, Ottawa, Montreal, and Quebec City.

The founding teachers were Thom Hansen, Kit Fortune, Marge Jones, and Lynn Cobb. There was no principal and the staff reported directly to Dr. Clinton. The teachers ran the school on a co-operative basis, but

19 Joanne Broatch and Thom Hansen, in Alan Etkin and Joshua Berson documentary, *City School: Twenty- Five Years of Alternative Education* (City School Productions, 1996).
20 VSB meeting, minutes, May 31, 1971.
21 VSB, Annual Report, 1971/72, 9.
22 Kay Alsop, "Every Block Is Their Blackboard," *Vancouver Province*, 1975.

the nominal head was Mr. Hansen who had been one of the teachers in Project SELF. From 1972 to 1976 seven other teachers taught at City School, including Daryl Sturdy, who had taught for four years at the New School.[23] By the third year, enrolment reached 125 students spanning grades four to twelve. Although the original conception was that the school would eventually include the primary grades, this was never implemented because some trustees were squeamish about placing young children in such an unstructured environment. At the end of the second year, the school went to a four-day week with Friday set aside for voluntary field trips or independent study.

City School was intended to attract well-functioning students who wanted more independence, and indeed some did apply because they wanted a less formal learning environment than what was found in traditional schools. However, according to Thom Hansen, two-thirds of City School's enrolment consisted of "students the principals wanted to get rid of" and who were having serious problems functioning in traditional schools.[24] Some of these students were referred by the Children's Aid Society and others by school principals or counsellors. This experience was typical of alternative schools.

Although the school had the backing of the district, it did incur some criticism from outside observers. One trustee visiting the school during the first year brought back reports about the "aimlessness and boredom of the students."[25] Another visitor observed that less than half of the students attended classes, while the others were "either wandering around, sitting in the smoking room, or not at school at all." This observer noted that "the ideology of freedom of choice (that a student cannot learn until he or she is ready to learn) is very strong," and there was "little evidence of attempts to get students involved in any academic work."[26] Some parents believed more teacher direction was necessary, and the staff decided to implement a "more structured curriculum plan and school organization as a result of

23 Other staff members to 1976 were Michael Day, Alan Crawford, Eva Zebrowski, Sue Arundel, Joanne Broatch, and Barbara McClatchie.
24 Thom Hansen, personal interview, March 12, 1997.
25 VSB meeting, minutes, April 24, 1972.
26 Peter Seixas, "Alternatives in Vancouver: To What? For Whom?" (unpublished paper, Simon Fraser University, July 1974), 14–15.

their experience at the school during the past year."[27] However, on the whole, most teachers, parents, and students connected with City School were satisfied with the program.

Almost from the outset, City School experienced organizational difficulties. In 1973 a parent delegation criticized the school board for insufficient staffing, inadequate science facilities, and the absence of a transportation budget even though activities in the community were to be a major aspect of the school. They submitted a brief claiming that the teachers had not been given enough planning time or administrative assistance to develop and implement a new program. They also suggested that an unclear admission policy resulted in some students who were not benefiting from the program. The parents further accused the board of setting up the school as a "token gesture" and claimed that "the school is regarded by many officials as a nuisance." The delegation asked the board to increase funding to hire more staff and improve the facilities. They believed City School to be a highly important program reaching beyond the one hundred students involved: "It is the nucleus of a very significant aspect of our educational system," providing "a unique and potentially successful answer to the growing disaffection of many of our young people with existing conditions."[28] The school staff also made several presentations to district officials, requesting budgetary improvements, upgraded facilities, and a realistic transportation budget. The district responded by leasing two vans, but the teachers continued to be concerned about their substandard building.

City School staff were also critical of the ineffective perfunctory channels of communication with district officials. During the first year Dr. Clinton, described by one teacher as the school's "spiritual advisor," kept in close touch with the staff, but each year a new district administrator was assigned to the school. The teachers felt ignored and powerless to make any decisions without permission and continued to appeal for more support and autonomy. Their conception of the school was as a collegial and community-oriented program entrusted with the responsibility for developing its own direction. The staff wanted to be more involved

---

27   VSB Education Committee, minutes, June 27 and September 12, 1972.
28   VSB Education Committee, minutes, May 31, 1973.

in decisions about the school's location and teacher hiring, and thought that the head teacher should be invited to attend principals' meetings. But these requests remained unanswered. A letter from the staff to the district superintendent in 1975 expressed distress at "what appears to be a breakdown in communication between the Vancouver School Board and City School."[29] That year the vice principal of a nearby secondary school was made responsible for City School. Although he rarely visited, he annoyed the staff by insisting on more traditional practices regarding attendance, report cards, and student supervision.

The school's administrative problems resulted from several contradictions. Although the district leadership was sincere in its desire for alternative high school programs, it did not want to commit the kind of funding necessary to guarantee success. Secondly, most administrators were nervous about such practices as voluntary attendance and student autonomy, which might result in bad publicity for the program and the district. Thirdly, the teaching staff's vision of City School as a democratic enterprise led to a predictable struggle with the district bureaucracy.

Despite these problems, most students found the program a success. At the end of the first year, a district evaluation of the school indicated that "students had achieved a better attitude toward school and had gained confidence."[30] A former student commented on his years at City School:

> City School taught me to be resourceful. The teachers would never give you the answers but they would give you some direction in how to find out what you needed to know. One of the things that was important for me was that the students really ran the school. Students decided what the direction was. That was a lot of responsibility for a young kid. There were times when it did good things for me.[31]

Other students remembered the emphasis on self-motivation. The school was "student oriented rather than teacher oriented"; its goal was

---

29　City School staff to Dr. Dante Lupini, Superintendent of Schools, May 8, 1975.
30　Alf Clinton, VSB Education Committee, minutes, September 12, 1972.
31　Rob Lando, in Alan Etkin and Joshua Berson documentary, *City School: Twenty-Five Years of Alternative Education* (City School Productions, 1996)

"teaching individuals how to learn."[32] However, not all students were self-motivated and one student recalled "playing guitar all year long."[33]

In September 1974 City School moved downtown to occupy one floor of the former Dawson School on Burrard Street, a building they would share with Ideal School. Although the building was considerably run down, the majority of staff and students liked the downtown location because of its proximity to the public library, law courts, and art gallery. However, after just over two years, in January 1977, the building was sold and the school was forced to move again. The school took up its new residence at the former Sacred Heart School on East Pender Street in Chinatown. Staff and students were never happy with this location due to the distance from downtown and the presence of a teenage gang in the neighbourhood.[34] The school eventually moved to the basement of King George Secondary School in the West End where it remained for many years. Classified as a minischool, it has continued to be administered by King George. In this setting the school has become a smaller and more traditional "academic enrichment program," although it retains some of its original "joie de vivre."

ALTERNATIVE PROGRAMS AND POLITICAL CHANGE

Other innovative projects were inaugurated in 1971.[35] At University Hill Secondary, students were responsible for organizing their own timetables, which included a compulsory integrated humanities course, regular scheduled classes, contracted individual work, and six-week mini-courses in such topics as creative writing, mythology, and ceramics. The school also encouraged parent involvement, and was so popular that over seventy applicants were turned away.[36] Bayview Elementary School, in the Kitsilano neighbourhood that had been home to Vancouver's

32   Alan Etkin and Joshua Berson documentary, *City School: Twenty-Five Years of Alternative Education* (City School Productions, 1996)
33   Steven Drake, former Whole School student, personal interview, March 26, 1997. Mr. Drake's guitar skills served him well. See Chapter 12, Footnote 30.
34   Karenn Krangle, "Alternative Schools Have Identity Crisis," *Vancouver Sun*, June 1, 1977.
35   Alf Clinton, Report on New Programs, VSB meeting, minutes, September 27, 1971.
36   .VSB, Annual Report, 1971/72.

countercultural community, developed a flexible approach to education that included team teaching and multi-age groups. The school encouraged an informal atmosphere as students worked together on thematic projects, addressed teachers by first names, and moved freely around the building. Charles Dickens Annex also established innovative programs based on the child-centred Integrated Day methods pioneered in England. In July 1971, Dr. Wormsbecker reported that thirteen Vancouver schools offered programs of "considerable change and innovation," while twenty-seven schools planned to implement new programs during the coming year.[37]

The rapid growth of alternative programs in the Vancouver School District after 1970 coincided with the emergence of The Electors Action Movement (TEAM), a reformist civic party founded in 1968. TEAM candidates won three seats on the nine-member school board in 1968 and 1970. The TEAM trustees proposed many new programs and policies and were often convincing enough to win the support of their more conservative colleagues.[38] The pace of reform increased when TEAM swept eight of the nine school board seats in 1972, along with the election of TEAM Mayor Art Phillips and a TEAM-dominated City Council.[39] Three of the new trustees were UBC faculty members, including Peter Bullen, a mathematics professor, who became chair in 1973.[40] The vice chair was Olive Johnson, a writer and child welfare worker. Two years later TEAM retained its majority on the board under Chair Katherine Mirhady, a pediatrician, and Vice Chair Elliott Gose, a UBC English professor. The increased number of educators and other professionals on the board concurred with a heightened interest in school programs.

37   VSB Education Committee, minutes, July 14, 1971.
38   Peter Bullen, personal interview, February 5, 1999.
39   Robert Sarti, "TEAM dominate trustee contest," *Vancouver Sun*, December 14, 1972, 53.
40   "Reformers Control the School Board," *Vancouver Sun*, January 9, 1973, 16. The other faculty members were Peter Oberlander and Fritz Bowers.

Olive Johnson and other TEAM trustees advocated for alternative schools in the Vancouver School District. *Vancouver Sun*, December 10, 1970

The TEAM trustees had campaigned on making the school system more democratic and responsive to the wishes of parents, and were enthusiastic about innovative programs.[41] Trustee Elliott Gose was a strong believer in Progressive education and had been a co-founder of the New School ten years earlier. Olive Johnson was equally committed to alternative schooling. She had experienced her children's schools as "rigid, authoritarian, and lock-step." She recalled: "I read everything I could get my hands on. I read about developmental psychology; I read John Dewey, Bertrand Russell, and *Summerhill*. I knew there was a better way to do this."[42] In 1967 Ms. Johnson had visited the Barker Free School and Knowplace, and her articles about them appeared in *Vancouver Magazine* and *Maclean's*. She was also a founding member of Citizens for Action to Reform Education and recalled that "we were all unhappy for our teenagers." Upon her election in 1970, she stated that her goal was to "increase

---

41   Dan Mullen "New TEAM School Board Open to Outside Ideas," *Vancouver Province*, December 15, 1972, 7.

42   Olive Johnson, personal interview, January 29, 1999.

flexibility in the school system so that students will have a wide variety of programs from which to choose."[43]

The 1972 school board election reflected a growing concern about the education system among the general public. Citizens groups of all kinds discussed new educational ideas. Even the Education Committee of the Greater Vancouver Regional District referred to the education system as "a hierarchic, self-perpetuating, self-serving system which no longer meets the needs of the community."[44] The Committee called for greater citizen participation in educational planning, more de-centralized decision-making, and a significant increase in "educational-cultural alternatives based on different philosophies and methods from those presently used."[45]

Public concern about education was part of a wider questioning of the role of all governing institutions. It grew out of the aftermath of the 1960s and reflected the public mood desiring change. Many Canadians wanted their society to be more democratic, less centralized, and more responsive to individuals. The civic victory of TEAM in Vancouver came just three months after the 1972 provincial election, in which the New Democratic Party swept to power under the leadership of Dave Barrett. As Ms. Johnson observed, the times were right for political and educational innovation: "Change was in the air. Young people were no longer prepared to be ordered about."[46]

BRITISH-STYLE OPEN CLASSROOMS

By 1970 many educators had heard about "open classrooms" in Britain, and some of the innovations in Vancouver were an attempt to incorporate features similar to those of the British primary school system.[47] The district's education staff was interested in "a more child-centred, open type of elementary school" and were particularly curious about "the Integrated

---

43 "City Voters Add an Olive to School Board Recipe," *Vancouver Sun*, December 10, 1970, 23.

44 Greater Vancouver Regional District Education Policy Committee, Report, December 1973, 1.

45 GVRD Education Policy Committee, Report, December 1973, 13–14.

46 Olive Johnson, personal interview, January 29, 1999.

47 Primary school is the British term for what Canadians call elementary school.

Day, multi-age grouping, and informal learning."[48] In 1971 trustee Olive Johnson and Vancouver's Primary Education Coordinator went to England to observe primary schools involved in "informal education." They visited twelve English schools using the Integrated Day approach and reported back to district staff on how teachers organized individualized instruction and supervised independent studies.[49] Ms. Johnson observed that most classrooms were organized into "activity areas," and that students "spend most of the day working individually or in small groups on a wide variety of activities involving all subject areas." She added that the learning is "interesting and enjoyable," and that teachers have few discipline problems. She found that children in informal schools "learn as individuals" in multi-age groups, with the teacher supplying "educational materials spanning a wide range of abilities." She also found that most subject areas were integrated into themes, that "rote learning and memorizing have been replaced by discovery, experience, and activity," and that evaluation was performed by observing and recording what work was done rather than by keeping marks.[50] School Board officials were intrigued by Ms. Johnson's findings on the British open-classroom concept, and Integrated Day methods were highlighted in the school district's 1971/72 Annual Report.

Ms. Johnson found her visits to the English schools "inspirational." She recalled that "the teachers knew about child development, they knew that individual children learn at different paces; it was really working." Her extensive report to the other trustees described "learning environments in which the child can learn for himself":

> Informal education is based on the premise that each child is an individual who learns in a unique way and whose development proceeds according to his own personal blueprint. It is based on the conviction that learning is more effective when it grows out of the needs and interests of the learner rather than the teacher. The goals of child-centred education and educating children as individuals are actually being realized in good British

---

48 VSB, Annual Report, 1971/72, 7–9.

49 Cynthia Taylor, report to VSB Education Committee, minutes, July 14, 1971.

50 Olive Johnson, "A Report on a Visit to Some British Primary Schools," presented to the VSB Education Committee, September 28, 1971.

> schools and that a child in a good English primary school
> is receiving a vastly superior education to that of his
> Vancouver counterpart.[51]

Olive Johnson and district staff recommended that the Vancouver School Board bring a British primary school expert to Vancouver to consult with interested teachers and school staffs about how best to implement aspects of "open education." Ms. Johnson also proposed that the board arrange an exchange between six Vancouver teachers and six teachers "from outstanding British primary schools." The proposal, entitled "Open Education in Vancouver Schools: A Proposal to Accelerate a Child-Centred Approach to Elementary Education," stated:

> There is a growing interest among Vancouver educators
> in a more child-centred, open type of elementary school.
> In open schools teachers seem to be more successful
> in translating into practice the theories of Montessori,
> Dewey, and Piaget about child development, learning
> from experience, exploration, and discovery.[52]

Acknowledging the impetus given to this approach in Vancouver by Progressive British primary schools, the authors of the proposal hoped an examination of open education principles would lead to changes in "our philosophy, curriculum, and methodology."

In 1972 Assistant Superintendent John Wormsbecker travelled to Britain to observe British primary schools, to examine in-service programs for practising teachers, and to arrange for teacher exchanges and the visit of a British consultant to Vancouver. He was impressed by "the emphasis upon the individual child rather than on the subject matter, the controlled freedom of pupils in integrated curriculum classes, the workshop atmosphere of most classrooms, and the role of the teacher as a learning coordinator working with individual pupils and groups."[53]

As a result of Dr. Wormsbecker's trip, the inspector of primary schools in Bristol visited Vancouver in the fall of 1972, making extensive recommendations about how "child-based, individualized, and open education"

---

51   VSB Education Committee, minutes, September 28, 1971.
52   VSB Education Committee, minutes, November 23, 1971.
53   Dr. John Wormsbecker, report to VSB Education Committee, February 29, 1972.

could be implemented in Vancouver elementary schools. She assured trustees and administrators that such a program offered many benefits for students. These included lessons in responsibility, self-control, wise choices, sound judgement, respect for other people, confidence and willingness to explore and master a new environment, and the ability to think in original and creative terms.[54] Vancouver began to actively recruit primary teachers from Britain, and several elementary schools, notably Charles Dickens Annex, began to use Integrated Day methods and individualized programs.

MINI-SCHOOLS, COMMUNITY SCHOOLS, AND REHABILITATION PROGRAMS

As the new programs at City School, University Hill, Bayview, and Dickens Annex were being established, the Vancouver School Board received a request for financial assistance from the independent alternative school Total Education. Alf Clinton supported this request and proposed that the school be given one teacher and the use of five bungalows at the former Model School at Twelfth Avenue and Cambie. He cited the school's "remarkable success" working with teenagers who had dropped out of Vancouver schools because of a "feeling that they did not fit in" and helping them "to rehabilitate themselves into the educational sphere":

> Some of these students have been referred by welfare agencies and others by Vancouver Schools. Educational officials were most impressed with the work being done by this organization which follows the curriculum of the Department of Education closely and, wherever possible, encourages students to re-enter the Vancouver school system. A low pupil-teacher ratio is necessary because most of the students need counselling and someone to take a personal interest in them. For some time education officials have been aware of the need for an institution of

---

54 Pamela McKeown, Schools Inspector, Bristol, UK, address to VSB Education Committee, October 24, 1972.

this kind, and the service being provided by this organization fills this void.[55]

The school trustees approved Dr. Clinton's recommendation in September 1971.[56] This was the first formal association between a school district and an independent alternative school in British Columbia.[57] In 1974 the board assumed "full responsibility for the educational component of Total Education" by providing four teachers, four teacher's aides, and other district services.[58] The same year the trustees brought Ideal School into the district as a "mini-school" to share the former Dawson School building with City School in downtown Vancouver.[59]

Between 1972 and 1975 an impressive number of alternative programs were developed in Vancouver. The first of Vancouver's mini-schools was established at Prince of Wales Secondary School in 1973 for eighty academically motivated and self-disciplined students.[60] The minischool featured an integrated curriculum, multi-age groups, flexible timetables, in-depth independent study, one-to-one consultation, enrichment experiences outside the school, parental involvement, increased student responsibility, and the opportunity for students to design their own programs.[61] The school board also designated Bayview and Champlain Heights Elementary Schools as "comprehensive community schools," a new idea in the 1970s that favoured more integration of school and community activities.[62] Vancouver's first bilingual school, l'Ecole Bilingue, and a wilderness education program, BC Quest, were other popular programs established in 1973.

---

55 VSB Education Committee, minutes, August 24, 1971.

56 VSB meeting, minutes, September 13, 1971.

57 Similar initiatives began about the same time in the Toronto School District. See Harley Rothstein, "Private to Public: Alternative Schools in Ontario, 1965–1975," in Nina Bascia, Esther Sokolov Fine, and Malcolm Levin, *Alternative Schooling and Student Engagement*, 71–94.

58 VSB meeting, minutes, July 15, 1974. For more on Total Education, see Chapter 9.

59 VSB meeting, minutes, July 15, 1974. For more on Ideal School, see Chapter 11.

60 VSB, Annual Report, 1972/73.

61 D. W. Renwick to Dr. John Wormsbecker, "Proposal for a Mini-school," presented to VSB Education Committee, May 16, 1973.

62 VSB Education Committee, minutes, April 17, 1973.

Many rehabilitation programs were developed for students who had dropped out of school or were identified as potential dropouts. These included the Britannia "8J9J" program, Operation Step-Up, the Vinery Project, Outreach School, the Grandview 7A program, the Bridge, the Cedar Cottage Project, and Chimo Place for learning-disabled students.[63] In 1975 alone six new rehabilitation programs were established.[64] Several of these were initiated by private organizations and run in partnership with the Vancouver School Board until eventually the school district assumed responsibility for them. Some received funding from the federal government or the provincial Human Resources Department. Most programs were housed in school buildings but a few, such as the Vinery at Kitsilano Neighbourhood House and Operation Step-Up in a Fourth Avenue apartment, were located in the community. Typically, rehabilitation programs enrolled from twenty to thirty teenagers and were attached to a mainstream school for administrative purposes. They provided instruction in basic academic skills but went beyond "remedial" programs by also offering personal counselling, interpersonal skills instruction, and assistance with family problems. Most rehabilitation schools were characterized by individualized academic programs, a low student/teacher ratio, informal but respectful relationships between teachers and students, and some degree of student autonomy regarding attendance and daily activities.

Rehabilitation programs adopted a variety of approaches. At the Vinery, associated with Kitsilano Secondary School, three staff members worked with twenty-five dropouts. Students spent each morning working on individualized mathematics or English according to weekly contracts. This was combined with a strong recreational component, counselling, and volunteer community service projects to help students "establish an idea of their own value."[65] The goal was to bring them up to the grade ten level or to give them the "social and academic skills to enable them to cope with society."

---

63   VSB, Annual Report, 1973/74.
64   These were the OK program, Strathcona Continuation, Hastings-Sunrise Learning Centre, Riley Park Rehabilitation Program, Byng Satellite, and KAT Class. VSB, Annual Report, 1974/75.
65   Lesley Krueger, "Some Alternatives to a World of Endless Defeat," *Vancouver Sun*, June 20, 1974, 47.

The 8J9J program with two staff members and twenty students was located on the grounds of Britannia High School. Founded by Mary Jo Campbell, 8J9J emphasized traditional academic work to enable students to return to the regular school. There were frequent field trips, and one day per week was set aside for the teachers to assist students with legal and family problems. Close peer group ties were encouraged and new students had to know someone already in the program to gain admittance.[66]

Some alternative programs, like Operation Step-Up, depended on volunteers.
Vancouver Sun, June 20, 1974

Operation Step-Up, for forty juvenile offenders on probation, was founded by a learning disabilities teacher, a probation officer, and a UBC professor. It offered a highly structured, incremental program in basic reading, writing, and arithmetic for three hours each day with twenty university volunteers who tutored the students on a one-to-two basis. A behaviour modification approach rewarded progress while ignoring unsocial behaviour.[67] The goals for these programs varied; some students were

---

66   Peter Seixas, "Alternatives in Vancouver: To What? For Whom?" (unpublished paper, Simon Fraser University, July 1974).
67   Peter Seixas, "Alternatives in Vancouver: To What? For Whom?"

prepared for re-entry into mainstream schools, while others were steered toward employment or training programs. In all cases, though, rehabilitation schools sought to improve academic skills while also addressing the social problems caused by disengaged and idle youth.

ADMINISTRATION OF DISTRICT ALTERNATIVE PROGRAMS

Public interest in alternative schooling was high in the early 1970s. Although a few parents still hoped to start their own independent unstructured school, most were now content to accept the school district's new alternative offerings.[68] Vancouver newspapers kept the public informed about new approaches to public education in numerous articles. The writers discussed individualization, continuous learning, non-competitive grading, and children learning from each other.[69] Others reported on organizational forms such as team-teaching, open-area classrooms, and multi-age groups. Some reporters noted changes in atmosphere that made high schools more democratic, and attempts to make school environments "pleasant and enjoyable" rather than authoritarian.[70] Due to keen parental interest in alternatives, the Vancouver Parent-Teacher Council organized a conference in 1974 to make the public aware of the full range of innovative programs available in Vancouver.[71] In May 1975, several Lower Mainland school districts sponsored a three-day Conference on Alternatives in Education.[72] However, the interest in alternative education was mainly a middle-class phenomenon. When school district officials surveyed parents on Vancouver's East Side about an alternative school in their area, most

---

68 Mike Graham, "Parents Hope to Organize Low-Cost Free School in City," *Vancouver Sun*, February 18, 1971, 28.
69 "City's School System Eyes New Approach to Learning," *Vancouver Sun*, July 24, 1971, 16, in which Mike Graham quotes Dr. John Wormsbecker.
70 Leslie Peterson, "Would You Goof Off in School Now?" *Vancouver Sun*, October 2, 1971, 32.
71 Wyng Chow, "Vancouver Offers Alternatives in Schooling," *Vancouver Sun*, February 22, 1974, 16.
72 VSB, Annual Report, 1974/75.

cited "skill development and basic literacy" as their main priorities, and the idea was not pursued.[73]

Alternative programs became so numerous in Vancouver that in 1973 the school board created a special committee, the "Administrative Coordinating Team on Alternative Education" (ACT) to supervise existing alternatives and to evaluate proposals for new ones.[74] The committee of administrators and teacher association representatives was headed by Alf Clinton. The establishment of the ACT was a response to public interest in educational alternatives and board officials emphasized that there should be "continuing community involvement" in developing new programs.[75] To this end, the committee was assisted by a broad-based advisory group with representatives from business, labour, religious organizations, Canada Manpower, Family Court, counselling services, Children's Aid, and Citizens' Action to Reform Education. The ACT undertook a "comprehensive assessment to determine the causes and needs for alternatives in the Vancouver school system." District officials encouraged Vancouver teachers to recognize and accommodate a variety of learning styles present among the children in their classrooms. A few district leaders hoped the introduction of alternative programs would not only create diversity but would influence the rank and file teaching staff, thus acting as a catalyst for widespread change within the system.[76]

The Administrative Coordinating Team took the lead in consolidating the school district's alternative programs. One of the important tasks was to inspect such independent schools as Total Education and Ideal School and to determine how they could best be incorporated into the system. One member of the committee recalled, "What we were really doing was to preserve the essence of their program, what was unique about it, maintain its identity. It was exciting visiting the schools. You never knew what you were going to see."[77] Committee members were concerned about

73   VSB Education Committee, minutes, "The Establishment of a Second Alternative Open Education Secondary School," April 9, 1973 and December 4, 1973.
74   VSB Education Committee, minutes, January 22, 1973.
75   VSB Education Committee, minutes, June 5, 1973.
76   John Uzelac, VSB administrator, and President of the Vancouver Secondary School Teachers' Association, personal interview, December 10, 1996.
77   John Uzelac, personal interview, December 10, 1996.

the untrained teachers and the highly countercultural or political nature of some of the programs. In asking, "Does this program really exist for the kids or does it exist for the teachers?" the committee had to be convinced that the teachers had a genuine interest in students. Ultimately, to be acceptable a program had to be able to work within the system.[78]

In the early 1970s the Vancouver School Board discussed other liberal ideas. In an effort to make Vancouver secondary schools less authoritarian, board members and administrators gradually relaxed hair and dress codes and instituted voluntary attendance for grade eleven and twelve students. Trustees Peter Bullen and Olive Johnson were committed to making the schools more "democratic," and the board encouraged the formation of parent and staff committees. The trustees also instituted an "open boundaries" policy, allowing parents to enrol their children in a school outside their local catchment area. In 1971 the board approved a statement on "professional freedom," assuring teachers that they were free to try experimental programs without fear of sanction. The official view of discipline was gradually changing, and in February 1973 NDP Education Minister Eileen Dailly outlawed the use of the strap in British Columbia schools with the enthusiastic support of the Vancouver trustees.[79] However, the board stopped short of adopting a student charter of rights, although this was debated for several years, and policies that would give students more control over their schooling were slow to be implemented.

OTHER DISTRICTS

Several years before alternative programs appeared in the Vancouver public schools, a small high school on northern Vancouver Island made news by allowing a substantial amount of freedom to its students and teachers. The Campbell River Senior Secondary School opened in 1965 under the principalship of John Young. Mr. Young, who grew up in New

78 The work of the ACT was similar to that of the Alternative and Community Programs Department of the Toronto School District during the 1970s under the leadership of Dale Shuttleworth. See Dale Shuttleworth, *Schooling for Life: Community Education and Social Enterprise* (Toronto: University of Toronto Press, 2010).

79 VSB meeting, minutes, February 19, 1973.

Brunswick, had been an idealist from an early age. After earning degrees in international development and education at UBC, he served as chief educational advisor in Sarawak, Borneo, in the late 1950s and, in the early 1960s, was a co-founder of the Canadian University Service Overseas (CUSO), an international development agency staffed by young adults. He had been principal of two schools in central BC before taking the position at Campbell River.[80] Mr. Young was familiar with the writings of well-known alternative educators such as Jonathan Kozol and John Holt, as well as with the British Columbia Teachers' Federation report, *Involvement: The Key to Better Schools*, Ontario's Hall-Dennis Report, *Living and Learning*, and the British Plowden Report. He had come to disagree with many traditional educational practices, including the rigid grade system, artificial divisions of subject matter, labelling of students, motivation by punishment, and the "obsession with order, control, and uniformity in our schools."[81] He also believed that teachers were not treated professionally.

At the Campbell River School, students were responsible for their own behaviour. Attendance at class was voluntary and students were free to move around the school without supervision. Students decided how many courses to take, chose their teachers, and arranged independent study. Flexible timetables permitted students to be employed, dress and appearance codes were eliminated, and there was no failure or punishment. Pregnant girls were permitted to continue in school, and many came from other parts of the province. The school also accepted some out-of-district students who disliked traditional high schools, and one former Knowplace student attended for a year. Staff decisions were made collegially, and teachers were permitted to decide how to teach their courses and whether or not to have examinations.[82]

Although the Campbell River experiment was educationally groundbreaking and popular with teachers and students, many conservatives

---

80   Biographical information from John Young, personal interview, February 11, 1997.

81   John Young, "Professional Perspectives and Educational Change," presentation to the British Columbia Principals and Vice Principals Association, October 28, 1970.

82   J. A. Young, "A Rural High School Tries Freedom," in *This Magazine is about Schools*, Winter 1967.

in the community questioned Mr. Young's reforms. An outspoken and forthright individual, he had angered some trustees and ministry officials for attracting too much attention to the school and for criticizing school board decisions. Ultimately, John Young was fired for insubordination in 1972 and the school reverted to traditional practices. As he was five to ten years ahead of his time in the world of public schooling, it was perhaps inevitable that his innovations would not last.

Many British Columbia school districts began to develop alternative programs by the mid-1970s, although none had the breadth offered in Vancouver. As a large urban district, Vancouver attracted young liberal educators, and parents in Vancouver had been more affected by the cultural and political ideas of the 1960s than in other parts of the province. Nevertheless, at the request of parents, West Vancouver developed a high school program, the Sentinel Satellite, which emphasized the humanities, drama, and the arts. It was led by teacher Barbara Shumiatcher (formerly a New School parent) and supported by Jim Carter, after he became principal at Sentinel Secondary School in the early 1970s.[83] As well, the North Vancouver School Board incorporated the alternative elementary school, Windsor House, into the district in 1975. This ensured that the school would remain financially viable and provided a ready-made alternative program for the district.[84]

VICTORIA: SUNDANCE SCHOOL

The Victoria School District developed its first alternative programs in 1973, despite its reputation as a conservative district. The change was driven by pressure from parents and district concerns about high school dropouts. The election of the New Democratic Party government in 1972 brought more "anti-establishment" people into the city. "Free schools had become a buzzword" by the early 1970s, according to Assistant Superintendent John Wiens, and district officials believed the public schools should offer more choice. Mr. Wiens was sympathetic to the "rebellious generation" and thought that many sound educational ideas

83   Barbara Shumiatcher, personal interview, June 13, 2021.
84   See Chapter 11.

had become discredited during the 1960s because they had been misunderstood.[85] Alternative schools were sold to the conservative trustees through a proposal to establish two "prototype" elementary schools, one "less structured" and one "more structured." The latter, called Sentinel, appealed to parents who wanted teacher-directed classrooms and traditional discipline but could not afford expensive private schools.

The "less structured" school, Sundance, generated immediate excitement when it opened in September 1973. There were 170 inquiries to the district's first advertisement, and parents "camped out overnight" to ensure their children would be accepted.[86] By the following June there were over two hundred children on the waiting list for the 1974/75 school year.[87] A year later there was still a waiting list of fifty-five. Some Sundance parents were educators and professionals, others were former hippies, and some were "pretty ordinary folks."[88] Parental demand was a major impetus behind the formation of Sundance School.[89]

Sundance opened with 125 students divided into four multi-age or "family" groupings in which older students were encouraged to take some responsibility for the younger children. Several teachers had experimented with "open classrooms" and the principal, George Olsson, had been principal of an open-area school in Cowichan. Teacher Donna Wooliams (who would become principal in 1976) had been influenced by the British primary system and by Summerhill. She recalled the enthusiasm with which teachers and parents embarked on the project: "On the first day of school we were walking on air and parents were hugging teachers."[90] Seeking to avoid hierarchy, the Sundance staff made decisions by consensus and the teachers worked as a close team.

One of the many distinguishing features of Sundance was the unusual level of parent participation, with as many as a dozen parents volunteering at the school on an average day. There was a great deal of discussion and

85 John Wiens, personal interview, March 6, 1997. Like Dr. Clinton, Mr. Wiens spent several years at the Ontario Institute for Studies in Education.
86 Dan Mullen, "Parents' Views on Education Lean to Free School Lines," *Vancouver Province*, April 12, 1973, 6.
87 "Even Small Babies Look to Sundance," *Victoria Times*, June 1, 1974, 27.
88 Donna Webb, personal interview, March 4, 1997.
89 John Wiens, personal interview, March 6, 1997.
90 Donna Webb, personal interview, March 4, 1997.

intellectual ferment, and parents participated actively in helping to shape the educational philosophy. But as often occurred in alternative schools, the parents knew what they disliked about the public school system but could not agree on what kind of education they wanted.

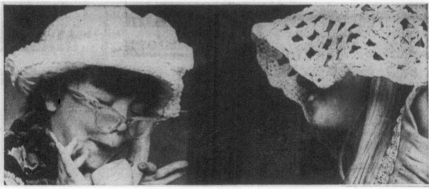

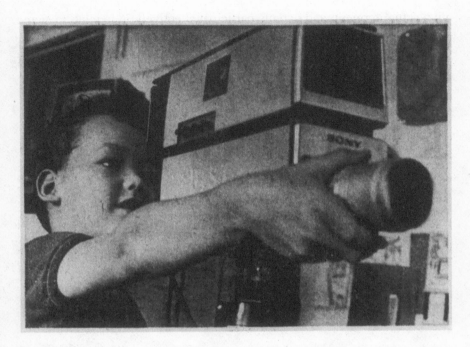

Sundance School emphasized the creative arts, which students were encouraged to explore through music, drama, and film-making. *Daily Colonist*, September 30, 1973

The curriculum was organized according to a "centres" approach, and students filled out contracts specifying their daily activities. The school emphasized "self-discovery, self-direction, and responsibility." Students moved freely around the building, and in late September one reporter observed, "It's noisy and a trifle chaotic, but the pupils look happy. So do the teachers and the principal. It seems strange to hear youngsters talk naturally among themselves while they work and see them structure their own work day with the guidance of teachers."[91] Basic language and mathematics skills were not ignored, but the school was "more concerned with the affective area than the cognitive" and with the creative arts. The school de-emphasized competition and tried to motivate students by allowing them to experience success. Mr. Olsson explained that "the success of each child attending the school is individually defined" and

---

91   Helen Hossie, "Sundance: An Experiment in Self-Responsibility," *Daily Colonist*, September 30, 1973, 19.

that progress is based on "individualized criteria agreed to by the child, the parent, and the teacher."[92] As the school brochure stated, "The core purpose of this school is to develop within each child a positive and realistic self-concept."[93]

In 1975 a district report on the school criticized "insufficient marking of students' work" and suggested the school maintain "systematic records of student progress, especially in basic mathematics and language skills." The report noted that "because of a desire on the part of staff to create positive non-threatening learning situations, at no time are students compelled to get down to work. In such a permissive environment there are some students who are unable to cope with this freedom and as a result are probably wasting time."[94] The evaluation concluded that students had to be highly motivated to achieve academically at Sundance. On the other hand, the report acknowledged that the objectives of the school had "for the most part been met" and the school appeared "highly successful." A survey of parents indicated that "they are extremely pleased with the school. Students are encouraged to be sensitive to the feelings and needs of those around them, to be independent, and to appreciate their own worth and abilities." As a result of the mutual respect and trust that exists between teachers and students, "Sundance is a very warm, open school—in every way a humanized environment for learning."[95]

Sentinel, the traditional school, received a strong endorsement from the evaluation team. Ironically, though, it closed after several years due to decreasing demand because it was not able to distinguish itself from mainstream public schools or existing private schools in Victoria.[96] Sentinel was also stretched because some district principals attempted to send their more challenging students there. Meanwhile, Sundance remained popular for fifteen years but declined in the late 1980s, as the school was unable to adapt to the changing expectations of parents who wanted the school to

92   Kit Collins, "Sundance Would Get A-Plus—If It Gave Grades," *Victoria Times*, October 24, 1975, 17.
93   Sundance Communicates, April 1977.
94   "Study Knocks Record System at Sundance," *Victoria Times*, October 23, 1975, 13.
95   "Sundance, Sentinel: Happy Structures on a Two-Way Street," *Daily Colonist*, October 24, 1975, 11.
96   John Wiens, personal interview, March 6, 1997.

be more academically accountable.[97] The school was never as successful academically as it had been in the affective domain. As well, mainstream schools had become more child-centred and Sundance School became largely superfluous. It closed in 1992.

VICTORIA: WAREHOUSE SCHOOL

While Sundance School catered to parents who wanted a more humanistic education for their young children, an independent rehabilitation school for high school dropouts also developed in Victoria during this period. The Warehouse School was founded in 1972 by two teachers at the Sisters of Saint Ann convent, Jacqueline Aubuchon and Charlotte Dauk. Both had considerable teaching experience, most recently at Saint Ann's Academy. Veronica Doyle, a teacher with an extensive background working with high school students, "street people," and prison inmates, joined the staff the following year and replaced Sister Aubuchon as co-director in 1974. Although Sister Aubuchon only remained at Warehouse for two years, her vision was the original driving force behind the school.

Warehouse School founder Sister Jacqueline Aubuchon enjoyed working with mature students. *Victoria Daily Times*, November 3, 1973

97   Donna Webb, personal interview, March 4. 1997.

Warehouse School taught basic skills to older motivated students.
Victoria Daily Times, May 3, 1975

Warehouse School offered to high school dropouts, street kids, teenage mothers, "free spirits" left over from the 1960s, and even a group of former prison inmates in their twenties an opportunity to continue their education.[98] Some lived with parents or relatives, many were in foster care or group homes, and some lived independently. Enrolment averaged fifty students, most of whom were working on their grade ten credentials, but some completed grade twelve or re-entered mainstream schools.[99] Some students heard about the school by word of mouth, while others were referred by social service agencies and many had social workers. Tuition was free and food was often provided. The school was run by a non-profit society and financed on a shoestring through Local Initiative Project grants and funding from the provincial Ministry of Human Resources.[100] In 1974 the staff increased to six teachers, all on minimal salaries of less than $500 per month.[101] There were also three part-time teachers and the school had the benefit of many dedicated volunteers.[102] The staff was a

---

98 Susan Ruttan, "Education on a Shoestring," *Victoria Times*, November 3, 1973, 29.
99 Susan Ruttan, "Warehouse School That Works Seeking New Home," *Victoria Times*, May 3, 1975, 37.
100 Eleanor Boyle, "Warehouse of Knowledge," *Victoria Colonist*, February 15, 1976, 51.
101 Warehouse School Society, Annual Financial Report, May 31, 1975; also Susan Ruttan, May 3, 1975 and Eleanor Boyle, February 15, 1976.
102 Sister Eileen King and retired teacher Ed McKeirahan were frequent volunteers.

close-knit group, made decisions collegially, and most enjoyed the experience.[103] In 1975 the Education Ministry began to contribute "adult education" funding through the Saanich School District until 1980, when the Victoria School Board formally incorporated the school into the district.[104]

The school's original home was the top floor of the St. Vincent de Paul warehouse in downtown Victoria. Students worked at long rough tables or sat on old couches, drinking coffee. They chose the subjects they wished to work on and the teachers they wanted to work with. Although the day-to-day operation of the school was informal, there was a strict policy against drugs, and students were expected to complete some work each day. Most were motivated enough that they made rapid progress.[105] All students were on self-paced "modular" programs in mathematics, basic English, and research skills, and there was no whole-group instruction. Formal attendance was limited to three and a half days per week, leaving time for field trips, social events, ping-pong games, and bowling outings. Students enjoyed the constructive environment and the sociability. Staff took a personal interest in the students' welfare, and there was a good deal of trust, caring, and mutual respect among students and teachers.[106]

The former Saanich firehall was one of several locations for Warehouse School during the 1970s. *Daily Colonist*, February 15, 1976

103 Bill Simpson, personal interview, March 5, 1977.
104 Warehouse School Society, Annual Financial Report, 1975–1981.
105 Jacqueline Aubuchon, personal interview, March 6, 1997.
106 Glen Pope, personal interview, February 27, 1997.

Alternative schools often had to move premises. Here, the Warehouse School principal
unpacks in a new location on Quadra Street in Victoria.
Victoria Daily Times, August 29, 1978

After being forced to move to several different locations, including a
church basement and the old Saanich fire hall, the school finally found
stability in the former Quadra Street School provided by the Victoria
School District. By 1977 the original teachers had left the school, and
Barbara Pelman, a former college instructor from Vancouver, became
director for five years. She was succeeded by Glen Pope, a Victoria district psychologist, and Bill Simpson, a teacher at the school since 1976.
The school remained an ongoing program in Victoria, enrolling over
eighty students until the district decided to close it in 1998.[107] Teachers
and former students were disappointed and some students protested, but
the decision stood.[108]

Similar to Total Education in Vancouver, the Warehouse School had its
roots in the social gospel tradition of service—as one founder expressed it,
"a bunch of people seeing a need."[109] Some students continued with their

107 Cindy E. Harnett, "School's 26-Year Service Ends," *Times Colonist*, June 25, 1998.
108 Marcy DeVries, "Parents Weren't Asked," *Times Colonist*, Letter to the Editor,
     February 8, 1998; Richard Watts, "Warehouse Students Stage Protest," *Times
     Colonist*, April 4, 1998; Martha Henry, "Rare Treasure Lost," *Times Colonist*, Letter
     to the Editor, June 21, 1998.
109 Charlotte (Dauk) Herkel, personal interview, April 2, 1997.

education after leaving Warehouse while others did not, but the school had a positive effect on the lives of most participants. As Veronica Doyle put it: "They knew they had accomplished something. It broke the pattern of discouragement and despair. It was the most intense educational experience I've ever had."[110]

Despite the popularity of alternative programs in Victoria, school trustees were far from unanimous about their value. In 1974 the school board refused to expand Sundance School despite a long waiting list and a presentation by almost one hundred parents.[111] A year later one trustee labeled the school a "complete circus," and plans for a similar secondary school were discontinued.[112] The board also withdrew funding for the teacher who worked with the Group Home Day Program for delinquent teenagers.[113] Moreover, despite numerous requests beginning in 1975 from the Departments of Education and Human Resources to incorporate Warehouse School into the district, Victoria trustees only agreed to do so under severe pressure in 1980. This reluctance of Victoria trustees to embrace alternative programs was partly due to financial constraints, conservatism, and the persistence of traditional educational values.

DEPARTMENT OF HUMAN RESOURCES

During the 1970s a few alternative schools, such as North Vancouver's Windsor House, the Vallican Whole School, and Sundance School in Victoria, continued to offer the humanistic, child-centred education that had been popular in the 1960s. But the proliferation of rehabilitation or Therapeutic schools was the dominant development in the 1970s. Schools like Total Education and the Warehouse School had less to do with theory than with addressing the needs of high school dropouts, potential dropouts, street kids, juvenile offenders, children from troubled families, and rebellious countercultural youth who would not accept traditional school

---

110 Veronica Doyle, personal interview, April 4, 1997.
111 "New System of Schools Big Success," *Daily Colonist*, June 21, 1974, 21.
112 Susan Ruttan, "Report on Sundance 'Cloud Nine Thing,'" *Victoria Times*, July 15, 1975, 13.
113 Peter Medwid, "Alternatives in Trouble," *Victoria Times*, August 15, 1975, 17; also Department of Human Resources correspondence, June to September 1975.

authority. As the number of rehabilitation schools grew dramatically in British Columbia between 1970 and 1975, many looked toward the Department of Human Resources for financial support.

When the New Democratic Party under the leadership of Dave Barrett ended the twenty-year reign of W. A. C. Bennett's Social Credit government in August 1972, there were great expectations from the educational and social services communities that long-ignored needs would finally be met. However, it was a challenge for Education Minister Eileen Dailly to satisfy widespread hopes for major innovation and change in the education system.[114] One of her initiatives was the appointment, amid much fanfare, of the American educator John Bremer as Commissioner of Education in February 1973. Mr. Bremer was well known among educators as the creator of Philadelphia's Parkway Program.[115] But little came of his ideas and he was abruptly fired eleven months later.[116]

Meanwhile, Human Resources Minister Norman Levi took the initiative for funding rehabilitation programs for school dropouts and students at risk. Some students were referred by school districts, others by the court system and probation officers. Mr. Levi's policy was to integrate all programs working with children, including local counselling services, daycare centres, group homes, diagnostic centres, foster homes, and residential treatment centres.[117] To this end he created the Special Services for Children Program, which provided child care workers to families, schools, and community projects.[118] This program grew out of a fundamental department policy to keep troubled youth in their communities and out of institutions: "to ensure that services are available to children so that they may remain in their own homes, schools, and communities."[119] A growing component of this network of children's services involved support for financially strapped alternative schools. Both Mr. Levi and the

---

114 See Lorne Kavic and Garry Nixon's history of the Barrett government, *The 1200 Days, A Shattered Dream* (Vancouver: Kaen, 1978), 169.
115 The Parkway Program was popularly called the "School without Walls," which had been the inspiration for City School.
116 Mr. Bremer was fired after Premier Dave Barrett pronounced his program "a flop" on province-wide television. Kavic and Nixon, *The 1200 Days, A Shattered Dream*, 165.
117 Department of Human Resources, "Report on Services to Children," April 1975.
118 Norman Levi, speech to Council for Exceptional Children, November 8, 1974.
119 Department of Human Resources, Press Release, July 26, 1974.

Department's Coordinator of Children's Resources, Marilyn Epstein, had a special interest in alternative education, having been founding parents of the New School in 1962. Their primary objectives, though, were limited to rehabilitation: "to enable young people who are experiencing difficulty at school or who have already dropped out to acquire basic academic skills. This would make it possible for such students to re-enter the school system or proceed to further training or employment" and "to promote the development of life skills and help in dealing with social and behavioural difficulties."[120]

By mid-1974 the department was contributing to forty-two rehabilitation and alternative school programs, and Mr. Levi approved an annual budget of more than one million dollars, a large sum at that time.[121] By the end of the year the number of programs had increased to fifty-five, and by the fall of 1975 Human Resources was supporting ninety-one programs with a total enrolment of 1,700 students.[122]

The largest number was in Vancouver and Victoria, where the department funded eleven programs in each district, but many of the province's school districts were represented. The diverse programs in Victoria included Warehouse School, the Group Home Day Program established in 1973 to provide education for "severely disturbed and hard core delinquent youth," the James Bay Girls' Alternative Program for female dropouts, the Boy's Club Work Activity Program, the Langford Alternative Program, the Victoria Autistic Society, the Native Friendship Centre, and the Victoria West Alternative Program. Some others around the province were the Northfield Alternative School in Nanaimo, the Quesnel District Alternative Program for very troubled students, the Aspire Program in Nelson, the Re-entry Program in Kamloops, Project Upgrade for foster children in Maple Ridge, the Sentinel Work Activity Project in West Vancouver, and the One Way School for "underprivileged and delinquent

---

120 Marilyn Epstein, "Proposed Guidelines for Alternative School Programs," April 30, 1975.

121 Marilyn Epstein, "Department Funding of Alternative School Programs," August 22, 1974.

122 Memorandum from Marilyn Epstein to Norman Levi, August 25, 1975, Human Resources Department file on alternative schools; Norman Levi document collection.

youth" in Surrey.[123] The Vancouver programs included two storefront schools: the Spring Street Program for disaffected teenagers and the East End Basic Training and Skill Development Centre, offering high school upgrading to teenagers and adults.[124]

Some programs were controlled directly by school districts while others were independently administered by non-profit societies. Many alternative programs had originally been funded by federal government Local Initiatives Project (LIP) grants. When those sources ran out by 1973, the Human Resources Department took over much of the funding. But with demands on its budget expanding, and under mounting political pressure to control spending, the department had to cut back on services in 1975. It established firm guidelines for alternative school funding, stipulating that educational staff and facilities had to be provided by local school districts or the Education Department.[125] Most school boards complied and gradually assumed responsibility for alternative programs.[126] After 1975 Human Resources continued to support rehabilitative educational programs, but only through the provision of child care staff. In a few districts where the number of alternative programs had stretched local school funds, some programs were cut back severely, to the dismay of professionals and parents.[127] For example, in Victoria the staff at one group home program was reduced from sixteen to four.[128] Human Resources officials tried to balance the financial needs of both the providers and recipients of these programs with the government's political need to appear financially prudent.[129]

Human Resources Minister Norman Levi and his staff were instrumental in the success of these numerous alternative and rehabilitation

---

123 Memorandum from Marilyn Epstein to Norman Levi, January 13, 1974.

124 The BSTD was affiliated with Vancouver City College and Canada Manpower.

125 Marilyn Epstein, "Guidelines for Alternative School Programs," April 30, 1975.

126 Norman Levi, personal interview, August 7, 1996.

127 Peter Medwid, "Alternatives in Trouble," *Victoria Times*, August 15, 1975, 17.

128 Department of Human Resources, alternative programs file, June to August 1975.

129 The concern about overspending came from a highly publicized "one hundred million dollar overrun" incurred by the Human Resources Department in 1974. See Geoff Meggs and Rod Mickleburgh, *The Art of the Impossible: Dave Barrett and the NDP in Power, 1972–1975* (Madeira Park, BC: Harbour Publishing, 2012); and Lorne Kavic and Garry Brian Nixon, *The 1200 Days: A Shattered Dream; Dave Barrett and the NDP in BC, 1972–75* (Coquitlam, BC: Kaen Publishers, 1979).

programs. In the early 1970s, such programs were just getting off the ground in a few forward-thinking school districts. But it was not clear where their funding would come from. Instead of risking their closure, Mr. Levi and his staff found ways to come up with the money. They provided a bridge of support at a critical time until individual districts became willing and able to support alternative programs after 1975.[130] Human Resources then facilitated a smooth transfer of funding from the province to school districts, in ways that did not unduly disrupt programs or schools.

The objectives of the rehabilitation programs were to reduce anti-social behaviour and to upgrade academic skills so that students could either return to regular classrooms or enter the work force. In their attempt to keep marginal students in school, rehabilitation programs achieved considerable success. One North Vancouver parent wrote to Mr. Levi that the alternative program "succeeded in helping our son become a self-confident, self-reliant boy. Previous to this time he was ready to quit school and considered himself a failure in the school system."[131] A Department field supervisor writing about an alternative program in Quesnel stated that "the improvement in the behaviour of the children is remarkable; the oldest boy is due to return to the regular school system next month."[132] A teacher in a Victoria program had "no doubt that without this program to guide them, a good many of these children would have been unable to adjust to a normal life within the school system and within society."[133]

CONCLUSION

By 1975 the educational landscape in British Columbia was considerably different from what it had been a decade earlier. This was particularly evident in Vancouver, the province's largest school district. Many elementary schools, such as Bayview and Charles Dickens, offered informal child-centred classrooms, secondary mini-schools were in place, and mainstream high schools like University Hill offered flexible programs with

---

130 The Human Resources Department file on alternative school programs contains a great deal of correspondence and testimonials regarding programs in jeopardy.
131 Alternative school parent to Norman Levi, April 30, 1975.
132 W. Prokop, to Norman Levi, December 20, 1974.
133 V. Sweeney to Norman Levi, June 16, 1975.

more student choice. In addition, three alternative secondary schools (City School, Total Education, and Ideal School) offered innovative programs for students who felt marginalized or bored at traditional high schools, and a myriad of rehabilitation programs were available to students who were at risk of dropping out. Parents were offered the opportunity to become more involved in their local schools, consultative committees were replacing the old parent-teacher associations, and community schools welcomed the public into their buildings. Teachers had developed a more significant voice through their professional associations and staff committees, and teachers were given more latitude to experiment with new programs. Although public schools were still hierarchical, students were treated with more respect, and the authoritarian nature of high schools was somewhat relaxed through voluntary attendance for older students, the elimination of dress codes and corporal punishment, greater choice of courses and programs, and open school boundaries. Alternative programs spanned the complete spectrum from informal and child-centred to highly therapeutic.

The transformation of the public school system between 1970 and 1975 exemplifies how rapidly change can be implemented when favourable conditions exist. In the case of liberalizing public education, some of those conditions were: parental demand for alternative programs and more choice in the public schools, increased self-confidence of youth, professional innovation with a critical mass of teachers trying new ideas, and supportive and effective leadership from liberal administrators and reform-minded school trustees. Also critical were the political and cultural movements of the times, which questioned accepted norms and values, and the inspiration of the pioneers who created the experimental schools of the 1960s.

By the 1970s many parents were demanding choice in the school system, particularly if they perceived that their children were not being well served by traditional classrooms and schools. Peter Bullen, Vancouver School Board chair from 1972 to 1974, cited parental demand as the most significant factor in the growth of alternative programs: "Many who complained were on the West Side and had children who were being picked on for long hair. The parents I talked to were thinking, 'Why is Vancouver so stodgy?' They wanted the whole thing loosened up."[134] As well, a significant number of teachers, influenced by liberation values of the 1960s or through their own experiences with students, wanted to implement a more humanistic and less coercive style of teaching. High school students, many influenced by counterculture values and rock music, were far less docile than they had been just a decade earlier, and if schools had not relaxed their standards of control to some degree, the tension could have become untenable. Finally, the public school system benefited from the political leadership shown by Vancouver TEAM trustees such as Peter Bullen, Olive Johnson, Katherine Mirhady, and Elliott Gose; by liberal administrators including Alf Clinton, Jim Carter, and John Wormsbecker in Vancouver as well as John Wiens in Victoria; and by provincial Human Resources Minister Norman Levi. They had the vision to address the needs of changing times.

The political mood that brought TEAM to power in Vancouver and the New Democratic Party to form the provincial government was rooted in principles of participatory democracy, de-centralization of institutions, individual freedom, and responsiveness to individual needs. Educational reformers rode this political wave that originated in the 1960s. Peter Bullen said, "There was something in the air at the time; people were dissatisfied." John Wiens explained the popularity of Victoria's Sundance School this way: "Sundance was doing something that was in tune with the times; there was a lot of excitement about the flower children."[135] Jim Carter described alternative schools as part of a "broad movement of cultural and social change in which people ceased to be rule followers."[136] And as Vancouver School Board Vice-Chair Olive Johnson put it, "The sixties had a big impact on everybody":

> Parents were demanding change. They felt emboldened
> to have expectations. Teachers were also emboldened
> by the sixties: the whole notion of getting away from
> authoritarian relationships to more respectful democratic

134 Peter Bullen, personal interview, February 5, 1999.
135 John Wiens, personal interview, March 6, 1977.
136 Jim Carter, personal interview, December 13, 1966.

relationships, greater self-expression, and more knowledge of child development.[137]

Although the independent alternative schools of the 1960s were in
decline by the early 1970s, they inspired innovators within the public
system to adopt many of their ideas. "The 1960s schools certainly had an
effect on me," Olive Johnson said. "They provided a kind of beacon. They
contributed to the critical few. Enough parents, enough kids, became familiar with these concepts; they helped change people's expectations."[138]

---

137 Olive Johnson, personal interview, January 29, 1999.
138 Olive Johnson, personal interview, January 29, 1999.

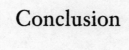

Conclusion

Chapter 16

CONCLUSION: THE LEGACY OF INDEPENDENT ALTERNATIVE SCHOOLS

By 1975 few independent alternative schools remained. All the Romantic schools of the late 1960s—the Barker Free School, Knowplace, and Saturna Island Free School—had closed by 1971. Craigdarroch School closed in 1969, and although other Progressive schools were longer-lived, the New School would eventually close in 1977, as would the Argenta Friends School in 1982. Total Education, Ideal School, and Windsor House had all joined the public school system by 1975. Only the Vallican Whole School in the Slocan Valley would remain independent and continue to serve its self-contained back-to-the-land countercultural community for many years. Alternative schools were short-lived for many reasons. They were hampered by parental divisiveness, financial instability, large numbers of special-needs students, the lack of a viable and realistic educational theory, and the normal challenges that come with pioneer enterprises. Perhaps the most important of all were the decline of the counterculture and, ironically, competition from new alternative programs within the public school system.

DECLINE

The founders of alternative schools often disagreed about the kind of education they wanted to offer. Parents were unclear about their educational goals and what they thought constituted effective teaching. These parents were better at articulating what they did not want than they were at agreeing about what they favoured. For example, parents (as well as teachers) couldn't agree on such fundamental issues as whether they wanted to be a Progressive or a Romantic (free) school, how structured or unstructured the curriculum should be, and whether their children should take at least some direction from the adults or remain free to do whatever they pleased. At the New School and Craigdarroch School the absence of agreement among parents was never resolved. Schools founded and led by teachers, such as the Barker Free School and the Saturna Island Free School, were more likely to be unified in their educational approach but were still faced with pressure from younger staff members to adopt more freedom for the students. Without a common vision among participants it was difficult for alternative schools to develop and grow.

A second factor in the decline of alternative schools was economic. Alternative schools relied on favourable student-teacher ratios to provide the individual attention that made their programs work. Most had ratios of one teacher to ten students or fewer. At the same time, alternative school founders wanted to keep tuition fees low to allow a wide cross-section of students to attend. The result was that teachers worked for barely subsistence salaries, making it difficult to sustain the considerable energy required to work with children and avoid burnout. The schools were therefore financially vulnerable to any kind of setback, whether it be a fire, a visit from the Health Department, or an unexpected withdrawal of students. Several schools simply went bankrupt while others lived on the edge for years.

A third factor that strained almost all alternative schools was the number of students with learning disabilities, emotional and family problems, or mental health and behavioural difficulties.[1] There was little choice available in the 1960s. Public school districts had few remedial programs to help such students, who often ended up at alternative schools as a last resort. But alternative school teachers had minimal expertise in

---

1   At the time such students were usually labelled "problem children." Today, debate continues as to which is the more respectful term: "children with disabilities" or "special needs children."

responding to disabilities. As students with special needs claimed a great deal of teachers' time and energy, the educational programs already in place were weakened. This was not a new concern, as resourceful and desperate parents of children needing more intensive help often sought out experimental schools. As early as the 1930s, Bertrand Russell realized that his Beacon Hill School was not equipped to handle what he described as "an undue proportion of problem children."[2] Some of Summerhill's early students had been in trouble with the law, and New York's City and Country School had students requiring therapy.[3] Ontario's Everdale Place was also stretched by too many students with complex needs, and the school's 1969 brochure warned that "the only entrance requirement for students is that they be emotionally stable enough to cope with our combination of freedom and community."[4] Similarly in British Columbia, the large proportion of students with disabilities detracted from alternative school programs and diverted staff energy from the schools' original purpose—to develop a new philosophy of education for the majority of students.

A fourth limitation of alternative schools was the lack of a comprehensive, systematic, and realistic educational theory. Allowing students to follow their own interests and to generate their own motivation was not a sufficient foundation upon which to build a functional learning program. As many as half of the staff members were not certified teachers and therefore did not have the benefit of formal professional training in how to motivate students or generate excitement about learning. Furthermore, of the teachers who were certified, very few had any training in Progressive methods. This absence of professionalism, while refreshing initially, was severely limiting to alternative schools in the long run. Consequently, the

---

2   Bertrand Russell, *The Autobiography of Bertrand Russell: The Middle Years: 1914-1944* (Boston: Little, Brown, and Company, 1968), 225; also published London: George Allen and Unwin, 1968. Also cited in Brian Hendley, *Dewey, Russell, Whitehead: Philosophers as Educators* (Carbondale: Southern Illinois University Press, 1986), 66.

3   A. S. Neill, Introduction to Homer Lane, *Talks to Parents and Teachers* (New York: Schocken, 1969); Aurie Felde, New School parent who had taught at City and Country School, personal interview, December 5, 1991.

4   Bob Davis, *What Our High Schools Could Be* (Toronto: Our Schools/Our Selves, 1990), 41.

teaching programs depended too much on the inclination and personal cha-
risma of individual staff members to develop any sort of consistency. As
a result, the overall educational programs didn't evolve to their potential.

Last, and perhaps most important, was the decline of the counterculture. With the fading of the 1960s, alternative schools lost their innocent
appeal. These 1960s schools depended too much on the special spirit of the
times. When the times changed most Progressive and Romantic schools
were not adaptable enough to change with them. However, some of the
Therapeutic schools were able to occupy a niche catering to alienated
teenagers who had dropped out of high school or were at risk of doing so.
This made these schools candidates for joining the public school system,
thus enabling them to survive.

By the mid-1970s most liberal parents wanted their children to learn
academic skills. At the same time, the public school system began to offer
a wider range of programs. As some districts developed child-centred
programs of their own, there was little demand for private alternatives.
By then parents and students could usually find the kind of education they
wanted in the public system.[5]

CURRICULUM CHALLENGES

Although curriculum development in the traditional sense was not usually
a priority of alternative schools, they did produce some significant innovations. They experimented with individualized learning programs, thematic
approaches, and integrated or inter-disciplinary subject material. They
emphasized co-operative and group learning, human relations, use of concrete materials, and the creative arts. Using the Project Method to teach
research skills, alternative schools encouraged students to follow and
explore topics that interested them in more depth than they would have
experienced in a traditional school. Alternative schools also demonstrated
the value of small classes and increased teacher attention, while others
showed how a relaxed and informal atmosphere could allow nervous or
discouraged students to approach learning without stress. Some schools

---

5   See, for example, Starla Anderson, "Mainstreaming Progressive Education," in
     Working Teacher 2, no. 3 (1978), 12.

had a political agenda, and all attempted to teach their students to be critical thinkers, questioning widely accepted social and intellectual values. One enduring contribution that influenced public schools arose from the extensive field trip programs developed at virtually every alternative school. Students spent large portions of time interacting with the outside community as well as acquiring outdoor skills and an appreciation for nature.

Most alternative schools were deficient in teaching basic educational skills. Despite this, students at moderate Progressive schools, for the most part, eventually returned to the public school system, went to university, and entered a variety of careers. Although many of these students missed basics such as spelling, grammar, and times tables, their reading and writing ability remained intact. Most already knew how to read, having been surrounded by books at home.

But for students who attended Romantic or free schools for several years or more, that experience often marked the end of their formal schooling. They fell too far behind and encountered too much freedom to return to public school. Some who tried became demoralized and frustrated. As a result, some of these former students reported that their educational and professional opportunities were limited. A few students also became side-tracked by drugs and sexual interest to a greater degree than they might have in more traditional schools. In the end, the theory was too simplistic, the young staff members were too inexperienced, and the ethos of the times did not value formal academic education.

Of course, there were exceptions. Some former Romantic school students eventually obtained high school diplomas, several became professional musicians, and a few attended university. One Knowplace student eventually earned a PhD in psychology, another became a self-taught art historian, a third trained himself to be a computer analyst, and another did graduate work at the University of Washington. Moreover, many former alternative school students reported having developed beneficial attributes such as self-reliance, ingenuity, tolerance, adaptability, and assertiveness as a direct result of their time spent in alternative schools. Others enhanced their critical thinking skills, problem-solving ability, and creativity, and also gained self-confidence, initiative, and responsibility. Some students appreciated the lack of academic pressure. As well, for students who had already decided to drop out of public school, alternative schools provided a refuge safe from the underworld of crime and drug addiction.

Alternative schools accomplished their curricular objects to some degree but proceeded in too unsystematic a manner, rarely developing lasting pedagogical tools. There was an unrealistic emphasis on students initiating their own learning, and not enough direction from adults. Alternative school proponents valued creativity but ironically neglected to teach the skills necessary to develop artistic or creative writing abilities. In some schools, educational activity was minimal. As James Harding, an original supporter of Knowplace, wrote in 1970:

> We do not have to abandon intellectual curiosities to have human freedoms, in fact the two are very much intertwined. In letting the kids do what they please and being supportive passively, rather than in a challenging way, something quite different from education is allowed to go on.[6]

GOVERNANCE AND LEADERSHIP

One of the principal goals among founders of alternative schools was to create organizations that were more democratic and participatory than was the norm in mainstream society. Alternative schools gave rise to a variety of governance structures and leadership styles. Several parent-founded schools, most notably the New School, began as experiments in co-operative governance and participatory democracy. This was successful in involving many parents in decision-making and volunteer activities, and in providing a sense of excitement and ownership. However, the co-operative model led to some serious problems. The decision-making structure did not clearly define the respective roles of teachers, board members, and parents. Parents spent too much time micromanaging and supervising teachers when they had little expertise to do so. The unreasonable scrutiny

---

6　James Harding, "Freedom From or Freedom To: Ideas for People in Free Schools," *Free School: The Journal of Change in Education* (Saturna Island Free School Press, 1970).

from parents made alternative schools difficult places in which to teach, and staff turnover at most schools was high.

Schools founded by teachers were more likely to provide continuity and a unified or shared sense of purpose. As a result, they experienced less dissension than schools run by parents. The most successful period of governance at the New School was when parents, tired of ongoing arguments, asked the teachers to take over administering the co-operative. This ushered in several years of peaceful governance and, by all accounts, the teacher co-operative ran very well. However, even in schools run by teachers, the directors often had to endure pressure from staff members who expected decisions to be made in a democratic manner. At the Barker Free School, for example, the founder was pressured by his young staff to adopt an even more laissez-faire attitude than he had originally established. The founders of Saturna Island Free School and Ideal School also sometimes found themselves at loggerheads with the teaching staff who wanted more input. At some schools, such as the Argenta Friends School and Total Education, as well as Ontario's Everdale Place, staff members (and in some cases students) attempted to use a consensus model with some success. This kind of decision-making was lengthy and emotionally draining, however, and took its toll on the participants. Except for Argenta, few schools had access to individuals experienced in the difficult art of achieving consensus.

As in any human organization, some individuals were more forceful, eloquent, or insightful than others, and those individuals usually got their way regardless of the governance structure. At the Argenta Friends School, for example, on paper students had decision-making authority equal to that of the teachers. However, students reported that policies were almost always decided by the most experienced and influential adults. Jonathan Kozol, a writer with years of experience with alternative schools in the United States, concluded in his classic 1972 book, *Free Schools*, that most compromise structures did not work: "There should either be a total commitment to full democratic participation of all people in the school or else there should be a straightforward, small, and honest power structure."[7]

---

7   Jonathan Kozol, *Free Schools* (Boston: Houghton Mifflin, 1972), 19.

In the end, most alternative schools adopted compromise procedures with resulting ambiguity.

The 1960s "do-your-own-thing" ethos made many people reluctant to exercise leadership.[8] This was certainly true in alternative school communities, where too many adults were afraid or unwilling to demonstrate the educational leadership necessary to inspire students. Jonathan Kozol argued that children deserve "teachers who are not afraid to teach." Although he believed that alternative schools should be "child-centred, open-structured, individualized, and unoppressive," he wrote:

> There has been too much uncritical adherence in [the free school] movement to the unexamined notion that you can't teach anything. It is just not true that the best teacher is the grown-up who most successfully pretends that he knows nothing. I think we must be prepared to strive with all our hearts to be strong teachers, efficacious adults, and unintimidated leaders in the lives of children.[9]

John Dewey expressed similar concerns near the end of his long career thirty-five years earlier: "Many of the newer schools tend to make little or nothing of organized subject matter of study, to proceed as if any form of direction and guidance by adults were an invasion of individual freedom."[10]

Above all, many of the parents and teachers who participated in alternative schools were too caught up in the times to provide effective leadership. The close adult communities that developed around most alternative schools were deeply important to the participants' lives. However, though idealistic and well-meaning, these alternative communities did not always provide a stable environment for education. For the parents and teachers, alternative schools became a focus for more than schooling, often acting as an expression of their own longings for political action, personal exploration, social connection, and community. They were busy sorting out their own lives. In the end, the educational goals were sometimes not a priority.

---

8   Michael Lerner describes a similar "cult of anti-leadership" in 1960s political organizations in "The Legacy of the Sixties for the Politics of the Nineties," *Tikkun*, January 1988.

9   Jonathan Kozol, *Free Schools* (Boston: Houghton Miflin, 1972), 31, 61.

10   John Dewey, *Experience and Education* (New York: Macmillan, 1938), 22.

THE 1960s

Ideas and values of the 1960s had a profound effect on the development of alternative schools. Following a period of optimism and reform in the early part of the decade, the late 1960s were characterized by a deepening radicalism that included increased protest of the Vietnam War and the emergence of the counterculture and alternative lifestyles. But eventually many activists realized that it was too difficult to challenge established mainstream politics and culture and that their hopes for revolution had been unrealistic. A few 1960s ideals remained alive into the 1970s and beyond, gaining widespread acceptance. These ideals found their way into the feminist, environmental, and human potential movements. Meanwhile, however, the more extreme activists remained outside mainstream culture.[11]

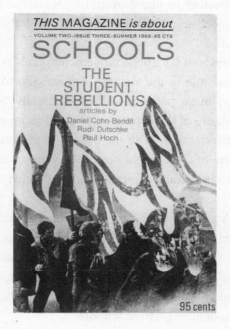

The alternative schools movement was partly a reflection of wider social activism during the 1960s. Cover of *This Magazine is about Schools*, Volume 2, Issue 3, Summer 1968

11   My conceptualization of these three alternative school stages roughly parallels the political developments described by historians Edward Morgan, *The Sixties Experience* (Philadelphia: Temple University Press, 1991); Kirkpatrick Sale, *SDS* (New York: Random House, 1973); and Richard Flacks, *Youth and Social Change* (Chicago: Rand McNally, 1971).

The life cycle of the alternative school movement was remarkably parallel to the social, cultural, and political shifts of the 1960s. Alternative schools in British Columbia began as moderate, reformist, Progressive enterprises. But by the late 1960s, most had adopted a Romantic and laissez-faire ideology, extending almost complete freedom to the children. These groups sometimes looked and behaved more like communes than schools and had political objectives ranging far beyond education. By the 1970s, however, the goals of alternative schools became more pragmatic, focusing on transmitting basic skills to discouraged teenagers and supporting marginal families in poor communities. Eventually almost all alternative schools still in operation joined the public school system. One weakness of many 1960s movements was that participants were reluctant to develop sufficient analysis to serve as a guide for action, for fear of being too intellectual or elitist. Activists neglected to create realistic and achievable objectives. The same could be said about the alternative schools movement.

The political ideals of the 1960s movements, such as peace and equality, played a central role in the visions of those who founded alternative schools. However, these political values eventually became overshadowed by the popularity of the counterculture and its emphasis on freedom and personal transformation. With the default to personal freedom as the ultimate goal, some of the original collective values were lost. This shift from communal to individual aspirations also affected the goals of alternative schools.

Many 1960s ideas and values were brought to Canada by the thousands of young Americans escaping the Vietnam War. They exemplified the political idealism and optimism of the 1960s. American ideas and individuals played a significant role in the alternative schools movement, as they did in Canadian society, and many American exiles became parents or teachers at Canadian alternative schools.

But the American participation was only part of the story. The American counterculture and emphasis on individual freedom was combined with Canadian democratic socialist traditions represented by individuals who had been active in the CCF/NDP, labour unions, co-operative enterprises, or religious organizations devoted to peace and humanitarian social action, often referred to as the Social Gospel. The rich diversity of British Columbia alternative schools was due to all of these influences.

LEGACY

The most enduring legacy of alternative schools was the adoption of many of their values and practices by the mainstream school system. By 1975 public schools had become less rigid, more imaginative in their teaching methods, and more accommodating of individual student needs and learning styles. Public school districts began to offer students and parents a wide range of choices including a myriad of alternative programs. Some of these alternatives were rehabilitative or practical, focusing on teaching basic academic and life skills. Others were informed by more innovative educational goals such as individualized learning and progress, an integrated curriculum, project research, and co-operative learning. Students were encouraged to follow their own interests, resulting in a deeper involvement in their education.

Cooperative, unstructured, and child-centred learning, pictured here at the New School, are now commonplace in the public school system.
1970 Photo courtesy of Daphne Harwood

The rapid development of alternatives in the public school system was due to a combination of factors: parental demand, new directions in the teaching profession, increased agency of students, leadership of liberal administrators and school trustees, and the ambience of the times. Parents were no longer willing to leave all the educational decisions regarding their children to school officials. Many teachers were excited by new humanistic and child-centred ideas about education. A significant number of high school students refused to accept authoritarian schools that left them feeling bored and marginalized. Public school officials recognized that a serious need existed and soon responded.

The small independent alternative schools that proliferated from 1960 to 1975 began as an attempt by groups of activist parents to create more humanistic and child-centred schools for their own children. Although many of these schools did not survive for the long term, they played a crucial role in demonstrating what was possible and, through their example, inspiring an avalanche of educational change by the middle of the 1970s.

Vancouver Sun columnist Bob Hunter wrote in 1969 that the alternative schools of the 1960s "have obviously had considerable influence. Something is happening in the public schools—a heightened awareness, a greater sensitivity on the part of the teachers. There appears to be considerably less repression and somewhat less authoritarianism than there used to be."[12] William Stavdal, education writer and former British Columbia Department of Education official, writing almost thirty years later, agreed: "It was beyond question a response to pressure from all sides for a more innovative kind of education. Everything was in ferment, everything was being questioned. Much that is occurring in today's education system can be traced to the challenges thrown up by the alternative schools of the sixties."[13] The pioneering example of independent alternative schools between 1960 and 1975 inspired educational change. These schools were a catalyst for the creation of more choice in public education and for the development of a more open, flexible and inclusive public school system.

---

12   Bob Hunter, *Vancouver Sun*, September 5, 1969, 19.
13   William Stavdal, letter to the author, March 29, 1997. Mr. Stavdal served as executive assistant to Deputy Education Minister Jim Carter for over ten years during the 1980s. He was also a parent at Craigdarroch School.

Bibliography

PRIMARY SOURCES: PRIVATE ARCHIVES AND DOCUMENT COLLECTIONS

ARGENTA FRIENDS SCHOOL ARCHIVE

Documents 1959–1982, belonging to the Argenta Friends Meeting and the family of John and Helen Stevenson. Photocopies in the possession of the author.

> Stevenson, Helen. "We're in This Together." Unpublished manuscript, 1993
> School publications: *The Whittler*, 1959–1962; *Stopped Press*, 1976–1980
> School Prospecti 1960, 1964, 1969, 1972, 1976
> Discipline for Argenta (school constitution)
> Philosophical statements, enrolment and staff lists, Staff and School Committee minutes, letters to parents and supporters, annual teacher reports, school newsletters, student handbooks, Staff Handbook, School Study, 1958, financial statements, teacher applications, Friends Meeting minutes

SATURNA ISLAND FREE SCHOOL ARCHIVE

Documents 1968–1971, donated to the author by the school's founder Tom Durrie.

> School prospecti, "Saturna Island Free School," 1968
> Prospectus, "Learning how to live; Learning how to learn," Free School Press, 1969
> Lynn Curtis, ed. *Free School: The Journal of Change in Education* (Saturna Island, BC: Free School Press, 1970); articles by Jim Harding, Brian Carpendale, and Paul Goodman
> Letters to and from parents, student files and applications, Tom Durrie lecture file 1968/9, requests to visit, 1969, correspondence about students, legal correspondence, Society papers, general correspondence 1968–1971, Health Department correspondence, 1969

WINDSOR HOUSE SCHOOL ARCHIVE

Documents 1971–2019, North Vancouver School District. Photocopies in the possession of the author.

> Hughes, Helen. "Windsor House: A History." Unpublished paper for Jean Barman, Educational Studies 426, circa 1984
>
> "What Windsor House Is All About," daycare funding brief, October 1973
>
> Windsor House School: A Report, June 1976
>
> An Interim Report: Windsor House, North Vancouver School District, February 1977
>
> Dr. Ray Williams, "Windsor House School: A Report," April 1975
>
> "25 Years of Windsor House History," 1971–1996
>
> Ray Williams, "Private Alternatives and the School System," brief to trustees, 1975
>
> Windsor House parents, "A Brief on Alternatives in Education," to North Vancouver school trustees, April 1975 (letter, Ms. Bratkowski)
>
> Enrolment lists, 1971 to the present; student records, 1972–1974; Parents' Handbook; day plans and curricula; papers on problem-solving; parent list, parent meetings; school meetings, minutes, newsletters; Helen Hughes, personal statements; operating budget, 1971/72

VALLICAN WHOLE SCHOOL ARCHIVE

Documents 1973 to the present, located in the Vallican Whole School, Vallican, British Columbia.

> Enrolment and staff lists, 1975–1980; school timetable, 1973; curricula, course outlines; papers of the Vallican Whole Community Centre; correspondence with the Nelson School Board; school meetings, minutes, and administration papers

CRAIGDARROCH SCHOOL DOCUMENT COLLECTION

William Stavdal and Carmen Stavdal document collection, 1966-1969, Victoria, loaned to the author by William Stavdal. Photocopies in possession of the author.

> Student reports; discussion papers of David Hummel; school prospecti, 1966, 1967; Board meeting minutes, 1968

Student reports belonging to Lori Williams, 1967–1969, in possession of the author.

New School Document Collections

Norman Levi document collection, 1962–1968, in the possession of the author.
Constitution and certification of incorporation: The New School, 1962,
revised 1964; The New School Teachers Society, 1968
Annual reports and financial statements, 1964–1972
New School Teachers Society, minutes, 1969–1986
New School Prospectus, 1962, 1963, 1964, 1972;
School enrolment lists, 1962/63, 1964/65, 1965/66
Staff lists, 1962–1966; philosophical papers written by members; curriculum, admissions, planning, and special committee reports; personal letters among members; newsletters, 1965/66; Director's Report, 1967/68; hiring papers; application form

Norman Epstein document collection, 1962–1966, in the possession of the author.
Finance Committee records, budgets, expenses, tuition scales; philosophical papers written by members; school newsletters; minutes of board meetings; Personnel Committee notes, minutes, reports; personal letters among members; hiring papers, 1964

Phil Thomas document collection, 1964/65, in the possession of the author.
Phil Thomas, personal correspondence, 1964/65
Teachers' Annual Report: Mr. Arntzen, Ms. Beck; Mr. Thomas, Ms. Gray
Student report cards: Mr. Arntzen, Ms. Gaba, Ms. Beagle
Correspondence, 1964/65; curriculum and philosophical papers; Committee minutes, 1964/65; newsletters, 1964/65; Prospecti, 1962, 1964

Sharon Van Volkingburgh document collection and Nora Randall document collection, 1969–1977, in the possession of the author.
Staff meeting minutes; student applications and records; newsletters, 1969–1977; curriculum papers; grant applications; building improvements; tuition scale; enrolment class list, 1969/70; funding proposal to Eileen Dailly

Photographs
Photographs loaned to the author by Daphne Harwood, Margot Hansen, Joan Nemtim, and Nora Randall

Photograph by Daniel Wood, in *Vancouver Sun*, July 8, 1972, 41.

Personal Journals
>   Julia Brown, excerpts from personal journal, 1962–1965
>   Mary Schendlinger, excerpts from personal journal, 1975–1977
>   Daniel Wood, excerpts from personal journal, 1971–1973

Total Education School Document Collection

Peter Seixas document collection, 1972–1980, donated to the author.
>   Vancouver Society for Total Education, Annual Report, 1972/73
>   Vancouver Society for Total Education Evaluation, 1975/76
>   Vancouver Society for Total Education, Curriculum Report, June 1974
>   "The Energy of Youth," Evaluation Report, LEAP program, 1974
>   Total Education yearbooks, 1974/75, 1979/80
>   Staff meeting minutes; school group evaluations; LEAP reports, 1973,
>   1974; course outlines; administrative papers, timetables, staffing; papers
>   relating to the farm, 1972–1976

Phil Knaiger, excerpts from personal journal, 1972–1975

Photographs on Vancouver School Board website: Archives and Heritage.

Ideal School Document Collection

Hugh Barr document collection, 1972–1976, in the possession of the author.
>   Ideal staff, "The Case for a Separate Facility for Ideal School," 1976
>   Prospectus, September 1972; staff list, 1972/73; letters from Garry Nixon to
>   parents; financial reports; enrolment lists, 1972–1975

Alan Best document collection, 1972–1974, in possession of the author.

Floating School Document Collection

Newsletters, 1969

Greenhouse School Document Collection

Carrie Shapiro Greschner, documents 1970-1973, donated to the author.
>   Prospectus and Philosophy; course descriptions; staff; tuition schedule

Saturday School Document Collection

>   The Saturday School: How It Began
>   Prospectus and Philosophy

Primary Sources: Public Documents

National Archives of Canada, Ottawa

Documents of the Company of Young Canadians regarding Barker Free School and Knowplace School, 1967–1969, Record Group 116, Volume 142, File 884.
Barker School Prospectus, 1968; Bob Barker, personal resume; CYC Project Application; Bob Barker, UNRRA Application (1945); Summerhill Society, Statement of Policy; Barker School correspondence; Barker School Operating Report; Bob Barker, Report to Parents

Correspondence among CYC staff, Vancouver and Ottawa; CYC funding applications; evaluation reports; financial statements; School Prospectus, 1968; memoranda; Vancouver Youth Project reports

Vancouver School District Documents, Vancouver Archives

Vancouver School Board (VSB) meeting minutes, 1966–1976
VSB Education Committee, minutes, 1966–1976
VSB, annual reports, 1966–1976

Registrar of Companies, Victoria

Incorporation documents, annual reports, financial statements for:
New School Society, 1962
New School Teacher's Society, 1968
Craigdarroch School Society, 1966
Society for Total Education, 1970
Ideal School Society, 1972
Rural Alternatives Research and Training Society, 1973
Waldorf School Society, 1969
Warehouse School Society, 1973
Relevant School Society, 1971
Saturna Island Free School—Community Projects Ltd., 1968

Department of Human Resources

Department of Human Resources documents: Alternative Schools Programs official reports, funding recommendations, and departmental correspondence, 1974–1975 (including letter from Ms. Morrice, 1975).

GOVERNMENT-COMMISSIONED AND OTHER REPORTS

British Columbia Teachers' Federation. *Involvement: The Key to Better Schools*. Vancouver: BCTF, 1968.

British Columbia Teachers' Federation. *Essential Educational Experiences*. 1977.

British Columbia Teachers' Federation. *Public Choice, Public Schools*. 1996.

Chant, S. N. F., J.E. Liersch, and R.P. Walrod. *Report of the Royal Commission on Education*. Victoria, BC: Government of BC, 1960.

Hall-Dennis Report. *Living and Learning*. Toronto: Government of Ontario, 1968.

Kirsh, Sharon, Roger Simon, and Malcolm Levin, eds. *Directory of Canadian Alternative and Innovative Education*. Toronto: Communitas Exchange, OISE, 1973.

Leslie, Susan, Jane Rosettis, and David Kaufman. *Total Education: An Evaluation*. Vancouver: Educational Research Institute of British Columbia; Victoria: Departments of Education and Human Resources, May 1974.

Middleton, M. A. *An Evaluation of Ideal School, 1974–75*. Research report 75–22. Vancouver: Vancouver Board of School Trustees, November 1975.

Putman, J. H., and G. M. Weir. *Survey of the School System*. Victoria: King's Printer, 1925.

Yip, Douglas. *SEED: A Preliminary Report*. Toronto: Board of Education, March 1971.

PRIMARY SOURCES: NEWSPAPER ARTICLES AND LETTERS

NEW SCHOOL

"Four Profs Plan Own School," *Vancouver Sun*, February 7, 1961, 1.

"New School Bases Fees on Income," *Vancouver Sun*, March 29, 1961, 12.

"City Progressive School Waives Rules," *Vancouver Sun*, September 10, 1962, 11.

"Exams Passé for Children at New School," *Vancouver Province*, June 12, 1963, 17.

"School Hires Boss," *Vancouver Sun*, June 22, 1965, 9.

"Conservative England Liberal in Education," *Vancouver Sun*, July 8, 1965, 38.

"No Exams, Reports at New School," *Vancouver Sun*, April 26, 1966, 27.

"It's Recess All Day at Vancouver's New School" *Vancouver Sun*, May 12, 1967, 14.

"Far-Out School to Be More Free," *Vancouver Sun*, August 17, 1967, 20.

"Free School Surge Called Spontaneous Development," *Vancouver Sun*, December 28, 1967, 16.

"Freedom Itself Not Enough," *Vancouver Sun*, December 28, 1967, 16.

"Free Schools Swap Ideas," *Vancouver Province*, December 29, 1967, 6.

"Boss System Hard to Shake Says Free School Teacher, *Vancouver Sun*, December 29, 1967, 13.

"Public Schools Turning Out Slaves or Rebels," *Vancouver Sun*, December 30, 1967, 13

"Free School Head Asks for Apology," *Vancouver Sun*, February 8, 1968, 11.

"MLA Erred," letter, *Vancouver Sun*, February 14, 1968, 5.

"Parents Split School, Disagree with Methods," *Vancouver Sun*, June 1, 1968, 7.

"We Took 24 Kids 1,500 Miles across BC," *Vancouver Sun*, July 8, 1972, 41.

"Students Do the Talking at New School," *Vancouver Province*, October 4, 1972, 41.

"Day Care Group Sues," *Vancouver Sun*, March 25, 1974, 70.

"Arsonist Burns School," *Vancouver Province*, June 11, 1975, 7.

"Public Invited to New School," *Vancouver Sun*, April 30, 1976, 30.

"Vandal-Damaged School Struggling to Survive," *Vancouver Sun*, March 15, 1976, 25.

"New School Changes View of Education," letter to the editor from Ms. Piltz, *Vancouver Sun*, March 23, 1976, 5.

CRAIGDARROCH SCHOOL

"Independent School Will Teach by New Methods," *Daily Colonist*, August 6, 1966.

"School Seeks Atmosphere of Freedom," *Daily Colonist*, August 10, 1966, 5.

"New School Accents Joy of Learning," *Victoria Daily Times*, May 2, 1967, 23.

"School Experiment in Freedom," *Victoria Daily Times*, June 1, 1967, 31.

"Craigdarroch Booked Solid for Second Term," *Victoria Daily Times*, August 25, 1967, 17.

"Progressive School Classes Full," *Daily Colonist*, August 25, 1967.

"Progressive System Used in New School," *Victoria Daily Times*, January 19, 1968, 19.

"Private School Expands Society," *Victoria Daily Times*, January 31, 1968, 35.

"She Thrives on Freedom," *Daily Colonist*, June 9, 1968, 5.

"Self-Disciplined Pupils or Ill-Mannered Brats?" *Daily Colonist*, June 9, 1968, 23.

"Free Education Brought to End by Money Woes," *Daily Colonist*, December 18, 1969, 15.

Barker Free School and Knowplace

"The Barker School," *County Citizen* (New City, NY), January 10, 1963, 5.
"This Is School?" *Vancouver Times*, June 7, 1965, 13.
"Students at Free School Just Don't Want to Quit," *Citizen* (North Vancouver), January 12, 1967, 1.
"Tell CYC to Go, Says Socred," *Vancouver Sun*, February 7, 1967, 14.
"Knowplace: An Answer to Boredom," *Vancouver Province*, October 14, 1967.
"22 Disgruntled Students Open Their Own School," *Vancouver Sun*, December 16, 1967, 33.
"Knowplace School Okay, According to Peterson," *Vancouver Province*, December 20, 1967, 14.
"Knowplace to Go?" editorial, *Vancouver Sun*, December 27, 1967, 4.
"School Never Like This," *Vancouver Province*, February 14, 1968, 21.
"Money Aid Denied," *Vancouver Sun*, March 18, 1968, 56.
"Column, Bob Hunter," *Vancouver Sun*, September 5, 1969, 19.

Saturna Island Free School

"Curriculum Unwanted," *Daily Colonist*, August 4, 1968, 25.
"Salt Air, Forest, Seashore, Saturna Free School Riches," *Daily Colonist*, September 22, 1968, 25.
"Health Inspector Visits School," *Victoria Daily Times*, May 14, 1969, 11.
"Free School Warned about Health Threat," *Daily Colonist*, May 14, 1969, 30.
"Meet Standards or Close Down" *Victoria Daily Times*, May 14, 1969, 4.
"Threat of Closure Haunts Free School," *Vancouver Province*, May 15, 1969, 22.
"Health Standards Now Met, Says Free School Head," *Vancouver Province*, May 23, 1969, 12.
"Head Hints Persecution," *Vancouver Sun*, May 23, 1969, 2.
"Free Schools Doomed," *Victoria Daily Times*, May 29, 1969, 23.
"Health Chief Hints Free Schools Doomed," *Victoria Daily Times*, May 29, 1969, 23.
"… And Suddenly the Clouds Gathered," *Victoria Daily Times*, May 30, 1969, 9.
"Free School Cleanup Extended," *Victoria Daily Times*, June 11, 1969, 41.
"Free School Conditions Set," *Vancouver Province*, June 12, 1969, 51.
"School Running Despite Decree," *Victoria Daily Times*, June 14, 1969, 2.
"Two Views on School," *Victoria Daily Times*, June 24, 1969, 5.
"Order Disputed," *Victoria Daily Times*, August 1, 1969, 19.
"Let Children Decide," *Daily Colonist*, August 7, 1969, 23.
"Artificial School Environment Avoided," *Victoria Daily Times*, August 7, 1969, 16.

"Red Tape in Schoolhouse," *Victoria Daily Times*, August 8, 1969, 4.

"No Closure Yet," *Victoria Daily Times*, August 23, 1969, 12.

"School Opening on Schedule," *Daily Colonist*, August 28, 1969, 40.

"Controversial School Enrols 20 Students," *Vancouver Province*, September 11, 1969, 17

"Informal Learning Best Way," *Vancouver Sun*, November 24, 1969, 18.

"Kripps Attacks Free School" *Victoria Daily Times*, April 17, 1970, 17.

"School Workshop Marathon Set," *Victoria Daily Times*, June 27, 1970, 12.

"School Completes Year," *Victoria Daily Times*, June 27, 1970, 12.

"Free School Head Plans Nation Tour," *Victoria Daily Times*, January 29, 1971, 35.

"Did Signal Tip-Off School?" *Victoria Daily Times*, September 27, 1972, 1.

"RCMP Agent at School," *Victoria Daily Times*, September 28, 1972, 1.

"Wall of Silence Surrounds Closing Free School," *Daily Colonist*, September 28, 1971, 1.

"Saturna Free School Wins Court Round," *Daily Colonist*, January 22, 1972, 1.

"School Fate Weighed," *Daily Colonist*, September 29, 1972, 26.

"Free School Closure Sticks," *Daily Colonist*, October 18, 1972, 19.

"Free School Loses Appeal," *Victoria Daily Times*, October 18, 1972, 33.

TOTAL EDUCATION

"Dropout School Just Too Popular," *Vancouver Province*, February 5, 1972, 15.

"Teachers Flock to School That Offers Life of Poverty," *Vancouver Sun*, June 14, 1972, 84.

"This School Looks for Bored Students," *Vancouver Province*, June 21, 1972, 10.

"Some Alternatives to a World of Endless Defeat," *Vancouver Sun*, June 20, 1974, 47.

"Students and Teachers Plan Alternative Education," *Mount Pleasant Mouthpiece*, March 12, 1975, 6.

"Everything's an Adventure," *Vancouver Sun*, November 27, 1976, 43.

IDEAL SCHOOL AND RELEVANT HIGH

"Dawson School to Be Reopened," *Vancouver Sun*, August 22, 1974, 41.

"An Ideal Is Adopted at Last," *Vancouver Sun*, September 7, 1974, 44.

"Ideal School Students Unjustly Treated," letter, *Vancouver Sun*, December 15, 1976, 5.

"Parent Feels Betrayed by School Relocation," letter to the editor from Dr. Stephenson, *Vancouver Sun*, December 15, 1976, 5.

"Students Mount Final Protest Over New Home," *Vancouver Sun*, January 4, 1977, 2.

"Situation is Less Than Ideal for Displaced Students," *Vancouver Sun*, January 7, 1977, 28.

"Ideal School Move to Byng Changed to Six-Month Test," *Vancouver Sun*, January 8, 1977, 12.

"New Downtown High School to Use Community Resources," *Vancouver Sun*, June 29, 1970, 27.

"Turning on—without Drugs," *Vancouver Province*, June 24, 1970.

"New School Teaches 'Four Rs,'" *Vancouver Province*, September 30, 1970.

"Classroom Tradition Challenged," *Vancouver Sun*, August 23, 1971, 2.

"The Best Way to Build a Barn Is in French," *Vancouver Sun*, September 2, 1971, 13.

"Ideal School Undermined," Ms. Williams, Vancouver Sun, January 6, 1977, 5.

Vallican Whole School

"Farm Communes Thriving in Flowery Slocan Country," *Vancouver Sun*, August 6, 1971.

"Urban Refugees Will Learn Rural Skills," *Nelson Daily News*, July 8, 1971, 2.

"Hippies, Deserters Cause Real Problems," *Vancouver Sun*, February 10, 1972, 12.

"Hippies, Nudies, and Hole in the Ground," *Vancouver Sun*, February 18, 1972, 11.

"Board Defers Action," *Nelson Daily News*, March 27, 1973, 2.

"Free Schools Meet Heavy Opposition," "Parents Desire Educational Choice," *Kootenay Miner*, March 29, 1973, 4.

"No Decision Yet on Free School," *Nelson Daily News*, April 4, 1973, 2.

"Unrest Sweeps Valley," *Nelson Daily News*, June 22, 1973.

"Freaks along the Slocan," *Vancouver Sun*, July 12, 1973, 37.

"Free School Starts Out in Bind," *Vancouver Sun*, November 9, 1973, 31.

"Public Funds to Be Denied," *Vancouver Sun*, September 27, 1973, 39.

Windsor House

"Parents Play Key Role in Private Education System," *The Citizen*, September 1972.

"School Tries Experiment," *The Citizen*, April 1974.

Sundance and Warehouse Schools

"Sundance: An Experiment in Self-Responsibility," *Daily Colonist*, September 30, 1973, 19.

"Even Small Babies Look to Sundance," *Victoria Daily Times*, June 1, 1974, 27.

"Report on Sundance 'Cloud Nine Thing,'" *Victoria Daily Times*, July 15, 1975, 13.

"Study Knocks Record System at Sundance," *Victoria Daily Times*, October 23, 1975, 13.

"Sundance Would Get A+, if It Gave Grades," *Victoria Daily Times*, October 24, 1975, 17.

"Sundance, Sentinel, Happy Structures on a Two-Way Street," *Daily Colonist*, October 24, 1975, 11.

"Education on a Shoestring," *Victoria Daily Times*, November 3, 1973, 29.

"Warehouse School That Works Seeking New Home," *Victoria Daily Times*, May 3, 1975, 37.

"Warehouse of Knowledge," *Daily Colonist*, February 15, 1976, 51.

VANCOUVER TRUSTEE ELECTIONS

"City Voters Add an Olive to School Board Recipe," *Vancouver Sun*, December 10, 1970, 23.

"TEAM dominate Trustee Contest," *Vancouver Sun*, December 14, 1972, 53.

"New TEAM School Board Open to Outside Ideas," *Vancouver Province*, December 15, 1972, 7.

"Reformers Control the School Board," *Vancouver Sun*, January 9, 1973.

OTHER SCHOOLS AND MISCELLANEOUS

"28 Students Off to Superschool," *Globe and Mail*, September 3, 1968.

"Parents Hope to Organize Low-Cost Free School in City," *Vancouver Sun*, February 18, 1971, 28.

"Parents' Views on Education Lean to Free School Lines," *Vancouver Province*, April 12, 1973, 6.

"Vancouver Offers Alternatives in Schooling," *Vancouver Sun*, February 22, 1974, 16.

"New System of Schools Big Success," *Daily Colonist*, June 21, 1974, 21.

"Alternatives in Trouble," *Victoria Daily Times*, August 15, 1975, 17.

"Alternative Schools Have Identity Crisis," *Vancouver Sun*, June 1, 1977.

"City's School System Eyes New Approach to Learning," *Vancouver Sun*, July 24, 1971, 16.

"Would You Goof Off in School Now?" *Vancouver Sun*, October 2, 1971, 32.

"Every Block Is Their Blackboard," *Vancouver Province*, 1975.

Primary Sources: Photographs

Selected photos by Dan Scott, Bill Cunningham, Dave Buchan, Charles Steele, Ralph Bower, Gordon Sedawie, Glenn Baglo, Mark van Manen, Ken Oakes, Brian Kent, George Diack, Ian Lindsay, and Powell Hargrave.

Primary Sources: Personal Interviews

In-person or telephone interviews conducted and recorded by Harley Rothstein between 1987 and 1999 and in 2015:

Argenta Friends School

Jonathan Aldrich, teacher; Brenda Berck, teacher; Ruth Boyd, parent; Phillip Carpendale, student; Charles Dyson, student; Jonathan Gregory, student; David Herbison, student; Hugh Herbison, teacher; Mary Holland, student, teacher; Pat Lawson, student; Judy Malek, student; Carolyn Mamchur, parent; Mickey Mamchur, student; Beth Martin, student; Erica Pfister, student; Dan Phelps, teacher; Jan Phelps, teacher; Lynn Phillips, teacher; Michael Phillips, teacher; Dick Pollard, student; Betty Polster, teacher; Arnold Porter, teacher; Barbara Pratt, student; Ann Rush, parent; John Rush, parent; Donna Sassaman, teacher; David Stevenson, student; Helen Stevenson, teacher; John Stevenson, teacher; Paul Tillotson, student; Ed Washington, student, teacher; Jack Wells, student; Polly Wilson, student; Mary Winder, student, teacher; Ruth Wolfe, parent

Barker Free School

Bob Barker, teacher; Kate Barlow, teacher; Galen Bellman, student; Cathleen Bertelsen, student; Mona Bertelsen, parent; Susan Bertelsen, student; Tony Bertelsen, student; Marilyn Carson, teacher; Michael Carson, student; Jan Fraser, teacher; Dan Jason, teacher; Rhody Lake, parent; Laura Landsberg, student; Gordon Yearsley, teacher; Kim Maclean, student; Robin Maclean, student; Shirley Maclean, parent; Wendy Maclean, student; Dave Manning, teacher; Marc McDougall, student; Jason Ridgeway, student; Kita Ridgeway, parent; Jennifer Tipper, student; Ray Valentine, student; Sharon Wiseman, teacher; Monica Yard, student

City School

Starla Anderson, teacher; Steven Drake, student; Thom Hansen, teacher; Daryl Sturdy, teacher

CRAIGDARROCH SCHOOL

Simon Andrews, teacher; Diane Brown, student; Bett Bugslag, teacher; Bernd Carrosseld, student; Betty Clark, parent; Beth Dickman, parent; John Dickman, parent; Ann Gregory, parent; Charles Gregory, parent; Jonathan Gregory, student; David Hummel, parent; Michael Hummel, student; Patricia Hummel, parent; Jesse Hyder, teacher; Mary Jamieson, teacher; Judith Koltai, parent; Tom Koltai, student; Kate McIntosh, student; Andy Mikita, advisor; Leah Muhleman, parent; Joan Ormondroyd, teacher; Ursula Peavy, student;
Vance Peavy, parent; Peter Schmidt, student; Claire Schwartz, student; Gordon Schwartz, student; Bill Stavdal, parent; Carmen Stavdal, student; Barbara Williams, teacher; Lori Williams, student; Phillip Williams, parent

FLOATING FREE SCHOOL

Don Babcock, parent; Garth Babcock, student; Tony Bertelsen, student; Jeremy Carpendale, student; Erica Dancer, student; Dave Manning, teacher; Thane Poole, student; Peter Vogel, student

IDEAL SCHOOL

Hugh Barr, teacher; Alan Best, student; Charles Campbell, student; Jono Drake, student; David Eaton, student; Meghan Ellis, student; Erin Harris, student; Meghan Hughes, student; Phil Knaiger, teacher; Laura Landsberg, student; Kim Maclean, student; Marc McDougall, student; Garry Nixon, teacher; Adelle Perry, student; Steven Pratt, student; Ken Spears, student; Barbara Stowe, student; Sandy Swanigan, student; Neil Tessler, student; Georgie Wilson, teacher; Rob Wood, teacher

KNOWPLACE SCHOOL

Bobby Barker, student; Monica Carpendale, student; John Doheny, student; Betty Griffiths, parent; Lloyd Griffiths, student; Jim Harding, teacher; Martha Jackson, student; Frances Long, student; Bob Makaroff, parent; Sonya Makaroff, student; Heather Maroney, teacher; David Orcutt, parent; Lowell Orcutt, student; Bruce Russell, student; Greg Sorbara, teacher; Ellen Tallman, parent; Karen Tallman, student; Hilda Thomas, parent; Mary Thomson, adviser; Rick Valentine, student; Peter Vogel, student; Rob Watt, teacher; Rob Wood, teacher

NEW SCHOOL

Lloyd Arntzen, teacher; Olive Balabanov, parent; Barbara Beach, parent; Mervine Beagle, teacher; Don Brown, parent; Julia Brown, parent; Don Burbidge, parent; Jim Carter, parent; Katherine Chamberlain, teacher; Charles

Christopherson, parent; Rita Cohn, parent, teacher; Gwen Creech, parent; Sandra Currie, parent; Tom Durrie, teacher; Eric Epstein, student; Marilyn Epstein, parent; Norman Epstein, parent; Aurie Felde, parent; Cara Felde, student; Elliott Gose, parent; Kathy Gose, parent; Gerry Growe, parent; Nomi Growe, parent; Barbara Hansen, teacher; Margot Hansen, student; Ron Hansen, parent; Margaret Hewitt, parent; Philip Hewitt, parent; Mark James, student; Jean Jamieson, parent; Laura Jamieson, student; Stuart Jamieson, parent; Beth Jankola, teacher; Olive Johnson, parent; Ross Johnson, parent; Jean Kamins, parent; Kiyo Kiyooka, student; Roy Kiyooka, parent; David Levi, student; Gloria Levi, parent; Norman Levi, parent; Tamar Levi, student; Anne Long, teacher; Dana Long, student; Ken McFarland, parent; Rob McFarland, student; Dewi Minden, student; Robert Minden, parent; Joan Nemtin, teacher; Hillary Nicholls, parent; Paul Nicholls, student; William Nicholls, parent; Aimee Promislow, student; Barry Promislow, parent; Nora Randall, parent; Jan Robinson, student; Phyllis Robinson, parent; Scott Robinson, student; Penny Ryan, student; David Schlendinger, parent; Karen Schlendinger, student; Mary Schlendinger, parent; Barbara Shumiatcher, parent; Cal Shumiatcher, student; Margaret Sigurgeirson, teacher; Fred Stockholder, parent; Kay Stockholder, parent; Peter Stockholder, student; Daryl Sturdy, teacher; Ellen Tallman, parent; Karen Tallman, student; Warren Tallman, parent; Hilda Thomas, parent; Phil Thomas, teacher; Alan Tolliday, parent; Elma Tolliday, parent; Jill Tolliday, student; Daphne Trivett, teacher; Sharon Van Volkingburgh, teacher; Ed Wickberg, parent; Jim Winter, parent; Else Wise, teacher; Mai Lai Wong, neighbour; Daniel Wood, teacher

North Delta Alternative School

Bruce MacDonald, teacher

Relevant High School

Erica Dancer, student; Rob Douglas, student, teacher; Grant Keays, student; Doug Smith, teacher; Neil Tessler, student

Saturna Island Free School

Anonymous, student; Jim Anderson, student; Emily Axelson, student; Lyn Bowman, teacher; Colin Browne, teacher; Lynn Curtis, teacher; Miles Durrie, student; Tom Durrie, teacher; Ron Forbes-Roberts, student; Rini House, teacher; Mary Hunt, student; Eugene Kaellis, parent; Jesse Kaellis, student; Rhoda Kaellis, parent; Tim Lucey, student; Kim Maclean, student; Mike McConnell, student; Susanne Middleditch, student; Judy Pruss, teacher; Bill Sheffeld, teacher; Kathy Sheffeld, teacher; Betty Spears, parent; David Spears, student;

Ken Spears, student; Peter Vogel, student; Dorothy Wheeler, teacher; Susie Wheeler, visitor

Sundance School

Jackie Bradley, teacher; Donna Webb, teacher

Sunshine School

Jezrah Hearne, teacher

The People School

Jan Fraser, teacher

Total Education School

Starla Anderson, teacher ; Tony Bertelsen, student; Scott Campbell, student; Doug Cochran, teacher; Liz Cochran, teacher; Jim Cruikshank, bishop, advisor; David Eaton, student; Ron Eckert, teacher; Virginia Eckert, teacher; Larry Haberlin, teacher; Charles Hill, teacher; Valerie Hodge, student; Phil Knaiger, teacher; Marc McDougall, student; Cathy Meakes, teacher; Dan Meakes, teacher; Richard Neil, teacher; Joan Nemtin, teacher; Bonnie Picard, teacher; Steven Pratt, student; Jason Ridgeway, student; Peter Seixas, teacher; Jane Shepherd, student; Annie Simmonds, teacher

Victoria Free School

Jeff Creque, student; Garth Dickman, student; Sally Kahn, student; Erica Peavy, student

Waldorf School

Colin Dutson, teacher; Elaine McKee, teacher

Warehouse School

Jacqueline Aubuchon, teacher; Veronica Doyle, teacher; Charlotte Herkel, teacher; Veronica Doyle, teacher; Glen Pope, teacher

Windsor House School

Jackie Bradley, teacher; Susan Brown, parent; Christina Cepeliauskas, student; Pam Douglass, teacher; David Elderton, student; Laura Elderton, student; Darcy Hughes, student; Helen Hughes, teacher; Meghan Hughes, student; Jenny Lawton, student; Susan Lawton, parent; Sharon Mason, parent; Ian

McNaughton, parent; John McNaughton, student; Sharon Prevette, parent; Glynis Sandall, student; Silvia Simpson, parent; Tamara Stillwell, student; Judy Stone, parent; Tanya Van Ginkel, student; Cindy Williams, parent; Katanya Woodruff, parent

Vallican Whole School

Pat Armstrong, parent; Alex Berland, teacher; Marcia Braundy, teacher; T. C. Carpendale, parent; Jeremy Carpendale, student; Phillip Carpendale, student; Caitlin de Jong, student; Jono Drake, student; Sally Drake, parent; Steven Drake, student; Tom Drake, parent; Carolyn Eaton, student; David Eaton, student; Ephraim Eisen, teacher; Bonnie Evans, teacher; Ailsha Grey, student; Freya Grey, parent; Ananda Harris, student; Erin Harris, student; Joel Harris, teacher; Marty Hykin, parent; Eric Lees, adviser; Barbara Pratt, student; James Pratt, student; Michael Pratt, parent; Steven Pratt, student; Pamela Swanigan, student; Sandy Swanigan, student; Liz Tanner, teacher; Cathy Woodward, parent; Jim Woodward, parent

School Trustees, Administrators, Cabinet Ministers

Peter Bullen, trustee, Vancouver School Board (VSB)
Don Burbidge, trustee, North Vancouver
Jim Carter, principal, Vancouver
Sally Clinton, spouse of Alf Clinton, Director of Education, Vancouver
Geoff Cue, regional director, Company of Young Canadians
Eileen Dailly, BC Minister of Education
Marilyn Epstein, BC coordinator, Special Services for Children
Elliott Gose, trustee, VSB
Olive Johnson, trustee, VSB
Norman Levi, BC Minister of Human Resources
Katherine Mirhady, trustee, VSB
Tomo Naka, principal, Nelson School District
John Uzelac, president, Vancouver Secondary Teachers' Association
John Wiens, assistant superintendent, Victoria
John Wormsbecker, assistant superintendent, Vancouver
John Young, principal, Campbell River Secondary trustee, Victoria

Other Provinces

Trustees and administrators
    Fiona Nelson, school trustee, Toronto; Dale Shuttleworth, senior administrator, Toronto

Everdale School, Hillsburgh, Ontario
Gail Ashby, teacher; Patricia Berton, student; Heather Chetwynd, student; Bob Davis, teacher; Jim Deacove, teacher; Rico Gerussi, student; Brian Iler, friend; Meredith MacFarquhar, friend; Judith McCormack, student; Naomi McCormack, student; Diana Meredith, student; Alan Rimmer, teacher; Wally Seccombe, friend; Ruth Shamai, student; Sarah Spinks, teacher; Helena Wehrstein, friend; Vera Williams, teacher

Greenhouse School, Regina
Carrie Shapiro Greschner, teacher; Eleanor Smollett, parent

Point Blank School, Toronto
George Martell, teacher; Satu Repo, teacher

Saturday School, Calgary
Robert Stamp, parent

SEED School, Toronto
Paul Shapiro, student; Murray Shukyn, teacher

Superschool, Toronto
Gail Ashby, teacher

This Magazine is about Schools, Toronto
Gail Ashby, assistant; Bob Davis, editor; George Martell, editor; Satu Repo, editor

LETTERS: TOM DURRIE AND SATURNA FAMILIES

Ms. Anderson, undated; Richard Bower, January 22, 1970; Ms. Brunner, October, 1969; Cam Dodds, August 27, 1970; Daniel Elam, October 29, 1968; Mina Fishell, April 14, 1970; Dorothy Forbes-Roberts, November 28, 1968; Julia Griffin, July 8, 1969; Patricia Henry, March 26, 1971; Ms. Hansen, January 16, 1970; Mr. Hunt, December 30, 1968; Irene Jeffery, April 16, 1969; Eugene and Rhoda Kaellis, March 25, 1968; Jesse Kaellis, April 29, 1970; Cielle Kollander, May 18, 1970; Ms. McClure, October 18, 1969; Vivian McConnell, June 1971; Joan Liknaitzky, October 8, 1969; Penny Marlatt, October 7, 1968; Danny Pelto, January 15, 1970; Marion Pelto, May 20, 1969; Mr. Powell, October 18, 1969; Ms. Proulx, December 5, 1968; Ms. Ralls, April 9, 1970; Ruth Wolfe, September 24, 1969

Secondary Sources: Books

Allen, Richard. *The Social Passion*. Toronto: University of Toronto Press, 1973.

Anastakis, Dimitry, ed. *The Sixties*. Montreal and Kingston: McGill-Queens, 2008.

Antler, Joyce. *Lucy Sprague Mitchell*. New Haven: Yale University Press, 1987.

Aronsen, Lawrence. *City of Love and Revolution: Vancouver in the Sixties*. Vancouver: New Star Books, 2010.

Ash, Maurice. *Who Are the Progressives Now?* London: Routledge, 1969.

Ashton-Warner, Sylvia. *Teacher*. New York: Simon and Schuster, 1964.

Axelrod, Paul, and J. H. Reid, eds. *Youth, University and Canadian Society*. Kingston: McGill-Queen's, 1989.

Barman, Jean. *Growing Up British in British Columbia: Boys in Private School*. Vancouver: UBC Press, 1984.

———. *The West beyond the West*. Toronto: University of Toronto Press, 1991.

———. *Exploring Vancouver's Past*. Vancouver: Centennial Commission, 1984.

Barrow, Robin. *Radical Education: A Critique of Freeschooling and Deschooling*. London: Martin Robertson, 1978.

Bascia, Nina, Esther Sokolov Fine, and Malcolm Levin, eds. *Alternative Schooling and Student Engagement: Canadian Stories of Democracy within Bureaucracy*. New York: Palgrave Macmillan, 2017.

Berman, Claudia. *The School around Us*. Kennebunkport, ME: School Around Us Press, 1993.

Bonham-Carter, Victor. *Dartington Hall*. London: Phoenix House, 1958.

Bowering, George. *Bowering's BC: A Swashbuckling History*. Toronto: Viking, 1996.

Braunstein, Peter, and Michael William Doyle. *Imagine Nation: The American Counterculture of the 1960s and 70s*. New York: Routledge, 2002.

Bremer, John and Michael von Moschzisker, *The School without Walls*. New York: Holt, Rinehart and Winston, 1971.

Brown, Justine. *All Possible Worlds: Utopian Experiments in British Columbia*. Vancouver: New Star Books, 1995.

Burton, Anthony. *The Horn and the Beanstalk*. Toronto: Holt, Rinehart, and Winston, 1972.

Byrne, Niall, and Jack Quarter, eds. *Must Schools Fail? The Growing Debate in Canadian Education*. Toronto: McClelland and Stewart, 1972.

Campbell, Laura, Dominique Clément, and Gregory S. Kealey, eds. *Debating Dissent: Canada and the Sixties*. Toronto: University of Toronto Press, 2012.

Carbone, Peter. *The Social and Educational Thought of Harold Rugg*. Durham: Duke University Press, 1977.

Carr, John, Jean Grambs, and E. G. Campbell, eds. *Pygmalion or Frankenstein: Alternative Schooling in American Education*. New York: Addison Wesley, 1977.

Chalmers, David. *And the Crooked Places Made Straight*. Baltimore: Johns Hopkins, 1991.

Chamberlain, Chuck, ed. *Don't Tell Us It Can't Be Done!* Toronto: Our Schools/ Our Selves, 1994.

Christou Theodore. *Progressive Education: Revisioning and Reframing Ontario's Public Schools, 1919–1942*. Toronto: University of Toronto Press, 2012.

Clark, Ronald. *The Life of Bertrand Russell*. London: J. Cape, 1975.

Clifford, Geraldine Joncich. *The Sane Positivist*. Middletown: Wesleyan University Press, 1968.

Cohen, Ronald, and Raymond Mohl. *The Paradox of Progressive Education*. Port Washington, NY: Kennikat, 1979.

Conley, Brenda. *Alternative Schools: A Reference Handbook.* Santa Barbara, ABC-CLIO, 2002.

Counts, George. *Dare the School Build a New Social Order?* New York: John Day, 1932.

Cremin, Lawrence. *The Transformation of the School: Progressivism in American Education, 1876–1957*. New York: Random House, 1961.

——. *American Education: The Metropolitan Experience*. New York: Harper & Row, 1988.

Croall, Jonathan. *Neill of Summerhill*. New York: Pantheon, 1983.

Cuban, Larry. *How Teachers Taught*. New York: Longman, 1984.

Curry, W. B. *The School and a Changing Civiization*. London: John Lane Bodley Head, 1934.

Darwin, Erasmus. *A Plan for the Conduct of Female Education in Boarding Schools*. London, 1797.

Davis, Bob. *What Our High Schools Could Be: A Teacher's Reflections from the 60s to the 90s*. Toronto: Our Schools/Our Selves, 1990.

Day, Thomas. *History of Sanford and Merton*. London: 1786.

De Lima, Agnes. *The Little Red School House*. New York: Macmillan, 1948.

Deal, Terrence, and Robert Nolan, eds. *Alternative Schools: Ideologies, Realities, Guidelines*. Chicago: Nelson-Hall, 1978.

Dennison, George. *The Lives of Children*. New York: Random House, 1969.

Dewey, John. *School and Society*. Chicago: University of Chicago Press, 1899.

————. *The Child and the Curriculum*. Chicago: University of Chicago Press, 1902.

————. *Democracy and Education*. New York: Macmillan, 1916.

————. *Education and the Social Order*. New York, 1934.

————. *Experience and Education*. New York: Macmillan, 1938.

————, and Evelyn Dewey. *Schools of Tomorrow*. New York: Dutton, 1915.

Dickie, Donalda. *The Enterprise in Theory and Practice*. Toronto: Gage, 1940.

Dickstein, Morris. *Gates of Eden: American Culture in the Sixties*. New York: Basic, 1977.

Duke, Daniel. *The Retransformation of the School*. New York: Nelson Hall, 1978.

Edgeworth, Richard and Maria. *Essays on Practical Education*. London, 1822.

Elizabeth Cleaners Street School. *Starting Your Own High School*. New York: Vintage, 1972.

Farber, David, and Beth Bailey, eds. *The Columbia Guide to America in the 1960s*. New York: Columbia University Press, 2001.

Featherstone, Joseph. *Schools Where Children Learn*. New York: Liveright, 1971.

Ferguson, Marilyn. *The Aquarian Conspiracy*. Los Angeles: Tarcher, 1980.

Fetherling, Douglas. *Travels by Night: A Memoir of the Sixties*. Toronto: Lester, 1994.

Flacks, Richard. *Youth and Social Change*. Chicago: Rand McNally, 1971.

Freinet, Celestin. *Co-operative Learning and Social Change*. Trans. Clandfield and Sivel. Toronto: Our Schools/Our Selves, 1990.

Friedenberg, Edgar. *Coming of Age in America*. New York: Vintage, 1965.

Froebel, Friedrich. *The Education of Man*. Keilhau, 1826.

Gamson, David. *The Importance of Being Urban: Designing the Progressive School District, 1890-1940*. Chicago: University of Chicago Press, 2019.

Gaskell, Jane, and Ben Levin. *Making a Difference in Urban Schools*. Toronto: University of Toronto Press, 2012.

Gitlin, Todd. *The Sixties: Years of Hope, Days of Rage*. New York: Bantam, 1987.

Goodman, Paul. *Compulsory Mis-education*. New York: Knopf, 1962.

Graham, Patricia A. *Progressive Education: From Arcady to Academe*. New York: Teachers College Press, Columbia, 1967.

Graubard, Allen. *Free the Children*. New York: Random House, 1972.

Greenberg, Daniel, and Hanna Greenberg. *The Sudbury Valley School Experience*. Framingham, MA: Sudbury Valley School Press, 1985.

Gross, Beatrice, and Ronald Gross, eds. *Radical School Reform*. New York: Simon and Schuster, 1969.

Hagen, John. *Northern Passage: American Vietnam War Resisters in Canada.* Cambridge: Harvard University Press, 2001.

Halpin, David. *Romanticism and Education: Love, Heroism, and Imagination in Pedagogy.* New York: Continuum, 2007.

Hamilton, Ian. *The Children's Crusade: The Story of the Company of Young Canadians.* Toronto: Peter Martin, 1970.

Hayes, William. *The Progressive Education Movement: Is It Still a Factor in Today's Schools?* Lanham, Maryland. Rowman and Littlefield Education, 2017.

Henderson, Stuart. *Making the Scene.* Toronto: University of Toronto Press, 2011.

Hendley, Brian. *Dewey, Russell, Whitehead: Philosophers as Educators.* Carbondale: Southern Illinois University Press, 1986.

Herndon, James. *The Way It Spozed to Be.* New York: Simon and Schuster, 1968.

Holmes, Edmond. *What Is and What Might Be.* London: Constable, 1911.

Holt, John. *How Children Fail.* New York: Pitman, 1964.

Horowitz, David, Michael Lerner, and Craig Pyes, eds. *Counterculture and Revolution.* New York: Random House, 1972.

Illich, Ivan. *Deschooling Society.* New York: Harper and Row, 1971.

Isaacs, Susan. *Intellectual Growth in Young Children.* London: Routledge, 1930.

Isserman, Maurice, and Michael Kazin. *America Divided: The Civil War of the 1960s.* Oxford: Oxford University Press, 2008.

Johnson, Marietta. *Thirty Years with an Idea.* Tuscaloosa: University of Alabama Press, 1974.

Katz, Michael. *Class, Bureaucracy, and Schools: The Illusion of Educational Change in America.* New York: Holt, Rinehart, and Winston, 1971.

Kavic, Lorne, and Garry B. Nixon. *The 1200 Days: A Shattered Dream.* Coquitlam, BC: Kaen, 1978.

Kaye, Michael. *The Teacher Was the Sea.* San Francisco: Links, 1972.

Kidel, Mark. *Beyond the Classroom: Dartington's Experiments in Education.* Bideford, Devon: Green Books, 1990.

Kilpatrick, William. *Foundations of Method.* New York: Macmillan, 1925.

———, ed. *The Educational Frontier.* New York: Appleton-Century, 1933.

Kohl, Herbert. *36 Children.* New York: New American Library, 1967.

———. *The Open Classroom.* New York: New York Review, 1969.

Kostash, Myrna. *Long Way from Home.* Toronto: James Lorimer, 1980.

Kozol, Jonathan. *Death at an Early Age.* New York: Houghton Mifflin, 1967.

———. *Free Schools.* New York: Houghton Mifflin, 1972.

Kurlansky, Mark. *1968: The Year That Rocked the World.* New York: Random House, 2004.

Lane, Homer. *Talks to Parents and Teachers*. New York: Schocken, 1928.

Lazerson, Marvin. *Origins of the Urban School*. Cambridge: Harvard University Press, 1971.

Leonard, George. *Education and Ecstasy*. New York: Delacorte, 1968.

Levitt, Cyril. *Children of Privilege*. Toronto: University of Toronto Press, 1984.

Liebschner, Joachim. *Foundations of Progressive Education*. Cambridge, UK: Lutterworth, 1991.

Lloyd, Susan. *The Putney School: A Progressive Experiment*. New Haven: Yale, 1987.

Lytle, Mark Hamilton. *America's Uncivil Wars: The Sixties Era from Elvis to the Fall of Richard Nixon*. New York: Oxford University Press, 2006.

Martell, George, ed. *The Politics of the Canadian Public School*. Toronto: James Lewis and Samuel, 1974.

Martin, Jane Roland. *School Was Our Life: Remembering Progressive Education*. Bloomington: Indiana University Press, 2018.

Marwick, Arthur. *The Sixties*. Oxford: Oxford University Press, 1998.

Miller, J. R. *Shingwauk's Vision: A History of Native Residential Schools*. Toronto: University of Toronto Press, 1996.

Miller, Ron. *Free Schools, Free People: Education and Democracy after the 1960s*. Albany: State University of New York Press, 2002.

Mills, Martin, and Glenda McGregor. *Re-engaging Young People in Education: Learning From Alternative Schools*. London: Routledge, 2014.

Mitchell, Lucy Sprague. *Our Children and Our Schools*. New York: Simon and Schuster, 1951.

Montessori, Maria. *The Montessori Method*. New York: Schocken, 1912.

Morgan, Edward. *The Sixties Experience*. Philadelphia: Temple, 1991.

Morrison, Kristan Accles. *Free School Teaching: A Journey into Radical Progressive Education*. NY: State University of NY Press, 2007.

Morrison, Terence, and Anthony Burton, eds. *Options: Reforms and Alternatives*. Toronto: Holt, Rinehart, and Winston Canada, 1973.

Myers, Douglas, ed. *The Failure of Educational Reform in Canada*. Toronto: McClelland and Stewart, 1973.

Neill, A. S. *Summerhill: A Radical Approach to Child Rearing*. New York: Hart Publishing Company, 1960.

Neima, Anna. The Utopians: Six Attempts to Build the Perfect Society. London: Macmillan, 2021.

Neumann, Richard. *Sixties Legacy: A History of the Public Alternative Schools Movement, 1967–2001*. New York: Peter Lang, 2003.

Novak, Mark. *Living and Learning in the Free School*. Toronto: McClelland and Stewart, 1975.

Nunn, Percy. *Education: Its Data and First Principles*. London: Edward Arnold, 1920.

Owram, Doug. *Born at the Right Time*. Toronto: University of Toronto Press, 1996.

Palaeologu, M. Athena, ed. *The Sixties in Canada: A Turbulent and Creative Decade*. Montreal: Black Rose Books, 2009.

Palmer, Bryan. *Canada's 1960s: The Ironies of identity in a Rebellious Era*. Toronto: University of Toronto Press, 2009.

Parker, Francis. *Talks on Pedagogics*. New York: John Day, 1937.

Parkhurst, Helen. *Education on the Dalton Plan*. London: Bell, 1923.

Pekin, L. B. *Progressive Schools: Their Principles and Practice*. London: Hogarth, 1934.

Perls, Frederick, Ralph Hefferline, and Paul Goodman. *Gestalt Therapy: Excitement and Growth in the Human Personality*. N.p.: Gestalt Institute Press, 1951.

Postman, Neil, and Charles Weingartner. *Teaching as a Subversive Activity*. New York: Delacorte, 1969.

Pratt, Caroline. *Experimental Practice in the City and Country School*. New York: Dutton, 1924.

———. *I Learn from Children*. New York: Cornerstone Library, 1948.

Priestley, Joseph. *Miscellaneous Observations Relating to Education*. London: 1778.

Punch, Maurice. *Progressive Retreat*. London: Cambridge University Press, 1977.

Quarter, Jack. *Student Movements of the Sixties*. Toronto: 1970.

Ravitch, Diane. *The Troubled Crusade*. New York: Basic Books, 1963.

Reid, Tim, and Julyan Reid, eds. *Student Power and the Canadian Campus*. Toronto: Peter Martin, 1969.

Reimer, Derek, ed. *Voices: A Guide to Oral History*. Victoria: BC Archives, 1984.

Reimer, Everett. *School Is Dead*. Middlesex: Penguin, 1971.

Repo, Satu, ed. *This Book is About Schools*. New York: Random House, 1970.

Ricard, Francois. *The Lyric Generation: The Life and Times of the Baby Boomers*. Toronto: Stoddart, 1992.

Rogers, Carl. *Freedom to Learn*. Columbus, OH: Charles E. Merrill, 1969.

Roszak, Theodore. *The Making of a Counter Culture*. New York: Doubleday, 1969.

Rotzel, Grace. *The School in Rose Valley*. Baltimore: Johns Hopkins Press, 1971.

Rousseau, J. J. *Emile*. London: Dent, 1911. First published, Paris, 1762.

Rugg, Harold, and Ann Shumaker. *The Child-Centred School.* Yonkers: World Book, 1928.

Russell, Bertrand. *The Autobiography of Bertrand Russell, Volume Two. The Middle Years: 1914–1944.* Boston: Little, Brown and Company and London: George Allen and Unwin 1968. Page references are to the Little, Brown and Company edition.

Sale, Kirkpatrick. *SDS.* New York: Random House, 1973.

Scott, Andrew. *The Promise of Paradise.* Vancouver, BC: Whitecap, 1997.

Selleck, R. J. *English Primary Education and the Progressives, 1924–1939.* London: Routledge and Kegan Paul, 1972.

Semel, Susan, and Alan Sadovnik, eds. *"Schools of Tomorrow," Schools of Today. What Happened to Progressive Education?* New York: Peter Lang, 1999.

Semel, Susan. *The Dalton School.* New York: Peter Lang, 1992.

Shannon, Patrick. *Progressive Reading Education in America: Teaching Toward Social Justice.* New York: Routledge, 2017.

Sheeran, Michael J. *Beyond Majority Rule: Voteless Decisions in the Religious Society of Friends.* Philadelphia: Philadelphia Yearly Meeting, 1985.

Shukyn, Beverley, and Murray Shukyn. *You Can't Take a Bathtub on the Subway: A Personal History of SEED.* Toronto: Holt, Rinehart, and Winston, 1973.

Shuttleworth, Dale. *Schooling for Life: Community Education and Social Enterprise.* Toronto: University of Toronto Press, 2010.

Silberman, Charles. *Crisis in the Classroom.* New York: Random House, 1970.

Silver, Harold. *English Education and the Radicals 1780-1850.* London: Routledge and Kegan Paul, 1975.

Skidelsky, Robert. *English Progressive Schools.* Middlesex: Penguin, 1969.

Snitzer, Herb. *Today Is for Children.* New York: Macmillan, 1972.

Socknat, Thomas. *Witness against War.* Toronto: University of Toronto Press, 1987.

Stamp, Robert. *The Saturday School: How It Began.* Calgary: Saturday School Society, 1973.

———. *About Schools.* Toronto: New Press, 1975.

Stewart, W. A. C. *Quakers and Education.* London: Epworth, 1953.

———. *The Educational Innovators: Progressive Schools 1881–1967.* London: Macmillan, 1968.

Stevenson, Hugh A., and J. Donald Wilson, eds., *Precepts, Policy and Process: Perspectives on Contemporary Canadian Education.* London, ON: Alexander, Blake Associates, 1977.

Stevenson, Hugh A., Robert M. Stamp, and J. Donald Wilson, eds. *The Best of Times, the Worst of Times: Contemporary Issues in Canadian Education.* Toronto: Holt, Rinehart, and Winston of Canada, 1972.

Sutherland, Neil. *Children in English Canadian Society.* Toronto: University of Toronto Press, 1976.

————. *Growing Up: Childhood in English Canada from the Great War to the Age of Television.* Toronto: University of Toronto Press, 1997.

Tait, Katharine. *My Father Bertrand Russell* (New York: Harcourt Brace Jovanovich, 1975), 74.

Teitelbaum, Kenneth. *Schooling for Good Rebels.* Philadelphia: Temple University Press, 1993.

Thompson, Paul. *The Voice of the Past.* Oxford: Oxford University Press, 1978.

Tisdall, Laura. *A Progressive Education: How Childhood Changed in Mid-Twentieth Century English and Welsh Schools.* Manchester: Manchester University Press, 2019.

Tomkins, George. *A Common Countenance.* Scarborough: Prentice-Hall, 1986.

Tyack, David. *The One Best System.* Cambridge, MA: Harvard Press, 1974.

Vaughan, Mark, ed. *Summerhill and A.S. Neill.* Maidenhead, England: Open University Press, 2006.

Verzuh, Ron. *Underground Times.* Toronto: Deneau, 1989.

Wallace, James M. *The Promise of Progressivism: Angelo Patri and Urban Education.* New York: Peter Lang, 2006.

Washburne, Carleton, and Sidney Marland. *Winnetka.* Englewood Cliffs, Prentice-Hall, 1963.

Welton, Michael, ed. *Knowledge for the People.* Toronto: OISE Press, 1987.

Westbrook, Robert. *John Dewey and American Democracy.* Ithaca: Cornell University, 1991.

Whitehead, Alfred North. *The Aims of Education and Other Essays.* New York: Macmillan, 1929.

Willinsky, John, ed. *The Educational Legacy of Romanticism.* Waterloo: Wilfred Laurier University Press, 1990.

Wilson, J. Donald, Robert M. Stamp, and Louis-Philippe Audet. *Canadian Education: A History.* Scarborough: Prentice-Hall, 1970.

Wood, B. Anne. *Idealism Transformed: The Making of a Progressive Educator.* Kingston: McGill-Queen's University Press, 1985.

Wood, Daniel. *Tales of B.C.: 50 Years of Wacky, Wild & Thought-Provoking Adventures. An Anthology.* Vancouver: OP Media Group, 2022.

Woodcock, George, and Ivan Avakumovic. *The Doukhobors.* London: Faber and Faber, 1968.

Young, Michael. *The Elmhirsts of Dartington.* London: Routledge, 1982.

Zilversmit, Arthus. *Changing Schools: Progressive Education Theory and Practice, 1930-1960*. Chicago: University of Chicago Press, 1993.

Secondary Sources: Articles

Anderson, Starla. "Mainstreaming Progressive Education." *Working Teacher* 2, no.3 (1978).

Axelrod, Paul. "The Student Movement of the 1930s." In P. Axelrod and J. H. Reid, eds., *Youth, University and Canadian Society*, 216–246. Kingston: McGill-Queen's, 1989.

Barman, Jean. "Accounting for Gender and Class in Retrieving the History of Canadian Childhood." *Canadian History of Education Association Bulletin* 5, no. 2, (1988): 5.

———. "Deprivatizing Private Education: The BC Experience." *Canadian Journal of Education* 16, no. 1 (Spring 1991): 12–31.

———, and Neil Sutherland. "Royal Commission Retrospective." *Policy Explorations* 3, no. 1 (Winter 1988): 6–16.

Berland, J., and D. McGee. "Literacy: The Atrophy of Competence." *Working Teacher* (Vancouver) 1, no. 1 (1977).

Berton, Patricia. "A Choice in Schools: Free—Everdale Place." In Hugh Stevenson, Robert Stamp, and J. Donald Wilson, eds., *The Best of Times, the Worst of Times*. Toronto: Holt, Rinehart, and Winston, 1972.

Bloomfield, Kate. "Free and Easy Sundance." *BC Teacher*, 1974.

Callwood, June. "Crisis in Our Classrooms." *Maclean's*, January 23, 1965.

Cremin, Lawrence. "The Free School Movement: A Perspective." In John C. Carr, Jean D. Grambs, and E. G. Campbell, eds., *Pygmalion or Frankenstein: Alternative Schooling in American Education*. New York: Addison Wesley, 1977. First published in *Notes on Education* (Columbia Teachers College) 2 (October 1973).

Durrie, Tom. "Saturna Island Free School." Victoria: Social Science Research, 1969.

———. "Free Schools: Threat to the System or Harmless Lunatic Fringe?" In Hugh Stevenson, Robert Stamp, and J. Donald Wilson, eds., *The Best of Times, the Worst of Times: Contemporary Issues in Canadian Education*. Toronto: Holt, Rinehart and Winston, 1972. First published in *BC Teacher*, 1969.

———. "Free Schools: The Answer or the Question?" In Niall Byrne and Jack Quarter, eds., *Must Schools Fail?* Toronto: McClelland and Stewart, 1972.

Ellis, Jason, and Ee-Seul Yoon. "From Alternative Schools to School Choice in the Vancouver School District, 1960s to the Neoliberal Present." *Canadian Journal of Educational Administration and Policy* 188 (2019): 86-103.

Gorham, Deborah. "The Ottawa New School and Educational Dissent in Ontario in the Hall-Dennis Era." *Historical Studies in Education* 21, no. 2 (Fall 2009).

Gray, Grattan. "What Happens When Parents Start Schools of Their Own." *Maclean's*, November 18, 1961.

Greer, Colin. "Romanticism, Rheumatism, and Public Education." In Colin Greer, ed., *Cobweb Attitudes*. New York: Teachers College Press, 1970.

Grescoe, Audrey. "Working Classrooms: Alternate Education in Vancouver." *Vancouver*, January 1975.

Harding, James. "An Ethical Movement in Search of an Analysis." *Our Generation* 3, no. 4/4:1 (May 1966): 20–29.

———. "From the Midst of a Crisis: Student Power in English Speaking Canada." In Gerald McGuigan, ed. *Student Protest* (Toronto: Methuen, 1968), 90–105.

———. "From Authoritarianism to Totalitarianism: Two Winnipeg Schools." *This Magazine is about Schools*, Autumn 1968. Reprinted in Tim Reid and Julyan Reid, eds., *Student Power and the Canadian Campus*. Toronto: Peter Martin Associates, 1969.

Heale, M. J. "The Sixties as History: A Review of the Political Historiography." *American History* (John Hopkins) 33 (2005).

Hentoff, Margot, and Nat Hentoff. "The Schools We Want." *Saturday Review*, September 19, 1970.

Hook, Sidney. "John Dewey and His Betrayers." In Cornelius Troost, ed., *Radical School Reform: Critique and Alternatives*. Boston: Little, Brown, 1973. Originally published in *Change*, November 1971, 22.

Hughes, Meghan, and Jim Carrico, "Windsor House." In Matt Hern, ed., *Deschooling Our Lives*. Gabriola Island, BC: New Society Publishers, 1996.

Janovicek, Nancy. "'The Community School Literally Takes Place in the Community': Alternative Education in the Back-to-the-Land Movement in the West Kootenays, 1959–1980." *Historical Studies in Education* 24, no. 1 (Spring 2012).

Johnson, Olive. "As a Cool School, There's No Place like Knowplace," *Maclean's*, December 1967.

———. "Free Schools: Tomorrow's Education or Passing Fad?" *Vancouver Life*, April 1968.

Kilpatrick, William. "The Project Method." *Teachers College Record* 19 (September 1918).

Kozol, Jonathan. "Schools for Survival." *This Magazine is about Schools*, Winter 1971.

———. "Free Schools Fail Because They Don't Teach." In J. Carr, J. Grambs, and E. Campbell, eds., *Pygmalion or Frankenstein: Alternative Schooling in American Education.* New York: Addison Wesley, 1977.

Leonard, George. "The Moment of Learning." *Look*, December 27, 1966.

Long, Anne. "The New School—Vancouver." In Beatrice Gross and Ronald Gross, eds., *Radical School Reform.* New York: Simon and Schuster, 1969.

Loo, Tina. "Flower Children in Lotusland." *The Beaver*, February/March 1998.

Mann, Jean. "G. M. Weir and H. B. King: "Progressive Education or Education for the Progressive State?" In J. Donald Wilson and David C. Jones, eds., *Schooling and Society in 20th Century British Columbia*, 91–118. Calgary: Detselig, 1980.

Martin, Jane Roland. "Romanticism Domesticated: Maria Montessori and the Casa Dei Bambini." In John Willinsky, ed., *The Educational Legacy of Romanticism.* Waterloo: Wilfred Laurier University Press, 1990.

Minden, Robert. "Sitting on the Bookshelf." *This Magazine is about Schools*, Autumn 1969.

Myers, Douglas. "Where Have All the Free Schools Gone? A Conversation with Bob Davis, Satu Repo, George Martell." In Douglas Myers, *The Failure of Educational Reform in Canada*, 75–94. Toronto: McClelland and Stewart, 1973. Also *This Magazine is about Schools*, Winter 1972/73, 90. First published in *Canadian Forum*, October 1972.

Nelson, Fiona, "Community Schools in Toronto: A Sign of Hope." *Canadian Forum*, October/ November, 1972. Also in Morrison and Burton, *Options: Reform and Alternatives for Canadian Educators*, 1973; and Douglas Myers, *The Failure of Educational Reform in Canada*, 1973.

Patterson, R. S. "Hubert C. Newland, Theorist of Progressive Education." In J. W. Chambers and J. W. Friesen, eds., *Profiles of Canadian Educators.* Toronto: Heath, 1974.

———. "Progressive Education: Impetus to Educational Change in Alberta and Saskatchewan." In Howard Palmer and Donald Smith, eds., *The New Provinces: Alberta and Saskatchewan.* Vancouver: Tantalus, 1980.

———. "The Canadian Response to Progressive Education." In N. Kach, K. Mazurek, R. S. Patterson, and I. Defaveri, eds., *Essays on Canadian Education.* Calgary: Detselig, 1986.

———. "The Implementation of Progressive Education in Canada." In N. Kach, K. Mazurek, R. S. Patterson, and I. Defaveri, eds., *Essays on Canadian Education.* Calgary: Detselig, 1986.

————. "The Canadian Experience with Progressive Education." In Brian Titley, ed., *Canadian Education: Historical Themes and Contemporary Issues*. Calgary: Detselig, 1990.

Prentice, Alison. "The American Example." In J. Donald Wilson, Robert M. Stamp, and L.-P. Audet, eds., *Canadian Education: A History*, 41–68. Scarborough: Prentice-Hall, 1970.

Rothstein, Harley. "Private to Public: Alternative Schools in Ontario, 1965–1975." In Nina Bascia, Esther Sokolov Fine, and Malcolm Levin, eds., *Alternative Schooling and Student Engagement: Canadian Stories of Democracy within Bureaucracy*, 71–94. New York: Palgrave Macmillan, 2017.

Sarti, Robert. "Decision Making in a Vancouver Alternative School." Unpublished paper for William Bruneau, University of British Columbia, late 1970s.

Shukyn, Murray. "Shared Experience, Exploration, and Discovery." *NASSP Bulletin* 55, 355, May 1971, 151.

Stamp, Robert M. "Paying for Those Free Schools." *Maclean's*, May 1973, 100.

Sutherland, Neil. "The New Education in Anglophone Canada." In George Tomkins, ed., *The Curriculum in Canada in Historical Perspective*. Vancouver, 1979.

————. "The Triumph of Formalism: Elementary Schooling in Vancouver from the1920s to the 1960s." *BC Studies,* Nos. 69/70 (Spring/Summer 1986): 175–210.

————. "Listening to the Winds of Childhood: The Role of Memory." *Canadian History of Education Association Bulletin* 5 (1988).

Wilson, J. Donald. "From the Swinging Sixties to the Sobering Seventies." In Hugh Stevenson and J. Donald Wilson, eds., *Precepts, Policy, and Process: Perspectives on Contemporary Canadian Education*, 21–36. London, ON: Alexander, Blake Associates, 1977.

Wood, Daniel. "The Fears of Public School Teachers." *BC Teacher*, (February 1974), 170.

Young, John. "A Rural High School Tries Freedom." *This Magazine is about Schools*, Winter 1967.

Secondary Sources: Theses and Dissertations

Gower, John. "The Impact of Alternative Ideology on Landscape: The Back-to-the-Land Movement in the Slocan Valley." Unpublished master's thesis, University of British Columbia, 1990.

McCreary, Gillian. "Greenhouse, 1970–1977: A Social Historical Analysis of an Alternative School." Unpublished master's thesis, University of Saskatchewan, 1978.

Mann, Jean. "Progressive Education and the Depression in British Columbia." Unpublished master's thesis, University of British Columbia, 1978.

Rothstein, Harley. "The New School, 1962–1977." Unpublished master's thesis, University of British Columbia, 1992.

Welton, Michael. "To Be and Build the Glorious World." Unpublished PhD dissertation, University of British Columbia, 1983.

The Vallican Whole School in BC's Slocan Valley opened in December 1972 with 25 students. *Images* (school publication), undated

Index

About the Author

Harley Rothstein is a Canadian educator and writer on the history of education and alternative schools. He has a PhD in the History of Education and has conducted extensive research in the development of alternative schools in Canada. After teaching at the elementary level for more than a decade, Harley taught music education and supervised student teachers at the University of British Columbia Faculty of Education. He contributed a historical chapter to the book *Alternative Schooling and Student Engagement: Canadian Stories of Democracy Within Bureaucracy* (Palgrave Macmillan, 2017) on alternative schools in the Toronto School District. He is co-author, with his wife Eleanor Boyle, of *Essentials of College and University Teaching: A Practical Guide* (ProActive Press, 2008). Also a musician, Harley has recorded two full length albums of folk music as a solo artist, and three albums of Jewish music, two of them with the group Shir Hadash. As a lay cantor, he has led synagogue services for forty years and now mentors younger aspiring leaders. Harley enjoys travelling, eating healthy food, and working out regularly at his local gym. Harley and Eleanor live in Vancouver.

Printed in Canada